Becoming the People of the Talmud

JEWISH CULTURE AND CONTEXTS

Published in association with the
Herbert D. Katz Center for Advanced Judaic Studies
of the University of Pennsylvania

David B. Ruderman, Series Editor

A complete list of books in the series
is available from the publisher.

Becoming the People of the Talmud

Oral Torah as Written Tradition in Medieval Jewish Cultures

Talya Fishman

PENN

UNIVERSITY OF PENNSYLVANIA PRESS

PHILADELPHIA

Publication of this volume was assisted by a grant from the Herbert D. Katz Publications Fund of the Center for Advanced Judaic Studies.

Published by
University of Pennsylvania Press
Philadelphia, Pennsylvania 19104-4112
www.upenn.edu/pennpress

Printed in the United States of America on acid-free paper
10 9 8 7 6 5 4 3 2 1

Library of Congress Cataloging-in-Publication Data
Fishman, Talya, 1955–
Becoming the people of the Talmud : oral Torah as written tradition in medieval Jewish cultures / Talya Fishman.—1st ed.
p. cm. — (Jewish culture and contexts)
Includes bibliographical references and index.
ISBN 978-0-8122-4313-0 (hardcover : alk. paper)
1. Talmud—History. 2. Talmud Torah (Judaism)—History. 3. Jewish law—Interpretation and construction. 4. Tosafists. I. Title. II. Series: Jewish culture and contexts.
BM503.F57 2011
296.1′2—dc22

2011002094

CONTENTS

PREFACE TO THE PAPERBACK EDITION

The University of Pennsylvania Press's decision to issue *Becoming the People of the Talmud* in paperback provides me with an opportunity to correct factual errors and to shed light on criticism that followed the book's publication. This Preface will highlight some of the book's challenges to entrenched perspectives in the hopes of promoting substantive conversation about the critical study of medieval rabbinic culture.

A work of intellectual and cultural history that relies on primary sources, *Becoming the People of the Talmud* attempts to reconstruct the process through which the Babylonian Talmud came to serve as Judaism's quintessential guide to law. The book focuses on ways in which the Talmud was used in disparate geographic communities between the tenth and twelfth centuries, by documenting its roles in the study hall and in legal decision-making and by tracing the shift from its oral to its written transmission. These matters are explored in conjunction with cultural features of the broader societies that the Jewish communities inhabited. A major finding of this work, revolutionary to some, is that the way in which the Talmud would be used as a guide to applied law was by no means predetermined. All Rabbanite Jews recognized the Talmud as an authoritative corpus, but, as late as the twelfth century, scholars from different regions disagreed about the supplementary texts that were to be consulted in order to facilitate use of the Talmud as a source of prescriptive law.

Students of rabbinic culture might understand this book as an investigation that focuses on the discrepancy between two categories recognized in the Talmud itself: "*halakha*," or received legal tradition, and "*halakha le-ma'aseh*," or received legal tradition that is implemented in deed, or practice. The distinction between the two is often obscured in common parlance. In considering their relationship, *Becoming the People of the Talmud* poses several historical questions: Did the boundaries between the categories denoted, respectively, by *halakha* and *halakha le-ma'aseh* become less stark during the period under consideration? Did the Talmud come to be construed as a guide to *halakha le-ma'aseh* during this period? If so, why, when, and how did this occur? Evidence discussed in Chapter 1 reveals that, in issuing rulings, the geonim—rabbinic scholars of the East whom medieval European Jews regarded as authority figures—complemented the authority of Talmud with that of *ma'aseh* (literally, deed), attesting thereby that the legal tradition in question was one implemented in practice. Chapter 2 notes that medieval Sefardi scholars were in possession of an explicit tradition that bridged the gap between *halakha* and *halakha le-ma'aseh*; it was this that enabled them to regard Talmud as a guide to applied law. In northern Europe, by contrast, the process of readying the Talmud for use as Judaism's guide to practical legislation was still under way in the High Middle Ages, even though the authority of that text was uncontested. The evidence for this is discussed in Chapter 4.

Over the course of the Middle Ages, some Jews read the text of Talmud, but others truly encountered it as Oral Torah, mediated by living masters through face-to-face instruction. The oral transmission of Talmud was not geared simply to memorization of the corpus; students hoped to so thoroughly internalize its content that they would be able to summon the apt talmudic tradition for application in any life situation. This book discusses the ways in which modalities of transmission—oral versus written—affected the cultural meaning of the knowledge in question, for its tradent-producers and for its recipient-consumers. Traditions were shaped by the manner in which they were relayed; their very packaging was a product of specific social and cultural realities.

Drawing on primary sources, the book notes that medieval Jews' growing perception of the Talmud's *written* text as the locus of religious authority was linked to significant changes in Jewish society and culture. Among the things that changed during the centuries in question was the very nature of religious authority. In this sense, *Becoming the People of the Talmud* challenges the notion that the Talmud played an unchanging role in Rabbanite Jewish life from the moment the corpus was completed.

The aforementioned notion is not only hard to square with the unmediated talmudic text, which leaves legal disputes unresolved; it is inconsistent with historical evidence of the tenth through twelfth centuries. Indeed, were it not for the remarkable accomplishments of the tosafists, Europe's talmudic glossators of the twelfth through fourteenth centuries, the ahistorical outlook might not have been possible. Through ingenious dialectical reasoning, the tosafists reconciled contradictions within the talmudic corpus, thereby revolutionizing the manner in which its text came to be studied and construed. The harmonistic approach to the study of Talmud and its commentaries is favored in certain traditional settings today, but more significant is the fact that halakhic adjudication itself depends on the perception of rabbinic literature as a unified and logically coherent system. Were it not for this presupposition, a decisor asked to render a legal ruling would be unable to subject the library of rabbinic teachings to scrutiny and analysis.

Yet the assumptions of internal consistency and conceptual coherence that some readers must, of necessity, bring to rabbinic writings may obscure the very markers that attest to a tradition's time and place of formation or transformation. In other words, when the tosafist, the rabbinic decisor, and the historian approach the very same texts, they do so with different aims. The historian reads rabbinic sources looking for its seams; these bits of conceptual, lexical, or stylistic evidence offer clues about the circumstances under which specific teachings came into being. The historian's approach is not merely deconstructive, for it ultimately weaves the evidence—including the testimonies to disjunction—into historically plausible narratives of *change*. In short, the motives that inform one's engagement of rabbinic sources may determine the lenses through which one reads them.

This should explain why impartiality in certain matters is not possible and why my discussion of academic debates about the interpretation of particular medieval cultural phenomena in *Becoming the People of the Talmud* has touched raw nerves. For each contested issue—the use of Scripture and Mishnah as prooftexts in North European responsa of the tenth and eleventh centuries; the slaughter of family members by Jews of the Rhineland as they faced Crusaders in 1096; the relative cultural importance of *Ḥasidei Ashkenaz*, Pietists of this region—I evaluate the data in light of *earlier* historical evidence. Only by extending the historical frame of reference backward—into the period of the geonim themselves—can the book escape the retrojected shadow of Tosafism and the harmonistic worldview that it facilitated. This long view refutes the notion that rabbis perceived Talmud as the exclusive source of legal authority from the moment they encountered it, and reveals that the nature of Rabbanite religious authority underwent change prior to the twelfth century. It is for these reasons, I believe, that the book is controversial.

Becoming the People of the Talmud also destabilizes an established view of the past that privileges Tosafism above all other developments in medieval rabbinic culture. It does so by scrutinizing developments in pre-twelfth-century Sefardi rabbinic culture (Chapter 2), discussing evidence that medieval Jews sensed a major change in their culture and society (Chapter 5), and framing Rhineland Pietism as a significant phenomenon in Ashkenazi culture (Chapter 6). The book's concerted effort to distinguish between peculiarly regional features of the medieval Jewish subcultures of Sefarad and Ashkenaz—and to explain these in light of developments in late Roman, Islamic, and Christian cultures—further distances its findings from those of the inherited narrative.

The plausibility of the interpretations presented in *Becoming the People of the Talmud* can and should be debated—in full awareness that no particular individuals or groups control access to the traditional Jewish library, or to the ways in which its riches can or should be read. One need not be invested in any given perspective to use these responsibly.

Introduction

> Transmission will never replace creation in the historian's romantic heart . . . but it does provide us with a set of hard, unromantic and revealing questions to ask about many received truths and tenets.
>
> —Anthony Grafton

The importance of the Babylonian Talmud in the lives of observant Jews is taken for granted. Yet when considered from certain vantage points, the Talmud's role as a guide to Jewish life is bewildering. Though construed as a legal reference work, a significant proportion of the Talmud's content does not pertain to law, and the legal traditions themselves are presented in the form of pending disputes. (Critical scholars have determined that the resolved disputes are actually late interpolations into the talmudic text.)[1] In other words, there is no evidence that the sages whose teachings are preserved in the Talmud, Babylonian amoraim of the third through sixth centuries CE, intended to produce a prescriptive guide to applied Jewish law. In the case of the Talmud, the ever-thorny problem of discerning authorial intent applies even at the level of genre. Does this voluminous repository of conflicting legal perspectives, legends, tall tales, and accounts of the sages' behavior (some quite unflattering) correspond to any known cultural or literary form that flourished in the Hellenistic or Persian societies with which rabbinic Jews had contact?[2] The cultural roles that the Babylonian Talmud came to play in the lives of medieval Jews are far better understood, but it would be anachronistic to retroject these onto rabbinic Jews of earlier generations, whether amoraim, saboraim, i.e., anonymous redactors, or geonim, the leaders of the post-talmudic rabbinic academies around Baghdad in the seventh through eleventh centuries.[3] The disconnect between the contents of the Talmud and the roles that it came to play in medieval Jewish culture (and beyond) is puzzling.

It is also difficult to understand why the Babylonian Talmud (unmediated by the commentaries and codes that transposed it into a reference work) has, for many centuries, enjoyed such prominence in Jewish education. As will be seen below, a range of medieval Jewish scholars plaintively argued that other textual products of Jewish culture were far better suited than the Talmud to assist students in their religious training and spiritual growth.

Another question about the Talmud's role in Jewish culture is best framed from the sociologist's perspective: As a rule, individuals learn proper comportment from living models—parents, teachers, and community members. It is unnatural to regard a (non-revealed) written text as the definitive guide to all socially and culturally desirable behaviors, for mimesis, rather than reading, is the primary guide to life. If anything, living life "by the book" is anomalous. The strangeness of regarding the Talmud as a guide to Jewish life comes into sharper focus when the scope of its teachings is compared with that of other legal systems. In most societies, huge swaths of life are left ungoverned by legal prescription; for example neither the spatial orientation of one's bed, nor the order in which shoes are to be donned is considered a matter to be monitored. Yet because the Babylonian Talmud—which came to be regarded as a prescriptive work—preserves advice about these matters, some rabbinic Jews have construed these arenas of life as ones that are subject to regulation.[4]

Each of these observations underscores the fact that students of Jewish history have little sense of what the Talmud was within its amoraic *Sitz-im-Leben*, before medieval Jews assigned it particular cultural meanings. Robert Brody, a scholar of rabbinics, affirmed this point: "We have no way of knowing to what extent, if at all, the 'editors' of the Talmud—as distinct from the authors of the legal dicta embedded within it—intended to create a normative legal work, rather than an academic or literary corpus."[5]

Why has scholarly ignorance about the Talmud's raison d'être gone largely unacknowledged? The most obvious answer is that there has been little room to even think about this question. The retrojective shadow cast by the medieval fashioning of the Talmud is enormous, and so generations of Jews who lived even earlier are presumed to have embraced the assumptions of their successors. The intellectual and compositional contributions of Rashi (1040–1105), the towering commentator on the Babylonian Talmud, and of the tosafists, its twelfth- and thirteenth-century glossators, have defined what are seen as "canonical" uses of this corpus in the arenas of education and adjudication. By the thirteenth century, these northern European approaches also transformed the classrooms of Sefarad,[6] displacing other ways of relating to the talmudic text.[7] In short, the "tosafization" of Talmud obscured earlier cultural realities. In Brody's words, "We are bound by a very specific perspective of the talmudic material—which springs from our talmudic education and draws upon Rashi and the tosafists in particular. It is difficult for us to free ourselves from this perspective."[8] Or, as Haym Soloveitchik put it, it is difficult to think "in a mode other than Tosafist" when approaching issues of Jewish law.[9]

The tosafist framing of the Babylonian Talmud seems to have contributed to anachronistic assumptions about the ways that Babylonian geonim of the seventh through eleventh centuries related to the Talmud (a topic to be considered in Chapter 1), and may even be discerned in certain historiographic representations of ancient Jewish culture. The retrojection of twelfth-century modes of Jewish study and decision making onto rabbis of the first centuries has fostered the impression that ancient "text-centered" Jews related to Scripture in much the same way that medieval Jews related to the Talmud, leading us to believe that medieval scholars who performed certain intellectual operations on the later text were following in the footsteps of forebears who had lived a millennium earlier.[10] Yet scholars are not at all sure that ancient Jewish sages were proto-scholastics who derived answers to all their legal questions from Torah itself.[11] Though Scripture was undeniably central to the lives of Second Temple period Jews, the label "text-centered" is of only modest descriptive utility, for it gives no information about a broad array of variables. Among these are the ways in which the text in question was encountered—through hearing, reading, or gazing, for example; the segment of the populace that had access to it; the occasions on which it was accessed; the text's status relative to other sources of cultural authority; whether its authority inhered in its particular material form or in its reproducible words, and whether it was interpreted and understood or revered in its inscrutability.

* * *

In attempting to think afresh about changes in the ways that the Babylonian Talmud was used over a discrete period of time and in specific places, the present study is very much a product of its own intellectual and cultural moment. Not long ago, the sheer breadth of the questions it attempts to address would have made the undertaking prohibitive. The possibility of painting on such a large canvas is only possible now because of the availability of secondary literature composed by scholars in an array of fields, most notably, in the recondite field of rabbinics. I could not have attempted to reconstruct historical narratives about changes in the ways that the Talmud was used over time and place, in both classroom and courtroom, without relying on secondary sources to guide me to the relevant primary sources, for I am neither a scholar of halakhah nor a historian of halakhah.

As a work of synthesis, the present study links scholarly findings encountered in a broad array of specialized disciplines in order to offer a plausible solution to a historical and cultural puzzle. Any new perspectives set forth in this book are not the fruit of pioneering archival research, but of thinking about known data in a fresh light; they were gained by bringing together works of scholarship from disparate fields—medieval Jewish and Christian cultural history, rabbinics, and anthropological and folkloric studies pertaining to orality and textuality—in new dialogues and concatenations. Like the medieval subjects of this study, I have scavenged widely and freely (though with attribution) and, like them, I have used the borrowed pieces in ways that diverge from the ways in which I encountered them. In order to open up particular riddles of medieval Jewish culture, I have used whatever tools and insights I have been able to gather—including ones generated in chronologically and geographically remote arenas of intellectual inquiry.

The anthropological turn in the study of history has left its mark on the present work by encouraging researchers to think about the ways that texts function within the societies that revere them, and by drawing attention to the ways that rituals inscribe boundaries, both affirming and altering power relations. The same can be said of studies that stress the difference between "tradition" and "traditionalism." Distinguishing between the two, Brian Stock wrote, "'Traditional' action consists of the habitual pursuit of inherited forms of conduct, which are taken to be society's norm. 'Traditionalistic' action, by contrast, is the self-conscious affirmation of traditional norms—and the establishment of such norms as articulated models for current and future behavior." Traditionalism, Stock explained, "is precipitated by the application of ratiocination to tradition. The past is thought about, codified and, as an abstraction, made a guide for action."[12] Medieval scholars who saw themselves as restoring some originary clarity formulated "past norms of conduct not as they were, but as they were thought to be." The version of the past that they affirmed was presented as a vision that was "more correct, truthful, and consistent than the welter of inherited customs which had been handed down from one generation to the next."[13] Scholarly emenders who imposed their own visions of a society's past were, in no small measure, recreating its culture and attempting to control its future.[14]

The field of orality-textuality studies, pioneered by anthropologists and literary scholars, has also shaped this work by reminding historians that orally transmitted testimonies and written texts give rise to different sets of questions. Readers who receive a communication in written form lose out on performative and nonverbal cues that clarify ambiguity—pauses, inflections, emphases, and gestures—and they wrestle with the text in order to extract its meaning. Inscribed data are thus highly susceptible to "logocentric" operations such as the parsing of words, the rearrangement of syntax, the elimination of perceived redundancies, and the harmonization of discrepancies through rationalization. Such reworkings of manuscript texts must be taken into consideration when attempting to reconstruct historical narratives. Indeed, before the technology of print imposed standardization, circulating manuscripts were continually rewritten by their readers. Manuscript readers held assumptions about reading and writing that could dramatically affect a text's discursive meaning, and often did. As one exponent of the New Philology put it, "Medieval writing does not produce variants; it is variance."[15] The longer a medieval manuscript was in circulation, the more its reception varied, for later readers often encountered a text that was quite different from what earlier readers had seen. Discussing this phenomenon, Stephen Nichols noted that since "almost all [medieval] manuscripts postdate the life of the author by decades or even centuries . . . what we actually perceive [in the text] may differ from what the . . . [writer], artist or artisan intended to express, or from what the medieval audience expected to find."[16]

One of the implications of this phenomenon is the likelihood that not all variants in medieval manuscripts of the same text are products of scribal error.[17] Indeed, the very impulse to search for a correct *ur*-text is often misguided.[18] Codicologist Malachi Beit Arié has stressed that these points apply in the case of medieval Jewish manuscripts: "Many principles and practices of classical textual criticism, such as the establishing of genetic relationships between manuscripts, stemmatic classification, the reconstructing of archtypes [*sic*] and the restoration of the original are not applicable in Hebrew manuscripts."[19] It is impossible to consider changes in the role that the Talmud came to play in the lives of observant Jews without internalizing this discomfiting insight.

It was not only the physical text that could be expected to change while in circulation. Changes made to the manuscript over time altered the way in which readers experienced it, and affected the cultural role(s) that it played within a society. Of these bi-directional dynamics, Gabrielle Spiegel wrote, "Texts both mirror and generate social realities, are constituted by and constitute the social and discursive formations which they may sustain, resist, contest or seek to transform."[20] For example, once a reader inserted some explanatory words in the manuscript that lay before him, subsequent readers of that manuscript would naturally embrace that meaning, and reject others. And inasmuch as the manuscript was presumed to be a representative of the past, such interpolations affected readers' understandings of the past. Corrective alterations to the manuscript had the same effect. A scholar who emended a text based on formulations that he encountered in earlier manuscripts may have assumed that he was restoring matters "as they were," but attempts to recapture the past can never succeed fully, given that people can only be in contact with a part of their cultural heritage at any given time.[21]

As a material and historical object at the nexus between consumers, merchants, scribes, copyists, and artisans (parchment preparers, ink manufacturers, line rulers, quire sewers, etc.) a medieval manuscript was the product of interlocking social, economic, and cultural networks. But whereas Christians established dedicated venues for the copying and sale of manuscripts (e.g., monastic scriptoria, ateliers, workshops connected with universities), Jews tended to copy books for personal use, in non-institutional settings.[22] In his study of 3,200 Hebrew manuscripts with dated colophons, Malachi Beit Arié discovered that half were produced for personal use.[23] The significance of this fact, noted Beit Arié, was that medieval Hebrew manuscripts were far less likely to be copied under supervision. Indeed, he suggested, an individual who copied a Hebrew manuscript for private use was more likely to alter the received text by inserting his own comments.[24]

Beit Arié's elucidation of this difference between manuscript production among Jews and Christians in medieval Europe suggests that Hebrew texts were even more vulnerable to variance than were their Christian counterparts. One might conjecture that the magnitude of variance may have been even greater when the text under consideration was one that had been transmitted for centuries as an oral corpus, and when Jews in disparate communities committed it to writing at different times. Such was the case with the Babylonian Talmud. Recognition that uncertainty is not the exception, but the rule, when attempting to reconstruct the cultural meaning and role of a medieval manuscript may make it somewhat easier to think about the Talmud (at least fleetingly) in a manner "other than tosafist." The medieval glossators' monumental enterprise, and the image of the Talmud that they made so indelible, constitute only one vision of the classical rabbinic past.

Changes in the "packaging" of tradition radically transform the mediated content. This is the case whether the transmitting scholar stitches together disjointed utterances so that they form a coherent narrative, systematizes received traditions in a particular written format, explains difficult words or passages by engaging ancient tradents in direct conversation, or comments upon them from the glossatorial sidelines. Awareness that such changes dramatically alter the embedded traditions, their place in society, and even the source of their legitimating power[25] may make it easier to discern how processes of transmission transformed the Babylonian Talmud into a reference work and a guide to Jewish life.

* * *

Earlier scholars of Jewish history and culture drew attention to the unprecedented prominence of the Talmud in the lives of medieval Jews; indeed, Ḥayyim Zalman Dimitrovsky asserted that the defining feature of "the Jewish Middle Ages" was the emergence of Talmud study as a cultural ideal.[26] Referring to the valorization of the Talmud in the Middle Ages, Naḥman Danzig claimed that it was in this period that Talmud came to acquire the status of a "book," a status that Jews had previously bestowed only on the Tanakh itself,[27] Haym Soloveitchik referred to the undertaking of the tosafists, the medieval talmudic glossators, as one that rewrote the entire Talmud anew,[28] and Colette Sirat asserted that North European Jews transformed six orders of ancient tractates into a unified and continuous text in the Middle Ages.[29] Common to these claims is the observation that medieval Jews experienced Talmud in ways that earlier Jews had not. Neither the corpus nor its constituent teachings were new, but the site of encounter between the student and talmudic tradition had changed dramatically. Unlike their amoraic and geonic predecessors, medieval Jews came to know Talmud as a written text, and they engaged it, not as auditors receiving oral tradition, but as readers studying a book.

Modern scholars have drawn attention to the greater availability of Jewish texts in medieval Jewish culture. Though a mere five percent of medieval manuscripts in Hebrew script are estimated to have survived,[30] Alexander Samely and Philip Alexander noted that medieval exemplars of Jewish texts composed in antiquity exist in unprecedented numbers. These texts, they wrote, appeared "with disconcerting suddenness on this side, as it were, of a great manuscript divide."[31] Roberto Bonfil referred to the transition of medieval Jewish societies from "orality" to "textuality,"[32] and Yisrael Ta Shma, drawing on the work of Brian Stock, spelled out some cultural ramifications of this shift. According to Ta Shma, the availability of written texts made it possible for readers to develop a "synoptic" perspective on tradition, and to hone the analytical tools needed for examining it.[33] He also noted that the way in which Talmud was used in the Middle Ages was unprecedented: in earlier times, it had constituted a focal point for exegesis, but Jews of medieval northern Europe came to relate to Talmud as a source for adjudication.[34] It was this radically different understanding of the text's function, wrote Ta Shma, that transformed Talmud into a guide for life.[35]

Though there is ample evidence that rabbinic culture underwent dramatic transformation in the Middle Ages, and that the expanded role of the Talmud was one of its foremost manifestations, the reasons for this change are far less obvious. Why did scholars decide to re-package received teachings in a particular way, at a specific time and place? Precedents for such acts might be detected in the Jewish past, but synchronic developments should clearly be given top consideration. Some decisions may have stemmed from concerns about the loss of tradition. Others may have been connected with the impulse to cultivate a regional, "subcultural," identity.[36] Ways in which medieval Jews related to data they encountered in the rabbinic archive, transmitted, and used it may also have been affected by the literary practices of non-Jewish neighbors. Finally, the very inscription of a formerly oral corpus may have generated its own dynamics. The visual encounter with a text that is a bearer of authority puts the onus on the reader to endow it with greater clarity and to bring it into line with what the reader knows to be true. In this sense, the inscription of the Talmud, a corpus of the Oral Torah, and the growing engagement with it as a written text constituted endogenous changes—and forces for change—within medieval Jewish culture.[37]

Comparable developments in medieval Christian culture, and the analyses provided by twentieth-century scholars, offer ways to think about this problem. Some of the relevant works of scholarship document changes in practice that occurred in specific regions of northern Europe in the eleventh century, and others offer insight into the ways that these changes played out more broadly in social and cultural arenas.[38] A body of influential research reveals that a significant—unnamed—cultural process transpired in northern Europe from the second half of the eleventh century through the middle of the twelfth. The present study therefore uses the term "textualization" to denote this slow and unconscious cultural process, during the course of which the society in question came to ascribe greater value to the authority of the inscribed word than it did to oral testimony, supported by gestures and props. The transition from the valorization of memory to the valorization of written records was not always a function of greater literacy. Textualization involved a change in *mentalité* that might be compared to changes triggered by the availability of a new technology.

The textualization of northern European Jewish culture in the eleventh and twelfth centuries should be examined within a broader regional context because nothing about the process itself was specific to one faith tradition.[39] Disparate societies and cultures within a given region may have formulated discrete rules to regulate the occasions and settings in which writing was used, but textualization affected all inhabitants within a given region without reference to the confessional boundaries that divided them.

In discussing the "tosafization" of Talmud, I have suggested why this narrative of cultural change remained untold, for so long, within the field of Jewish studies, but, in fact, the textualization process itself—and its irreversibility—must also be credited with having imposed a certain ineluctable, and amnesiac, vision of the past. Bound by unexamined cultural presuppositions, contemporary readers and, arguably, those of the past millennium, have mistakenly assumed that texts played the same roles in earlier societies that they play in our own. Yet this is hardly the case. As Brigitte Bedos-Rezak noted, the "assumed epistemological centrality of the [medieval] document . . . does not correspond to the role, significance and meaning of documentation in the time and place it was generated."[40]

Happily, scholarly writings produced over the last several decades by the medievalists Jean Leclercq, M.T. Clanchy, and Mary Carruthers have mediated access to cultures that ascribed oral testimonies greater authority than textual evidence, and shed light on the "oral-memorial" mindset that was eclipsed by the textualization process. By the same token, recent rabbinic scholarship has made it easier to dispel the deserved confusion wrought by the label "Oral Torah"—the referent of which is encountered today in the form of inscribed texts that occupy miles of bookshelves. Clarification of this seeming oxymoron has been greatly advanced by Ya'aqov Sussman, who noted in a voluminous study that Mishnah and Talmud, two of the corpora of Oral Torah, were transmitted in oral fashion throughout the period of the tannaim and amoraim,[41] and by Robert Brody and Naḥman Danzig, who concluded that oral transmission of Talmud remained the norm in the Babylonian academies for the duration of the geonic period.[42]

While historical evidence indicates that the corpora of Oral Torah were transmitted in oral form over the course of centuries, it is far harder to detect when they began to circulate as written texts. The difficulty in reconstructing the moment of cultural shift was well put by Sussman, who framed the problem in cross-cultural terms.[43] Within other cultures that had once vigilantly guarded the orality of specific corpora, he noted, the inscription of oral traditions triggered powerful protest. This was clearly the case among Zoroastrians when the *Avesta* was committed to writing, and among Muslims, when *hadith* were inscribed.[44] Yet, surprisingly, wrote Sussman, no comparable protest appears to have erupted within rabbinic society when Oral Torah was ultimately consigned to writing. Offering a compelling, if frustrating, explanation for this silence,[45] Sussman conjectured that Jews may well have raised objections between the fifth and eighth centuries, but that these reactions cannot be retrieved, having been expressed during the "Dark Ages" of rabbinic historiography.[46]

* * *

The present work demonstrates that when the Talmud, a corpus of orally transmitted traditions, was inscribed in the Middle Ages and disseminated as a written text, a process was set in motion that affected what Hans Robert Jauss called "the horizon of expectations," transforming Jewish culture and society in significant and lasting ways. In tracking cultural developments that transpired within geographically diverse rabbinic communities from the tenth century through the twelfth, this study "slows down" the textualization process that enabled Jews to construe the Talmud as the legal reference work par excellence, and as a prescriptive one at that. Awareness of some of the stages in this process should counteract the tendency to assume that the role Talmud came to play in Jewish culture and society from the twelfth century onward was teleologically determined. If anything, the historical narrative reconstructed here suggests that the changing roles of the Talmud in Jewish life were conditioned by contingent decisions and broader contextual circumstances.

Overview of Chapters

Chapter 1 begins by exploring the distinction that third-century Palestinian rabbis established between *written matters* and *oral matters*. Situating this distinction within a broader historical and cultural context, the chapter elaborates on the rules formulated for the treatment of corpora within each category and it attempts to explain why these discrete categories were created. Subsequent analysis of certain geonic-era writings reveals the doggedness with which later Babylonian scholars attempted to uphold these ancient regulations in their post-talmudic academies, notwithstanding the fact that this impulse was in tension with their efforts to disseminate knowledge of the Babylonian Talmud. The resoluteness with which geonim preserved the orality of *oral matters* is boldly illustrated in their eschewal of written transmission while living in the environs of Baghdad, a cosmopolitan, multicultural, and highly textualized society and in Sherira Gaon's late tenth-century *Epistle*. Certain Jewish communities far from the geonic heartland possessed the Talmud as a written text, but in their own domain, the geonim strove to transmit talmudic teachings orally for as long as they could.

Geonic correspondence with rabbinic Jews of eleventh-century Qayrawan, today's Tunisia, reveals that the leaders of the Babylonian academies did not view the talmudic corpus as the sole source of Jewish law, and did not even assign it pride of place over teachings imparted by living models. Moreover, among the regulatory vehicles through which the geonim asserted their authority, talmudic exegesis had a surprisingly low profile. Given the tenor of these findings, the production of halakhic compositions in Babylonia during the geonic period is particularly puzling. In line with earlier geonic scholarship, this chapter portrays the capitulation to written law as a late and concessionary development in geonic culture, prompted by the need to offer guidance to far-flung Jewish communities. But it also stresses the ambivalence that geonim felt about the works in question, whether the omnibus Aramaic compilations that were composed outside the academies, or the Judeo-Arabic legal monographs that were composed by geonim themselves. The cultural authority—or meaning—that later rabbinic Jews ascribed to both types of halakhic compositions probably did not mirror geonic perceptions.

Inasmuch as the geonim familiarized the rest of the Jewish world with the talmudic oeuvre, it seemed reasonable, in this study, to regard the place of the Babylonian Talmud in geonic culture as something of a baseline with respect to subsequent developments in rabbinic culture.[47] Yet strikingly, Jewish communities of the eleventh century—the Sefardi ones of Qayrawan and al-Andalus, the eastern and western ends of the Maghreb, and the Ashkenazi ones of northern Europe—developed ways of relating to the Talmud that were dramatically different from from that of the geonim, as well as from one another. Noting the distinctive approaches that were characteristic of these discrete regions, this study offers some preliminary ruminations on why Sefarad and Ashkenaz, Jewish subcultures that first emerged in the Middle Ages, engaged the Babylonian Talmud in disparate ways.

Chapter 2 explores the roles that the Talmud played in eleventh-century Qayrawan and al-Andalus, Jewish communities whose rabbinic contributions were formative of Sefardi culture. Jewish students in these locations encountered the Talmud as a written text, and they related to the written Talmud as the preeminent source for adjudication. Yet when it came to transposing a confusing corpus of received teachings into applied law, the Jews in these two regions adopted different compositional formats. Scholars of Qayrawan who, among other things, pioneered the creation of study aids for the Talmud, wrote commentaries on the Talmud that steered each passage of the text to its concrete legal endpoint, that which was to be practiced. By contrast, rabbinic leaders of the pre-1088 Andalusian Jewish community composed digests of applied law. Speculation about why these two rabbinic communities cultivated the post-talmudic genres that were specific to their respective regions identifies possible analogues in the realms of Islamic jurisprudence.

Chapter 2 also explores the broader cultural ramifications of two claims that were unique to the Jews of Sefarad: the tradition that local ancestors had acquired the Talmud as a written text centuries earlier, and the assertion that "our Talmud," namely, the text known by the Jews of Spain, had been inscribed in generations past for the express purpose of teaching applied Jewish law. It also notes that the roles played by the Talmud in Sefardi pedagogy and adjudication stand in marked contrast to those it played in these two arenas in Ashkenazi Jewish communities from the twelfth century onward. Medieval Sefardi society's tiered educational curriculum was designed to accommodate the varying abilities of a broad segment of the male Jewish population, and therefore offered Talmud study only to the most intellectually gifted. By the same token, the very difficulty of the talmudic corpus led rabbinic scholars of Sefarad to encourage judges (*dayyanim*) to consult geonic digests of applied law, rather than Talmud itself, when issuing decisions.

Without developing a new genetic explanation for the emergence of the Ashkenazi and Sefardi Jewish subcultures in the Middle Ages, Chapter 3 opens by suggesting that the specific characteristics of each may be partly explained with reference to the political, institutional, and cultural histories of each region. Just as Jewish communities of Sefarad were situated in areas that had been at the heartland of the Roman Empire, those of Ashkenaz were located at its frontier, an area that had been affected by imperial military and fiscal policies but was only superficially "Romanized." Cultural manifestations of *Latinitas* in pedagogy and law, manifest in the continued reliance on written documents as sources of evidentiary and dispositive legal authority, persisted in regions south of the Loire River long after the empire's collapse at the end of the fifth century, but matters were quite different in northern lands. Outside the barbarian courts themselves, societies north of the Loire tended to rely on the spoken word for administrative and legal practices into the eleventh century.

Chapter 3 continues by singling out formative social, economic, and religious developments in Christian societies of northern Europe from the eighth to the tenth centuries that may shed light on particular social, political, religious and pedagagic features of Ashkenazi Jewry. It also explores several developments within northern European society that shed light on distinctive characteristics of Ashkenazi Jewry's legal culture. Once the Carolingian Empire had disintegrated, legal professionals who could be trusted to interpret and apply written law ceased to be trained, and societies fell back on a range of non-written strategies for self-regulation.

In order to set the stage for the following chapter, Chapter 3 reviews evidence pertaining to the textualization of northern European societies over the course of the eleventh century. It summarizes possible precipitating causes of textualization that have been identified by specialists in medieval Christian cultural history, and it spells out some of the ramifications of the textualization process on classroom practices, pedagogic ideals, and the society's assessment of cultural worth. It also considers ways in which the ascription of authority to written texts led to the rise of new literary genres, new juridical practices, and an altered understanding of how individuals were to live their lives. For some medieval thinkers, the privileging of ancient documents awakened an awareness of the discrepancy between past and present—and it compelled them to develop strategies for bridging the gap between then and now.

In broad strokes, Chapter 4 intimates the contours of the textualization process that transformed Ashkenazi Jewry, from the time of Rabbenu Gershom at the turn of the millennium through the first generation of the tosafists in the twelfth century. Focusing specifically on the changing place of the Talmud in this society, it highlights shifts in text-related behaviors and attitudes, in readers' assumptions and practices, and in compositional activities, curricular emphases, pedagogic ideals and approaches to adjudication.. In keeping with earlier historiography, Chapter 4 adopts as an organizational device the palpable divide between rabbinic cultural phenomena that were characteristic of the period before the First Crusade (1096) and those that emerged thereafter. And in considering the earlier period, this chapter brackets its discussion of developments in the realm of pedagogy from those that transpired in the arena of adjudication.

This chapter reads Rabbenu Gershom's inscription projects, along with the ordinances ascribed to him, as symptoms of the textualization process. It reflects on the cultural significance of early Ashkenaz's omniverous curricular proclivities, and explores the phenomenon of textual tampering, in which the reader re-created received tradition through active engagement as tradent. The anthologistic and aggregative tendencies of both the Mainz Talmud commentary and Rashi's Talmud commentary are mapped onto the historical narrative of textualization, and Rashi himself is shown to have consciously adopted the role of self-appointed mediator between "old" and "new" assumptions about rabbinic texts. Novel compositional features of Rashi's Talmud commentary occasion reconstruction of the learning conditions that prevailed in his time and ruminations about other classroom practices that his opus may may have set in motion. Chapter 4 also reviews the disparate scholarly assessments of the role that the Talmud played in the lives of eleventh-century Ashkenazi Jews by recapitulating radically divergent interpretations of the grisly events of 1096, when Rhenish Jews killed their own children and committed suicide. At stake in this debate is the possibility that non-talmudic sources of tradition, biblical and post-biblical, may have influenced their decisions to undertake these deeds.

Moving on to the twelfth-century, the chapter examines the project of the talmudic glossators who already held certain assumptions about what an authoritative text should be, and thanks to Rashi, had come into possession of a semantically comprehensible talmudic narrative. The tosafists' concern to determine the correct version of the Talmud, a project they pursued through intense archival research, and their presumption that the corpus was a unified whole, such that any unclear passage could be explained with the help of a clearer one, are emblematic of their immersion in a culture that now regarded texts as preeminent bearers of authority. The range of activities undertaken by the tosafists—their system of cross-referencing Talmud, and their resolution of ostensible conflicts within the text—would insinuate the Talmud into Jewish life with an omnipresence that was previously unknown. Through the activities of Rashi and the tosafists, the Talmud was transformed into a logically coherent corpus, one that a Jewish population newly hungry for textual guidance could construe as a universal reference work and a blueprint for life.

The vitriolic exchange between Rabbenu Tam, the leading tosafist of northern France, and Rabbenu Meshullam of southern France reveals that the assumptions undergirding the tosafists' attempt to bridge the discrepancy between the Talmud and life were not universally accepted in the second half of the twelfth century. Relying heavily on recent scholarship by Rami Reiner, this altercation is seen as a witness to the live and unsettled issues that needed to be addressed before the Talmud could serve as a reference work of prescriptive import.

Corollary developments of the textualization process that transformed northern European Jewish society and culture are spelled out in this chapter Social transformation was evident in the decline of an older ethos of discipleship and in the rise of a cultural hierarchy that privileged the most adept logician. As the Talmud acquired the status of a prescriptive text, discrepancies between talmudic teachings from the past, and life as practiced in the present, provoked anxiety—and triggered disparate solutions. Strikingly, all solutions to this problem worked on the assumption that life needed to be brought into congruence with the inscribed word. In their approach to this problem, the tosafists took as axiomatic that both reference points—the talmudic text and the behaviors of pious Jews—were authoritative, and they harmonized ostensibly conflicting positions in dialectical *tours de force*. This stands in marked contrast to the way in which a different group of twelfth-century Jews dealt with the newly awakened sense of cultural discontinuity between the textual past and the lived present. Whereas the tosafists acknowledged the "newness" of their own time, their contemporaries, the Rhineland Pietists (subject of Chapter 6) affirmed the illusion of "omnitemporality," maintaining that "things had always been the same." In order to ensure that their own practices were perfectly aligned with those of the past, they engaged in acts of historical ventriloquism and created hitherto unknown textual pasts. The chapter concludes by considering the impact of textualization on genres other than the Talmud—the preservation of responsa, standardization of liturgy, commitment of esoterica to writing, and inscription of customs.

The array of internal Jewish evidence considered in the first part of Chapter 5 underscores the fact that modern historians are not the only ones to have discerned changes in medieval rabbinic culture; some medieval Jews were well aware of the range of changes that had already transformed their societies and were continuing to do so. Certain evidence of this awareness takes the form of reportage, while other testimonies are outright protests. Jews who resented the new prominence, and in some places, virtual monopoly, of the Talmud in the classroom lamented the narrowing of the curriculum and marginalization of other subjects. The talmudocentric course of study was faulted for its preoccupation with irrelevant legal minutiae and its failure to address spiritual education. Arrogance and hunger for fame were cited as unsavory side effects of Talmud study, particularly as students, inspired by the tosafists, invested intellectual energy in dialectical gymnastics. Some critics claimed that the seductiveness of tosafistic casuistry actually resulted in greater ignorance of the Talmud itself. Other medieval Jews noted that the master-disciple etiquette was no longer observed, because books had become substitutes for teachers. One medieval scholar attempted to reconstruct the conditions that had prevailed within rabbinic cultural in earlier times, and to speculate about the cause of change.

The second part of Chapter 5 hypothesizes that a well-documented development in contemporaneous Christian culture may also have been triggered by the textualization of rabbinic Judaism. Historians are well aware that the Christian encounter with Talmud in the 1140s marked a turning point in the history of church attitudes toward the Jews and in the focus of anti-Jewish polemic. The old tolerationist Jewry policy associated with Augustinian theology had been predicated on the assumption that Jews would eventually come to understand that Hebrew Bible prophecies had been fulfilled in the life and death of Jesus of Nazareth. However, when Christians discovered the Talmud, some theologians argued that the church's policy failed to take into account the obstructionist role that the Talmud played in shaping Jewish beliefs and perspectives. In attempting to explain why this Christian realization of the Talmud's importance occurred as late as it did, historians have focused on internal developments within the church, on trends in Christian theology, and on the growing importance of certain clerical orders. By contrast, this study posits that Christians only became aware of the Talmud when they did because it was not until the twelfth century that this corpus, as a written text, became a universal Jewish reference work. In an effort to support this conjecture, Chapter 5 briefly recapitulates the work of earlier scholars who reconstructed what Christians knew about extrabiblical Jewish traditions, when they came to know it, and how they encountered the information in question. This section of the chapter concludes with the (seemingly tautological) observation that Church's *physical* assault on the

Talmud could only occur once a standardized text of that name was in widespread circulation.

The final part of Chapter 5 suggests that certain Jewish cultural phenomena of the Middle Ages may be construed as ones that evolved in reaction to developments that were part of the textualization process. The explosion of customary literature in Ashkenaz, and that subculture's heightened sensitivity to custom, are explained not only with reference to the non-written legal culture that prevailed in northern Europe over the course of centuries, but as a reaction to an unprecedented development in the history of Jewish law. After all, earlier generations of Jews had not regarded talmudic teachings, on their own, as prescriptive; a received legal teaching (*halakhah*) could only be seen as a mandate if a master attested to having seen it implemented in practice (*le-ma'aseh*). However, once the—unalloyed—talmudic text came to be construed as a prescriptive source of law, the latter requirement was overlooked, and halakhah on its own, without the vetting of any living witness, rose to a position of legal preeminence. Under these novel circumstances, the authority that had always been ascribed to communal practice asserted itself in the (new) genre of customary literature. Jews who lamented the distortion of juridical equilibrium insisted that the authoritative status of communal practice not be dwarfed by the Talmud's new role in adjudication.

Chapter 6 suggests that Rhineland Pietism, its practices, claims, and attitudes, and even the poorly understood circumstances of its appearance and disappearance, assume greater historical clarity when viewed in relation to the textualization process. Researchers have described certain Pietist practices as revivals of those that prevailed in Ashkenazi Jewish culture prior to the First Crusade, but this chapter suggests that the practices in question had never actually died out. Though the Pietists fashioned themselves as representatives of the past by championing and emphasizing certain cultural practices that were being eclipsed, they, like the tosafists, were asserting their own particular vision of the past. This chapter frames certain features of Pietism as perpetuations of longstanding practices and attitudes that were now under attack, some as acts of protest, and some as acts intended to accommodate northern European Jewry's new cultural standards. In an age in which a textual witness became the hallmark of cultural authority, Rhineland Pietists, consciously or unconsciously, engaged in acts of literary bricolage that simultaneously bear witness to their extraordinary erudition and to their inventiveness. The resulting fabrications supplied the evidence of a "textual past" that helped Pietists to legitimate and defend some of their contested practices.

After recapitulating examples of this phenomenon that were analyzed in earlier scholarship, Chapter 6 reconstructs the way in which medieval Pietists created a hallowed literary pedigree for their extreme penitential practices. The penances in question were analogues of contemporaneous Christian practices that developed in the medieval Rhineland under the influence of Irish monasticism, but by engaging in historical ventriloquism, Rhineland Pietists endowed them with inscribed ancestral legitimation The chapter also hypothesizes that the many passages about book manufacture, its tools and its agents in *Sefer Ḥasidim*, a Pietist compilation of exempla, were designed to repair a cultural logic disturbed by textualization. After all, the Talmud was a corpus of *oral matters*, yet Jews of medieval northern Europe encountered it as an inscribed text. This alteration in the material status of the Talmud blurred the longstanding taxonomic distinction between *oral* and *written matters*. The miscellany of Pietist-generated rules governing the treatment of "books" had the effect of redrawing existing taxonomic boundaries and of bringing the talmudic text into the category of a sacred artifact—a category that had previously included only the Torah scroll itself. The reclassification of the Talmud as a sacred work had bearing on the way in which that text's content might be read.

The widespread inscription of liturgy, and its standardization in a particular textual form in the twelfth century, posed a comparable problem for Pietists. Not only were blessings traditionally classified as *oral matters*, but reliance on a written book might reduce the worshiper's experience of prayer to that of a mechanical undertaking. Chapter 6's analysis of a peculiar Pietist prayer praxis described in *Sefer Ḥasidim* reveals that some Jews of medieval northern Europe found ways of ensuring that worship would never become a rote activity. Examination of this strange practice within its diachronic and synchronic contexts facilitates reconstruction of its mechanics—and exploration of Pietist prayer commentaries promotes speculation about the cultural meaning ascribed to this practice by its practitioners. Exploration of another compositional *novum* pioneered by the Rhineland Pietists, Masorah commentary, suggests that it too was a response to textualization and was intended to prevent yet another recently inscribed corpus of *oral matters*, the Masorah itself, a body of tradition stipulating precisely how a Torah scroll is to be written, from losing its living, oral quality. As in the case of prayer commentary, the Pietists' commentary on Masorah transformed the now-inscribed data into a venue for oral, recollective meditation.

The chapter concludes by explaining Rhineland Pietism's disappearance after a mere three generations with reference to the larger historical narrative of textualization. Once all the relevant corpora of *oral matters*—Pietist exempla, prayer praxes, Masorah commentary, and esoteric theological teachings—had been committed to writing, the Rhineland Pietists obviated their very *raison d'être*: they wrote themselves out of existence. Moreover, certain eccentricities of Pietist behavior were "culturally domesticated" once they were included in normative rabbinic compositions. Though Rhineland Pietism died out as a movement, many of its characteristic practices and attitudes, indigenous to the region's Jewish culture, were simply resorbed into mainstream Ashkenazi culture.

1

The Place of *Oral Matters* in Geonic Culture

By the eighth century, when the entire Babylonian Talmud was written out—from memory—at the request of Jews living far from the rabbinic academies of Iraq,[1] some Jewish communities had come into possession of an oxymoron: an inscribed corpus of *oral matters*. The distinction between *written matters*, i.e., Scripture, and *oral matters*, extra-scriptural tradition, had been made by tannaitic sages of late antiquity. One of their several dicta regulating the transmission and use of these disparate categories of Jewish knowledge explicitly stated: "Words/matters that are oral—you are not permitted to say them in writing."[2] It is clear from ancient rabbinic literature that there were instances of non-compliance, but, at a rhetorical level, even these accounts served to reinforce the strictures themselves.[3] The geonim [literally "Eminences"][4] who led the post-talmudic academies around Baghdad from the seventh through eleventh centuries were thus engaged in a sensitive balancing act: while attempting to disseminate teachings of the Babylonian Talmud to Jewish communities throughout the world, they strove to uphold the ancient prohibition against the inscription of *oral matters*. The discipline exhibited by the geonim in preserving the orality of Talmud was all the more remarkable in that the broader culture of Baghdad, from at least the ninth century, was highly "textualized," having come to privilege written texts more highly than orally transmitted traditions.[5]

The two topics that comprise the focal themes of this chapter—pedagogic encounters with Talmud in the Babylonian yeshivot and the place of Talmud in geonic legislation and governance—offer ample evidence of this tension at the core of the geonic enterprise. As will be seen, rabbinic Jews outside of the academies were the first to capitulate by studying from inscriptions of *oral matters*, but with the passage of time, the geonim made concessions too, responding to geographic, cultural, and economic exigencies. Examples discussed in this chapter illuminate the larger claim that modes of transmission—in this case, encountering Talmud as a written text and not as an orally relayed tradition—have considerable bearing on the ways that tradition is understood.

Rabbinic Regulations Concerning the Transmission and Use of *Oral Matters*

Third-century rabbis who claimed that Oral Torah, extra-scriptural tradition, had been revealed at Sinai, along with Scripture itself,[6] promulgated rules to regulate the production, handling, transmission, and use of *written matters*, on the one hand, and of *oral matters*, on the other. Their prescriptions for each corpus are mirror images of one another; regulations stipulated for one type of knowledge are proscribed for the other. "R. Judah ben Naḥmani, the interpreter of Resh Laqish, discoursed as follows: It is written: [Ex. 34:27], '*Write you these words/matters,*' and it is written [ibid.], '*for according to the mouth of these words/matters.*'[7] What are we to make of this? It means: The words/matters that are written you are not at liberty to say by heart, and the words/matters that are oral you are not permitted to say them in writing."[8]

The peculiar locution of the final phrase, "*i atta rashai le-omran be-khtav*" ("you are not permitted *to say them in writing*"), was taken to mean something quite specific: It did not prohibit the inscription of *oral matters* per se, but the public declamation or recitation of these matters from a written text. As was the case in other Hellenistic period societies that distinguished between a *syngrama*, an authorized inscription accorded official status, and a *hypomnema*, written notes for private use, Jews distinguished between texts that were intended for public reading and those that were mere jottings, *aides de memoire*.[9] From the perspective of rabbinic culture, inscriptions in the latter category were "phantom texts"; these could be seen and silently read, but they merited no particular cultural attention and could not be adduced as sources of authority. Sages of the classical rabbinic period, geonim and medieval scholars, designated inscriptions in this latter category as "*megilot setarim,*" "scrolls to be sequestered"—a term misunderstood by some later researchers.[10] Unlike official writings, which were often posted on walls, the cultural status of *megilot setarim* was made evident in the fact that they were kept out of the public view and hidden in private recesses [*setarim*].[11]

Rabbinic culture's designation of its own extra-biblical traditions as "Oral Torah" (a subset of *oral matters*)[12] and its assignment of certain inscriptions to the category of "*megilot setarim*" have given rise to a number of erroneous assumptions. One is the radical hypothesis that rabbinic culture's pointed distinction between *written matters* and *oral matters* was articulated as a response to Christianity;[13] another is the claim that rabbinic sources harbored a "hostility toward writing."[14] While it is indeed the case that "Oral Torah" was brandished as a sign of pedigree within a particular polemical context,[15] both of the above-mentioned claims overlook the fact that the rabbinic regulations pertaining to *written matters* and to *oral matters* were formulated within the context of sectarian debates over the definition of the biblical canon. Following the Second Temple's destruction in 70 CE, Jews of disparate theological orientations produced writings that were said to have been divinely inspired, and some sought to integrate them into the corpus of Scripture. It was this expansive impulse that prompted rabbinic Jews to formulate the first of the mirror-image dicta. By asserting that only certain ancient Jewish writings could be "read," which is to say, liturgically chanted, the rabbis made the boundaries of the biblical canon knowable in performative terms. Thus, when the second-century tanna R. ʿAqiva condemned [M. San. 10:1] one who "*qoreh* ["reads"] in 'the external books,'" he did not censure the simple act of reading books of the Apocrypha[16] (those excluded from the scriptural canon by rabbinic Jews), but the act of reading aloud from them with melodic chanting in a liturgical setting.[17] R. ʿAqiva's censure of this public gesture was designed to obviate any lingering confusion about the scriptural canon: the texts in question were distinctly out-of-bounds.

Rabbinic Jews did not deny that Jewish knowledge was produced even after prophetic inspiration had ceased, but they wished to make the non-canonical status of this knowledge dramatically evident. For this reason, they formulated a diametrically opposed rule for the treatment of extra-prophetic knowledge. The observance of these regulations in public practice made the map of Jewish knowledge something other than a purely academic construct, for disparate corpora of tradition were encountered and experienced in different ways. The parallel formulations of these rabbinic dicta also fulfilled another cultural function: by granting *oral matters* equal billing with *written matters*, the dicta themselves accorded considerable authority to the bearers of Oral Torah, the rabbis themselves.

Rabbinic rules not only circumscribed the manner in which *oral matters* were to be transmitted, but also the way in which they could be used: "A tanna of the school of R. Ishmael taught: It is written [Ex. 34:27], '*for according to (the mouth of) these words I have established a covenant with you.*' *These* [scriptural words] you write, but you do not write *halakhot* [legal traditions]. And one who learns from them [*ve-ha-lomed mehem*] receives no reward."[18] The somewhat opaque terms in this passage, "*halakhot*" and "learns from them," are illuminated by a related tannaitic dictum: "The sages taught: We do not learn *halakhah*—not from *mishnah*, nor from *talmud* [a lesson derived from *mishnah*], nor from *ma'aseh* [a practical case] unless they [one's masters] tell him, 'this is an applied law [*halakhah le-ma'aseh*].' If he asked and they told him, 'it is an applied law,' he should go and perform it in practice."[19]

As is clear from this passage, the term "halakhah" was used by ancient rabbis to designate all received legal teachings, and not exclusively (or necessarily) applied law; indeed, the rabbis knew of a variety of *halakhot* that were not to be implemented in practice.[20] Yet even *halakhot* that are devoid of prescriptive import were deemed worthy of investigation, for from antiquity onward, the enterprise of *talmud torah*, the study of tradition, was conceived as a sacred activity, something quite separate from the search for legal guidelines or the adjudication of applied law.[21] On the other hand, only legal traditions designated "*halakhah le-ma'aseh*" prescribe actual practice. As its compound name suggests, a teaching bearing this distinction has been vetted by complementary sources of authority: it is not only a legal tradition ("*halakhah*"), but one whose implementation in practice (*le-ma'aseh*) has been witnessed by a living master.

Sherira Gaon's *Epistle* on the Orality of *Oral Matters*: A View from the Millennium

In the late tenth century, R. Ya'aqov ben Nisim of Qayrawan (today's Tunisia) wrote to the head of the rabbinic academy of Pumbeditha (in Baghdad) asking a series of questions about the origins of Mishnah, Tosefta, and Talmud, foundational corpora of rabbinic Judaism—which the Jews of Qayrawan possessed as written texts.[22] Both the questions they posed (on this occasion and others) and the answer they received reveal that members of their community made assumptions about *oral matters* that the geonim of Babylonia did not share. The reply to their questions, Sherira Gaon's *Epistle* of 987, shaped all subsequent rabbinic notions about the formation and transmission of early extra-scriptural tradition. The *Epistle* circulated in two recensions, designated respectively as "*Ẓorfati*" (or French) and "*Sefardi*" (or Spanish), referring to the lands in which each version predominated. Contemporary geonic scholars regard the "French" recension as the version that most accurately reflects geonic perspectives.[23]

As Sherira makes clear to his questioner, the consolidation of the rabbinic corpora in question—Mishnah, Tosefta, and Talmud—had nothing to do with their inscription. Echoing a tradition that Sa'adya Gaon had voiced a century earlier,[24] Sherira writes that the ancient sages responsible for the creation of these corpora had scrupulously adhered to the rabbinic injunction regulating the treatment of *oral matters*: "And that you wrote: 'How was Mishnah written, and how Talmud?' Talmud and Mishnah were not written, but they were arranged. And the sages were careful to recite them by heart, but not from written versions."[25]

Offering documentary evidence for his claim, Sherira refers his questioners to a talmudic passage which demonstrates that the second-century crafter of the Mishnah, Rabbi Judah the Patriarch, had learned tradition not from any inscribed text, but only through oral instruction. According to the Talmud, after reciting a memorized question pertaining to the extension of Sabbath boundaries,[26] Rabbi Judah had wondered aloud about the spelling of one of its key words. The word *me'abberin*, "extend," he noted, was a homonym[27] whose orthographic variants have subtly different etymological connotations. Spelled one way (with an *'ayin*), it would be related to the word "pregnancy" (*'ibbur*); spelled another way (with an *alef*), it would be a cognate of the word for "limb" (*ever*). Rabbi Judah's uncertainty prompted Sherira to comment on the Patriarch's pedagogic *Sitz im Leben*: such a question, notes Sherira, could only have arisen if Rabbi Judah had never seen the tradition (and the word *me'abberin*) in written form. In other words, writes Sherira, Rabbi Judah (known simply as "Rabbi") had learned this question about the extension of the Sabbath boundaries by listening to it as an oral teaching:

> Our Mishnah says [M. Eruv. 5:1], "How are the [Sabbath boundaries of] cities *extended*?" And we say [BT Eruv. 53b], Rabbi said: "Who is there to inquire of the Judeans, who are meticulous about

> language, whether our Mishnah teaches *ma-avrin* [from the word 'limb'] or *me-'abberin* [from the word 'pregnancy']?" . . . Which is to say that even Rabbi himself, who arranged the Mishnah, was uncertain how we recite it . . . From this we hear that it was said in this language in Rabbi's presence. There were some who recited it in this manner, and some who recited it that way.[28]

Sherira's analysis of this passage displays the type of historicist insight associated with later humanists of early modern Europe. Through close reading, he was able to reconstruct two important points: (a) lexical ambiguity arose because tradition had been relayed solely through oral transmission. At the same time, (b) uncertainty about which of two homonyms was intended had no bearing on the passage's semantic or legal meaning.

Sensing that his Qayrawanese interlocutors did not fully grasp the ideology that had motivated rabbinic sages to orally preserve and transmit copious amounts of tradition, Sherira pointedly emphasized the overriding commitment to oral transmission that had prevailed over a millennium of rabbinic history. Prior to the year 70 CE, wrote Sherira, extra-scriptural tradition had been transmitted in oral, face-to-face encounters between masters and pupils, without the mediation of any written text. Moreover, only deeper meanings of Torah were transmitted orally to these early rabbinic sages:

> For those Early Ones[29] who were before the Destruction of the Temple had no need for this,[30] since it was Torah of the mouth [*torat peh*] and its known meanings were not said to them, as is the case with Written Torah; rather, they gathered meanings in their hearts [orally].[31]

The earliest sages refrained from standardizing their teachings because it was unnecessary. They had, Sherira claimed, "no need to link matters [in standardized concatenations, in order] that they be recited in one [single standardized] formulation."[32] Indeed, Sherira explained, in earlier times, the sequence of teachings varied from one master to the next,[33] with each freely transmitting oral teachings to his students in an unscripted manner, "in the words that he strung together at that moment" and as he saw fit.[34] "Each one teaches them to his students like one who talks with his friend, in whatever formulation he likes."[35]

Sherira's *Epistle* emphasized that early sages used this latitude in formulation in order to address the pedagogic needs of each student:

> This is how it was in the beginning: Just as we today explain our [own] explanations [so], each and every one of the sages, as he saw it, would teach all his students, each one as needed and in accord with his capabilities. There were some to whom he said [transmitted] topic headings and principles, and the rest he [the student] would understand on his own. And for others it was necessary to spell things out plainly and to draw comparisons for them.[36]

Notwithstanding the fact that the students of early sages were exposed to divergent oral formulations of the *mishnayyot*, the meanings they gleaned, claimed Sherira, "amounted to the same thing."[37] Thus, for example, all students in these early generations agreed on which decisions were unanimous and which disputed; which teachings were those of individuals and which were teachings of the many.[38] Still, because each master had his own way of transmitting the traditions of the *mishnayyot*, the insights derived from them varied. Sheira noted that these insights, referred to collectively as "*talmud*"—literally, "that which is derived from study"—had been a fixture of rabbinic instruction even before the Temple's destruction: "*Talmud* is the wisdom of the Early Ones who used it to explain the meanings of the *mishnah*."[39]

Staking out a theme that would command considerable attention in writings of medieval Sefardim,[40] Sherira makes the commonsense observation that when tannaim, sages who flourished prior to the year 200, used the term "*talmud*," they must have been referring to something other than the corpus of that name, since the latter contains teachings by named sages who lived as late as the sixth century. (Indeed, Sherira adduced several examples in order to impress this upon his Qayrawanese questioners.)[41] And since each early sage transmitted tannaitic traditions using somewhat different formulations, there were comparable variations in the formulations of *talmud*, in the lessons derived from them: "The studies of each student occurred in the presence of his [own] master. And before the Mishnah was arranged, the *talmud* of each and every one accorded his *mishnah*."[42]

Elaborating on these differences, Sherira alludes to the teaching style that prevailed in the geonic academies of his own time. His comment testifies to the fact that Talmud was not a lexically fixed corpus in the second-to-last decade of the tenth century.

> Those Early Ones [who flourished] up to the death of Rabbi did not recite in one [single] formulation, but rather, the way that we, today, explain matters and the like to our students, all of whom learn it. This is how they would explain their *mishnayyot* and they called their explanations "*talmud.*"[43]

The Qayrawanese questioners had asked Sherira why the Mishnah contains so many more teachings by later tannaim, and why there is relatively little mention of earlier ones. He explained that "Early Ones" had no need to spell out all the implications and ramifications of a given teaching, because "their hearts were broad and they needed only principles."[44] Their restraint did not mean that early sages were unfamiliar with all the nuances of a tradition teased out and articulated by later sages. On the contrary, asserted Sherira, earlier sages had already possessed all the insights articulated by later sages, but only the latter had felt the need to formulate them. "Not that the Early Ones did not know this, but [rather,] what? They left room for those who came after them to distinguish themselves. For the world did not need this in their days."[45] In warning students not to mistake changes in the formulation of *oral matters* for changes (or innovation) in the content of *oral matters*,[46] Sherira affirmed that while the packaging of tradition changes over time, the content of tradition does not change.

According to Sherira, oral transmission and the private inscription of talmudic insights continued in rabbinic classrooms up until the turn of the third century. At that time, Rabbi Judah the Patriarch ["Rabbi"] became alarmed by manifestations of cultural decline that had been set in motion by the Temple's destruction two generations earlier: "When Rabbi saw that there were so many differences in the *mishnayyot* of the sages, in spite of the fact that their meanings all came out to the same thing—he was concerned lest it not work out and some loss might come from it." In order to convey Rabbi Judah's fear that tradition would be forgotten, Sherira invoked a number of rabbinic tropes lamenting the loss of erudition and decline in mnemonic ability:

> For he saw that the heart was being diminished and that [BT Sot. 49b] the wellsprings of wisdom were being stopped up, and that the

> Prince of Torah[47] was leaving. And like that which we say [YT Demai 1:3], "If the Early Ones are angels, we are humans. And if the Early Ones are humans, we are donkeys." And like that which R. Yoḥanan said [BT Eruv. 53a], "The hearts of the Early Ones were like the opening of the [Temple's] Great Hall [*ulam*], the Later Ones like the opening of the [Temple's smaller] Sanctuary [*heikhal*]." And we say [there], "The fingernail of the Early Ones is greater than the bellies of the Later Ones."[48]

In order to staunch the loss of knowledge, Rabbi Judah created an official *ḥibbur*, literally, a "composition" or "concatenation." This work, the Mishnah, standardized the formulation of the legal traditions (*mishnayyot*) that had been transmitted, until then, in diverse, and equally valid, formulations.[49]

> And he [Rabbi Judah] agreed to arrange the halakhah that all recited—that it be in one voice and one formulation, and not that each and every one should recite the language to himself [as he pleased].[50]

According to Sherira, standardization of the language of tradition did nothing to alter the taxonomic status of *oral matters*. For whether or not Rabbi Judah's Mishnah was written down (a point over which the *Epistle*'s two recensions diverge),[51] his *ḥibbur* was too tersely worded to be taught without oral elaboration: "for Rabbi Judah recalled . . . their main points, and did not lay out examples."[52]

Indeed, writes Sherira, until the end of his life, Rabbi Judah demonstrated by personal example that Mishnah was to be transmitted in face-to-face encounters, as was appropriate in relaying *oral matters*: "And after it [Mishnah] was arranged, throughout the days of Rabbi, he would explain to each one the Mishnah, and teach his pupils their meanings."[53] In other words, Judah the Patriarch's imposition of lexical standardization did nothing to alter the oral transmission of this (now scripted) body of tradition or to affect its taxonomic status as a corpus of *oral matters*.

The Ideology and Strategies of Oral Transmission: Sherira's Reconstruction

Sherira made a concerted attempt to illuminate a cultural outlook that was alien to the Jews of Qayrawan, a community that relied on the written text of Talmud as a source of authority.[54] Invoking rabbinic traditions known to his North African correspondents, he pointedly chose ones that valorized the cultivation of memory, idolized living repositories of tradition, and endorsed the discipleship model of instruction. The overarching aim of rabbinic education, after all, was to fashion scholars who might become links in the chain of tradition. Those who internalized the copious body of received knowledge and who could retrieve and apply the appropriate teaching to address any life circumstance were, in effect, embodiments of tradition.[55]

Along with other cultures of late antiquity that celebrated mnemonic prowess, Jews paid tribute to scholars who were distinguished by their prodigious powers of retention. Like their Greek, Roman, and Christian counterparts, tannaim and amoraim likened such people to harvesters, sponges, plastered cisterns, baskets full of books, and even Sinai itself, the source of all sacred knowledge.[56] The sage most valued in society was not the one who applied logic most adeptly in order to ferret out implicit information, but the one who had internalized the treasures of tradition and embodied its plenitude. Sherira portrays this as an emblematic bias of rabbinic culture:

> And even though the one who could recite did not know how to engage in the casuistic extraction of some *novum* or [of a] ramification that he had not explicitly recited, [and] did not know how to create analogies and to foreground its underlying principles [of the passage recited]—nonetheless, *he* was preferable to the one who could engage in casuistry and reason, [but who] had not learned that which was recited and that which was said. For the one who *had* learned could teach these matters of those which he heard, *halakhah le-ma'aseh* [as applied law]. And the one who [merely] reasoned could not.[57]

Seeking to impress this cultural hierarchy on his correspondents, Sherira cited a decision made hundreds of years earlier, when a vacancy at the head of the talmudic academy had necessitated a search for the ideal leader. One candidate, Rava, was a dialectician whose powers of textual analysis had earned him the epithet "uprooter of mountains"; the other candidate, Yosef, was renowned or his erudition and graced with the epithet "Sinai." In order to drive home a larger point about epistemological priorities, Sherira reconstructs this pivotal fourth-century showdown:

> For this reason, when they had the problem, which of the two [candidates] was preferable? [After all,] the world needs Rava, who is *the*

> *uprooter of mountains*, and R. Yosef, who is *Sinai*, for it is said that he applied to himself [Prov. 14:4], '*a rich harvest comes through the strength of the ox.*' They sent from there: *Sinai* is preferable, since all need the master of wheat.[58]

The point of this episode—echoed elsewhere in geonic writings[59]—is clear: without command of the "stuff" of tradition, dialectical refraction or analysis is impossible.

Sherira draws attention to certain oral-memorial strategies that had enabled earlier sages to acquire knowledge, retain it, and expedite its retrieval from memory.[60] One of these was regular review of one's learning, even when there was no need to apply it in a practical context:[61] "In each and every one of those generations . . . they would arrange them continually, as we say [BT Ber. 35a; Ḥul. 86b], 'R. Ḥiyya bar Abba would arrange his talmud before R. Yoḥanan every thirty days.' And we also say [BT Pes. 68b], 'Rav Sheshet would arrange his *talmud* every 30 days, and he would stand and lean at the doorway and exclaim, *Rejoice, O my soul. For you I read [Scripture], for you have I recited [Mishnah].*' "[62]

Another ancient strategy, use of audible vocalization during study to strengthen the imprint on memory,[63] is illustrated in a talmudic account of how R. Judah the Patriarch was able to reclaim knowledge that he had forgotten during an illness.[64] Recounting this anecdote in his *Epistle*, Sherira writes that after R. Judah had studied all thirteen "facets" of Mishnah, seven of which he taught to R. Ḥiyya,

> Rabbi got sick, and they were uprooted from him. Then R. Ḥiyya reviewed before him the seven he had learned. But the other six facets were gone. There was this launderer who would listen to Rabbi when he would recite them. R. Ḥiyya went to the launderer, learned them from him and established them, and then restored them to Rabbi. When Rabbi saw the launderer he said to him: 'You made me and R. Ḥiyya.' And some say that he said, 'You made Rav Ḥiyya and Rav Ḥiyya made me.' "[65]

Sherira also emphasizes the importance of arranging oral traditions in succinct and well-crafted formulations for mnemonic ease. Explaining why Rabbi Judah the Patriarch had chosen the formulation written for private use by Rabbi Meir (rather than the formulation of another student) as the basis of the standardized Mishnah, Sherira notes that R. Meir's words were distinguished by their brevity and general stylistic excellence:

> In the matter of *halakhot*, Rabbi Judah took the way of Rabbi Meir, which was the way of Rabbi 'Aqiva [R. Meir's teacher]—since he saw that it was succinct and easy to learn.[66] And its matters were linked in an elegant concatenation, each and every matter with that which was similar to it [and] far more precise than [the ways of] all the [other] tannaim. And there was no excess verbiage in them; each and every word achieves its meaning without saying unnecessary synonyms, and without anything lacking in their information, except in a few places. Great and wondrous things are in each and every word. Not every wise person knows how to compose in this manner, as it is written [Prov. 16:11], "[*A man may arrange his thoughts, but*] *what one says depends on God.*"[67]

The *Epistle*'s reference to the "elegant concatenation" celebrates R. Meir's compositional skill, his ability to preserve tradition by binding it in memorable patterns.[68] The ease with which stored material can be retrieved and accessed depends upon the creation of mnemonic links that are clear and compelling. Rabbi Meir's formulation of tannaitic teachings lent itself to oral instruction—and easy recall—because its chain of associations made sense; he had linked its many subjects to one another in ways that drew upon their affinities [*kol davar ve-davar 'im ma she-domeh lo*]. In updating R. Meir's formulation, writes Sherira, Rabbi Judah created a similarly elegant, thoughtfully arranged construction.[69] In this sense, the Mishnah was a *ḥibbur*—literally a work of *catenae*, or links, bound together in a pattern that lent itself to memorization and to easy retrieval.

Like their counterparts in other cultures of late antiquity, rabbinic teachers trained students to create mental cubbyholes that would correspond to ideational, rhetorical, or numeric categories; not surprisingly, the images of mnemonic organization that pervade tannaitic and amoraic teachings—like "rings," "rooms," and "honeycombs"—parallel those found in contemporaneous pagan and Christian sources.[70] If a student was to retrieve the apt tradition at the appropriate time, he would need to store it properly when it was first "harvested." Proper storage required the construction of a durable system of mental filing, predicated on careful sorting and arrangement of the bounty. Sherira highlights the special acclaim reserved for the sage who could organize vast quantities of received tradition by ordering and binding it into clusters:[71]

> "Our sages praised one who learns his Mishnah well, for to him are revealed the meanings of Torah. . . . Like that tradition [BT San. 42a]: R. Aḥa bar Ḥaninah said, R. Ami said, R. Asi said, R. Yoḥanan said: Why does Scripture say [Prov. 24:6], '*For with wise advice* [*taḥbulot*] *you shall make your war*?' In whom do you find [skill] of Torah's battle? In the one who has in his possession bundles [*ḥavilot*] of mishnah."[72]

The Oral Transmission of *Oral Matters* in Geonic Culture

Sherira drew upon ancient rabbinic literature in glorifying oral transmission and its strategies, but, in expressing these attitudes, he was also endorsing the outlook that prevailed in the Babylonian academies. Sar Shalom, gaon of Sura in the mid-ninth century, emphasized that responsiveness to students' learning styles was possible only in face-to-face instruction. Only then could the teacher tailor content and pace to the needs of the learner, discern his errors in comprehension and correct them, anticipate his questions and answer them. Responding to a student's written inquiry, Sar Shalom lamented the inadequacy of learning by correspondence: "If . . . you were before us, it would be possible to explain them very well, and distinguish between one and another, like [Prov. 25:11] *a word fitly spoken*. For when a student sits before his master and discusses a matter of law, his master perceives the trend of his thoughts, and what he has overlooked and what is clear to him, and what stubbornly eludes him, and explains to him until his eyes light up. . . . but in writing, how much is possible?"[73] And in another responsum of the tenth century, Gaon Aaron Sarjado asserted that the vocal inflection—declarative or interrogative—appropriate to a particular tradition was known through the teachers' recitation: "Whatever the students know is from the mouths of their rabbis, and most of them don't know what a book is."[74]

Even when later geonim made adjustments in order to accommodate the needs of Jewish communities far from Baghdad (as discussed below), they nonetheless remained committed to the oral transmission of *oral matters*[75] and strove to uphold the tannaitic stricture against "speaking" from inscriptions of *oral matters*, in keeping with the locution "*i atta rashai le-omran bikhtav.*"

Like their rabbinic predecessors, geonim employed tannaim for the transmission of Mishnah, "repeaters" who played the role of human tape recorders.[76] Geonim also relayed talmudic traditions through oral instruction, not from text. They seem to have done so by imparting tradition in two distinct stages, a practice that may have originated with the amoraim.[77] In the first stage, students memorized the *oral matters* in question by repeatedly reciting lessons taught by their teachers (who did not consult texts). In the second stage, where students practiced "opening up" or "exposing" the memorized traditions, they posed questions about the material in question in order to exhaustively grasp its meanings and ramifications.[78] This, too, was was done without consultation of any inscribed text. An allusion to these two stages of instruction appears in Sherira Gaon's reference to the instructional roles played by his son at the Pumbeditha academy. Speaking of the future Hai Gaon, Sherira write that his son was diligent in "putting [the traditions] in their mouths—and in teaching the students to pose objections/questions [*qushiyyot*]."[79]

Geonic-era writings distinguish the "recitation" of the talmudic tractate, an activity denoted by the verb *g-r-s* [chew, or ruminate], and the "exposure" of the tractate, denoted by the verb *g-l-y* [expose or uncover]. Describing the biennial *kallah* convocations of rabbinic scholars held at the yeshivot, Sherira Gaon refers to the tractate that was the current focus of study as one that was being "recited," and to the tractate that would be the focus of the following convocation as the one that was to be "uncovered":

> We gather the leaders and the wise men at each and every convocation, and recite the tractate of that convocation and expose another tractate, and assign chapters and grasp the fence that it not be splintered, and are aided by God our Lord.[80]

"Exposure" of the subsequent tractate to be studied may have entailed preparing students for their next subject by discussing the tractate's topics and raising questions to be borne in mind.[81]

* * *

Toward the end of the geonic period, the heads of the Baghdad academies acknowledged that it was impossible to abide by the tannaitic dicta in their own times. "Now that the heart has become diminished, and everybody needs to consult written versions, we say [cf. BT Tem. 14b], *better that one letter of the Torah be uprooted [than that the entire Torah be forgotten].*"[82] Indeed, a particular tannaitic ruling was updated—presumably because of the growing prominence of inscribed texts of *oral matters*. Where the Talmud had asserted that inscriptions of prayers and *halakhot* were not to be saved from a (non-life-threatening) conflagration on the Sabbath,[83] the geonim ruled differently: "We save books of aggadah and of Talmud, for it is now permitted to write them all."[84] This accommodation, explained Hai Gaon, was a concession to forgetfulness: "The stricture against writing *halakhot* no longer applies because hearts have become diminished and we need the written version. Therefore it is good to write *halakhot*."[85] In fact, certain late geonim—Sa'adya (882–942), Samuel ben Ḥofni Gaon (d. 1034), and Hai Gaon (939–1038)—did compose monographs on discrete topics of Jewish law. Apart from these works (whose status will be discussed below), there were also *nusḥaot*, inscriptions of Talmud, in the geonic academies;[86] their quality, noted Sherira Gaon, varied greatly.[87]

If none of the above-mentioned evidence deterred Sherira Gaon from asserting in his *Epistle*, without qualification, that *oral matters* were relayed only through oral transmission, this may have been because scholars in the geonic environment regarded halakhic monographs on discrete topics, and even *nusḥaot* of Talmud, as inscriptions that fell below the radar screen of "formal writing." Only such an assumption would explain why, in one scholar's words, Sherira was "apparently . . . unaware of the need . . . to bridge the discrepancy between a postulated oral transmission and the written literary corpus which existed in his own time."[88]

Yaakov Elman and Dafna Ephrat drew attention to the fact that the geonic yeshivot zealously guarded oral transmission of *oral matters* at a time when broader Baghdadi culture increasingly privileged the authority of the written word over that of oral testimony.[89] The manufacture of paper in the Middle East, beginning in the mid-eighth century,[90] had a dramatic impact on the broader culture in which the yeshivot flourished. A paper mill was established in Baghdad in 794, and by the late ninth century Baghdad boasted private libraries established by wealthy patrons, *Suq al Warraqin*, a book market with more than one hundred bookstalls, and *Bayt 'al-Hikma*, a government-funded library. Like the later stationers of medieval Paris, scribes and copyists in Baghdad prepared some manuscripts in bulk copies, though they also made single copies on demand.[91] The cultural value ascribed to writing was apparent not only in the growing availability of written texts, but also in society's growing reliance on them. A select collection of *ahadith*, oral traditions about the Prophet Mohammed's behavior and teachings, was compiled in the *Muwatta* of Malik ibn Anas in the eighth century, and other compilations of *ahadith* were committed to writing and disseminated in topically arranged form (*musannaf*) beginning in the early ninth century.[92] A pioneering work on Islamic legal theory composed at this time set out to define the interpretive methodologies and epistemological sources of Islamic law.[93]

Local Jews of the scholarly class were not insulated from these technological, economic, social, intellectual, and compositional developments. Like their educated Muslim counterparts, they cultivated behaviors and styles that conformed to the ideals of *adab*, literate culture. Certain exilarchs and geonim even participated—as representatives of the Jews—in official *majlis* debates with members of other faiths on topics of theological import.[94] Yet, for quite awhile, neither familiarity with broader environmental patterns nor recognition that Jews far from Baghdad needed legal guidance led the Babylonian geonim to break with a longstanding cultural pattern of oral transmission. Indeed, even when geonim permitted the inscription of certain *oral matters* (namely, prayers and lists of *halakhot*), they nonetheless made strenuous efforts to avoid committing talmudic teachings to writing. Elman and Ephrat portrayed this stance as an act of "conscious resistance" on the part of the geonim; they argued that the geonim were intentionally parsimonious about sharing the Talmud in writing because this enabled them to retain monopolistic control of legal authority.[95]

While it is true that geonim often tailored their explanations to what they thought their correspondents could grasp,[96] the assumption that they withheld talmudic information appears to be predicated on the unproven assumption that geonim "should have" adjudicated on the basis of Talmud, as did later rabbinic adjudicators. It is this assumption—a retrojection, I would argue, from attitudes and practices that only became prevalent in the Middle Ages—that deserves reexamination. Questioners who consulted with the geonim were not always seeking to to align their lives with the dictates of the talmudic text;[97] at least in the earlier geonic period, some sought guidance about how to live Jewishly, asking questions such as, "How should we pray?"[98] Moreover (as will be seen), when questioners did seek to align their lives with talmudic dictate and turned to the yeshivot for guidance, geonim (over several centuries) actually responded by championing the authority vested in the community over that of the talmudic text.[99] In other words, contemporary amazement at manifestations of geonic independence vis-à-vis amoraic predecessors may stem from the unspoken (or unexamined) assumption that Jews had always regarded the Talmud, in its unalloyed state, as the preeminent source of legal authority. Yet this perspective seems to have been a product of post-geonic medieval Jewish culture. The geonic stance vis-à-vis Talmud only appears to be radical when viewed anachronistically, that is, when it is evaluated with reference to a perspective that only came to prevail later.[100]

This is not to ignore or deny the fact that the geonim articulated new adjudicatory principles (*kelalei pesiqa*); more than seventy new geonic rules have been identified as supplements to those set forth in the Talmud itself.[101] Yet if the heads of the Baghdadi academies were thinking about ways in which the talmudic text could yield legal guidance, the very scattered and non-comprehensive way in which they formulated these principles of adjudication[102] suggests that the transposition of Talmud into a corpus of decided law was not a concerted part of the geonic agenda.

Finally, the fact that geonic status and power were aggrandized when Jews throughout the world sought legal guidance from the yeshivot does not mean that the academy leaders had sought to foster such reliance as part of a premeditated (Machiavellian) policy. Their reticence about sharing talmudic teachings may be seen as an organic expression of geonic adherence to the tannaitic dicta pertaining to the transmission and use of *oral matters*. Thus, for example, during study sessions in the academies, greater weight was always ascribed to a *girsa*, a version of a talmudic tradition heard directly from the mouth of a master, and less weight to a *nusḥa*, a written version of a tradition. The axiological priority of orally transmitted traditions was reflected in the sequence of citation: variant oral versions were adduced prior to variant written versions.[103] Inscriptions were ultimately of some utility, but they were perceived more as ephemera and not deemed as trustworthy as recensions known by heart. According to the geonim, authority did not reside in the texts of tradition, but only in its living tradents.

Corrollaries of Oral Transmission in Geonic Culture

Reliance on the authority of human transmitters of tradition (rather than texts) goes hand in hand with a particular cultural understanding of literary anonymity. When asked by the Qayrawanese why the names of the earliest tannaitic sages were not preserved in the rabbinic corpora, whereas those of later generations are mentioned in great numbers, Sherira explained that anonymity was an indicator of unanimity: where all are in agreement about a given matter, it may be asserted without ascription to any individual.[104] In other words, a work's authorlessness and/or anonymity can be seen as a sign of cultural health, for it testifies to the absence of dissent. And just as the trustworthiness of tradition (or one of its units) is inseparable from its status as a collective inheritance, the ascription of a teaching to a particular figure marks it as one that had not been endorsed by *consensus omnium.*[105]

Building on the principle of consensus, Sherira's comments on anonymity and ascription certainly evoke contemporaneous Islamic notions of *ijma'*, the consensus of scholars, but they may also have been inherited from earlier rabbis and conditioned by the pressures of Karaite polemic. When, in the twelfth century, Maimonides defended his *Mishneh Torah* against the charge that he had failed to ascribe cited teachings, he portrayed this omission as a consciously adopted tactic. Writing to Rabbi Pinḥas, *dayyan* [judge] in the Alexandrian Jewish community, Maimonides explained that he had purposefully omitted the names of the sages responsible for promulgating various laws lest identification of each by name play into the hands of Karaite critics: "For this reason, I have chosen not to leave room for the heretics to prevail, who after all, say, 'You [Rabbanites] rely on the words of [mere] individuals.' But this is not so, but rather, thousands and tens of thousands from thousands and tens of thousands. . . . And my aim and intention was that each halakhah would be encountered without attribution, to say that it is [reflects] the words of all."[106] It is possible that earlier Karaites (of Sherira's time) also perceived the predilection for anonymity as a trademark of Rabbanite literary culture.[107]

The *Epistle*'s untroubled reference to the correction of difficulties encountered in inscribed texts of Mishnah may disturb modern readers who would view this activity as tampering with a sacred text: "Wherever we find something distorted in the Mishnah, and need to erase from it a difficulty that doesn't come out right, we say, 'erase from here such and such' . . . And if something is excess in our Mishnah, we remove it. . . . And if it requires ordering, we order it. And if there is a distortion in [the formulation of] our Mishnah, and the *beraita* is preferable, we clarify the matter."[108] It is not clear whether Sherira was speaking only of the amoraim or was including himself in this first-person formulation—but either way, the passage affirms that those responsible for transmitting tradition must correct errors that they detect.

A similar claim had been sounded earlier by Sa'adya Gaon, notwithstanding his break with the reigning pattern of literary anonymity, and his introduction of the *ḥibbur* model of writing into rabbinic culture.[109] Because Sa'adya conceived of tradition as a collective treasure, he invited "shareholders" to improve on its literary presentation.[110] In a direct address to his readers—from his (new!) authorial vantage point[111]—Sa'adya implored them to correct any mistakes they might find in his philosophical treatise:

> I also adjure by God, Creator of the Universe, any scholar who, upon studying this book, sees in it a mistake, that he correct it. Or should he note an abstruse phrase, that he substitute for it a more felicitous one. Let him not feel restrained therefrom by the fact that the book is not his work, or that I had anticipated him in explaining what had not been clear to him. For the wise have a tender solicitude for wisdom, entertaining for it a sympathy similar to that entertained for one another by members of the same family, as Scripture says, [Prov. 7:4], "*Say to Wisdom, you are my sister.*" Although the fools, too, are devoted to their folly and are loathe to forsake it, as Scripture says [Job 20:13], *"He saves it and does not let it go."*[112]

Sa'adya's remarkable invitation to readers to improve upon his work should be seen against the backdrop of Arabic literary culture which, at that time, was preoccupied with scribal error, unauthorized borrowings, and outright plagiarism.[113] A distinguished roster of geonic and later Jewish scholars in the Andalusian cultural orbit echoed Sa'adya's request that readers share in the production and transmission of truth; some even invited readers to add their own insights before transmitting the manuscript to others.[114] Nobody who produced a written work, author or compiler, named or unnamed, had a monopoly on wisdom; the effort to "get it right" was understood to be a collective effort.

Geonim immersed in a pedagogic environment that guarded oral transmission knew from their own experience that when traditions were handed down in unwritten form over long periods of time, tradents and copyists alike introduced alterations for such (laudatory) purposes as clarification, concatenation, and harmonization. Awareness that this was an inevitable corollary of oral transmission informed Sa'adya Gaon's keen historicist observation that a similar process had affected passages of Scripture that had been orally transmitted, over a long period of time, before their consignment to writing. Commenting on the term "*he-'etiqu*," "they copied"—or "they moved from place to place"—in Proverbs 25:1, "*These too are proverbs of Solomon which the men of King Hezekiah of Judah copied*," Sa'adya Gaon noted,

> The words of this book teach us that our ancestors transmitted many matters from one to another over time in unwritten form, until they were [finally] written afterward. For it is said explicitly that these proverbs were said by Solomon, peace be upon him, and that they remained unwritten over the course of time until the men of Hezekiah wrote them.[115]

In the Introduction to his commentary on *Sefer Yeẓira*, Sa'adya explicitly compares the circumstances under which the Written and Oral Torah were transmitted:

> These [matters, the teachings of *Sefer Yeẓira*, articulated by the patriarch Abraham] did not cease to be transmitted in the midst of our nation in their unwritten form, just as the Mishnah was transmitted when it was not written. And even some of Scripture remained, for many years, transmitted, but not written, like [Prov. 25:1] "*proverbs of Solomon which the men of King Hezekiah of Judah copied.*"[116]

This assertion about the literary formation of Scripture is notably untroubled; Sa'adya's candor and directness in making this comment contrasts sharply with the patent discomfort evinced by later scholars who felt constrained to veil comparable historicist insights.[117] Along with other Jewish scholars of Byzantium, sages of early Ashkenaz, and rabbinic thinkers in the Islamic orbit prior to the time of Maimonides,[118] Sa'adya carefully distinguished between the sacred content of tradition and its historically contingent formulations.

Sherira's *Epistle* on the Inimitability of Mishnah

A single leitmotif—the fear that tradition might be lost—shapes the *Epistle*'s description of both Mishnah and of Talmud.[119] Yet nothing Sherira says about Talmud (or Tosefta) in the *Epistle* parallels his encomiastic portrait of the Mishnah's creation.[120] Mishnah is portrayed as the premeditated compilation of one individual, while Talmud is portrayed as an unauthored corpus of far less orchestrated formulation.

According to Sherira, a confluence of rare circumstances—and, above all, divine assistance—contributed to the inimitable qualities (and powers) of the mishnaic corpus. To begin with, its agent, Rabbi Judah the Patriarch, was uniquely endowed:

> Heaven bestowed upon Rabbi, at one and the same time, His Torah and grandeur. For all those years [of R. Judah's leadership], all those generations were subject to him. As they say [BT Git. 59a], . . . "From the days of Moses until Rabbi, we never found Torah and grandeur in one place."[121]

According to Sherira, the time in which the Mishnah's standardization took place was unusually fortuitous: "In those days, the sages rested from all destruction, because of [the Roman Emperor] Antoninus's compassion for him [Rabbi Judah]."[122] Under the leadership of Rabbi Judah the Patriarch, there was even a miraculous restoration of the intellectual clarity that had prevailed in bygone generations.

> And in the days of Rabbi, it came to pass that the words of our Mishnah were as if they had been said from the mouth of the Almighty. And they seemed like *a sign and a witness* [Isa. 19: 20]. And Rabbi did not compose these from his heart, but from the matters which some of the Early Ones had been reciting before him.[123]

This marked a distinct reversal in a trend that had begun earlier, for when the students of Hillel and Shammai failed to fulfill their obligations as disciples, disputes proliferated in the rabbinic academies. Now, several generations later, claims Sherira, all scholars saw eye to eye.[124] With divine assistance, Rabbi Judah the Patriarch and his rabbinic cohort regained the sense of certainty and lucid comprehension of *oral matters* that sages living prior to the Destruction had possessed. "And [because] heaven helped them, the meanings of Torah were as clear to them as *halakhah le-Moshe mi-Sinai*. And there was no division nor dispute."[125] Moreover, writes Sherira, were it not for divine intervention, the Mishnah could never have attained its linguistic perfection and semantic power:

> Had Rabbi wished to say everything that was taught, the matters would have been long and [ultimately become] uprooted.[126] But Rabbi only arranged the principles of matters, so that even from a single matter one might learn several principles and terse formulations and great and wondrous meanings and numerous details. For our Mishnah was said with the aid of heaven.[127]

Ultimately, the most compelling evidence of the Mishnah's wondrousness was that it was accepted by all Israel. According to Sherira, Rabbi Judah's standardization of *oral matters* spread immediately[128] and was received to unanimous acclaim. The Mishnah's most effective marketing agent was its own linguistic, organizational, and stylistic perfection; other formulations of *oral matters* simply could not compete with such a compelling product.

> And when everyone saw the beauty of the Mishnah's arrangement and the truth of its meanings and the precision of the words, they abandoned all those [other] *mishnayyot* that they had been reciting. And these *halakhot* spread throughout Israel and became our *halakhot*. And all the others were abandoned, and became, for example, *beraita*,[129] which one hears and analyzes as an interpretation or an auxiliary remark. But Israel relies on these *halakhot* and all Israel accepted them with faith, once they saw them. And no one differs with this.[130]

In enumerating the many "signs" that point, singly and collectively, to the Mishnah's miraculousness, and in repeatedly asserting that Rabbi Judah had benefitted from divine assistance, Sherira makes claims about the Mishnah that parallel (and imitate) Muslim claims about the Qur'an. The doctrine of *I'jāz*, or "inimitability," refers to the qur'anic document itself: The literary and stylistic perfection of this written text constitutes incontrovertible proof of its divine origin. According to this doctrine, elaborated by the Mu'tazilites, scholastic theologians of Islam, the qur'anic text itself is incapable of imitation—because it is a paragon of eloquence and a work of unparalleled rhetorical genius, formulated with consummate economy. The Qur'an's superlative literary standards render all other literary aspirants impotent and speechless.

Little wonder, asserted the theologians, that the Qur'an came to be accepted by the consensus of all Muslims. The doctrine of *i'jāz* acquired its technical meaning in the mid-ninth century, but was still being elaborated in Sherira's time.[131]

The *Epistle*'s emphasis on the Mishnah's miraculous nature (unparalleled in any remarks about the Talmud's etiology, style, or reception) suggests that Sherira was either involved in "sacralizing" the text of Mishnah or in reaffirming an already extant tradition about its literary perfection and inimitability that put this text off-limits to any criticisms or improvements. Such an undertaking may have been seen as necessary to parry Karaite critiques, on the one hand, and Muslim critiques on the other.[132] The *Epistle*'s special arguments about the Mishnah may also be a testimony to the fixed language of this corpus (and to Sherira's consciousness of its fixity) at a time when the language of Talmud had not yet acquired a comparable measure of stability.[133] In this sense, the discrepancy between Sherira's portraits of the two works offers a valuable snapshot of a particular historical moment in the formation of rabbinic literary culture, one whose accuracy has been corroborated in recent scholarship.[134] Brody has suggested that the variant formulations of talmudic traditions that circulated in geonic times[135] might best be understood as "reflecting different oral 'versions' and 'performances' of a single recension."[136] While the geonic variants of this corpus possessed a stable "dialogic skeleton," the Talmud they knew still exhibited considerable lexical latitude, and it continued to be reworded through the geonic period, the middle of the eleventh century.[137] Writing in 987, Sherira could hardly have articulated any claims about the Talmud's linguistic and stylistic inimitability.

How Geonim Used and Did Not Use the Talmud

In a spatial, as well as cultural sense, the geonim of the Iraqi yeshivot who "sat on the chair of Rav Ashi" were the heirs of the amoraim whose traditions were preserved in Talmud, and they portrayed themselves as such.[138] Their access to traditions transmitted by earlier generations was the source of geonic cultural authority, and the academy heads disseminated the Babylonian Talmud to Jews living in far-flung communities. For all this, modern scholars have been struck by the temperate, even half-hearted way in which geonim marketed Talmud. They explained obscure words in the Talmud, analyzed the structure of textual units, and attempted to establish which version among many was correct,[139] but geonic engagement in talmudic exegesis was limited.[140] Indeed, the geonim continued to comfortably showcase divergent formulations of amoraic tradition—even in situations where these had bearing on the legal outcome of the matter at hand.[141] Moreover, while geonim quoted Talmud in their applied legal rulings, they did not present Talmud as a stand-alone source of prescriptive authority. As discussed below, they understood Talmud to be authoritative in tandem with living testimony.[142]

Geonim related to talmudic traditions in a decidedly more cavalier manner than they did to those of Mishnah.[143] When asked about the textual basis for certain laws, geonim occasionally ignored talmudic interpretations outright; in other cases, they used Mishnah in ways that deviated from the approaches of the amoraim.[144] And when geonim adduced talmudic passages, they did not always select the most relevant ones. They disagreed freely with amoraic predecessors and, from time to time, noted that they were in possession of a tradition declaring that a particular amoraic teaching did not correspond to halakhah.[145] Brody summed up the geonic relationship to the amoraim by noting that the geonim did not subscribe to any "doctrine of binding precedents—even with respect to the Talmud."[146]

The seemingly independent stance that the geonim brought to their encounter with the talmudic text is startling when compared with later rabbinic attitudes and practices (explored in Chapters 2 and 4). Yet when seen in its proper historical and "compositional" context, the geonic reliance on extra-talmudic traditions is more easily understood. Since legal deliberations in the Talmud (with the exception of some late interpolations) are generally presented as unresolved disputes, the geonim, of necessity, had to invoke interpretive traditions they had received from their teachers in order to arrive at legal decisions. In their unalloyed form, the legal traditions transmitted in Talmud could not serve as the sole source of applied law.

I would suggest, however, that the importance of extra-talmudic traditions in the geonic decision-making process was not simply a concession necessitated by the Talmud's ambiguities. The need to factor extra-talmudic teachings into adjudication, alongside of talmudic teachings, was, for the geonim, a matter of principle, and an expression of an epistemological outlook that was most boldly expressed in their altercations with Karaites. In countering the latter's claims that Torah was the lone source of Jewish legal authority, geonim affirmed that the text of Torah was not self-sufficient; it needed to be coupled with extra-scriptural teachings. It was this very outlook,

I suggest, that shaped the geonic understanding of the Talmud's role in the decision-making process. Though transmitted orally, the Talmud was, nonetheless, a finite corpus of tradition, and the teachings it preserved were those of sages who had lived centuries earlier. As such, the Talmud, on its own, could not bear witness to the ways in which its teachings had been understood by generations of post-amoraic Jews. Only the living testimony of one's masters could distinguish between the talmudic teachings that were implemented in practice and those that were not. The overarching conceptual perspective of the geonim was that no text, whether written (Torah) or oral (e.g., Talmud), could adequately represent the acquired wisdom of a culture's most learned practitioners.

This outlook may shed some light on the way that rationalist geonim understood *midrash halakhah*. Unlike Maimonides, who later claimed that ancient sages had produced rabbinic law by applying inferential operations to words and passages of Torah,[147] Sa'adya, Samuel ben Ḥofni, and Hai Gaon did not think that extra-biblical laws had been generated in this manner. Indeed, these geonim did not regard the thirteen modes of inference ascribed to R. Ishmael as exegetical algorithms whose application to the biblical text would bring new laws to light.[148] As Hai Gaon put it, the midrashic interpretation of a scriptural verse must not be mistaken for the source of the law.[149]

Two corollaries of this perspective should be highlighted. The first is that the geonim in question did not believe that ancient rabbinic sages had used scholastic pathways to generate law; they were (merely) its transmitters. The second corollary is that when Sa'adya (among others) insisted that the biblical text on its own was not a sufficient source of law, he was not assuming that logic-driven exegesis was the missing component. Lived tradition was that complement which, in tandem with Torah, would comprise an "adequate" source of law.

The geonic insistence that ancient rabbis were transmitters and not generators of law was undoubtedly precipitated by epistemological concerns that prevailed in the Muslim environment and by theological challenges posed by Karaites.[150] Yet it is not clear whether this geonic perspective was actually novel. Students of Jewish history do not (at present) know whether the sages of antiquity were consciously engaged in creating law (at least for their own generations);[151] thus, before adopting assumptions about the ancient rabbis that were articulated so compellingly by later tosafists, they should seek evidence indicating that Jews, prior to the time of Sa'adya, regarded tannaim and amoraim as charismatic initiators of tradition.[152]

Geonim on the Distinction between Halakhah and *Halakhah Le-Ma'aseh*

As noted above, the geonim could not have relied exclusively on talmudic formulations in arriving at their legal decisions, since legal deliberations in the Talmud are generally presented as unresolved disputes. When drawing on Talmud in issuing applied rulings, the geonim had, of necessity, to invoke interpretive traditions they had received from their teachers, and to establish as their gold standard of adjudication the "compound" phenomenon of *halakhah le-ma'aseh*—that is, a legal tradition known to have been implemented in practice. When the Jewish community of early ninth-century Qayrawan adopted certain practices associated with Palestinian Jews, Pirqoi ben Baboi (who had studied with Yehudai Gaon's student) wrote an impassioned letter attempting to convince the Qayrawanese that the religious authority of "Babylonia" (Baghdad and its environs) was superior to that of Palestine. In framing the contrast between the two rabbinic centers, Pirqoi asserted that their disparate legal claims and practices stemmed from the fact that they privileged different epistemological pathways.

Pirqoi may not have been the first to frame the cultural clash in this way; if Pirqoi's testimony is to be trusted,[153] Yehudai Gaon of Sura had said something similar in his criticism of Palestinian Jewish practices—and even he may have had predecessors.[154] When Yehudai attempted, in the 760s, to uproot certain "customs of persecution" practiced by earlier Palestinian Jews, he had emphasized that teachings encountered in Talmud could not, on their own, be seen as authoritative. They received this vetting only if living masters, links in the chain of tradition, attested to their actual implementation, *halakhah le-ma'aseh*.[155] According to Pirqoi, the Jews of eighth-century Palestine had rebuffed Yehudai's overtures, and responded by justifying their own (text-driven) approach to adjudication. Exhibiting the very epistemological bias for which Yehudai criticized them, Palestinian Jews had affirmed the validity of their own perspective by brandishing a particular talmudic phrase: "*minhag mevattel halakhah*," "custom overrides law." In its two appearances in the Jerusalem Talmud, this original phrase is devoid of tendentious connotations,[156] but the Jews of Palestine at this time evidently brandished it as a slogan of cultural combat, a proclamation of the superiority of local practice to centralized legislation. The Palestinians thus shifted the terms of the debate to one over regional jurisdiction, ignoring the Babylonian critique of Palestinian legal epistemology.[157]

Whatever the historical accuracy of his screed, Pirqoi took up the mantle of Yehudai Gaon and begged Jews of ninth-century Qayrawan to recognize that Babylonian legal perspectives, unlike those of Palestine, were not simply derived from the academic study of texts. In order for any teaching to be authoritative, claimed Pirqoi, it needed to be rooted in Talmud, on the one hand, and in living testimony on the other:

> And Yehudai, of blessed memory, also said that, never, when you asked me something, did I ever tell you anything other than that which has a proof from the Talmud and that I learned as a *halakhah le-ma'aseh* from my teacher, and my teacher from his teacher. But any matter for which there is proof in the Talmud, but for which I did not have [testimony] from my teacher or from his teacher, as a *halakhah le-ma'aseh*, I did not say to you. Only that which has a *halakhah* in the Talmud, and that I had received as a *halakhah le-ma'aseh* from my teacher—in order to uphold the tannaitic teaching [cf. BT BB 130b], "one does not derive applied *halakhah* from Miqra, nor *halakhah* from Mishnah, nor *halakhah* from Talmud, until they instruct him that it is a *halakhah le-ma'aseh*—and *then* he should go and perform the deed."[158]

Pirqoi claimed that Babylonian legal perspectives fulfilled the two epistemological criteria which, together, endow a claim with legal authority, but that those of Palestine fulfilled only one: Jews of Palestine derived applied law solely from the inscribed talmudic text, without acquiring corroboration from living sources of authority. This had occurred, according to Pirqoi, when persecution forced the Jews of Palestine to alter longstanding practices, rupturing a chain of tradition that had been faithfully transmitted until that time.[159] In the absence of living tradents, charged Pirqoi, the Jews of Palestine had come to rely on written texts; they even ascribed authority to inscriptions that had been intended as nothing more than private jottings, writings that Pirqoi labels "hidden" texts.[160]

> Some of them found texts of Mishnah and parts of Talmud that were hidden [*genuzin*], and each one engages with it [the text] and interprets it in accord with his own ideas [and with] whatever arises in his heart. For they did not apprehend it from earlier sages who would teach them *halakhah le-ma'aseh*.[161]

The epistemological battle waged by Yehudai and Pirqoi continued through the end of the geonic period. As Jewish communities throughout the world became more familiar with the written Talmud, and discerned discrepancies between their own practices and those inscribed in the text, they turned to the Baghdadi academies for clarification. The geonic response—which unsettled later medieval European scholars[162]—was consistent over the course of centuries: leaders of the yeshivot fiercely opposed the derivation of applied law solely from the talmudic record. When perturbed questioners in the late ninth century observed that their manner of reciting the Hallel prayer at the Passover Seder diverged from the Talmud's prescription, R. Ẓemaḥ Gaon responded by invoking a tannaitic teaching [BT Eruv. 27a]: "Rabbi Yoḥanan ruled: No inference may be drawn from general rulings, even where an exception is actually specified."[163]

Commenting on this matter more than a century later, Hai Gaon invoked his predecessor and reaffirmed the primacy of received practice: "He also spoke well when he said that we do not learn from general rulings. And since the whole world does this [recites the Hallel in this manner at the Seder] and this is also how Israel inherited it from their ancestors, we do not learn from general rulings in order to reject [*lidḥot*] their deeds."[164]

A similar point was made in the late tenth century by Hai's father, Sherira Gaon, when he wrote disparagingly about certain students who claimed that evidence they had found in a text, presumably a text of Talmud, flouted geonic teachings:

> You have written that there are students among you who are little foxes[165] in which there is no substance.[166] And they dispute and say, regarding the geonim, pillars of the world: "How do they know this?" And they take out their books [to show that its teaching differs from that of the geonim]. They have no concept of divine activity![167]

When Sherira Gaon learned that some rabbinic students in Qayrawan were deriving applied law solely from the academic study of the talmudic text, he was outraged. The students in question were studying a talmudic passage that preserves the playful repartee of ancient sages vying with one another in a rhetorical contest to see who could best convey the baseness of the *'amei ha-areẓ,* the "ignoramuses" vilified as nemeses of the rabbinic scholars.[168]

> R. Eleazar said: An *'am ha-areẓ* [ignoramus]: It is permitted to stab him [even] on the Day of Atonement which falls on the Sabbath. Said his disciples to him, Master, say, 'to slaughter him [ritually]'? He replied: This [ritual slaughter] requires a benediction, whereas that [stabbing] does not require a benediction. . . . Rabbi Samuel ben Naḥman said in R. Yoḥanan's name: One may tear an *'am ha-areẓ* like a fish! Said R. Samuel ben Isaac: And this means along his back.[169]

Notwithstanding the obviously ludic nature of this banter, some Qayrawanese students decided that one of the claims made in this passage—"some say, we do not proclaim their losses"[170]—was a legal prescription. Thus, when they came across the lost money of anyone whom they regarded as an *'am ha-areẓ*, the students did not feel obligated to broadcast its discovery; instead, they took it for themselves.[171] The writer of the inquiry asked Sherira for clarification of the talmudic tradition "permitting the mamon of the ignoramuses,"[172] and indicated that some colleagues in the Qayrawan study house had already availed themselves of such funds.

Sherira not only condemned those who behaved in this manner, he excoriated them for their outrageous misunderstanding of rabbinic juridical procedure. Derivation of applied law directly from the talmudic text was a travesty, he thundered; it highlighted the students' own ignorance and glaringly revealed that they themselves had never practiced discipleship. Had they actually learned from masters, living sources of tradition, they would have known that not everything preserved in the talmudic corpus is of legal value, writes Sherira; some are instructive without being prescriptive. The gaon concludes by labeling the students who drew this conclusion as the real ignoramuses; it is they who richly deserve the abusive treatment described in the ancients' banter about the *'amei ha-areẓ*:

> And you have explained that some of the students there rely upon these external matters [*ha-ḥiẓonot halalu*] and permit themselves the mamon of the ignoramuses. [But] these are not matters of prohibition and permission, such that one is required to tell, based on them, what is *halakhah* and what is not *halakhah*! Rather, they are "extra matters"—like the rules of etiquette—telling about the depravity of ignoramuses, and [other] vain talk. And if these were *halakhot* [legal traditions] that were to be regarded as authoritative in keeping with

> their sense, these students whom you have mentioned would be worthy of being excommunicated on Yom Kippur that falls on the Sabbath, and of being torn like fish! And if the mammon of the *'am ha-areẓ* is permitted, the mammon of these students is permitted, for they are like the ignoramus! For even if he read [Talmud] and he repeated it—but did not serve rabbinic scholars [as disciples]—this is an ignoramus. For if these students had served sages [as disciples], they would never have said this.[173]

Sherira's son, Hai Gaon, addressed another celebrated case, in which talmudic teachings were mistaken construed as prescribing applied law. The Qayrawanese scholar, R. Ya'aqov ben Nisim, turned to Pumbeditha for clarification of a matter that had first arisen in 998, when Jewish immigrants from Italy raised questions about the local Qayrawanese performance of the shofar blasts on Rosh HaShanah. According to the questioner, when local Qayrawanese students read the relevant talmudic text, they found corroboration for the challenge of the newcomers.[174] This awareness had shaken Qayrawanese confidence in their own local traditions. How could they know, wrote R. Ya'aqov, which practice was truly correct?

At the outset of his lengthy response, Hai Gaon informed the Qayrawanese that they were making the matter unnecessarily complicated:

> That practice by which we fulfill our obligation and the will of our Creator is established and certain in our hands. That which we do is a legacy which has been deposited, transmitted, and received in tradition—from fathers to sons—for continuous generations in Israel, from the days of the prophets unto the present time. Namely, that we blow [the shofar] while sitting according to custom, and [then,] while standing during the order of the Benedictions, we again blow three blasts, three times. This is the widespread law throughout all of Israel. Since we have this in our hands [as a received legacy] as an implemented practice [*ma'aseh zeh be-yadenu*], it is correct, [and] a law transmitted to Moses on Sinai. And since they have fulfilled their obligation [in following this practice], any difficulty vanishes.[175]

Proceeding to the larger epistemological issue, Hai impresses on his readers the larger stakes involved:

> How do we know *at all* that we are commanded to blow [the shofar] on this day? [For that matter,] regarding the essence of the written Torah: How are we to know that it is *indeed* the Torah of Moses, that which he wrote from the Mouth of the Almighty, if not through the mouth [attestation] of the Community of Israel! After all, those who testify to it are the same ones who testify that, through this deed, we have fulfilled our obligation; and [who testify that] they received this by means of tradition, from the mouths of the prophets, as Torah transmitted to Moses at Sinai. *It is the words of the multitudes that testify to [the authority] of each mishnah and every gemara.*[176]

According to Hai, the consensus of the Jewish people is the ultimate guarantor of the authority of any belief or practice. No source of jurisprudence, be it Torah, Mishnah, or Talmud, can be authoritative, claims Hai, if authentication is lacking:

> Greater than any other proof is: [BT Ber. 45a] "*Go out and see what the people do.*'" *This* is the principle and the basis of authority! [Only] *afterward* do we examine everything said about this issue in the Mishnah or Gemara. Anything that arises from them and that can help to explain what we want is fine, but if there is nothing in it [Mishnah or Gemara] which aligns with our wishes, and if it is not clarified through proof, this [textual teaching] does nothing to uproot the principle [of following the consensus of the Jewish people].[177]

Legal teachings in the talmudic text are only to be taken into account, asserts Hai, when they corroborate tradition as practiced. Custom and consensus, both non-textual criteria, determine the legal applicability of a talmudic opinion.

Impressing this point on his readers, Hai urges them to reflect in a more philosophical vein on the reasonableness of this hierarchy, without reference to issues of applied law.

> We must acknowledge this principle even when we are not compelled by need on the occasion of performing a commandment. After all, it is in this [principle] that we find the great proof that it

> [the practice in question] was fulfilled in keeping with the law transmitted to Moses at Sinai.[178]

Hai's claim that consensus is a source of law (a claim that may parallel the status of *ijma* in Islamic legal theory)[179] seems to describe a geonic *modus operandi* that had been in effect for generations. Though Hai's remarks were prompted by the Qayrawanese Jews' somewhat obsessive impulse to align their behavior with Talmud, he shifted the focus from an assertion that the *talmudic* corpus needed an external referent, to an assertion that Scripture itself needed one as well. In doing so, Hai was echoing Sa'adya Gaon, who had insisted, in response to Karaite claims, that Scripture was *not* "self-sufficient."[180] It is tempting to see the geonic adoption of an "anti-fundamentalist" posture with regard to both Scripture and Talmud as closely allied with the Babylonian leaders' repeated assertions that talmudic teachings needed to be vetted by living attestation in order to qualify as legally prescriptive. Little wonder that numerous geonic responsa—earlier as well as later—conclude with a programmatic affirmation that the decision just rendered is informed by both of the necessary conditions: "This is the halakhah and this is the custom."[181]

The struggles of Yehudai Gaon, Pirqoi ben Baboi, Ẓemaḥ Gaon, Sherira Gaon, and Hai Gaon were to recur, under different historical and cultural circumstances, in Jewish communities of northern Europe in the late eleventh and twelfth centuries. The contested subject was nothing less than the epistemological grounds for the authority of rabbinic law: What forms of attestation and transmission were necessary and sufficient in order for a given teaching to be deemed legally authoritative? Could a teaching rooted only in the inscribed text of Talmud be legally binding, or did it also need the vetting of an external referent? Geonim decried both the assumptions and the practices of Jews who regarded the talmudic text as a stand-alone source for practical adjudication, unsupported and untempered by attestations of implemented practice, but by the twelfth century, it was this very approach that had become the norm in rabbinic culture.

Halakhic Compilations of the Geonic Era

A number of contemporary scholars have noted that the composition of halakhic works in the geonic period broke sharply with tradition. What motivated the composition of these works, and what cultural meaning was ascribed to them by their creators?[182] Use of these works by later medieval adjudicators in Sefarad and Ashkenaz cannot substitute for an understanding of the juridical standing they possessed in their own times and places of composition.[183] One clue to their status in geonic times may be found in a ninth-century comment by Natronai Gaon. Explaining the term "*megilat setarim*," literally "a sequestered scroll," which appears in several talmudic passages,[184] Natronai set up a juxtaposition between this type of inscription and Talmud. (The ambiguity of the unpunctuated first sentence has been intentionally retained in the following translation): "*Megilat setarim* in which there are decided laws like a book of *halakhot* which is unlike the Talmud which every person has. And this is why it is called *megilat setarim*."[185]

What is it that "every person has"? Scholars of geonica have understood this passage to mean that what is widely found is the Talmud itself, and not the "sequestered scroll."[186] Yet Talmud, a voluminous corpus, is far less likely to have been widely found in the ninth century than the shorter compilations of halakhah that were written in the geonic period. As noted above, there was nothing arcane or esoteric about the content of a "sequestered scroll"; the verb *s-t-r* referred only to the fact that it was to be stored out of sight. Were it not secreted away, the *megilat setarim* might have been mistaken for an official writing worthy of public declamation, a text that, in ancient times, might have been inscribed on a wall. I believe that Natronai's remarks are more plausibly rendered, "*Megilat setarim*: in which there are decided laws, like a book of *halakhot*—which is unlike the Talmud—*and* which every person has. And this is why it is called *megilat setarim* [because it is kept in inner chambers]."

Natronai clearly regarded "a book of *halakhot*" as a type of *megilat setarim*. More than a century later, Hai Gaon described a *megilat setarim* as a private, unofficial, and non-authoritative text, in which one writes for himself the recollections of what he heard [*zikhronot shemu'otav le-'aẓmo*].[187]

The remarks by Natronai Gaon in the ninth century and by Hai Gaon in the eleventh strongly suggest that, whatever other Jews may have thought, the geonim themselves regarded inscribed halakhic collections as unofficial writings.[188]

Of the two different sorts of halakhic writings produced during the geonic period,[189] those composed by the geonim themselves were monographs on discrete topics of law, and were written in Judeo-Arabic. By contrast, halakhic compilations composed outside the Babylonian academies during the geonic era—the *Sheiltot*, wrongly attributed to the mid-eighth-century Rav Aḥai of Shabḥa,[190] *Halakhot Pesuqot* (also known as *Halakhot Qetu'ot*) attributed to Yehudai Gaon,[191] and the more derivative *Halakhot Gedolot*, attributed to R. Shimon Qayyara[192]—were written in a combination of Hebrew and Aramaic.

There are ample grounds for assuming that earlier geonim were displeased by the widespread circulation of these Aramaic compilations and by the ways in which they were being used.[193] Writing from Pumbeditha in the mid-ninth century, Paltoi Gaon was critical of the way in which *Halakhot Pesuqot*—or perhaps digests of decided law in general, since this, too, is the meaning of "*halakhot pesuqot*"—were being used. Works of this sort, he asserted, were only intended as mnemonic prompts for the highly accomplished, namely, those who were capable of studying Talmud and had already done so:

> And that it is written: Which is preferable and more praiseworthy, to delve deeply into the laws, or to study *Halakhot Qetu'ot* [either *Decided Laws* or decided laws]? And we would not have asked, but for the fact that most people incline to *halakhot qetu'ot*, and say: what need do we have for talmudic dialectic? What they do is not right, and it is forbidden to do so, because they are diminishing Torah and it is said [Isa. 42:21], *He will* [in this context, *we must*] *make the Torah great and glorious*. And not only that, but they are causing [the activity of] *talmud torah* to be forgotten, God forbid. And these *halakhot qetu'ot* [decided laws] were not arranged [for the purpose of] recitation [*lo nitqenu le-shanen ba-hem*]. Rather, if one who has studied the entire Talmud and is engaged in it is in doubt about something and does not know how to explain it, he consults them.[194]

Paltoi Gaon did not categorically oppose the use of *Halakhot Pesuqot* (or of digests of applied law); he affirmed its utility as a reference work for erudite scholars who were already conversant with Talmud. The problem, as he saw it, was its deleterious effect on Jewish education and religious life: because it was so much easier to understand than Talmud itself, it was proving far more popular. Yet the knowledge thus acquired was only superficial; only the exertionary study of Talmud could be construed as a sacred activity.

Paltoi's counterpart at Sura targeted the inappropriate use of *Halakhot*

Pesuqot in the realm of adjudication. Chastising correspondents who had ascribed to it the weight of *ma'aseh*, lived tradition, Gaon Sar Shalom wrote:

> That which you [pl.] have inscribed before us in *Halakhot Qetu'ot* . . . we have never heard it either in writing or orally. And you should not do this, for it is not practiced, but only that which I have explained to you. And let the *halakhot* not mislead you.[195]

Notwithstanding these significant reservations, later Babylonian Jewish leaders (particular at the Suran academy) held both *Halakhot Pesuqot* and *Halakhot Gedolot* in high regard; it is even possible that Hai Gaon used the latter as a classroom textbook.[196] Still, neither compilation was explicitly designed as a guide to applied law,[197] and it is unlikely that later geonim would have ascribed them the adjudicatory stature that they came to hold for later Jews.[198] Yet because they were written in Hebrew and Aramaic, *Sheiltot, Halakhot Pesuqot,* and *Halakhot Gedolot* reached Jewish readers far from the Babylonian academies who knew little or nothing of the concerns expressed by ninth-century geonim.

By contrast, the topic-specific legal monographs produced by geonim themselves were written in Judeo-Arabic. This choice of language is striking, given that Sa'adya, Samuel ben Ḥofni, and Hai Gaon, like their geonic predecessors, authored their responsa in Aramaic. Why, then, did they compose their halakhic monographs in Judeo-Arabic? I suggest that this language choice may be seen as significant within the contexts of geography, education, and cultural "coding."

These monographs were not designed for all Jews, for unless they were translated, Judeo-Arabic writings remained incomprehensible to Jews living outside the Islamicate orbit.[199] Nor were the geonim who composed these works targeting rabbinically learned Jews. In a culture described as "perennially diglossic," in which each of the language options had its own literary system and internal dynamics,[200] learned Jewish writers communicated in Judeo-Arabic, rather than in Hebrew and Aramaic, when they wanted the text to reach Jews who were not rabbinic scholars. This point, explicitly stated in polemical exchanges between Rabbanites and Karaites in the generation of Sa'adya Gaon and his students,[201] was still valid in the eleventh century. Andalusian Jews of this time noted that halakhic writings composed in Judeo-Arabic were intended for Jewish readers who were mere beginners in the study of Jewish law (though they may have been educated in the *'adab* of Arabic culture).[202]

In short, when late geonim prepared halakhic monographs in Judeo-Arabic, they saw themselves as writing for Jews who were *not* learned in Talmud. Their compositions were designed to play a very different role from that which (at least earlier) geonim had ascribed to compendia like *Halakhot Pesuqot* and *Halakhot Gedolot.* Geonim had criticized the early Hebrew-Aramaic compilations, composed outside the academy, on the grounds that they were being used by Jews who were not learned in Talmud. The geonic monographs, by contrast, were designed for precisely this population. Hai Gaon alludes to this in justifying his composition of a halakhic monograph on oaths.

> Our God knows that I would not have not explained [by means of] this writing were it not to bring understanding to one who does not understand, and to enable one who does not learn, to be taught—and one who does not know, to know. For I have seen the dearth of understanding on the part of most who are becoming learned [or, who consider themselves wise] [*ha-mitḥakkemim*] in Gemara nowadays.[203]

As is clear from Hai's caustic response to the students of Qayrawan, access to written texts of Talmud evidently led some Jews outside the Babylonian academies to (incorrectly) assume their own competence in determining applied law.

There is reason to surmise that the halakhic monographs of late geonim were designed to address a situation specific to Jews in Muslim lands far from the gaonate. Though the evidence for this conjecture is slightly late, circumstances known to have existed in the eleventh century may also have prevailed in the tenth. In Spanish communities of the eleventh century, legal administration fell to two different types of Jewish professionals. Some locales were fortunate in having a resident *ba'al hora-a,* a rabbi whose talmudic learning qualified him to render applied halakhic instruction, but even these communities required other functionaries to maintain social order. *Dayyanim* [judges] were selected by parties to a dispute or appointed by the Jewish community itself to discharge regulatory tasks, and they lacked grounding in the study of Talmud. Local *dayyanim* determined the appropriateness of witnesses, validated documents, administered oaths, and appointed guardians and proxies. Beyond this, *dayyanim* rendered legal decisions in monetary cases.[204] In order to fulfill these duties, *dayyanim* did not need to be talmudic scholars, but they did need to learn certain essentials of Jewish law.

The topic-specific halakhic monographs composed in Judeo-Arabic by the geonim presented relevant legal material in systematic fashion, breaking it down into chapters and subsections and explaining the underlying legal sources. And unlike the earlier halakhic compilations composed outside the geonic academies, these writings were internally consistent. They enabled a *dayyan* who read them as an auto-didact to acquire the modicum of applied halakhic knowledge he would need in order to manage specific civic functions—even if he had never studied Talmud.

According to this conjectural reconstruction, the topic-specific halakhic monographs that late geonim composed in Judeo-Arabic were designed to enable Jewish communities remote from the center of scholarship to regulate themselves according to Jewish law. Far from promoting more intensive contact with the talmudic corpus, these compositions relieved the greater part of Jewish communal leadership of the need to consult the Talmud directly.

Some later Jews were troubled by what they perceived as the geonic violation of tannaitic strictures against the "saying of *oral matters* in writing", and they surmised that the earliest post-talmudic halakhic writings had never been designed to circulate. This hypothesis (to be considered in Chapter 5) may not have been correct, but the conjecture that geonic halakhic writings were composed for use by people who were not scholars of Talmud may have been right on the mark.

* * *

A final speculative rumination concerns the geonic use of Judeo-Arabic in their halakhic monographs. If the geonim who committed halakhic material to writing were concerned that they not violate tannaitic dicta that respectively warned against the "saying" of *oral matters* in writing, and of deriving halakhah from Talmud, their decision to use Judeo-Arabic in these monographs may have signaled (or been intended to signal) that these compositions possessed a very modest status within the hierarchy of Jewish cultural authority. Since neither Talmud, nor any other corpus of *oral matters*, had been transmitted in Judeo-Arabic, the inscription of halakhic information in this language may have enabled geonic authors to avoid the problem of taxonomic boundaries which the dicta were designed to enforce.[205]

* * *

The question of why the geonim began to compose halakhic monographs when they did, and why they did so in this specific compositional style, inevitably draws attention to Sa'adya Gaon, who pioneered this genre, along with so many other forms of Jewish literature. Introducing the new concepts of "*sefer*" [literally, "book"] and "*ḥibbur*"[206] [literally, "composition"] into Rabbanite literature and culture in the beginning of the tenth century, Sa'adya adapted Arabic compositional models and created Jewish genres that became the norm for many Jewish writers (including geonim) who followed him.[207] Modern scholars attempting to account for Sa'adya's position as a literary maverick have cited (apart from his personal arrogance) the influence of geography and his involvement in cross-cultural conversations. Unlike earlier and later geonim who hailed from Abbasid Iraq (a.k.a. "Babylonia"), Sa'adya was from Egypt, "on the periphery of the rabbinic world."[208] The years he spent in Palestine prior to serving as gaon exposed Sa'adya to regionally specific cultural phenomena that contributed to his own intellectual orientation. Sa'adya's studies with a prominent Masorete in Tiberias, a center for Hebrew language study and the place where authorized scriptural texts were prepared for use throughout the Jewish world,[209] undoubtedly shaped his (highly influential) attitudes toward biblical Hebrew.[210] And it is likely that Sa'adya encountered Arabic literary models and theories in the course of interactions with Muslim intellectuals in Tiberias, which was not only the caliphate's administrative seat in the province of al-Urdun at this time, but also the site of a school for the training of Muslim bureaucrats, where students received a broad-ranging education in Arabic literature.[211] Finally, as the first Rabbanite to respond polemically to the challenge of Karaism, Sa'adya was certainly familiar with the writings of Karaites, whose Judeo-Arabic works already employed structural and stylistic conventions of Arabic writing.[212]

If the above-mentioned phenomena help to contextualize Sa'adya's initiatory role in Jewish literary composition in general, his decision while serving as gaon to produce topic-specific halakhic monographs seems to reflect his familiarity with developments in Islamic law. Researchers have noted that the fullest set of halakhic monographs, those composed by Shmuel ben Ḥofni Gaon (of which forty-three titles have been retrieved to date), closely parallel the divisions and nomenclature of Islamic law books of various genres.[213] The growing importance of texts in Baghdadi society and the opportunities for interaction between Jewish and Muslim literati in *majalis* (convocations of intellectuals), in bookstalls, and in Baghdad's great library, the *Bayt al-Hikma*, may well have had an impact on the geonic composition of halakhic monographs. As arabicized Jews became familiar with systematic writings in other realms, geonim concerned about the paucity of Jewish legal knowledge moved to repackage traditional rabbinic knowledge in ways that made it more easily accessible. Just as works on Islamic legal theory may have served as literary models for the introductions to Talmud written for beginners in the geonic era,[214] the topical arrangement of *hadith* collections may have influenced the breakdown of subjects in the halakhic compilations of the geonic era.[215]

Subsequent geonim persisted in the legal literary endeavors pioneered by Sa'adya not only because they were receptive to the penchant for systematizing that was dominant among rationalists in their environment, but because they recognized that the gaonate's relevance depended upon its ability to educate Jews who lived far from the academies of Iraq. Indeed, historians have linked the proliferation of halakhic writings by later geonim to declining economic conditions that affected the academies from the mid-tenth century onward.[216] As the yeshivot struggled to attract funding from far-flung Jewish communities, geonim turned their unparalleled command of the Babylonian Talmud into a commodity. Intent upon wooing patrons, Sherira, Samuel ben Ḥofni and Hai Gaon invited Jews in other lands to write to the academies with questions about matters of applied law or about the meaning of difficult texts, and they dedicated halakhic works to wealthy merchants and courtiers. Late geonim also displayed their powers of reasoning and prodigious erudition in new textual fora.[217]

While it is obvious that these cultural developments could only occur once the broader Jewish environment was saturated with respect for Talmud, the geonic role in promoting the reputation of Talmud may not have been matched by their role in promoting knowledge of Talmud.

The Preferred Legal Instruments of Geonic Culture

Until the last several decades of the twentieth century, the image of geonim in Jewish historiography was that of micromanaging tyrants, eager to impose their will on communities far from Baghdad.[218] Though this reputation seemed to be consistent with Babylonian critiques of Palestinian traditions, and with strident calls for donations to the academies, the portrait of the geonim as autocrats may reflect little more than the biases of certain reporters. One such figure was the twelfth-century Andalusian chronicler, Abraham ibn Daud, who tendentiously portrayed the Jews of Spain as having triumphantly declared independence from Babylonian hegemony.[219] Early twentieth-century Jewish historiographers reinforced this negative portrait of the geonim by contrasting the hierarchy of Jewish society in Babylonia with the (idealized) egalitarianism and democracy that, in their imaginations, had prevailed in the Jewish communities of ancient Palestine and of medieval northern Europe.[220] More recent scholarship on the geonim has challenged this image, however; not only were the leaders of the Babylonian academies ill-equipped to see their will enforced, but, in many cases, they affirmed the power of local communities to regulate their own affairs.[221]

Analysis of the instruments and institutions that geonim utilized in making legal decisions and in asserting their legal authority supports this revised perspective. More than this, it suggests that geonim were profoundly reticent about formulating prescriptive laws that would be binding on all Jews. A surprising number of geonic legal decisions were effected through legislative mechanisms whose enforceability was predicated on communal consent.

Numerous "communal ordinances" [*taqqanot ha-qahal*] were enacted in geonic times, and these were understood as expressions of popular will. Thus, even when geonim formally approved such longstanding behaviors, they did not, strictly speaking, alter the de facto status quo.[222] These ordinances were legally binding not because they had been granted the geonic seal of approval, but because they were understood to be rooted in communal assent.[223]

In contrast with the large number of communal ordinances that they instituted, geonim were very sparing in the promulgation of other ordinances [*taqqanot*], that is, of legal rulings that are not exegetically linked to the teachings of tradition. As Brody showed in a seminal and thought-provoking study, geonim implemented only two such pieces of legislation over the course of five centuries.[224] Paltry geonic use of this juridical vehicle stands in sharp contrast with the large numbers of *taqqanot* passed by later medieval rabbis.

The impression that geonim were either reluctant to enact legislation or possessed limited ability to do so[225] is reinforced by their reliance upon patently nonlegal strategies of social control, like court procedure. One such example was an oath-taking ceremony described by Hai Gaon. Replete with smoke and mirrors, this frightening ritual was carefully choreographed to terrify the would-be perjurer with threats of waiting torments:

> When a person becomes obligated to take an oath, and you wish to have him take an oath, let them take out a Torah scroll [from the ark] and prepare it [so that it is open] to the curses [Deut. 28], and let them lie it . . . in the ark. And have them bring a bier upon which the dead are transported, and let them spread upon it the items [clothing?] that are spread upon the dead. And have them take out shofars. And have the children of the synagogue bring inflated goatskins [*nodot*] and cast them in front of the bier. And let the court say to this man who is being adjured, "Know that, on the morrow, this man will be cast off like these goatskins [*nodot*]." And they bring chickens and they also light candles and bring ashes. And they stand the one obligated to take an oath upon the ashes and blow the shofars and they threaten him with ostracism [*u-menadin befanav*], saying, "You, so and so, son of so and so, if person X claims that you owe him this money, and you deny it, all the curses written in this book will stick to you." And they threaten him with this entire ostracism, and blow the shofars. And all the children and those standing say, "Amen."[226]

Technically speaking, nothing about the ceremony's choreography had bearing on the oath's legal efficacy. Rather, the entire frightening pageant was designed to impress upon the assembled the *tremendum* of the oath and the dire consequences that would befall its violator. Situating the ceremony in the synagogue made oath-taking a public act witnessed by the entire Jewish community, and it gave participants a sense that the experience itself fell within the realm of the sacred.[227] Children played a central role in this ceremony, not only because the young connote purity and innocence, but because their presence ensured that they—as future oath-takers—would be duly impressed by the solemnity of the act. The intensely sensory quality of the ceremony—its sights, sounds, smells—made it more likely that all present would remember its specifics, and be able to bear witness to them, should the act ever be questioned in years to come. As was the case in other ancient and medieval societies that valorized the authority of oral testimony, the geonim made administrative procedures and dispositive legal acts mnemonically indelible by maximizing their somatic impact.[228] The inflated goatskins (which might have exploded loudly when flung before the bier) helped make the threat of ostracism more concrete: As hollow shells of former lives, these props were menacing on their own, but their very name, *nodot*, punningly evoked the threat of *niddui*, ostracism—a point emphasized in the ceremony's liturgy.

The instrument of jurisprudence most closely associated with the geonim is the responsum, a written reply to a specific question posed in writing by correspondents.[229] Responsa often discuss actual issues that had arisen in specific communities at specific times;[230] compared with other vehicles of legislation, they are distinguished by their specificity. Though responsa preserve the anonymity of the involved parties, their description of *realia* make them valuable windows into Jewish social life, especially when their time and place of composition are known. Unlike prescriptive legal tools of the code-constitution model, responsa do not seek to extract or articulate principles of jurisprudence; they are crafted, stylistically and methodologically, to address the circumscribed case at hand.

Growth in the use of responsa in the geonic period may be attributed to the Muslim conquest—which brought the majority of the world's Jewish population under a single political dominion, to the importation of paper technology into the Arabic speaking world, and to the growing importance of inscription in Muslim legal culture.[231] Yet as a legal instrument, the responsum was part of the rabbinic heritage. The determination of case law through written correspondence is well attested in the Talmud,[232] and there is reason to assume that the Jews' use of this vehicle paralleled a legal practice used in the Roman Empire from the birth of the republic until the mid-third century CE.[233] Roman responsa have their origins in oral consultations between jurisconsults and the litigants who approached them in the Forum, but the first written anthologies of Roman responsa, the *Digesta* (which, like their Jewish counterparts, guarded the anonymity of the litigants),[234] were compiled as early as the first century BCE.[235] Some Roman responsa were granted the special designation of *ius respondendi*; these were written by jurists who had received an imperial license to answer in the name of the Emperor. Yet even this mark of distinction did not compel litigants or lawyers to accept the decision set forth in such a responsum, and parties were free to seek more favorable judgments from other jurisconsults, licensed or unlicensed.[236] In other words, Roman responsa had some clout in the determination of law, but they were hardly sources of unquestionable authority.

Micha Perry has discussed later Jews' revaluation of geonic responsa.

Embedded in compilations and removed from real-life settings, dialogues become monologues and conclusions were elevated over the deliberative process. Later Jews construed geonic responsa as universal imperatives, precedents for future legal decisions.[237] How different from the geonic period itself, in which the responsum occupied "a sort of no-man's-land between the realms of literary, historical and administrative documents."[238]

Rina Drory suggested that the responsum may have had the status of an "epistle," a document accorded a negligible place in the hierarchy of inscription. As Drory noted, a celebrated rabbinic passage designates the epistle as a type of writing that is devoid of authority. Commenting on Rabbi 'Aqiva's assertion (in the Mishnah) that "one who reads from heretical books" has no share in the World to Come, the Jerusalem Talmud considers some of the writings in question: "These are, for example, the books of Ben Sira and the books of Ben La'anah. But as to the books of Homer and all books written henceforeward, he who reads from them is as one who reads from a [mere] epistle."[239]

If, as Drory suggested, a responsum was seen as an epistle, a form of writing that ancient rabbis deemed to be of negligible importance, then the geonic predilection for this genre would support the impression that the Babylonian leaders were highly restrained (if not utterly reticent) adjudicators. Moreover, because of the responsum's specificity—its composition for a particular interlocutor, and its focus on a particular case—adjudicators who chose to use this legal mechanism were, in effect, refraining from enacting legislation that would be universally binding on Jews of all times and places.[240]

In a study of the legal standing of the rabbinic responsum across many centuries and geographic locales, Berachyahu Lifschitz concluded that its legal force has always been determined by a complex network of social interests and pressures that affect the responding scholar.[241] During the geonic period, when geonim were not the only scholars to write legal responses to posed questions,[242] the authority of academy-generated responsa was undoubtedly enhanced by the setting in which they were promulgated. Inquiries sent to the geonic *yeshivot* were shared and discussed in an international forum of rabbinic scholars that convened in Baghdad twice a year, during the final week of the two *yarḥei kallah*, "months of convocation." Noting that the academies only operated "at full strength" during these *kallah* months,[243] Robert Brody emphasized that the convocations' participants played a consultative role; they helped to shape the final product through discussion and persuasion. According to a highly stylized early tenth-century chronicle by Nathan the Babylonian, the geonic academy during these seasons was like the (defunct) Sanhedrin: inquiries that had been sent to the academy at Sura were read aloud to the scholars attending the *kallah*, and following collective discussion, the answer—the responsum itself—was read aloud to all present.[244] This public reading of the responsum would have marked its "publication"[245] (an act with cultural parallels in medieval Islam and Christianity).[246]

Whatever its reliability as a source of documentary history,[247] Nathan's chronicle portrays the geonic responsum as a creation of the international House of Israel, a decision shaped and ratified by a quorum of scholars who represented the Jewish collective.[248] Or, as Brody puts it, "the Gaon's habit of speaking in plural was not an empty gesture."[249]

The geonic preference for *minhag*, custom, as a "juridical bridge" also reflects the impulse to root legal enactments in the popular will. Gideon Libson noted the rise in the number of customs that were acknowledged in the geonic period, and he suggested that this development reflects not only the growing need for social and legal regulation within geonic societies, but the geonic impulse to draw legal authority from broad-based social assent.[250]

* * *

The preceding overview of the ways in which *oral matters* were transmitted and utilized in the Babylonian academies suggests that the geonim strove, sometimes ingeniously, to uphold the tannaitic dicta pertaining to *oral matters*. Ya'aqov Sussman's observation that, "up to the very end of the geonic period, Talmud remained literally in the category of Oral Torah"[251] testifies to the seriousness with which the academy leaders adhered to the prohibition against "saying *oral matters* in writing." Awareness that the geonim never regarded the corpora of Mishnah or Talmud as the sole source of authority in making legal decisions—but instead, insisted on *halakhah le-ma'aseh* as the standard for applied law—speaks to their adherence to the other tannitic dictum. Finally, examination of the range of vehicles employed by the geonim in asserting their legal authority suggests that talmudic exegesis was only one adjudicatory strategy among many, and that Babylonian Jewish leaders often preferred to govern through mechanisms of social coercion. Many life circumstances that called for legal guidance could be addressed without reference to the Talmud itself—and they were.

Over the course of six centuries, geonic perspectives and practices were hardly static. As heirs to amoraic traditions, the geonim could claim an authority rooted in the past, but the passage of time brought with it growing consciousness of the overwhelming task they faced. Ninety percent of the world's Jews lived in the great geographic swath of Islamic lands at the time of Hai Gaon's death in 1048, and their communities differed as widely in their social, economic, and political conditions as they did in their intellectual and cultural orientations. Later geonim were far more cognizant than earlier ones of the need to forge something like a unifying reference work that would address the needs of all Jews, and the challenge they faced led them to take into consideration juridical tools and approaches that would help them in this undertaking. The very strains that led geonim like Sa'adya, Sherira, Shmuel ben Ḥofni, and Hai to adapt, for Jewish needs, certain developments in Islamic jurisprudence[252] also forced them to compromise their adherence to tannaitic strictures, and to deviate from intellectual, institutional, and juridical patterns that had been established by their amoraic predecessors.

Yet, with all its dynamism, the broad contours of geonic culture nonetheless offer a baseline from which to evaluate subsequent developments in medieval Sefarad and Ashkenaz. Later Babylonian leaders implemented certain changes—as concessions—where the transmission of *oral matters* was concerned, but the geonim never ceased being conscious of the ancient dicta regulating the transmission and use of *oral matters,* and they strove to uphold them within the precincts of the academies themselves.

2

Oral Matters among Jews of Qayrawan and al-Andalus: Framing Sefarad

While late geonim conceded the necessity of inscribing *oral matters*, in contravention of a tannaitic prohibition, they saw no reason to disavow the tannaitic dictum stipulating that applied law could only be derived from Talmud once a master attested that the relevant teaching was to be implemented in practice. As seen in the previous chapter, Hai Gaon had reacted with rage when he learned that rabbinical students in Qayrawan were treating the talmudic text as a prescriptive legal source, privileging its authority over that of orally transmitted tradition, and permitting its teachings to undermine longstanding patterns of communal behavior.[1] Yet the very availability of Talmud as a written text in certain locales seems to have awakened an impulse to regard it as an unalloyed guide to applied law, or at least as the pre-eminent one. While Qayrawan was not the only Jewish community to have used the Talmud in ways unsanctioned by the Baghdadi academies in the tenth and eleventh centuries, it left an unusually strong archival imprint because of the unique role it played in the dissemination of geonic communication.

From 711 on, the city of Qayrawan linked the Abbasid caliphate of the Babylonian east with the Umayyad province of Al-Andalus in the west,[2] and in the ninth century, when Muslim conquests of Byzantine ports transformed the Mediterranean into "an Arab Sea," Qayrawan's location made it a natural entrepot linking the Mediterranean north and the sub-Saharan south.[3] Because Qayrawan was less vulnerable to attack than the fortified harbor of

Maḥdiyya, it served as Ifriqiyya's capital and as the administrative, military, diplomatic, and commercial headquarters of the Maghreb from 800 until its destruction in 1057.[4] The complex network of political alignments maintained by Qayrawan's rulers also ensured that Qayrawan's residents were privy to the flow of goods, people, and ideas from many geographic regions in the tenth and eleventh centuries. Between 909 and 1171, when Ifriqiyya was technically under Fatimid rule, it was linked with the Ismailis of Cairo and Fostat. At the same time, Ifriqiyya's local governors, the Banu Ziri tribe, shifted their allegiance from the Fatimid caliphs in Cairo to the Abbasid caliphs in Baghdad. This move may have facilitated more intense contact between Qayrawan's Jews and the Babylonian geonim.[5] Yet another political alignment that began in 945 linked Qayrawan more closely to al-Andalus; in that year, certain powerful residents sent delegations offering submission to Abdul-Rahman III, the Umayyad ruler of Spain.[6]

Babylonian geonim took full advantage of existing commercial and postal routes (a legacy of the Byzantines and Persians), and they relied upon Jews in Ifriqiyya's capital city to relay messages from the yeshivot to Jewish communities situated north and east of Qayrawan—in Palestine, Egypt, Sicily, and Italy, and to those situated to its west and south—in Tahert, Sijilmasa, Fez, Lucena, and Cordoba.[7] The unique role that Qayrawan's Jews played in facilitating international correspondence for the Baghdadi academies may explain why this community is disproportionately represented in geonic correspondence,[8] and why its non-geonic approach to rabbinic adjudication is more easily reconstructed than those that may have prevailed in other Jewish communities far from Baghdad.

Qayrawan's scholars maintained an extensive, bi-directional correspondence with Babylonia,[9] taking care not to exacerbate tensions between the rival academies.[10] According to Menaḥem Ben Sasson, most of the questions sent from Qayrawan to Babylonia in the tenth and eleventh centuries were academic in nature.[11] R. Ya'aqov ibn Shaḥin (d. c. 1006) and his son R. Nisim (d. c. 1062) asked for geonic help in identifying which of several variant recensions of a talmudic unit should be deemed authoritative, and they requested clarification of the legal relevance of social conditions.[12] In laboring to derive rules of administration and management from the Talmud, Qayrawanese scholars consulted the geonim about matters of court procedure, civil procedure, legal aid, and corporal punishment.[13] They also sought geonic help in identifying principles of adjudication, i.e., the rules to be followed in disputes between particular amoraim.[14] Once they were in possession of these tools, Jews of Qayrawan employed them as they studied the talmudic text and derived applied law on their own. Indeed, as Menaḥem Ben Sasson noted, the failure of Qayrawanese scholars to pose questions of applied law to the geonim suggests that they made such decisions themselves.[15] Nothing in the posture of the Qayrawanese suggests that they regarded themselves as legally subservient to the leaders of the Babylonian academies (or deprived by them of juridical autonomy). Yet, by the same token, the Qayrawanese do not appear to have thought of themselves as rebels against the geonim, and they certainly were not perceived as such.[16] Geonic correspondence with Qayrawan is suffused with respect,[17] and for a period of two decades (between the death of R. Hai in 1038, and the sacking of Qayrawan in 1057) the rabbinic academy in Ifriqiyya was seen as a proxy of Baghdad and bore the mantle of geonic authority.[18]

Rabbinic Compositions in Qayrawan

Though of different literary genres, the rabbinic works produced in eleventh century Qayrawan appear to have had two overlapping aims: to make the written Talmud accessible to readers who lacked access to a master, and to enable readers to understand the practical legal implications of the text's often meandering discourse. These writings were not wholly without precedent; if anything, they fused aspects of two types of geonic writing. The geonim themselves had undertaken talmudic exegesis, though they did so only in piecemeal fashion,[19] responding to specific requests and tailoring their answers to what they thought their questioners could comprehend.[20] Late geonim also composed topic-specific halakhic monographs, which, like the Qayrawanese writings, set forth the law to be followed. Yet whereas the geonim had composed their monographs in Judeo-Arabic (targeting the rabbinically unlearned, and possibly signaling as well that these works were not to be viewed as instantiations of *oral matters*),[21] the Qayrawanese compositions were written explicitly for students of Talmud, and in Aramaic, the language of Talmud.

Jews of Qayrawan acquired renown elsewhere in the Jewish world as meticulous copyists of rabbinic texts—not unlike Muslim scholars of the city, who, from the end of the eighth century, acquired reputations as prodigious and precise copyists of jurisprudential writings.[22] Under the leadership of R. Nisim, Qayrawanese Jewish scholars compared variant manuscripts of Talmud in order to establish the optimal textual iteration.[23] (The same activities were undertaken later by Rashi and the tosafists in northern Europe.)[24] At a time when the geonic academies were not issuing any "official" or "approved" exemplars of the rabbinic corpora,[25] scholars in Jerusalem and in European lands designated particular manuscripts produced in the Qayrawanese academies of Rabbis Ḥushiel, Ḥananel, Ya'aqov, and Nisim as ones that were "*mugahim*," "corrected."[26] The exemplars in question seem to have been regarded as "fair copies," manuscripts whose exactitude and textual reliability was guaranteed by the master himself.[27]

Qayrawanese scholars created a pedagogic apparatus of written instructional aids that would make the student's encounter with the talmudic text less confusing. (Some works of this sort were planned, but may never have been executed.)[28] R. Nisim explained that he composed his *Sefer Mafteaḥ Man'ulei ha-Talmud* (Key to the Locks of the Talmud) because students who encountered an allusion to an anonymous tannaitic or amoraic statement without any sense of its fuller context would fail to grasp its meaning.[29] The very problem identified by R. Nisim suggests that at least some students were studying Talmud without the guidance of a master who could have supplied the needed reference points.

While the rabbinic community of Qayrawan ultimately made its own legal decisions, it was, for the most part, aware of developments in the Baghdad academies.[30] North African scholars were familiar with many geonic works, and they commissioned the composition of others.[31] Under the leadership of R. Ya'aqov ben Nisim, Qayrawanese Jews helped to disseminate geonic writings: they drew up lists of geonic responsa, collected responsa from other lands, copied them, and bundled them into compilations that were sent to Jewish communal leaders and merchants in other lands.[32] The fact that the geonic responsa in these anthologies were pegged to the order of the Babylonian Talmud[33] suggests that the sequence of this corpus was fixed and well known.[34] This organizational scheme also had a profound influence on subsequent architectonic mappings of rabbinic knowledge.

The first sustained Talmud commentaries were composed in eleventh-century Qayrawan by Rabbenu Ḥananel ben Ḥushiel (d. c. 1050) and R. Nisim ben Ya'aqov (c. 990–1062). Like the talmudic exegesis of the geonim, R. Ḥananel's Talmud commentary was not comprehensive; its compiler may have thought that material he omitted was self-explanatory. Nonetheless, he acknowledged that readers of his generation required far more assistance than had been needed by predecessors.[35] Both the scope and the texture of Rabbenu Ḥananel's Talmud commentary suggests that it reflected insights that had been honed in Qayrawan's rabbinic academy over many teaching cycles.[36] The commentary's explanation of difficult Aramaic and Hebrew locutions with reference to Greek, Arabic, and Persian words, and its references to the locations of *mishnayyot* or *beraitot* embedded in the talmudic text, offer clear evidence of its pedagogic orientation. Rabbenu Ḥananel's overview of the *sugya* (the talmudic literary unit) in the commentary, made it far easier for readers to see "the big picture", and follow meandering talmudic discussions replete with embedded narratives.[37]

One of the most striking features of Rabbenu Ḥananel's commentary is its overarching concern with applied law. Indeed, his explanation of a particularly enigmatic talmudic passage programmatically states that the Talmud is to be studied as a guide to Jewish practice.[38] A talmudic tradition (BT BM 33a) asserts that engagement in Scripture is less meritorious than engagement in Mishnah, and engagement in Mishnah is less meritorious than engagement in Talmud. Clarifying the logic behind this hierarchy of merit, Rabbenu Ḥananel explained that the study of Mishnah warranted greater merit than the study of Scripture because tannaitic traditions (those preserved in Mishnah) do double duty: Like Scripture, they set forth the commandments, but unlike Scripture, they also set forth traditions that explain the commandments and clarify how they are to be implemented. By the same token, wrote Rabbenu Ḥananel, the Talmud ranks even higher in the curricular hierarchy:

> One who engages in *talmud*, and instructs and explains the *mizvot* in their proper manner [*ke-taqqanan*] and who imparts law as it is practiced (*halakhah le-ma'aseh*)—there is no merit greater than this. For in the Talmud is found the meaning [*pitaron*] of the Torah and of the Mishnah and of the *mizvah* that are in the Tradition, law given to Moses at Sinai [*halakhah le-Moshe mi-Sinai*].[39]

For Rabbenu Ḥananel, Talmud is the most valuable of the three corpora of tradition because it is the vehicle through which readers can most fully understand the how and why of Jewish legal practice. Rabbenu Ḥananel made this same point when he appropriated a rabbinic tradition from the Bar Kokhba era and invested it with a radically different meaning. The talmudic narrative in question (BT AZ 17b) ponders why the Romans had meted out a cruel death to one sage whose only "crime" was Torah study, while they spared another sage whose five "crimes" included Torah study and the performance of acts of lovingkindness (*gemilut ḥasadim*). As if to make sense of this inequitable treatment, the amora R. Huna had offered a (purely) rhetorical explanation in a midrashic *coda*: Torah study could be construed as a crime, he suggested, if it were not applied in practice, that is, if not accompanied by deeds of lovingkindness: "One who engages only in Torah, is like one who has no God, as it says [II Chron. 15:3], '[*Now for a long season Israel had been*] *without the true God . . . and without Torah.*' "[40]

It was this passage that Rabbenu Ḥananel appropriated in affirming the Talmud's adjudicatory function. Citing the remainder of the scriptural verse adduced by R. Huna, Rabbenu Ḥananel asserted that the only person who can be said to possess Torah is one who knows how to extract information about applied law from the text of Talmud:

> "[II Chron. 15:3] '*without the true God and without an instructing priest and without Torah.*' What is '*without Torah*'? Anyone who engages solely in Torah and does not engage in miẓvot, and does not [labor to] extract the truth of the law [*le-hoẓi din le-amito*], and does not offer proper instruction—it is as if he has no Torah."[41]

By citing geonic principles of adjudication and formulating others, Rabbenu Ḥananel's commentary created bridges between exegesis and adjudication, between the talmudic text and the law to be practiced.[42] The agenda of making Talmud useable as a corpus of applied law was exceptional in the case of Shmuel ben Ḥofni Gaon, but North African Jews beginning with Rabbenu Ḥananel seem to have embraced this mission wholeheartedly. The number of adjudicatory principles that he (and his towering student, Rabbi Isaac Alfasi) articulated dramatically exceeded those formulated by the geonim.[43]

Rabbenu Ḥananel (like his student and colleague, R. Nisim) did not always note the places in which he was citing geonic perspectives, but where he did, he freely noted his points of agreement and disagreement. And even when he rejected a geonic position as unacceptable,[44] he nonetheless called it a "*melekhet shamayyim*," i.e., "a labor of heaven."[45] When he and and R. Nisim dismissed certain geonic rulings, they noted that these teachings were not rooted in Talmud, and described the rejected positions as ones that stemmed from "the custom of the yeshiva."[46]

The Talmud commentary composed by R. Nisim b. Ya'aqov also spelled out practical legal ramifications, but it took the form of a talmudic paraphrase.[47] A student reading this commentary could now grasp the content of

Talmud without opening the talmudic text itself.[48] Whether its paraphrastic form is seen as an accomodation to the social reality of study without a master, or was a catalyst to autodidactism, R. Nisim's Talmud Commentary made the presence of a teacher unnecessary.[49] This single innovation in the packaging of knowledge could both reflect—and trigger—changes in the social and institutional transmission of tradition.

Ties between the Jews of Qayrawan and the Jews of al-Andalus

Links of family, scholarship, commerce, and correspondence connected the Jewish communities at the eastern and western poles of the Maghreb: Qayrawan and al-Andalus.[50] Writing to Jews in Qayrawan from Babylonia in the first quarter of the ninth century, Pirqoi ben Baboi took it for granted that the rabbinic academies in Spain were linked to those in North Africa: "We have heard that God granted you merit [*zikah etkhem*] and established houses of study [*batei midrashot*] in all the lands of Ifriqiyya and in all the places of Sefarad, and that God granted you the privilege to utter and engage in Torah day and night."[51] Ties between these communities persisted until Qayrawan's destruction in 1057. Shmuel HaNagid of al-Andalus (c. 993–1056) wrote to R. Ḥushiel of Qayrawan (father of Rabbenu Ḥananel) with halakhic queries, eulogized him eloquently upon his death, and wedded his own son, Yehoseph, to the daughter of R. Nisim of Qayrawan;[52] the latter's Talmud commentary refers to "a student from Spain."[53] And before R. Isaac Alfasi (1013–1103) emigrated to Spain in 1088 and assumed leadership at the rabbinic academy at Lucena,[54] he studied in Qayrawan with R. Ya'aqov bar Nisim and Rabbenu Ḥananel and composed the seminal (and multiply revised) *Halakhot Rabbati*.[55]

In referring to their land as "Sefarad," Jews of al-Andalus identified it with a place mentioned in Obadiah 1:20 as a land settled by exiles from Jerusalem, associated by the Targum with the Roman province of Hispania. Yet, as Jonathan Decter noted, the boundaries of "Sefarad" changed over time not only because of military and political realignments, but because they were reimagined. "In essence," writes Decter, "it was the extension of a Sefardi cultural model that determined the physical borders of Sefarad, and not vice versa."[56] The rabbinic subculture of "Sefarad" may be understood as a fusion of practices and attitudes developed by Jewish scholars in al-Andalus itself—and in North Africa prior to the destruction of Qayrawan.

According to Haim Zev Hirschberg, much of what is regarded as medieval Sefardi culture was indebted to North African Jewry.[57] Certain developments that are regarded as characteristically Sefardi—Hebrew poetry[58] and Hebrew (and comparative) philology,[59] for example—may have been exported to al-Andalus from the Maghreb. The interest of medieval Sefardim in philosophy (known as "external wisdom" or "external science") can be traced to Qayrawan, with some precision. The writings of Isaac Israeli (d. 955), which synthesized Greek, Arabic, and Jewish sources, were an important conduit of neoplatonic thought for subsequent Jewish philosophers in Andalusia;[60] and those of his disciple, Dunash ben Tamim (885–955), influenced a roster of Spanish Jewish notables who produced work in philosophy, poetry, philology, exegesis, and law.[61] (Dunash ben Tamim saw himself as linked to the Jews of al-Andalus by patronage; he dedicated one of his works to the Iberian benefactor, Ḥasdai ibn Shaprut.)[62] Additional study may facilitate more precise reconstruction of the place of Qayrawanese rabbinic accomplishments—such as the establishment of a definitive recension of Talmud, composition of academic analyses of the Talmud's language and method, and the collation, summation, arrangement, and analysis of the geonic oeuvre—in the development of subsequent Sefardi rabbinic culture.

Sefarad's Early Reception of Written Talmud, "Our Talmud," and Its Sacrality

Like the Qayrawanese, Jews of al-Andalus used written texts of Talmud at a time when Babylonian geonim resolutely persisted in the oral transmission of this corpus. In the case of the Andalusian Jews, reliance on written Talmud was not only dictated by necessity, but was justified by a tradition (in several variants) claiming that Spanish ancestors had been early recipients of this inscription.[63] Some narratives that circulated within al-Andalus identified Paltoi Gaon[64] as the Eastern scholar who had provided Spanish Jews with written Talmud; others mentioned Natronai bar Ḥakhinai.[65] According to a narrative recorded by R. Judah al-Barceloni in the late eleventh or early twelfth century, after many centuries of partly oral and partly written transmission, the entire Talmud was ultimately inscribed by a scholar from the East.[66]

> For the Talmud is received tradition transmitted by [*qabbalah u-masoret be-yede*] the yeshivah heads, generation after generation,

> from the days of the exile of Yehoyakhin King of Judah and the Prophet Ezekiel, whose yeshivah was on the Euphrates River. And the Talmud was transmitted, orally, by the prophets, from the days of that yeshivah of Yehoyakhin's exile, one yeshivah after another, and by the sages of each generation, until Rav Ashi and Ravina. And in their days, Talmud was closed [*nistam*] to further additions. And each yeshivah transmitted it, orally, in its closed state, to the next yeshivah, and the sages of each and every generation—part of it in writing, and part of it by heart [*miqẓato katuv u-miqẓato 'al peh*]—from the days of these early ones up until [the time of] Isaac, the son of the Exilarch's sister, through whom it was arranged and transmitted [*she-hayya 'arukh u-masur be-yaddo*]. And he wrote the Talmud for the diaspora [Jews] of Spain.[67]

The end of this narrative (echoed in other Hebrew writings composed in medieval Spain and Provence) evokes a talmudic passage [BT Yeb. 115b] referring to the death of the exilarch, R. Isaac, while en route from "Qortva" to "Asfamya." Modern scholars have debated whether "Asfamya" designates all of Spain, or only part of it, and whether "Qortva" refers to a place inside or outside that land,[68] but medieval Andalusian Jews entertained no such uncertainty: they regarded this talmudic passage as one that documented their community's early acquisition of written Talmud.[69]

* * *

It is not clear whether or not Sefardi scholars ever invoked this tradition in order to argue that they had been "released from" the tannaitic dictum prohibiting the recitation of *oral matters* from a written text;[70] what is clear is that their regional "memory" of the Talmud's purposeful inscription informed the Spanish rabbis' perception of this corpus as a self-sufficient source for adjudication, notwithstanding the tannaitic prohibition against deriving applied law from "*talmud*." In his late eleventh- or early twelfth-century comment on the tannaitic passage in question [BT BB 130b], "one does not learn halakhah from *talmud*,"[71] R. Joseph ibn Migash made a philological observation that had been noted earlier in Sherira's *Epistle*.[72] According to Ibn Migash, when the tannaim who formulated this dictum used the term "*talmud*," they could not possibly have been referring to the written composition bearing this title, since it did not yet exist. This being the case, he reasoned, "*talmud*" for the ancient rabbis was something quite different from what he himself called "our Talmud." Elaborating on this point, Ibn Migash asserted that

> this Talmud of ours ["*ha-Talmud shelanu*"] is [a corpus of] applied law [*halakhah le-ma'aseh*], for it was not written/consigned to writing until after several generations of investigation and scrutiny ['*iyyun ve-diqduq*], and after several redactions [*mahadurei*]. And it is as if that which they told us in it is applied law. After all, they wrote it down for the explicit purpose of [guiding] practice [*she-hare la'asot bo ma'aseh ketavuhu*].[73]

According to Ibn Migash, "our Talmud" differs from the earlier "*talmud*" not simply because it is transmitted in a different manner—which is to say, in writing. "Our Talmud" is also distinct in content. Unlike unwritten "*talmud*," "our Talmud" consists of selections that were judiciously winnowed from the oral corpus, so that all its teachings possess the doubly vetted status of *halakhah le-ma'aseh*, applied law. From Ibn Migash's perspective, the act of inscription entailed more than a simple change of medium; it reshaped the corpus of tradition itself.

The theory of "our Talmud" articulated by Ibn Migash may have been held earlier by Shmuel HaNagid as well; the latter's student, Judah al-Barceloni, made a passing reference to "Talmud transmitted to us, which is *halakhah le-ma'aseh*."[74] And though the later Maimonides (whose father studied with R. Isaac ibn Migash) does not seem to have explicitly articulated the "our Talmud" theory, his defense of the decision to omit discarded minority opinions from his legal code relies on precisely this theory: "Since . . . the Talmud has already settled every law either specifically or generally, by means of the general principles of decision-making, and there is no longer divergence in the law as applied in practice, why should I mention the name of one whom the law does not follow?"[75] It is conceivable that Maimonides avoided the "our Talmud" theory articulated by Ibn Migash (a scholar he greatly admired) because he was more wary of Karaite polemics than his Spanish counterparts. Living in the east, where he was more intensely exposed to the Karaite claim that Written Torah was the sole source of Jewish law (an early iteration of "*sola Scriptura*"), Maimonides may have felt it prudent to avoid mentioning that the Talmud on which Rabbanites relied was not identical to the "*talmud*" mentioned in ancient teachings. Yet even without this explanation,

Maimonides articulated a theory of Talmud that justified its use as a corpus of applied law.[76] Like Sherira and Hai Gaon before him, Maimonides argued (in the introduction to *Mishneh Torah* and the introduction to his *Commentary on the Mishnah*) that proof of the Talmud's authority lies in the fact that its teachings had garnered the near-universal assent of the community of Israel.

The theory of "our Talmud" continued to shape Sefardi culture at least into the thirteenth century. Writing in Toledo, R. Meir Halevi Abulafia (1170–1244) sharpened the contrast between the term "*talmud*" in the tannaitic dictum in question and the body of writing known as "our Talmud":

> This [ancient rabbinic prohibition against deriving applied law from *talmud*] applies to *their talmud*, which they recited orally. But *our* Talmud, once it was/which is written, was written for purposes of applied law [*halakhah le-ma'aseh*]. . . . For when it was written, it was written in order that applied law might be derived from it.[77]

The notion that the text known as "our Talmud" was specially composed as a repository of practical adjudication (and that it was not to be confused with the earlier, unwritten corpus of that name, mentioned in the tannaitic prohibition) may have released the above-mentioned medieval Sefardi scholars from a challenge that was felt keenly by their North European counterparts: the need to negotiate the relative legal authorities of talmudic and non-talmudic traditions.[78]

* * *

It is not clear precisely when the Jews of medieval Sefarad came to regard the written Talmud as a sacred artifact, but the emergence of this notion might be detected by tracking successive rabbinic explanations of why post-biblical tradition was to be trusted.[79] Writing in Babylonia, Sa'adya Gaon, Shmuel ben Ḥofni Gaon and Hai Gaon concluded that the consensus of the Jewish people was the guarantor that tradition was authentic and authoritative.[80] As Hai famously put it, were it not for the vetting of living tradents, we could not even be certain of Scripture's authenticity.[81] Writing in Spain, HaNagid implicitly equated tradition with Talmud, and while he echoed the argument from consensus in affirming the authority of Talmud, he also added another claim that Sherira Gaon had (implicitly) made only about the Mishnah.[82]

According to HaNagid, Talmud is authoritative because it belongs in the category of Scripture itself: "The Talmud is [authoritatively] accepted [*muḥzaq*] and clear to the entire Diaspora of Israel—to the point that it is [authoritatively] accepted [*muḥzaq*] by all Israel, and is upheld in our hands [*u-mequyyam be-yaddeinu*] like Written Torah and Prophets."[83] A century later, the association of Talmud with Scripture was made far more strongly in *Sefer ha-Qabbalah*. In describing Shmuel HaNagid's contribution to the propagation of rabbinic culture—his hiring of copyists, dissemination of biblical and rabbinic texts throughout the Jewish world, and creation of a personal library—Ibn Daud wrote:

> And he performed [acts of munificence] for Israel in Sefarad and in the Land of the Maghreb and in Ifriqiyya and in the land of Egypt, and in Sicily and as far as the Babylonian academies and as far as the Holy City. All Torah scholars in these lands benefited from his wealth. And he acquired many books of sacred writings—and of Mishnah and Talmud, *which are also sacred writings*.[84]

In adding the qualifying words at the end of this passage, Abraham ibn Daud pointedly altered the category of "sacred writings" (generally thought to refer to the twenty-four books of Tanakh) and expanded it to include Mishnah and Talmud as well, corpora of *oral matters*.

Andalusian Jewry, the Babylonian Geonim, and Andalusian Rabbinic Compositions

Twentieth-century scholars produced disparate pictures of the relationship that prevailed in the early eleventh century between Andalusian Jews and Babylonian geonim. According to one perspective, tension between these two centers began when R. Ḥanokh, an emigrant from Bari to al-Andalus, failed to answer letters sent him by the Babylonian Sherira Gaon,[85] and it continued when R. Ḥanokh's young student, Shmuel HaNagid, disputed some of Hai Gaon's legal decisions.[86] The foremost proponent of this viewpoint, Mordecai Margalioth, claimed that Jews of eleventh-century al-Andalus (the poet Shlomo ibn Gabirol among them) were keenly aware of their region's competition with Babylonia and took pride in local "triumphs."[87] Margalioth found evidence for this rivalry in several comments made by HaNagid at the time of Hai Gaon's death in 1038: a poetic assertion of newfound parity between the foremost centers of rabbinic leadership—"Bavel, Ifriqiyya, and Spain are now all even,"[88] an invitation to others to turn to him with legal queries, and an elegiac claim that the celestial beings themselves had come to avert their faces from the East once Torah came to dwell in the West.[89]

Shraga Abramson took issue with many of Margalioth's claims, rejecting (among other things) the notion of a rivalry between al-Andalus and Babylonia.[90] This perspective finds some corroboration in the fact that early Andalusian rabbinic literature is highly dependent upon geonic writings,[91] and in Gerson Cohen's analysis of Abraham ibn Daud's *Sefer ha-Qabbalah*, a Hebrew chronicle, composed in 1161, more than a century after HaNagid's death. One section of that chronicle, Ibn Daud's "Tale of the Four Captives," portrays Cordoba's Umayyad rulers as eager to see local Jews attenuate their relationship with the geonim in the rival Abbasid empire.[92] According to this narrative, when Jews in al-Andalus redeemed R. Moshe of Bari who had been taken captive by pirates on the high seas, the ship's captain was furious; he could have demanded far more money for the release of the hostage had he known that he was a prominent scholar. Moreover, wrote Ibn Daud, R. Moshe's arrival in Spain was of great political importance, for it reduced the local Jewish community's dependence on the geonim: "the King . . . was delighted by the fact that the Jews of his domain no longer had need for the people of Babylonia."[93] Both the substance and structure of *Sefer ha-Qabbalah* emphasized that God Himself willed this *translatio studii*, the shift in the geographic center of rabbinic learning from Babylonia to al-Andalus.[94]

In his analysis of this chronicle (and of the "Tale of the Four Captives" in particular), Gerson Cohen questioned its portrait of animosity between the Andalusian Jewish community and the Babylonian geonim, and he demonstrated ways in which Ibn Daud had engaged in historical distortion. A plethora of evidence, and even a statement by the chronicler himself, undermined *Sefer ha-Qabbalah*'s assertion that Jews of al-Andalus and Qayrawan stopped sending funds and questions to the Babylonian yeshivot.[95] Moreover, noted Cohen, the enmity between Hai Gaon and R. Ḥanokh of Bari was greatly exaggerated in the chronicle, and the image of Shmuel HaNagid was manipulated in order to fashion him into the icon of Sefardi Jewish culture.[96] According to Cohen, Ibn Daud magnified the rivalry between the rabbinic centers in the West and the East at a time when there was no longer a commanding Gaonate[97] in order to enhance the power of a particular rabbinic faction in twelfth-century Spain.[98]

* * *

The caliber of rabbinic learning in al-Andalus prior to the late eleventh century has been debated by twentieth-century scholars,[99] but all agree that it was greatly enhanced by the arrival of the septuagenarian Rabbi Isaac Alfasi in 1088. Shmuel HaNagid had done much to promote greater access to Talmud in the early eleventh century, commissioning copyists and sending manuscripts to Jewish communities throughout the world,[100] but he had nothing but scorn for the ignorant Andalusian rabbis of his time, who fancied themselves Talmud instructors: "One needs, it seems, only fringes, a turban and beard to head the Academy now."[101] In the poem, "*Ha-yirhav ha-zeman*" ("Would Time Dare?"), HaNagid presents himself as defending Rav Ashi, the amora of the late fourth and early fifth centuries amora who was the last to transmit applied legal instruction. Some rabbinic contemporaries, implies the poet, are benighted fools. Not only do they misunderstand Talmud and egregiously abuse it, but their piety is belabored. HaNagid's caustic portrait (replete with misogynistic overtones) of a pompous, boorish, and unqualified instructor takes center stage in the poem, but the "populist" nature of Talmud study is also a target of his critique. The poet thought it preposterous that Talmud study should be undertaken by the masses, as if it were a pursuit appropriate for all Jews.[102] The very behavior of Talmud students was esthetically offensive, an assault on decorum. Describing their swaying in the study hall on Hoshana Rabbah, a festival when willow branches are beaten on the ground, HaNagid writes witheringly that "their heads bob up and down like the knocking of willows." Worse, the very manner in which Talmud is studied in this *beit midrash* evokes a barnyard holding pen:

> My brother,
> remember the day we passed the House of Prayer, the Day of
>   Willows,
> and heard up close a donkey bray
> and cows cry and low? And I asked:
> "Is the Lord's House now a dairy?
> This is a sin and disgrace."
> And they told me: "There are no fatlings or mules
> in the House of the Lord;
> they are reading in the Tractate and the *Gate*."[103]

In another poem, HaNagid identified what he saw as the challenges facing rabbinic Jews in al-Andalus, and he set forth specific desiderata. After nearly losing his life in battle,[104] he composed "*Elohim he-erikh li peh ba-torot*" ("The Lord has enabled me to expound on the Torahs") In the spring of 1049. Expressing gratitude for his deliverance, HaNagid took an oath to compose a work that would "anoint those parched for *nomos* [*dat*] and Mishnah and Talmud with the dew of God's testimony [*te'udah*, presumably Torah] and with counsels in the adjudication of *halakhot*."[105] In the first (and longer) part of this rhymed poem, HaNagid offers a brief historical overview of the rabbinic corpora that resembles the narrative in Sherira Gaon's *Epistle*, while moving beyond it chronologically. According to the poet, details of the miẓvot had, for generations, been preserved in the heart and transmitted orally. At a certain crisis point, however, the "unleashing of tribulations, formerly bound" led to scarcity in both the "bread" and "water of understanding." It was in response to these conditions, wrote HaNagid, that "R. Judah the Patriarch arose and collected Oral Torah in six granaries [i.e., Orders]; . . . he recalled the disputes known in his generations and resolved them."[106] Once the Mishnah and other tannaitic teachings (*beraitot*) were inscribed, they were interpreted by God-fearing people with the aim of deciding applied law. So successful were they in this restorative enterprise, asserted HaNagid, that "doubts vanished from the lips of teachers, male and female."[107] Yet turbulent external conditions once again led to the rise of doubts, and ultimately to the disappearance of the "secrets of *halakhot* that had been resolved for Early Ones." Fortunately, amoraim found clues in the Mishnah, and thus made it possible for Jewish law to flourish again. Over a period of time, they "gathered laws/*nomoi* [*datot*] like eggs" [cf. Isa. 10:14] and "plucked *miẓvot* like sprouts" [cf. II Kings 4:39], until

> Rav Ashi and Ravina set them in this Talmud,
> and built a wall and towers for this Torah,
> erecting a rampart and dwellings for the law [*dat*].
> They winnowed every surprising matter through [the sieve of] Torah
> [*ba-te'udah*]
> Like one who presses the grapes and vintage of the vine.[108]

Until this point, HaNagid's rhymed history had described the episodes of confusion that disrupted rabbinic transmission as ones triggered by forces outside the Jewish community. At this juncture in the narrative, however, the poet directed blame at internal Jewish developments. According to HaNagid, the absence of legal clarity in his own time was to be traced to the rabbinic teachers who came after the amoraim.

Many after them who ranged far and wide [cf. Dan. 12:4] . . .
instructed people using sayings that flout Talmud.
They wrote their compositions, in which a few words were allied to distortions.
Unfit sayings were [thus] said in the names of fit and noble leaders.
And, today, responsa in their name are spread, removing many from the just path.
[Though] they never said these, they are spoken, today, in their name![109]

According to HaNagid, the legal confusion that prevailed within his own rabbinic society was caused by halakhic works that contravened Talmud and masqueraded as geonic writings.[110] In order to restore the needed clarity, HaNagid would compose a new guide to applied Jewish law, one that would rely on two sources: Talmud and the teachings of Hai Gaon:

I place the Talmud above my words
as [cf. Ezek. 16:3] a birthplace and land of origin.
And in that which I lay out and write, I will rely on choice geonic sayings,
setting before me the wonders of Rav Hai, greatest of them all,
diadems in which to glory.
From his well I draw and his bread I eat, finding nothing bitter.
And from his clouds I will slake the parched.[111]

HaNagid's student, Judah al-Barceloni, preserved some of his teacher's halakhic teachings in his own,[112] but the fact that HaNagid's *Hilkheta Gavrata* (Aramaic for *Halakhot Gedolot,* Great [Compendium of] Laws), did not survive led to a dramatic disagreement between two twentieth-century scholars about what it was that the Granadan leader had actually written—or intended to write. According to Mordecai Margalioth, HaNagid's lost work was highly influential: a topically arranged, comprehensive code of Jewish law, and the forerunner of subsequent Andalusian codes—including Maimonides' *Mishneh Torah,* which has been mistakenly described as the first of its kind.[113] Shraga Abramson vehemently disputed many of Margalioth's assertions, especially his claim about HaNagid's influence on subsequent halakhists. According to Abramson, the most that HaNagid would have attempted would have been the resolution of disputed legal questions.[114]

Recent studies of particular *genizah* fragments by David Sklare and Yehuda Ẓvi Stampfer have added to the portrait of rabbinic culture in eleventh century al-Andalus. Their analysis of *al-Hawwi*, a six-volume Arabic halakhic compilation produced in Spain in the second quarter of the eleventh century, and of the correspondence between its author, Rabbi David ben Sa'adya and Shmuel HaNagid, confirms that the caliber of rabbinic learning in al-Andalus improved significantly upon Rabbi Isaac Alfasi's arrival from North Africa a few decades after HaNagid's death. *Al-Hawwi* (fragments of which have been found in multiple copies) was designed as a textbook for would-be *dayyanim*, Jewish judges who rendered binding legal decisions.[115] The author's introductory remarks reveal that he did not design his work for a readership learned in Talmud; his aim was to "establish basic concepts of law and clear exposition of all the ordinances from the sources of halakhah," and to present readers with "whatever *dayyanim* need of the science of legislated law [*madda' ha-mishpat ha-neḥqaq*] for purposes of judging [*lishpot bo*]."[116] Because of its systematic arrangement, its elaborate explanation of the laws, and the attention it paid to the sources of the law (along the lines of *usul al fiqh*, the Islamic science of jurisprudence),[117] even readers who lacked access to a master—the preferable mode of education—would be able to acquire this knowledge autodidactically.[118] Nor was the language of its composition an accidental choice. R. David explained that he composed *al-Hawwi* in Arabic so that it might be used by Jews educated in Arabic culture who were beginners in the study of halakhah.[119] A later work composed in Saragossa echoed the notion that works of halakhah written in Arabic were designed for novices in this field. After listing rabbinic scholars of various lands who had composed halakhic works in Arabic, R. Shlomo ben Yosef noted, "Most of their *perushim* [interpretations] and responsa are in Arabic—in order to make it easy for the questioners and the students."[120]

Shmuel HaNagid thought well of *al-Hawwi* and held its author in esteem. The Granadan Jewish leader praised Rabbi David ben Sa'adya's halakhic talents in one of his poems, noted Sklare, and he even encouraged Rabbi David to assume the office of *dayyan*.[121] Yet not long after HaNagid's death, when Rabbi Isaac Alfasi, head of the Lucena yeshivah, was asked about a passage in R. David's *al-Hawwi*, he asserted that its author had not properly understood either the underlying talmudic passage or the relevant material in *Halakhot Gedolot*.[122] Indeed, wrote Alfasi, *al-Hawwi* could be fruitfully used only by learned scholars who could distinguish between the correct and incorrect parts of its content. Under no circumstances was R. David's work, or any other Arabic halakhic manual for *dayyanim*, to be used as a guide to applied law, warned Alfasi: "And whoever communes with one of these Arabic monographs and gives instruction on its basis, without consulting the Talmud, will face a future reckoning. And if he is in a place that has rabbinic scholars, and he [nonetheless] instructs, he is in the category of what they [ancient sages; BT San. 7b] mentioned in the matter of [Deut. 16:21] *You shall not plant an* ashera *or any tree near God's altar*."[123] A century later, R. David ben Sa'adya's manual elicited even harsher criticism from Alfasi's student, R. Isaac ibn Albalia.[124] These changing assessments of Rabbi David's *al-Hawwi* indicate, as Sklare suggested, that rabbinic scholars in Spain held themselves to ever higher standards of learning over the course of the eleventh and twelfth centuries.[125]

Future research may help to resolve one of the bones of contention that divided Margalioth and Abramson: the question of whether eleventh-century Andalusian Jews composed, or aspired to compose, comprehensive codes of Jewish law. Abramson rejected this notion outright,[126] but it is hard to ignore the fact that the programmatic guidelines spelled out in HaNagid's oath poem of 1049 correspond to features of the *Mishneh Torah* that Maimonides took pains to emphasize 130 years later in his introduction to that work: omission of legal dispute, use of clear and accessible language, inclusion of the latest opinions, comprehensiveness of scope, and preemption of the need for any other legal work. Explaining that his work would omit legal debates and employ an easily accessible language and style, HaNagid announced that he would

> promulgate [matters that are] undisputed,
> in limpid language and clear ways,
> Removing each matter of probity from graves,
> and entombing every distortion.[127]

In referring to "limpid language and clear ways," HaNagid was championing the use of Hebrew, endorsing a cultural ideal that had begun with Sa'adya Gaon and that remained a hallmark of Andalusian Jews over the next several centuries.[128] Maimonides' avoidance of talmudic Aramaic is better known, but HaNagid preceded him in expressing a strong linguistic preference for the use of Hebrew in a halakhic composition.[129]

HaNagid also asserted that his compendium of applied Jewish law would take into account *all* authoritative rabbinic traditions that had been generated up to his own time.

> In my book you will see the words of ancients and moderns,
> And you will not need to labor in search [for them].[130]

When read with historical hindsight, these remarks seem to presage those written by Maimonides when he proclaimed his *Mishneh Torah* to be a work so up to date that it would relieve the student of the need to consult any other rabbinic text.[131]

It is not known whether HaNagid created anything resembling a comprehensive code of Jewish law, but the compositional goals that he articulated in his oath poem may be read as countenancing a project of this sort. This interest in codification ought not be taken for granted; it is quite different, after all, from the orientation of Qayrawanese rabbinic scholars of the eleventh century, who preferred to transmit applied law through Talmud commentary. Nor was the impulse to codify law a legacy of the geonim. The omnibus Hebrew-Aramaic halakhic compilations produced in the geonic period did not bear the imprimatur of the academies, and the systematic Judeo-Arabic treatises on particular topics of law composed by later heads of the yeshivot were not comprehensive codes of Jewish law.

If it is fair to speak of Andalusian Jewry's predilection for the codification of applied law,[132] cross-cultural analysis would suggest that this generic preference may have been part of a broader regional orientation.[133] The Maliki legal scholars of Umayyad al-Andalus, a politically powerful "clerical aristocracy," took a position oblique to many of their Islamic colleagues. Unlike other legal scholars of their time, the Andalusian Malikis declared that *ijtihad*, intellectual exertion, could not be applied in *hadith* study. Their prohibition not only preempted the derivation of new legal interpretation; it even forbade *ijtihad* for purposes of personal reflection.[134] For this reason, the Malikis of al-Andalus championed the study of manuals of jurisprudence, *furu*, and they produced a distinct type of legal writing, in codificatory form.[135] In North Africa, on the other hand, Maliki legal scholars did not forbid the application of *ijtihad*; they continued to study (written) *hadith*—and to regard these units of tradition as religiously useful sources. Further investigation may shed light on the noteworthy coincidence of generic preferences in the Jewish and Muslim legal cultures of these two geographic regions: the production of codes of applied law by rabbinic scholars and Islamic jurists of al-Andalus,[136] and the willingness of Qayrawanese legal scholars, both Jews and Muslims, to persist in the interpretation of post-scriptural tradition.

Differences in cultural orientation between the rabbinic communities of Qayrawan and al-Andalus became moot after the destruction of Qayrawan in 1057,[137] and the Lucena-trained students of Rabbi Isaac Alfasi greatly facilitated the blending of North African and Andalusian traditions into Sefardi rabbinic culture.[138]

Sefardi Culture's Preservation of the Oral Transmission of *Oral Matters*

The "Spanish" version of Sherira Gaon's *Epistle* emphasizes two points not found in its "French" counterpart. For this reason, Maimonides, like other readers of the "Spanish" recension, learned not only that Rabbi Judah the Patriarch had actually written the Mishnah (and not merely "arranged" it);[139] he also read that this inscribed Mishnah was transmitted by Rabbi Judah in a very specific way. One noteworthy detail (absent from the *Epistle*'s "French" recension) was that Rabbi Judah the Patriarch amplified the Mishnah's teachings in unscripted, oral exposition even after he had committed this corpus to writing. The second detail (found only in the "Spanish" recension) was that Mishnah continued to be learned by heart and transmitted from memory even after it was written.[140] In short, like other careful readers of the "Spanish" recension of Sherira's *Epistle,* Maimonides understood that even if written, a corpus of *oral matters* might still be transmitted through oral performance.[141] This awareness is evident in some of Maimonides' remarks about his fashioning of the *Mishneh Torah*, and in his references to the manner in which his code was to be studied and transmitted. Together these comments strongly suggest that Maimonides conceived of his own legal code as a work of *oral matters.*

As Isadore Twersky noted, Maimonides drew attention to the intentionally skeletal style of his code, referring to *Mishneh Torah* as a work he had composed "in the way of the Mishnah." Since teachings formulated in so truncated a fashion could not be grasped by anyone attempting to learn on his own, a student encountering the code's elliptical style would need to have a teacher reconstitute the body of tradition compressed therein.[142] In other words, Maimonides designed the *Mishneh Torah* to be studied in living encounters between teachers and students, which is to say, through oral transmission. (This process had been modeled by R. Judah the Patriarch, according to the "Spanish" version of Sherira's *Epistle.*) Maimonides also noted in several passages that he had designed the *Mishneh Torah* as a work to be memorized. He drew attention to various compositional choices that were intended to render the work "easy to know . . . by heart," and he quite consciously decided to "divide every chapter into short *halakhot* in order that they be arranged in memory."[143] The Talmud could not be memorized, but the *Mishneh Torah* could, wrote Maimonides.[144] Indeed, noted Twersky, the code's very title contained an allusion to the oral-memorial goal of study.[145]

Maimonides' obvious concern for the manner in which the *Mishneh Torah* would be studied can be understood as an expression of a cultural system that assigned discrete "performative markers" to the transmission of *oral matters*. Notwithstanding the fact that teachings within this category had been committed to writing, the behaviors connected with their transmission (such as memorization and oral elaboration) helped to preserve their status, along with the existing taxonomic distinction between *oral matters* and *written matters*. Some of the vehement criticisms leveled against the *Mishneh Torah* (and against other codes of Jewish law) reflect the failure of critics to pick up on these behavioral clues. While critics were offended by the code's omission of underlying disputes and by its failure to name tradents, the codifier assumed that the omitted material would be recalled through the exertionary activity of oral dialogue.[146]

A later legal code produced in the Sefardi orbit, Joseph Qaro's *Shulḥan 'Arukh*, was also designed by its author for memorization—which is to say, for oral transmission and living amplification. In the introduction to the first edition of this code, a pocket-sized text printed in Venice in 1565, the author gave explicit directions about how the work was to be used: "The young pupils will utter it at all times, and will recite its language by heart, and this formulation of childhood will be arranged in their mouths, as applied law [*halakhah le-ma'aseh*]. And thus [cf. Prov. 22:6] '*they will not swerve from it, even in old age.*'"[147] Qaro's assumption that his code would be memorized reinforces the conjecture that the ancient distinction between *written matters* and *oral matters* was kept alive in Sefardi culture over the course of centuries by specific behaviors of transmission.[148] Within pockets of this rabbinic society, it was not the absence or presence of writing per se that indicated whether a corpus of tradition belonged in the category of *written matters* or *oral matters*, but rather, the behaviors and practices of the texts' readers and teachers. Qaro's remarks in the *Shulḥan 'Arukh*'s first edition suggests that these distinctions were perpetuated among Sefardi students even after the notion of *megilot setarim* ("scrolls to be sequestered") had been rendered unimaginable by the advent of print. Through activities of learning, performance, and transmission, Sefardi rabbinic culture prevented the category of *oral matters* from falling into disuse or from becoming a mere academic construct.

Andalusian Jewish Anxiety about the Sources of Applied Rabbinic Law

Eleventh-century Jewish scholars in both Qayrawan and al-Andalus shared a common agenda. Though the rabbinic leaders of these regions approached their work in somewhat different ways, all were engaged in the mission of translating the text of the Babylonian Talmud into a system of applied law. This project was far less important in Babylonia itself, where applied law was heard from the mouths of living tradents; it was they who indicated whether or not talmudic teachings had been implemented in practice. However, outside of the geonic academies, where students accessed the Talmud through the written text, the need to transform Talmud into an operative system of applied law was keenly felt.

The written corpus that eleventh century scholars possessed was not laid out in a manner that lent itself to this practical goal. After all, much of the Talmud's content does not concern law, and the legal material it does contain is transmitted in the form of unresolved disputes. An even more acute problem for Jews outside Babylonia was the Talmud's distinction between halakhah, a received legal teaching, and *halakhah le-ma'aseh*, a received legal teaching whose implementation in practice is attested by a living tradent; as noted above, one talmudic passage cautioned against presuming that what one learned from "talmud" was prescriptive.[149] Hai Gaon had warned the Qayrawanese Jews that lived Jewish experience could not be reconstructed from the text alone, and he rebuked them for their fundamentalist reliance upon the text. How, then, were non-Babylonian rabbinic scholars to derive applied law from the Talmud?

The transposition of Talmud into a legal reference work, a process that took place over the course of the eleventh and twelfth centuries, was in no way straightforward, already-scripted or predetermined. Disputes between rabbinic scholars that erupted in the eleventh century (and that continued to resonate into the early modern period) bear witness to the methodological, epistemological, and sociological challenges encountered along the way. If the talmudic text was not the sole guide to applied law, how were its prescriptions to be tempered by other sources of tradition, and what, precisely, were these other sources? How much weight was to be granted to geonic mediations of Jewish law? Who was entitled to discern applied law?

Some of these concerns can be discerned in Shmuel HaNagid's claim that the halakhic confusion of his time had been bred by the circulation of "faux" geonic writings. The work whose composition he announced in the oath poem, a guide to applied Jewish law, would rely only on Talmud itself, mediated by the interpretations of Hai Gaon. Yet a century later, esteemed Jews in al-Andalus still disagreed about the sources that were to be consulted in determining applied law. An early twelfth-century altercation, known from a responsum and from (an immoderately worded) epistolary correspondence, reveals that the disputants themselves understood that they were arguing about epistemology. Rabbi Ya'aqov Alacal'i, a Spaniard, relied on Talmud alone in arriving at a particular legal decision, while Abu Said Ḥalfon Ha-Levi, a wealthy Egyptian merchant of Damietta who had studied at the Lucena yeshivah,[150] relied on the talmudic interpretations of the geonim.

The responsum occasioned by this dispute, written by Rabbi Joseph ibn Migash, affirmed that judges [*dayyanim*] rendering legal decisions were to rely on geonic writings, not on Talmud itself. Yet it would be wrong to infer that Ibn Migash regarded geonic writings as ones that bore greater "legal weight" than the Talmud.[151] On the contrary; the head of the Lucena yeshivah tailored his remarks to suit the sociological and curricular circumstances described in the question posed. The inquiry concerned a *dayyan*, a judge charged with issuing legal decisions, who had never studied Talmud with a master. Whether selected by the parties to a dispute or appointed by the community itself, *dayyanim* were arbitrators, and many of the tasks they oversaw were of a regulatory nature. They determined the appropriateness of witnesses, validated documents, administered oaths, and appointed guardians and proxies. *Dayyanim* also rendered legal decisions in monetary cases.[152] However, unlike *ba'alei hora-a*, masters of applied halakhic instruction, *dayyanim* were not expected to be learned in Talmud.

Keying his response to this particular demographic, Ibn Migash advised that the judge in question ought not attempt to derive his decisions from

Talmud, but should instead consult geonic responsa or legal compilations. The latter two were designed as reference works, whereas the former was not:

> [Question:] What would our master say about this man, who never in his life read a halakhah with a master, who knows neither the way of halakhah nor its interpretation, nor even how to read it—though he has seen many of the geonic responsa and books of *dinim* [regulations]. . . . Answer: . . . One who instructs on the basis of geonic responsa and relies upon them—even if he cannot understand Talmud—is more proper and praiseworthy than a man who thinks that he knows Talmud and relies upon himself. . . . It is better to permit him to give instruction than many other people who have established themselves as teachers in our time.[153]

The approach to practical adjudication taken by R. Ya'aqov Alacal'i, the party whose perspective was dismissed by Rabbi Joseph ibn Migash (and by the Egyptian merchant Ḥalfon), does not seem to have been anomalous in Spain, either in his own time or among subsequent generations. For some Sefardim (as for the Qayrawanese students who wrote to Hai Gaon), the default assumption was that adjudication was to be made solely with reference to the talmudic text. This would seem to explain why, from the time of Shmuel HaNagid onward, distinguished Spanish and Provençal scholars expressed amazement that the geonim had not rooted their own rulings in "the foundations of Talmud."[154] While certain scholars of the twelfth through fourteenth centuries (Naḥmanides foremost among them) made a point of inserting overlooked geonic perspectives into their glosses on rabbinic law,[155] the late medieval Ottoman scholar, R. Elijah Mizraḥi (1455–1525), summed up the more characteristic Sefardi perspective after anthologizing the statements of many of his predecessors: "You already know that several matters of the geonim have been pushed aside because it seems that these matters are not founded on the principles of Talmud—even though [you know that] the stature of the geonim is very great, and that we live by their words and their Torah. . . . But the world does not rely upon them."[156]

When rabbinic adjudicators of medieval Spain explicitly diverged from known geonic rulings in order to uphold talmudic guidelines, they might have been emulating the geonim themselves, who themselves freely deviated from predecessors' legal decisions. Yet in eschewing geonic teachings, medieval Sefardim might also have been relying on their belief that "our Talmud" was the quintessential guide to applied law, a work that transmitted *halakhah le-ma'aseh* and not only halakhah; that is, legal teachings that had been—and were to be—implemented in practice.

Approaches to Talmud: Sefarad versus Ashkenaz

Rabbi Joseph ibn Migash's allusion to the inadequacy of some Talmud instructors in the above-cited responsum lacks the bite of HaNagid's earlier poetic critique, but it does not differ vastly in import. In the Andalusian environment, where many (or perhaps most) of the Jews who served as *dayyanim* did not have had the opportunity to study Talmud with a master, rabbinic scholars opted for pragmatism and a division of labor.[157] When *dayyanim* consulted the systematic legal monographs composed by Sa'adya, Shmuel ben Ḥofni and Hai Gaon, they encountered the end-products of the process by which Talmud was transposed into applied law, and were relieved of the need to undertake the transposition themselves.

The study of Talmud proper remained a fairly rarified activity in medieval Sefarad, and the scholarly rabbinic class there was much smaller than in Ashkenaz.[158] Moreover, as was not the case in northern Europe, medieval Sefardi culture maintained discrete educational programs for laymen who did not aspire to the rabbinate. A typology of Jewish students set forth by Baḥya ibn Paquda in eleventh-century Spain distinguished between nine different classes on the basis of intellectual abilities and spiritual goals, and articulated for each the corresponding curricular focus. It is noteworthy that Talmud was studied only by students in the three highest classes.[159] A document from twelfth-century Egypt also describes the grouping of students into different levels, based on their abilities and needs. Some would study only the foundational curriculum of the prayer book and the Pentateuch, others would add to this the study of the Prophets and Hagiographa and Alfasi's *Halakhot*.[160] Only students at the highest level would undertake the study of Mishnah, Talmud, and talmudic commentaries (like that of Rabbenu Ḥananel).[161] Jews of medieval Spain never adopted the cultural assumption of their North European counterparts, who more strongly encouraged male students to undertake Talmud study.[162]

Nonetheless, the growing prominence of Talmud study among northern European Jews, and the intensification of contacts between Jews living in different lands, presented Sefardi culture with certain challenges.[163] Yet even after the thirteenth century, when Naḥmanides and his students channeled the tosafist oeuvre (produced by northern Europe's talmudic glossators) into the Sefardi rabbinic curriculum,[164] the study of Jewish law in Spanish rabbinic academies never assumed the adversarial quality that was characteristic of yeshivot to the north. Writing in early fifteenth-century Spain, Rabbi Joseph ibn Ḥabiba contrasted the pedagogic ambiences of the two regions: "Today in the Kingdom[s] of Ashkenaz and France . . . there are students who know as much halakhah as the rabbi, . . . they at times best him in debate. . . . But in our regions, the Kingdom of Aragon and Spain, where the rabbi is very accomplished and much more erudite than the students, where the students at times don't understand the language, and the rabbi teaches them, it would not be appropriate for them to enter into this."[165] The disparate ways in which Talmud was studied and used in Sefarad and in the lands of northern Europe are not only emblematic of the broader differences between these two Jewish subcultures that emerged in the Middle Ages; they were formative of these subcultures as well.

3

Framing Ashkenaz: Cultural Landmarks of Medieval Northern European Societies

It has been fashionable in Jewish historiography to account for the subcultures of Sefarad and Ashkenaz in genealogical terms: Sefarad has been portrayed as the cultural heir of Babylonia, and Ashkenaz as the cultural heir of ancient Palestine.[1] Yet scholars of the last several decades have raised questions about the adequacy of this explanatory paradigm, particularly where Ashkenaz is concerned.[2] To complement the reigning hereditary perspective, the present chapter will consider features of non-Jewish cultures that left their marks on northern Europe, the territory that became identified with Ashkenaz.[3]

Though the Roman Empire came to an end in 476, its impact on patterns of civic administration, social organization, and cultural pursuits continued to be felt over wide swaths of territory well into the Middle Ages. Pierre Riché described the period from 500 to 750 as "characterized by the persistence of fragments of classical order: institutions, techniques, ideas—though it lacked the network that gave them imbedded meaning."[4] Features of topography—the Loire River and the Langres plateau, a massive limestone elevation forming a watershed between rivers flowing to the Mediterranean and to the English Channel—formed the geographic boundary that divided the latinized southern regions of the former Roman Empire from the more heavily barbarian regions on the empire's northern borders. The most germanized of these was eastern Gaul, an area that extended from Reims to the Rhineland.[5] Residents of these areas were highly sensitive to the differences in culture that were geographically determined; until the middle of the eighth century, Franks of northern Gaul called the Germanic residents of Aquitaine, on Spain's northeast border, "Romani," and the latter, though aware of their tribal identity, "were proud that they did not belong to the [b]arbarian world."[6]

Even after the collapse of Rome, senatorial families continued to live on estates in the highly latinized areas that had constituted the empire's heartland, and their uninterrupted residence under the rule of Byzantines[7] and barbarians ensured the continuation of Roman cultural patterns in Italy, Spain, North Africa, Aquitaine, Narbonne, and Provence.[8] Students in southeastern Gaul were trained in the classical *paidea* until at least the mid-seventh century,[9] in Aquitaine until the early eighth century,[10] in Spain until the end of the Visigothic period,[11] and in North Africa, throughout the period of the Vandal occupation up until the Arab conquest of Carthage in 698.[12] Roman legal and rhetorical studies never really disappeared in Italy or southern France,[13] and scholars like Boethius (480–524), Cassiodorus (490–585), Isidore of Seville (530–636), and Gregory the Great (540–604) acquired training in the (pagan) arts of grammar, rhetoric, and dialectic.[14]

Many features of Roman legal practice survived in lands south of the Loire after the empire's collapse; indeed, residents continued to speak of themselves as living under Roman law.[15] Tenacious attachment to written law ensured an ongoing need for professional scribes and notaries in this region and, for awhile, the continued importation (through Marseilles) of Egyptian papyrus.[16] Pierre Riché's map of the regions in which the use of written legal documents prevailed in the sixth through eighth centuries vividly illustrates the persistence of *Romanitas* in lands south of the Loire.[17] In this area, written documents did not merely serve an evidentiary function, but a dispositive one; in other words, the act of writing or signing a document brought the legal transaction into effect.[18] Documents containing autographs of involved parties and witnesses continued to be publicly posted in Rome and Ravenna in the sixth century,[19] and in southern Gaul, where Roman administrative practices were retained, the writing of documents clinched a broad range of transactions: sales, donations, and exchanges of property, dowries, wills, loans, payments of fine, oaths, acts of adoption and manumission.[20] Documents of legal import were registered and stored in chests so that they could be consulted if disputes arose and reproduced verbatim if lost, stolen, or destroyed.[21]

Roman culture even shaped barbarian notions and practices of government for some time after the fall of the Empire. Certain kings of the Ostrogoths, Burgundians, and Visigoths fashioned themselves rulers in the Roman mold; these commissioned German aristocrats who were trained in Roman law to create written codes—in the Latin language!—of their respective legal traditions.[22] Descendants of the Roman senatorial aristocracy were appointed administrators of the barbarian courts, where all legal and administrative transactions were effected through writing. In the Roman fashion, barbarian documents of state were sealed with signatures and preserved in *scrinia* so that they might be consulted if questions arose.[23]

Yet, outside the royal barbarian courts, practices of inscription were not widespread during the Merovingian period in lands north of the Loire. As borderlands of the empire, Britain, northern Gaul, and outlying Germanic lands had been affected more intensely by Rome's later policies of provincial organization than by its literary or legal culture. Moreover, by the end of the fifth century (by which time Italian influence on local politics in these areas had sharply declined),[24] the resident populations of Celts and Germans, supplemented by new migrations, reasserted their own, earlier, patterns of organization.[25]

The claim that northern Europe "did not belong to the area of written civilization" from the fall of Rome through the Merovingian period may be somewhat overstated,[26] but administrative and legal practices in northern Europe certainly relied on the spoken word up until the eleventh century.[27] Texts were far less important in northern than in southern Europe; fewer were produced, and those that were had meaning for a smaller percentage of the population. When priests produced Germanic writings in this period, they used runic script for talismanic purposes and not for documentary import.[28] Most important, these documents possessed no dispositive legal authority in this time and place; they did not enact the associated transaction.[29]

* * *

Not surprisingly, the topographic boundary that demarcated the characteristic patterns of social organization, educational practices, cultural propensities, and legal orientation in southern and northern Europe following the fall of Rome also had meaning for medieval Jews living in these lands. Earlier scholars of Jewish history have recognized that the Loire was a boundary of more than purely geographic importance,[30] but they made little effort to explore the impact of this boundary on regional attitudes and practices, or to ruminate on its significance for the medieval Jewish subcultures known as Sefarad and Ashkenaz.[31] This chapter takes some rudimentary steps in this direction,

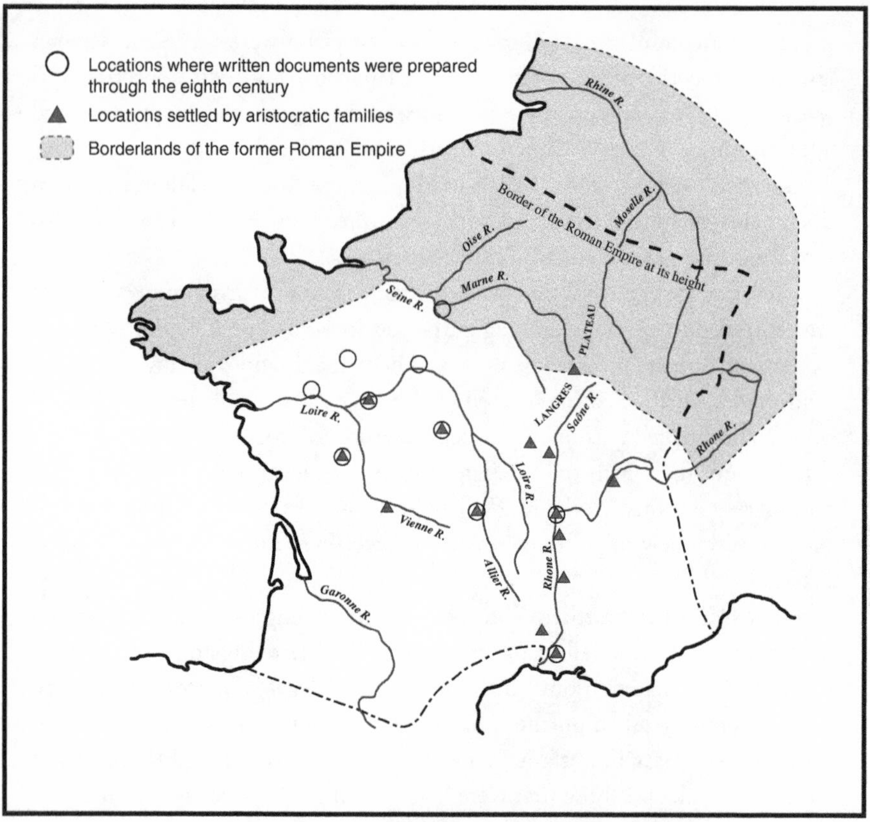

Figure 1. Following Pierre Riché in *Education and Culture in the Barbarian West,* this map offers evidence of Roman culture's enduring impact on populations living south of the Loire River and west of the Langres Plateau. In this region, settled by senatorial families, the Roman practice of preparing written documents in order to effect legal transactions continued at least through the eighth century. During this same period, documentation was not an essential part of legal culture north of the Loire and east of the Langres Plateau, an area in which there was no aristocratic settlement. In these borderlands of the former Roman Empire, populations effected status-changing events through oral declarations and prop-aided public performances. The disparate cultural orientations of these two discrete regions, so deeply defined by topography, may shed light on the density of Ashkenazi rituals and their richly performative quality. Like other populations living in the former borderlands, medieval Jews cultivated practices that were rich in semiotic significance to ensure mnemonic imprint and easy recall.

focusing exclusively on Ashkenaz.[32] Its first part highlights prominent features of Christian life and society north of the Loire, the "cultural landmarks" that serve as reference points in the chapter's second part, an overview of distinctive features of Ashkenazi society and culture in the tenth and early eleventh centuries. The chapter's third and final part discusses a major cultural shift that occurred in northern Europe in the late eleventh and twelfth centuries and highlights certain developments that have been identified as contributing factors. Because the changes that transformed many aspects of life were not theological in nature, they affected all residents of northern Europe, irrespective of confessional affiliations and religious identities. In presenting evidence for these changes, in reflecting on possible precipitating causes, and in tracing the broader impact of these changes in the social, pedagogic, and cultural arenas, this final section sets the stage for Chapter 4, which examines broad-ranging changes that transformed northern European Jewish culture in the same period.

Orienting Features of Northern European Society and Culture

Social and Religious Features of Franco-Germany up to the Year 1000

Notwithstanding their disparate histories, populations, and cultures, the contiguous lands of Gaul and Germania were forcibly united under the reign of Charlemagne. Recognizing the difficulty of creating a single entity out of this territory, the emperor identified noblemen with international connections, appointed them to positions of power, and married them off to members of the Carolingian royal family.[33] As a result of this carefully orchestrated process, the Franks, a small group of leading families, gained ascendancy over purely local nobles in the ninth-century East-Frankish kingdom.[34] Taking up residence in towns, the leaders of the Frankish aristocracy benefited from international commerce and stimulated it; they acquired and displayed exotic luxury items as markers of their wealth and status.[35] Not surprisingly, international merchants who brought Frankish rulers the wonders of the East were extended special favors and protection.[36]

The extraordinary overlap between the lay aristocracy and the religious leadership in the Carolingian Empire, unparalleled in other regions, developed under very specific circumstances. In order to avoid the fragmentation of patrimony, the wealthiest Germanic families opted not to distribute family lands among all the heirs, but to pass it on to only one. The disenfranchised siblings were provided for in a different way: cloisters were built for them on family land. This arrangement ensured the continued social standing of the non-land-owning relatives, and it redounded to the "spiritual credit" of the clan [*sippe*] as a whole. It was through this inheritance practice that siblings and cousins of lay noblemen came to assume the leadership of rural religious communities (including great abbeys) throughout Carolingian lands.[37] And since women were seen as part of the larger clan in Germanic cultures, aristocratic Frankish women also accumulated inheritances and had claims on patrimony. Like their disinherited male kinsmen, disinherited noblewomen were installed as the leaders of female cloisters established by their families. Both the legacy of Germanic tribal culture and its successful adaptation within the Christian environment of the Carolingian Empire enabled aristocratic women to wield exceptional religious—and economic—power.[38]

Monastic leaders were barred from the exercise of civil or military authority, but they wielded a spiritual currency that was ascribed great value in medieval northern Europe from Carolingian times onward—what Karl Leyser called "purchasing power in heaven."[39] Indeed, thousands of noblemen donated money to abbeys in order to have their names inscribed in those institutions' *Libri Memoriales* and to have the monks pray on their behalf.[40] Out of concern for the fate of their souls in this world and in the next, members of noble families continued to donate property, moveable goods, and luxury items to monasteries long after their initial establishment. Since such gifts were generally bestowed upon the institution's patron saint—often its deceased founding figure—the donations, in effect, aggrandized the sanctity of the donor's own ancestor and enhanced the religious stature of the entire family.[41] Such acts of charity, deemed useful as a "precautionary practice in a conflict-ridden society,"[42] affirmed and solidified family relations between lay noblemen and those of their kinsmen who wielded spiritual authority in the region. Monasteries came to serve as political and religious headquarters for family units in Frankish Europe, and material and spiritual transactions involving the cloister had considerable impact on the local social and political status quo.

The unique linkage between Frankish aristocrats and powerful monasteries helps to explain why monasticism had a far greater impact on Christian culture in northern Europe than it did in other parts of medieval Europe. Nor was the monasticism that took hold in this region as temperate as it was elsewhere. Since bishops of late antiquity and the Merovingian period had concentrated their ministries on urban centers, paying little attention to rural areas (much of northern Europe),[43] the Franks proved enormously receptive to the mission of St. Columbanus, who came to the Rhineland from Ireland in the late sixth century. According to Patrick Geary, "the list of people influenced by Columbanus reads like a *Who's Who* of Frankish aristocracy."[44] The monasticism that took root among German-speaking Christians shared with its Irish counterpart an intoxication with penance.[45] And unlike the originary hermits of the Egyptian, Syrian, and Palestinian deserts, the cloistered men and women of northern Europe were deeply enmeshed in the life of the community and centrally involved in regional power plays. It was this "vigorous" Frankish-style monasticism, writes Geary, that spread throughout Europe in the Middle Ages.[46]

The northern European monastery was novel in its social and political engagement, and obsessive in its courting of penance, but its religious and pedagogic goals were consistent with those of the Desert Fathers and of cloisters that had already been established in Italy and Provence.[47] Frankish monks of the Carolingian era privileged purity of the heart and contemplation of God over cultivation of the intellect; indeed, the latter faculty was regarded as a source of impiety.[48] Charisma, rather than erudition, was the source of an abbot's power, and the best evidence of his pedagogic prowess was the desire of students to emulate their teacher's behavior.[49]

The Cathedral Schools that were established under the Ottonian successors (919–1024) to the Carolingian dynasty shared this educational orientation. Beginning in the second half of the tenth century, Cathedral Schools were established as training grounds for clerics who would serve as governors and administrators of what had come to be regarded as the "imperial church system."[50] Mainz, Worms, and Regensburg housed such schools, and later, under Salian rule (1024–1125), the Cathedral School in Speyer became the preeminent school for diplomats of the Holy Roman Empire.[51] Like monasteries, the Cathedral Schools were distinctly anti-intellectual in outlook and emphasized the cultivation of personal qualities.[52] "Given this orientation of studies" in the Cathedral Schools, wrote Stephen Jaeger, "an inventory of the books read and the intellectual goals pursued has only a secondary value. We have to put aside the conception of school learning as primarily the transmission of knowledge."[53]

Cathedral Schools did integrate the liberal arts into the curriculum,[54] but their pedagogic emphasis was on "moral discipline," the inculcation of qualities deemed effective in regulating social and political life.[55] Since comportment was seen as the external evidence of "virtue," the quality essential to governance, manners were deemed far more important than knowledge. Speaking of the towering figures in these schools, Jaeger noted, "It mattered less what they knew than what they were."[56] As was the case in monasteries, tenth- and eleventh-century Cathedral Schools regarded emulation of the master's qualities as the goal of pedagogy.[57] His "living presence" was authoritative; he modeled the *habitus*—the gestures, gait, motions, facial expression, voice, speech, and conduct—that students were to internalize and make their own.[58] In speaking of Brun of Cologne, the first educator-statesmen of the Ottonian period, Jaeger writes that he "was the text that students studied."[59]. One of Brun's students recorded the details of this master's personal comportment in a biography lest subsequent generations lose access to his instructive life.[60]

Developments in Franco-Germany at the Turn of the Millennium

With the disintegration of Charlemagne's dynasty in the last quarter of the tenth century, members of the Frankish aristocracy who had inculcated a sense of "internationalism" in their children by maintaining contact with geographically distant relatives now cut off all but local allegiances in order to save what they could.[61] Armed warlords arose in the ensuing power vacuum; these claimed the right to appoint abbots and bishops, pillaged sanctuaries and monasteries, terrorized the populace, and triggered widespread migrations. It was against this backdrop that the church, through its clergy, assumed the role of "absentee sovereign."[62] The absence of any other strong centralized authority capable of reining in the lawlessness was only one factor that contributed to the church's appeal and power at this time; another was the growth of eschatological fears as the millennium of the Passion drew near.

Drawing on earlier Carolingian edicts that had upheld "the King's Peace" by defending society's most vulnerable groups, church leaders convened "peace councils" in the 990s among the clerics of southern Europe; these councils imposed spiritual sanctions on anyone who stole from churches or monasteries, or who harmed the clergy, the poor, and the unarmed. As terrors about the imminent eschaton mounted in the early eleventh century, the Peace of God councils evolved into a penitential movement that spread northward.[63] The chronicler Raoul Glaber describes how, in the year 1033, the millennial anniversary of Christ's crucifixion, bishops and abbots in Aquitaine collected people in synods, and in the presence of relics and of saints' bodies created a solemn pact with God. Pledging to undergo spiritual purification, the people prayed that God, in return, would spare them from famine, plague, and other manifestations of His wrath.[64] It was also around 1033 that the church offered armed warriors the possibility of participating, as Christians, in the renunciations of the penitential movement. Just as ascetically inclined parishioners could make a commitment to forego wine on Thursdays and meat on Fridays for the purification of their souls, arms-bearing men could choose to abstain from warfare during certain periods (for example, Wednesdays through Sundays) in order to become parties to the "Truce of God."[65]

Scholars have claimed that northern European Christians of the early eleventh century experienced a growing sense of "the divide between guilt and the punishment of sin"; as the Final Judgment drew nearer, they feared that they might not be able to adequately atone for their transgressions. This anxiety had institutional ramifications, for while the Church itself had limited penitential resources to offer terrified Christians,[66] monastic communities, influenced by Irish practices that had penetrated the continent in the Merovingian period, had highly developed approaches to penance.[67] Under the leadership of Abbot Hugh (1049–1109), the monks of Cluny offered eschatologically fearful Christians opportunities to ready themselves for the End of Days and to gain shelter from its devastations. Mobilizing a range of sermonic, liturgical, and artistic resources, Cluniac monks emphasized the protective power of good deeds and of penitential practices that could commute sin. Well before the First Crusade (1096) and the establishment of a Frankish Crusader Kingdom in the Holy Land (1099), these penances included pilgrimage to Jerusalem.[68]

By enabling early eleventh-century Europeans to better prepare themselves for the anticipated apocalypse, monastic Christianity reinforced the sense that life in the present world was a treacherous place, and the notion that the only asylum was the abbey itself.[69] For this reason and others, the power of the monasteries increased dramatically in the eleventh century. The pioneering role of the Cluniacs in the Peace of God and Truce of God movements enhanced their credibility and power in the broader society, and monks came to be seen as spiritual authorities for both the unarmed and armed classes of Christians.[70] The growing importance of monastic Christianity after the collapse of the Carolingian Empire was also abetted by Pope Gregory VII, who implemented significant church reforms between 1050 and 1080, utilizing Cluny's monks as his agents.[71] As an expression of his gratitude, Cluniac monasteries in both France and Germany were granted special papal privileges that enhanced their liberty within the ecclesiastical hierarchy and the political power they wielded within their own geographic locales.[72]

The Rise of Custom in Franco-German Legal Culture

At the beginning of the ninth century, Charlemagne introduced into his empire many of the cultural practices that had prevailed in Roman times. Legal writing was ascribed considerable weight in all arenas of society,[73] and the ancient *mallus publicus*, or "common judicial assembly," was reinstated as a neutral venue for arbitration.[74] These borrowings from Roman culture did not long survive the disintegration of the Carolingian Empire, however.[75] Without an infrastructure of trained legal professionals—readers of Latin who could be trusted to apply and rationally interpret a set of impersonal rules when deciding law, judging civil suits or punishing lawbreakers[76]—the maintenance of a community's stability increasingly came to depend on social coercion. The complete breakdown in public order was avoided only by the adoption of certain strategies. One of these was to make larger groups of people culpable for the behavior of individuals. Since it was in the interest of all to maintain the peace, especially in disputes between upper-class litigants who possessed large military retinues,[77] practices like compurgation evolved, to shore up the judgments of the court by harnessing the power of the collective. Fear of the supernatural was also exploited, and horrific imprecations were called down on anyone who failed to uphold a judicial decision.[78] Finally, local custom, a body of practice regarded as authoritative because it had been modeled by revered ancestors, came to constitute the default system of governance. Unlike a priori legislation, custom, by its very nature, was not dependent on any procedural norms; it could be observed but not enacted.[79] The public as a whole was both the source of custom's binding power and the means for its enforcement. The preeminent repository of information about the practices of the past in any given community was not a written record but a human "remembrancer"; this figure held knowledge of the region's customs—and of the transactions they effected—in living memory.[80]

The gestures enacted and the formulae recited in socially regulatory gatherings were part of the legacy of Germanic tribes, and had even been used during the Carolingian period, though in tandem with legal documents.[81] Now, in the absence of centralized authority, these practices of social regulation and management came to constitute the core of the legal process. All of the strategies deployed in maintaining public order involved some element of public performance. Contractual obligations, whether of a social, financial, or military nature, were not only formalized, but effected through the performance of gestures and the recitation of formulae. Physical acts, witnessed by eye and ear, brought into being such legal transactions as marriage, vassalage, manumission, ordeals, feuds, and the "alienation" of property or of moveable goods through sale or donation.[82]

Bodily movements—kisses, prostrations, handclasps—were all semiotically laden, and the concrete (at times symbolic) objects used in these rituals of legal enactment—e.g., rod, knife, book, glove, hammer, censer, bell, candlestick, coin, fork, gage, piece of sod—left durable impressions on the memories of all bystanders, whether the object in question was transferred, thrown, struck, or merely displayed.[83] The presence of children at these rituals was crucial to the durability of the legal record. When disputes arose regarding legal enactments of the past, people in their dotage could call to mind the vivid spectacles they had witnessed in their youth: the transfer of a yoke or a key, the placement of an object on an altar, the casting down of a gauntlet, the marking of territorial boundaries by physically bumping up against trees and boulders.[84]

Even when written documents were used, they were not the agents of the transactions in question. A written charter might be used as a symbolic prop in a choreographed ceremony; its placement on the altar when a family member was alienating his property indicated that God, too, was a witness to the transaction.[85] A document might be used as a record of what had transpired—and it might even be "performed," with the involved parties reciting certain parts and witnesses offering appropriate responses. The use of written texts might also signal (rather than effect) some realignment of power within a family. While a *laudatio parentum*—the document signed by a donor's relatives indicating that they would not challenge his right to "alienate" what might have been a family inheritance—was devoid of legal authority, Stephen White noted that it could reflect a reconfiguration of the region's social and spiritual hierarchy.[86] In short, while written documents continued to be produced in northern Europe after the breakdown of the Carolingian Empire, their mere use ought not be construed as evidence of the cultural or legal authority of text in that time and place.

Post-Millennial Regionalism and Its Manifestations

Some cultural blending did take place between the Gallic and Germanic populations within the Carolingian Empire. This was evident in the Lotharingians' gallicized pronunciation of certain German words, and in the curriculum that was common to all the Cathedral Schools, whether situated in German- or French-speaking lands. Cathedral Schools that were founded in French areas or revived there in the eleventh century were no less devoted to the cultivation of personal qualities than were the Cathedral Schools of German lands.[87] Writing about these eleventh-century schools, Stephen Jaeger stressed that "the perspectives of local history have severe limits for our period. The cathedral schools formed a cultural unity and need to be studied from that perspective."[88]

With the breakdown of the confederation of Gaul and Germania, however, the regionalism that had been characteristic of the earlier Merovingian period reemerged—though in new ways.[89] Apart from the most obvious political indicators of separateness—the rule of the Capetian dynasty (987–1328) in French lands, and of the Ottonian (919–1024) and Salian (1024–1125) dynasties in German lands—cultural differences between the two regions became increasingly apparent. In times of greater Latin literacy, people of disparate tribes had been governed by the law of their tribal kin, no matter where they lived. The Franks, in particular, adhered to the legal "principle of personality" that had prevailed in the multi-tribal Roman world; though complex, this arrangement facilitated the coexistence of many peoples within a given locale.[90] However, with the decline in literacy that accompanied the breakdown of the Carolingian Empire, regional practices came to be perceived as the norms that governed every person who resided within certain geographic boundaries, irrespective of his ethnic or tribal affiliation. In this way, the inhabitants of any given region came to be subject to "territorial law," and not to the "law of person" that had once identified them by ancestral heritage.[91]

The reassertion of regionalism was discernible in a number of arenas. Over the course of the twelfth century, the Cathedral Schools of France responded to growing criticism by scholastics at the University of Paris and adopted the study of liberal arts.[92] And while Cathedral Schools in Germany continued to embrace the time-honored curriculum and pedagogic orientation, their students, who were being groomed to serve at the imperial Salian court, were subjected to new challenges. As the ruling dynasty became increasingly extravagant, masters and students of the Cathedral Schools wistfully invoked the ideal of "moral discipline" and cultivated a plaintive rhetoric that Jaeger describes as "nostalgia for the cloister."[93]

* * *

In highlighting particular features and developments, the foregoing sketch was designed to help contextualize parallel—and prominent—aspects of Jewish society and culture in medieval northern Europe. Ashkenazi Judaism was shaped not only by diachronic influences, the legacies of Palestinian, Babylonian, and Byzantine rabbinic cultures, but also by its synchronic context as well. The following remarks refer only briefly to features of Ashkenazi life that parallel the above-mentioned cultural landmarks of medieval northern Europe; they are not intended to discuss each phenomenon in a comprehensive manner

Social and Cultural Features of Medieval Ashkenazi Jewry

The name "Ashkenaz," which appears three times in Scripture, was equated by the talmudic sages with "*Germamia*" [*sic*],[94] and was used in Jewish writings to refer to Germany by the tenth century.[95] In its expansive sense, however, "Ashkenaz" refers to the lands of Gaul and Germania, confederated under the short-lived Carolingian Empire.[96] That the Jews of this region partook of a unified cultural milieu (particularly until the First Crusade of 1096) is suggested by their gallicized pronunciation of German words,[97]and, more anecdotally, by the travels undertaken by Rashi, Rabbi Shlomo Yiẓḥaqi (1040–1105), from Troyes to Worms in order to pursue Jewish studies before returning to teach in France. The more narrow use of "Ashkenaz" to designate only the communities of German-speaking lands became increasingly pertinent in the twelfth century, when cultural differences between Jews of northern France and of Germany became far more noticeable.[98] Just as the Cathedral Schools of both regions partook of a common curriculum and orientation in the eleventh century and grew in regional distinctiveness in the twelfth, the Jewish subculture of northern Europe that had seemed a unity in the eleventh century became increasingly differentiated in the twelfth century. The divergent directions taken by Jews in these regions also parallel those of their Christian neighbors: when rabbinic academies of northern France came to valorize the exercise of logic in the twelfth century, those of the Rhineland exhibited a form of nostalgia, pining for a bygone era when the master's living presence had been all powerful. Throughout the course of the twelfth and thirteenth centuries, what had seemed to be a single Jewish subculture became identifiable as the more narrowly regional Jewish communities of Ashkenaz (Germany) and Ẓorfat (northern France), each with its distinct customs.[99]

* * *

The civic leaders of early Ashkenaz came from only a few aristocratic families; Avraham Grossman identified five leading families that exercised leadership in all Jewish communal affairs over the course of several generations until the devastations of 1096.[100] Noting that the concentration of administrative, social, commercial, and religious authority in the hands of so few was a phenomenon unprecedented and unparalleled in Jewish history, Grossman hypothesized that it may have mirrored the leadership pattern of the broader environment.[101] As discussed above, the consolidation of all forms of leadership in the same families was, indeed, a feature of Frankish society that had emerged under specific political and economic circumstances.

Not unlike their Christian counterparts in the region, Jewish women from aristocratic families in Ashkenaz were entrusted with financial powers that were exceptional when compared with those of women in other Jewish communities. Their kinship with the male educational elite and their enhanced economic status even had bearing on the religious behavior that was expected of Jewish women in this region. The Talmud had declared that women belonging to the category of "important women" (*nashim ḥashuvot*) were to undertake a particular ritual practice (namely, reclining at the Passover seder) that was otherwise obligatory only for men.[102] In explaining what set a woman in this category apart from others, medieval Jewish commentaries identified several characteristics. One might be designated an "important woman" because she enjoyed unusual independence—whether this was granted by her husband,[103] or because she was no longer bound to serve him, having been widowed or divorced,[104] or because she possessed great wealth.[105] A woman's social class, and specifically her status as "the daughter of the great of the generation"[106]—which is to say, her birth into the spiritual aristocracy—might also bring her into this category. Yet another defining characteristic, one's identity as "a woman of valor and God-fearing,"[107] might enable even a lower-born Jewish woman of character and piety to be included in the category of "important women." Rabbinic scholars of twelfth-century northern France and thirteenth-century Germany designated all their female relatives as "important women." Echoing a comment made by earlier talmudic glossators of the region, R. Mordecai b. Hillel declared that, "in our times, all women are to be considered *nashim ḥashuvot*."[108]

The aristocratic Jewish families of the Rhineland were successful merchants; individual Jews appear to have been present at the courts of Charlemagne and Louis the Pious in the ninth century,[109] and in the eleventh century, Christian bishops and noblemen issued *privilegia* that granted Jews rights of residence in the hopes that their settlement would stimulate commerce and the local economy.[110] Michael Toch has noted that the many references in Ashkenazi responsa to the *ma'arufia*, a legal arrangement granting a particular Jew sole rights to deal with a given Christian client (and precluding other Jews from approaching him with business or trade propositions),[111] bespeak an environment in which small numbers of Jewish agents were effecting large-scale commercial transactions on behalf of extremely wealthy Christian patrons, namely noblemen.[112] As Toch makes clear, such an arrangement would have been essential to the security and well-being of the Jewish community itself.

The international business dealings of medieval Ashkenazi merchants[113] at times involved Jews in other lands. A Hebrew letter of the tenth century describes an undertaking that joined Jewish partners located in Italy and Germany with ones living in cities of North Africa and Egypt,[114] and geonic correspondence reveals that northern European Jews living in "Faranjah," Frankland, had contact with the Baghdadi academies even in the ninth century.[115] There is also reason to assume that Ashkenazi traders had relatively easy access to Palestine, for the contacts Charlemagne initiated with Muslim rulers and with representatives of the Byzantine Church in the Holy Land persisted up through (and beyond) the turn of the eleventh century, when the Crusader Kingdom was established in Jerusalem.

Civic and spiritual authority was not merely closely intertwined in northern European Jewish communities (as it was in the Christian dominant society); individual leaders were the repositories of both types of power. Later rabbinic writings made reference to this unusual confluence, noting that the very qualities that had been combined in the third-century tanna, Rabbi Judah the Patriarch, Torah and *gedulah* (scholarship and political stature), were once again visible "in one and the same place" in the leaders of medieval Ashkenaz.

The affinities that have been noted between features of Ashkenazi Jewish culture and of medieval monasticism[116] probably existed before the twelfth-century emergence of *Ḥasidut Ashkenaz*, Rhineland Pietism. As discussed in

Figure 2. "In our times, all women are to be considered *nashim ḥashuvot* [important women]." In this scene from the fifteenth-century Darmstadt Haggadah, bearded and unbearded Jewish men are studying with women and girls, perhaps instructing them. It is not clear what books are being studied, but the women can clearly read and are engaged in animated conversation about the text. Darmstadt Haggadah, Cod. Or. 8, fol. 37v. Universitats- und Landesbibliothek Darmstadt, Technische Universitat Darmstadt.

Chapter 6, some extremist practices associated with that short-lived group gave heightened expression to tendencies that were already widespread among the Jews of the region. Just as monasticism played a disproportionate role in Frankish Christianity, an inclination toward stringency and self-abnegation was characteristic of medieval Jewish culture in Ashkenaz. Whether or not medieval Ashkenazi culture in general shared the Rhineland Pietists' profoundly pessimistic worldview is somewhat less clear, however.[117] Referring to their fears of "aloneness in the face of God and His Judgement," Haym Soloveitchik inverted a classical biblical image of protection to describe the Pietists' sense of almost inexpiable culpability: "The cloud of guilt did not budge from their tents."[118]

The pedagogic ideals of Jewish education that prevailed in northern Europe through the first half of the eleventh century may well have resembled those that shaped Christian classrooms in this time and place. The most prominent Cathedral Schools of the eleventh century, the educational institutions that produced the empire's diplomats, were situated in the very cities that comprised the heartland of Ashkenazi Jewry, Mainz, Speyer, Worms, and Regensburg.[119] (A mapping of the geographical relationship between the major centers of Jewish residence in Ashkenaz and France in the Middle Ages and the most influential monasteries of the era remains a desideratum.) There is reason to speculate that the master was the text in the classrooms of pre-Crusade Ashkenaz, and while there is not sufficient data to confirm this conjecture, this was certainly the case for later Rhineland Pietists, who pointedly perpetuated cultural practices that had prevailed earlier in the region.[120] It was not until the twelfth century that Ashkenazi Jews produced written records of the master's daily comportment (for the benefit of those who were not privileged to have witnessed it themselves),[121] but the disciples' practice of rehearsing the minute details of a master's conduct presumably predated the impulse to commit such details to writing.

Finally, like their German Christian counterparts, medieval Ashkenazi Jews ritually dramatized status-changing events using recitation, props, and gestures.[122] Some performative acts possessed dispositive authority; others complemented the use of written documents. A striking (and therefore memorable) example of the latter may be adduced from *Sefer Maharil*, a highly influential Ashkenazi customary, in which R. Zalman of St. Goar recorded the practices of his teacher, Rabbi Jacob ben Moshe Levi Moellin (1365–1427).[123] In its lengthy discussion of marriage customs, *Sefer Maharil* refers to the importance of using very specific types of winecups in order to distinguish between a bride who was marrying for the first time and one who had already been married. The different styles of goblet to be ritually used in the two cases allude with a disturbing lack of subtlety to the virginity of the first-time bride and the sexual experience of the veteran. In situations where the bride had never been married, stipulates *Sefer Maharil*, a narrow-rimmed goblet was to be used, while a wide-rimmed one was to be used in situations where the bride was a widow or divorcee. Contemporary readers may be unsettled by the indelicacy of this allusion to the bride's sexual history, but when understood within the context of the times, this detail of the ceremony assumes more than semiotic meaning.[124]

The spread of epidemics and fires (and in certain times and places, outbreaks of lawlessness) made impermanent residence a fact of life in northern Europe. Jews may have been exceptionally attuned to the tenuousness of their living conditions; their rights of residence were revoked at times of expulsion, and they were targets of mob violence in times of unrest. In the course of migration and resettlement, documents were lost, and the inability to produce these when needed created a range of legal problems. Medieval rabbinic writings attest to the ways in which the absence of documents affected people's lives: Could new arrivals in a Jewish community who claimed that the *ketubah* (marriage contract) was lost live together as man and wife?[125] Could an alleged divorcee who claimed that the writ of divorce (*get*) granted by her former husband had been destroyed in a fire remarry in her new place of residence? When considered in the light of such social and legal realities, the important mnemonic purpose served by distinctive props becomes clearer. When an individual's personal status was contested and no relevant legal documents could be produced, the acts performed and props used served as components of a "back-up system" for the maintenance of social order. Inasmuch as the details of the public ceremony encoded legally significant information, the spectacle as a whole could function, if necessary, as a recoverable archive of unwritten data. Of course, under normal circumstances, Jewish weddings were documented; the *ketubah* clearly spelled out the economically significant details of whether or not the bride had been married before. But if this marriage document were ever to be lost, and if the husband died and the widow moved to a new community where she claimed to be virgin and sought to remarry, how could anybody disprove her claim? The elaborate and meticulously choreographed details of medieval Ashkenazi customs possessed cultural and even legal meaning—both for the actors and for the witnessing Jewish public. Rather than supplanting documentation, the esthetic and symbolic details of a ceremony formed a social and legal safety net, a mnemonic backup of the written record.

Nonetheless, where commercial transactions were concerned, Jews of early medieval Ashkenaz may have preferred verbal agreement to written documentation. Reflecting on northern European rabbinic responsa of the tenth and eleventh centuries, the economic historian Robert Sabatino Lopez wrote, "Though written contracts were fairly often produced, a large proportion of the agreements seem to have been verbal, and the courts seem to have relied more upon the oath of the parties than on any verbal record. This, even at such an early period, would indicate carelessness on the part of merchants and Jews; written proof prevailed in the Mediterranean countries."[126] The contrast noted by Lopez, between the practices of medieval Jewish merchants who operated in the Mediterranean basin and their northern European counterparts, has been amply corroborated over the past few decades in the study of written commercial documents generated by Jewish traders from Qayrawan and Gabes,[127] and in scholarly analyses of the role that writing played in medieval communities south and north of the Loire River.[128] Ultimately, any attempt to account for Ashkenazi Jewry's failure to use written contracts—at a time when their use was de rigeur for Jewish and non-Jewish merchants of the Mediterranean basin—must take into account not only the "culture of orality" that prevailed in northern Europe between the breakdown of the Carolingian Empire and the twelfth century, but also the reliance of Ashkenazi Jews on the dictates of the Babylonian geonim, who themselves refrained from using written documentation to effect financial transactions.[129]

* * *

At a time when Christians of the erstwhile Carolingian Empire began to stress their more local identities, Ashkenaz (Germany) and Ẓorfat (northern France) emerged with greater clarity. The foundation myth that traced Jewish settlement in Ashkenaz to an invitation tendered by the Emperor Charlemagne in the eighth century was not inscribed until the twelfth century.[130] This ennobling narrative, recorded by R. Elazar of Worms, accounted for the Jewish presence in northern Europe, but it was also an important tool in the construction of Ashkenazi identity. The conceptualization of a regional kinship purveyed in this tale of founding fathers enabled Jews in twelfth-century Ashkenaz to affirm their common heritage and their common cause.[131] But while the identities of Jews from Ashkenaz and Ẓorfat became more distinct in the twelfth century, their residence in different political kingdoms did not sunder the close ties of scholarship and culture that bound them. Before the First Crusade, French Jews went to the Rhineland to study and returned home to disseminate what they had learned; during the twelfth and thirteenth centuries, the pattern of movement shifted, and rabbinic students from Germany were more likely to study in French academies.[132]

Cultural Transformation of Northern European Societies

In his monumental study *From Memory to Written Record*, Michael Clanchy emphasized that the making of records was actually viewed with distrust in tenth- and eleventh-century England; written proof would only be demanded of someone who had fallen under suspicion. The prevailing legal assumption in England at this time was that a witness giving oral testimony possessed greater credibility than any written document.[133] By the twelfth century, however, greater authority was ascribed to the written word. Clanchy's juxtaposition of parallel legal cases that took place in England in the eleventh and twelfth centuries spotlights this development.

In each of the centuries, two litigants presented themselves before a court of arbitration, each claiming to be the owner of a plot of land. In asserting his ownership, Litigant A reported that the land in question had been acquired by his grandfather and had passed to him by inheritance. This litigant supported his claim with two types of evidence: a vessel and a very old man. Testifying before the members of the court, the old man stated that in his childhood he had witnessed the transfer of the land from its prior owner to Litigant A's grandfather. Referring to the vessel brought as evidence, he stated that the land's former owner had handed it to the new owner while reciting a particular formula. Litigant B, who made the same legal claim as Litigant A, brought with him only one piece of supporting evidence: a bill of sale naming him the land's owner. According to Clanchy, the court of arbitration at the beginning of the eleventh century would have decided the case in favor of Litigant A, but in the twelfth century, Litigant B would have been deemed the plaintiff with the stronger evidence. In eleventh-century England (and in earlier times), when unwritten customary law constituted the legal norm, remembered traditions, oral testimonies, and the artifacts used to mark transactions were the privileged bearers of cultural authority. By the twelfth century, however, the power of text had become preeminent; the written word now trumped these other sources as the preferred and most reliable vehicle of cultural and legal authority. And by the second half of the thirteenth century, writes Clanchy, "memory, whether individual or collective, if unsupported by clear written evidence, was ruled out of court."[134]

Though Clanchy's data is culled exclusively from British archives, it offers an unusual window onto a gradual and unconscious process of cultural transformation that also transpired in northern France and Germany in the eleventh and twelfth centuries.[135] I use the term "textualization" to refer to this process: one that led a given society to ascribe greater authority to the written record than to oral testimonies and witnessed acts. While growth in literacy and an increase in the number of texts a society produced may, at times, have been linked to textualization, neither of these developments was a necessary indicator that the process was underway. Evidence for the presence (or absence) of textualization is best sought in the ways that people and communities related to texts—and in the roles that texts played within a given society: the circumstances under which texts were produced, the uses for which they were intended, the manner in which they were treated, the ways that they were viewed and read, and their relationship to other expressions of cultural meaning and authority.

A society's attitudes toward texts in general or in particular may be imbued with theological meaning, and its regulation of the ways in which they are to be handled, transmitted, and used can be of intense religious significance, as seen in the preceding chapters. Nonetheless, there is nothing inherently religious about the decision to privilege written documentation over oral testimony—or vice versa. Critics who decried specific developments that were set in motion by the textualization process sometimes did so on religious grounds, but the dynamics that abetted the trend toward textualization in northern Europe were only tangentially linked to religion per se.[136] In the end, a society's preference for one mode of transmission or another was theologically neutral. Once this shift in cultural orientation had taken root in a particular locale, it spread on its own, aided by hosts of agents, many of them unaware of the larger significance of their acts. There is no historical evidence that any salesman consciously marketed this transformative process. Textualization traversed confessional boundaries and affected all inhabitants of a region, irrespective of their religious identities.[137]

Causes of Textualization

That northern European communities underwent textualization is well documented, but why they did so when they did is far less clear. If anything, the wide range of possible precipitating factors identified by historians underscores the fact that textualization affected virtually all arenas of medieval society and culture. Indeed, some developments cited as causes might actually have been symptoms of textualization. In recapitulating some of the developments that have been cited as contributing factors, the following overview does not argue that any one of them was either a necessary or sufficient cause of the textualization process.

* * *

The significant number of northern European manuscripts that date from the late eleventh century contrasts sharply with the documentary paucity of the preceding six centuries. Was this due to an actual increase in the number of texts produced, or was greater effort exerted in this period to retain and preserve writings?[138] In their efforts to account for this discrepancy, some scholars have noted that the textual bounty of the late eleventh century coincides with the first extended period of tranquility experienced by the region's inhabitants since the breakdown of the Carolingian Empire, and perhaps even since the fall of Rome. Between the fifth century and the end of the eleventh, aggressive cultivation of wasteland and marshes led to a dramatic rise in agricultural yield. Toward the end of this period, old cities were revived at the junctures of overland routes and waterways, and markets that had fallen into disuse were reestablished. The northern European nobility's appetite for luxuries was whetted and fed by international imports; specialized craftsmen like viticulturists and masons emerged locally in new villages and in new markets in order to supply the growing demands of their palaces.[139] The sheer complexity of economic life may have necessitated greater reliance on documentation. Once exchange was remonetarized,[140] record keeping became de rigeur.

The impetus to summarize the contents of land charters and copy them became particularly acute following the collapse of the Carolingian Empire, especially in areas where the monarchy had laid claim (through *mainmise*) to lands that had previously belonged to local dukes and barons.[141] It was not until the early eleventh century that the restoration of more stable conditions made it possible for residents of northern Europe to demonstrate possessory right to their land.[142]

* * *

The "Peace of God" and the "Truce of God," church-led movements of the eleventh century, have been cited for their indirect roles in the textualization process. Not only did they contribute to the social stability that was a precondition for other economic, political, and administrative developments,[143] but the penitential fervor they channeled stimulated an outpouring of donations to monasteries and churches—from aristocrats and knights alike.[144] The careful recording of all these grants resulted in what Brigitte Bedos-Rezak called a "documentary explosion," in which laymen were as involved as clerics.[145]

* * *

The general revival of jurisprudence in the twelfth century, and the growth of canon law in particular, would seem to be manifestations of the textualization process, and some scholars have suggested that these were precipitated by the rediscovery in 1070 of Justinian's *Digest*, a corpus of civilian Roman law compiled in late antiquity.[146] Yet other scholars have challenged this hypothesis: according to Charles Radding, the magisterial activities of the canonist, Irnerius (Guarnerius) of Bologna, could never have occurred if Roman and Lombard law had not continued to flourish in the legal culture of early eleventh-century Ravenna and Pavia. According to Radding, trained legal professionals in these cities put Justinian's *Digest* (a difficult work that could only be read by specialists) back into circulation once interest had shifted from delineating legal norms to the elaboration of a scientific approach to law.[147]

Brian Stock has wondered whether the "accidental" discovery of Justinian's *Digest* in this particular time and place, and the attention paid to it, may have been a symptom of an already-heightened receptivity to written texts prevailing in northern European culture rather than its cause.[148] After all, cultural factors, and not merely accidents of discovery, determine whether a society neglects, or studies, documents of the past; indeed, the very quest to recover texts from the past may reflect a new understanding of what writing is for.[149] The rediscovery of a long-forgotten text is rarely a monocausal trigger of a multifaceted cultural development; as Clanchy observed, "Neither archives nor archivists originated from disinterested historical research."[150] Recovery of older texts in this period may have been a manifestation or byproduct of the textualist impulse and not its spark. In this case, the acutely felt need for unifying legislation may have primed northern Europeans to accept an overarching system. The authority of custom may have been unquestionable in any given area, but its sphere of jurisdiction was limited by geography. Moreover, this was a region in which feudal law, commercial law, customary law, and the codes of different Germanic tribes overlapped—and were all deemed valid. Only canon law could offer universal legal coverage for all Christians.[151]

* * *

Harold Berman has argued that the Investiture Contest of 1076, a controversy pitting emperor against pope, triggered a rash of developments associated with textualization, among them the revival of jurisprudence. When each of the contending powers challenged the authority of the other to oversee ecclesiastical offices, they adduced texts to support their claims; indeed, one legal defense of the emperor's position was drawn from Justinian's *Digest*. Inasmuch as logical analysis of sources was universally recognized as the most effective tool of investigation, asserted Berman, the very showdown between empire and papacy spotlighted the privileged status of the written word as the ultimate arbiter of legal authority.[152]

* * *

Developments connected with Pope Gregory VII's reformist enactments of 1050–80 have also been identified as factors in and agents of the textualization process. The new Carthusian and the Cistercian orders established during his pontificate called for the establishment of libraries in each of their monasteries, and the heightened demand for bibles, breviaries, hymnals, saints' lives, and interpretations of Christian doctrine stimulated widescale book production. Copies of the statutes created by each monastic order were disseminated among its allied houses, and each kept its own financial records of contractual obligations, lands acquired and rented, and produce yielded, bought, and sold. Like other parties to business transactions, monasteries needed to produce their written records when representing their interests in legal disputes.[153]

Reliance on the authority of written text has been seen as a general characteristic of Gregory VII's papacy. The chancery expanded under his pontificate, and his own letter writing standards are credited with setting "new standards of documentation both in output and quality—which compelled secular governments to follow suit."[154] Gregory VII also replaced charisma-based church leadership with leadership rooted in the authority of the office. His establishment of written law and procedural transparency as the basis of ecclesiastical administration set the stage for widespread bureaucratization of northern European society in the twelfth century.[155] The reformist pope's overarching belief "that law, as opposed to custom, was the equivalent of truth"[156] was a stimulant to the development of canon law in general, and to its many constituent activities: compilation, authentication, organization, editing, and interpretation. Once the written text was construed as the ultimate source of legal authority, and its interpretation came to depend upon linguistic and logical analysis, hermeneutic principles needed to meet criteria of transparency, replicability, and socially useful rationality.[157]

The Impact of Textualization

Between the late eleventh century and the end of the twelfth, the range of people using documents expanded dramatically—and clerics lost their monopoly on the production and preservation of texts. Habits of writing that had initially been the province of specially trained monks working in the scriptoria of abbeys and in the papal chancery spread first to the nobility and later to the nontitled.[158] When universities and Cathedral Schools of the twelfth century made the inscribed word the backbone of their respective educational enterprises, even students who were not destined for the clergy studied from compendia that had been prepared for classroom use in multiple copies. The inscription of the prayer book introduced written liturgy into lay households and transformed a practice that had once been the monopoly of clerics into a domestic activity.[159] In short, the growing use of writing was connected with dramatic changes in social patterns.

Growing reliance on the written word in medieval northern European communities also brought about changes in the assessment of social worth; it enhanced the status of people who could interpret texts in ways that addressed societal needs. Cultural power had once been associated with charismatic figures—whether the king or emperor, who were believed to be the embodiments of law, or ecclesiastical leaders and monastic masters, who were seen as living repositories of tradition. Now, however, the most valued figures were those who could understand the authoritative texts, apply them judiciously, delimit their applicability, and tease out their implications, offering transparent interpretations to which all could assent.[160] Models of leadership changed in every realm of medieval society: literate professional administrators succeeded charismatic civic and ecclesiastical rulers,[161] abbots and bishops ascended to church office through election,[162] and the virtuoso logician replaced the master as the most revered person in the classroom.

Stephen Jaeger describes how the pedagogic ethos that prevailed in the northern European Cathedral Schools of the eleventh century was supplanted in the twelfth:

> Reasoning and proof, when pitted against venerable authority, textual or personal, were pernicious instruments of pride that invited discrediting and were seen as deserving it. But gradually, knowledge, reasoning, success in disputation and in proof become ends in themselves. . . . Thought frees itself from its subordination to discipline. By the early twelfth century, the discipline of manners has been largely displaced at the schools and replaced by definitions and systematizing, frameworks of argumentation and harmonizing of inconsistencies.[163]

Writing in 1065, a one-time teacher in the Cathedral Schools of Liége and Mainz bitterly attacked the changes that he was witnessing. Both the students and the new teachers in the classroom, fumed Goswin of Mainz, "seek to encompass God within the boundaries of nature, and to confine within human reason that which surpasses the reason of any rational creature."[164]

The privileging of reason and logic was also fomenting a social change in classroom hierarchy. As was already the case in universities, Cathedral Schools in both French and German lands were becoming sites of contentious learning—and the new combative rhetoric was directed not only at fellow students but at teachers as well.[165] Intellectually arrogant students contradicted their teachers and attempted to show them up in logical virtuosity, and the disputatiousness of scholastics came to permeate the Cathedral School environment.[166] Though preservation of the master's honor remained a topic of discussion,[167] the laws of *reverentia* and *pieta* were violated with impunity.

* * *

As written texts came to be construed as reference points for everyday activities, bodies of tradition that were once transmitted exclusively through practice (e.g., penances, or oral judiciary procedures) underwent inscription in edited compilations.[168] People not only allowed texts to inform and shape their experience, they sought to bring their lives into congruence with them. Since written references lacked the malleability of traditions stored in memory, societies tended to become less tolerant of variation; anything short of conformity to the text came to be seen as deviant.[169]

As text came to be ascribed greater cultural weight, time-honored oral practices, authorized by custom, came under scrutiny. Something similar had occurred in the Carolingian period, when Germanic peoples began to consult codes of law. Discussing a case from the ninth century, Fritz Kern described what transpired when Franks discovered that some of their communal practices deviated from inscribed legal prescriptions:

> In the year 819, for example, in a question of marriage law, the Franks detected disagreement between the [unwritten] rules of customary law and those laid down in the *Lex Salica*. Were they to repudiate and reverse the current usage as an evil innovation in view of the express testimony of the ancient folk-law, which was the law of their fathers? On the contrary, the Franks simply decided that the marriage custom was to be treated "as our forebears have treated it heretofore," and "not as it stands written in the *Lex Salica*."[170] The Franks . . . perceived no conflict between the unfettered legal feeling of their own day and the recorded custom of their forebears. An ancient custom, actual and conscious in a living tradition, triumphs over a "dead" Latin record, over a written legal dictum which the Franks of 819 may have conceived to have been introduced into the *Lex Salica* . . . perhaps as a slip in writing, of interpolation, or possibly of a wrongful custom adopted by the author. . . . It seems, at any rate, that practice knew how to find a way out, without violating theory.[171]

Whereas ninth-century Franks had been able to camouflage the clash between competing systems of legal authority, one written and one oral, this option was no longer open to northern Europeans of the High Middle Ages, who, with near universality, valorized the written text. As legal compilations became known to a larger body of readers, there was growing recognition that community behaviors were not in synch with written prescriptions. One solution to this problem was to level the playing field by committing custom itself to writing. In the eleventh century, principalities and monasteries throughout northern Europe began to produce cultural oxymorons: texts of "customary law" that codified the very body of unwritten tradition that had always been transmitted through modeled behavior.[172] The earliest customaries, produced by the monastery at Cluny between 1000 and 1030, were not so much descriptive as prescriptive; they were written, noted Barbara Rosenwein, "in the subjunctive and/or imperative modes." Their treatment of the monk's daily activities—from the sublime heights of liturgy to the mundane acts of eating, sleeping, washing, and donning shoes—reflected the assumption that "the ritualization of norms—divinely ordained norms—was the corrective to the human condition."[173]

The peculiar array of consequences triggered by custom's inscription have been discussed in works of historical and legal scholarship pertaining to medieval Germany, France, and England.[174] Before the composition of consuetudinal writings, custom possessed considerable flexibility; its mandates in any particular time and place depended on "the living legal sense of the people."[175] As long as the community's remembrancer was accepted as the authoritative repository of local tradition, "social management" of collective memory tended to go unnoticed. Whether consciously or unconsciously, this figure accommodated change; he responded to the demands of the present by refashioning the past.[176] As long as these circumstances prevailed, customs functioned as vital "instruments for legal change,"[177] for communal memory was consistently responsive to the needs of the present. Changes and metamorphoses went undetected and the past remained indistinguishable from the here and now.[178] In the words of Fritz Kern, "being neither enacted nor annulled, [unwritten law] was not so much actual as timeless. . . . The law itself remains young, always in the belief that it is old."[179]

As long as customs—or unwritten laws—left no indelible traces, communities could accommodate change while continuing to profess fidelity to time-hallowed tradition·[180] Once inscribed, however, customs could no longer evolve undetected; the textual iteration of a custom came to be construed as a precise record of a practice that had existed for all time. And as written customaries circulated over wider geographic expanses, regional variations were homogenized; ironically, the very manifestations of localism that had spawned the proliferation of custom in the first place were now flattened or obliterated.[181] Once custom was construed as written law, it lost its moorings in popular consent,[182] and "customary law" became just another contender in the welter of written legal corpora—feudal law, canon law, Roman law—that jockeyed for juridical preeminence in medieval communities.

Awakening to the Chasm Between Present and Past—and Establishing Filiation

As people and communities became increasingly reliant on written texts, discrepancies between the present and the past became harder to ignore. The encounter with old writings destroyed the illusion of "omnitemporality," a characteristic of cultures indifferent to the pastness of the past.[183] In its place came notions of archaism and historical change. Describing this as "the idea of modernity . . . in medieval terms," Brian Stock referred to "the awareness on the actor's or narrator's part that, for reasons difficult to specify, the present had become unlike the past, a fact which, in itself, demanded reflection and explanation."[184] The awakening of a sense of cultural discontinuity experienced by eleventh-century northern Europeans was reflected in the strenuous efforts made by both clerics and laymen to explain how contemporary circumstances were connected to the past, and validated by its authority.[185] The new circumstances of stability (following generations of lawlessness and migration) brought people into contact with "the material, social, political and mental residue" of social and cultural systems that had once flourished in the region, which they no longer understood. It was these dislocated fragments, inherited from the past, that people embraced as the basis of their own newly constructed identities.[186] The ability to explain the present with reference to the past endowed their lives with a sense of order, meaning, and purpose. The eleventh-century impulse to establish lines of chronological filiation can be discerned in the document writer's use of a dating system, an act that "required the scribe to express an opinion about his place in time,"[187] and in the proliferation of chronicles that cited precedents for the practices of their own times.[188] Eleventh-century historical compositions legitimated monastic claims to ancient abbeys that had fallen into disuse during the mayhem of the tenth century,[189] and local chronicles affirmed existing power structures through foundation myths that, more often than not, starred the Emperor Charlemagne.[190]

The need for "usable pasts," ones that would validate the precise conditions or claims that people wished to assert in the present, also fueled the composition of forgeries. These could be bridge texts that linked present to past by supplying narratives of transition, or fabrications that made the past look precisely like the present.[191] For the writers of such works, observed Mary Carruthers, "the present itself became a sort of recycled, updated past."[192] Or, as Michael Clanchy noted, once a written evidentiary trail had become all important, posterity needed to know "what really should have happened. . . . Truth was too important to leave to chance."[193]

Still a different route of filiation was adopted by jurists of the twelfth century. Eleventh-century canonist scholars who labored to bring internal coherence to the legal corpus (and to church doctrine) had developed critical methods for discerning the quality of a manuscript recension: they scrutinized variants for authenticity, identified textual problems, and resolved inconsistencies. Their twelfth-century successors strove to establish "external" coherence—by affirming the compatibility between life as practiced and the legal prescriptions of the textually refined corpora. Unlike Carolingian-era scholars, those of the twelfth century did not—and could not—pretend that there were no discrepancies between the two realms. Instead, they acknowledged the gaps, but diminished them very considerably by circumscribing the applicability of the written law. By applying logical distinctions to the legal passage in question, scholastic lawyers could claim that a seemingly unqualified mandate was only practicable under very limited circumstances of person, time, place, or condition. By executing these logical maneuvers, jurists cleared spaces in which unwritten practices did not clash with written laws, but could coexist with them as arbiters of cultural authority.

* * *

The very precipitants that prompted northern European Christians to undertake a broad range of literary activities beginning in the second half of the eleventh century, and the newly experienced need to filiate with the recovered fragments of the cultural past, affected Jews in the region as well. Through analysis of discrete developments, the following chapter attempts to reconstruct both the course of textualization and its impact on the Jews of medieval Ashkenaz from the late tenth through the twelfth centuries.

4

Textualization of Northern European Rabbinic Culture: The Changing Role of Talmud

European Jewry's shift from an "oral" culture to a "written" one in the Middle Ages has not gone unnoticed.[1] Observing that Jewish works composed in late antiquity became available at this time "with disconcerting suddenness—on this side, as it were, of a great manuscript divide,"[2] historians of Hebrew codicology noted that more Hebrew manuscripts are extant from the eleventh century than from any previous century,[3] and that a far greater number of manuscripts have been preserved from the twelfth century.[4] How is this data to be explained? One (now discredited) hypothesis suggested that the trauma of the First Crusade led northern European Jews to commit orally transmitted traditions to writing,[5] but, in fact, inscription and related activities of textualization were underway in northern European Jewish communities well before 1096.[6] A different line of reasoning would explain the unprecedented quantity and variety of Hebrew texts in the twelfth century as a function of the new conditions of stability that prevailed in this region, following centuries of invasions. This theory presupposes that earlier generations of Jews who were forced to flee from danger abandoned their material property, books included.[7] Yet another theory would link the greater availability of Hebrew manuscripts in northern Europe to a shift in *mentalité*, that is, to the growing sense among local Jews that inscribed texts were bearers of cultural authority. According to this last hypothesis, the earliest medieval citation of an older Jewish source would not be construed as evidence that the quoted work had just become available in the region; it might just as easily point to the society's newly awakened interest in older texts that had long been accessible, but not painstakingly explored.[8] Awareness that both of the latter lines of reasoning (with their starkly different methodological assumptions) are tenable should serve to remind readers that any narrative that aspires to interpret the existing data is a speculative reconstruction, at best.

* * *

By connecting information unearthed in a range of specialized studies and presenting it in a historically plausible pattern, the present chapter aims at intimating the contours of the textualization process that transformed rabbinic culture in medieval northern Europe from the time of Rabbenu Gershom at the turn of the millennium, through the second generation of tosafists, the talmudic glossators, in the thirteenth century. This cultural transformation, which occurred throughout northern Europe, affected Jewish communities as well as Christian ones, because it was devoid of theological meaning. By tracing developments that transpired over time in the rabbinic culture of this region, the following remarks attempt to map out some of the shifts that occurred in text-related attitudes and behaviors. The data reveals changes that occurred in the roles that texts came to play in Jewish society, in readers' assumptions and practices, in compositional activities, in the popularity of particular genres, in curricular emphases, in pedagogic ideals and methods, and in modes of rabbinic adjudication. While many corpora of tradition came to play new roles within medieval Jewish culture under the impact of textualization,[9] this chapter will focus specifically on changes in the ways that Talmud was used—first in the realm of pedagogy and subsequently in the realm of adjudication. I would argue that, in the case of north European Jewish culture, the growing prominence of the talmudic corpus in the classroom, and its growing importance in adjudication and in the shaping of Jewish life, were functions of its commitment to writing.

The process of textualization that transpired in northern Europe is not relevant to the cultural history of Sefarad. Not only were the territories in question always in the zone of writing (whether in Roman or Visigothic or Muslim times), but Sefardi Jews possessed two traditions that the Jews of northern Europe did not: the tradition of the Talmud's early inscription, and the notion that "our Talmud," which is to say, the talmudic text in its written form, was explicitly designed as a source of applied law.[10] Medieval Sefardi

Jews raised with these traditions would have had little need to labor over the talmudic text itself in order to elicit applied law. Unlike their Ashkenazi contemporaries, they could avail themselves of digests or codes that set forth applied law in far more accessible literary venues than the Talmud itself. In other words, up until the thirteenth century (when Naḥmanides and his students imported the tosafist method of Talmud study, thereby "homogenizing" the rabbinic world), Talmud played different roles in the lives of Sefardi and Ashkenazi Jews.

Not only was the memory of the Talmud's commitment to writing still "fresh" for the Jews of northern Europe (as will be seen below), but the broader society in which the Jews of Ashkenaz participated had relied on the authority of custom over the course of generations in which there was neither strong centralized government nor written legislation. Though Yisrael Ta Shma speculated that the earliest Ashkenazi settlers brought a sophisticated legal culture (the precursor of Tosafism) with them, in that they hailed from Lucca, Italy, an area under Lombard rule where notarial records were kept from the 850s, this hypothesis is hardly robust. According to Charles Radding, the "stirrings of a critical legal science" in Lombardy (and in Pavia, in particular) only began in the 1020s;[11] thus, when the Ashkenazi community's founders departed for the Rhineland in the ninth century or the tenth,[12] their emigration would have predated these developments in Lombardy.

Reconstruction of cultural developments that transpired within northern European rabbinic society (and that were specific to this region) tends to bolster the impression that there was nothing inevitable about the Talmud's transformation into the preeminent guide to Jewish law. If anything, it reveals the array of of historical circumstances and contingent decisions that paved the way. Analysis of developments in a number of arenas, pedagogy and adjudication among them, may shed light on the ways in which the shift from the oral transmission of Talmud to its written transmission reshaped rabbinic tradition itself.

The Place of Talmud in Northern European Jewish Pedagogy

Rabbinic Culture in Pre-Crusade Northern Europe

Jews lived in Ashkenaz, a territory coincident with the Carolingian Empire, for at least five generations prior to the First Crusade of 1096, but Jewish writings from this area were produced only during the last three generations, from the time of Rabbenu Gershom ben Meir, active in Mainz around the year 1000, through that of Rashi, who left the Rhineland in the 1070s to return to his native Champagne.[13] This historical record need not mean that writings had not been produced by the first two generations of Jewish settlers in the Rhineland; only that their descendants did not know of them. The contrast between the modes of cultural expression that prevailed in Ashkenaz and in Sefarad at this time is impressionistically conveyed by comparing Rabbenu Gershom of Mainz with his Andalusian contemporary, Shmuel HaNagid. At around the same time that HaNagid was amassing a personal library that would be renowned for generations[14] and arranging for the large-scale copying of Bible, Mishnah, and Talmud manuscripts to be sent to students in Babylonia and Mediterranean Jewish communities, Rabbenu Gershom was demonstrating concern with inscription (and textual accuracy) in a more modest way, writing out a copy of the Bible and a copy of the Talmud in his own hand.[15]

Though Rabbenu Gershom was not the promulgator of the ordinances ascribed to him, the rulings recorded in his name reflect the concerns of Jews who lived only slightly later.[16] The ordinance prohibiting the clipping of blank manuscript margins for reuse reveals that parchment was a valued commodity,[17] and the imposition of a ban on anyone who withheld relevant documents while engaged in a legal dispute indicates that (at least) some texts possessed evidentiary authority.[18] The anathema that Rabbenu Gershom is alleged to have proclaimed against anyone who engaged in textual emendation[19] similarly presupposes that written texts possessed some sort of cultural weight; uncontrolled changes could distort received tradition. Yet in Rabbenu Gershom's own time, this stricture would most likely have been an expression of wishful thinking. Not only was it normal for those transmitting tradition to graphically rectify what they saw as textual errors,[20] it was also natural for them to respond, in writing, to the texts they read, as if in conversation. If the aim of Jewish education was to fashion students into repositories of tradition, it would hardly have seemed inappropriate for an erudite scholar to engage in direct conversation with tradition and to speak in its name.

The perception of written tradition as "authorless" texts that belonged to all[21] supported an active, forceful, or, in the words of Yisrael Ta Shma, "aggressive" practice of reading: one who encountered a written text might engage it by putting pen to page. Not only did corpora of ancient tradition accumulate anonymous exegetical strata in this manner,[22] they were prone, in the words of Alexander Samely and Philip Alexander, to an "unusually high degree of re-creation."[23] In this sense, the process that affected written Hebrew texts in the Middle Ages mimicked a process that had affected units of tradition during their prolonged period of oral transmission. Indeed, features of sedimentation that have been detected in written texts of Mishnah,[24] Tosefta,[25] and Talmud[26] constitute evidence that each corpus underwent multiple acts of reworking. In discussing the phenomenon of ongoing reformulation, Ya'aqov Sussman wrote: "These matters are surprising and perhaps even a bit shocking. But it seems to me that more than making us recoil from our conclusions, they teach us a larger principle about the process of transmission of traditions of texts in our literary sources. Parallel passages . . . were transmitted in disparate literary frameworks, during which the transmitters, redactors and students, inserted into the different frameworks other passages that were interwoven with them in the formulation and language (*versio*) of the tradition that they had received [as authoritative]."[27]

The alteration of written texts—perceived by later generations as "tampering"—was hardly unique to Jews in medieval northern Europe, however;[28] there is evidence that Hebrew manuscripts were emended by Jews in Italy,[29] the Muslim East,[30] and perhaps even Andalusian Spain.[31] Philological studies by Menaḥem Kahane, Pinḥas Mendel, Peter Schäfer, and others[32] support the conjecture that "forceful reading" was the norm among medieval Jewish readers and demonstrate that re-creation of traditions was part and parcel of the transmission process over the course of centuries.[33] Reflecting on this same phenomenon within contemporaneous Christian culture, Mary Carruthers observed, "The medieval understanding of the complete process of reading doesn't observe . . . the basic distinction we make between 'what I read in a book' and 'my experience.' "[34]

In a similar vein, C. S. Lewis described the "characteristic activity of the medieval . . . author" as " 'touching up' something that was already there":

> We might equally well call our medieval authors the most unoriginal or the most original of men. They are so unoriginal that they hardly ever attempt to write anything unless someone else has written it before. They are so rebelliously and insistently original that they can hardly reproduce a page of any older work without transforming it. . . . We always tinker [with our drafts]. . . . But in the Middle Ages, you did that as cheerfully to other people's work as to your own. . . . When we are treating the Middle Ages, . . . for many of

the texts there is no one human being who can be called the author in the full sense.[35]

At a time when written texts of rabbinic tradition were not yet seen as either the definitive or the sole *loci* of religious and legal authority, transmitters engaged tradition directly, and not from the margins, for they were, in effect, its living embodiments.

* * *

Prior to the First Crusade, the Rhineland yeshivot pursued a curriculum that has been described as "omnivorous."[36] Talmud was but one of the subjects studied there, alongside the Bible,[37] Masorah,[38] aggadic and halakhic midrash,[39] Mishnah, and prayer.[40] The earliest Jews of northern Europe had inherited Jewish traditions from Palestine, Babylonia, Byzantine Italy, and Provence—and they showed little inclination to harmonize discrepancies they encountered in the accumulated teachings.

This anthologistic embrace of even incompatible traditions is evident in several features of northern Europe's earliest Talmud commentary.[41] Though the composition in question came to be known as *Rabbenu Gershom's Commentary on Talmud*, it was not, in fact, the product of a single author.[42] The earliest work to cite it, the *'Arukh*, a Hebrew lexicon produced in twelfth-century Rome, knew of this commentary as a compilation of traditions transmitted by anonymous scholars of the Mainz academy.[43] While it shows some signs of having been reworked (perhaps during use in different academic cycles),[44] the Mainz *Commentary*'s presentation of multiple interpretations without attempting to reconcile them or to identify a single one as correct[45] contributes to the impression that Talmud study in the Mainz yeshivah was geared toward transmitting tradition in its copiousness, and not toward the determination of applied law.[46] Features of the Mainz *Commentary on Talmud* reflect the pedagogic assumptions of the classroom and may be seen as written instantiations of oral practices.[47]

* * *

In the generation following Rabbenu Gershom, additional Hebrew written materials were prepared for classroom use in both German- and French-speaking lands. Rashi's Rhenish teachers dictated works for students to copy,[48] and one introduced the term "*quntres*" to designate the notebook in which a student recorded his teachers' comments on an underlying text. (The term itself was derived from the Latin *quinternus*, because the pamphlet was constructed of five folio pages that were bound together.)[49] In the next generation, Rashi's commentaries on Scripture and Talmud displaced others that had previously circulated in Ashkenaz, Provence, and Spain; this fact elicited the chagrin of critics.[50] Though hardly the instigator of the textualization process, Rashi was undoubtedly its most formidable agent.

Rashi's Historiographic Account of the Talmud's Formation and Inscription

Rashi's comments about the formation of the rabbinic corpora added several historical claims that were not found in Sherira Gaon's *Epistle*, a work whose "French" recension Rashi knew and cited.[51] It was he who noted that "*talmud*," an oral corpus containing explanations of mishnaic traditions that had been studied in tannaitic times,[52] "was the template of Gemara set up by the amoraim."[53] Rashi also taught that legal decisions were not to be derived from either Mishnah or *beraita*, because the exponents of tannaitic teachings were not as meticulous in their explanations as were later amoraim.[54] Finally, Rashi explained that the talmudic corpus was not given its shape and its texture until the turn of the sixth century, when amoraim associated with "the end of instruction" undertook certain activities:

> Ravina and Rav Ashi arranged the amoraic heard teachings [*shemu'ot*] that they had before them. And they established them in the order of the tractates, each and every one next to the appropriate Mishnah that was recited with it. And they posed questions that needed to be answered, and uncoupled matters that were in need of [re]arrangement, they and the amoraim who were with them. And they established everything in Gemara.[55]

Whether Rashi assumed that the "heard teachings" of the amoraim, the *shemu'ot* that Ravina and Rav Ashi "had before them," were units of oral tradition or existed in written form as unofficial *megilot setarim*,[56] he understood that Rabbi Judah the Patriarch had engaged in "arranging" the orders and tractates of Mishnah at the turn of the third century,[57] and that Ravina and Rav Ashi performed one additional task three centuries later, one that had not been necessary before: they "filed" amoraic teachings in their appropriate places.[58]

Apart from relaying these post-Sheriran traditions about the formation of the rabbinic corpora, Rashi's commentary conveys information that explicitly links Talmud to the adjudicatory process. According to Rashi, one stratum of talmudic material—its anonymous teachings—are sources of applied law: "In the yeshivah of the last ones, these anonymous *halakhot* were decided [*nifsequ*] in the Talmud/Gemara."[59]

The different portraits of *talmud* offered by Sherira Gaon and by Rashi may bear witness to the standardization of Talmud during the century that separated the two scholars, to changes in the image of this corpus, or to both. Writing in the late tenth century, Sherira had offered an encomium to Mishnah,[60] but had said nothing about the ordering activities of the last amoraim. Rashi, by contrast, placed Talmud in the limelight. So great is the discrepancy between the two portraits of Talmud that the modern scholar, Yonah Frankel, was moved to ask, "What compelled Rashi to go and aggrandize the role of the generation of Ravina and Rav Ashi?"[61]

An attitudinal change appears to have transpired during the hundred-year interval that separated the two scholars. For Rashi, it was Talmud rather than Mishnah that was the consummate rabbinic creation of antiquity.

* * *

Jewish communities in medieval northern Europe were not privy to anything like the medieval Sefardi tradition(s) that located the Talmud's inscription in the distant past. If anything, the rhetoric of the northern European tradition portrayed the inscription of Talmud as a relatively recent development, though it offered no substantive chronological reference points.[62] Rashi touched upon this when he contrasted the transmission practices of amoraim with those of later generations:

> For in their days, the Talmud was not in writing, nor was it permitted to write it. However, because the hearts have become diminished, our generations have begun to write it.[63]

Echoing the leitmotif of Sherira Gaon's *Epistle*,[64] Rashi portrayed the Talmud's inscription as a concession to the frailty of memory. (This perspective contrasts sharply with the medieval Sefardi tradition of "*ha-Talmud shelanu*," which understands the Talmud's inscription as an event undertaken, unapologetically, for the purpose of imparting applied law.) Still, Rashi's formulation (unlike that of Sherira) evinced neither regret nor nostalgia about the changes that had occurred. If anything, he seemed to be adopting the role of a historical anthropologist as he tried to explain the alien assumptions and practices of a now defunct culture to his bewildered contemporaries.[65] One of Rashi's bridge-building explanations was occasioned by the puzzling ranking of three corpora of Jewish learning in the following talmudic passage: "Our rabbis taught: Those who occupy themselves with the Bible [alone] are of but indifferent merit; with Mishnah are indeed meritorious; with Gemara—there can be nothing more meritorious."[66] Commenting on this enigmatic statement, Rashi accounted for the gap between the assumptions of the present and a now-forgotten mindset by supplying a missing puzzle piece: In earlier times, he explained, oral transmission was the cultural norm, in deference to the tannaitic prohibition. Instructors relayed tradition through oral formulae, and students memorized these teachings. For this reason, the corpora that were deemed more difficult to learn were accorded greater value:

> Mishnah and Gemara are finer [more desirable] than it [Bible] because they are dependent upon oral recitation, and are susceptible to being forgotten. For in their days, the Gemara was not in writing, nor was it permissible to write it.[67]

If the attitudes of ancient rabbinic sages were sometimes hard to grasp, noted Rashi, it was because they, unlike contemporary Jews, did not encounter *oral matters* in written form. The inscription of *oral matters* was a watershed event that made it hard for later students to grasp the assumptions and perspectives of their predecessors. For this reason, Rashi commented on every occurrence of the term *megilat setarim* ["a scroll to be sequestered"] in the Talmud, taking pains to clarify the role played by such "phantom texts" in the culture of earlier Jews. His comments explain why the writing in question was to have been concealed, and what it contained:

> They hid it because it was not permitted to commit it to writing [as an official document]. And when one hears the innovative words of an individual that are not taught [as applied law] in the rabbinic academy[68] and writes them down that they not be forgotten, one hides the scroll.[69]

According to Rashi, a writing in the category of *megilat setarim* was merely a mnemonic aid; it was to be kept out of the public view lest it be construed as an authorized and official text. The sequestration of a writing that was in the category of *megilat setarim* signaled to anyone who read or possessed it that it was a text that lacked authority.[70] Rashi glossed every single talmudic reference to a written text that occurs in the Babylonian Talmud because he was aware that contemporary Jews would not (otherwise) understand cultural assumptions held by the ancient rabbis. In each case, explained Rashi, the inscribed text was either scriptural, or it was a private epistle.[71] As Ya'aqov Sussman noted, Rashi missed no opportunity to remind readers that tannaim and amoraim would never have dreamed of inscribing *halakhot*.[72] He also vigilantly distinguished between terms denoting oral transmission (e.g., "*shana*," "*garas*," "*sidder*," "'*arakh*," "*qava*'") and terms denoting written transmission (e.g., "*katav*," "*qara*"). Rashi's determination to sensitize contemporaries to the disparate cultural assumptions that separated his generation from that of the ancient rabbis was, in Sussman's words, "almost obsessive."[73]

Rashi's unremitting reminders made readers of his Talmud commentary aware that a shift had occurred, but the implications of this shift for Jewish practice were not spelled out; these would only become palpable as Rashi's labors, linked with those of the tosafists, transformed the talmudic text into the legal guide for Jewish life. In the absence of clear geonic guidelines, Rashi, like his predecessors in Mainz, Qayrawan, and al-Andalus, had to make (historically contingent) decisions about how the Talmud would be "deployed"—in the classroom and beyond. And as is clear from earlier counterexamples like the Mainz commentary of the tenth century and the Qayrawanese commentaries of the eleventh, no feature of Rashi's commentary was "inevitable"; the author faced a variety of options for every parameter of composition. In the end, the cultural changes set in motion by Rashi's commentary were not the result of any predetermined Jewish understanding of the role(s) that Talmud was intended to play in the lives of rabbinic Jews, or of how it was to do so.

Rashi's Commentary on the Talmud

Before attempting to explain the meaning of the Talmud's narrative, Rashi needed to establish its precise wording. He did so by examining variant formulations of talmudic passages that he encountered in a range of writings, both European and Eastern.[74] Some formulations were from manuscripts of Talmud; others were talmudic phrases embedded in post-talmudic compositions. Though Rashi declared, "This is how we recite" ("*hakhi garsinan*"), in more than 1,500 places in his Talmud commentary, he only occasionally shared the deliberations that led him to establish a particular lexical formulation as definitive.[75] Yet recent scholarship has greatly advanced our understanding of the process by which Rashi came to establish precise wordings in the talmudic text. Building on Vered Noam's discovery of the strong degree of correspondence between the talmudic formulations chosen by Rashi and those found in talmudic manuscripts from the East,[76] Rami Reiner has surmised that Rashi scrutinized Babylonian texts in which passages from Talmud were cited—works like *Halakhot Gedolot* and geonic writings—in order to ascertain (or recover) "authentic" wordings of the talmudic text.[77]

The form of Rashi's commentary on the Talmud lends itself to several historical observations. The decision not to explain the talmudic text in paraphrastic form reveals that Rashi designed his commentary to be used as an accompaniment to the open talmudic text, and not as a substitute for it. A reader would need to visually track a written—and lexically stable—text of Talmud in order to successfully use Rashi's explanatory composition. For reasons pertaining to both pedagogy and composition, a commentary of this sort could not have been produced in the geonic academies. Not only were pains taken in the Babylonian yeshivot to maintain the oral transmission of *oral matters*, but the wording of the talmudic corpus itself was not yet fixed in the geonic period. The cueing device adopted by Rashi (and by certain predecessors)[78]—the *dibur ha-matḥil* [Latin, *incipita*], the word or words from the Talmud that occasioned the explanation—could only have been effective in a study environment where the Talmud's precise formulation was standardized and in which the text itself was accessed in written form.

Rashi's presentation of multiple explanations for a given talmudic word or passage[79] may reflect the experience of studying the same material in different academic cycles, at times under the tutelage of different teachers. And his inclusion of interpretations that are, at times, mutually exclusive, may be seen as consistent with the anthological orientation of the Rhineland classrooms, which strove to transmit tradition in its plenitude. Variant manuscripts of Rashi's Talmud commentary suggest that this work was itself shaped by some of the same pedagogic conditions. Each time Rashi taught a given tractate in the classroom, he encountered it with fresh eyes and comfortably altered his earlier comments—adding, emending, and at times even erasing.[80] But because students who had attended the academy in earlier semesters were often unaware of these alterations, they continued to disseminate—and teach—versions of Rashi's commentary that they had copied while studying with the master, not knowing that these, in effect, had been "recalled."[81] The multiple recensions of Rashi's Talmud commentary bear witness to the commentator's dynamic review of material and to his discovery of disparate formulations of Talmud encountered in "old texts" that came to his attention.[82]

Like the geonim, Rashi paid careful attention to the pathways through which traditions were transmitted, pointedly using the distinct terms "*shama'ti*" (I heard) and "*maẓati*" (I found), to introduce teachings that he heard in oral instruction and those he had encountered in writing.[83] The copious collection of *le'azim,* vernacular translations of obscure terms, in his Talmud commentary[84] may reflect Rashi's immersion in the environment of the eleventh-century schoolroom, where, in the words of Mary Carruthers, scholarly tools and commentaries "sprang up virtually formed" after generations of oral dissemination.[85]

Rashi's commentary supplied the talmudic text with a connective tissue that wove its utterances into a comprehensible discourse. This project is indicative of a particular stage in the transition from oral to written transmission, in that live speech (as was captured in talmudic phrasing) requires less formal articulation than written communication.[86] As a running (rather than an intermittent) gloss that unpacked every unclear term in the Talmud in sequential fashion, Rashi's commentary on Talmud made it possible for literate Jews (including those who lacked access to a master) to make sense of the talmudic text's truncated and epigrammatic formulations. Throughout his commentary, Rashi addressed the reader as if in a live encounter (though not in the second person); his remarks presage what is to come next and grant assurance that an unclear talmudic passage will be illuminated by one soon to follow. Rashi also indicated when the unpunctuated talmudic utterance should be read as an interrogative or an expression of astonishment, and not in the (default) declarative mode. In cases like these—which would normally be known only through oral transmission—Rashi gave written instruction about the proper vocal inflection. These stage directions, along with Rashi's vernacular translation of arcane talmudic terms and his description of the *realia* from the amoraic age,[87] made it exponentially easier for Jews to undertake home study of Talmud when they lacked access to a master. By disseminating traditions that had been preserved and orally transmitted in the Rhineland over the course of generations, Rashi's Talmud commentary contributed, wittingly or unwittingly, to the attenuation of discipleship and the weakening of its many collateral assumptions.

The Tosafists' Comments on the Talmud

Though Rashi's commentary on the Talmud had the effect of "authorizing" this specific version of the text,[88] Rashi's grandsons and their disciples, the talmudic glossators active in France and Germany in the twelfth and thirteenth centuries, felt that the most correct formulation of the talmudic text had yet to be identified. Following in the path initiated by Rashi,[89] these tosafists, so-called because of the *tosafot* or "additions" that they composed,[90] propelled the process of textual rectification into higher gear by scrutinizing variant formulations of talmudic passages that were embedded in a broader array of old compositions.[91] Linking the novel insights of the tosafists to their archival undertakings, the thirteenth-century Catalonian scholar Naḥmanides, observed: "The tosafists were able to reveal that which was hidden because they were master collectors."[92] It has been suggested that the tosafists undertook their unique project when they did because the older compositions they consulted had just become available in northern Europe,[93] but (as discussed above) this claim relies on an unproven assumption. We cannot be sure whether the eleventh-century Qayrawanese Talmud commentary by Rabbenu Ḥananel was cited in early twelfth-century France because Jews in this area now had acess to it, or because they were now more keenly interested in textual evidence from the past.[94] Either way, both the ability of the tosafists to improve on the accuracy of the Talmud's formulation and their drive to do so distinguish their assumptions about Talmud and its uses from those held by their rabbinic predecessors. Tosafist concerns and activities contrast dramatically with those of the transmitters of Oral Torah portrayed in Sherira's *Epistle*, who had focused on relaying the meaning of tradition, but not on specific wording—and even with Rabbenu Gershom, who observed, at the turn of the millennium, that the talmudic text before him was not precise ("*lav davka kol kakh*").[95] The tosafists' quest for older compositions that could bear witness to talmudic phraseology, and their comparison of lexical variants speak volumes about their assumption that there was a correct formulation to be recovered, and that this iteration (and not merely the ideas it expressed) was of crucial importance.

The tosafists' mimicry of the Talmud's language and style was so convincing that later scholars portrayed them as *amoraim redivivus*.[96] Their fluency in this regard points to the importance of memorization in the tosafist classrooms and to their "total immersion" in the talmudic oeuvre. The comfortable adoption of talmudic phraseology that was evident in Shmuel Ha-

Nagid's Andalusian poems of the late tenth century became a feature of northern European rabbinic culture in the early twelfth.[97]

The tosafists' panoptic approach to Talmud was built on an assumption held by Rashi. Where he had clarified obscure passages with reference to clearer ones that appeared elsewhere in the talmudic tractate,[98] the tosafists regarded the entire Talmud as a unified and internally coherent corpus. Relying on this notion, they put scaffolding into place that would enable students reading the Talmud to compare and contrast related utterances that occur throughout the corpus. Even before pagination was standardized, the tosafists identified textual parallels and created a comprehensive system of cross-referencing.[99] An idealized account of the way Talmud was studied in the academy of the tosafist R. Isaac of Dampierre[100] offers some sense of the manner in which these cross-references may have been generated. According to R. Menaḥem b. Aharon b. Zeraḥ of fourteenth-century Spain, each of the sixty scholars studying with R. Isaac of Dampierre committed a different talmudic tractate to memory, so that when they convened together in the classroom, "the entire Gemara was between their eyes."[101] Whatever its accuracy, this tradition offers a glimpse into how collaboration between scholars of considerable mnemonic prowess may have facilitated cross-referencing of the entire Talmud.

The tosafists could never have retrieved relevant talmudic passages had they not developed the ability to skip around within the corpus, deploying the mnemonic agility that Mary Carruthers calls "the proof of a good memory."[102] Still, a material feature of book production—one that distinguished twelfth-century northern European Jews from their counterparts in the East—may also have helped the tosafists in this enterprise and contributed to their cultural and pedagogic sense of the Talmud's unity. A codicological testimony preserved in *Sefer Ḥasidim* reports that while the Jews of Babylonia bound each tractate of Talmud separately, the Jews of Germany bound together all talmudic tractates within one Mishnaic order: "The [practice of] binding together the entire order in this kingdom is because we need to investigate another tractate while in the academy, and how could one bring each tractate separately?"[103] Though the first generation of tosafists were French, the book-binding practice that prevailed in the Rhineland academies may well have been adopted by students who studied there before returning to France.

The tosafists did not always agree with everything written by Rashi in his Talmud commentary, but his mammoth contribution was the precondition of their own. They were only able to identify certain problems and resolve them because Rashi had produced a semantically comprehensible talmudic narrative. The tosafists appended their comments to far fewer selections from the talmudic text than had Rashi, and they used these glossatorial sites to entertain a wider range of concerns. Apart from offering exegesis, comments by the tosafists set forth alternative readings of the talmudic text, challenged Rashi, noted the recurrence of particular phrases in other *sugyot* (units) of the Talmud, drew attention to ostensible contradictions between talmudic passages, and resolved them by means of dialectical reasoning. This last activity, reminiscent of the give and take of the amoraim, involved the systematic comparison of related talmudic passages, the identification of conflicts between them, and, ultimately, the dissolution of the problems raised. In this final stage of the activity, the tosafists would reveal that the circumstances treated in the apparently incompatible talmudic passages were, in fact, hardly identical. The undertakings of the tosafists affirmed two assumptions about the Babylonian Talmud on which their logocentric activity was predicated: the notion that the Talmud's language was fixed and authoritative, and the notion that the Talmud was internally consistent.

* * *

Beginning at the turn of the millennium, northern European scholars took steps toward making the Talmud more useable in the classroom, and each generation's contributions paved the way for those of the next. The text-centered activities of copying and dictation that were begun in the time of Rabbenu Gershom made the written talmudic text available to subsequent students in the region; Rashi's Talmud commentary made it possible for literate Jews to read the Talmud as a comprehensible narrative; and the tosafists' dialectical operations resolved ostensible textual inconsistencies such that, as a sixteenth-century rabbinic scholar said, they "made of the Talmud one ball."[104]

The Place of Talmud in Medieval Northern European Rabbinic Adjudication

Each of these developments, in its own historical moment, altered the cultural status quo. As students in the region came to read the Talmud in new ways (e.g., as a comprehensible narrative and, later, as an internally consistent text), the corpus itself assumed new roles in northern European Jewish society. Scholastic engagement with the Talmud increasingly displaced the ethos of discipleship. As long as talmudic teachings had been imparted orally, students acquired knowledge of applied law from living links in the chain of transmission, from masters who could attest to the *halakhot* that were implemented in practice. However, as the written text of the Talmud acquired the status of a reference work, applied law increasingly came to be learned though textual analysis and the application of a growing number of procedural rules.[105] While this shift may not have brought about any significant changes in the specifics of applied law, the process through which applied law was derived was now bared for the scrutiny of any reader capable of following the articulated reasoning. This had not been the approach taken by the scholars of Qayrawan, for while their Talmud commentaries built bridges between the underlying text and the applied law to be practiced, the actual feats of connective engineering were not on display. The social ramifications of this northern European development were gargantuan. Whereas students of the geonim and of the Rhineland masters were conditioned to accept the practical guidelines transmitted by their teachers, northern European rabbinical students from the twelfth century onward possessed exegetical tools and procedural rules that enabled them to challenge their teachers' conclusions and to derive the applied law themselves. A student's ability to discern new meanings through logical analysis of the talmudic text enhanced his social status.

* * *

The following historical overview of the roles that Talmud played in the realm of adjudication from the late eleventh century through the late twelfth is both sketchy and speculative. Because it seeks to draw conclusions about the Talmud's relative importance in adjudication from evidence of its presence (or absence) in the writings or behaviors of northern European rabbinic Jews, this undertaking itself may be seen as prejudicially predetermined. This is a valid methodological criticism. Having come up with no alternative method for assessing the desired information, I can only attempt to compensate for the bias implicit in the following remarks by including the voice that is critical of this investigative approach and by attempting to represent its perspective with accuracy.

Sources of Ashkenazi Adjudication Prior to the Twelfth Century: A Debate

What sources of tradition played a role in the process of legal decision making for northern European Jews prior to the twelfth century? The earliest rabbinic scholars of Germany seem to have been less attuned than their French contemporaries to the geonic legacy, and up through the mid-eleventh century, Ashkenazi legal decisors do not appear to have relied on decisions articulated in geonic-era Babylonia.[106] Yet other features of this period's adjudicatory writings are even more surprising when judged by the standards of later rabbinic jurisprudence. In some cases, a rabbinic decisor would cite the relevant talmudic teaching yet indicate that it was not upheld, because a contrary perspective was engrained in popular practice.[107] In others, a decisor might ignore obviously pertinent passages from the Babylonian Talmud when building an argument,[108] and instead invoke prooftexts from Torah[109] or Mishnah,[110] or even *midrash aggadah*.[111] When viewed from the perspective of subsequent rabbinic adjudication, such rulings are striking, even shocking. Only a few generations later, the use of such non-talmudic sources would come to be regarded as wholly inappropriate to the project of legal decision making. How is the above-mentioned phenomena to be understood?

Some researchers would conclude from this data that, in eleventh-century northern Europe, the Talmud was not yet playing the definitive role in legal decision making that it would come to play in the twelfth century. The failure of eleventh-century rabbis to recognize talmudic teachings as the lone determinants of applied law might even be seen as echoing the adjudicatory approach of the Babylonian geonim, who had ascribed weight to communal behavior and attested practice.[112] In several celebrated exchanges with the Jews of Qayrawan (discussed in Chapter 1), the geonim counseled reliance on ancestral practice even when the latter appeared to flout explicit talmudic teachings, and Hai Gaon boldly exposed the logical rationale behind this epistemological ranking of the sources of tradition.

This same interpretive perspective would portray the willingness of pre-Crusade rabbis to utilize non-talmudic prooftexts in legal decision making as indicative of the procedural immaturity of rabbinic adjudication in eleventh-century northern Europe.[113] Scholars of the time had inherited an array of methodological rules for adjudicating from Talmud itself (some articulated by tannaim, others by amoraim, and still others by the geonim themselves), but these *kelale pesiqa*, principles of adjudication, were at best inconsistent and hardly comprehensive.[114] For this reason, northern European decisors who needed to imbue their decisions with authority (and who did not have stature of the Baghdadi geonim) availed themselves of all the resources they had at their disposal; they drew upon well-known corpora of cultural authority—like Scripture, Mishnah, and Midrash—in bolstering their judgments.[115] It was only in the twelfth century, when the procedural principles for adjudicating from Talmud had been augmented and refined, that rabbinic scholars would make that corpus into the sole basis for their legal decisions and forego the use of other sources of tradition.

An opposing interpretive viewpoint would explain the peculiar features of eleventh-century northern European adjudication in the light of later developments in the region's rabbinic culture, and claim that scholars of the pre-Crusade period were no different from their twelfth-century successors. According to this perspective, the procedurally anomalous rulings of the eleventh century need not be seen as inconsistent with their decisors' perception of the Babylonian Talmud as the definitive and sole legal authority.[116] In fact, an eleventh-century adjudicator who upheld communal practice that conflicted with talmudic legislation did so in keeping with the Talmud's own counsel, given the advice (BT Beẓ. 30a) that it was preferable to keep people in ignorance of a particular law if the population was unlikely to heed it, inasmuch as sinning without awareness of one's transgression is less egregious than sinning with consciousness.

This same interpretive perspective would explain the appeal to non-talmudic prooftexts as a strategy adopted by eleventh-century decisors for rhetorical reasons. Knowing that their less-learned Jewish contemporaries were not very familiar with the Babylonian Talmud, these rabbinic scholars crafted their decisions in manners that would maximize their suasive impact. Appeals to the Talmud were simply less compelling at this time than were appeals to better-known sources of cultural authority. For this reason, when they needed to address issues of foundational importance for young, decentralized, and fractious Jewish communities, eleventh-century adjudicators consciously invoked passages from Scripture, Mishnah, and aggadah, all well-known and revered repositories of cultural authority, whose citations would be easily recognized.[117]

* * *

These disparate theories are represented in a vigorous debate among contemporary scholars over the interpretation of an episode in Jewish history that is as hermeneutically challenging as it is grisly. Jews of the Rhineland, a population distinguished by its adherence to legal stringencies, chose to murder their children and themselves in 1096 rather than submit to the Crusaders.[118] Because they performed these acts with full knowledge that homicide and suicide violated Jewish law, modern scholars have struggled to make sense of their deeds. According to one interpretive perspective, the (seemingly) transgressive behavior of these pious Jews can be explained with reference to a distinct cultural logic, and it offers historical evidence about legal decision making in the eleventh century. According to the opposing interpretive perspective, it would be both inappropriate and foolish to draw from these deeds any historical conclusions about adjudicatory practices of the time, since legal thinking, per se, had nothing to do with the behavior of a community *in extremis*.

Scholars taking the former approach have argued that eleventh-century Rhenish Jews found inspiration and justification for their deeds in texts from the Jewish past that they perceived as authoritative, and permitted these extra-talmudic sources to influence their legal reasoning.[119] According to this hypothesis, Jews of the Rhineland found role models for their own behavior of 1096 in the first century Zealots who committed homicide-suicide at the mountain fortress of Masada. They had encountered an account of this self-inflicted massacre in the *Sefer Yosippon*, a tenth-century Hebrew adaptation of the histories of Josephus Flavius, and assumed that this was actually the work of a tanna, a rabbinic sage of mishnaic teachings, since its author was witness to the Temple's destruction.[120] Jews of medieval northern Europe could also have found inspiration for their extreme deeds in aggadic narratives recounting the suicide of pious Jews. Contemporary scholars who are of the opinion that law-abiding Rhineland Jews did engage in legal deliberations and seek juridical justification before killing their children and themselves have identified a number of literary sources that could have provided inspiration for their horrific deeds.[121]

Vehemently rejecting this theory, Haym Soloveitchik has asserted that the gruesome massacres of 1096 cannot, and should not, be evaluated through the prism of juridical analysis. In his opinion, it would be foolish to assume that legal concerns were on the minds of Jews who were overwhelmed by their circumstances as they faced the Crusaders. Little wonder, argues Soloveitchik, that attempts made by later talmudic glossators to render the acts of 1096 legally defensible are casuistically strained and "of dubious legal worth."[122]

This twenty-first-century debate over whether the behavior of Rhenish Jews in 1096 offers insight into contemporaneous practices of rabbinic adjudication seems destined to remain at a stalemate, because the parties to the dispute approach the question with diametrically opposed assumptions about the purview of halakhic reasoning. Scholars who cannot imagine pious Jews undertaking any act without careful legal deliberation will find the eleventh-century tragedy instructive, while those who believe that halakhic reasoning is not invoked in grave and abnormal situations of crisis assume that the aberrant deeds committed by the Rhineland's Jews in 1096 yield no data that could be useful for reconstructing the history of Jewish legal practice.

The Place of Talmud in Rashi's Applied Adjudication

Contemporary assessments of the role that Talmud played in Rashi's adjudicatory activities are far less polarized, though there are slight differences in emphasis and nuance. Rashi generally used his Talmud commentary as a venue for clarifying the text's meaning and, less frequently, to convey practical adjudication.[123] Most of Rashi's legal decisions appear, not in his Talmud commentary, but in his responsa and in compilations of his oral teachings that were transcribed by his students in works like *Sefer ha-Orah*, *Sefer ha-Pardes*, *Isur ve-Heter shel Rashi,* and others—writings designated collectively as *sifrut devei Rashi*, "literature of Rashi's school."[124] The most prominent exception, a digest of applied law that is appended to Rashi's Talmud commentary on the fourth chapter of tractate 'Avodah Zarah, need not be seen as undermining this generalization. Where other tractates were concerned, Rashi (like other scholars) was the beneficiary of exegetical interpretations and legal decisions that had accrued over many cycles of academic study, but he was northern European Jewry's pioneer in subjecting this tractate to rigorous study. Rashi's systematic articulation of a body of applied law that stemmed from this tractate—much of it pertaining to gentile involvement in different aspects of Jewish wine production—was thus a response to a gaping need. Wine production was crucial to the economic life of northern European Jews, yet before Rashi's time, it had received relatively little rabbinic attention.

Even if this newly articulated body of applied law, dictated by Rashi to his grandson, R. Samuel ben Meir, known as Rashbam, and appended to the Talmud commentary, is construed as an exception that proves the rule;[125] and even if Rashi, in fact, demonstrated a preference for rendering applied legal decisions in genres other than Talmud commentary, there is no question that he regarded the Babylonian Talmud as the sole authority in matters of law, the standard by which he evaluated other legal traditions embedded in writings of the geonic era.[126]

The Place of Talmud in the Adjudicatory Activity of the Tosafists

The tosafists were born into a Jewish educational aristocracy that regarded the Talmud as an accessible and internally coherent text, and into a broader environment in which the activities of daily life were being aligned with systematically articulated laws.[127] Because historical circumstances had granted them both the necessary tools and the requisite motivation, the tosafists were able to bring Talmud into immediate conversation with applied Jewish law with a thoroughness, and to a degree, that had not been possible for their scholarly predecessors (assuming that this had been desired at all). A particular comment by Rashbam (1085–1174) offers dramatic evidence of northern European Jews' increasingly "instrumentalist" view of Talmud. As the first of the region's scholars to draw on perspectives encountered in the Qayrawanese Talmud commentary of Rabbenu Ḥananel,[128] Rashbam claimed that the talmudic statement (BT BB 130b) asserting that a given received legal tradition (halakhah) could not be construed as applied law (*halakhah le-ma'aseh*) until a master attested to its implementation in practice was merely the stringent position of a lone individual, and not a universally endorsed opinion. Concluding this comment with an unacknowledged borrowing from Rabbenu Ḥananel, Rashbam negated the import of the tannaitic dictum—and declared that the sole authoritative source of applied law was Talmud: "And whom can we still consult in the midst of a deed, if we do not rely upon the *halakhot* adjudicated in Talmud [*ha-pesuqot ba-Talmud*] as Rav Ashi arranged them?!"[129]

Once they saw the talmudic text as an "inescapable referent," the tosafists, already leaders in their communities, were positioned to "predispose" the region's Jews to rely more heavily on applied law derived from Talmud. Unlike Rashi, who had largely refrained from attacking or uprooting popular behaviors that were inconsistent with the Talmud, the tosafists grappled head-on with the discrepancies that separated lived practice from the talmudic text.[130] At the same time, the tosafists did not definitively resolve all the questions they posed in their talmudic glosses; they often left the reader with multiple solutions. As was the case in the school of Rashi, applied law was inscribed in digests compiled by the tosafists' students.[131]

Northern European scholars of the twelfth century discussed a number of methodological and procedural issues with considerable intensity. Was Talmud the only text in the Jewish canon to be consulted before issuing legal decisions? If not, what other sources were to play a role in adjudication, and how were the disparate sources to be weighted? When talmudic dictate was found to be in conflict with well-established practices, how was law to be decided? Analysis of relevant passages in medieval rabbinic writings may offer a window onto these discussions.

A celebrated and pugnacious correspondence between Rabbenu Tam and R. Meshullam ben Natan of Melun, a Provençal scholar who had moved to northern France in the 1130s, reveals that the relative rankings of Judaism's juridically authoritative texts were being debated into the mid-twelfth century. The lively epistolary exchanges between the two, preserved in Rabbenu Tam's *Sefer ha-Yashar*,[132] point to the vastly disparate assumptions each scholar held about the purpose of the talmudic text, its formation, and its role in the determination of applied law. The immoderate tone that Rabbenu Tam adopted in these letters offers a visceral impression of his personality, and it reflects the cultural acceptability of barbed debate and rancorous "mock combat" in epistolary exchanges of the time,[133] but it may also attest to the gravity of the debate and to the writer's awareness that the stakes were sky-high in this contest to define Jewish legal epistemology.

In his valuable study of Rabbenu Tam's juridical methodology, Rami Reiner demonstrated that many of this tosafist's more puzzling legal decisions stemmed from consistently applied principles; they were neither makeshift responses to "exigencies of the time" nor reflections of the author's personal eccentricities.[134] Building on Reiner's insights, the following remarks attempt to frame the divergent perspectives and methods of Rabbenu Tam and R. Meshullam within a broader geographic context and against the backdrop of a longer historical continuum.[135]

Rabbenu Meshullam based his jurisprudential conclusions not only on Talmud, but on Torah and Mishnah as well; indeed, he ascribed a similar cultural status to all three of these corpora.[136] Other works of Jewish tradition, on the other hand—such as midrashic compositions, *Massekhet Sofrim*, and writings by earlier scholars from Babylonia, Qayrawan, al-Andalus, and Ashkenaz—were, in his opinion, irrelevant to the adjudicatory process. What was the logic behind Rabbenu Meshullam's taxonomy? In the absence of any clear information, the following is offered as a speculative conjecture. If Provençal Jews of his time were privy to (and influenced by) the Andalusian tradition[137] teaching that written Talmud ("our Talmud") had been designed, a priori, as a guide to applied law,[138] and if they were heirs to the "Sefardi" recension of Sherira's *Epistle*, according to which Rabbi Judah the Patriarch had committed the Mishnah to writing, then they may have thought that the Talmud and Mishnah, like the Torah itself, were authoritative guides to applied legal practice. Other texts of *oral matters*, which had not been inscribed with the same purposeful intention—whether midrashim, the geonic era *Massekhet Sofrim*, or post-talmudic writings like *Halakhot Gedolot*—might have been conceived as mere *megilot setarim*, that is, as "phantom texts," works that did not possess comparable authority. (The fact that a later Provençal scholar, R. Menahem HaMeiri [1249–1316], claimed that post-talmudic halakhic writings were never intended for circulation, and were not to be treated as prescriptively authoritative,[139] may offer a sliver of support for this speculation.)

By contrast, Rabbenu Tam, a resident of northern France who was not privy to the Sefardi tradition declaring "our Talmud" a work explicitly inscribed as a guide to applied law, could not as easily discount the importance of other sources of Jewish tradition.[140] Though he, too, regarded Talmud as the consummate source of Jewish law, Rabbenu Tam may have shared the geonic assumption that legal traditions preserved in the Talmud could not be vetted as *halakhah le-ma'aseh*, applied law, unless there was corroboration that they had been implemented in practice.[141] Whereas the geonim (like the tannaim before them) expected living masters to supply this corroboration, Rabbenu Tam sought the evidence of lived Jewish practice not in human embodiments of tradition but in older texts, like midrashim and the written legacies of earlier scholars. In his view, these sources, which he referred to as "old books," offered insight into what had actually been practiced by earlier Jews, who, after all, knew Talmud. According to Rabbenu Tam, it was this documentary trove that supplied the needed corroborating testimony, and that vetted a given received legal tradition (halakhah) as one that was to be implemented in practice (*halakhah le-ma'aseh*).[142] Because he regarded extra-talmudic writings such as midrashim, works of the geonic period, texts written earlier in Ashkenaz, *Sefer Yosippon,* and even the apocryphal book of Judith as necessary complements to Talmud,[143] Rabbenu Tam insisted that they play a role in the adjudicatory process:

> Whoever is not proficient in the *Seder Rav 'Amram* and in *Halakhot Gedolot* and in *Massekhet Sofrim* and in *Pirqe de-Rabi Eliezer*, and in *Rabbah* and in *Yelammedenu*,[144] and in the other books of aggadah,

> must not destroy the words of the Early Ones and their customs where they do not conflict with our Talmud, but add to it. And many of the customs that we possess follow them.[145]

Indeed, for Rabbenu Tam, these writings were far more trustworthy than any verbal claims: "Anyone adducing a support requires seeing [a text] and not [simply] hearing [a teaching], for some offer the defense that such and such a great man said this, and that so-and-so recited it. And often, this is not found [in writing]."[146] According to Rabbenu Tam, the Talmud itself affirmed the necessity of consulting extra-talmudic Jewish tradition, for both the anonymous redactors of this corpus and their successors in the geonic yeshivot regarded communal practice—and not the Babylonian Talmud—as the touchstone of applied law:

> For we have seen that the sages of Talmud chose for themselves the Talmud of Jerusalem, as we say [BT BM 85a], "R. Zera undertook 100 fasts to forget the Babylonian Talmud." . . . And again we say [BT BB 158b], "the atmosphere of *Ereẓ Yisrael* makes one wiser." And our *minhag* [custom] is Torah. And our *minhag* in Babylonia accords with the Sages in the Land of Israel, who are the prime [authorities] in applied legal instruction. And for this reason, we must rely on our geonim and on our masters the saboraim.[147]

Notwithstanding its collation of anti-Babylonian *topoi*, it would be a mistake to read this passage as an expression of (putative) northern European Palestino-centrism.[148] Both "Babylonia" and "the Land of Israel" function here as synecdoches; the former refers to theoretical or academic learning devoid of practical application, and the latter refers only to practical legal decisions. In this passionate outburst, Rabbenu Tam affirms that northern European Jews, like their Babylonian role models, hold living instruction about applied law in higher esteem than any theoretical or academic statement in the Talmud. If saboraim and geonim, Jewish scholars who were knowledgeable in the Babylonian Talmud, deferred to a different source as one that imparted information about actual practice (in which Jews of ancient Palestine were expert), claimed Rabbenu Tam, then anyone (like R. Meshullam) who would rely more heavily on talmudic teachings than on those preserved in "old books," repositories of lived practice, was actually flouting the Talmud! In Rabbenu Tam's formulation, the appreciation that northern

European Jewry had for the instructional clarity of Palestinian traditions was a legacy of Babylonian Jewish culture itself.

When seen as a contest between the authority of talmudic legal teachings and of applied law, the dispute between R. Meshullam of Melun and Rabbenu Tam may be seen as loosely parallel to the exchanges between the Jews of Qayrawan and the Babylonian geonim (discussed in Chapter 1). Like the Qayrawanese, R. Meshullam derived applied law directly from the talmudic text, and, like the geonim, Rabbenu Tam held that applied law required supplementary testimony about the implementation of legal teachings in practice. For the geonim, this corroboration was supplied by the verbal affirmation of a living master; for Rabbenu Tam, the corroboration was supplied by literary evidence that testified to what earlier Jews had practiced. Whether consciously or unconsciously, Rabbenu Tam's very framing of his epistemological dispute with Rabbenu Meshullam echoed the rhetoric of R. Hai's challenge to the Qayrawanese community more than a century earlier:[149] "And if you don't believe the words of the Early Ones and our customs, don't believe the *Bavli* [Babylonian Talmud] either!"[150]

Rabbenu Tam regularly brought extra-talmudic sources of tradition into conversation with talmudic teaching in *Sefer ha-Yashar*, using midrashic traditions to illuminate difficult passages in Talmud[151] and declaring that the stringency of extra-talmudic tradition should prevail over the Talmud's leniency.[152] The disparate valuations of Jewish sources that divided his perspective from that of Rabbenu Meshullam are boldly reflected in *Sefer ha-Yashar*'s record of their divergent legal conclusions. One such dispute concerned candlelighting at the outset of the Sabbath, a practice for which there is no talmudic mandate.

According to R. Meshullam, since there is no talmudic teaching that designates Sabbath candlelighting as a precept, the practice itself should not be accompanied by a blessing.[153] Rabbenu Tam countered this position by noting the practice of his female relatives (discussed below)[154] and by appealing to an aggadah: According to a tradition preserved in ancient and medieval sources, women were singled out to perform three gender-specific commandments, Sabbath candlelighting among them, so that they might atone in perpetuity for the sin of Eve, who induced Adam to eat from the forbidden tree. (The precept of candlelighting was described as an apt counterweight to the deed of Eve, for in bringing mortality into being she "extinguished the first light of the world.")[155] From Rabbenu Tam's perspective, the authority of this tradition was sealed by the fact that it was attested to in "old books":

"And even more so, because it is written in books of aggadah and in sermons that are preached on Shabbat."[156] In a related exchange, Rabbenu Tam indignantly rejected R. Meshullam's assertion that if a candle was already burning in a Jewish home before sunset on Friday, there would be no need to extinguish and relight it merely to mark the Sabbath's entry.[157] In this case, Rabbenu Tam adduced the testimony and deeds of his female contemporaries as a source of legal authority:

> Our women hold the custom [*nashim shelanu minhag be-yadam*] of extinguishing and lighting. And I saw this with my eyes and I asked them and they said so. And if they are not prophetesses, they are the descendants of prophetesses.[158]

* * *

Like certain other figures and groups in the history of Jewish culture who believed in the self-sufficiency of (some) text, R. Meshullam was a "reformer"; he sought to bring life experience into conformity with the texts he identified as authoritative.[159] When he encountered customs and behaviors inconsistent with the Talmud, he labeled them erroneous and attempted to expunge them.[160] And if the Talmud's role as a guide to life was not adequately reflected in certain passages, Rabbenu Meshullam altered the text to bring it into accord with life. His textual emendations were the target of Rabbenu Tam's ire in *Sefer ha-Yashar*: "Just as you erase this, so you might also say about each and every halakhah that it was never said! Had another said this, I would have decreed that he be ostracized, for this is close to the act of the *Cuthim* [Samaritans] who raised torches and hired [messengers] to testify [falsely] about the [new] moon, in order to destroy the order of the holidays."[161]

Yet Rabbenu Tam's critique of textual emendation, a reaction to the intensive and widespread alteration of talmudic manuscripts, was hardly categorical. These texts, he wrote, were highly unreliable because they were already rife with conjectural emendations. In such cases, advised Rabbenu Tam, derivative sources might contain more reliable iterations of the talmudic passages, for such manuscripts were not as likely to have been subjected to aggressive emendation.[162] In short, Rabbenu Tam understood that emendation was a ubiquitous activity,[163] he indulged in it himself,[164] and he believed it to have merit when properly practiced. He acknowledged that his brother,

Rashbam, was wrong to have been profligate in making textual emendations,[165] but felt that, in his case, there were several exculpatory factors. Not only was Rashbam distinguished by "the grandeur of his heart" (perhaps a reference to the capaciousness of his memory) and by "the depth of his dialectical acuity," wrote Rabbenu Tam, but some of his brother's emendations were based on his consultation of "old books." By contrast, asserted Rabbenu Tam, R. Meshullam had misled unsuspecting readers because he failed to alert them to his alterations,[166] and because his emendations were made needlessly, that is, without consulting "old books."[167] Nor was Rabbenu Tam willing to believe R. Meshullam (among other rabbinic correspondents)[168] in cases when the latter claimed to have based his emendations on manuscripts he had seen. Responding to one such claim with incredulity and scorn, Rabbenu Tam wrote, "You say that . . . you saw this version [*nusḥa*], and you are lying. Send it there, and I will send it [too], and I will pay half the travel costs; we will wonder and see.[169] . . . And even if the version of your kingdom *were* like that, it's [only] because it has been conquered by bandits/brigands like you!"[170]

* * *

By the following generation, the canon of authoritative sources was no longer a contested issue. Rabbenu Tam's students perpetuated his epistemological assumptions, and they brought an even broader range of early Jewish sources into the "big tent" to be considered—not only for clarifying the meaning of the Babylonian Talmud, but even for arriving at legal decisions.[171] Employing techniques he had learned from his uncle, Rabbenu Tam, R. Isaac of Dampierre systematically fulfilled projects toward which his uncle had only gestured.[172]

The tosafists greatly expanded the Talmud's usability as a source of applied law by demonstrating its relevance even in life situations that the text did not explicitly address. Continuing a process that had begun generations earlier in northern Europe (and that had already occurred, at a conceptual level, in Sefarad), the tosafist enterprise transformed the talmudic text from a collection of legal and nonlegal traditions into a prescriptive blueprint for Jewish life.[173] Within a matter of generations, it was hard for northern European Jews to imagine that the Talmud had ever been regarded as anything but the definitive reference to be consulted when deciding applied Jewish law. Indeed, by the thirteenth century, northern European Jewish scholars (like earlier rabbis of Sefarad and Provence) expressed astonishment that Babylonian geonim could have knowingly deviated from talmudic teachings.[174] The Talmud had come to play the same role in northern European Jewish life that it already played, rhetorically, if not textually, in the lives of Sefardi Jews.[175]

Historicist Sensibility in Northern European Rabbinic Culture

As the talmudic text assumed growing authority in their lives, certain Jewish scholars in medieval northern Europe came to experience a newly awakened sense of "cultural discontinuity."[176] The realization that the practice of Jewish life in their own communities differed from practices of the past as recorded in Talmud raised questions about the legitimacy of contemporary behaviors. To a certain extent, this was a new problem. Never before had the talmudic text been so accessible, and never before had Talmud been seen as the standalone prescriptive source of Jewish law. Nor does this problem seem to have arisen in the lands of Sefarad, where Jews were far more reliant on legal codes for adjudication. Only at this particular historical and geographical juncture did the glaring disparities between text and practice come to demand immediate attention.[177]

Tosafists began by recognizing the newness of their own time, even emphasizing the ways in which it differed from the past. Like later Humanists of the early modern period, the tosafists used their unparalleled familiarity with ancient sources to reconstruct earlier approaches to learning. They discerned that rabbinic study had once occurred through chanting,[178] surmised that the Mishnah's arrangement had been designed to facilitate easy recall,[179] and were able to explain the presence of conflated and spurious biblical verses in the Talmud.[180] The tosafists even realized that some textual discrepancies in Talmud stemmed from the fact that early traditions were not known to all scholars of later generations. Having studied variant manuscripts of Tosefta and Talmud, Rabbenu Tam had come to realize that the Talmud's compilers had incomplete knowledge of certain *beraitot* (tannaitic teachings not found in Mishnah). He also realized, as he wrote in the introduction to *Sefer ha-Yashar*, that "since the reasons [of the early ones] were not made known, the later ones did not understand their heard-teachings."[181]

Social Ramifications of Textualization

As logic was increasingly used to resolve contradictions and harmonize incompatibilities, the production of Jewish knowledge ceased to be restricted to those with the greatest erudition and the right educational pedigree. With analytical acuity the quality most highly valued in the rabbinic scholar, and with processes of reasoning bared for examination, claims to adjudicatory power within the Jewish world came to be worked out in "public"—over texts and through texts. In this sense, the Tosafists were, paradoxically, non-elitist.[182] The parchment trail they created made it possible for later textual analysts to join in the conversation about Jewish law, and even to reopen earlier decisions.[183] With authority now vested in texts that were accessible to the literate Jew, the dissemination of knowledge, its interpretation, and its very production were not easily restricted. In earlier generations, members of the northern European Jewish community would not have been in a position to question the master's presentation of the way things had been done and how they were to be done—nor would they have been inclined to do so. But with the rise of reasoning as the ultimate arbiter of textual meaning, the teacher's charisma became largely irrelevant. Through their own powers of analysis, twelfth-century students of the talmudic text could, and did, articulate legal perspectives that differed from those they had been taught.

One expression of discipleship, a rule prohibiting a student from issuing a practical legal decision in the geographic environs of his teacher, fell into disuse.[184] A leading tosafist who noted this turn of events identified it as a consequence of the inscription of *oral matters*. Now that students could access legal teachings through written texts, wrote R, Isaac of Dampierre (d. 1184), they accorded less respect to their teachers.

> In the times of the tannaim and the amoraim who derived instructions from depth [of analytical reasoning] and from *pilpul* [casuistry] and from knowledge [erudition], the master assumed a crown in giving this instruction. But now the *pesaqim* [applied legal judgments] and the *hora-ot* [applied legal instructions] are written. And [now that] all can look in the books of *pesaqim*, the master no longer has a crown as much as he did in those days, if he [the student] is no longer actually in his [the master's] presence.[185]

A century later, R. Asher ben Yeḥiel affirmed that this feature of discipleship etiquette (refraining from the issuance of legal rulings in the presence of one's teacher) was abandoned in the generation of Rashi's grandchildren.[186] With the passage of time and the growing transparency of the adjudicatory process, the established religious hierarchy found itself challenged by what Brian Stock referred to as the "disinterested market of ideas."[187]

The Impact of Textualization on Other Oral Matters

The process of textualization also affected the roles that corpora of Jewish knowledge other than Talmud played in the life of the community. At the end of the thirteenth century, French Jews chose, for the first time, to compile responsa (and those of Rabbenu Tam in particular) for preservation and dissemination; previously, these epistles, occasioned by an individual's query and tailored to the questioner's specific circumstances, were understood to be of only ephemeral utility.[188] As Rami Reiner pointed out, there was no prior tradition in this region of preserving responsa, of promoting their circulation, or of treating them as universally prescriptive legal documents.[189]

Jewish prayer was also dramatically transformed by the process of textualization, for prayer fell within the category of *oral matters*, and the earlier norm in northern Europe had been for Jews to recite the liturgy by heart.[190] A written text was only consulted on Rosh HaShanah and Yom Kippur, when the liturgy included many less-familiar prayers—and then only by the congregation's prayer emissary, who recited the occasion-specific prayers and liturgical poems for the benefit of all.[191] Beginning in the second half of the eleventh century, however, most of Rashi's students inscribed their own prayer books, and, in the 1130s, northern European Jewish liturgy became far more standardized with the compilation of *Maḥzor Vitry*.[192] Like earlier models used in Eastern Jewish communities, and like contemporaneous Christian customaries and ordinaries, Jewish prayer texts of medieval northern Europe mixed passages of prayer with directions for their proper performance in "how-to" manuals that described the celebrations and ritual practices of the liturgical year.[193]

However, because these prayer props—inscriptions of *oral matters* that were recited aloud—flouted tannaitic prohibitions, their very use posed a legal problem. R. Isaac of Dampierre explained that a concession had been made in response to changed conditions: though prayers were of the category of *oral matters*, their inscribed versions had come to be accorded cultural weight. The touchstone for this assessment, set forth in an ancient *beraita*, was whether a given writing could be saved from a conflagration that broke out on the Sabbath. In the days of the amoraim, he wrote,

> they forgot nothing, and therefore wrote neither Talmud nor prayer—in keeping with "*oral matters* may not be inscribed." But

> we, later generations, who write down every word—because of [Ps. 119:126] "*It is time to act for the Lord [lest] Your teachings be nullified*"—we save prayers and Talmud and all sacred writings from a conflagration.[194]

Reiteration of R. Isaac Dampierre's comment in the fourteenth century suggests that later northern European Jews also wondered about their own failure to uphold ancient dicta.[195] In short, it would seem that at least some Jews in medieval Europe sought to explain why the practices of communal worship in which they engaged were in violation of an ancient rabbinic injunction.

Once inscribed, the prayers themselves became subjects of commentary; this was true not only of the "fixed prayers," those recited regularly, but also of the *piyyutim*, the novelty liturgical poems that were crafted according to form-specific conventions to conform with occasion. The magnitude of this cultural change is boldly illustrated in a twelfth-century *maḥzor* composed by one of Rashi's students. When R. Ya'aqov ben R. Shimshon adorned the *piyyutim* he had composed with their own explanatory commentary, he both created and authorized his own work in one fell swoop.[196] There is considerable irony in the latter development, for *piyyutim* (at least the early ones) were designed as ephemeral compositions, to be performed only once. In contrast with the fixed prayers, *piyyutim* were, by definition, displays of innovation that satisfied the demand (and the rabbinic call) for freshness in worship.[197]

In the textualized environment of twelfth-century northern Europe, the prevailing culture demanded that even the most esoteric of *oral matters* undergo inscription. Guardians of hidden Jewish lore capitulated to these expectations in the twelfth century by committing these traditions to writing, but (as discussed in Chapter 6) they inscribed esoterica in an enigmatic way, thereby ensuring the indispensability of face-to-face instruction from a master who could unpack the encoded material.

As texts came to structure all aspects of experience, arenas of life that had been only lightly regulated—like mourning[198] and charity[199]—were now subjected to dense and systematic written guidance. Even practices that had traditionally been learned through apprenticeship came to acquire the authorizing mantle of a textual apparatus. Yisrael Ta Shma drew attention to this development when he noted the unprecedented composition, in the thirteenth and fourteenth centuries, of how-to manuals for circumcision, ritual slaughter, and scribal arts—skills traditionally acquired not through textual study, but though observation and guided practice.[200] The new mark of legitimacy was behavioral conformity to the dictates of a text.[201]

Within this environment, even custom—a body of authoritative tradition transmitted through behavior—was consigned to writing. Where *Ma'aseh ha-Geonim*, the earliest compilation of Jewish custom in northern Europe, had cited conflicting explanations for particular customs and admitted ignorance about the reasons for others,[202] later rabbinic scholars from this region subjected custom to more stringent standards of assessment and rationalization. Some offered logical explanations for customs, and others linked customs to ancient rabbinic sources that would enhance their textual legitimacy. Within this new, and inescapable, hermeneutical environment, "scholasticism overcame its most ardent opponents by forcing them to struggle against it on its own terms."[203] Indeed, Jews of medieval Provence came to regard custom as but one more corpus of Jewish tradition whose authority was vetted in legal texts. Once co-opted into the heart of the legislative system, custom lost its defining epistemological identity.[204]

Persistence of **Memoria** *in Ashkenazic Pedagogic and Legal Culture*

The changes in northern European rabbinic culture in the late eleventh and twelfth centuries mapped in this chapter ought not obscure the many cultural continuities that connected tosafists (and their successors) with northern European Jews who lived prior to the Crusades. The accomplishments of Rashi and the tosafists, robust agents of textualization, would never have been possible had they themselves not been steeped in the assumptions and practices of a culture that privileged the oral transmission of tradition.[205] Though textualization precipitated distinct shifts in curricular emphasis among Jews of subsequent generations (particularly the "talmudocentrism" that is discussed in the next chapter), the tosafists themselves studied and composed works of grammar, lexicography, biography, Bible commentary, midrash commentary, *piyyut* and *piyyut* commentary, *masorah*, mysticism, and magic.[206]

Some of the behaviors prescribed in antiquity for the treatment of *oral matters* seem to have been meaningful in northern European Jewish culture (as in the culture of medieval Sefarad) even after these corpora underwent inscription.[207] Digests of applied halakhah continued to be dictated to students by the teacher (and designated *mipi rav*, "from the master's mouth"),[208] and distinctions continued to be made between oral and written transmission. Menaḥem b. Aharon b. Zeraḥ's portrait of the learning practices that had prevailed two centuries earlier in R. Isaac Dampierre's academy may be of questionable reliability,[209] but there is little doubt that the thirteenth-century Spaniard who reported this tradition believed that the realms of oral and written transmission were carefully circumscribed in a particular rabbinic classroom of twelfth-century France:

> My French teachers testified to me, in the names of their masters, that it was known and publicized that sixty rabbis studied before him [R. Isaac of Dampierre]. Each one heard halakhah when he said it [*ke-she-hayya magid*], and also learned by himself [by reading] a tractate that his friend had not learned.[210] Isaac would not say [*lo hayya magid*] any halakhah that they did not all know orally [had not all committed to memory].[211]

Testimonies from later centuries offer further evidence of Ashkenazi Jewry's continued dedication to the oral transmission of *oral matters*. The fifteenth-century Ashkenazi R. Judah Mintz made a clear distinction in his Paduan yeshivah between the propadeutic study activities that involved study of the open Talmud and those that occurred subsequently when that book was closed. Describing the regimen of this institution in his sixteenth-century chronicle, Elijah Capsali wrote that the rabbis and students of the Padua yeshivah would assemble after morning prayers for around an hour to engage in an activity called "*mishpat ha-Talmud*" (literally, "judgment of Talmud"):[212]

> The rabbi would begin to pose questions, and each individual would respond to him, each in accord with his stature. And then each one would pose questions and resolutions so that they shed light on that which was obscure.[213] This was called the *pilpul* [casuistry] of the yeshivah . . . and this *pilpul* was done 'from the outside,' by which I mean without opening a book. For everyone was fluent in the halakhah, and there was nothing with them except for the gemara of the rabbi, in which he would show them the halakhah of the [next] day. . . . And in the end, the rabbi of the yeshivah, our Master, the aforementioned Rabbi Judah Mintz, would open his book and show them the point from which they should investigate the halakhah, neither adding to it nor detracting from it.[214]

Even once the advent of print and publication of rabbinic works made inscriptions of *oral matters* ubiquitous, at least one Ashkenazi scholar sought to guard jottings of his legal insights in the form of a *megilat setarim*, a private inscription designed solely for his own use. Not long after the 1559 publication of the *Shulḥan 'Arukh* law code with the glosses of R. Moses Isserles, R. Ḥayyim ben Beẓalel referred to this work and its carefully circumscribed role. Years earlier, he wrote, he had created his own collection of laws on forbidden foods by culling from many rabbinic writings, imposing his own arrangement, and writing with utmost brevity. Then, when this private composition was "*all put away, sealed up in my storehouses*" (Deut. 32:34), some adolescent boys (presumably rabbinical students) who were staying in his house at the time found the work in question and copied it. When R. Ḥayyim discovered what had occurred, he became extremely angry and confiscated their unauthorized copy, "for I only composed it for myself, to be an aid and to be effective against forgetting. Not that any other person should rely on it!"[215]

Though R. Ḥayyim ben Beẓalel did not use the term *megilat setarim* in referring to the composition in question, it is clear from the anger he expressed—and from his decision, years later, to share this incident for instructional purposes—that he expected rabbinical students to know that a private work of halakhic insights could not be deemed authoritative. By the same token, the distinctive practices of Rabbis Jacob Pollack and Shalom Shakhna of mid-sixteenth-century Poland bear witness to Ashkenazi society's continued sensitivity to ancient rabbinic regulations pertaining to *oral matters*. Fearing that subsequent rabbinic decisors would regard any written judgments they issued as the "the final word," in keeping with the principle of *hilkheta ke-vatraei* ("the law follows the last-named decisor"),[216] these two adjudicators refused to consign their legal decisions to writing. According to Pollack, this was necessary in order to ensure that Jewish law would continue to be responsive to the particular circumstances of each case.[217] The rationale invoked for their oral adjudication was a halakhic principle that had acquired particular relevance by the mid-sixteenth century, but the *policy* adopted by Pollack and Shakhna was one that resonated within early modern Ashkenazi society because of its ongoing attunement to the cultural meaning of oral transmission.[218]

5

Medieval Responses to the Textualization of Rabbinic Culture

By the twelfth century, northern European Jewish communities had come to determine applied Jewish law solely with reference to the Talmud. This approach differed considerably from that of the Babylonian geonim, who understood living tradition to be a necessary complement to the teachings preserved in Talmud. As noted earlier, the geonim concluded many of their responsa by acknowledging these two sources of authority, affirming that "this is the *halakhah* and this is the custom."[1] It seems unlikely that most rabbinically learned Jews of medieval Europe would have been aware that their own approach to adjudication deviated from the approach taken by geonic predecessors, but a small number of scholars *did* realize that their modes of engaging Jewish law were new—and some sought to account for the changes that had occurred. Strikingly, a number of medieval Jewish reflections on transformations that had occurred in the curricular, pedagogic, adjudicatory, and social arenas traced these changes to the inscription of *oral matters.*

Medieval Jewish Cognizance of Change

Talmudic glossators were most likely to comment on the move toward transmitting *oral matters* in writing when discussing passages that had direct bearing on this matter. As noted in the previous chapter, R. Isaac of Dampierre had acknowledged this change in commenting on the talmudic passage stipulating which writings could be saved on the Sabbath from a conflagration without violating rabbinic law. The practice that prevailed in his own time—of salvaging blessings, Targum, and *halakhot*, all *oral matters*—flouted rabbinic regulations, he noted. This, explained Rabbi Isaac, was because a concession had been made in deference to changed conditions.[2] R. Isaac of Dampierre's comment was echoed by Jewish scholars throughout medieval Europe: the northern French rabbis, Simḥa ben Samuel and Barukh, author of *Sefer ha-Terumah*;[3] the Provençal rabbis, Abraham ben Isaac (1110–79),[4] Zeraḥya Halevi (1125–86), Isaac ben Abba Mari (1122–93), Meshullam of Beziers (early thirteenth century), and Menaḥem HaMeiri (1249–1316);[5] the Ashkenazi rabbis, Isaac ben Moses of Vienna (1200–1270) and Mordecai ben Hillel (1250–89);[6] the Sefardi rabbis, Meir Halevi Abulafia (1170–1244) and Asher ben Yeḥiel (1250–1328);[7] and the Italian rabbi Ẓidqiyahu ben Avraham 'Anav (1230–1300).[8]

A talmudic passage referring to books that were loaned out or rented for a fee[9] occasioned other medieval Jewish reflections on the change that had occurred, as did a discussion of the proper etiquette for handling a borrowed Torah scroll. According to the Talmud, one was permitted to "open" and "read" from a borrowed Torah scroll, but not to lend it to anyone else or to "learn from it."[10] The activities of "opening" it and "reading" it—both connected with liturgical chanting[11]—were permitted, because neither entailed aggressive handling of the scroll. "Learning from it," on the other hand, would subject the physical artifact to excessive wear and tear, since a student searching for particular passages would need to roll the parchment backward and forward. Commenting on this passage in thirteenth-century Spain, Rabbi Moses ben Naḥman (Naḥmanides) prefaced his remarks with an acknowledgment of the historical shift that had occurred in his own time: "But now that it is the custom to write Talmud, if he lent him a tractate . . . all people are equal with regard to it. For one who recites his chapter 100 times and one who has never recited it—all touch them and finger them. For there isn't a person who does not require additional analysis and thought in order to investigate/analyze, and to pull further and further, and to [figuratively?] roll it from its beginning to its end and from its end to its beginning, in order to analyze the *halakhot* that he requires, [looking] for that *halakhah* that he is reciting."[12]

* * *

Sherira Gaon had said nothing in his *Epistle* of 987 about the standardization of Talmud's language, nor about the commitment of this corpus to writing, but several medieval Jewish scholars felt the need to update the historical record, as Rashi had.[13] In his early thirteenth-century description of the "establishment" of the Babylonian Talmud by the amora Rav Ashi (352–427), R. Moses of Coucy used Sherira's remarks about the Mishnah as a template for the "establishment" or "arranging" of Talmud, and went on to portray the subsequent inscription of this corpus as a concession to tumultuous times and forgetfulness: "And afterwards many troubles occurred and the sages of Israel were scattered widely and hearts were diminished—and they began to write the Talmud in a book."[14]

A late fifteenth-century commentary on Moses of Coucy's work by R. Isaac Stein underscored the distinction between these two stages of cultural formation.

> Rav Ashi arranged the Talmud, and he [Moses of Coucy] did not write that he 'wrote' the Talmud. Not until the hardships multiplied and the sages were scattered and hearts were diminished—*then* Talmud was written in a book. And these hardships and the scattering of the sages were not in the time of Rav Ashi. . . . After the days of all the amoraim, in the days of the saboraic teachers, the Talmud was written. . . . And this is a straightforward matter and there is no doubt about the matter.[15]

The basis of R. Isaac Stein's claim about the saboraic inscription of Talmud is not clear; it is certainly not derived from Sherira's *Epistle*. Yet the two writers, separated by half a millennium, were both concerned to remind readers that rabbinic Jews had, for centuries, transmitted *oral matters* solely in oral form.

Medieval Jewish Testimonies to the Growing Prominence of Talmud Study

Several medieval Jewish voices testify to changes in the classroom that were linked to the growing prominence of Talmud study. Most of these are laments over the abandonment or loss of other disciplinary pursuits, or pleas for the implementation of a broad curriculum that would accommodate the disparate learning styles and interests of a range of students. Curricular preoccupation with Talmud, at the expense of other subjects, was a distinctly medieval development that originated in northern Europe; there is no reason to assume that it was the curricular norm in antiquity or in geonic times, and it was clearly not the norm in either Sefarad (prior to the time of Naḥmanides)[16] or in the Jewish communities of Byzantium.[17] As Talmud study encroached on the pursuit of other subjects, it was most volubly resisted by pockets of Jews living in Germany and Spain.[18] Their many critiques bear witness to the novelty of this phenomenon, for which Isadore Twersky coined the term "talmudocentrism."[19]

An eleventh-century responsum bears witness both to the constriction of the Jewish curriculum in Andalusian communities, as Talmud study assumed greater importance, and to the social tension that accompanied this development. When the Jews of a particular Spanish community invited a visiting French Jew to stay and teach them, they drew up a weekly schedule that their new instructor would follow: four days of the week would be set aside for the study of Talmud, one day for the study of Scripture, and one day for the study of scriptural exegesis linked to the weekly Torah reading. Once it was implemented, however, this plan of study fomented division within the community. Some of the locals found its emphasis on Talmud to be excessively taxing:

> And then Yissakhar, one of them, shouted at his friends, and said: "I cannot understand the depth of the *halakhah* [Talmud study], and I don't want this. Rather, you [the teacher] should tell them three lines of Talmud, and then go back and tell them three lines of Mishnah." And his friends said to him, "We don't want this." Therefore, Yissakhar stood up and said, "If so, then I don't want to read, and I don't want to pay salary."[20]

The impression conveyed by this lone anecdote, that talmudocentrism was exported to al-Andalus from northern Europe, finds blunt corroboration in a comment made in early fifteenth-century Spain by Profet Duran (known as Efodi). The Talmud, he wrote, is a work of enormous difficulty, and preoccupation with this one subject "is an illness, one that has spread from Ashkenaz and France to Spain."[21]

* * *

As Talmud came to assume the instructional limelight, other curricular subjects were displaced. Of course, curricular adjustments, prompted by a broad array of challenges, were nothing new. Though a talmudic dictum mandated the division of study into thirds—"one-third Scripture, one-third Mishnah, one-third Talmud"[22]—Natronai Gaon of mid-ninth-century Babylonia wrote that economic pressures—at some unspecified time in the past—had made it impossible for scholars to follow this ideal curricular division. "And since poverty and penury increased, and it became necessary for scholars[23] to earn a living from the work of their hands, and they were not always able to engage perpetually in Torah and to divide every day into thirds, they came to rely solely on the Talmud, and abandoned Scripture and Mishnah. [In so doing] they relied on their saying, '[Eccl. 1:7] *All streams flow into the sea*: Scripture, Mishnah, and Midrash [*yet the sea is never full*: this is Talmud].' "[24] Whereas Natronai portrayed the narrowing of the Jewish curriculum as a regrettable concession to economic reality, the leading tosafist of twelfth-century France did not see this as a liability. According to Rabbenu Tam, one could fulfill the rabbinic mandate to divide one's study into three by studying nothing but Talmud, for Talmud contains Scripture and Mishnah within it.[25]

Profet Duran forcefully disagreed. Attacking the curricular imbalance that prevailed in his time, he observed that contemporary Jewish students were so focused on the study of Talmud that they even neglected the study of Scripture itself.

> And that which has led people to laziness regarding engagement with Scriptures is the investigation of the wisdom/craft of the Babylonian Talmud, which is deep and wide—and people's inadequacy in grasping it, given its depth and difficulty. They terminate their days in its pursuit and have totally abandoned Scripture, throwing it behind their backs.[26]

A more subtle attempt to redress a perceived curricular imbalance may be discerned in Maimonides' "restatement" of the talmudic passage that counsels a Jew to divide his study time into thirds. Boldly redefining the explicitly named disciplines, Maimonides managed to include arenas of inquiry that the Talmud had not mentioned:

> The time allotted to study should be divided into three parts. A third should be devoted to the Written Torah, a third to the Oral Torah, and the last third should be spent in reflection, deducing conclusions from premises, developing implications of statements,

> comparing dicta, studying the hermeneutical principles by which the Torah is interpreted—until one knows the essence of these principles, and how to deduce what is permitted and what is forbidden from what one has learned traditionally. This is called "Talmud."[27]

The claim that the term "*talmud*" did not designate the written corpus of Talmud, but rather that which is derived inferentially from one's studies, the fruit of reasoning, was actually very much in sync with Sherira Gaon's understanding of "*talmud*." Through this act of "translation," Maimonides enabled the term "*talmud*" in this ancient dictum to represent the discipline of philosophy, and he portrayed philosophical inquiry as a religiously mandated activity.[28] Critics of the *Mishneh Torah*, the legal code in which this passage appeared, did not fail to note that Maimonides' radical redistribution of the Jewish curriculum significantly displaced the study of the talmudic text itself. In presenting the second topic of study in the triad as "Oral Torah," Maimonides seems to have been advocating the study of his own legal code as a substitute for the study of Mishnah, Talmud, and all post-talmudic halakhic writings.[29] Though Maimonides demurred, the storm of protest that accompanied the circulation of the *Mishneh Torah* indicated that disapproving contemporaries understood this work as a composition that had been designed to deflect students from the study of Talmud.[30]

Medieval Jewish critics of the new curriculum who expressed themselves less cautiously than Maimonides openly identified disciplines that they deemed of greater consequence for intellectual and spiritual growth than Talmud. Writing in early fourteenth-century Provence, the rationalist philosopher Joseph ibn Kaspi expressed astonishment that the study of talmudic law had come to be valued above all other subjects, including those touching on human knowledge of the divine. How could his own field of expertise, "knowledge of the existence of the Creator," be perceived as less important than the specialized knowledge of applied Jewish law? Ibn Kaspi made this rhetorical point in the concluding anecdote of the ethical will he composed for his son. There he relates that he had once needed to delay the start of a feast he was hosting, because his kitchen maid had accidentally used a dairy spoon in the meat pot. Having forgotten the halakhah stipulating the proportions of dairy and meat that render a dish of intermingled foods unfit for kosher consumption, Ibn Kaspi left his guests waiting and went to consult the local rabbi. When he returned home, he told the assembled all that had happened and made no effort to cover up his own ignorance about the legal minutiae in question. Addressing his son, Ibn Kaspi wrote:

> The invited ones, the poor and indigent, were there awaiting me, and I told them the entire episode, for I was not ashamed that I am not an expert in this particular craft. But I am an expert in other crafts. And why should a verse or instruction [concerning] knowledge of the existence of the Creator or His great unity not be equal to a small dairy spoon?[31]

Perhaps the most potent of all medieval Jewish critiques of the new curriculum was that which questioned whether the study of Talmud made any contribution to a person's spiritual formation. Writing in twelfth-century Spain, Baḥya ibn Paquda noted that the technical knowledge about executing a writ of divorce (a topic whose minutiae are discussed in the Talmud) hardly brings a devotee closer to God. Zeroing in on the underlying issue—the purpose of religious education—Baḥya wrote with considerable trenchancy:

> One of the sages was asked about an arcane issue in the laws of divorce, and he replied to his questioner: "You who ask me about something, your ignorance of which cannot harm you at all. Have you already completed the study of those duties that you must not neglect, that you find leisure to turn to these arcane questions and their difficulties, whose knowledge would not add anything to your faith and religion, nor correct any of your soul's vices? As for me, I swear that, for 35 years, I have taken upon myself the obligation to investigate that which my religion imposes upon me personally. You know my efforts and the opportunities I have had to acquire books. And, to this point, I have not found the time to spare that you have freed up to pose this question."[32]

Addressing readers in his introduction to *The Book of Direction to the Duties of the Heart*, Baḥya explained that he had decided to compose a work about cultivating and performing the "duties of the heart" because it was these that were overlooked by his contemporaries—rabbis preoccupied with the fine points of the law.

> I turned to the traditions of our ancient righteous forefathers, and I found that their devotion to the duties specific to them [to the souls]

> was much stronger and more stringent than was their engagement in the details of statutory laws or their posing questions about rare cases. Their exertions were toward [understanding] the principles of law and the foundations of what is lawful and unlawful. After this, they turned their investigation and engagement to the purification of their deeds and the duties of their hearts. And any time there arose among them a question regarding a detail of the law and of rare matters, they would investigate in keeping with their power of judgment. . . . And they would learn its law from the accepted principles, but would not trouble their thinking to consider this ahead of time, given their disdain for this world and for its matters.[33]

Other medieval Jewish writers drew attention to unsavory side effects that were occasionally linked to Talmud study, particularly when students became enamored of the dialectical method of the tosafists.[34] The Rhineland Pietist R. Judah (1140–1217) accused students who specialized in the formulation of *quaestiones* of being motivated by arrogance,[35] and his student, Elazar of Worms (1176–1238), called *pilpul* (talmudic casuistry) a trap for those who are not pious.[36] Would-be scholars were rebuked by their teacher for bringing tosafist glosses to synagogue and reading them when they should have been reciting liturgical poems.[37] Medieval Jewish writings are filled with charges that students who pursued the dialectical study of Talmud were motivated by hunger for fame and recognition, knowing that their casuistic prowess could be leveraged into a form of communal power.[38] In the words of Profet Duran, "I saw that even he who did interest himself in the study of the law applied himself only to those things that would make him wise in the eyes of fools, or would make him seem learned to those who pretend to be scholars. . . . And many attempt to apprehend the depth of the give and take, posing *quaestiones* and making thousands and tens of thousands of distinctions—not for the attainment of the goal of knowing the Torah's laws and that which can be derived from the talmudic *sugyot*, but only in order to vie with one another and lord it over the other."[39]

The *way* in which Talmud had come to be studied was also targeted for censure. Some medieval Jewish critics complained that the tosafist's dialectical method, whose seductive appeal made it the favored (and, often, sole) approach to Talmud study, actually heightened ignorance of the talmudic text itself.[40] Writing in twelfth-century Germany, R. Eliezer of Metz asserted that the casuistic posing of *quaestiones* distorted the true purpose of *talmud*, which had traditionally been understood as an exertionary activity through which a student would discern the "roots of the *mizvot*."[41] A century later, Moses bar Ḥasdai Taqu of Regensburg lamented the fact that the tosafist method was misleading students who were insufficiently learned.[42]

Other medieval Jewish critics lamented the absence of masters, living repositories of tradition who were qualified to impart *halakhah le-ma'aseh*. Writing in al-Andalus in the eleventh century, the Hebrew grammarian and lexicographer Jonah ibn Janaḥ identified this as the cause of the ignorance that prevailed among contemporary students of Talmud: "And they take this lightly [upon their souls] for what they learn from Talmud, they learn with error. . . . But they don't sense [this] because they are lacking *qabbalah* [received tradition] and [because] they didn't learn from men of instruction."[43]

Even Naḥmanides, the thirteenth-century Catalonian scholar who admired the elegance and intellectual utility of the northern European glosses and who (along with his students) disseminated this approach to Talmud study throughout the lands of Sefarad and Provence,[44] refused to embrace a cardinal change that was generally a corollary of the tosafist approach to Talmud. Unlike others drawn to this method, Naḥmanides clung fiercely to the old ways and refused to derive applied law from the inscribed text of the Talmud; indeed, he felt no compulsion to follow talmudic prescriptions at all if they flouted geonic perspectives and practice.[45] Notwithstanding his appropriation of the tosafists' approach to Talmud, Naḥmanides continued to distinguish between the study of the talmudic text and the adjudication of law.[46] As a transitional figure (in more than one arena of thirteenth-century rabbinic culture),[47] Naḥmanides was well positioned to comment on broader changes that he had observed. He lamented the abandonment of a traditional mode of rabbinic decision making, and claimed that R. Isaac Alfasi (d. 1103) had been the last scholar whose decisions in applied law were consonant with the traditions that he had received, orally, from his masters. Since Alfasi's death, wrote Naḥmanides, instruction—and even adjudication—had come to be derived from texts, and not from face-to-face encounters.[48] Jews had come to substitute the inscribed text of *oral matters* for the living repository of tradition.

The Provençal scholar Menaḥem HaMeiri elaborated on this problem at the end of the thirteenth or beginning of the fourteenth century. His comments on a passage in the Babylonian Talmud evince reverence for the vanishing *paidea* of oral culture: "[*BT*, *BB* 130b] 'One doesn't learn *halakhah* from

Talmud': this means, even though we sometimes find that it says, 'And the *halakhah* accords with his words,' we do not rely on this. . . . And we rely only on a matter of practice about which a person has asked, and about which the master [*rav*] relays [as] *halakhah le-ma'aseh*."[49] HaMeiri noted with sadness that many of his rabbinic contemporaries had jettisoned one of the needed conditions implied in the term "*halakhah le-ma'aseh*" (law to be applied in practice): "And the important thing which the enlightened one must implant in his heart—and this is among the things in which this generation fails—is that . . . it is not appropriate to teach in accord with what is written by one sage or author, or by one who interprets with great novelty. . . . Unless there is proof."[50] Indirectly chastising rabbinic colleagues who seemed more impressed by novel interpretations than by erudition, HaMeiri alluded to an anecdote found in the Talmud.[51] An ancient sage was describing a near-death experience to his colleagues and reported that the denizens of the Other World—unlike the living—cannot be fooled by appearances. Elaborating on his claim, the sage explained that when a scholar at the end of his mortal life arrives in their domain, the dead do not assess the intellectual merit of the new arrival by surveying his library, but by appraising what he brought with him, which is to say, that which he had internalized.[52]

HaMeiri was not only pained by the fact that the study of Talmud had become too dependent upon the written text, he was distressed by his contemporaries' reliance on halakhic digests. Ridiculing the absurd graphocentrism in the rabbinic academies of his day, HaMeiri caricatured students who applied dialectical reasoning to fragments of text, but were totally ignorant of their broader contexts: "And they rely upon making *distinctiones* with shreds of *novellae* and snippets of phrases. And like a crane they shriek, 'Look, I found that so and so wrote this!'—without knowing or even checking to see if it was said properly or not, and without relying on the Talmud."[53]

* * *

HaMeiri was highly attuned to the impact that modes of transmission—oral versus written—had on pedagogy, literary genre, and spiritual formation. Valorization of "holistic" Talmud study, in which legal traditions are never isolated from their literary contexts or from their embeddedness in lived Judaism, permeates his reconstruction of rabbinic cultural history. The geonim, asserted HaMeiri, had transmitted tradition solely through oral-mnemonic strategies, in strict observance of the rabbinic dictum prohibiting the inscription of *oral matters*. Indeed, he claimed, the geonim had no need to commit traditions to writing, for they themselves had cultivated prodigious memories. This, asserted HaMeiri, is why the geonim left few writings to posterity.

> You should know that, until this point, the *yeshivot* were great and honored, and the students were numerous. Torah was their craft—and how much more so [was this the case with] the heads of the great and respected academies and those ordained into the Gaonate, who were not accustomed to leave the tent [of Torah] day or night. And they knew the entire Talmud by heart, or close to it. And the words of all of Torah and Talmud were arranged in their mouths as [is for us] the passage of *Shema'* ["*Hear O Israel*"]. And therefore they didn't find it necessary to go on at length in their compositions, for the explanation was all arranged in their mouths [in memory]. And in their eyes, writing down the explanation of [these] matters would have been like one who, in our times, writes down the vernacular of the words.[54]

HaMeiri's remarks combine an idealized vision of a bygone oral past with nuggets of historical information about rabbinic culture in his own time and place. His familiarizing analogues preserve data about the note-taking practices of his rabbinic contemporaries, their use of the vernacular to clarify difficult Hebrew or Aramaic words, and, above all, their estrangement from the practices and values of the geonic classroom. When viewed as part of an ongoing rabbinic conversation, however, HaMeiri's recreation of the post-talmudic academies' *Sitz im Leben* offers a perspective quite different from that of Maimonides, who had been critical of the paltry geonic writings on Jewish law.[55] As HaMeiri presented it, the sparse literary output of the geonim—which Maimonides portrayed as a shortcoming—was actually a symptom of their remarkable (and now, practically unimaginable) mnemonic virtuosity. In effect, implied HaMeiri, Maimonides had been insensitive to cultural nuance, for he evaluated the written legacy of oral geonic culture using the anachronistic standards of textualized twelfth-century society.[56]

According to HaMeiri, undesirable developments in rabbinic pedagogy and adjudication had emerged in the geonic period quite by accident. In two separate cases, he claimed, inscriptions of *halakhot* that had been designed for the exclusive and private use of particular individuals—and that were specifically tailored to address their respective limitations—took off in ways never intended by their creators. HaMeiri makes some striking claims in discussing the circumstances under which two such works were composed: the *Sheiltot,* a halakhic work of the eighth or ninth centuries written by Rabbi Aḥa of Shabḥa, and *Sefer ha-Piqqadon*, one of the topically specific halakhic monographs written in the tenth century by Sa'adya Gaon:

> And this is what caused them to write only a little bit, both in explanation and in adjudication. And even this was not for their own need, but [only] for their children or relatives who lacked the competence of the other students. And they wrote for them short compositions [*ḥiburim*] to be a mouth for them, some regarding forbidden and permitted matters, and some laws pertaining to a requested subject.
>
> We received a clear tradition regarding R. Aḥa of blessed memory: He had a son who was not at all inclined to be diligent [in his studies]. And [so] he [R. Aḥai] compiled for him *Sefer ha-Sheiltot* so that, each and every Sabbath, when the Torah portion would be read, known *halakhot* from the Talmud [connected with the weekly Torah reading] would be explained in this [work].[57]
>
> We have similarly received [a tradition] regarding our Master, Sa'adya, of blessed memory, regarding *Sefer ha-Piqqadon*—that he compiled it for one who was appointed a judge in his town. . . . And this judge was sometimes perplexed, and pleaded with him [Sa'adya] to explain to him the laws of bailment in general.[58]

If HaMeiri's etiological account is of dubious historical worth,[59] its message is unequivocal: neither of these early halakhic digests had been designed for circulation. That these works nonetheless came to be perceived as guides for all Jews was not simply unplanned, implied HaMeiri; it was wrong. From his perspective, a practice that prevailed in his own time—the treatment of halakhic digests as legally authoritative—was rooted in error.

* * *

One of the most elaborate reflections on the consequences of textualization appears in a thirteenth-century testimony from France by Rabbis Moses and Samuel Shneur of Evreux, Normandy. Whether their remarks describing interconnected pedagogic, social, and institutional changes that had been set in motion by the inscription of *oral matters* are to be read as a celebration of the new order or as a lament over the displacement and loss of an older one may be debated.[60]

> From the day that we were exiled from our land, and our Temple was destroyed, and the lands became distorted, and hearts were diminished, the ruling that "awe of your teacher should/must resemble awe of heaven"[61] is no longer said [upheld]. So, too, the rulings that obligate a disciple to his teacher have been nullified. For books[62] and compositions and commentaries—they are [now] those that teach us. And [now] everything depends upon one's mental acuity, and on reasoning. And for this reason, each student is accustomed to establishing an academy for himself in their [his] city. So, too, one can no longer say to a student that he must not give halakhic instruction [in the presence of his teacher, or without the latter's permission],[63] and a student, through powers of casuistry, can contradict the words of his teacher.[64]

Until this upheaval, asserted the Shneur brothers, greatest respect had been accorded to masters who were trusted links to the past. But this social hierarchy was overturned as Jews came to rely on inscribed *oral matters*. The ability to analyze a written text was now prized more than erudition, and young casuists lacking in life experience were accorded the esteem that had formerly been reserved for seasoned repositories of tradition. With logical acuity the new key to institutional prominence, new rabbinic academies were springing up all over, each headed by a young dialectician.[65] In short, the very locus of religious authority had shifted:[66] Written texts—and those most adept at teasing new meanings from them—now commanded greater respect than living tradents.

Christian Responses to the Textualization of Rabbinic Culture

The well-documented shift in Christian anti-Jewish polemic that began in the twelfth century might be construed as circumstantial evidence for the talmudic text's growing prominence in Jewish life.[67] From Christianity's inception, its critiques of Judaism had focused on the inadequacy of Jewish doctrines and on the failure of Jews to grasp the meaning of Hebrew Scriptures,[68] but this modus operandi of long duration underwent a dramatic change shortly before the mid-twelfth century. When Christian polemicists became cognizant of the Talmud's existence, they identified this text as the greatest barrier to Jewish conversion. The Christian encounter with Talmud did not merely add another focus to anti-Jewish polemic; it caused the Church to reevaluate its understanding of Judaism's place in a Christian world, and to reformulate its Jewry policy. Up until this turning point, Augustine's perspective had set the tone: Jews in Christian lands could be subjected to legal constraints, but they were not to be killed. After all, reasoned Augustine, while Jews, in their blindness, failed to acknowledge that certain scriptural prophecies had already been fulfilled, their tenacious adherence to Torah bore witness to Scripture's truthfulness and authenticity. Moreover, wrote Augustine, if Jews were allowed to live unharmed, and were shown the error of their ways, they might well come to acknowledge the truth of Christianity.[69]

The Christian encounter with Talmud in the 1140s challenged the very assumptions of Augustine's doctrine and the policy that stemmed from it. It now became apparent to Christians that the church, over the course of centuries, had not taken into account the looming presence of the Talmud in Jewish life, nor reckoned with the fact that this text constituted a monumental, and perhaps insurmountable, impediment to Jewish conversion.[70] Subjection of the Talmud to inquisitorial trial in the thirteenth century only confirmed Christian fears. The Augustinian assumption that Judaism was not a heresy had failed to take "talmudic Judaism" into account. Unlike "biblical Judaism," this phenomenon was construed as "an ideational danger to the church"—even in places where there were no Jews.[71] The church accordingly acted on this threat in the thirteenth century; through the agency of the friars, they confiscated talmudic texts from Jewish homes and synagogues and burned them.

The multiple explanations offered for the shifting focus of Christian anti-Jewish polemic situate this development in contexts that highlight social, economic, legal, theological, and institutional changes within Christendom.[72] Common to all the interpretations, however, is the recognition that the Christian "discovery" of Talmud drastically altered the Western Church's attitude toward the Jews. But why did it take so long for the church to understand the prominent and powerful place of Talmud in Jewish culture? Or, as Jeremy Cohen put it, "If European Jews had always lived according to the Talmud, as indeed they had, what suddenly led to the development and acceptance of the new attitude that rabbinic Judaism was heretical and had no place in Christendom?"[73] Developments described in the preceding chapters suggest that this question should be answered not only with reference to new trends in Christian thought[74] and to the powerful roles played by the new orders of urban friars,[75] but also with reference to changes that occurred within Jewish culture itself. We might hypothesize that Christians did not mention "Talmud" until 1146 because the written text of this name had simply not been regarded by northern European Jews as the stand-alone source of legal authority. It was not until the talmudic text came to be widely perceived as *the* guide to Jewish life that Christians would have needed to consider how it affected, or altered, the Jews' relationship to Scripture. In an effort to flesh out this claim, the following remarks will review what is known about Christian familiarity with post-biblical Jewish traditions, whether written or oral.

Studies by Ḥen Merḥavya, Avrom Saltmann, and Bat-Sheva Alpert identify extra-biblical Jewish traditions and sources that were mentioned by Christian writers in the centuries before the first Christian reference to "Talmud."[76] In some cases, such knowledge was acquired from sources written by earlier Christians, and in others from conversation with Jews. New Testament writings clearly know of post-biblical Jewish practices, but it is unclear whether the ancestral traditions referred to with disparagement in the Gospels and Pauline Epistles were encountered as written sources. The *Didache* and the *Epistle of Barnabas* mention extra-biblical Jewish practices,[77] and the fourth-century church fathers, Epiphanius and Jerome, made reference to the Jews' *paradosis*, "tradition."[78] Writings by Greek and Latin church fathers make reference to some midrashic teachings, and ridicule other extra-biblical Jewish traditions as "myths" and "fables."[79] Many later Christian writers echoed Jerome's disparagement of these teachings: "How numerous are the traditions of the Pharisees, called today, '*deuteroses*' ["second teachings"] and how inane their stories, I cannot even begin to recount. Most are so repulsive that I blush to tell them."[80]

In 553, the Emperor Justinian issued a decree asserting that Jews throughout the Byzantine Empire were to be allowed access to Hebrew Scripture in Greek, Latin, or any other translation.[81] A part of this legislation prohibited Jews from engaging in "what they call '*deuterosis*,' which is not part of the Sacred Writings, and which was not transmitted earlier through the mediation of the Prophets, but is the invention of people whose words are [derive authority] only from the mundane, and have nothing divine about them."[82]

Whatever its precise content,[83] the prohibited *deuterosis* to which Justinian referred was not inscribed; it circulated as "empty unwritten matters—which are known to mislead the simple people."[84]

Christians do not seem to have known the names of any post-biblical Jewish compositions,[85] but they do refer to non-scriptural Jewish texts.[86] Visigothic legislation forced Jewish converts to Christianity to surrender all their non-biblical works to the authorities, and forbade both Jews and converts to read Jewish books that had been deemed off-limits by Visigothic ecclesiastical authorities.[87] By 680, ecclesiastical councils in Spain had compiled a list of anti-Christian statements extracted from extra-biblical Jewish writings.[88] Around a century and a half later, the biblical exegete Heimo of Halberstadt (or perhaps of Auxerre) made reference to Hebrew books that do not contain Torah or Prophets,[89] and alluded to "Jewish books, by means of which they shore up their lies."[90] Yet none of these Christian references to post-biblical Jewish writings name the works in question, and historians cannot be certain whether these inscriptions were ephemeral jottings, compilations of teachings, or discrete compositions.

Though some church fathers referred mockingly to rabbinic oral teachings about the Bible,[91] ninth-century Christian scholars like Claudius of Turin and Rabanus Maurus revered the *Hebraica veritas* as an essential tool for establishing the Latin text of Scripture, and garnered information about extra-biblical Jewish exegetical traditions from Jerome's writings and from contemporary Jewish converts.[92] References to post-biblical Jewish beliefs and practices also appear in writings by Angelomus (fl. 845–55), a monk of Luxeuil,[93] and by Lyonnaise clerics of the Carolingian era. Bishop Agobard,[94] his assistant Archdeacon Florus,[95] and his successor Bishop Amulo all sought out Jewish informants because of their interest in the *Hebraica veritas*. Nonetheless, whereas Carolingian predecessors (along with Italian and English contemporaries) had portrayed extra-biblical Jewish traditions (including mystical and messianic notions)[96] as ridiculous, the ecclesiastics of Lyons regarded them as noxious elements that were to be eradicated. Their virulent anti-Judaism has been explained with reference to regional origins: Agobard, Angelomus, Florus, and Amulo were all Visigoths influenced by Visigothic legislation. Unlike other Christian societies of the Merovingian period, Visigothic Spain did not embrace the Jewry policy set forth by Augustine, but actively forced conversion upon the Jews within its own domain.[97] The writings of Agobard and of Amulo reflect their largely unsuccessful attempt to shape Carolingian Jewry policy in the image of Visigothic precedents, particularly after the establishment of the new Western Frankish Kingdom in 840.[98]

Descriptions of Jewish beliefs and practices appear in a series of letters written by Bishop Agobard in the 820s and 830s, and by Bishop Amulo in the 840s, and sent both to ecclesiastical leaders and to Emperors Louis the Pious and Charles the Bald. Outraged by the freedoms Jews enjoyed in Lyons and by their friendly relations with Christians, Agobard and Amulo exhorted Christians to cease all economic interactions with Jews, and they called for the imposition of imperial legislation to restrict Christian contact with them.[99] A prominent cleric's conversion to Judaism in 838 offered particularly disturbing evidence of the absence of social barriers, for the convert in question, the monk Bodo (later known as Elazar), had once served as Chaplain to the Imperial Court.[100] Hoping to shock Christians into recognizing that Jews were to be detested and shunned, Agobard and Amulo collected Jewish beliefs and practices that they regarded as abominable. None of their testimonies make reference to literary sources, however, and some of their descriptions of extra-biblical Jewish beliefs are prefaced with the phrase, "the Jews say."[101]

* * *

The first Christian writer to refer to a literary composition recognizable as the Talmud began life as Moses the Sefardi (1062–1140), a Jew of Aragon. Upon embracing Christianity in 1106, he assumed the name Petrus Alfonsi and composed *Dialogus Petri et Moysi Iudaei*, a work justifying his conversion.[102] At the crux of this work was the argument that Christianity was by far the more rational of the two religions, for the *aggadot* of Judaism depict God in shockingly anthropomorphic terms.[103] Alfonsi did not actually use the term "Talmud" in this work, but the intended referent of "the Book of *Doctrina*" or "*doctrinarum liber*[104] is clear, for he described the opus in question as a work that depends upon *lex* [= Scripture],[105] that contains four *sedarim* [orders] of which *Zera'im* and *Mo'ed* were included in one volume,[106] and that opens with a section called "*Berakhot.*"[107] Several of Alfonsi's remarks refer to traditions that are written, but scholars are not certain whether he drew directly upon Talmud or adduced examples from some anthological intermediary.[108]

It was not until 1146 that the "*Talmud*" was mentioned by its name in a Christian anti-Jewish treatise.[109] According to Peter the Venerable (1094–

1156), Abbot of Cluny from 1122, the actual name of this work had been revealed to him by Jesus.[110] The final chapter of his polemic, *Tractatus adversus Iudeaorum inveteratam duritem*, concerns "the ridiculous and most stupid fables of the Jews," and aims, in the author's words, to expose and attack "the monstrous beast." Identifying the *portuentuosa bestia* with the Talmud, Peter the Venerable claimed that it was this book that caused the Jews to be something less than human.[111] Peter the Venerable knew no Hebrew; he drew some of his talmudic quotations from a French version of the Hebrew *Alphabet of Ben Sira*, but lifted most, almost verbatim, from the work of Petrus Alfonsi.[112]

It may not be insignificant that Petrus Alfonsi, the erstwhile Moses the Sefardi, was reared in Spain, or that Peter the Venerable wrote his *Tractatus adversus Iudaeorum inveteratam duritem* after spending two years (1142–43) there.[113] Jews of twelfth-century Spain could have been sensitized to the irrationality of rabbinic *aggadot* through a number of channels. They were, after all, cultural heirs to the late geonic rationalists of Babylonia—Sa'adya, Sherira, Shmuel ben Ḥofni, and Hai—all of whom had declared that *aggadot* were devoid of authority.[114] Moreover, Jews of al-Andalus were exposed to the corrosive attacks on aggadah leveled, on the one hand, by Karaites like Samuel al-Maghribi, and, on the other, by Muslims like Ibn Ḥazm.[115] (In one of his autobiographical remarks, Petrus Alfonsi described himself as having "always been nurtured among the Muslims," because he had learned the Arabic language and read Arabic books while growing up.)[116]

The subsequent history of the trial, burning, and ultimate censorship of the Talmud follows directly from the twelfth-century undertakings of Peter Alfonsi and Peter the Venerable.[117] Their works and those of successor polemicists[118] drew attention to talmudic passages deemed blasphemous of Christianity and the Holy Family, and to preposterous *aggadot* that were said to demonstrate the irrationality of the Jews. Ultimately, however, the weightiest charge against talmudic Judaism was that rabbinic Jews relied more heavily on the teachings of their sages than they did on the teachings of God Himself.[119] If it was indeed the case that Jews valued Talmud over Scripture and regarded it as the foremost source of authority, asserted the polemicists, it was pointless for Christians to continue hoping that Jews could be brought round to embracing the correct understandings of biblical prophecies.[120] This point was stressed in a missive that Pope Gregory IX sent to European clerics and noblemen in 1239, enlisting them in the campaign to confiscate local copies of Talmud:

> If what is said about the Jews of France and of the other lands is true, no punishment would be sufficiently great or sufficiently worthy of their crime. For they, so we have heard, are not content with the Old Law which God gave to Moses in writing; they even ignore it completely and affirm that God gave another law which is called "Talmud," that is, "Teaching," handed down to Moses orally. Falsely, they allege that it was implanted in their minds, and unwritten, was there preserved until certain men came, whom they call "Sages" and "Scribes," men who, fearing that this law may be lost from the minds of men through forgetfulness, reduced it to writing. And the volume of this far exceeds the text of the Bible. In this is contained matters so abusive and so unspeakable that it arouses shame in those who mention it and horror in those who hear it. Wherefore . . . this is said to be the chief cause that holds the Jews obstinate in their perfidy.[121]

Christian polemicists pointed out that Jewish preoccupation with Talmud had come at the expense of scriptural study. A charge leveled against the Jews in 1236 by the apostate Nicholas Donin echoed critiques that had been voiced within the Jewish community itself. In this more public context, however, it led to the confiscation and burning of the Talmud in 1240: "The Jews prevent their children from studying the Bible, placing the Talmud at the center of their educational curriculum."[122] Christians also blamed Talmud, and the unique manner in which it was studied, for the seeming inability of geographically dispersed Jews to endorse a single doctrinal perspective. In sermons delivered between the 1240s and 1270s, Berthold of Regensburg criticized the Jews for embracing a diverse array of theological perspectives. According to Berthold, this potpourri of ideas was decidedly noxious, and wholly out of keeping with biblical religion. It was, he declared, a chaos born of immersion in Talmud study, and fanned by the distortions of rabbinic pedagogy and adjudication:

> The Jews, who are most diverse in their faith, are not in harmony with the faith which their ancient forefathers believed. Whence they believe in one land many things regarding their faith which they do not in another—even in one city and not in another, and even in an individual home. The reason for this most diverse credulity of the Jews is that whatever their blind modern teachers dream up and

tell them to believe, they believe. And in order that they [the teachers] might receive greater honor from them, that say that what a sage maintains is to be believed was given by God at Mt. Sinai, so that people must believe [it]. Consequently, whatever this blind doctor says must be believed, [the Jews] immediately believe, and whatever a doctor of other [Jews] similarly says to his people must be believed, they likewise believe—and thus in each individual case. Therefore, since one of the Jews' teachers says that one thing is to be believed and another teacher [says] another thing and a third, still another thing—and so, in many instances, there is a great diversity of belief among the Jews, even in matters pertaining to the faith of the Old Testament."[123]

* * *

Polemical Christian testimonies about the Talmud and about talmudocentrism not only corroborate the evidence from Jewish sources, they help to sharpen certain insights about the history of cultural transmission. A number of the historical observations made by Ḥen Merḥavya in his monumental study of citations from rabbinic literature in medieval Christian sources are quite subtle;[124] the following hypothesis, by contrast, is obvious: Christians could not have confiscated and burned the Talmud before a standardized text of that name was in widespread circulation. As long as the transmission of the Talmud was effected through face-to-face instruction, and as long as talmudic inscriptions were of the status of unofficial "phantom texts," it would have been strategically pointless for the church to attempt to uproot the Talmud through eradication of any material artifact. Widespread availability of the talmudic text was an essential precondition of the church's physical assault on Talmud. By the same token, the medieval Jewish perception of the talmudic text as an artifact indispensible to their *modus vivendi* was a precondition for mourning once physical sacrilege was committed.[125]

Medieval Jewish Attempts to Parry Talmudocentrism

The central place of Talmud in medieval Jewish life did not preclude some Jews from attempting to parry what they perceived as the unwelcome new developments wrought by talmudocentrism. Maimonides' inventive reinterpretation of the talmudic injunction to divide one's study into three parts, Scripture, Mishnah, and Talmud,[126] was one such response. Profet Duran approached the problem differently. Writing in Aragon at the turn of the fifteenth century, he set forth a historicist argument in order to convince Jews that Talmud should be relegated to a more marginal place in the curriculum. Drawing attention to a passage in rabbinic literature that praises Rabbi Yoḥanan ben Zakkai for his devotion to a number of subjects, *talmud* among them,[127] Efodi made the following point: Since the sage in question lived in the first century, when there was not yet a fixed corpus called "Talmud," is it not obvious that the term "*talmud*" in the passage referred to something other than the eponymous composition? Moreover, wrote Efodi, if it were true that this one text was truly indispensable to a Jew's spiritual perfection, how could earlier towering figures of Jewish history have been able to attain their religious stature?

> What is intended by "the craft of *talmud*" is *not* everything that appears in this composition [which is called "Talmud"]. For if this were so, what was the merit of David and Solomon and all the sages of Israel who lived prior to the closure of this composition? Do you think that the wisdom of Solomon consisted of the apprehension of the knowledge of *this* composition—that was composed more than 1300 years after him?! . . . This being the case, that which is intended by "*talmud*" must mean something other than this![128]

Assuming the voice of a hypothetical critic, Efodi highlights features of the Talmud that compromise its effectiveness and that make it an unlikely guide to the *summum bonum*:

> [Some] say that it is impossible that this talmudic composition alone should be the sole one capable of enabling man to acquire the ultimate success, given that this composition includes many matters that couldn't possibly be a necessary cause of human felicity. This is the case with many of the *aggadot* that are included therein, and some of the incidents [*ma'asiyyot*]. Also because this composition includes the great disputes which fell between the sages of Israel regarding the statutes/laws of the Torah.[129]

As thinkers within the Andalusian orbit who were separated by two and a half centuries, Maimonides and Efodi focused on the curricular impact of the Talmud's growing importance, and attempted to defuse it by illuminating the lexical ambiguity of the term "*talmud.*" One would not have expected either of these Sefardi Jews to comment on the Talmud's growing prominence in the process of adjudication, for Andalusian Jews had long relied on codes or legal handbooks—and possessed the tradition that "our Talmud" had been inscribed as a guide to applied law. In northern Europe, however, some Jews decried the marginalization of sources that had once played a greater role in the making of Jewish legal decisions.

"Custom Trumps Legislation": A Critique of Talmud's New Role in Adjudication

Noting the prominent role played by custom (*minhag*) in medieval Ashkenaz and the explosion there of customary literature [*sifrut ha-minhagim*], Yisrael Ta Shma offered a narrative in several writings that attempted to explain these phenomena as symptoms of a reawakened *Kulturkampf* between the heritages of rival Jewish cultures in antiquity. According to Ta Shma, the Jewish community of medieval Ashkenaz was heir to the cultural proclivities of ancient Palestinian Jewry, a population, he claimed, that had always ascribed greater authority to *ma'aseh*, literally "deed"—which Ta Shma equated with *minhag*, custom—than to legislation. The former was transmitted through lived behaviors, and the latter, through inscribed texts. The Jews of medieval Ashkenaz perpetuated this orientation, claimed Ta Shma, because their founding family hailed from Italy, which was in the cultural orbit of ancient Palestine.[130] According to Ta Shma, custom—and not the Babylonian Talmud—was the default reference point for Jews of early Ashkenaz. In tenth-century Ashkenaz, wrote Ta Shma, "custom did not yet have a particular status vis-à-vis *halakhah*, because it itself [custom] was the entire essence of *halakhah* and its energizing force."[131] This, he asserted, was "how *halakhah* had always been established [in ancient Palestine] . . . from its outset, as *ma'aseh-minhag* ["deed-custom"], whether written in a book or not."[132] In their "originary period," Ta Shma claimed, the Jews of Ashkenaz were guided by "the principle of deed-custom" (*ha-'iqqaron ha-ma'aseh-ha-minhag*), which "was still known as the living principle of Hebrew law [*ha-halakhah ha-'ivrit*]; its primary reliance was on widespread practice and accepted precedent, and only secondarily on generative and abstract analysis."[133] But beginning in the eleventh century, he wrote,"the tension became more palpable between the custom-deed principle [*ha-'iqqaron ha-minhag-ha-ma'aseh*] and the demands of analysis, explanation, and creative adjudication based on the written sources—and of decision making on their basis."[134] It was during this period, claimed Ta Shma, that the Babylonian orientation triumphed over that of Palestine, forcing Jews of Ashkenaz to accommodate to the new reality. "The infiltration of the Babylonian Talmud and fortification of its status brought about a diminution in the force of Palestinian *halakhah* there . . . and gradual adaptation to it [the Babylonian Talmud]."[135] The subjection of Ashkenazi assumptions and practices to evaluation by the standards of the Babylonian Talmud proved devastating, he wrote,[136] and the Jews of the region succumbed to the legal orientation of Babylonia. Yet with the passage of time, Ashkenazi Jews alit upon a way of reaffirming their beleaguered, if not suppressed, Palestinian heritage. They made custom into a sacrosanct entity, "defined . . . in exceptional terms."[137] "The ancient Palestinian *halakhah*, living and oral, was 'pushed upward' and became a type of meta-*halakhah*, [in the form of] 'the custom of our fathers is Torah'; its status was greater than that of the Babylonian Talmud, which was simply '*halakhah.*' "[138] In Ta Shma's narrative, custom's rise to a position of unprecedented importance in medieval Ashkenazi society marked the return of the repressed Palestinian element, and compensated for the Babylonian Talmud's triumph in this region.

In short, Ta Shma explains the prominence of custom in Ashkenaz as a byproduct of a geographically rooted contest between Palestine and Babylonia that had been in play for centuries. Little wonder, he noted, that the two ancient iterations of "*minhag mevattel halakhah*" (custom trumps or nullifies legislation), a phrase used by Jews of medieval Ashkenaz, appears only in the Jerusalem Talmud and not in its Babylonian counterpart. According to Ta Shma, when medieval Ashkenazi Jews affirmed the cultural authority of custom, theirs was an agonistic posture challenging talmudic legislation.

A number of claims made in Professor Ta Shma's multipronged thesis are simply incorrect and others rest on unproven assumptions. Lest other scholars ingest this narrative uncritically, several of its problems will be noted here.

In using a newly-fabricated term, "the *minhag-ma'aseh* principle", Ta Shma was equating *minhag* with *ma'aseh*. Yet Palestinian Jews from mishnaic times onward did not use the term *ma'aseh* to designate an act that was practiced, but a legal decision rendered in a court case.[139] There are therefore no grounds for equating or conflating *ma'aseh* and *minhag*, or for positing that the conjunction of the two constituted a form of guiding legal "principle". Beyond this, when Professor Ta Shma asserted that reliance on *ma'aseh* was quintessentially Palestinian, he referred to *Sefer ha-Ma'asim*, a post-talmudic compilation of court cases from Palestine discovered in the *genizah* which he called "the archetypical book of Palestinian laws."[140] While the existence of *Sefer ha-Ma'asim* certainly proves that Palestinian Jews preserved case law, it does not prove that Jews of this region took no other approach to the resolution of legal problems. Nor does the existence of *Sefer ha-Ma'asim* warrant Professor Ta Shma's claim that the use of case law was quintessentially Palestinian. On the contrary, court-rendered legal decisions were preserved as case law in a broad array of societies and cultures.

Scholarship produced over the last three decades has demonstrated the inadequacy of Professor Ta Shma's overarching genealogical claims.[141] While certain practices of medieval Ashkenaz are related to those of ancient Palestine,[142] Jews of northern Europe saw themselves as the cultural heirs of both Palestine and Babylonia,[143] and they recognized the authority of the Babylonian geonim.[144]

Professor Ta Shma's claims about the disparate forms of legal authority that Palestinian and Babylonian Jews privileged is also in need of careful reconsideration, not least because the rabbinic literary units he portrayed as emblematic of these differences lend themselves to vastly other readings.[145] The phrase "*minhag mevattel halakhah*" does not function as a combative slogan pitting custom against law in either of its two occurrences in the Jerusalem Talmud,[146] and it was not used as a battle cry in either of the medieval cases cited by Ta Shma, both of which occur in writings by the twelfth-century rabbi Isaac bar Judah. In one case, the phrase appears in a context more lackadaisical than defiant,[147] and in the second, its message is explicitly presented as one shared by both the Jerusalem and Babylonian Talmuds![148] In short, it would seem that "*minhag mevattel halakhah*" was not used as an agonistic slogan in medieval Ashkenazi writings; like other rabbinic references to the importance of custom in this literature (e.g., "*minhag avotenu hu*," it is a custom of our fathers),[149] it signaled sensitivity to custom, a regional phenomenon well described in the work of Ta Shma and other scholars.[150]

A consideration of the relationship between legislation and custom in the broader cultures to which Jews had access tends to support the notion that out-and-out clashes between the two realms of authority were unlikely. Scholarly investigation of classical and post-classical Roman law has not unearthed any cases in which custom actually abrogated law; on the contrary, this research confirms that custom and legislation complemented one another,[151] at least through the twelfth century.[152] Following the breakdown of the Carolingian Empire, custom became increasingly important in medieval northern Europe because it filled lacunae left by the cessation of legislation. Classically understood (and epitomized in Justinian's *Digest*) as the product of tacit, popular, and unwritten consent, custom granted legitimacy to the practices of medieval institutions like the family and the feudal order.[153]

It was not until the thirteenth century that interpreters of Roman law debated the relative rankings of custom and law. This discussion might have been warranted on purely academic grounds, inasmuch as classical and post-classical texts contradicted one another on the matter[154]—but it undoubtedly took place when it did because this was a time when discrete bastions of authority—papacy, royalty, empire—were attempting to work out their jurisdictions not only with respect to one another but vis-à-vis popular practice.[155]

If there is no historical basis to the claim that legislation and custom were sources of cultural authority that operated at cross purposes in Jewish antiquity, and if one discards the hypothesis that a feud between the two was rekindled in the Middle Ages because of genealogically ingrained predilections, what can account for the heightened sensitivity of medieval Ashkenazi Jews to the authority of custom? Eschewing hereditary explanations that fall back (anachronistically) on centers of Jewish life far removed from Ashkenaz in space and time, and that posit the eruption of suppressed subterranean elements, historians may wish to think about the Jews of this region in their synchronic context. If Jewish settlement in Ashkenaz was indeed initiated in the ninth century (as claimed in a Jewish foundation narrative inscribed in the twelfth century),[156] it is hard to imagine that the descendants of the earliest Jewish immigrants, living in the region centuries later, would not have accommodated their own traditions to aspects of the local legal culture. As discussed before, North Europeans ritually dramatized their legal acts in order to leave durable mnemonic records. These performances were enshrined in custom.[157]

As long as the Talmud was not construed as the lone reference work for applied Jewish law, the legal traditions (halakhot) preserved therein were not in competition with living Jewish practice. (As discussed in Chapter 1, this had been the case in geonic society.) However, as the logical operations undertaken by the tosafists led to reliance on the Talmud alone as the source of applied law, the longstanding linkage at the heart of *halakhah le-ma'aseh* was uncoupled, and "unalloyed" halakhah, that which was written in the Talmud, was catapulted to a position of legal primacy. It was at this point that the homeostasis between law and custom was disturbed, and that custom appeared to be in conflict with law itself. The process of textualization, which transformed medieval Ashkenazi society into one that privileged teachings inscribed in the Talmud and devalued the authority of living tradition, occasioned the new prominence of custom in written sources of the time.

Jews of Ashkenaz, whose familiarity with tradition had been shaped by ritual experience and by the counsel and behavior of elders, did not suddenly abandon a worldview in which mimesis was normative and memory an unquestioned source of authority. When one of the most dramatic byproducts of textualization, the divorce of *halakhah* and *ma'aseh*, left modeled behavior without a textual advocate, Ashkenazim responded in several ways.

One strategy was to create a level playing field by composing customaries, writings that made the authority of custom visible in the textual arena.[158] The impulse to put *minhag* on a footing comparable to that of talmudic halakhah produced the surge in Jewish customary literature in medieval Ashkenaz. Yet, ironically, the commitment of custom to writing also led to its ossification. Scholars of medieval Jewish and Christian societies (Yisrael Ta Shma among them) have discussed how custom, prior to its inscription, had maintained its vitality over the course of centuries by undergoing needed metamorphoses without leaving any written traces. Whether consciously or unconsciously, the "remembrancers" who served as the guardians of custom in each community, had traditionally responded to the demands of the present by refashioning the narratives of the past. Since this form of social management was exercised without oversight, checks, or transparency, custom was able to to remain both powerful and forever current. Adjustments made by local remembrancers ensured that recollections of "what had been" remained indistinguishable from contemporary community practices; they enabled societies to accommodate change while continuing to profess fidelity to time-hallowed traditions.[159] However, once these customs were inscribed and accessible for consultation, their static records could not easily be manipulated. Changes that continued to occur in communal practice now had to be justified, exegetically, with reference to the text of the customary itself.

A second northern European Jewish strategy for bridging the now considerable gap between the prescriptions of Talmud and the authority of custom was developed by the tosafists. Their many feats of dialectical harmonization were designed to assure readers that custom was in line with halakhah. Though the talmudic glossators of northern France, Germany, and Italy did not assign custom an address within the halakhic system (as did R. Zeraḥya Halevi of Lunel and other Provençal scholars),[160] their very approach to harmonization subordinated *minhag* to halakhah.

A third response[161] of northern European Jews to the experienced discrepancies between inscribed halakhah and orally transmitted *minhag* was that of the Rhineland Pietists, known as *Ḥasidei Ashkenaz.* Strongly disapproving of many of the changes that were associated with textualization, this group found novel ways of conveying criticisms and of expressing cultural resistance.[162] Some Pietist perspectives and practices overtly protested social and cultural changes, while others related to textualization more indirectly—by perpetuating patterns of social hierarchy, pedagogy, and transmission that had come under siege. Still other Pietist innovations attempted to compensate for textualization's impact on Jewish society and culture by adapting older traditions so that they would continue to be resonant in a world whose standards of authority had changed. In responding to the challenges of textualization, the Rhineland Pietists—like the tosafists and the compilers of Jewish customaries—became agents of textualization in their own right.[163]

6

Rhineland Pietism and the Textualization of Rabbinic Culture in Medieval Northern Europe

On the Simultaneity of Significant Cultural Developments

The chronological proximity of disparate cultural developments in medieval Jewish history has attracted a fair amount of scholarly attention, some of it quite productive.[1] The present chapter attempts to account for the simultaneous emergence of Tosafism and Rhineland Pietism in northern European Jewish communities by situating both within the broader historical narrative of textualization. It stops short of trying to tell an even larger (and longer) story, one that would link textualization to the emergence of Kabbalah. Happily, the contours of this omitted narrative (and a great amount of detail) may be found in studies by Moshe Idel, Elliot Wolfson, Ḥaviva Pedaya, Daniel Abrams, and Moshe Halbertal.[2] Their works, which are sensitive to proximate historical triggers, acknowledge that the appearance of kabbalistic writings was causally linked to the inscription of other texts. The process of textualization ought not be credited—or blamed—for every development in medieval Jewish culture, but the impulse to inscribe esoteric teachings that had previously been transmitted only through oral communication was crucial to the rise of Kabbalah, its dissemination, and its subsequent development.

Tosafism and Pietism: Twelfth-Century Claims on the Jewish Past

Tosafism and Pietism emerged concurrently in twelfth-century northern Europe, centuries after the beginnings of Jewish settlement in Ashkenaz, and both had formidable impact on subsequent Jewish culture. It has been natural to assume some relationship between these two movements,[3] for talmudic glossators (tosafists) and Rhineland Pietists were products of the same time and place.[4] Rabbi Isaac of Dampierre, a tosafist, is reported to have spoken approvingly of Jews who adopted a particular stringency because of their desire to be "cunning in their awe" for the Divine.[5] While the phrase "*'arum be-yirah*" is of talmudic origin (BT Ber. 17a), it was closely associated, in this time and place, with the Rhineland Pietists, who used the phrase to describe their own extraordinary efforts to discern the inscrutable Divine Will.[6] Scholars speculating about the linkage between the two groups posited that certain features of Pietism—most notably, its attitude toward dialectics and its stress on humility—were reactions to Tosafism.[7] The present study places the two groups within a longer (and broader) historical context in order to indicate how Tosafism and Pietism may be understood both as manifestations of the textualization process and as responses to it. Both groups faced a newly recognized problem: the need to affirm an organic continuity between the Jewish present, known from communal behavior, and the Jewish past, whose written record had become the subject of intense scrutiny. More specifically, both tosafists and Pietists needed to legitimate the present by linking it to the past. As was the case within Christian society around a century earlier, Jews of medieval northern Europe chose between two alternatives. Those who acknowledged the discrepancy between present and past built plausible historical or logical bridges between the two. Those who denied that anything had changed reshaped the past in the image of the present.[8] Tosafists took the first approach: they frequently emphasized the ways in which the present differed from the past, but affirmed the continuity of Jewish tradition by using dialectical reasoning to spotlight the common denominator between then and now. Pietists took the second approach: whether consciously or unconsciously, they manipulated inherited tradition so that allegedly ancestral sources gave voice to perspectives which they themselves embraced. Pietists used historical ventriloquism to mask the differences between present and past.[9]

Pietism in Its Synchronic and Diachronic Contexts

It has been suggested that Tosafism and Pietism have typological parallels in particular cultural phenomena of medieval Christian society, namely, scholasticism and monasticism. Ephraim Kanarfogel noted that monks and Jewish

Pietists took similar approaches to pedagogy, articulated largely parallel critiques of the excesses of dialectic, and shared an emphasis on memorization through repetition at a time when large numbers of students, lured by dialectics, were flocking to the academies of scholastics on the one hand and of tosafists on the other.[10]

Studies of the relationship between medieval monks and Christian scholastics may, at the very least, lead students of medieval Jewish culture to ask new questions about the relationship between Pietism and Tosafism. To give but one example, analysis of the vitriolic exchanges between the abbot Bernard of Clairvaux and the Parisian dialectician Peter Abelard in the twelfth century has shown that the antagonism between monasticism and scholasticism[11] had little to do with doctrinal matters and much to do with the locus of religious authority.[12] Whereas monasticism located spiritual authority in human masters whose teachings were to be memorized and whose behaviors emulated, scholasticism located authority in the written text and in its most gifted analysts. Monasticism, a development of late antiquity,[13] emphasized prayer and contemplation, while scholasticism, a twelfth-century *novum*, emphasized the scrutiny of texts and their deconstruction.

Like others in a long tradition of pagan, Jewish, Christian, and Muslim thinkers,[14] medieval monks and Rhineland Pietists preferred living memory and experience to the artificial memory of written record. In an environment where written transmission had become indispensable, their respective capitulations to inscription were dictated by necessity, not preference. *Sefer Ḥasidim*, a compilation of exempla and tales to guide the Jewish Pietist that was composed before 1225,[15] contains many references to memory-training,[16] and, as discussed below, the Pietist oeuvre as a whole reflects both the assumptions and the practices of the culture of *memoria*.[17] From the perspective of Jewish Pietists and Christian monks, texts might serve as supplements to the authority that inhered in orally transmitted traditions.[18] And at a time when scholastics and tosafists applied themselves to the harmonization of disparate traditions, Pietists and monks reveled in the copiousness of tradition, making little effort to reconcile disparities or conflicts.[19] Jewish Pietists and Christian monks were both suspicious of students whose learning was tinged with pride,[20] and both believed, to paraphrase Stephen Jaeger, that what they knew was less important than what they were.[21]

* * *

Noting that certain aspects of Pietist culture seem to be more characteristic of pre-Crusade than of post-Crusade rabbinic society, some scholars of medieval Ashkenaz have argued that Rhineland Pietists consciously revived outmoded practices and perspectives.[22] I would posit, instead, that the practices and attitudes in question had never died out; they featured prominently in Pietism only because the leaders of that group chose to consign them to writing. Whereas Ashkenazim of earlier generations had felt no need to leave written records of their memory-intensive attitudes and practices, Pietists felt compelled to do so. In the newly textualized world, even a seasoned worldview needed documentary bona fides if it was to viably compete in defining the Jewish present (and future). I would argue that Rhineland Pietism, as a discrete phenomenon, was "born" of the impulse to inscribe teachings and traditions that had previously been transmitted through oral and performed instruction. Neither the practices nor the attitudes of this group were novel in the region; what was new was the vehemence with which they were expressed—in written venues. Awareness that many of Rhineland Pietism's characteristics were autochthonous helps to explain why this seemingly eccentric phenomenon had such a significant impact on subsequent Ashkenazi culture, notwithstanding its relatively late emergence and (as discussed below) its brief, three-generation life span.[23]

Similarities between the behaviors and attitudes of twelfth- and thirteenth-century Rhineland Pietists and those of Rhenish Jews prior to the Crusades suggest that many of Pietism's peculiarities may have been indigenous to Ashkenazi society.[24] For example, the term "*ḥasid*" was applied to at least some Jews of Ashkenaz even before the First Crusade, for Rabbi Yeḥiel of tenth-century Rome referred to the talmudic commentators of Ashkenaz as "*ḥaside Magenẓa*," "the Pietists of Mainz."[25] In this case, the precise meaning of this term can only be the subject of conjecture,[26] but the *Chronicle of Aḥima'aẓ*, a work of tenth-century southern Italy, used the term "*ḥasidim*" to designate particular Jews in that region who were renowned for their connection to higher worlds,[27] and Qayrawanese sources of the same century used the term "*ḥasidim*" to refer to wonder workers.[28] In his scholarly discussion of developments in Ashkenaz after the First Crusade, Yosef Dan noted that the term "*ḥasid*" denoted individuals affiliated with an array of subgroups, all of whom had access to esoteric knowledge drawn from particular traditions (e.g., *Sefer Yeẓirah* and its commentaries).[29] Medieval sources composed after the First Crusade attest to the existence of "*ḥaside Ẓorfat*" (the Pietists of France) and "*ḥaside Provinẓa*" (the Pietists of Provence), alongside "*ḥaside Alemania*" (the Pietists of Germany).[30] Whatever its precise referents, it seems likely that *ḥasid* (Pietist) was one of the labels[31] used by medieval Jews to designate individuals who focused on the interconnection between the mundane and divine worlds, and who attempted to draw the latter into their daily lives through practices of contemplation and theurgy.[32]

The cultivation of self-abnegation, a hallmark of Rhineland Pietism, also seems to have been practiced by extraordinary individuals in the region before the First Crusade; Rashi's teacher, R. Ya'aqov ben Yaqar, stands out in this regard.[33] Moreover, the appellation "*perushim*," "those who set themselves apart," was applied to some Ashkenazi Jews who lived prior to the Crusades. Not only was R. Ya'aqov ben Yaqar labeled a *parush* (as was Rashi's student, R. Shlomo ben R. Shimshon),[34] but subgroups of Jews, and even entire northern European Jewish communities, were known for embracing practices of "*hafrasha*" (separatism) before the emergence of Rhineland Pietism.[35] Members of R. Yehudah HaKohen's family, referred to as "*kohane Magenẓa*" ("the levitical priests of Mainz"), took certain positions on matters of Jewish practice that were not universally held,[36] as did those called the "*perushim* of Speyer."[37] Though the earliest records of these separatist practices date from the twelfth century, when Rashi's students consigned them to writing, Rhenish Jews had been engaging in supererogatory behaviors that were not prescribed by Jewish law well before the appearance of *Ḥaside Ashkenaz*. Their designation of themselves as a "*qehila qedosha*," "consecrated community," may also be an indication of medieval Ashkenazi Jewry's self-image.[38]

Awareness that these particular features—all deeply resonant of Rhineland Pietism—characterized pockets of Jews who lived in the region prior to the Crusades helps to explain why the movement's impact on subsequent Ashkenazi culture was disproportionate to its brief, three-generation lifespan. The "packaging" of Rhineland Pietism—its textual self-presentation, in particular—was decidedly new, but there is reason to assume that many of the perspectives it promoted were indigenous to and engrained in the region's Jewish culture.

Why, then, did Rhineland Pietism emerge under the leadership of R. Samuel the Pietist in the mid-twelfth century, flourish under the leadership of his son Rabbi Judah the Pietist (d. 1217), and recede from view following the death of Judah's disciple, Elazar of Worms in 1238? I would suggest that Rhineland Pietism came onto the scene when certain learned Jews of the region who disapproved of the pedagogic and social changes that were eclipsing the status quo put up a fight. As part of their combative strategy, they inscribed their—now beleaguered—perspectives and practices for the very first time. As was true within Christian society, where "scholasticism overcame its most ardent opponents by forcing them to struggle against it on its own terms,"[39] Ashkenazi defenders of the old ways had no choice but to adopt the tools of textualization. Exigencies of the time prompted them to abandon the prevailing code of orality, and to make parts of their world accessible in writing.[40] It was only at this point that Rhineland Pietism, richly textured and fully formed, gained the notice of readers (historians among them). The literary undertakings of the Rhineland Pietists illuminated regional customs that were already well entrenched and that had long been practiced by individuals, if not by whole groups of Jews. If Rhineland Pietism's three generations of standard bearers are seen as the consolidators and scribes of these earlier attitudes and practices, rather than as their originators, it is easier to understand how and why the short-lived phenomenon could have had an impact so disproportionate to its brief lifespan. A penchant for self-abnegation and separatism had always been indigenous to the area, but because *Ḥaside Ashkenaz* profiled it and preserved its specifics in writing, subsequent Jews mistakenly identified Rhineland Pietism as the source of these eccentricities.

Just as this theory explains the timing of Rhineland Pietism's "sudden" emergence into literary visibility and accounts for its disproportionate cultural impact on subsequent Ashkenazi life, the context of textualization helps to explain Pietism's equally sudden disappearance from the historical picture. Though Rabbi Judah b. Samuel of Pietism's second generation had made the decision to inscribe formerly oral traditions (esoteric *sodot* among them), he was able to ensure the continued need for the master-disciple relationship by composing his works in an intentionally elliptical style.[41] Unless or until Rabbi Judah's writings were elucidated—through oral instruction—readers could not grasp their meaning. However, in the third generation of *Ḥaside Ashkenaz*, R. Elazar of Worms consciously abandoned the esoteric register of writing that had been used by his teacher, and inscribed Pietist teachings in genres that could be understood even by readers who had no living masters to guide them. Through compositions like *Sefer ha-Roqeaḥ*, a compendium that blended halakhah with Pietist traditions, R. Elazar "domesticated" attitudes and practices that had previously been associated with an elite community. His literary activity "dissolved" the boundaries that had ensured the Pietists' social distinctiveness, and made it possible for many of Pietism's features to be absorbed—or resorbed—as Ashkenazi cultural norms.

Why was Rhineland Pietism such a riveting and ferocious literary presence for a brief historical moment? Insights from the study of medieval Christian culture may help to address this question. Few creative works of painting, sculpture, or literature were produced by Christians in eleventh-century Europe, while many were produced in the twelfth. Stephen Jaeger accounted for this discrepancy by explaining that Christian seekers of the eleventh century would not have been contented with representation of their ideals. "That age," he wrote, "had—or sought—the thing itself."[42] When, by contrast, Christian cultural productivity skyrocketed in the next two centuries, asserted Jaeger, it was because Christian seekers no longer experienced "the real presence" of the master as the authentic "bearer of culture." Under these circumstances of loss, the best that could be done was to create souvenirs: "Many of the great artifacts of the twelfth century are born out of the nostalgic urge to recapture the incomparable personality and moral heroism of the eleventh century."[43] Jaeger's interpretation may help to explain two intertwined phenomena: why the *ḥasidim* and *perushim* of pre-Crusade Ashkenaz did not make it onto the radar screen of readers, and why historians encountering the monuments to the Pietist worldview mistakenly assumed that this group had emerged as a *sui generis* cultural phenomenon in the twelfth-century Rhineland. The intense awareness on the part of Pietists that an entire cultural orientation was being eclipsed impelled them to make of charisma "an object for study and reading,"[44] and inspired them to capture their worldview for posterity.

Pietist Responses to Textualization

Various poorly understood features of Rhineland Pietism come into clearer focus when they are seen as reactions to the textualization process and its cultural corollaries. Some Pietist perspectives overtly protest social and cultural changes; others pointedly perpetuate attitudes and practices that were displaced or under attack. Certain claims reflect the Pietists' need to accommodate to the new standards of textualization, others "compensate" by integrating new cultural developments into the framework of an older cultural logic, and still others carve out new arenas of behavior in which the assumptions and practices of *memoria* culture would continue to prevail.

Pietist Protest

Pietism's critique of authors who claim credit for their compositions can be construed as one of its frontal attacks on the changes wrought by the textualization process. Noting the absence of historical precedent for this practice, several passages in *Sefer Ḥasidim* emphasize its novelty and implicitly challenge its legitimacy.[45]

> After all, Rabbi [Judah the Patriarch] arranged the *mishnayyot* and he did not write, "I did them." Nor did [the composers of] *beraitot* and *midrashot* say who wrote them, "I, so and so, son of such and such, composed them; I made them."[46]

According to *Sefer Ḥasidim*, revered authors of the past chose to remain anonymous because they knew that a closed economy of merit operates in the life of every individual.[47] They understood that any rewards received in one's lifetime—whether the satisfaction of having one's authorship acknowledged, or the birth of male children—consumed some of the finite resources of reward allotted to an individual during his time on earth and in the hereafter. It was for this reason, explains *Sefer Ḥasidim*, that early writers guarded their anonymity: to refrain from courting reward.

> For this reason, early sages did not write books in their names, nor would they permit [others] to write their names in their books . . . lest he derive benefit from this world, and [in so doing,] damage his reward in the next world. Or they [the accountants of Fate?] might diminish his [reward] in this world—through his offspring and the good reputation of his offspring, in keeping with the measure of benefit that he derived in this world from his reputation, having derived benefit from his name.[48]

Beyond this, notes *Sefer Ḥasidim*, anyone who claims credit for his composition engages in self-praise and nourishes pride, a characterological flaw with dire consequences:[49] "About these it is said: [Prov. 10:7], 'the fame of the wicked rots,' and [Ps. 9:7] 'their very names are lost forever.' "[50] While *Sefer Ḥasidim* reserves its sharpest censure for contemporary composers of liturgical poetry [*paytanim*] who—unlike their modest, anonymous predecessors[51]—showcase their authorship by weaving their names into poems,[52] it also attacks writers of other Jewish genres (including tosafist glosses on Talmud)[53] who pride themselves on their compositional activities: "If a sage wrote many books, like *Tosafot*, let him not think well of himself, saying that he will be saved from Gehenna."[54]

Pietist criticism of dialectic largely targets the baser motives that attracted some of its devotees.[55] *Sefer Ḥasidim* cautions that a teacher must refrain from giving instruction to those who participate in "competitive learning—for example, two who engage in debate in order to best the other";[56] it encourages a person in a position to offer financial help to contribute to "righteous people who will engage Torah" and avoid those "who split *qushiyyot* [*quaestiones*] in order to display their acuity."[57] Unless the pursuit of dialectics has some higher goal, declares *Sefer Ḥasidim*, even rote learning of the laws is of greater value. Referring to the verse (Eccl. 4:6), "Better a fistful of gratification than two fistfuls of labor—which is pursuit of wind," *Sefer Ḥasidim* comments: "Better to know the rulings of applied laws [*pisqe halakhot le-ma'aseh*] than to know how to engage in talmudic casuistry—in order to show off."[58] While *Sefer Ḥasidim* speaks of a scholar "who reviles his own Torah,"[59] and of logicians who are wicked,[60] its attack on the attention-craving exhibitionism of some talmudic dialecticians is not a preemptive attack on *pilpul* (talmudic casuistry) per se. The term *dialeqtiqa shel goyyim*, literally "gentile dialectic," specifically denotes the inappropriate uses of dialectical reasoning.[61] The Pietists' critique of dialectic was qualified and in no way an attack on analytical engagement with the talmudic text or a blanket indictment of tosafist literature.[62] In fact, *Sefer Ḥasidim* emphasizes the importance of acquiring the glosses of the Tosafot (along with other commentaries) if these texts are not available in a particular location,[63] and it refers approvingly to a Pietist who, for the benefit of the many, hired a scribe to make copies of talmudic commentaries, novellae, and Tosafot.[64] *Sefer Ḥasidim* may well have appreciated the tosafists' rigorous analysis of the underlying texts, for it heartily encouraged students who were capable of doing so to undertake active, inferential learning:[65]

> Why is it said [*Sifra, Meẓora'*, 3] that one neither teaches a *ḥakham* [wise one] nor explains to a *ḥakham*? Because it says [Prov. 1:5], "*the wise one, hearing them, will add more wisdom.*" Since he is wise, if he [the instructor] were to explain to him, he would not apply himself to understand one matter from another.[66]

Like medieval monks who criticized its excessive use yet still employed it in the service of "mystery,"[67] Rhineland Pietists understood that dialectic was a tool that enabled trained students to draw non-explicit information from a text. *Sefer Ḥasidim* was realistic about the range in student abilities, but it identified creativity in learning as the ideal for one who could discover new insights in the body of tradition and make them his own: "Insofar as he is engaged with Torah and is innovating within it, it is as if it [Torah] is his, and it came from him.[68]

Pietist Perpetuation of Older Cultural Patterns

At a time when the religious authorities for most northern European Jews were rabbis renowned for their dialectical prowess, Rhineland Pietists reserved their highest esteem for different types of authority figures: the charismatic advisor (*ḥakham*) and the wonder worker (*ba'al shem ma'asim*). Valuing something quite distinct from intellectual ability in their leaders, Pietists sought masters who were "conveyors of the real presence,"[69] individuals who embodied the lessons to be learned. A legend that appears in the Yiddish *Maysebukh* offers a stark assessment of the relative cultural worths of two different types of Jewish leaders. Though this work was not published until 1602, analyses of earlier manuscripts led Sara Ẓfatman to determine that the work's most coherent unit, the twenty-five tales about R. Samuel the Pietist and his son Judah the Pietist, may have been told by the Pietists themselves.[70] The tale in question pits the charismatic wonder worker, renowned for his connection to higher worlds, against the *rosh yeshivah,* head of the rabbinic academy.[71] According to this legend, when the students of R. Samuel the Pietist teased him about his younger son's wild behavior, he put both his children to a "trial"—in order to divine their potential for learning. The reactions of the two boys revealed to R. Samuel that the undisciplined younger child (later to be known as R. Judah the Pietist) had greater aptitude for engaging the mysteries of the Divine than did his brother. Upon making this discovery, R. Samuel broke the bad news to his older son: "Abraham my son: The hour is propitious for your brother Judah! Know that you will be a *rosh yeshivah* all your days, but your brother Judah will know what is above and what is below, and nothing will be hidden from him, and he will be a Master of the Name and of wonders [*ba'al shem ma'asim*]."[72] At a time when the authority of the *rosh yeshivah* had eclipsed that of the charismatic Jewish leader, Pietists pointedly affirmed a different social hierarchy, one that reflected their own ideals.

Rhineland Pietists rejected many of the curricular changes that were concomitant with the new prominence of Talmud in study and adjudication. Though the tosafist Rabbenu Tam had claimed that the obligation to study Mishnah was fulfilled through the study of Talmud, Pietists continued to pursue Mishnah as a separate subject of study.[73] Moreover, *Sefer Ḥasidim* encouraged students to create their own mnemonic arrangements of tradition, citing a geonic-era compilation as one such example: "And even if he does not innovate within it [tradition], but [only] arranges it, as did Mar Yehudai Gaon when he saw that hearts were becoming diminished, and he made *Halakhot Gedolot* in brief . . . that a person might know."[74]

Though tosafists themselves commented on talmudic passages pertaining to the sacrificial cult and to purity regulations that could not be upheld in the Temple's absence, it would seem that this was not the pedagogic practice of all Jews at this time.[75] This can be seen in the Pietists' chastisement of others for allowing utilitarian considerations to guide their rabbinic curriculum and in Rabbi Samuel the Pietist's brilliant revaluation of the term "*met miẓvah*," literally "dead miẓvah." In ancient rabbinic sources, this phrase denotes the supreme obligation of giving a proper burial to a Jew who died in a place where there was no established Jewish community to perform this activity.[76] Exhorting Pietists to study portions of Oral Torah that others neglected, R. Samuel refers to them as precepts that have been given up for dead: "When you see a dead miẓvah, in which none engage—for example, you see the people of your town studying *Seder Mo'ed* and *Seder Neziqin* [which treat of utilitarian matters]—you should study *Seder Qodashim* [whose laws cannot be implemented in the Temple's absence]."[77] The Pietists' programmatic credo (which was implemented as curricular policy in the rabbinic academy of Evreux)[78] affirmed that no component of tradition could possibly be discarded. This, of course, was consistent with the "omnivorous" cultural proclivities of northern European Jews that predated Rhineland Pietism's emergence and that persisted after its demise.

Pietists who continued to embrace the plenitude of received tradition did not shy away from acknowledging non-talmudic sources of legal authority. Indeed, they appealed to Mishnah as a source of practical halakhah,[79] and they invoked aggadah in defending certain legal decisions.[80] It is tempting to imagine that their appreciation for the thought of Sa'adya Gaon was based, in part, on the fact that he insisted that "the text" alone could not impart the entirety of tradition.[81] The similarity between the perspectives of Sa'adya and of Rhineland Pietists, who accepted the authority of Talmud but did not regard it as a self-sufficient text, did not go unnoticed: Sa'adya Gaon and Judah the Pietist were among the thinkers singled out for excoriation by R. Moses ben Ḥasdai Taqu, a tosafist of thirteenth-century Bohemia, who vehemently opposed the use of "outside writings" to interpret either Scripture or Talmud.[82] Apart from regarding non-talmudic texts as repositories of cultural authority, the Rhineland Pietists recognized a higher, and non-written source, to which they had supreme allegiance: *reẓon ha-Boreh*, the will of the Creator.[83]

* * *

The poorly understood practice of textual tampering associated with medieval Ashkenaz in general and with Rhineland Pietist circles in particular[84] assumes considerable clarity when seen in the context of the textualization process. Manuscripts of the Jerusalem Talmud's tractate *Sheqalim* that circulated in Pietist circles constitute the most widely discussed example of this phenomenon.[85] As Ya'aqov Sussman showed, the erasures, interpolations, and alterations made in this family of manuscripts tended to bring the Jerusalem Talmud's perspectives into greater accord with those of the Babylonian Talmud—and these emendations continued to be made over a prolonged period of time. In Sussman's opinion, this family of manuscripts bears witness to a process that had once shaped all rabbinic writings.

> It seems to me that the account of the incarnations of versions of [the Jerusalem Talmud's tractate] *Sheqalim* does not only teach about itself, but also teaches about the manner in which rabbinic literature was transmitted, and about the manner in which manuscript versions/traditions came into being.[86]

In other words, Jews of the medieval Rhineland who boldly altered manuscripts of the Jerusalem Talmud tractate *Sheqalim* were keeping alive a once ubiquitous practice that other Jews of their environment had abandoned. While the tosafists were striving to produce a "correct" exemplar of the Babylonian Talmud, unknown scholars connected with Pietist circles perpetuated an older practice; they engaged tradition (in this case, the Jerusalem Talmud) not as curators, but as tradents. At a time when tosafists chose to comment on tradition from the margins, some Pietist scholars brought the text into line with their own lived reality by inserting their own voices directly into the accumulated body of learning.

An exhortation made in the first generation of Rhineland Pietism by R. Samuel, father of Judah, may offer insight into the mindset of scholars who felt that they were welcome to improve upon existing formulations of tradition. The curious blend of perspectives captured in R. Samuel's written remarks (later incorporated into *Sefer Ḥasidim*) marks a particular moment in the textualization process, for while he envisioned a reading public for his work, he did not claim absolute ownership of its content:

> I have arranged this *Sefer ha-Yirah* [Book of Reverence] in order that one who fears God's word might be cautious. . . . And if I have erred in it, let the wise one correct it and understand it [make it understandable to others], in order that he fear God all his days, in truth.[87]

Like ancient and geonic predecessors who were influenced by the assumptions and practices of late antiquity,[88] Samuel the Pietist assumed that tradition was the shared inheritance of all. Thus, when he attempted to represent tradition in writing, he welcomed (and even encouraged) learned readers to make whatever changes were needed to make this written simulacrum more accurate.

Pietist Accommodation: The Invention of a Textual Past

As texts came increasingly to be regarded as bearers of cultural authority, Jews of northern Europe sought to link their undocumented practices to ancient written sources. Even Pietists, who so valued the ideals of oral culture, had to capitulate, for, as Brian Stock explained, once "the sole means of establishing a position's legitimacy is the discovery of a written precedent, the rules of the game are radically altered."[89] Though Pietists continued to valorize instruction through oral teaching and behavioral modeling, the very inscription of *Sefer Ḥasidim* irrevocably altered the status quo ante. This written work—which presents itself as a teacher!—is an outright oxymoron.[90] Whether or not the inscription of *Sefer Ḥasidim* transformed Pietists into a text-based community whose readers knew one another personally, its circulation created a kinship among readers who were linked by their recognition of a common heritage and of a shared text of stature.[91]

Unlike tosafists, who acknowledged the gap between present and past, and who bridged it through dialectical filiation of text and practice, Rhineland Pietists denied the existence of any temporal gap. In support of the claim that nothing in Jewish life had changed, the Pietists adduced ancient texts that would endow their own attitudes and practices with unquestionable legitimacy. When such texts did not exist, Pietists brought them into being by cobbling sources together in literary pastiches.

Three examples will be cited to illustrate the Rhineland Pietists' invention of a textual past. In his pathbreaking analysis of post-biblical Jewish traditions about the actual slaughter and subsequent resurrection of the patriarch Isaac, Shalom Spiegel demonstrated that the constituent details of this narrative had ancient rabbinic precedents, but their resulting medieval assemblages were wholly new creations.[92] In the twelfth century, at a moment of psychological and spiritual crisis in Ashkenazi history, R. Ephraim of Bonn's poetic narrative of the *completed* sacrifice of Isaac, stitched together from ancient aggadot, gave comfort to fellow Jews and endowed their suffering with theological meaning. The ostensibly ancestral template he offered his Jewish contemporaries helped them make sense of their own travails and strengthened their faith.

The use of literary interpolation to create a usable textual past was also discerned by Ivan Marcus in his study of medieval Jewish rites of pedagogic initiation.[93] When, in Pietism's final generation, Elazar of Worms first wrote about a Shavu'ot (Pentecost) ceremony initiating a young Jewish boy into study, he described it as an old practice, an ancestral custom. As Marcus explained, the decision to describe this ceremony in writing seems to have been triggered by a specific negative stimulus: the tosafists' claim that age alone should determine when a Jewish boy would begin his course of study. Pietists, who wanted to ensure that the onset of Jewish education would be construed as a sacred rite of passage and not a mere biological function of age, disagreed; they prescribed the performance of this educational initiation ceremony on Shavu'ot, the festival of Revelation.[94] As the tosafists' perspective gained ground, Elazar enhanced the legitimacy of the Pietist ceremony by linking it exegetically to a biblical passage and giving it a textual basis.[95]

Finally, the Rhineland Pietists invented a textual past to justify their ascetic behaviors and acts of self-mortification, penitential undertakings that had considerable impact on subsequent Ashkenazi culture and on Jewish practices in many other regions.[96] While some researchers assumed that these behaviors reflected Christian influence,[97] others argued that the Pietists' penitential practices were rooted in ancient Judaism.[98] Scholars holding this opinion drew attention to accounts of ascetic practice in tannaitic sources, some of which were motivated by the impulse to atone, and others by the desire to prophylactically stave off future calamity.[99] Yet *Sefer Ḥasidim*'s depiction of Adam as a penitent who, for 130 years, stood up to his neck in the waters of the Giḥon river[100] conflates disparate rabbinic traditions in order to root one of the Pietists' more bizarre penances in sacred history.

Why was such a literary pastiche necessary at this time? And why were accounts of penitential practices plucked from the rabbinic archive (e.g., ancient legends about the atonement of Judah[101] and the self-mortification of Naḥum of Gamzu and Yaqim of Ẓerorot)[102] ascribed such prominence and authority in this time and place?[103] After all, the extreme acts of atonement practiced by ascetics had long been part of the rabbinic heritage, yet it was only this Jewish subculture of the medieval Rhineland that glorified such acts as social ideals. What was the proximate cause?

In her literary analysis of *Sefer Ḥasidim*, Tamar Alexander identified one particularly unsettling passage, the "Tale of the Three Penitents" (SḤ 52–53) as a sui generis creation of the Rhineland Pietists.[104] In this passage, each of three men relating his story to a confessor figure explains how he had withstood extraordinary temptation over a long period of time. More than this, each had assiduously cultivated the temptation in question—theft, murder, and adultery, respectively—by engineering the conditions and circumstances that would make transgression most likely. As each man confessed his deeds, he inquired of the *ḥakham* (wise man) whether he might expect to be rewarded for his forbearance.

Both the eyebrow-raising behaviors of the three men and their hopes of receiving reward indicate that they were attempting to fulfill one of the four methods of penance identified by Rhineland Pietists, that known as "*teshuvah ha-ba-ah*," probably a truncation of "*teshuvah 'al 'averah she-ba-ah le-yado*," "repentance for a sin which comes one's way."[105] According to the Talmud, *teshuvah ha-ba-ah* could be performed if an individual managed to steer clear of sin when he found himself in a situation identical to one in which he had previously transgressed—when he was, in the language of the Talmud, "with the same woman, at the same time, in the same place."[106] Still, while *teshuvah ha-ba-ah* has talmudic roots, the situations depicted in *Sefer Ḥasidim* hardly conform to the Talmud's definition of this form of penance. Indeed, as Asher Rubin pointed out in an undeservedly neglected article, when *Sefer Ḥasidim* translated the Talmud's Aramaic question, "How can a penitent be described?" (*heikhi damei ba'al teshuvah?*) into "How should one repent/perform penitence?" (*keizad ya'aseh adam teshuvah?*), it transformed the talmudic description of a penitent into a programmatic guide, a prescription for penance in general.[107] One crucial difference separates this mode of Pietist penance from the talmudic perspective: each of the would-be penitents in *Sefer Ḥasidim* assiduously flirted with sin by (repeatedly) revisiting the "scene of the crime," yet in none of the cases had any sin actually been committed! If anything, the underlying logic of the *teshuvah ha-ba-ah* penance seems quite similar to that of the ordeal.

Was there any Jewish precedent for construing such behavior as a form of penance? Various Jewish sources laud the fortitude shown by men (from the biblical Joseph onward) who withstood overwhelming sexual temptation, and two ancient rabbinic traditions describe instances in which temptation was intentionally courted by figures who wished to withstand it.[108] Yet none of these passages have anything to do with penance or atonement. Medieval Christian sources provide more obvious parallels to the activities of the penitents in *Sefer Ḥasidim*'s narrative. Twelfth- and thirteenth-century Latin documents from England and Gaul reflect the attempt to expunge the practice of *syneisaktism* (literally, the introduction of a spiritual companion of the opposite sex)[109] which, under Irish influence, had become a form of penance.[110] Medieval sources testify to the fact that certain male ascetics explicitly sought out the company of women in order to have the opportunity to incite lust and conquer it.[111] The practice of this penance by Robert of Arbrissel (d. 1117), wandering hermit, preacher to men and women, and founder of the monastery at Fontevrault, made his ecclesiastical contemporaries anxious. While the bishop of Rennes and the abbot of Trinité de Vendôme expressed admiration for Robert's zeal (and evangelical success), they implored him to renounce practices that were perilous to his own virtue and to that of others. It seems that, in order to atone for the sins of his youth, Robert regularly undertook a "*martyrium*," a practice in which he slept, chastely, among the women whom he had converted from a life of sin.[112] Evidence of such a practice—designed to promote spiritual progress by arousing, and withstanding, temptations of the flesh—also comes from a thirteenth-century Christian cleric who lived closer to the locale of the Rhineland Pietists, though, historically speaking, his condemnation is somewhat late.[113]

A book that appeared one century before the emergence of Rhineland Pietism transformed the nature of Christian penance; its ecclesiastical author was closely connected to the towns of Speyer, Mainz, and Worms. One book of Bishop Burchard of Worms' *Decretum*, a twenty-volume canonical collection, undoubtedly enhanced both the popularity and the cultural cachet of some of the more extreme Christian penitential practices—including the conspicuous penances undertaken in public spaces, such as immersion in icy rivers.[114] The Nineteenth Book of this compilation was itself a penitential tract, called *The Corrector*, and it ended four hundred years of church opposition to the penitential literature that the Irish had exported to the continent.[115] Burchard appropriated material from earlier penitentials—texts of dubious authority—but he circumspectly hid their original sources and invented more reputable attributions.[116] Not only did the inclusion of penitential traditions in a canonical anthology bend the boundaries of genre, it launched a new phase in Christian penitential culture.[117] Burchard's *Decretum* dominated the canonical tradition until the composition of Gratian's own collection in the mid-twelfth century,[118] and its penitential component, *The Corrector*, continued to be used into the thirteenth century, especially where sexual sins were concerned.[119] Guided by confessors who consulted penitential tracts, Christians in many European lands had long engaged in acts of penance, but Burchard's *Corrector* granted them a new respectability by bringing penitential traditions into the ecclesiastical mainstream and catapulting them to greater visibility, not only among Christians, but among Jews as well.

It was within this broader environment that Rhineland Pietists legitimated their own practices of self-mortification by producing previously unknown Hebrew texts, replete with putative antecedents. When Pietists unconsciously appropriated some of the demanding penitential practices of their Christian neighbors that had gained new visibility in the medieval Rhineland, they fused disparate elements of Jewish tradition in order to create for these practices a hallowed Jewish pedigree. At a time and place when it would have been unthinkable to acknowledge the influence exerted by the despised majority culture, Ashkenazi Pietists produced a usable textual past.[120]

The Pietists' Interest in the Book as Artifact

Pietists decried the displacement of certain practices associated with memory culture, but they greatly valued the transmission of knowledge that the written book made possible. Thus, for example, *Sefer Ḥasidim* strongly endorses the lending of books, even while it can imagine the possibility of vandalism:

"Better . . . that people learn from his books and erase them, than that the books be in a private place [*maqom muẓna'*] and nobody learns from them."[121]

The Pietists were also profoundly interested in the technology and paraphernalia of book production, and they paid close attention to the cultural status of the written artifact. Scholars of Hebrew codicology have noted that *Sefer Ḥasidim* is exceptional among medieval writings in the amount of detailed information it offers about the book as a material object.[122] Hundreds of its passages refer to different stages of book production, to the many implements used in pricking, ruling, inking, erasing, binding, covering, and fastening books,[123] and to the artisans' work habits.[124] *Sefer Ḥasidim* also relates to the book as a commodity; it describes which bound manuscripts are best suited to the rental market, stipulates the conditions under which a purloined book may be ransomed for more than its fair price, and describes a range of economic and social interactions in which Christians and Jews came together over books.[125] *Sefer Ḥasidim*'s admonitions to copyists not to invert the order of words,[126] add colophons, inscribe their names in acrostic form, or include written invocations for God's help underscore the Pietists' valorization of the written artifact.

These warnings also reflect *Sefer Ḥasidim*'s perception of people involved in the manufacture of books as agents of higher matters.[127] Whether the artisan prepares the parchment, pricks the holes used for ruling lines, plumbs the lines, stitches the quires together, or binds the book, his labors build and maintain written vessels of the sacred. And when compared with earlier writings, *Sefer Ḥasidim*'s formidable anthology of regulations regarding "*sefarim*"—literally "books," but in this case, a term whose referent will need to be clarified—stands out. The Pietists were clearly familiar with regulations designed to promote the principle of *kevod Sefer Torah*, "reverence for the Torah scroll," and *kevod ha-sefer*, "reverence for the book"—and to discourage its opposite, *bizayon ha-sefer*, "disrespect for the book,"[128] that were all found in Talmud[129] and in the later *Massekhet Sofrim*;[130] these rabbinic passages discussed the treatment to be accorded inscribed texts—mostly Torah scrolls and their accoutrements—in the synagogue, study hall, and home.[131] Yet the behavioral standards imposed in *Sefer Ḥasidim* for the treatment of *sefarim* are more stringent than those found in earlier sources, and the array of life situations involving *sefarim* that *Sefer Ḥasidim* seeks to regulate is far broader. For example, it is forbidden to use a *sefer* to hide from another, or to shield one's face from sun or smoke (SḤ 504–6). One may not touch a *sefer* if he has just wiped his nose (SḤ 252), nor kiss a *sefer* after having kissed his dirty children (SḤ 274). A teacher may not hit a student with a *sefer*, nor may a student use a *sefer* to shield himself, unless the blows are life-threatening (SḤ 276). An intensification of earlier regulations is particularly evident in *Sefer Ḥasidim*'s stipulations regarding the *sefer*'s accessories. Toddlers may not walk on a low table that is designated to hold *sefarim* (SḤ 520). A *sefer* may not be closed over a pen, nor may it be used to store one's notes (SḤ 499). If tallow drips onto a *sefer*, it may not be scooped up and put back onto the candle (SḤ 495). If a large *sefer* with a latch cannot be closed easily, one may not squeeze it shut with his knees in order to fasten it (SḤ 656). One who wishes to ease the pressure of a blister may not open it using a pen, an awl, or a needle used in binding a *sefer* (SḤ 1755). The margins of a *sefer* may not be used for recording debts, for doing calculations, or for trying out one's pen, for these are not in keeping with the principle of *kevod ha-sefer* (SḤ 102, 645; cf. 661, 665).[132] In some cases, *Sefer Ḥasidim* appropriates existing rabbinic regulations and widens the spatial zone in which taboos are to be applied. For example, the Talmud (BT Shab. 14a) forbids one to appear naked in a room containing a Torah scroll, but *Sefer Ḥasidim* even prohibits the placement of *sefarim* on pillows and bedcovers, since one sits on them unclothed (SḤ 648).

The sheer density of regulations, all novel with respect to earlier legislation, if not sui generis, suggests that the Pietists were attempting to alter something within the cultural or legal status quo. But what, precisely, was at stake, and how did this miscellany of rules benefit or affirm the Pietist worldview?

Preserving the Old Cultural Logic: Sacralizing the Texts of Oral Matters

Rhineland Pietists were aware that a long-prevailing cultural logic had been disturbed: Notwithstanding the ancient proscription against "saying *oral matters* in writing," Jews of their time routinely read aloud from written texts of Talmud and other corpora in the category of *oral matters*. Pietists could not reverse this development, but they could restore the integrity of the rabbinic regulations that governed the treatment of *written matters* and *oral matters* by tweaking the existing taxonomy of Jewish knowledge. Rhineland Pietists reaffirmed the coherence of the traditional cultural logic by assigning the newly inscribed writings a different address on the map of sacred texts.

As the first northern European Jews to introduce non-scriptural writings into a longstanding rabbinic conversation about "*sefarim*" (singular, "*sefer*"), "books," Rhineland Pietists do not appear to have known that this step had already been taken by Sefardi contemporaries.[133] Rhineland Pietists made the taxonomic point that certain inscriptions of *oral matters* belonged squarely in the category of sacred texts, *kitvei qodesh*, by articulating the cluster of regulations itemized above. It is here that the referent of the terms "*sefer*" and "*sefarim*" become all important. Earlier rabbinic prescriptions pertaining to the treatment of *sefarim* seem to have had only scriptural writings in mind—whether this term designated the tripartite Tanakh or its constituent parts,[134] but *Sefer Ḥasidim* expressly applies the term "*sefarim*" to non-scriptural writings, and specifically to the written texts of Mishnah and Talmud.[135] Thus, it asserts, worn-out pages of Talmud, like those of Scripture, may not be thrown away but must be put into a *genizah*, a chamber for texts containing the name of God that have become unusable (SḤ 698).[136] In setting forth the rationale for expanding the domain of sacred texts, *Sefer Ḥasidim* invokes a law pertaining to ritual impurity, notwithstanding the fact that laws of this sort do not apply in the absence of the Temple. The Talmud (BT Shab.14a) had forbidden the storage of sacred (scriptural) writings in the place of the *terumah*, the heave offering of grain or wine or oil, lest the texts be nibbled by mice. Noting that inscriptions of Oral Torah contain the Divine Name, *Sefer Ḥasidim* asserts that the same rule applies to texts of Oral Torah: "And even though [laws of] ritual impurity do not apply in our time . . . so, too, nowadays, one must not put books [*sefarim*] with foods, so that the mice not eat them. And it says [Deut. 12:4], 'You shall not do this to the Lord your God,' and in order that one not cause God's Name to be erased [cf. BT Shab. 120b], as in [Lev. 22:21], 'No blemish shall be upon it'—that he not cause this to happen to God's Name."[137]

In some cases, *Sefer Ḥasidim* maps out regulations pertaining to inscriptions of Mishnah and Talmud by building upon existing hierarchies of sanctity articulated by earlier rabbis. These include distinctions between Pentateuch, Prophetic, and Hagiographic writings on the one hand[138] and between scroll and codex on the other.[139] According to *Sefer Ḥasidim*, Written Torah is to be saved before Oral Torah in case of a fire (SḤ 603),[140] and Oral Torah is to be sold before Written Torah in case of financial need (SḤ 666). Texts of Oral Torah possess a lesser degree of sanctity, and should ideally be housed in separate bookshelves from texts of Written Torah (SḤ 646). Yet while the artifacts of Oral Torah may be of lower rank, they are nonetheless sacred: a text of Talmud must not be used as a placemarker in a Pentateuch (SḤ 1748).[141]

The Pietists' reference to texts of Oral Torah as "*sefarim*" was not simply a sleight of nomenclature; the insertion of Talmud into the category of *sefer* and the subjection of this text to a range of regulations signaled the redefinition of its ontological status.[142] Indeed, the Pietists' placement of the talmudic artifact in the category of the sacred implicitly put them at odds with the tosafists. Whereas the tosafists believed (and demonstrated) that the Talmud's authority was a function of its logic, the Pietists (implicitly) claimed that Talmud's authority stemmed from its essence as a sacred artifact. Inaugurating a move that was further developed by certain Jewish mystics,[143] Pietists acknowledged the power of written Talmud as a "charismatic text,"[144] and insisted that its authority had nothing to do with logic or with the process of human reasoning. By emphasizing the sanctity of the material artifact itself, Pietists, in effect, dismissed the Talmud's discursive meaning as being of little or no import.

A legend preserved in the *Maysebukh,*[145] depicting an apocryphal encounter between R. Samuel the Pietist, recently returned from many years in self-imposed exile,[146] and Rabbenu Tam, may allude to this opposition. Upon coming to the home of the great tosafist, R. Samuel introduced himself as "Samuel the Parchment Maker" and refrained from speaking words of Torah. Nonetheless, one of Rabbenu Tam's students discerned that the wayfarer was a person of great learning, and he shared this insight with his master: "Rabbenu Jacob, my master and teacher: Yesterday, when you asked the guest who lodged with you what his name was, he answered you correctly, 'Samuel who prepares skins which are called parchment.' That is because he is thoroughly familiar with their contents."[147] While Rabbenu Tam's student clearly understood more than his teacher, there is no way of knowing whether he perceived the full significance of Samuel's chosen moniker. Given his belief in the sanctity of the material artifact itself, the leader of Rhineland Pietism's first generation may not only have been exhibiting modesty when he introduced himself as "Samuel the Parchment Maker."

The Pietists' strategy of sacralization had a potent counterpart in medieval Christian culture. At a time when their *sancta*-based power was being threatened by the growing authority of text, medieval churchmen sacralized deeds of sale, charters, and other legally binding documents by placing them on church altars.[148] Rhineland Pietists performed an analogous cultural maneuver when they applied the principle of *kevod sefarim* to the written texts of Oral Torah.[149] Through this strategy of "enchantment," Pietists made it possible for a cultural framework of long duration to accommodate a new technological reality.

Pietist "Re-Memorialization" of Prayer

As noted in Chapter 4, the composition of *sidurim* (weekday and sabbath prayer books) and *maḥzorim* (festival prayer books) in the eleventh and twelfth centuries, and their growing use,[150] necessitated certain cultural adjustments, since prayer (like Talmud) is a corpus in the category of *oral matters.*[151] Tosafists reacted in one way, by acknowledging the change that had occurred and by justifying it.[152] Rhineland Pietists reacted to the inscription of Jewish liturgy in quite a different manner, sensitive to the fact that one of the clearest victims of the textualization process was the spontaneity of prayer.[153] While acknowledging the ubiquity of prayer texts, *Sefer Ḥasidim* expressed an implicit preference for worship that does not rely upon props of this sort: "One who cannot pray with *kavvanah* [intention] without a *sidur* in which the prayer is written—and so, too, a sated person who cannot concentrate on *birkat ha-mazon* [Grace after Meals]—should read from a book in which *birkat ha-mazon* is written."[154] The availability of the written prayer book had made it possible for any literate Jewish male of majority age—or as a responsum of the early thirteenth century put it, any Tom, Dick, or Harry—to serve as the prayer emissary [*sheliaḥ ẓibbur*]: "But nowadays . . . it is an everyday occurrence that Reuben prays [leads] *Shaḥarit* [the morning prayer], Simeon reads Torah, and Levi prays [leads] *Musaf* [the additional prayer for Sabbaths or Festivals]."[155] *Sefer Ḥasidim* decried this slippage into an egalitarianism of all Jewish males, for it regarded the prayer emissary as the officiant of a sacrament. The emissary, insisted *Sefer Ḥasidim*, cannot simply be any literate male selected by the majority; he must be someone appointed by consensus. If one were to assume this (sacramental) role without being acceptable to *all*, his prayers might prove dangerous—to the community as well as to himself.[156]

A distinctive Pietist prayer practice that piqued the curiosity of scholars[157] can be understood as one that parried some of the unwelcome byproducts of liturgy's inscription. The practice in question is described in a *Sefer Ḥasidim* narrative about a *ḥakham* (sage) who came to a town and tried out both its synagogues before choosing to worship in the smaller one rather than the one frequented by many people of rank. When asked why, the *ḥakham* explained that he preferred the small synagogue because its congregants recited the blessings and Psalms in a drawn-out fashion (*bi-meshekh*), a pace he found more comfortable given what he himself did during prayer:

> I am groaning to/enlarging the Holy One blessed be He [*va-ani marviyyaḥ la-Qadosh Barukh Hu*] when I draw out, counting on my fingers how many *alef*'s and *bet*'s in that Psalm, how many of each and every letter. And afterward, when I return to my house, I come up with a reason why [there are] such and such [quantities of each letter].[158]

According to the *ḥakham*, his activity was undertaken in two stages that did not need to be carried out in the same setting.[159] During communal prayer, while others (or at least the prayer emissary) recited the prayers aloud, the Pietist made a count of the words and letters of prayer, keeping a physical record. When he later got home, he did something with the numerical data he had collected.

How are we to understand this praxis—both its mechanics and its religious-cultural meaning? Ruminations on the latter must remain in the realm of speculation, but a range of medieval sources, Jewish and non-Jewish, facilitate reconstruction of the activity itself. From antiquity to the present, people in both Christian and Muslim lands have used their fingers for record keeping and computation.[160] Writing in early eighth-century England, the Venerable Bede recommended "the language of fingers" (*manualis loquela*) as a mode of communication that could be used in the presence of persons who were indiscreet or dangerous,[161] and his treatise on the ecclesiastical calendar, *De Temporum Ratione*,[162] opened with an excursus on finger reckoning that was based on earlier tracts from Ireland.[163] Manuscripts of this manual, *De Computo Vel Loquela Digitorum*, circulated independently of the calendrical treatise itself, and some included illustrations.[164] As Bede explained, the numbers from 1 to 9,999 can be physically represented using the fingers of both hands. The positions assumed by the second to fourth fingers on the left hand—erect, bent straight down, or bent from the middle joint—mark the integers from one to nine. Positions assumed by the thumb and index finger of the left hand indicate the number of tens (from 10 to 90). Hundreds (from 100 to 900) are indicated on the second to fourth fingers of the right hand (following the same positions used to denote the integers on the left hand), and thousands (from 1000 to 9000) are indicated by the particular position taken by the thumb and forefinger of the right hand.[165]

Latin manuals of finger reckoning—distinguished from their Arabic counterparts only in the choice of the left hand to count lower numbers, and the right hand to count higher ones[166]—spread from the British Isles to the European continent. Rabanus Maurus, Abbot of Fulda (who studied with Bede's student, Alcuin of York, and who served as the "educational minister" of the Carolingian kingdom),[167] composed his own chapter on finger reckoning in the *Liber de Computo*. This mode of computation was unlikely to have been merely an academic curiosity, for clergy were heavily involved in financial transactions pertaining to the properties of the church and monastery, and to the produce grown on the lands of these institutions. An abacus would presumably have been present in official places of business, but it is not unreasonable to imagine that medieval Europeans also undertook financial negotiations spontaneously and in a broad array of settings, when they had no access to this device. In 850, Rabanus Maurus assumed the position of Archbishop in Mainz, a town that would later become the heartland of Jewish Pietism.

If finger computation was widely used in Rhenish commerce, it is unlikely that the technique would have been known only to Christians. Jewish vintners in the Rhineland (as in France) depended upon interaction with Christians—at times common laborers, and at times monastery abbots—at every stage of wine production and distribution.[168] Twelfth-century Jews might even have encountered written descriptions of digital reckoning in Hebrew sources. An unidentified source cited in the early twelfth-century commentary on *Sefer Yeẓirah* composed by Rabbi Judah ben Barzilai of Barcelona—a work which refers to the use of toes, as well as fingers, for digital reckoning—presupposes the reader's familiarity with the practice:

> He who knows how to count by the fingers is able to count by the ten fingers of the hand ten thousand, which is one myriad, and by the ten toes of the foot, up to ten myriads, which is the end of numeration [*ve-hu gemirat ha-ḥeshbon*.][169]

In short, there is no reason to think that the finger-reckoning technique alluded to by the *ḥakham* in *Sefer Ḥasidim* was an esoteric or arcane practice in the Middle Ages.

On the other hand, the use of this computational technique in the context of prayer is anything but self-evident. Fortunately, the Pietists left fuller textual records pertaining to each stage of this prayer praxis: the numbers

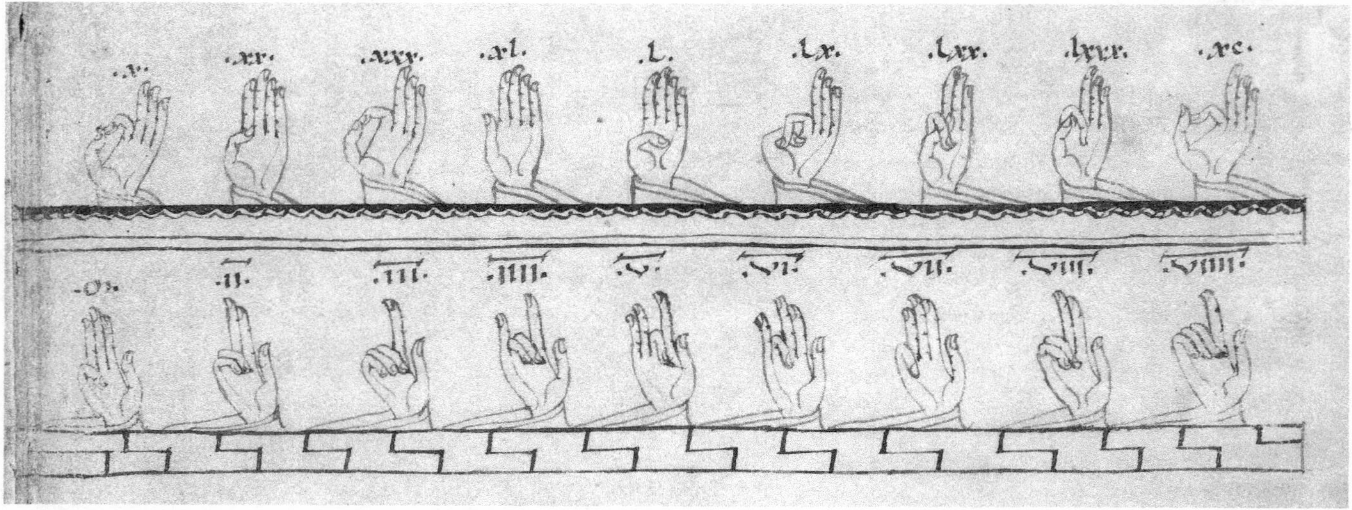

Figure 3. "I am groaning to/enlarging the Holy One blessed be He when I draw out [my prayers], counting on my fingers how many *alef*'s and *bet*'s in that Psalm, how many of each and every letter." This guide to digital computation from twelfth-century Rouen illustrates how the numbers from 1 to 9,999 can be physically represented using the fingers of both hands. This strategy of numerical reckoning was known to medieval Jews in both Ashkenazi and Sefardi lands. Leber ms. 1157 (3055), fol. 4. Collections of the Bibliothèque municipale de Rouen. Photograph by Thierry Ascencio-Parvy.

that resulted from the tabulation of distinct letters and words, and the meanings of those numbers. Rabbi Judah the Pietist's *Sodot ha-Tefilah* (Mysteries of Prayer)[170] can be construed as a written record of the first stage; it gives the count of the letters and words extracted from the raw material of prayer in different sections of the liturgy, along with certain scriptural verses that hint at the significance of these matters. But though Rabbi Judah asserts that every given number is "connected by clasps and loops, and they all have reasons and many mysteries,"[171] these connections are not spelled out. It is not until the second phase of the praxis that meaning is ascribed to—better, constructed of—this numerical data. Examples of these constructions fill two Pietist prayer compositions of the thirteenth century, the *Perush ha-Tefilah* (Explanation of Prayer) by Rabbi Elazar of Worms, disciple of Rabbi Judah the Pietist, and the *'Arugat ha-Bosem* (Bed of Spices) prayer commentary by Rabbi Avraham ben 'Azriel, a student of Rabbi Elazar's.[172] These works are designed to assist any literate worshiper in prayer, but they also transmit Rabbi Judah the Pietist's esoteric teachings about the numbers of liturgy.

The following lengthy illustration from Elazar of Worms's *Perush ha-Tefilah* gives a sense of what the worshiper might call to mind when reflecting on the prayer known as *'Amidah*—or, with some inaccuracy, "Eighteen Benedictions."[173] Given the operative number in this prayer, one who engages in the numeric practice strives to recall any fragment of tradition that is associated with the number eighteen.

> I will now write for you the correspondences [that explain] why they [the rabbis of antiquity] established the Eighteen Benedictions: [The word] "voices" appears eighteen times: thirteen [mentions of] "voice" in [Scriptures' account of] Revelation, and five [mentions of] "voices" which makes seventeen [*sic*][174] and one [mention of] "with the voice," which makes eighteen. And once in conjunction with the Tabernacle [Num. 7:82], "and he heard the voice speaking to him"—which corresponds to the nineteenth benediction, "And for the apostates."
>
> There are eighteen vocalization marks which appear underneath [the letters]. [There follows a listing of all the vowels, linked to the letter *alef*, in which each unconnected stroke, whether a point or a line, counts as one mark.] This makes eighteen [marks below the letter] below, and one above, which corresponds to nineteen.
>
> There are eighteen festive days: seven [days of] *Mażot*, one *'A-*

ẓeret, one Rosh HaShanah, one Yom Kippur, seven Sukkot, one Shemini [*'Aẓeret*], which makes eighteen from the Torah, and one received from Tradition, Purim.

It is written [Gen. 28:17], "and this is the gate to heaven": the Upper Temple is eighteen miles taller than the Lower [Temple].[175]

The verse [Deut. 3:23], "And I pleaded" has eighteen letters, not counting the [Divine] Name.

There are eighteen years in the cycle of Aries.

It is written [Num. 8:4], "This is the work of the menorah," teaching that [BT Men. 29b] the menorah was eighteen spans high. For this reason, three [scriptural appearances of the word] "the menorah" are [written] in *plene* spelling [with the optional letter *vav*, whose numerical equivalent is six]. . . .

The spine has [BT Ber. 28b] eighteen links, and one tiny one called "*luz*."

There are eighteen [mentions of] "teachings" in Psalms between [Ps. 25:4] "teach me" and [Ps. 94:10] "He that teaches," referring to the Shekhinah. And corresponding to [the nineteenth benediction] "and for the Apostates," [Ps. 132:12] "and I will teach them my testimony."

Eighteen Benedictions correspond to the Redemption from Egypt; therefore [BT Ber. 28b] the [prayer discussing] Redemption must be proximate to the *'Amidah* prayer: ". . . who redeems Israel. Lord, open my lips."

There are eighteen [scriptural mentions of] strengthening Pharaoh's heart and of making it heavy, and one [Ex. 7:3], "And I will harden Pharaoh's heart," or [Ex. 14:17] "strengthening the heart of Egypt."[176]

This passage, with its haphazard, possibly random, train of thought,[177] gives some sense of the *modus operandi* of Pietist prayer praxis, and perhaps even of its function. The devotee uses the numbers extracted from prayer as "collational sites," places to gather together elements of tradition that are (ostensibly!) associated only through their common numeric denominator. This selection alone, a small part of a larger encyclopedic excursus on the number eighteen, gives a sense of the range of associations that might be retrieved from memory. Data pertaining to the natural world are bound together with teachings from aggadah, halakhah, midrash, the order of liturgy, and the craft of vocalization—and also with *Masorah*, the body of oral, scribal tradition that fixes the precise count of Scripture's words and letters, its prescribed spacing and its orthographic anomalies. In describing the encyclopedic scope of R. Avraham's *piyyut* commentary, Yosef Dan wrote that its compiler, through his exegetical ruminations, attempted "to exploit all knowledge, in all arenas of religious literature—halakhah and aggadah, philosophy and mysticism, language and exegesis."[178] Ephraim Urbach adumbrated the purpose of this undertaking in discussing the wide-ranging mnemonic connections made in *'Arugat ha-Bosem*. The worshiper who exerted himself in this manner, wrote Urbach, would have needed not only to know the meaning of the words of prayer, but also "to gather in his mind/intention, those matters that are not explicitly stated, but that are somehow appropriate to the explicitly stated words."[179] In short, the numbers of prayer functioned as mnemonic triggers, and a worshiper using the Pietist praxis who labored to be mindful of all possible associations made himself into a conduit for tradition.

Some meditational praxes (Jewish as well as Christian) used graphic images of things (Latin, "*res*"; Hebrew, "*devarim*") as springboards to invention,[180] but ancient and medieval pedagogy regarded the ability to recognize and reconfigure patterns that were devoid of conceptual meaning (e.g., numeric patterns) as a skill that "made thinking possible."[181] Early Christian writings—by Jerome, Augustine, and Isidore of Seville—give a sense of the ways in which Scripture's numbers had been used, in calculational games, for largely exegetical purposes,[182] and intensive memory work was practiced in cloisters from the eleventh century onward, as demonstrated in the scholarship of Jean Leclercq and Mary Carruthers.[183] There is little question that the Pietist prayer practice described in *Sefer Ḥasidim* used numbers as "machines of the mind."[184]

In referring to himself as one who is "*marviyyaḥ* the Holy One, blessed be He," the *ḥakham* of this narrative may be utilizing a cognate of the word "*ravḥati*," "my groan," a biblical *hapax legomenon* that appears in Lam. 3:56, "*Hear my plea. Do not shut Your ear to my groan, to my cry.*"[185] In this sense, the phrase "I am *marviyyaḥ* the Holy One blessed be He when I draw out each number" may be a poetic reference to the practice of making prayer, that is, to thinking about God continuously.

Yet it is also tempting to think about the verb *marviyyaḥ* as a term of expansion, as a cognate of the term *revaḥ*, meaning "space."[186] The reading "I am enlarging the Holy One blessed be He" is particularly intriguing in light of the Pietists' familiarity with *Shi'ur Qomah* traditions.[187] In giving quantitative expression to the gargantuan dimensions of the Divine body, *Shi'ur Qomah* may have intended to emphasize God's unknowable grandeur, emphasizing the unbridgeable chasm that separates man from God,[188] and intensifying the devotee's desire for the unattainable. One wonders whether some similar idea was not at work in the second stage of the prayer praxis, when the Pietist amassed associations that were triggered by a given number, heaping up traditions about God and His teachings. Seen in this light, the second stage of Pietist prayer praxis, *harvaḥa la-Qadosh Barukh Hu*—perhaps "expansion for the sake of the Holy One, blessed be He"—may express not only the emotionally charged and prayerful state of longing, but the manipulative technique of "longing" as well.[189]

The Pietist's mental exertion while engaged in this praxis transformed the quotidian act of worship from passive recitation of a rote formula into an active, creative, personal experience. After performing these feats of recollection, the devotee labored to weave together the disparate strands of tradition he had summoned in ways never seen before; this creative act made him into a living bearer of Revelation.[190] At a time when the growing use of written prayer books in northern Europe threatened the living, straining, voice of worship, the Pietist's prayer praxis turned liturgy's written text into the pretext for a highly strenuous activity: memory-intensive meditation. In this sense, Pietist praxis ensured that the prayer experience retained an unscripted component, as was only fitting for *oral matters*.

This and more. When the Rhineland Pietists' prayer commentaries are compared with *piyyut* commentaries composed earlier, in both Germany and France, the later ones stand out in that they subject the *liturgical text itself* to the type of word count performed by the *Masorah* for the text of Scripture.[191] Earlier *piyyut* commentators had paid close attention to the word count in scriptural verses,[192] but R. Elazar of Worms (in the wake of his teacher, Rabbi Judah) lists the word count of prayers themselves.[193] This unusual feature of Pietist prayer commentary can also be explained with reference to the textualization process. Once the growing use of written *sidurim* and *maḥzorim* brought Jews of northern Europe into contact with the liturgical formulations of different locales, a prayer emissary could choose from an array of prayer versions, including some that were not native to the area. Pietists were enraged; they declared that there could only be one proper formulation of prayer, and even dismissed variants that had been tolerated in earlier generations.[194] Attacking the liturgy of French and English Jews, Pietists criticized the order of its passages, its words, letters, vowels, and even its punctuation. Not content to label French liturgy as imprecise, Pietists condemned it as destructive:

> You invent from whole cloth and add several words in your prayers which never arose in the hearts/minds of early *ḥasidim*, who established the prayers for us in place of sacrifices. And every prayer and blessing that they established is like (!) [them] in measure, and meter, in letters and words.[195]

The conception of prayer as a substitute for sacrifice is standard in rabbinic Judaism,[196] but Pietists of R. Judah's generation presumed an exact dimensional (!) equivalence between the formal characteristics of a given Temple offering and those of its corresponding prayer. The Pietists' preoccupation with the precision of liturgy had nothing to do with concerns for semantic accuracy; errors were to be avoided because they marred the sacred, and thus sabotaged the efficacy of the prayer act itself.

By applying the preservationary tactics of *Masorah* to the words of liturgy, Rhineland Pietists marked the corpus of prayer as sacred and unalterable. Just as the enterprise of *Masorah*, with its careful tabulations of words, letters, and orthographic anomalies, fixed the precise text of Scripture and ensured the uniformity of all Torah scrolls, the Pietists' *masorah* of prayer—found in Rabbi Judah the Pietist's concordance of liturgical numbers and in the later Pietist prayer commentaries—affirmed one particular version of prayer as authoritative, to the exclusion of all others.[197] In an age when texts had become an indispensable reference system, the numerical "masoretization" of the prayer affirmed the authority of one liturgical formulation and eliminated all other contenders.

Christian sermons that circulated in Germany, England, and France from the eleventh through thirteenth centuries describe an encounter between a cleric and a particular devil, called, in some versions, "Tutivillus." When asked about the bulging sack on his back, the devil gleefully responded that he had filled it with "syllables and slurred utterances and verses of Psalms which the clergy had stolen from God when they enunciated their prayers incorrectly." M. T. Clanchy described this tale's heightened concern for liturgical precision as emblematic of twelfth-century monastic culture,[198] but he might well have been referring to a contemporaneous Jewish development. From the Pietists' perspective, deviant versions of prayer were devoid of sacramental value; they were, as Tutivillus might have described them, words stolen from God.

Pietist Re-Memorialization of Masorah

Fearing that any corpora of *oral matters* that were left unwritten would be consigned to oblivion, Rhineland Pietists inscribed teachings pertaining to *Masorah*, the corpus of details pertaining to spelling, orthography, spacing, and layout that render a Torah scroll valid for liturgical use. Rabbi Judah the Pietist's *Ta'ame Masoret ha-Miqra* (roughly, "Meanings of the *Masorah* of Scripture") is the earliest written commentary on the masoretic corpus,[199] and the technique applied in this work bears a distinct resemblance to the approach found in Pietist prayer commentary. Some detail of *Masorah* is noted, whether lexical, grammatical, orthographic, or numeric (such as the number of times a word or phrase appears in Scripture), and the associations evoked are then embedded within a larger narrative (sometimes of homiletical import) that facilitates easy recall. Several brief examples may suffice.

A scriptural phrase used in describing the imminent death of the patriarch Jacob is identical to the language that appears in an unsavory episode in the Book of Esther. This datum is preserved in the repository of *Masorah*; what the Pietist commentary adds is a homiletical rubric that transforms this piece of information into a theological lesson:

> [On Gen. 48:2] "*And he sat on the bed*": [This phrase] appears twice [in Scripture], and the second refers to Haman falling on the bed that Esther was on [Est. 7:8]. This hints [at the notion] that the merit of Jacob, who sat on the bed, stood Esther in good stead.[200]

Another passage in R. Judah the Pietist's commentary seems less focused on masoretic data than on the desire to employ recollection as an occasion for a homiletical lesson:

> "*For you are coming to the land*" [Num. 34:2]: The *gematria* [numeric] value of [the word] *ba-im* ["are coming"] is fifty-three. And there are fifty -three pericopes in the Pentateuch. [In other words], they are coming to the land because of the merit of Torah.[201]

A particularly dense passage in the *Masorah* commentary might easily be mistaken for one from the Pietists' prayer commentaries—were it not for the fact that the "trigger" is a piece of masoretic information: the four-fold recurrence of a particular phrase in Scripture.

> [On Num. 33:1] "*These are the journeys*": Four scriptural passages begin with "*these are*": [Gen. 6:9] "*These are the line of Noah*"; [Ex. 38:21] "*These are the records [of the Tabernacle]*"; [Num. 33:1] "*These are the journeys*"; [Deut. 1:1] "*These are the words.*" In *gematria*, these four [occurrences of the word "*eleh,*" whose numerical value is 36] add up to 144, which corresponds to the number of hours in the [six] days of Creation, counting the nights. And the length of the earth is 144,000 days journey. How is this known? Egypt['s expanse] is a journey of forty days, and this is one-sixtieth of [the length of] Kush, and Kush is one-sixtieth of [the distance of the world], which comes to 144,000 days [journey].[202]

As in Pietist prayer commentary, Rabbi Judah the Pietist's *Ta'ame Masoret ha-Miqra* draws upon all the corpora of tradition that were accepted and revered by the omniverous Pietists: Scripture, Midrash, Talmud, *Masorah*, and natural, astronomical, and mystical lore. Though it might have been assumed that only *sofrim*, the professional scribes concerned with the orthography, calligraphy, and layout of the Torah scroll, would immerse themselves in the highly technical apparatus of *Masorah*, Pietists plumbed this body of *oral matters* for purposes of recollective contemplation. Their creative engagement with the traditions of *Masorah* transformed seemingly technical data into engines of religious praxis. The Pietists not only preserved and transmitted *oral matters* by engaging the details of *Masorah*; they used its data to reveal the interconnectedness of all realms of divine wisdom.[203]

Rhineland Pietism's Disappearance, Domestication, and Persistence

The preceding discussions reinforce Ivan Marcus's observation that Rhineland Pietists were impelled by a desire to conserve,[204] and they underscore the prominent roles that Pietists themselves played as agents of textualization. Apart from prayer commentary and *Masorah* commentary, Pietists inscribed bodies of esoteric lore: *Shi'ur Qomah* traditions, the *Hekhalot* literature, and the lore of "Special Cherub"; indeed, it was only through their efforts that later generations had access to these mysteries.[205] It is hard to imagine that the inscription of many previously unseen corpora of *oral matters* within a relatively short period was anything other than a conscious decision. In a cultural environment that privileged the authority of the written word, Pietist leaders adopted the dominant *modus operandi* in order to ensure that these troves of tradition would not be eclipsed or forgotten.

But if Pietists wrote down their lore and praxes to prevent them from falling into disuse, they did not fully attain their goal. The act of inscription created historical records of Pietist behaviors, but it could not ensure their continued practice.[206] In the fourteenth century, R. Jacob ben Asher referred to the Rhineland Pietists in the past tense. Recording a teaching of his deceased brother Yeḥiel ben Asher, he identified the "*dorshei reshumot*," "those who explicate material inscribed in lists," with "*Ḥaside Ashkenaz*, who used to weigh and count the number of words in prayer and blessings, and their correspondences [*ki-negged ma nitqenu*]."[207] And in an autobiographical remark from the same century, the Spanish liturgical commentator David ben Joseph Abudraham explained why he had chosen to abandon the praxis that he had learned at an Ashkenazi yeshivah in Toledo. Having encountered the prayer texts of Jews from many regions, Abudraham came to regard liturgical variations as inevitable.

> There are people who counted the words in each and every blessing of the *Eighteen* [*Benedictions*], and, for each blessing therein, they brought verses whose words add up to the number of words in the blessing. I, too, made a computation like this at first, and then I saw that it had no foundation or root. For you will not find any place in the world in which they all say the same thing regarding each and every word of the *'Amidah*. Rather, there are those who add words or delete. Therefore, this count doesn't help anybody but the one who made it, and nobody else. So why should we burden the scribes by having them write it?[208]

Why did Rhineland Pietism "disappear" after three only generations? Any explanation, I believe, must acknowledge the integral place of this phenomenon in Ashkenazi culture. In the first generation of *Ḥasidut Ashkenaz*, R. Samuel the Pietist (presented in the Parchment-Maker legend as the foil to Rabbenu Tam) found it necessary to protest many of the changes that were displacing time-honored practices and assumptions, but by the time of

Rabbi Elazar of Worms, in the movement's third generation, there was a willingness to "domesticate" many of Pietism's perspectives and practices in order to bring them into the region's cultural and legal mainstream. At a time when northern European Jewish society had come to associate cultural authority with written texts, Rabbi Judah the Pietist, leader of Pietism's second generation, struggled to achieve two goals that were in tension with one another. In deference to the new textualist criterion of authority, he inscribed many traditions that had previously been communicated only in oral transmission. (Indeed, Rabbi Judah's boldness comes into relief when compared with the perspective of Rashi, who had unpacked the numeric data of many *piyyutim* one century earlier,[209] but took a principled position against transmitting esoteric number-linked teachings.)[210] On the other hand, R. Judah the Pietist preserved and transmitted these mysteries in a most elusive manner, so that they remained enigmas to anyone who did not have access to a master's explanations. When positioned between the earlier prayer commentaries of Rashi, and the later commentaries of R. Elazar of Worms and R. Avraham ben 'Azriel, Rabbi Judah the Pietist's *Sodot ha-Tefilah* appears to be something of a compromise, perhaps even a stage in an evolutionary process. It divulges data that Rashi had refused to convey in writing, yet it has none of the fuller written exposition found in the later Pietist prayer commentaries. Like Maimonides, who had adopted a skeletal type of writing knowing that it would require the "rehydration" of oral explication,[211] Rabbi Judah the Pietist's highly elliptical style forced devotees to bring pedagogic, or even spiritual, meaning to similarities that, in and of themselves, were rather dry. No matter what body of teachings was concerned, recollective meditation required the adept to create his own oral synthesis from the gathered strands of tradition.

However, in Rhineland Pietism's third generation, R. Judah's student, Elazar of Worms, undertook various projects that diminished the distinctiveness of Pietism and deflated its aura of mystery. Not only did R. Elazar (and later, his student R. Avraham ben 'Azriel) knowingly transform the Pietist praxis of meditation into a canonical commentary on prayer, which is to say, into an authorized, academic text, he also discontinued the practice of confession to a *ḥakham*, an act whose importance had been emphasized by his teacher.[212] Beyond this, in order to bring greater transparency to the transmission of knowledge, Elazar of Worms enjoined every author to inscribe his name in books he wrote.[213] In his Introduction to *Sefer ha-Roqeaḥ* (The Book of the Blended Compound), R. Elazar explained that the book's title was an allusion to his own name,[214] and he noted that authorial attribution—albeit in encoded form—had long been the norm, even in seemingly anonymous works of antiquity.[215]

In his introduction to *Sefer ha-Ḥokhmah*, a work of esoterica composed thirty years after he had begun his prayer commentary,[216] R. Elazar portrayed the decision to commit oral traditions to writing as a conscious choice. The proximate causes for this work's composition were the death of his teacher, Rabbi Judah the Pietist, and the murder of his own son by Crusaders.[217] There had been religious giants until quite recently, wrote R. Elazar, sages whose erudition bridged the teachings of Torah and Talmud and wonder workers who were versed in the interconnection of higher and lower worlds. Now, however, he lamented, his generation was bereft: "for men of deed [*anshe ma'aseh*] are no more, and hearts have become diminished such that there is no understanding of how the Talmud comes out of the five books of the Torah." Elazar's remarks acknowledge that the deaths of two great individuals contributed to the "orphaning" of his own generation, but they also suggest that the decline in the culture of *memoria* was due to the deluge of written works illuminating the relationship between Talmud and Scripture. Describing the emergence of an entire rabbinic literary industry, Elazar painted a picture of informational overload:

> Talmud gives rise to [literally, "makes"] many books without end, for the offshoots of the Talmud are more than 1,000 books, with the Oral Torah[218] and dialectics and clarification of the miẓvot and laws and [regulations pertaining to that which is] prohibited and permitted. But . . . the hearts [memories] of people cannot contain all this—because of the tribulations and Exile and financial loss and [need for] sustenance.[219]

Elazar's decision to use written compositions to transmit various hermeneutical techniques of letter and number manipulation—first in prayer commentary, and later in *Sefer ha-Ḥokhmah*—was hardly precipitous; it may even have had the approval and encouragement of Rabbi Judah the Pietist himself.[220]

Two centuries after Bishop Burchard transformed Christian culture by integrating the once disparaged penitential literature into an official church anthology, Elazar of Worms made an analogous move by including the penances of Rhineland Pietists in his *Sefer ha-Roqeaḥ*, a mainstream halakhic compendium. Just as Burchard's canonical text had endowed previously marginal penitential practices with new legitimacy, Elazar of Worms' codification of Pietist penitential practices granted them a visibility and an audience they had not possessed when the exempla of *Sefer Ḥasidim* constituted their only literary venue. The mere transposition of these practices from one genre to another "tamed" the legacy of a self-styled sociological elite and brought it into the cultural mainstream.[221] When Pietist practices were integrated into the *Sefer ha-Roqeaḥ*, they attained wide dissemination, lost the separatist valence that had characterized them initially, and became part of Ashkenazi society's new behavioral norm.

Judah the Pietist's inscription of previously oral traditions, and R. Elazar of Worms' positioning of these teachings in the "public domain" of Hebrew readers, obviated Rhineland Pietism's very *raison d'être*. Pietism had emerged to protest the marginalization of the charismatic master's power and to do what it could to preserve it, but it also advanced the textualization process itself. The very cultural circumstances that had summoned Rhineland Pietism into existence, "compelling" it to assume the literary instantiation that historians equate with its beginnings, were also responsible for its end. Having consigned various besieged oral traditions to writing, the Rhineland Pietists, for all intents and purposes, wrote themselves out of existence. Rhineland Pietism was a casualty of its own inscriptive agenda; it died at its own hand, but not without leaving a weighty legacy.

The cultural propensities that had been present in Ashkenaz before the emergence of *Ḥasidut Ashkenaz* and that were intensified, magnified, and placed at center stage by Pietism's exponents over the course of three generations were subsequently "resorbed" into "mainstream" Ashkenazi culture, where they continued to shape attitudes and practices. The expressions of "neo-Pietism" in Ashkenazi culture of the later medieval and early modern periods all meshed smoothly with the halakhic framework erected by the tosafists.[222]

Epilogue

Little is currently known about why the amoraim generated, and preserved, the traditions found in the Babylonian Talmud. What *is* clear is that Jews who lived in the centuries following the last of the Talmud's named tradents focused on the legal traditions of this orally transmitted corpus and, over time, "transposed" them so that they came to be construed as guidelines for living a Jewish life. A range of activities made this transposition possible: unclear words and phrases were explained, conflicting passages were harmonized, and adjudicatory principles, *kelale pesiqa*, were articulated. Principles of this sort, establishing (for example) that the law always accorded with Rabbi X whenever he disputed with Rabbi Y, functioned as algorithms; they helped to make unresolved data in the Babylonian Talmud usable in situations of applied law.

The saboraim, anonymous redactors of the sixth century, began the process of transposing Talmud into a "usable" corpus, but it is easier to speculate about the motives of those who continued this process through the mid-eleventh century, the Babylonian geonim. Rabbinic Jews of the post-talmudic era were spread throughout a vast geographic diaspora in communities shaped by dramatically disparate political, economic, and social circumstances. Working with the amoraic teachings that they had inherited, geonim embarked on a project to provide Jews throughout the world with a single and unifying legal system. The geonim undertook these labors in the environs of Baghdad, capital of the Abbasid caliphate, at a time and place where Muslim jurists and scholars of tradition were collecting, scrutinizing and systematizing inherited teachings so that the now far-flung community of Muslims, united by belief, could function and flourish as a single political entity, guided by clear legal norms.

Though the geonim advanced the process of transposing the Babylonian Talmud into a legal reference work, their own legal decisions continued to rely heavily on a non-talmudic source of authority, namely, lived tradition backed by trustworthy attestation. The comprehensive remodeling of Talmud as a legal reference work was only completed outside of the geonic academies, in Jewish communities of the eleventh and twelfth centuries. Whether through the use of bridging commentary (as was the case in Qayrawan, and later, Sefarad) or through the baring of intermediating operations of transposition (as was the case in the tosafist glosses of northern Europe), the Babylonian Talmud's legal material came to be portrayed and construed as applied law.

This study has linked the "tosafization" of the Babylonian Talmud to northern European Jewry's (relatively late) encounter with this corpus as a written text. It has suggested that the full-scale apprehension of Talmud as a prescriptive reference work—and the range of bridge-building activities that made this apprehension possible—occurred in this time and place for specific historical reasons. The textualization process that transformed the cultures of this region in the eleventh and twelfth centuries led resident populations to ascribe greater cultural authority to the written word than to mimetically transmitted teachings, and it motivated them to demonstrate that their own behaviors were guided by texts and aligned with them. The panoptic encounter with the written text of Talmud made it possible for readers to work with it in ways that were only possible when granted visual (and not solely auditory) access. These included a panoply of redactional, comparative, analytical, and harmonizing operations. In short, the change in the way that the Babylonian Talmud was transmitted affected that way that its traditions were perceived, understood, and used.

Other Cultural Shifts Linked to Changes in the Transmission of Jewish Tradition

This conclusion (which can barely be mentioned without acknowledging Marshall McLuhan's adage "The medium is the message") brings to mind several other moments of cultural transition that were linked to modal changes in the transmission of Jewish tradition. The twelfth-century composition of the *Mishneh Torah* was one such instance, for, according to its critics, Jews of little training could now use Maimonides' code to make legal decisions without consulting rabbinic authorities.[1] Like observers of the textualization process described in this book who commented (neutrally or with nostalgia) on the decline of discipleship, observers of Jewish legal codification noted that cultural values had shifted, and that the prodigious mastery of tradition had come to carry less authority than had previously been the case. Once tradition was encountered in a different venue than had previously been the case—whether in writing, or in codificatory form—existing configurations of cultural, political, and social power were destabilized and, in some cases, redrawn.

Another comparable development was the consignment of Jewish traditions to print. If the medieval inscription of Talmud had made it difficult for rabbinic elites to control the role that this corpus of *oral matters* played vis-à-vis other sources of cultural authority, the problem was greatly exacerbated by the use of early modern technology. Print granted all readers who were literate in Hebrew access to both *written* and *oral matters*, and it placed particular bodies of knowledge squarely in the public domain. A Christian reader could now mine the Zohar to abet his conversionary agenda,[2] and a non-expert Jew who read the printed edition of the *Shulḥan 'Arukh*, replete with the Ashkenazi glosses of R. Moses Isserles, might assume that he could forego the consultation of a rabbi. Writing in the second half of the sixteenth century, R. Ḥayyim ben Beẓalel lambasted contemporaries "lacking in sense who are convinced that they can give instruction from anything they find in the name of any book, whatsoever—because '*we are all sages*'—without consulting any *ḥakham* [wise man]."[3] According to Ḥayyim ben Beẓalel, the perfunctory representation of Ashkenazi perspectives in this published work impugned the rich scholarship of earlier generations, and would contribute to its further neglect. Print would have a deleterious effect on erudition, for Jews who knew that they could consult a book stored on their shelves would no longer exert themselves to determine the law.[4] Excoriating certain authors of his own time, Ḥayyim ben Beẓalel wrote that these fame-seekers claimed credit for innovative halakhic insights that had been known all along.[5] Comparing the overexposure of the halakhic corpus in the printed edition of the *Shulḥan 'Arukh* to the publication of medical arcana, Ḥayyim ben Beẓalel asserted that Jewish law, like medicine, was a specialized body of knowledge that was only to be applied by rigorously trained experts.[6]

The standardization of Jewish traditions brought about by print also had the effect of narrowing readers' perceptions of the Jewish past. Just as reliance on the inscribed Talmud marginalized extra-talmudic traditions, the early modern printing of Jewish works necessarily represented only a chosen sliver of the historical archive, and in this sense created a "new canon," as Elḥanan Reiner has shown in his research.[7]

A third historical development that shares some features with the instance of textualization examined in this book was the subject of Haym Soloveitchik's justly famous essay, "Rupture and Reconstruction: The Transformation of Contemporary Orthodoxy." Beginning in the second half of the twentieth century, noted Soloveitchik, observant American Jews came to ascribe greater authority to written texts than to living repositories of tradition. Nourished by geographic dislocation following the Holocaust, he suggested, this shift in *mentalité* was indicative of a lack of confidence in (human) religious authority. "Rupture and Reconstruction" situated this contemporary instance of preferring the written word to modeled behavior within the diachronic context of earlier reassessments of the locus of Jewish cultural authority. Not unlike the comments of the Shneur brothers of thirteenth-century Evreux,[8] Soloveitchik's ruminations on the ways that this shift has reshaped the attitudes and practices of contemporary of observant Jews is inflected with a palpable sense of nostalgia.[9]

Other "Indices of Packaging" and Their Impact on Jewish Traditions

Awareness that shifts in modes of transmission have enormous impact on shaping the relayed content is not new in the study of classical rabbinic literature. Scholars of rabbinics, for example, have long understood that oral transmission made the corpora in question prone to specific types of change. Writing about the Mishnah, Saul Lieberman spoke of the "fusion and confusion of the *lemmata* with the commenting text,"[10] and Meir Ish Shalom made a similar point about Talmud: "The Gemara you are used to already has commentaries and additions mixed in!"[11] Eliezer Shimshon Rosenthal noted that it was hard to draw a clear line between the actual "tradition" and its redaction or arrangement,[12] and Ya'aqov Sussman programmatically rejected the search for a stable *ur* tradition: "There are no defined boundaries between coming into being, arrangement and transmission; between the history of (a text's) arrangement/editing and the history of its formulation."[13] Orality and textuality as distinct modes of transmission represent just one set of binaries among a vast array of variables that have been used for "packaging" units of Jewish knowledge. It would be wrong for twenty-first century readers, accustomed to the media of print and internet, to assume that "lack of technical development narrowed the range of choices available to the transmitters" of antiquity and the Middle Ages.[14] In fact, earlier generations of Jews ingeniously ascribed different cultural meanings to disparate units of knowledge by assigning them different "indices of packaging." Indeed, the contemporary historiographic debate (discussed in Chapter 4) about how the deeds of Rhenish Jews in 1096 are to be interpreted hinges on the question of whether the Jews of this time and place assigned equal, or unequal, cultural "weight" to units of halakhah and aggadah.

Along with the above-mentioned indices—oral versus written, and the taxonomic designation of a tradition as halakhah or aggadah—a broad array of rabbinically generated rules that regulate the "packaging" of Jewish knowledge tag the relayed content with a specific cultural meaning or cultural worth. This is as clear in the ancient rabbis' likening of certain compositions to "a mere epistle"[15] as it is in the geonic assertion that Jews need not rely on aggadah. There are rules regulating variables such as the type of Hebrew font to be used; the material format—e.g., scroll or codex—to be employed for the inscription of the work in question; the use of parchment or of paper; the question of whether pricking and ruling needed to precede the writing of a particular text; the designation of certain written works as texts that "defile the hands" (that impart ritual impurity when touched); and the question of whether, or how, the text in question was to be preserved. Each rule articulated by rabbinic scholars for the transmission or treatment of a specific type of Jewish knowledge encoded a message about the cultural significance of the datum in question.

Other "indices of packaging" can be discerned even where no explicit rules have been found. Analysis of Jewish writings has led scholars to infer that only some types of Jewish literary production were to be rhymed, just as only some were to be written in Hebrew,[16] or with vocalization (*niqqud*), or with scribal flourishes (*tagin*). In generation after generation, new conventions of transmission—pertaining to the material artifact, to constraints of composition and genre, to paratextual markings, and to performative guidelines—transformed a body of Jewish tradition that predecessors had perceived as homogeneous into a differentiated and stratified legacy, replete with hierarchical rankings and coded cultural meanings.

Fresh Thinking about Medieval Jewish Regionalisms

In the present study, I have chosen not to rely on the tenacious historiographic portrait of medieval Sefarad and Ashkenaz as the genealogical descendants of the ancient Jewish centers of Babylonia and Palestine, respectively.[17] Ongoing efforts to identify the geographic lineages of certain traditions will undoubtedly yield new and interesting insights, but in the course of my own studies, I have come to suspect that preoccupation with this line of inquiry has, at times, impeded clear observation and interfered with the processing of evidence. An example of such an overlooked, or ignored, observation may be drawn from this study: Examination of the ways in which the approaches to Talmud (in pedagogy and adjudication) developed by medieval Sefardi and Ashkenazi Jews, respectively, compared with those used by the geonim, reveals that the stronger phenomenological parallels are between the approaches taken in Babylonia and in northern Europe.[18] Like the geonim, the Jews of Ashkenaz perpetuated the oral transmission of *oral matters* long after Sefardim had ceased to do so, and, like the geonim, Jews of medieval northern Europe were far more explicit about factoring in extra-talmudic sources of Jewish authority before arriving at their applied legal decisions. With the exception of Naḥmanides (who exerted tremendous efforts to uphold geonic perspectives even when they conflicted with Talmud, and who was the first Sefardi to fully grasp the tosafist revolution), medieval Sefardim tended to align applied law with the perspectives of Talmud.[19]

This study does not offer any comprehensive alternative explanatory paradigm to account for the emergence of the subcultures of Ashkenaz and Sefarad in the Middle Ages, but it does start from two core observations. One is that the medieval Jews of Ashkenaz, as well as Sefarad, received the teachings of the Babylonian Talmud and the Jerusalem Talmud from geonim of the Baghdadi academies. (Palestinian traditions did circulate in Ashkenaz, but Jews of medieval northern Europe had no stronger sense of allegiance to that ancient center than they did to Babylonia.)[20] The second core observation is that the Jewish communities of medieval Sefarad and Ashkenaz map, geographically, onto the heartlands and borderlands of the ancient Roman Empire, respectively. As discussed in Chapter 3, this cartographic perspective helps to explain certain cultural characteristics that were discernible in regional practices of writing and in regional attitudes toward texts. In and of themselves, the political boundaries of the Roman Empire do not supply a satisfactory, comprehensive etiology of (two of) the medieval Jewish subcultures, but they may shed some light on why Jews of Sefarad had a more positive attitude toward inscribed law than did the Jews of Ashkenaz.

Future studies will surely want to consider developments in the Christian legal culture of Visigothic Spain and in the Islamic legal cultures of al-Andalus and Qayrawan—and, if possible, address a far more elusive question: What cultural universes were displaced by the growing prominence of Talmud within the medieval Jewish societies known as Ashkenaz and Sefarad? Any synthetic overview of Jewish culture in pre-Crusade society north of the Loire River would need to grapple seriously with its vivid imaginarium. In making law the centerpiece of Jewish culture, "tosafization" did much to marginalize other rich dimensions of Jewish life.

Finally, forthcoming research into the origins of Sefarad and Ashkenaz will certainly want to focus on the mechanics of cultural formation in the Middle Ages. While the original Jewish settlers in the Rhineland, members of the Qalonymos family who had emigrated from Italy, shared a common history and common traditions, it is hard to imagine that a sense of kinship could have been inculcated among much larger numbers of unrelated northern European Jews living in a vast geographic expanse were it not for their sharing of a common library. It is unlikely that this could have occurred solely through the oral transmission of ancestral lore, but by modeling their lives on the same revered texts, people who did not live in the same cities or descend from common ancestors could nonetheless embrace a shared communal identity.[21] Wherever they lived, Jews of Ashkenaz relied on the same Talmud commentaries, the same halakhic digests, the same compilations of custom—and, ultimately, the same foundation myth. Their common textual references helped them fashion shared patterns of thought that, in Brian Stock's words, "inevitably [fed] back into the network of real interdependencies."[22]

GLOSSARY

adjudication: the act of rendering a legal decision.

aggadah (s.), *aggadot* (pl.) [Heb.]: narrative, non-legal passage(s) in the classical sources of rabbinic Judaism.

amora (s.), *amoraim* (pl.) [Aram.]: rabbinic sage(s) of the third through sixth centuries C.E. whose teachings are recorded in the Talmud.

applied law: law as it is actually implemented; distinguished from legal teachings that are part of the rabbinic archive, but are not implemented in practice

Ashkenaz (n), *Ashkenazi* (adj.) [Heb.]: a Jewish subculture that emerged in the Middle Ages in the region of the Carolingian Empire (Franco-Germany). By the twelfth century, the term was being used to refer specifically to Jewish communities in German-speaking lands. Genesis 10:3 names Ashkenaz as a descendent of Noah's son Japheth.

beraita (s.), *beraitot* (pl.) [Aram.]: tradition(s) of the *tannaim* not included in the Mishnah.

codicology: the study of books as physical objects, especially bound manuscripts written in codex form.

consuetudinal: pertaining to custom.

dayyan (s.), *dayyanim* (pl.) [Heb.]: literally, "judge(s)." Functionaries in medieval Jewish communities of al-Andalus and North Africa whose study of certain essentials of Jewish law enabled them to discharge regulatory tasks, though they were not experts in Talmud.

deuterosis [Gk.]: literally, "second teaching." Some scholars presume that this Greek term designates Mishnah. According to *Novella* 146 issued by Emperor Justinian in 553, the term "*deuterosis*" refers to a corpus of human teachings that were not divinely inspired, and Byzantine Jews were forbidden to impart it.

Ereẓ Yisrael [Heb.]: the land of Israel.

gaon (s.), *geonim* (pl.) [Heb.]: literally, "eminence(s)." Scholar(s) who headed the post-talmudic rabbinic academies from the seventh through the early twelfth centuries. The most influential geonic academies were those of "Babylonia" (Iraq), though there were also geonim in the land of Israel and in Egypt.

Gemara [Aram.]: Talmud. Corpus of orally transmitted teachings generated by rabbis of the third through sixth centuries C.E. in Palestine and Babylonia. See "Talmud."

girsa (s.), *girsaot* (pl.) [Aram.]: recited utterance(s), relayed solely through oral transmission. Distinct from *nusḥa*.

ḥadith (s.), *aḥadith* (pl.) [Arab.]: oral narratives describing the words and deeds of the Prophet Muḥammed.

ḥakham [Heb]: literally, a wise man. In the culture of medieval Jewish Pietists, a charismatic master, versed in *sod*.

halakhah (s.), *halakhot* (pl.) [Heb]: received legal tradition(s).

halakhah le-ma'aseh [Heb.]: received legal tradition whose implementation in practice has been attested by a living master.

ḥasid (s.), *ḥasidim* (pl.) [Heb.]: Pietist, Pietists.

Ḥaside Ashkenaz [Heb]: Jewish Pietists of the medieval Rhineland.

Hebraica veritas [Lat.]: literally, "truth of the Hebrew doctrine." A term that denotes respect on the part of medieval and early modern Christian scholars for the masoretic text of the Hebrew Bible, and for the ways in which the rabbis understood it.

ḥibbur (s.), *hibburim* (pl.) [Heb.]: composition, from the verb meaning "to link."

I'jāz [Arab.]: literally, "the [act of] rendering incapable, powerless." An Islamic theological doctrine affirming the Qur'an's inimitability in both content and form.

kallah (s.), *yarḥei kallah* (pl.) [Heb.]: convocation; months of convocation. In geonic times, Jews from around the world attended rabbinic study sessions at the Babylonian *yeshivot* in the months of Adar and Elul.

ketubah [Heb.]: a Jewish marriage contract.

ma'aseh [Heb.]: a real case decided in a law court that might be cited as a precedent when deciding law. Literally, "deed."

maḥzor (s.), *maḥzorim* (pl.) [Heb.]: prayer book(s) containing the liturgy for holidays.

mainmise [Fr.]: seizure; stranglehold.

majlis (s.), *majalis* (pl.) [Arab.]: meeting, assembly. A term used to denote interfaith conversations between intellectuals in medieval Baghdad.

Masorah [Heb.]: body of Jewish tradition stipulating precisely how a Torah scroll is to be written and how it is to be read liturgically.

megilat setarim (s.), *megilot setarim* (pl.) [Heb.]: literally, "a scroll to be sequestered."

Midrash (s.), *midrashim* (pl.) [Heb.]: rabbinic scriptural interpretation; also, discrete compilations of such interpretation.

midrash aggadah [Heb.]: rabbinic narrative connected with a scriptural passage that yields no legal information.

midrash halakhah [Heb.]: rabbinic narrative linking a scriptural passage with law. Scholars debate whether the scriptural passage is the source of the law, or a mnemonic for a law that was already in existence.

minhag (s.), *minhagim* (pl.) [Heb.]: custom(s).

Mishnah (s.), *mishnayyot* (pl.): [Heb.] Corpus of orally transmitted rabbinic legal traditions whose form was fixed by Rabbi Judah the Patriarch in Palestine in 200 C.E. and which serves as the foundational text of the Talmud. Also, unit(s) of this corpus.

miẓvah (s.), *miẓvot* (pl.) [Heb.]: commandment(s).

nusḥa (s.), *nusḥaot* (pl.) [Aram.]: teaching(s) relayed in writing.

parush (s.), *perushim* (pl.) [Heb.]: separatist(s).

piyyut (s.), *piyyutim* (pl.) [Heb.]: liturgical poem(s).

quaestiones [Lat.]: a term used in rhetorical theory and in dialectics for debatable points around which disputes are centered.

responsum (s.), responsa (pl.) [Lat.; Eng.]: written reply (or replies) by a rabbinic authority to specific questions posed in writing by correspondents.

rosh yeshivah [Heb.]: leader of a rabbinic academy.

saboraim (pl.) [Aram]: anonymous sages of the sixth and seventh centuries who redacted the Babylonian Talmud.

scrinia (pl.) [Lat.]: cylindrical containers used in ancient Rome to hold papyrus rolls.

Sefarad [Heb.]: Jewish subculture shaped in medieval al-Andalus and North Africa. The place name appears in Obadiah 1:20.

sefer (s.), *sefarim* (pl.) [Heb.]: book(s).

Sefer Yeẓirah [Heb.]: literally, "Book of Formation." An esoteric Hebrew work of the early ninth century devoted to speculations about God's creation of the world, whose authorship is ascribed to the patriarch Abraham.

Shema' Yisrael [Heb.]: "Hear O Israel," a liturgical passage drawn from Deuteronomy 6:4.

Shulḥan 'Arukh [Heb.]: comprehensive sixteenth-century Jewish code of law which is used to this day.

sidur (s.), *sidurim* (pl.) [Heb]: prayer book(s).

sod (s.), *sodot* (pl.) [Heb]: literally, "secret(s)"; esoteric teachings that are taught only to initiates.

sugya (s.), *sugyot* (pl.) [Aram]: unit(s) of Talmud.

Talmud [Heb.]: a term denoting two orally transmitted Aramaic corpora of rabbinic (legal and non-legal) teachings uttered and relayed by amoraim who lived between the third and sixth centuries. The latest named tradents of the Jerusalem (or Palestinian) Talmud flourished at the turn of the fifth century, and the latest named tradents of the Babylonian Talmud flourished around the turn of the sixth century. Both Talmuds were later consigned to writing.

talmud [Heb.]: literally, "that which is derived from study." In amoraic times, this referred to the body of insights derived from the study of Mishnah.

tanna(s.), *tannaim* (pl.) [Aram.]: rabbinic sage(s) who lived in Palestine between the first century B.C.E. and 200 C.E., and whose teachings are recorded in the Mishnah and Tosefta.

taqqanot (pl.) [Heb.]: rabbinic ordinances that are not derived through exegesis of Talmud.

Tosafot (pl.), Tosafists [Heb.]: medieval Jewish glosses—and glossators—of the Babylonian Talmud.

Tosefta [Aram.]: corpus of tannaitic teachings that serves as a supplement to the Mishnah.

yeshivah (s.), *yeshivot* (pl.) [Heb.]: rabbinic academy; academies.

Ẓorfat [Heb.]: France. The place name appears in Obadiah 1:20.

ABBREVIATIONS

AJS Review	*Association for Jewish Studies Review*
AZ	*'Avodah Zarah*
BB	*Bava Batra*
Bekh.	*Bekhorot*
Ber.	*Berakhot*
Beẓ.	*Beẓah*
Bik.	*Bikkurim*
BK	*Bava Kama* (properly spelled "*Qama*")
BM	*Bava Meẓia*
BT	Babylonian Talmud
Cant. R.	Canticles Rabbah
EH	*Even Ha'Ezer*
Eruv.	*'Eruvin*
Exod. R.	Exodus Rabbah
Gen. R.	Genesis Rabbah
Git.	*Gittin*
Guide	*Guide for the Perplexed*
Ḥag.	*Ḥagigah*
Hil.	*Hilkhot*
HM	*Hoshen Misphpat*
HTR	*Harvard Theological Review*
HUCA	*Hebrew Union College Archives*
Hul.	*Ḥulin*
JQR	*Jewish Quarterly Review*
JSS	*Jewish Social Studies*
Ket.	*Ketubot*
Lev. R.	Leviticus Rabbah
Meg.	*Megilah*
Men.	*Menaḥot*

MQ	*Mo'ed Qatan*
Ned.	*Nedarim*
Nid.	*Nidah*
Num. R.	Numbers Rabbah
OḤ	*Oraḥ Ḥayyim*
PAAJR	*Proceedings of the American Academy for Jewish Research*
Pes.	*Pesaḥim*
PIASH	*Proceedings of the Israel Academy of Sciences and Humanities*
PL	*Patriologia Latina*
Qid.	*Qidushin*
REJ	*Revue des Études Juives*
RH	*Rosh HaShanah*
San.	*Sanhedrin*
SH	*Sefer Ḥasidim*
Shab.	*Shabbat*
Shev.	*Shevu'ot*
Sot.	*Sotah*
Suk.	*Sukkah*
Ta'an.	*Ta'anit*
Tem.	*Temurah*
YD	*Yoreh De'ah*
Yeb.	*Yebamot*
Yom.	*Yoma*
YT	Yerushalmi Talmud; Palestinian Talmud

NOTES

INTRODUCTION

The epigraph comes from Anthony Grafton, "Introduction: Notes from Underground on Cultural Transmission," *The Transmission of Culture in Early Modern Europe*, ed. A. Grafton and A. Blair (Philadelphia, 1990), 4.

1. Uziel Fuchs, "Darkhe ha-hakhra'a, samkhut shel teqstim u-muda'ut 'aẓmit: Hirhurim 'al darkhe ha-pesiqa bi-shalhe tequfat ha-geonim," in *Sugyot be-Meḥqar ha-Talmud* (Jerusalem, 1991), 100, and bibliography in note 2; Y. Spiegel, "Leshonot perush ve-hosafot meuḥarot ba-talmud ha-bavli," *Te'udah* 3 (1983): 91–112; Shamma Friedman, "Mavo 'al derekh ḥeqer ha-sugya," *Meḥqarim u-Meqorot* 1 (New York, 1978), 282ff.; Y. Sussman, "Ve-shuv le-Yerushalmi Neziqin," *Meḥqere Talmud* 1 (1990): 108n204; Y. Brody, "Sifrut ha-Geonim ve-ha-teqst ha-talmudi," *Meḥqere Talmud* 1 (1990): 266–67.

2. In the words of one scholar, "We are better off positing that the Talmud is literature, and asking what genre of literature it is. . . . What other literature is this literature like, and in what ways is it different?" David Kraemer, *Reading the Rabbis: The Talmud as Literature* (New York, 1996), 7. On the heterogeneous contents of the Babylonian Talmud, see Richard Kalmin, "The Formation and Character of the Babylonian Talmud," in *The Cambridge History of Judaism*, vol. 4, *The Late Roman Rabbinic Period*, ed. Steven Katz (Cambridge, 2006), 841. Among Yaakov Elman's many pathbreaking writings on the impact of Middle Persian culture on the Babylonian Talmud, see "Middle Persian Culture and Babylonian Sages: Accommodation and Resistance in the Shaping of Rabbinic Legal Tradition," in *The Cambridge Companion to Rabbinic Cambridge Literature*, ed. C. E. Fonrobert and M. S. Jaffee (Cambridge and New York, 2007), 165–97. I encountered a new attempt to think about the Talmud's genre in light of Hellenistic literature only as the present work was going to press. See Daniel Boyarin, *Socrates and the Fat Rabbis* (Chicago, 2009). On 24 (and in one of the opening epigraphs), Boyarin recalls that his teacher, Professor Saul Lieberman, had claimed that the Greek work of Lucian, a second-century rhetorician and satirist, "holds the key to the Talmud."

3. If anything, suggested Robert Brody, "the ambitions which the Geonim entertained on behalf of the Talmud were probably greater than those of its creators." Brody, *The Geonim of Babylonia and the Shaping of Medieval Jewish Culture* (New Haven, Conn., 1998), 161.

4. BT Shab. 61a stipulates that one should put on the right shoe first, but tie the left shoe first. According to BT Ber. 5b, one's bed should be aligned along a north-south axis.

5. Brody, *The Geonim of Babylonia*, 161.

6. On Naḥmanides as a conduit for Tosafism, see S. Abramson, *Kelale ha-Talmud be-Divre Ramban* (Jerusalem, 1971), 8–9; Y. Ta Shma, *Ha-Sifrut ha-Parshanit la-Talmud be-Eropa u-ve-Ẓefon Afriqa*, (Jerusalem, 1999), vol. 2, 38–45; Ẓvi Groner, "Darkhe hora-a shel rishonim u-geonim," in *Meah She'arim: 'Iyyunim be'Olamam ha-Ruḥani shel Yisrael be-Yeme ha-Benayyim le-Zekher Yiẓḥaq Twersky*, ed. E. Fleischer et al. (Jerusalem, 2001), 267–78; M. Halbertal, "Ha-Minhag ve-ha-historia shel ha-halakhah be-torato shel ha-Ramban," *Ẓion* 67 (2002): 25–56.

7. This claim requires some qualification, for kabbalists did develop other ways of approaching Talmud. Kabbalistic readings of Talmud differed primarily in their epistemological assumptions about the text and in the range of hermeneutic techniques they were willing to use. Where kabbalists differed regarding the the legal status quo, they advocated greater stringency. See T. Fishman, "A Kabbalistic Perspective on Gender-Specific Commandments: On the Interplay Between Symbol and Society," *AJS Review* 17 (1992): 199–245.

8. R. Brody, "Sifrut ha-geonim ve-ha-teqst ha-talmudi," 251.

9. H. Soloveitchik, "Halakhah, Hermeneutics and Martyrdom in Medieval Ashkenaz," *JQR* 94:1 (2004): 78.

10. See Moshe Halbertal, *People of the Book: Canon, Meaning and Authority* (Cambridge, Mass., 1997), introduction, passim, esp. 15.

11. Modern scholars of *midrash halakhah* remain uncertain about whether its hermeneutic webs were designed to serve a generative function or "merely" a mnemonic one. The two perspectives on *midrash halakhah* are are denoted as *midrash yoẓer*, or "generative midrash," and *midrash meqayyem*, or "affirming midrash." The presumption that masters of *midrash halakhah* generated law through their exegetical efforts (rather than giving existing laws mnemonic links to Scripture) fails to reckon with the role of ancestral tradition as a source of authority alongside Scripture—an important issue as early as the second century BCE.

12. Brian Stock, "Tradition and Modernity: Models from the Past," in *Modernité au Moyen Age: le défi du passé*, ed. Brigitte Cazelles and Charles Méla (Geneva, 1990), 39.

13. Ibid., 39–40.

14. This closely follows ibid., 36.

15. Bernard Cerquiglini, *Éloge de la variante: Histoire critique de la philologie* (Paris, 1989), 111.

16. Stephen Nichols, "Introduction: Philology in a Manuscript Culture," *Speculum* 65 (1990): 9.

17. Manuscript variants also project social attitudes and systemic rivalries onto the parchment. A scribe who intentionally (rather than inadvertently) reworked a text may have assumed that he had superior judgment or understanding. Stephen Nichols, "Introduction: Philology in a Manuscript Culture," *Speculum* 65 (1990): 3, 7–8.

18. On the mistaken belief that literature is "referential mimesis where reference begins with its origin," see ibid., 7.

19. Malachi Beit Arié, "Transmission of Texts by Scribes and Copyists: Unconscious and Critical Interferences," *Bulletin of the John Rylands Library of Manchester* 75 (1993): 51.

20. Gabrielle Spiegel, "History, Historicism and the Social Logic of the Text," *Speculum* 65 (1990): 77.

21. Brian Stock, "Tradition and Modernity: Models from the Past," 38.

22. Beit Arié, "Transmission of Texts by Scribes and Copyists," 38.

23. Ibid., 39.

24. Ibid.

25. Ibid., 36.

26. This point is made by H. Z. Dimitrovsky in "Ha-yesh yeme ha-benayyim yehudiyyim?" in *Meḥqarim be-Madda'e ha-Yahadut*, ed. M. Bar Asher (Jerusalem, 1986), 265.

27. Naḥman Danzig, "Mi-talmud 'al peh le-talmud be-khtav," *Sefer ha-Shana Bar Ilan* 30–31 (2006): 108. I have offered more detailed ruminations on this topic in T. Fishman, "The Rhineland Pietists' Sacralization of Oral Torah," *JQR* 96 (2006): 9–16. And see Chapters 2 and 6 below.

28. Cited in Yisrael Ta Shma, "The Library of the French Sages," in *Rashi, 1040–1990: Hommage à Ephraim E. Urbach*, ed. Gabrielle Sed-Rajna (Paris, 1993), 536, and see Ta Shma's own claim in *Ha-Sifrut ha-Parshanit la-Talmud be-Eropa u-ve-Ẓefon Afriqa*, 2 vols. (Jerusalem, 1999), 1: 72–73.

29. Colette Sirat, *Hebrew Manuscripts of the Middle Ages*, trans. Nicholas de Lange (Cambridge, 2002), 65.

30. Ibid., 234.

31. Alexander Samely and Philip Alexander, "Artefact and Text: Recreation of Jewish Literature in Medieval Hebrew Manuscripts," *Bulletin of the John Rylands University Library* 75 (1993): 8, 9.

32. Reuven Bonfil, "Mitos, retorika, historya? 'Iyyun be-Megilat Aḥima'aẓ," in *Tarbut ve-Ḥevra be-Toldot Yisrael be-Yeme ha-Benayyim*, ed. R. Bonfil, M. Ben Sasson, and J. Hacker (Jerusalem, 1989), 114.

33. Ta Shma, *Ha-Sifrut ha-Parshanit*, 1:32.

34. Ibid., 1:16.

35. Ibid., 1:76.

36. As Brian Stock noted in "Tradition and Modernity: Models from the Past," 37: "The organization of tradition reflects the need to give an intellectual definition to a socio-geographical reality."

37. Ibid., 39, and cf. 43. Stock uses this phrase to designate cultural changes that are not precipitated by forces external to the society in question, such as war, famine or migration.

38. The following list of studies is not intended to be exhaustive: Fritz Kern, *Kingship and Law in the Middle Ages*, trans. S. B. Chrimes (Oxford, 1939); Frederick Cheyette,

"Custom, Case Law and Medieval Constitutionalism: A Reexamination," *Political Science Quarterly* 78 (1963): 362–90; Harold J. Berman, *Law and Revolution: The Formation of the Western Legal Tradition*, (Cambridge, Mass., 1983); Emily Z. Tabuteau, *Transfers of Property in Eleventh-Century Norman Law* (Chapel Hill, N.C., 1988); Brigitte Bedos-Rezak, "Diplomatic Sources and Medieval Documentary Practices: An Essay in Interpretive Methodology," in *The Past and Future of Medieval Studies*, ed. John Van Engen (Notre Dame, 1994), 313–43; Stephen D. White, *Custom, Kinship, and Gifts to Saints* (Chapel Hill, N.C., 1998). Studies that interpret the broader cultural ramifications of these changes include M. T. Clanchy, *From Memory to Written Record* (London, 1979); Brian Stock, *The Implications of Literacy* (Princeton, 1989); and Mary J. Carruthers, *The Book of Memory: A Study of Memory in Medieval Culture* (Cambridge, 1990).

39. In other words, I am making no claim about the "influence" of the dominant Christian culture, nor about "osmosis" (an explanatory model that focuses attention on the boundaries traversed), nor about "*zeitgeist*" (which lamely evades questions of simultaneity or contemporaneity).

40. Bedos-Rezak, "Diplomatic Sources and Medieval Documentary Practices: An Essay in Interpretive Methodology," in *The Past and Future of Medieval Studies*, ed. John Van Engen (Notre Dame, Ind., 1994), 314.

41. Ya'aqov Sussman, "'Torah she-be-'al peh'—peshutah ke-mashma'a: Koḥo shel qoẓo shel yod," *Meḥqere Talmud* 3 (2005): 209–385.

42. Brody, *The Geonim of Babylonia and the Shaping of Medieval Jewish Culture* (New Haven, Conn., 1998), 156; Brody, "Sifrut ha-geonim vi-ha-teqst ha-talmudi," *Meḥqere Talmud* 1 (1990), 290–91; Danzig, "Mi-talmud 'al peh le-talmud be-khtav."

43. Sussman, "'Torah she-be-'al peh'—peshutah ke-mashma'a," 320–22, 325.

44. On the inscription of the *Avesta*, see Mary Boyce, *A History of Zoroastrianism* (Leiden, 1999), 123. On the inscription of *hadith*, see Gregor Schoeler, "Writing and Publishing: On the Use and Function of Writing in the First Centuries of Islam," *Arabica* 44 (1997): 423–35; Gregor Schoeler, "Oral Torah and Hadit: Transmission, Prohibition of Writing, Redaction," in *The Oral and the Written in Early Islam*, ed. James E. Montgomery (Abingdon, 2006), 111–41; Michael Cook, "The Opponents of the Writing of Tradition in Early Islam," *Arabica* 44 (1997): 437–530. See also Talya Fishman, "Claims about the Mishna in Sherira Gaon's *Epistle*: Islamic Theology and Jewish History," in *Border Crossings: Interreligious Interaction and the Exchange of Ideas in the Islamic Middle Ages*, ed. D. Freidenreich and M. Goldstein (Philadelphia, forthcoming).

45. Sussman, "'Torah she-be-'al peh'—peshutah ke-mashma'a," 320. In leaving open the possibility that Jews did protest, Sussman's formulation strikes me as preferable to that of Ignaz Goldziher, who asserted that no debate ever arose in Jewish society over the inscription of oral matters. See Nehemiah Brüll, "Die Enstehungsgeschichte des babylonischen Talmuds als Schriftwerkes," in *Jahrbuch für jüdische Geschichte und Literatur* 2 (1876): 8; Gregor Schoeler, "Oral Torah and Hadit: Transmission, Prohibition of Writing, Redaction," 113–14.

46. Sussman, "'Torah she-be-'al peh'—peshutah ke-mashma'a," 322, 324n17.

47. The Talmud they disseminated was first and foremost that of Babylonia, but the geonim, and especially Sa'adya, were instrumental in mediating Palestinian traditions to the Jews of medieval northern Europe. Brody, *The Geonim of Babylonia*, 121–22.

CHAPTER 1

1. On the earliest (eighth century) evidence of inscribed Talmud, see D. Rosenthal, *Mishnah 'Avodah Zarah: Mahadurah Biqortit be-Ẓeruf Mavo* (Jerusalem, 1980), 96–106; D. Rosenthal, "Lishna de-kalla," *Tarbiẓ* 52 (1983): 305; M. M. Kasher, *Torah Shelemah Massekhet Pesaḥim min Talmud Bavli* 1 (Jerusalem, 1960), introduction, 17–18; R. (Y.) Brody, "Sifrut ha-geonim ve-ha-teqst ha-talmudi," *Meḥqere Talmud* 1 (1990): 280. Traditions regarding the Talmud's inscription are reviewed in Chapter 2.

2. BT Tem. 14a–b. The earliest source of this claim is a *beraita* of the school of Rabbi Ishmael; it is also found in BT Git. 60b. See Saul Lieberman, *Yevanim ve-Yevanut be-Ereẓ Yisrael* (Jerusalem, 1962), 213–24; Y. N. Epstein, *Mavo le-Nusaḥ ha-Mishnah* (Jerusalem, 1963), 2:692–706; M. Elon, *Mishpat ha-'Ivri: Toldotav, Meqorotav, 'Eqronotav*. (Jerusalem,1973), 1:208–10; J. M. Baumgarten, "The Unwritten Law in the Pre-Rabbinic Period," *Journal for the Study of Judaism* 3 (1972): 7–29; B. Gerhardssohn, *Memory and Manuscript: Oral Tradition and Written Transmission in Rabbinic Judaism and Early Christianity* (Copenhagen, 1961), 122ff.; Solomon Gandz, "Dawn of Literature: Prolegomena to a History of Unwritten Literature," *Osiris* 7 (1939): 440–63; Dov Zlotnick, "Memory and the Integrity of the Oral Tradition," *JANES* 16–17 (1984–85): 229–41. The question of whether the rabbinic dicta in question are actual prohibitions has been widely discussed in scholarly literature. In addition to the aforementioned sources, see Ya'aqov Sussman, "'Torah she-be-'al peh'—Peshuta ke-mashma'ah," *Meḥqere Talmud* 3: 227; Y. N. Epstein, *Mevo-ot le-Sifrut ha-Tannaim* (Jerusalem, 1957), 17; N. Brüll, "Die Enstehungsgeschichte des Babylonischen Talmuds als Schriftwerkes," *Jahrbücher für Jüdische Geschichte und Literatur* 2 (1876): 114. It seems likely that different Jewish sects of the Second Temple period had disparate perspectives on this matter.

3. An inscription of aggadah is mentioned in BT Tem. 14b and an allusion to a large volume of inscribed aggadot appears in BT Pes. 62b. Uses of the term "halakhot" to refer to an inscribed compilation are collected in Yehudah Aryeh Blau, "Shemot ha-ḥiburim shel Torah she-be'al peh," *Sefer ha-Zikkaron le le-khevod ha-Doktor Shmuel Avraham Posnanski* (Warsaw, 1927; reprint, Jerusalem, 1969), 8. See also Sussman, "'Torah she-be-'al peh,'" 217n28. Inscriptions of *halakhot* had existed as mnemonic aids even when the Temple stood, and ancient sages were unequivocal in condemning their use for adjudicatory purposes. See, e.g., *Megilat Ta'anit,* chap. 4, on why fasts cannot be declared on 14 Tammuz.

4. The translation is that of Robert Brody, in *The Geonim of Babylonia and the Shaping of Medieval Jewish Culture* (New Haven, Conn., 1998), 4.

5. A fuller discussion of "textualization" appears in Chapter 3. On the growing importance of writing in ninth-century Baghdad, see Shawkat M. Toorawa, *Ibn Abī Ṭāhir*

Ṭayfūr and Arabic Writerly Culture: A Ninth-Century Bookman in Baghdad (London, 2005).

6. Martin Jaffee, "Oral Cultural Context of the Talmud Yerushalmi: Greco-Roman Rhetorical Paideia, Discipleship, and the Concept of Oral Torah," in *The Talmud Yerushalmi and Greco-Roman Culture,* ed. P. Schäfer (Tübingen, 1999), 1:54; Martin Jaffee, *Torah in the Mouth: Writing and Oral Tradition in Palestinian Judaism, 200 BCE–400 CE* (Oxford, 2001), 140–46.

7. The term "*devarim*" can mean both "words" and "matters."

8. BT Tem. 14a–b. The earliest source of this teaching is a *beraita, Tanna devei Rabi Ishmael.* This teaching also appears in BT Git. 60b.

9. During the entire amoraic period, only the Bible was a *syngramma.* On Jewish students' note-making activities during lessons, and their use of *pinaqsiyyot* (*pinaxes*) and *megilot setarim* (literally, "scrolls to be sequestered") as mnemonic aids, see S. Lieberman, *Hellenism in Jewish Palestine: Studies in the Literary Transmission, Beliefs and Manners of Palestine in the I Century B.C.E.-IV Century C.E.* (New York, 1950), 87–88, 204–5; Lieberman, *Yevanim ve-Yevanut,* 213–24; B. Gerhardsson, *Memory and Manuscript,* 159ff.

10. Unfortunately, some scholars unfamiliar with this feature of ancient diplomatics imagined from the phrase that the scrolls in question contained esoteric teachings, whereas nothing in their content was arcane; they were veiled only in their manner of storage.

11. Post-Second Temple period traditions that use the term *setarim* to denote a hidden chamber include M.Sot. 1:2. See also the Hebrew version of 1 Maccabees.

12. Rina Drory identified a range of corpora that would have been regarded as *oral matters* in antiquity (and beyond). They include prayers; translations of Scripture (see *Tanḥuma Vayera* 5; *Pesiqta Rabbati* 10:5; *Tanḥuma Ki Tissa* 34); lists of *halakhot,* lists of the dignitaries in geonic academies; chronologies of yeshivot; lists of *nusḥei,* or "crib notes" for lectures on Talmud; *pesaqim* (legal decisions); Saboraic explanations acknowledged as such by later geonim; anonymous Masoretic compositions (which appear by the mid-eleventh century and are referred to as *divrei ha-qadmonim*); and mystical teachings. Rina Drory, *Reshit ha-Magga'im shel ha-Sifrut ha-Yehudit 'im ha-Sifrut ha-'Aravit ba-Meah ha-'Asirit* (Tel Aviv, 1988), 33. And see Blau, "Shemot ha-ḥiburim shel ha-Torah she-be-'al peh," 5.

13. This is argued in Daniel Boyarin, *Border Lines: The Partition of Judeo-Christianity* (Philadelphia, 2004), e.g., 171–72, 196. Israel Yuval does not directly address the emergence of the notion of Oral Torah, but he claims that rabbinic Judaism evolved in dialogue with Christianity: see *Two Nations in Your Womb: Perceptions of Jews and Christians in Late Antiquity and the Middle Ages* (Berkeley, Calif., 2006).

14. Thus, for example, Michael Cook asserted that the opposition to *hadith* inscription in the early Islamic community could be traced to the "hostility toward writing" found in Palestinian rabbinic Jewish sources. Michael Cook, "The Opponents of the Writing of Tradition in Early Islam," *Arabica* 44 (1997): 500. See now Talya Fishman, "Guarding Oral Transmission: Within and Between Cultures," *Oral Tradition* 25:1 (2010).

15. A midrashic motif that was popular in medieval Jewish culture stated that, when Christians claimed to be *Verus Israel*, having already usurped the Written Torah, Jews gloated over the fact that they alone possessed the *mysterion*, the oral teachings that God granted to His true children. Variants of this motif appear in YT Peah 2:16; YT Meg. 4:1; YT Hag. 1:8 and elsewhere.. On this theme, see P. Schäfer, "Das 'Dogma' von der Mundlichen Torah im rabbinischen Judentum," in Schäfer, *Studien zur Geschichte und Theologie des Rabbinischen Judentums* (Leiden, 1978), 166–79; J. Neusner, *What, Exactly, Did the Rabbinic Sages Mean by "The Oral Torah"? An Inductive Answer to the Question of Rabbinic Judaism* (Atlanta, 1999), 40–46; Jaffee, *Torah in the Mouth*, 142–46, Marc Bregman, "Mishnah ke-mysterion," *Meḥqere Talmud* 3 (Jerusalem, 2005), 1:101–9.

16. Had this in fact been the import of R. 'Aqiva's statement, it would be hard to explain why medieval Jews continued to read—and cite—aprocryphal writings such as the *Wisdom of Ben Sira*. See, for example, the introduction to Baḥya ibn Paquda's *Book of Direction to the Duties of the Heart.*

17. M. San. 10:1. See Menaḥem Haran, "Mi-ba'ayot ha-qanonizaẓya shel ha-miqra," *Tarbiẓ* 25 (1956), 247. As Haran notes in a footnote, this observation had previously been made by Yeḥezqel Kaufman and Naḥman Krochmal. Cf. Yisrael Moshe Ḥazan, *Iyye HaYam* Gloss on *She-elot u-Teshuvot ha-Geonim: Sha'arei Teshuva* (Livorno, 1869), 76ff.

18. BT Tem. 14b; BT Git. 60b.

19. BT BB 130b. On the variant recensions of this tradition—some of which replace "*talmud*" with "*limud*," or even "*gemara*," see E. Urbach, *Ha-Halakhah, Meqoroteha ve-Hitpatḥuta* (Jerusalem, 1984), 229–30.

20. On the distinction between "halakhah" on the one hand and "decided law" on the other, see Urbach, *Ha-Halakhah, Meqoroteha ve-Hitpatḥuta*, 91–92; N. Danzig, *Mavo le-Sefer Halakhot Pesuqot* (New York, 1993), 138n99 (middle paragraph); D. Sklare, *Samuel ben Ḥofni Gaon and His Cultural World* (Leiden, 1996), 44. And see S. Mirsky, introduction to *Sheiltot de-Rav Aḥai Gaon* (Jerusalem, 1960), 17–18. Examples of non-practiceable *halakhot* include those designated as *hilkheta le-meshiḥa* and those in the category of *halakhah ve-eyn morin ken.*

21. The sages indicate that this meritorious activity brings its own reward, "*derosh ve-qabbel sakhar.*" See Norman Lamm, *Torah Lishmah: Torah for Torah's Sake in the Works of Rabbi Ḥayyim of Volozhin and His Contemporaries* (Hoboken, N.J., 1989).

22. On the Qayrawanese Jews' use of written texts of Talmud, see Chapter 2.

23. Both recensions appear in B. M. Levin, ed., *Iggeret Rav Sherira Gaon Mesuderet be-Shne Nusḥa-ot: Nusaḥ Sefarad ve-Nusaḥ Ẓorfat 'im Ḥilufe Girsaot* (Haifa, 1921). On the identification of the "French" recension as the version more compatible with geonic cultural assumptions, see, e.g., Moshe Beer, "'Iyyunim le-Iggeret Sherira Gaon," *Shenaton Bar Ilan* 4–5 (1967): 181–95; M. A. Friedman, "'Al terumat ha-genizah le-ḥeqer ha-halakhah," in *Mada'e ha-Yahadut* 38 (1993): 277–94. The claim that all "Spanish" manuscripts of Sherira's *Epistle* are late and were subject to "heavy-handed reworking" in order to bring them into accord with the writings of Maimonides appears in Sussman, "Torah she-be'al peh," 234n26.

24. In several of his writings, Sa'adya Gaon attempts to correct his mistaken Rabbanite brethren who don't understand that Mishnah and Talmud had been transmitted orally. In his *Commentary on Proverbs*, Sa'adya refers to the Mishnah and Talmud as having been written down long after their traditions had been in circulation. In Sa'adya Gaon, *Mishle 'im Tirgum u-Ferush ha-Gaon Sa'adya ben Yosef Fayumi,* ed. Yosef Kafaḥ (Jerusalem, 1975–76), introduction to Chapter 25, 134. And in his introduction to the *Commentary on Sefer Yeẓirah* (Kafaḥ translation [1972], 33)] , Sa'adya writes: "And when it was the time that the sages of the nation gathered togetherand consolidated the matters of the Mishna and dressed them in their own words and fixed them. . . . " Cf. Sa'adya, *Sefer ha-Galuy*, in A. Harkavy, *Ha-Sarid ve-ha-Palit* (St. Petersburg, 1891), 153. And see Sklare, *Samuel ben Ḥofni Gaon*, 93 and n. 86.

25. This is the language in the Spanish and French versions. Levin, *Iggeret Rav Sherira Gaon*, 71.

26. These boundaries, *'eruvin*, circumscribe the area within which a Jew may carry on the Sabbath. The Mishnah is concerned with the way in which the 2,000 cubits of the "Sabbath domain" were to be measured from the houses at the periphery of a settlement.

27. It would seem from this passage that the consonants *alef* and *'ayin* were not clearly distinguished in the environment of R. Judah the Patriarch.

28. Levin, *Iggeret Rav Sherira Gaon*, 24–25.

29. Sherira's designation of sages who lived before and after the Temple's Destruction as *rishonim* and *aḥaronim*, respectively, may be the earliest medieval periodization of rabbinic history. On this topic, see I. Gafni, "Concepts of Periodization and Causality in Talmudic Literature," *Jewish History* 10 (1996): 21–38; Y. Ta Shma, "Hilkheta ke-vatraei: beḥinot historiyyot shel kelal mishpati," *Shenaton ha-Mishpat ha-'Ivri* 6–7 (1979–80): 405–23; Yisrael Yuval, "Rishonim ve-Aḥaronim, Antiqui et Moderni," *Ẓion* 57 (1992): 369–94; S. Z. Havlin, "'Al ha-ḥatimah ha-sifrutit ke-yesod ha-ḥaluqah le-tequfot ba-halakhah," in *Meḥqarim be-Sifrut ha-Talmudit* (Jerusalem, 1983): 148–92; E. Kanarfogel, "Progress and Tradition in Medieval Ashkenaz," *Jewish History* 14 (2000): 287–316.

30. I have translated here in keeping with the Sefardi recension (and one French manuscript) that reads "*la iẓterikhu le-hakhi*," rather than "*la iẓterikhu le-hakhin*." Dr. David Sklare was kind enough to point out to me that this is the more plausible reading.

31. Levin, *Iggeret Rav Sherira Gaon*, 21–22. Thanks to Dr. David Sklare for helping me with this passage.

32. Ibid., 31.

33. Ibid., 18.

34. Ibid., 9, 10, 48, 62.

35. Ibid., 22. Thanks to Dr. David Sklare for improving this translation.

36. Ibid., 58.

37. Ibid., 20, and cf. 48. On the possible connection between Sherira's claim and the Muslim theological discussion about transmission of *hadith* according to its meaning or *ipsissima verba*, see T. Fishman, "Claims about the Mishna in Sherira Gaon's *Epistle*: Islamic Theology and Jewish History," in *Border Crossings: Interreligious Interaction and*

the Exchange of Ideas in the Islamic Middle Ages, ed. D. Freidenreich and M. Goldstein (Philadelphia, forthcoming).

38. The importance of this distinction was magnified under the influence of Islamic legal theory. See J. Goldin, "The Freedom and Restraint of Haggadah," *Studies in Midrash and Related Literature,* ed. Judah Goldin, Barry L. Eichler, and Jeffrey H. Tigay (Philadelphia, 1988), 253–55.

39. Levin, *Iggeret Rav Sherira Gaon,* 51.

40. Later Sefardi scholars found it necessary to reaffirm this point, which was not always grasped by students of Talmud. See Chapter 5.

41. For example, M. Avot 4:3: "Rabbi Judah says, be careful in [the endeavor of] *talmud,* for [the culpability incurred for] unintentional errors in *talmud* is as great if they were intentional errors." Cited in Levin, *Iggeret Rav Sherira Gaon,* 50. Other passages highlighted by Sherira include the catalogue of disciplines in which R. Yoḥanan ben Zakkai was said to have been proficient [BT Suk. 28a], and the ranking of disparate Jewish disciplines according to the merit that accrues to those who study them [BT BM 33a]. This last passage is discussed in Chapter 4.

42. Levin, *Iggeret Rav Sherira Gaon,* 58–59.

43. Ibid., 51–52.

44. Ibid., 52.

45. Ibid., 67.

46. Compare Brody's observation that Sherira's *Epistle* distinguishes between the content of tradition and its literary crystallization. Brody, *Geonim,* 278.

47. The "Prince of Torah," *Sar Torah* (or *Sar ha-Torah*), is understood to be an angel who imbued those he graced with knowledge of Torah and the supernatural ability to retain it. The phrase about *Sar Torah* is found in *Seder 'Olam, Seder Hakhamim,* 1:173; *Massekhet Kallah Rabbati,* 8; *Tosefta 'Atiqta.* On *Sar ha-Torah,* see Michael Swartz, *Scholastic Magic: Ritual and Revelation in Early Jewish Mysticism* (Princeton, 1996), 22–26; Ivan Marcus, *Rituals of Childhood: Jewish Acculturation in Medieval Europe* (New Haven, Conn., 1996), 45.

48. Levin, *Iggeret Rav Sherira Gaon,* 20–21. A gloss on the last saying explains that "the Early Ones" refers to Rabbi 'Aqiva, while "the Later Ones" refers to 'Aqiva's student Elazar b. Shamu'a.

49. Scholarly efforts to define the Mishnah are helpfully surveyed in Y. Elman, "Order, Sequence, and Selection: The Mishnah's Anthological Choices," in *The Anthology in Jewish Literature,* ed. David Stern (Oxford, 2004), 53–80.

50. Levin, *Iggeret Rav Sherira Gaon,* 21.

51. According to the "French" version (which contemporary scholars deem more reflective of Geonic language and attitudes), Rabbi Judah the Patriarch composed the Mishnah but never actually inscribed it. According to the "Spanish" version of the *Epistle,* he wrote it down. Ibid., 71. Many scholars, including Yisrael Moshe Ḥazan, Y. N. Epstein, S. Lieberman, S. Abramson, D. Weiss Halivni, and Y. Sussman, have written on the question of whether R. Judah inscribed the Mishnah.

52. Ibid., 43.

53. Ibid., 59. On the exposition of inscribed texts as an activity of oral transmission, see E. Wolfson, "Beyond the Spoken Word: Oral Tradition and Written Transmission in Medieval Jewish Mysticism," in *Transmitting Jewish Traditions: Orality, Textuality, and Cultural Diffusion*, ed. Y. Elman and I. Gershoni (New Haven, Conn., 2000), 193–202. And cf. the discussion of Maimonides' intentions in Chapter 2.

54. See below in this chapter, and Chapter 2.

55. Mary Carruthers has written eloquently in *The Book of Memory* about how educational ideals and practices of antiquity shaped medieval pedagogy. The abilities to store information in one's memory and retrieve from it when appropriate marked one as a person of prudence and good judgment. The aim of religious education was thus not so much to analyze tradition as it was to embody it and model it for others. Students who sought to become living authorities not only learned cognitively from the learned discourse of the master, they also learned mimetically—from his comportment and from what he did not say. Acquisition of knowledge was a means to the higher goal of personal transformation. See Mary Carruthers, *The Book of Memory: A Study of Memory in Medieval Culture*. Cambridge: Cambridge University Press, 1990.

56. These images appear throughout tannaitic literature. See, for example, M. Avot 5:15; *Avot de-Rabi Natan* A 40; *Avot de-Rabi Natan* B 45 (Schechter, 127); *Sifre Deuteronomy*, Finkelstein ed., 110:3–5, 8–12; 338:9–13; R. Hammer edition, paragraphs 48 and 306. See S. Fraade, *From Tradition to Commentary: Torah and Its Interpretation in the Midrash Sifre to Deuteronomy* (Albany, N.Y., 1991), 18, and Chapter 3 there, especially 100–121. Carruthers noted that writings about the lives of saints make recurring references to the prodigious memories of celebrated figures such as Francis of Assisi and Aquinas, because this characteristic marks them as individuals of superior moral character. Carruthers, *Book of Memory*, 12, 173–74.

57. Levin, *Iggeret Rav Sherira Gaon*, 44–45.

58. Ibid., 46, citing BT Hor. 14a and BT Ber. 64a .

59. This theme, of clear importance to the geonim, is also discussed in a comment on a *beraita* in BT BB 145a that appears in *Teshuvot ha-Geonim, Qohelet Shelomo*, 23. Parallels appear in *Teshuvot ha-Geonim* (Kisch), 12–13, 97.

60. On the centrality of memory in antiquity and the fear of forgetting, see Sussman, "'Torah she-be-'al peh,'" 255. On techniques for acquiring and preserving knowledge in memory, see Sussman, 245–46, 249–50, 252 and n. 30, and 359–61. Though Sussman (252n30) echoed earlier researchers (e.g., José Faur) in writing that there is "no *mishna sedura* of *ars memoria* among Jewish sages, as there were elsewhere in the ancient world," he nonetheless acknowledged Shlomo Naeh's pathbreaking article, "Omanut ha-zikkaron: Mivnim shel zikkaron ve-tavniyyot shel teqst be-sifrut ḥazal," *Meḥqere Talmud* 3 (2005): 543–89.

61. For example, in distinguishing between (Deut. 1:13) those who are *ḥakhamim* ("wise") and those who are *nevonim* ("discerning"), midrash describes the successful moneylender as one who makes himself mindful of his collection even when there are no

customers. (*Sifre* on Deuteronomy, Finkelstein ed., 22:1–5; Hammer ed., paragraph 13.) The image of the successful moneylender also appears in Jerome, *Apol.*, 1:16, cited in H. F. D. Sparks, "Jerome as Biblical Scholar," in *The Cambridge History of the Bible*, ed. P. R. Ackroyd and C. F. Evans (Cambridge, 1970), 536. The importance of constant review of one's learning is also conveyed in descriptions of the farmer who toils in his fields even when he has nothing to show for it: "Whoever studies but does not labor [review] is like one who sows but does not harvest" (YT Para 4:7; cf. YT Oholot 16:8; BT San. 99a, end). Saul Lieberman noted that the rabbinic contrast between the "*ḥakham*" and the "*navon*" parallels its contrast of "Sinai" and "the uprooter of mountains." S. Lieberman, "Biqoret Sifre," *Qiryat Sefer* 14 (1937–38): 325–26. And cf. *Sifre* Deut., Finkelstein ed., 84:7–15; Hammer ed., paragraph 41.

62. Levin, *Iggeret Rav Sherira Gaon*, 62. The distinction between the liturgical reading of Scripture while reading from a text and the recitation of Mishnah by heart is designated in the distinct verb choices. See above.

63. Thus, for example, in BT Meg. 32a, R. Yoḥanan claims that the phrase "bad statutes and laws according to which they do not live" (Ezek. 20:25) refers to the practice of reading without a chant and reciting without melody." Cf. the reference to Rabbi Yoḥanan ben Zakkai and Vespasian in Lam. Rabbah 1:5 and the description of Moses' repeated recitations in BT Eruv. 54b. Manuscripts of Mishnah and Talmud that have cantillation marks offer codicological evidence that these corpora were recited with melody. See Y. Yeivin, "Hat'amat ha-torah she-be-'al peh ba-te'amim," *Leshonenu* 24 (1960): 47–69, 167–78, 207–31.

64. BT Ned. 41a. On the trope itself, see Sussman, "'Torah she-be-'al peh,'" 257 and n. 47.

65. Levin, *Iggeret Rav Sherira Gaon*, 19–20, referring to BT Ned. 41a. On launderers' tales in rabbinic literature, see Eli Yassif and Jacqueline Teitelbaum, *Hebrew Folktales: History, Genre, Meaning* (Bloomington, Ind., 1999), 217, 222.

66. According to the eleventh-century French commentator Rashi, 'Aqiva had recited these repeatedly until they were arranged in his mouth. Rashi on BT Git. 67a, "*oẓar balum.*"

67. Levin, *Iggeret Rav Sherira Gaon*, 28–29. Though the *Epistle* as a whole is written in geonic Aramaic, the paean to R. Meir's formulation is written in Hebrew and may preserve older, embedded, traditions.

68. "*U-devareha meḥubarim ḥibur yafeh.*" On the poet as a mnemotechnician who preserves "the useful by binding it in verse," see J. A. Notopoulos, "Mnemosyne in Oral Literature," *Transactions and Proceedings of the American Philological Association* 69 (1938): 469.

69. Levin, *Iggeret Rav Sherira Gaon*, 30.

70. Thus, the comparison of Rabbi 'Aqiva to a laborer who collected all sorts of grains and legumes, which he subsequently converted into "rings" may refer to this tanna's gifts as a master of midrash. One who is adept at this genre amasses seemingly unrelated traditions and groups them in discernible patterns. See Fraade, *From Tradition*

to Commentary, 18. Exhorting students not to be like the "sated person" of Proverbs 27:7, who "disdains a honeycomb," midrash encourages them to "make the heart like chambers within chambers . . . and bring into it both the words of the House of Shammai and the words of the House of Hillel" (YT Hag. 7:12). Cf. Shlomo Naeh, "'Aseh libkha ḥadre ḥadarim: 'Iyyun nosaf be-divre ḥazal 'al ha-maḥloqet," in *Meḥuyyavut Yehudit Meḥudeshet: 'Al 'Olamo ve-Haguto shel David Hartman*, ed. Z. Zohar and A. Sagi (Tel Aviv, 2001), 851–75; D. Zlotnick, *The Tractate Mourning* (New Haven, Conn., 1966), 6. Organizing categories include teachings associated with a particular sage, teachings with common rhetorical features (such as "*eyn beyn . . . ella*"; "*bo bayom darash*"), numeric categories, acronyms, and so on. On the image of the honeycomb in Latin writings, see Carruthers, *Book of Memory*, 33, 35–36.

71. *Avot de-Rabi Natan* A, chap. 18 (Schechter, 34a). Cf. the description of the "disciple of the sages" who, like a filter, "separates flour, bran and meal . . . sits and sorts words of Torah and weighs them" (*Sifre, Deuteronomy*, Finkelstein ed., 109:13–110:3; Hammer ed., paragraph 48). Other references to the sage as filter appear in M. Avot 5:15; *Avot de-Rabi Natan* A 40; *Avot de-Rabi Natan* B 45; BT Hag. 3a–b.

72. Levin, *Iggeret Rav Sherira Gaon*, 43–44. Later rabbinic sages were also renowned for their activities of aggregation, classification, and assemblage. Talmudic passages (e.g., BT AZ 42b and BT Shab. 138a, top) credit the amoraim Abaye and Rav Sheshet with collecting rings of Mishnah and linking them into a chain. Carruthers (*Book of Memory*, 5–6) describes the *catena*, a staple of the monastic *lectio divina*, as a "very old medieval genre."

73. Cassel, *Teshuvot Geonim Qadmonim*, 46, translation by Brody, in *Geonim*, 55.

74. "For one who knows a *sugya* of Gemara and the language of the rabbis and its recitations [*ve-gursehon*] knows it best." Gaon Aaron Sarjado, in *Oẓar ha-Geonim*, ed. B. M. Levin, vol. 7, *Teshuvot* Yeb., responsa 170, 71; Brody, "Sifrut ha-geonim ve-ha-teqst ha-talmudi," 24; Elman and Ephrat, "Orality and the Institutionalization of Tradition: The Growth of the Geonic Yeshiva and the Islamic Madrasa," in *Transmitting Jewish Traditions: Orality, Textuality, and Cultural Diffusion* (New Haven, Conn., 2000), 127–28. This point is fully (and forcefully) articulated in Sussman, "Torah she-be-'al peh." On Aaron Sarjado, see Levin, *Iggeret Rav Sherira Gaon*, 120; Moshe Gil, "R. Aharon HaCohen Gaon ben Yosef u-vanav 'Eli ve-Avraham," *Sefunot*, n.s. 1 / o.s. 16 (1980): 9–23. The testimony of Natan HaBavli regarding the oral transmission of Talmud is adduced in Naḥman Danzig, "Mi-talmud 'al peh le-talmud be-khtav," *Sefer ha-Shana Bar Ilan* 30–31 (2006): 77.

75. On the orality of geonic learning, see E. S. Rosenthal, "Lishna aḥarina," *Proceedings of the Second World Congress of Jewish Studies* (1957), 14–15 (Hebrew); 18–19 (English); Y. N. Epstein, *Mevo-ot le-Sifrut ha-Amoraim* (Jerusalem, 1962), 140–41; Brody, "Sifrut ha-geonim ve-ha-teqst ha-talmudi," 290–91; Brody, *Geonim*, 156; Sussman, "'Torah she-be-'al peh,'" 239–40nn49a and 50, 241n51, 298n65, 302n8.

76. On the tannaim connected with the geonic academies, see Brody, *Geonim*, 42, 50, 155, 166; Y. N. Epstein, *Mavo le-Nusaḥ ha-Mishnah*, 673–88, 690; Y. N. Epstein, *Perush*

ha-Geonim le-Seder Tohorot (Jerusalem, 1982), 45; Sussman, "Kitve yad u-mesorot nusaḥ shel ha-Mishnah," *Proceedings of the Seventh World Congress of Jewish Studies* (1981), 238–39n92 re earlier literature on this subject. On the tannaim in the mishnaic academies, see Lieberman, *Hellenism in Jewish Palestine*, 88; Dov Zlotnick, *The Iron Pillar—Mishnah: Redaction, Form and Intent* (New York, 1988), 14–15.

77. Like their amoraic predecessors, geonic yeshivot distinguished between two (sequential) stages of study. According to talmudic sages, the student's first task was to memorize the material in question in order to be able to recite it (*shinun, gerisa, gemira*). Only then was he equipped to to undertake critical investigation (*limud, ḥaqira, sevara*) of that which had been stored in memory. As the Talmud counsels in BT Shab. 63b and AZ 19a, a student should first memorize and recite the material in question, and then return to understand it rationally. A report of the study practices of the Palestinian amora, R. Yoḥanan, offers a case in point: after learning *Sifra* by heart in three days, it took him three months to understand it (BT Yeb. 72b). The rabbinic tradition that describes Moses as having studied Written Torah in the daytime and Oral Torah at night (e.g., *Pirqe de-Rabi Eliezer*, quoted in S. Schechter, *Saadyana* [Cambridge, 1903], 15–16) may well be related, since study from the open text (of Scripture) could only be done in the daylight, while critical examination of teachings stored in memory (Oral Torah) could be undertaken even in the dark.

78. In his reconstruction of the role of written texts in the academies of ancient Palestine, Martin Jaffee posits that jottings of *oral matters* were used in *progymnasmata* drills designed to hone rhetorical agility. Students presented with received traditions were asked to reconfigure them, shaping the pertinent teachings so that they could address any situation that might arise. See Jaffee, *Torah in the Mouth*, 130, and cf. E. Wolfson, "Beyond the Spoken Word: Oral Tradition and Written Transmission in Medieval Jewish Mysticism," in *Transmitting Jewish Traditions*, 35.

79. Schechter, *Saadyana*, 118–21; Brody, *Geonim*, 55.

80. In Levin, *Iggeret Rav Sherira Gaon*, appendix, xxviii; S. Assaf, *Tequfat ha-Geonim ve-Sifrutah* (Jerusalem, 1955), 70n6; S. D. Goitein, *Sidre Ḥinukh be-Yeme ha-Geonim u-Vet ha-Rambam* (Jerusalem, 1962), 161; S. Abramson, *Rav Nisim Gaon, Ḥamishah Sefarim* (Jerusalem, 1965), 133–34, 531; Brody, *Geonim*, 44n40. Another reference to students who first recite and subsequently "expose" (*megalim*) appears in Sherira's responsum in Schechter, *Saadyana*, 118. See also Moshe Gil, *Malkhut Yishma'el be-Tequfat ha-Geonim* (Jerusalem, 1997), 73–74.

81. Might the use of the term "expose" in conjunction with preparing the next tractate have been intended in a literal sense as well, in the sense of showing the written text? Though Shraga Abramson does not endorse this hypothesis, he does cite one use of the verb "*gale*" which would support it. A passage in Midrash Tehilim, Ps. 59 (Buber ed., *gimel*), describes how the wife of R. 'Aqiva's son aided her husband in study by "opening a book and *revealing it* from beginning to end" (S. Abramson, *R. Nisim Gaon, Ḥamishah Sefarim* [Jerusalem, 1965], 531).

82. B. M. Levin, ed., *Oẓar ha-Geonim: Teshuvot Geone Bavel u-Ferushehem 'al pi*

Seder ha-Talmud, (Jerusalem), Shab., responsa 311. Cf. Tos. Shab. 115a, "*aliba*"; *Hagahot Maimuniyyot,* MT Hil. Shab. 23:27, letter *shin*; *Mordecai,* Shab. chap. 16, 396. This passage is cited in *Sefer Ḥasidim* 1751, in the introduction to *Or Zaru'a, Alpha Beta* 49, and in Beẓalel Ashkenazi's *Shita Mequbeẓet,* Tem. 14b. with a "*Lishna aḥarina.*" See Y. N. Epstein, *Mavo le-Nusaḥ ha-Mishnah,* 669, 696; Y. N. Epstein, *Mevo-ot le-Sifrut ha-Amoraim,* 143; S. Schlesinger, "'Al ketivat torah she-be-'al peh be-zeman ha-talmud," *Sinai* 117 (1996): 46; Danzig, *Mavo le-Sefer Halakhot Pesuqot,* 4; Sussman, "'Torah she-be-'al peh,'" 299n76; Danzig, "Mi-talmud 'al peh le-talmud be-khtav," 51–52.

83. According to Tosefta Ber. 13:4 (in the Zuckermandel edition) and BT Shab. 115b, "Those who write down *berakhot* are like those who burn Torah—because these writings cannot be saved from a conflagration on Shabbat." See Schlesinger, *'Al ketivat Torah she-be-'al peh be-zeman ha-talmud,*" 47. Earlier rabbinic prescriptions pertaining to the treatment of *sefarim* seem to have had only scriptural writings in mind, whether the tripartite TaNakh or its constituent parts. Stefan Reif, Malachi Bet Arié, Meir Bar Ilan, Colette Sirat, and Catherine Heszer are among the scholars who have discussed Jewish use of the codex before the Moslem conquest.

84. Levin, *Oẓar ha-Geonim,* Shab., responsa 310, cited in HaMeiri, *Bet ha-Beḥira,* Shab. 115a.

85. Hai Gaon, in Epstein, *Mevo-ot le-Sifrut ha-Amoraim,* 140–43. On the extension of this ruling by the twelfth-century tosafist R. Isaac of Dampierre and his students, see Chapter 4 below.

86. A question posed to Natronai Gaon in the mid-ninth century reveals that the questioner hoped to use the illumination of the synagogue oil lamp (*ner tamid*?) for reading Talmud. Levin, *Oẓar ha-Geonim,* Shab., responsa 21; Natronai Gaon, *Teshuvot Rav Natronai bar Hilai Gaon* (Jerusalem, 1994), 155–56. Generations later, when asked by Qayrawanese Jews whether it was permissible to read by the light of a candle on the Sabbath, Hai Gaon reponded that use of the candle was permitted but that, in Babylonia, Talmud was not studied from books on the Sabbath. In Levin, *Oẓar ha-Geonim,* Shab., responsa 17. On the use of *nusḥaot,* written versions of *oral matters,* within the Baghdadi academies at the end of the geonic period, see S. Abramson, "Ẓerufe teshuvot geonim," in *Minḥah le-I"sh: Sefer Yovel le-R-Aleph Yod Dolgin* (Jerusalem, 1991), 196n11. On geonic references to *nusḥaot* and to "old books," see Sussman, "'Torah she-be-'al peh,'" 297.

87. See Brody, "Sifrut ha-geonim viha-teqst ha-talmudi," 283–84, 288–89.

88. M. Schlueter, "Was the Mishna Written? The Answer of Rav Sherira Gaon," in *Rashi 1040–1990: Hommage á Ephraim E. Urbach,* 218. In a personal communication, David Sklare suggested that Sherira may have been articulating an ideological stance that was no longer reflective of reality precisely because he was attempting to bind the Qayrawanese community more tightly to the gaonate.

89. Elman and Ephrat claim that the amoraim were not comparably zealous about guarding oral transmission, but cf. the opinion of Sussman in "Torah she-be'al peh," 296.

90. See Toorawa, *Ibn Abī Ṭāhir Ṭayfūr and Arabic Writerly Culture,* 56.

91. See ibid., chap. 4; J. Lassner, *The Topography of Baghdad in the Early Middle Ages*

(Detroit, 1970), 155–77; J. Lassner, *The Shaping of Abbasid Rule* (Princeton, N.J., 1980), 194–204. On the stationers of medieval Paris, see, e.g., Richard and Mary Rouse, *Manuscripts and Their Makers: Commercial Book Producers in Medieval Paris, 1200–1500,* 2 vols. (Turnhout, 2000).

92. See, e.g., Harald Motzki, "The Author and His Work in the Islamic Literature of the First Centuries: The Case of Abd al-Razzaq's *Musannaf*," *Jerusalem Studies in Arabic and Islam* 28 (2003): 28, 1–31; Scott Lucas, "Where Are the Legal *Hadith*? A Study of the *Musannaf* of Ibn Abi Shayba," *Islamic Law and Society* 15 (2008): 283–314. I am grateful to Professor Joseph Lowry for offering bibliographical guidance. Geonica scholars are now beginning to investigate whether the Islamic compilation and inscription of *hadith* literature is in any way related to the inscription of Talmud, to the composition of topically arranged compilations of halakhah, or to the creation of legal monographs in the geonic period. See, for example, Sklare, *Samuel ben Ḥofni Gaon,* 51n41, and 55n57, where he mentions an introduction to *hadith* by al-Naysaburi (933–1014) as a possible model for Samuel ben Ḥofni's introduction to the Mishnah and Talmud. See also David Sklare, "R. David ben Sa'adya al-Ger ve-ḥiburo Al-Ḥawwi," *Te'udah* 14 (1998): 103–23; Gideon Libson, "Ha-monografiyot ha-hilkhatiyyot shel ha-Rav Shemuel ben Ḥofni," *Te'udah* 15 (1999): 221; Yehuda Ẓvi Stampfer, "Ha-mishpat ha-'Ivri be-Sefarad ba-meah ha-11: Bein geonim le-rishonim ('al pi Kitab al-Ḥawwi le-R. David ben Sa'adya)," *Shenaton ha-Mishpat ha-'Ivri* 38 (2008): 217–36.

93. On al-Shafi'i's *Risala,* see Majid Khadduri, trans. and ed., *Islamic Jurisprudence: Shafi'i's Risala* (Baltimore, 1961); J. Robson, ed. and trans., *An Introduction to the Science of Tradition* (London, 1953), and now, Joseph E. Lowry, *Early Islamic Legal Theory: The Risāla of Muḥammad ibn Idrīs al-Shāfi'ī* (Leiden, 2007).

94. Jewish literati, like Sa'adya Gaon, even studied Hellenistic texts in interfaith colloquia. On the *majalis,* see J. Kraemer, *Humanism in the Renaissance of Islam* (Leiden, 1986), 7, 54–60; Sklare, *Samuel ben Ḥofni,* 73, 100–101; Ḥava Lazarus-Yafeh, ed., *The Majlis: Interreligious Encounters in Medieval Islam* (Wiesbaden, 1999).

95. Elman and Ephrat, "Orality and the Institutionalization of Tradition." This perspective dovetails with the perspectives of earlier scholars who speculated about why the geonim undertook so little Talmud exegesis. A summary of these ruminations appears in A. Grossman, *Ḥakhme Ẓorfat ha-Rishonim* (Jerusalem, 1995), 429–36.

96. Referring to Samuel ben Ḥofni's commentary written for readers who lacked rabbinic education, David Sklare describes it as a "simplistic" work, whose use of talmudic passages "would elicit a protest from any educated talmudist." Sklare, *Samuel ben Ḥofni,* 17, 93–94 and n. 17. Cf. Brody, *Geonim,* 190, 286.

97. The questions posed by the Qayrawanese Jews, discussed below, are obvious exceptions.

98. It was this request from the Jewish community of Spain that prompted Rav 'Amram Gaon to produce his *Seder* in the second half of the ninth century.

99. These examples, to be analyzed below, add to the growing body of evidence that point to the necessity of revising the historiographic image of the geonim as overreaching,

micromanaging despots. See Brody, *Geonim*, 147; Menaḥem Ben Sasson, *Qayrawan*, xi, xii.

100. Cf. Brody's formulation in "Sifrut ha-geonim ve-ha-teqst ha-talmudi," 251: "We are, to a great extent, shackled to a very specific vision of the talmudic material, [one] which stems from our talmudic education and [that] is nourished, in particular, by the heritage of Rashi and the Tosafot. It is difficult for us to free ourselves from this point of view and to appreciate the many other interpretive possibilities that are latent in the talmudic material." In citing Professor Brody, I do not mean to imply that he himself has posed the question that I present here: whether the Talmud itself, when not allied to attested practice, had always been regarded as the preeminent source of Jewish legal authority.

101. Some guidelines for adjudication appear in BT Eruv. 46b–47a, Yeb. 42b, Ber. 9a; Bekh. 49a; Beẓ. 4a. Simḥa Assaf found seventy more adjudicatory principles in geonic writings, and Shraga Abramson notes that others have since been identified. However, as Abramson notes, some of these adjudicatory principles were reworked by multiple later hands. See Assaf, *Tequfat ha-Geonim ve-Sifrutah*, 223ff.; S. Abramson, *Perush Rabbenu Ḥananel la-Talmud* (Jerusalem, 1955), 148–49.

102. Abramson, *Perush Rabbenu Ḥananel la-Talmud*, 148–49.

103. See, e.g., Levin, *Oẓar ha-Geonim*, BK, responsa 100, 37; Suk., responsa 96, 45; Brody, "Sifrut ha-geonim ve-ha-teqst ha-talmudi," 290–91; Brody, *Geonim*, 156–57.

104. Levin, *Iggeret Rav Sherira Gaon*, and see below.

105. Thus, in tannaitic times, an anonymous mishnah was deemed more authoritative than the opinion of a named rabbi, for a ruling without a name was presumed to be the voice of the majority. See Yeb. 42b, noted in Brody, *Geonim*, 142n14.

106. Letter to Pinḥas ha-Dayyan, in Moses Maimonides, *Iggerot ha-Rambam*, ed. Yiẓḥaq Shilat (Jerusalem, 1988), 2:442.

107. The eleventh-century Karaite Nisi ben Noaḥ portrayed the absence of authorial attribution as a tactic deliberately undertaken by Rabbanites to hoodwink readers and avoid questions of accountability: "Don't wear yourself out reading the works of the errant ones [*ha-to'im*] that are ascribed to *ẓaddiqim* [the righteous] and *ḥasidim* [the Pietists]." Quoted in Rina Drory, *Reshit ha-Magga'im*, 97. Toorawa notes that a comparable disdain for anonymous and pseudonymous works was expressed in Ibn al-Nadim's tenth-century *Fihrist*. Though I raise the issue of Karaism in considering formulations in Sherira's Epistle, I am in agreement with recent scholars who understand this work as a response to questions that troubled the Qayrawanese Jews, and not as a defense of Rabbanism against Karaism. See Menaḥem Ben Sasson, *Ẓemiḥat ha-Qehilah ha-Yehudit be-Arẓot ha-Islam: Qayrawan, 800–1057* (Jerusalem, 1996), 41–46; Brody, *Geonim*, 20.

108. Levin, *Iggeret Rav Sherira Gaon*, 56–57. See Sussman, "'Torah she-be-'al peh,'" 266–68nn34–35, 276–77, 279, and n. 74. Sherira is presumably describing how the amoraim responded to problematic formulations in Mishna, but he also seems to identify with them.

109. On the novelty of authorship see Drory, *Reshit ha-Magga'im*, 97, 172; Danzig,

"Mi-talmud 'al peh le-talmud be-khtav," 109; Brody, *Geonim*, chap. 15; Sklare, *Samuel ben Ḥofni*, 77, and, in general, Jed Wyrick, *The Ascension of Authorship* (Cambridge, Mass., 2004). Sa'adya's status as a maverick within Jewish culture is affirmed in studies by Henry Malter, Rina Drory, Robert Brody, Diana Lobel, and others. On the practice within oral Arabic culture of emulating—and lifting from—from the work of predecessors and peers, see W. Heinrichs, "An Evaluation of *Sariqa*," *Quaderni di Studi Arabi* 5–6 (1987–88): 357–68.

110. Had any inscribed iteration of tradition been viewed as authoritative, later voices could never have joined in the conversation, but would, at most, have commented from the sidelines. In *From Tradition to Commentary*, Steven Fraade analyzed the cultural and literary process whereby creative engagement with tradition gradually moved from frontal encounter and unrestrained emendation to the more deferential posture of glossing tradition from the margins, without attempting to alter it.

111. Fine contextualizations of Sa'adya's maverick innovations appear in Brody, *Geonim*, 65, 235–44, 247, and 260–65, and in Drory, *Reshit ha-Magga'im*.

112. Sa'adya Gaon, introduction to *The Book of Beliefs and Opinions*, trans. Samuel Rosenblatt (New Haven, Conn., 1948), 8. I have translated the last line in keeping with the suggestion made in Shraga Abramson, "Mehem u-vahem," in *Sefer Shalom Sivan*, ed. A. Even-Shoshan (Jerusalem, 1979), 3n1, *aleph*.

113. On the many works about poetic plagiarism, see Toorawa, *Ibn Abī Ṭāhir Ṭayfūr and Arabic Writerly Culture*, chap. 2.

114. The geonic figures include Rav Natan Av HaYeshiva, Nisim Gaon, and Hai Gaon, and the Andalusians include Avraham bar Ḥiyya, R. David Kimḥi, R. Yeḥiel bar Yequtiel, R. Ḥananel b"r Shmuel, Isaac ibn Sahula, and Maimonides. In Shraga Abramson, "Mehem u-Vahem," 3–7.

115. Sa'adya Gaon, *Mishle 'im Tirgum u-Ferush Sa'adya ben Yosef Fayumi*, trans. Y. Kafaḥ (Jerusalem, 1975–76), 194.

116. Sa'adya Gaon, introduction to *Commentary on Sefer Yeẓira*, trans. and ed. Y. Kafaḥ (Jerusalem, 1972), 33.

117. See, e.g., A. ibn Ezra on Deut. 1:2 and Gen. 12:6; *Ẓofnat Pa'neaḥ* on Deut. 1:2 and Gen. 22. Cf. Moses Alashqar, *She-elot u-Teshuvot* (Jerusalem, 1984), no. 74, 42a; Nahum M. Sarna, "The Modern Study of the Bible in the Framework of Jewish Studies," in *Proceedings of the Eighth World Congress of Jewish Studies* (Jerusalem, 1983), 22; Jon Levenson, "The Eighth Principle of Judaism and the Literary Simultaneity of Scripture," *Journal of Religion* 68 (1988): 205–25; D. Weiss Halivni, *Peshat and Derash: Plain and Applied Meaning in Rabbinic Exegesis* (New York, 1991), 218n31; Shalom Rosenberg, "Ḥeqer ha-miqra ba-maḥshavah ha-yehudit ha-datit ha-ḥadashah," in *Ha-Miqra ve-Anaḥnu* (Ramat Gan, 1979), 86–119; Jakob Petuchowski, "The Supposed Dogma of the Mosaic Authorship of the Pentateuch," *Hibbert Journal* 57 (1959): 356–60; A. J. Heschel, *Torah min ha-Shamayim ba-Aspaqlaryah shel ha-Dorot* (London, 1962), 2:71–99; Louis Jacobs, *Principles of the Jewish Faith: An Analytical Study* (London, 1964), 216–301; Marc Shapiro, *The Limits of Orthodox Theology: Maimonides' Thirteen Principles Reappraised* (Oxford, 2004), 91–121.

118. A lucid explanation of why Jews in disparate regions embraced different understandings of Scripture's literary-editorial formation appears in an important article by Richard Steiner, "A Jewish Theory of Biblical Redaction from Byzantium: Its Rabbinic Roots, Its Diffusion and Its Encounter with the Muslim Doctrine of Falsification," *Jewish Studies Internet Journal* 2 (2003): 123–67. And see Ḥaggai Ben Shammai, "'Al 'Mudawwin', 'orekh sifre ha-miqra be-farshanut ha-miqra ha-'aravit ha-yehudit," in *Rishonim ve-Aḥaronim: Meḥqarim be-Toldot Yisrael Mugashim le-Avraham Grossman*, ed. J. Hacker, B. Z. Kedar, and Y. Kaplan (Jerusalem, 2010), 73–110.

119. Levin, *Iggeret Sherira Gaon*, 9–11, 18–31, 48–49, 51–52, 58–59, and 63–64. Comparable claims made in rabbinic antiquity traced the decline to the deaths of great scholars or to weakened conditions of discipleship (e.g., *Tosefta*, *Ḥag.* 2:9; YT San. 19c; BT San. 88b). The latter was presumably linked to the proliferation of legal disputes because inattentive students would not necessarily know whether a master had revised an earlier teaching. See S. Lieberman, *Greek in Jewish Palestine: Studies in the Life and Manners of Jewish Palestine in the II–IV Centuries C.E.* (New York, 1942), 92n71; Jaffee, "Oral Cultural Context of the Talmud Yerushalmi," 58. Whereas Sherira attempted—with some awkwardness—to link the decline to the Temple's destruction, some of the ancient rabbinic etiologies trace cultural deterioration to events that occurred *prior* to 70 CE. See BT Sot. 47b; Rashi on BM 33b, "*be-yeme.*" Whether or not he sensed inconsistency in Sherira's narrative, Maimonides supplies a missing link (not found in the *Epistle*): the claim that the national calamity had diminished contact between masters and pupils. According to Maimonides' introduction to *Mishneh Torah,* as Jews sought to escape local hardships, there was widescale emigration from Palestine.

120. See T. Fishman, "Claims about the Mishna in Sherira Gaon's *Epistle.*"

121. Levin, *Iggeret Sherira Gaon*, 21. As is seen below, the term "grandeur" refers to the Patriarch's wealth and political might and is connected with his easy access to the Roman powers of the time.

122. Levin, *Iggeret Sherira Gaon*, 21. The friendly conversations between the Emperor Antoninus and Rabbi Judah on matters pertaining to the relationship of body and soul, the evil inclination, and governmental affairs are recounted in BT San. 91a–b; YT Meg. 3:2.

123. Levin, *Iggeret Sherira Gaon*, 23.

124. Ibid., 22. Yet the rabbinic tradition that roots decline in the generation of the students of Hillel and Shammai suggests that this crisis occurred before the Temple's destruction.

125. Ibid., *Iggeret Sherira Gaon*, 22. Where one version of the "French" recension of the Epistle reads "*ḥiluq*," others, and the "Spanish" recension, read "*ḥiluf*," "alteration" of tradition. This latter term was used in Muslim anti-Jewish polemics to charge Jews with having falsified the Hebrew Bible that they had received as an authentic revelation; rabbinic teachings would not even have merited this charge. Thanks to Dr. David Sklare for helping me clarify this formulation.

126. I have opted for the "French" variant "*it'aqqerin*," which is the dominant locution in the "Spanish" version.

127. Levin, *Iggeret Rav Sherira Gaon*, 36.

128. Ibid., 41–42. According to Sherira, Mishnah spread within Israel from the time of its arrangement, which was hardly the case with *midrash halakhah*.

129. The term *beraita* designates a tannaitic teaching that was not included in the Mishnah. *Beraitot* were collected in the Tosefta, however, and they were brought back "into play" in the legal deliberations of the amoraim.

130. Levin, *Iggeret Rav Sherira Gaon*, 30.

131. See Richard C. Martin, "Inimitability," in *Encyclopedia of the Qur'an*, ed. J. D. McAuliffe (Washington, D.C., 2008), 2:526, columns 2ff. The term *I'jāz* was originally used in the context of a poetic duel, in which the defeated opponent was rendered incapable of speech, incapacitated, impotent. The doctrine of *I'jāz al-Qur'an* acquired its technical meaning sometime between 855 and 919. Late tenth-century discussions concerned the role of the Qur'an in establishing Muhammad's prophethood, and early eleventh-century writings perfected the literary rationale for the claim that the Qur'an was inimitable. See R. C. Martin, "The Role of the Basran Mu'tazila in Formulating the Doctrine of the Apologetic Miracle," *Journal of Near Eastern Studies* 39 (1980): 175–89; Issa Boullata, "The Rhetorical Interpretation of the Qur'an: *I'jāz* and Related Topics," in *Approaches to the History of the Interpretation of the Qur'an*, ed. Andrew Rippin (Oxford, 1988), 141–42; Yusuf Rahman, "The Miraculous Nature of Muslim Scripture: A Study of Abd al-Jabbar's *Ijaz al-Quran*," *Islamic Studies* 35 (1996): 415.

132. On Sherira's possible motives in fashioning this argument, see Fishman, "Claims about the Mishna in the *Epistle* of Sherira Gaon." On the sacralization of texts in Sefarad, see Chapter 2; in Ashkenaz, see Chapter 6.

133. Ẓemaḥ b. Mar Ḥayyim, gaon of Sura, had also referred to the precision of Mishnah's language, even when compared with the language of Scriptures, "which are fixed in writing." Noted in Sussman, "'Torah she-be-'al peh,'" 234n26; cf. 278, 304, 319, 342n57; and 344n61.

134. According to contemporary scholars of geonica, Talmud continued to be transmitted in a lexically fluid state in the Babylonia academies through the end of the geonic period. See Brody, "Sifrut ha-geonim ve-ha-teqst ha-talmudi," 279n172, 238–40; Sussman, "'Torah she-be-'al peh,'" 278, 304, 319, 342n57, 344n61; Danzig, "Mi-talmud 'al peh le-talmud be-khtav."

135. The claim that Talmud had never been transmitted in one unified form appears in E. S. Rosenthal, "Toldot ha-nusaḥ u-va'ayot 'arikha be-ḥeqer ha-talmud ha-bavli," *Tarbiẓ* 57 (1988): 1–39; E. S. Rosenthal, "Le-leshonoteha shel Massekhet Temura," *Tarbiẓ* 58 (1989): 317–56; E. S. Rosenthal, "'Iyyunim be-toldot ha-nusaḥ shel ha-talmud ha-bavli," *Sefer ha-Yovel le-khvod Mordecai Breuer*, ed. M. Bar Asher (Jerusalem, 1992), 2:571–91. This view was challenged in Shamma Friedman, "Le-hithavut shinuyye ha-girsaot ba-talmud ha-bavli," *Sidra* 7 (1991): 68–102.

136. Brody, *Geonim* 160, and cf. pp. 7, 39; 159–62. On variations in language between different *nusḥaot* that should not be attributed to copyists' errors: see Brody's citation from E. S. Rosenthal, in "Sifrut ha-geonim ve-ha-teqst ha-talmudi," 277.

137. Brody notes that the Babylonian Talmud never actually underwent lexical redaction. See Brody, "Sifrut ha-geonim ve-ha-teqst ha-talmudi," 279n172, 238–40. Yet this did not prevent later geonim from composing commentaries on Talmud, as David Sklare noted in correspondence with me.

138. On continuities between the geonim and amoraim, see Assaf, *Tequfat ha-Geonim ve-Sifrutah*, 133–71; Y. Gafni, "Yeshiva u-metivta," *Ẓion* 43 (1978): 12–37; David Goodblatt, "Hitpatḥuyyot ḥadashot be-ḥeqer yeshivot Bavel," *Ẓion* 46 (1981): 14–38; Y. Gafni, Review of David Goodblatt's article, *Ẓion* 46 (1981): 52–56; Jeffrey Rubenstein, "The Rise of the Babylonian Rabbinic Academy: A Re-Examination of the Talmudic Evidence," in *Jewish Studies: An Internet Journal* (*JSIJ*) 1 (2002): 55–68.

139. Y. Ta Shma, *Ha-Sifrut ha-Parshanit*, 1:23.

140. Brody, *Geonim*, 268–73. A list of the geonic responsa that contain talmudic exegesis appears in D. Rosenthal, "Le-toldot Rav Paltoi Gaon," *Shenaton ha-Mishpat ha-'Ivri* 11–12 (1984–86): 593n34. An overview of theories on why the geonim engaged in so little talmudic exegesis appears in Grossman, *Ḥakhme Ẓorfat*, 429–36. Cf. A. Grossman, "Ha-ziqa bein ha-mivneh ha-ḥevrati le-yeẓira ha-ruḥanit be-qehilot Yisrael be-tequfat ha-geonim," *Ẓion* 53 (1988): 259–72. However, in private correspondence, David Sklare has noted that this characterization does not accurately reflect the approach of R. Samuel b. Ḥofni, whose talmudic exegesis points to a much broader pedagogic agenda.

141. See, e.g., Levin, *Oẓar ha-Geonim, Perushim*, Shab. 3; *Teshuvot*, Meg. 56–58, 20; *Teshuvot,* Git. 35, 15; *Perushim*, Ber. 167, 53. And see Brody, "Sifrut ha-geonim ve-ha-teqst ha-talmudi," 238–40.

142. Brody formulated it this way: "As a practical rule, the Babylonian Talmud constitutes the source of authority on which the Geonim rely in their decisions, but in theoretical terms, the Talmud itself requires validation from without, which is found in the realm of consensus and tradition within Rabbanite Judaism." Brody, *Geonim*, 178.

143. Uziel Fuchs, "Darkhe ha-hakhra'a, samkhut shel teqstim u-muda'ut 'aẓmit: Hirhurim 'al darkhe ha-pesiqa be-shalhe tequfat ha-geonim," in *Sugyot be-Meḥqar ha-Talmud* (Jerusalem, 1991), 105; and cf. Y. Frankel, *Darko shel Rashi be-Ferusho la-Talmud ha-Bavli* (Jerusalem, 1980), end of Chapter 2.

144. On Samuel ben Ḥofni's neglect of talmudic interpretations and sources, see Sklare, *Samuel ben Ḥofni,* 94n88. On his innovative uses of *mishnayyot* in the *Treatise on the Commandments*, see 208, line 194; 212 line 22; 214–15n132. As Sklare emphasizes (94), Samuel ben Ḥofni adopted these approaches because of his sensitivity to the needs of a particular arabicized population.

145. Fuchs, "Darkhe ha-hakhra'a," 100–123; Brody, *Geonim,* 165 and n. 36. This was also the case when questioners requested clarification of passages in Gemara. Examples of requests to geonic yeshivot from communities for *girsa u-sevara* are collected by S. Abramson in *Ba-Merkazim u-va-Tefuẓot be-Tequfat ha-Geonim* (Jerusalem, 1965), 125–26.

146. Brody, *Geonim*, 149–50. The geonim, writes Brody, seem to have seen themselves as bearing institutional authority equivalent to that of the amoraim, though "compositionally distinct" from them. He also notes (180) that "some decisions that conflicted with those of Talmud circulated alongside Talmud and were absorbed by geonic texts."

147. Thus, e.g., Maimonides claimed that *midrash halakhah* actually *generated* rabbinic law. Maimonides, introduction to the *Commentary on the Mishnah*; Introduction to *Sefer ha-Mizvot.* See Jay Harris, *How Do We Know This? Midrash and the Fragmentation of Modern Judaism* (Albany, N.Y., 1995), 86–90.

148. The thirteen modes of inference, enumerated in the *Beraita of Rabbi Ishmael,* appear in the introduction to the *Sifra.* The geonim may have considered these as thirteen strategies used to link the Oral Torah mnemonically to the Written Torah. Moshe Ẓucker wrote that, in Sa'adya's view, "the sages determined that these principles were operative in the law by examining and observing the laws' inner workings in the same manner that the Masorah tells us a word occurs so many times in the Bible, or that rules of grammar are discovered by examining a language." Sa'adya's *Commentary on Leviticus,* published in Moshe Ẓucker, "Qeta'im mi-Kitab Tahsilal-Shar'ia al-Sama'iyah," *Tarbiẓ* 41 (1972): 378, cited in Sklare, *Samuel ben Ḥofni,* 45. And see M. Zucker, *Perushe Rav Sa'adya Gaon le-Vereshit* (New York, 1984), introduction, 13n9. The perspectives of Sa'adya, Sherira, and Hai Gaon on *midrash halakhah* are discussed in Harris, *How Do We Know This?,* 73–81; Sklare, *Samuel ben Ḥofni,* 44, 93–94.

149. Hai's comment, *Oẓar ha-Geonim,* BK, 28, responsum 68, is cited in Sklare, *Samuel ben Ḥofni,* 45n25.

150. Sklare, *Samuel ben Ḥofni,* 159.

151. While Sklare suggests (*Samuel ben Ḥofni,* 45) that Sa'adya's anti-Karaite polemic may have led him to "distort the reality of talmudic hermeneutics," it is possible to see Sa'adya's perspective on *midrash halakhah* as one adumbrated in Rabbi Ishmael's exchange with Rabbi 'Aqiva over the process—and import!—of scriptural interpretation: "And just because you interpret the superfluous [letter *vav*], should we take her [the married daughter of a *kohen* who prostitutes herself] to be burnt?" BT San. 51b.

152. See Sklare, *Samuel ben Ḥofni,* 43.

153. According to Menaḥem Ben Sasson, "not everything that Pirqoi described as a *minhag shmad* [custom that developed under circumstances of persecution] was one, and not everything that he described as a custom of Ereẓ Yisrael was in fact unique to Ereẓ Yisrael and without [parallel] practice in Babylonia, and not everything that he described as practiced in Ifriqiyyah was really practiced." M. Ben Sasson, *Ẓemiḥat ha-Qehilah ha-Yehudit be-Arẓot ha-Islam: Qayrawan,* 171, 241n287. Cf. Louis Ginzberg, *Ginze Schechter* (New York, 1929), 2:504–44.

154. Brody, *Geonim,* 117n57, writes that the same claim was also made earlier (as well as later) in the Babylonian tradition!

155. In Ginzberg, *Ginze Schechter,* 2:556–60.

156. The import of this phrase has been misrepresented in scholarship pertaining to medieval Ashkenaz. See Chapter 5 below.

157. Though Pirqoi rejected the Palestinian practices as "invented traditions," the Jews of Palestine did not address this charge. Instead, they claimed that the local trumps the general.

158. Translation in Brody, *Geonim,* 179. Pirqoi ben Baboi, in Ginzberg, *Geonica,*

2:53; Ginzberg, *Ginze Schechter,* 2:559; Levin, "Mi-seride ha-genizah 'B': Ma'asim le-vene Yisrael"," *Tarbiẓ* 2 (1931): 403; Danzig, *Mavo le-Sefer Halakhot Pesuqot,* 19–22.

159. Menaḥem Ben Sasson noted that many customs attacked as "Palestinian" by Pirqoi were actually those of Babylonia, in *Ẓemiḥat ha-Qehilah ha-Yehudit be-Arẓot ha-Islam: Qayrawan,* 171. Cf 242n287.

160. Though Louis Ginzberg assumed that Pirqoi had invented this detail, both Mordecai Friedman and Naḥman Danzig asserted that this was "undoubtedly" a reference to written manuscripts of the Jerusalem Talmud found in eighth-century Palestine. See Ginzberg, *Ginze Schechter,* (New York, 1939), 2:504ff; Mordecai A. Friedman, "'Al ta'anat Pirqoi ben Baboi be-divre meẓiat sefarim genuzim shel ha-Yerushalmi," *Sinai* 82–83 (1977–78): 250–51; Danzig, "Mi-talmud 'al peh le-talmud be-khtav," 65. Yaakov Elman observed that all mentions of *megilat setarim* (sequestered scrolls) in the Babylonian Talmud are connected with the circle of R. Ḥiyya in Palestine. See Elman, "Orality and Redaction in the Babylonian. Talmud," *Oral Tradition* 14 (1999): 52–99.

161. In S. Spiegel, "Le-farashat ha-polmos shel Pirqoi ben Baboi," *Harry Austryn Wolfson Jubilee Volume,* ed. Saul Lieberman (Jerusalem, 1965), Hebrew section, 245, 272–73.

162. Thus, Rabbi Meir of Rothenburg and Rabbi Zeraḥya Halevi expressed outrage that Hai Gaon could have declared a particular talmudic ruling non-authoritative. See Fuchs, "Darkhe ha-hakhra'a," 104. And see Chapter 4 below.

163. Levin, *Oẓar ha-Geonim,* Pesaḥim, responsa 347, 125.

164. Ibid., 348.

165. An allusion to Cant. 2:15, "Catch us the little foxes that ruin the vineyards."

166. Cf. BT AZ 55a: "An idol, there is no substance to it."

167. The last phrase alludes to Ps. 28:5. Quoted in M. A. Friedman, "'Al terumat ha-genizah le-ḥeqer ha-halakhah," 285n29. On the contested ascription of this responsum to Sherira, see 286n35.

168. On *'amei ha-areẓ,* ignoramuses, in ancient rabbinic writings, see Aharon Oppenheimer, *The 'Am Ha-Aretz: A Study in the Social History of the Jewish People in the Hellenistic-Roman Period,* trans. I. H. Levine (Leiden, 1977).

169. BT Pes. 49b.

170. Ibid.

171. This was not sanctioned by the prevailing opinion in the Talmud, however, which reasoned (BT Pes. 49b) that "virtuous seed may sometimes issue from him [the *'am ha-areẓ*] and they will enjoy it, as it is said [Job 27:17], '*He will prepare it and the just shall put it on.*'"

172. Our edition of the Babylonian Talmud has no such claim; my assumption is that the Qayrawanese were referring to the claim that one need not proclaim the discovery of their lost property.

173. Avraham E. Harkavy, *Teshuvot ha-Geonim* (facsimile of Berlin, 1887), responsa 240, 117; 380, 197–98; M. Ben Sasson, *Ẓemiḥat ha-Qehilah ha-Yehudit be-Arẓot ha-Islam: Qayrawan,* 237.

174. They discovered that their own practice reflected compliance with an ordinance that had been implemented by the amora, R. Abbahu, mentioned in BT RH 33b. A later Qayrawanese inquirer, Rav Bahloul, refers to the fact that R. Ya'aqov b. Nisim, now deceased, had also posed this question to Rav Hai, since it disturbed the Jews of their community every year. See M. Ben Sasson, *Ẓemiḥat ha-Qehilah ha-Yehudit be-Arẓot ha-Islam: Qayrawan*, 173.

175. Levin, *Oẓar ha-Geonim*, RH, responsa 117, 61–62. My translation of this passage differs from the overlapping sections translated in Ẓvi Groner, *The Legal Methodology of Hai Gaon* (Chico, Calif., 1985), 16–17.

176. Levin, *Oẓar ha-Geonim*, RH, responsa 117, 62. Emphases are mine.

177. Ibid.

178. Ibid.

179. Notwithstanding the rabbinic injunction to "go out and see what the people do," consensus does not seem to have had the status of a formal source of law in the Talmud. See M. Ben Sasson, "Ha-Qehilah ha-Yehudit be-Ẓefon Afriqah—Ḥevrah u-Manhigut: Qayrawan 800–1057" (Ph.D. diss., Hebrew University, 1983), 2:20n18. On the geonic conjoining of "consensus" with "tradition," see Gideon Libson, "Halakha and Reality in the Geonic Period: Taqqanah, Minhag, Tradition and Consensus," in *The Jews of Medieval Islam: Community, Society and Identity* (Leiden, 1995), 95; Sklare, *Samuel ben Ḥofni*, 162–64 (and cf. 55). Sklare notes (164) that Rabbanites took the position of the majority as indicative of consensus, whereas Karaites did not.

180. Citing Ps. 19:8, "The Torah of the Lord is perfect," Karaites argued that if the specifics of a commandment were not stipulated in Scripture, then they did not need to be regulated. The essence of Sa'adya's "strongest argument" against the Karaites was that the authority of Scripture itself was predicated on the existence of an external, validating referent. See the introduction to Sa'adya's *Commentary on Genesis*, in Zucker, *Perushe Rav Sa'adya Gaon le-Vereshit*, 181–84, and Brody, *Geonim*, 92.

181. "*Ve-khen halakhah, ve-khen minhag*" or "*ve-kakh halakhah, ve-kakh minhag.*" The phrase appears, for example, in Levin, *Oẓar ha-Geonim*, Ket., responsa 474; Git., responsa 162; *Seder Rav Amram*, Sukkot, "*ve-hakhi de-amar.*" See G. Libson, "Halakha and Reality in the Geonic Period," 91.

182. Sklare, *Samuel ben Ḥofni*, 51; Grossman, *Ḥakhme Ẓorfat ha-Rishonim*, 429–36; Brody, *Geonim*, 242, 281; Ephrat and Elman, "Orality and the Institutionalization of Tradition," 125; Danzig, "Mi-talmud 'al peh le-talmud be-khtav," 129–31, 140; Gideon Libson, "Terumat ha-genizah le-ḥeqer ha-monografiyyot ha-hilkhatiyyot shel ha-Rav Shmuel ben Ḥofni," *Te'udah* 15 (1999): 190.

183. Instances in which medieval Jews (and especially northern Europeans) related to halakhic writings as if they were compilations of applied law are cited in Danzig, "Mi-talmud 'al peh le-talmud be-khtav," 438, 445–49, 476–501. But see the qualifications about the place of *Halakhot Gedolot* in early Ashkenaz in Rami Reiner, "Le-hitqabluto shel Sefer Halakhot Gedolot be-Ashkenaz," in *Limud ve-Da'at be-Maḥshavah Yehudit*, ed. Hayyim Kreisel (Beer Sheva, 2006), 2:95–121. On an eleventh-century Judeo-Arabic work of hala-

khah that cited *Halakhot Gedolot* as if it were a talmudic source, see Stampfer, "Ha-mishpat ha-'Ivri be-Sefarad ba-meah ha-11," 225–26. In any event, conclusions about authorial intention cannot be drawn from later uses made of *Halakhot Gedolot* (or other works).

184. BT Shab. 6b; Shab. 96b and BM 92 refer to a *megilat setarim* of R. Ḥiyya. See also YT Ma'aserot 50a.

185. "*Megilat setarim: Megilah she-yesh ba halakhot pesuqot ke-'eyn sefer halakhot she-eyno ka-Talmud she-matzuy etzel kol adam. Lefikhakh niqra megilat setarim,*" in *Teshuvot Rav Natronai bar Hilai Gaon*, Y. Brody, ed., #385; L. Ginzberg, *Geonica*, 2:319; Levin, *Oẓar ha-Geonim*, Shab., *Perushim*, 3.

186. This is how the passage was understood by S. Assaf, "Sefer Megilat Setarim le-Rav Nisim bar Ya'aqov me-Qayrawan," 229n7. Much has been written about the term *megilat setarim* and the type of writing it designates. See, e.g., *'Arukh ha-Shalem*, 4:75, "*m-g-l*"; Yisrael Moshe Ḥazan, *Iyye HaYam* glosses on *She-elot u-Teshuvot ha-Geonim: Sha'are Teshuvah* (Livorno, 1869), 133ff. Simḥa Assaf described the *Megilat Setarim* by R. Nisim b. Ya'aqov of Qayrawan as a commonplace book: "a large collection/anthology into which he entered innovations on different occasions during his studies in two Talmuds, midrash, halakhah, aggadah, questions asked." See also Assaf, "Sefer Megilat Setarim le-Rav Nisim bar Ya'aqov me-Qayrawan," 229–31; Lieberman, *Yevanim ve-Yevanut*, 216, 301–5; Ginzberg, *Geonica*, 1:73–75, 117–18; *Geonica* 2:319; Epstein, *Mavo le-Nusaḥ ha-Mishna*, 692–706; Julius Kaplan, *The Redaction of the Babylonian Talmud* (Jerusalem, 1973), 261ff.; Goitein, *Sidre Ḥinukh be-Yeme ha-Geonim u-Vet ha-Rambam*, 163; Abramson, *Rav Nisim Gaon*, 37n2; 181–86; S. Abramson, *'Inyanot be-Sifrut ha-Geonim* (Jerusalem, 1974), 268–69; Drory, *Reshit ha-Magga'im*, 38; Schlesinger, "'Al ketivat Torah she-be-'al peh be-zeman ha-talmud," 47. Abramson reconstructs the circumstances that led some to be confused by the meaning of this term. Cf. Danzig, *Mavo le-Sefer Halakhot Pesuqot*, 6–7; Sussman, "'Torah she-be-'al peh,'" 321. This rendering of R. Natronai's remarks seems to rest on two arguments: that something "secret" is unlikely to be widely found, and that all talmudic references to *megilat setarim* appear to designate one single inscription. See Sussman, "'Torah she-be-'al peh,'" 216n26.

187. Hai Gaon, cited in Judah ben Barzilai, *Sefer ha-Shetarot*, ed. S. J. Halberstamm (Berlin, 1898), 126.

188. Sklare, *Samuel ben Ḥofni*, 50n40, 51. See also Drory, *Reshit ha-Magga'im*, 59; Assaf, *Tequfat ha-Geonim ve-Sifrutah*, 133–71. This understanding was echoed in the later writings of Rashi (Shab. 6b, 13b, 96b, 138b; BM 33a, 92a) and was also embraced by Maimonides. Without using the term "*megilat setarim*", Maimonides refers to the practice of private note taking in earlier times and to the "non-official" status of the resulting text. Maimonides emphasizes that such private jottings were subjective and of varied quality; when used for public instructional purposes, their contents were never read but were transmitted from memory in face-to-face encounters: "Our saintly Master [Rabbi Judah the Patriarch] compiled [*ḥibber*] the Mishnah. And from the days of our Master, Moses to our saintly Master, they had not compiled compilations [*lo ḥibberu ḥiburim*] in Oral

Torah for public teaching. Rather, in each and every generation, the head of the court or the judge of that generation would write for himself a recollection of the auditory teachings [*zikhron ha-shemeu'ot*] that he had heard from his masters, and he would teach that in public, by heart/orally. Thus, each and every one would write for himself, in keeping with his abilities, of the explanation of the Torah and of its laws, as he had heard." Maimonides, introduction to *Mishneh Torah*, ed. Kafaḥ (Jerusalem, 1993), 1:40. Cf. Maimonides, Introduction to *Commentary on the Mishnah*, in section "*aḥar keyn ra-a lehistapeq*": "But for one who was less [qualified] than he [who could use Mishnah to sharpen his intellect], this was [excessively] profound, for the early sages only compiled for themselves."

189. On these two types of Jewish legal writing in the geonic period, see Stampfer, "Ha-mishpat ha-'ivri be-Sefarad ba-meah ha-11," 218.

190. This collection of structured homilies is the earliest indirect witness to the preservation of large quantities of Talmud. See Brody, *Geonim*, 212; Brody, *Le-Toldot Nusaḥ ha-Sheiltot* (Jerusalem, 1991).

191. Danzig, *Mavo le-Sefer Halakhot Pesuqot*, 132 and n. 81. The Hebrew version of this work is known as *Hilkhot Re-u*.

192. Ezriel Hildesheimer, ed., *Halakhot Gedolot* (Jerusalem, 1971). See Danzig, *Mavo le-Sefer Halakhot Pesuqot*, chaps. 6 and 7.

193. See Assaf, "Sefer Megilat Setarim le-Rav Nisim bar Ya'aqov me-Qayrawan," 229–31; Goitein, *Sidre Ḥinukh*, 163; Sklare, *Samuel ben Ḥofni*, 50n40, 178–79, and n. 36; Libson, "Terumat ha-genizah le-ḥeqer ha-monografiyyot ha-hilkhatiyyot shel ha-Rav Shmuel ben Ḥofni"; Brody, "Meḥqar sifrut ha-halakhot mi-tequfat ha-geonim," *Tarbiẓ* 64 (1994): 143–44; Drory, *Reshit ha-Magga'im*, 59–60. Danzig, however, believes that the halakhic compilations of the geonic era were designed by their creators to be used for purposes of adjudication.

194. There are two versions of the question posed to R. Paltoi Gaon: *Sefer Ḥemdah Genuzah* (Jerusalem, 1863), *Teshuvot ha-Geonim*, no. 110, and Assaf, *Teshuvot ha-Geonim* (Jerusalem, 1927), no. 158, p. 81 This is translated in a "slightly free" manner in Brody, *Geonim*, 231; Elon, *Mishpat ha-'Ivri*, 2:955–57, 964, 1017; Urbach, *Ha-Halakhah, Meqoroteha ve-Hitpatḥuta*, 92; Rosenthal, "Le-Toldot Rav Paltoi Gaon," 359ff.; Drory, *Reshit ha-Magga'im*, 60n1; Danzig, *Mavo le-Sefer Halakhot Pesuqot*, 285–86. Danzig, however, attempts to minimize the significance of this testimony by suggesting (137) that Paltoi is not a reliable witness regarding the intentions of the compiler of *Halakhot Pesuqot*.

195. Sar Shalom in Y. D. Bamberger, *Sha'are Simḥa la-Rav Yiẓḥaq ben Ghiyyat* (Fuerth, 1861), vol. 2, *daled*.

196. Brody, *Geonim*, 232. This use of *Halakhot Gedolot* might correspond to the use for which Paltoi Gaon had expressed approval, since the students in Hai's academy were clearly being trained in Talmud.

197. As Danzig noted, the compilers of these works were more inclined to anthologize than to offer advice about applied law. Danzig, *Mavo le-Sefer Halakhot Pesuqot*, 141.

198. The debate over whether Hai Gaon related to *Halakhot Gedolot* as a work of

adjudication is reviewed by Fuchs, "Darkhei ha-hakhra'a," 110n43. Fuchs concludes that Hai held the work in esteem but did not regard it as authoritative. Though Yisrael Ta Shma had claimed that scholars of early Ashkenaz regarded *Halakhot Gedolot* as an authoritative work, Rami Reiner has qualified this portrait in "Le-hitqabluto shel Sefer Halakhot Gedolot be-Ashkenaz," 2:98–100.

199. This point is illustrated by the exceptional case. Because Hai Gaon's monograph on commerce was translated into Hebrew quite early, it reached not only Spain but Ashkenaz as well. Libson, "Terumat ha-genizah le-ḥeqer ha-monografiyyot ha-hilkhatiyyot shel ha-Rav Shmuel ben Ḥofni," 223.

200. Drory, *Reshit ha-Maggaim*, 23, 47–48; Rina Drory, "'Words Beautifully Put': Hebrew vs Arabic in Tenth Century Jewish Literature," *Genizah Research after Ninety Years: The Case of Judeo-Arabic*, ed. J. Blau and S. Reif, 53–57.

201. In his refutation of Jacob b. Samuel, a student of Sa'adya, Sahl b. Masliaḥ indicates that he had been goaded to write in Hebrew, suggesting that it was a harder skill, and that it made the content far less accesssible to others: "And you also wrote: 'Your responses should be in the holy tongue.' . . . I have done as you requested, though I did not wish to, nor is it fit in my eyes to write as you have done, for I desired that the reader might read it easily. Perhaps I shall write a copy of this epistle in Arabic too, so that those who do not know the Jewish tongue may also read it." S. Pinsker, *Lickute Kadmoniot: Zur Geschichte des Karaismus und der karäischen Literatur* (Vienna, 1860; Jerusalem, 1968), 2:25. Discussed in Drory, *Reshit ha-Magga'im*, 47–48, and Drory, "'Words Beautifully Put,'" 57–58.

202. R. David shows his awareness that different languages are used for different genres of writing: The Arabic was for beginners who needed to understand the basic concepts. The Aramaic was a mnemonic prompt for readers who already understood the underlying issues and needed reminders about the law itself. See Sklare, "R. David ben Sa'adya al-Ger ve-ḥiburo Al-Hawwi," 122–23. The latter claim corresponds to the assertion that Paltoi Gaon had made in the ninth century, and the former notion—that halakhic works in Arabic were designed for beginners to the discipline—was echoed in a work composed in medieval Saragossa. Having listed rabbinic scholars of various lands who had composed halakhic works in Arabic, R. Shlomo ben Yosef noted, "Most of their *perushim* and responsa are in Arabic—in order to make it easy for the questioners and the students." Quoted in Sklare, "R. David ben Sa'adya al-Ger," 103. In the introduction to the *Mishneh Torah*, Maimonides made a similar observation. He described the geonim as having designed their monographs so that they would "be easy to know by those who cannot delve into the depths of Talmud." See Libson, "Terumat ha-genizah le-ḥeqer ha-monografiyyot ha-hilkhatiyyot shel ha-Rav Shmuel ben Ḥofni," 220.

203. Hai Gaon, *Mishpetei Shvu'ot* (Venice, 1602), end of part 1, 10b, cited in Libson, "Terumat ha-genizah le-ḥeqer ha-monografiyyot ha-hilkhatiyyot shel ha-Rav Shmuel ben Ḥofni," 228. Sa'adya Gaon also felt the need to justify his bold compositional undertaking, but he was less explicit than Hai about the precipitating factors. He referred to one particular monograph as "that which I was compelled to do, given the magnitude of the

nation's need for it, and my knowledge of the great benefit they will receive from it." Awareness of his Jewish contemporaries' legal ignorance prompted Sa'adya to make a comparable remark in the introduction to his monograph on the laws of sale: "I decided to write this . . . because I have seen the nation's powerful need for it, and I know how great its utility will be." Quoted in M. Ben Sasson, "Seridim mi-Sefer ha-'Edut ve-ha-Shtarot le-Rav Sa'adya Gaon," *Shenaton ha-Mishpat ha-'Ivri*, 11–12, 163.

204. On the distinction between *dayyanim* and *ba'alei hora-a* in the responsa of Rabbi Isaac Alfasi, see Y. Ta Shma, "Shiput 'ivri u-mishpat 'ivri ba-meot ha 11–12 be-Sefarad: Le-yedi'at maẓav limud ha-torah 'al pi Shut ha-Rif," reprinted in his *Knesset Meḥqarim* 2:247–48.

205. It was also not to be the case in al-Andalus, where halakhic information was inscribed in Hebrew works, even before the composition of Maimonides' *Mishneh Torah* in the twelfth century. I would suggest that Jewish scholars in the Andalusian orbit were not subject to the constraints of the tannaitic dicta because of the Sefardi concept of "our Talmud." See Chapter 2 below.

206. Drory lists the characteristics of the *ḥibbur* as a composition (a) which has a defined topic, generally referred to in the title; (b) a systematic structure and subdivision; (c) a methodological introduction for preface; (d) is written in the first person; and (e) is attributed to the author who composed it (rather than being anonymous or pseudonymous). Drory, *Reshit ha-Magga'im*, 172.

207. Thus, for example, Sa'adya pioneered the creation of Scripture-focused genres, including an Arabic translation of Targum, biblical exegesis, a biblical lexicon, guidance for poets (*Sefer ha-Egron*), and *piyyutim* (liturgical poems) that took scriptural language as their model. Drory, *Reshit ha-Magga'im* 162, 60. According to Drory (172), the few compositions that were produced in Rabbanite culture prior to the time of Sa'adya were (a) mnemonic aids; (b) designed for private use; (c) preparatory to subsequent oral composition; and (d) always occasioned by some specific circumstance.

208. Drory, *Reshit ha-Magga'im*, 159; Drory, "'Words Beautifully Put,'" 53 and n. 3.

209. Drory, *Reshit ha-Magga'im*, 3, 35, 138.

210. See, e.g., Abraham Halkin, "The Medieval Jewish Attitude toward Hebrew," in *Biblical and Other Studies*, ed. A. Altmann (Cambridge, Mass., 1963), 233–48.

211. Drory, *Reshit ha-Magga'im*, 31.

212. Ibid., 158.

213. These include legal writings by Sahnun, Shafi'i, Kharqi, and Tahawwi. See G. Margoliouth, "A *Fihrist* of Works by the Gaon Samuel ben Hofni," *JQR* 14 (1902): 311; Boaz Cohen, "The Classification of Law in the *Mishneh Torah*," *JQR* 25 (1935): 526; Libson, "Terumat ha-genizah le-ḥeqer ha-monografiyyot ha-hilkhatiyot shel ha-Rav Shmuel ben Ḥofni," 200; Brody, *Geonim*, 262.

214. On introductions to the study of Talmud written expressly for beginners by Samuel ben Ḥofni—and perhaps by Hai Gaon, who expressed his intent to write a guide that would be "*moreh derekh ve-afilu le-megasheshe be-raḥame Elohim*," Sklare writes: "These works not only met the needs of a certain population, but also fit into the long-

term plan of the gaonim to spread knowledge of the Babylonian Talmud and make it the authoritative base for Jewish practice." In Sklare, *Samuel ben Ḥofni*, 95; see 55 and also M. Ben Sasson, "Shivre iggerot me-ha-genizah: Le-toldot ḥidush ha-qesharim shel yeshivot Bavel 'im ha-ma'arav," *Tarbiẓ* 56 (1987): 183–84 and n. 38.

215. Sklare compares the structure of *hadith* collections with halakhic compilations produced outside the yeshivot, in *Samuel ben Ḥofni*, 51n41. See also Libson, "Terumat ha-genizah le-ḥeqer ha-monografiyyot ha-hilkhatiyyot shel ha-Rav Shmuel ben Ḥofni," 200, 221.

216. The economic downturn has been traced to the poor agricultural policies of the Abbasids, which impoverished the tax-paying base of Jews living within the *reshuyyot* (domains) of the academies. See Sklare, *Samuel ben Ḥofni*, 71.

217. See Ẓ. Groner, "Ha-Maghreb ve-yeshivot ha-geonim be-bavel be-re-i ha-she-elot u-teshuvot ba-meot ha-9–11," *Peamim* 38 (1989): 49–57; Sklare, *Samuel ben Ḥofni*, 84–86; M. Ben Sasson, "Shivrei iggerot min ha-genizah," 186–88; Danzig, "Mi-talmud 'al peh le-talmud be-khtav," 63; Brody, *Geonim*, 131–32.

218. It is not only the reigning portrait of geonim as power hungry tyrants that needs to be reevaluated; the impression that the geonim glorified their own local customs to the disparagement of others is also not borne out by the evidence. See Brody, *Geonim*, 147, 151, 153; Ben Sasson, *Ẓemiḥat ha-Qehilah ha-Yehudit be-Arẓot ha-Islam: Qayrawan*, xi; Libson, "Halakha and Reality in the Geonic Period," 74, 76.

219. See Chapter 2.

220. Consider, for example, the romanticized portraits of the democratic and consensus-driven northern European Jewish communities in works by Jacob Agus and Louis Finkelstein, two scholars writing in America in the first half of the twentieth century. And see Y. Baer, "Ha-hatḥalot ve-ha-yesodot shel irgun ha-qehilot ha-yehudiyyot be-yeme ha-benayyim," *Ẓion* 15 (1950): 1–41. Cf. Johannes Heil, "Deep Enmity and/or Close Ties? Jews and Christians before 1096: Sources, Hermeneutics and Writing History in 1996," *Jewish Studies Quarterly* 9 (2002): 259–306, esp. 261–67.

221. As seen in this chapter, when Qayrawanese Jews turned to Babylonia for guidance in a matter of custom, the geonim sanctioned the authority of the local Jewish community. The campaigns undertaken by Pirqoi and Sa'adya may be seen as exceptions, and at least the latter may have been fueled by anxiety about Karaism. See M. Ben Sasson, *Ẓemiḥat ha-Qehilah ha-Yehudit be-Arẓot ha-Islam: Qayrawan*, 270.

222. Aharon Naḥalon, *Qahal ve-Taqqanot Qahal be-Toratam shel ha-Geonim* (Jerusalem, 2001); M. Elon, "Le-mahutan shel taqqanot ha-qahal ba-mishpat ha-'Ivri," *Meḥqere Mishpat le-Zekher Avraham Rosenthal*, ed. Guido Tedeschi (Jerusalem, 1964), 1–55; Elon, *Mishpat ha-'Ivri* (Jerusalem, 1973), 2:558ff. On the occasionally interchangeable use of the terms *taqqanah* and *minhag* in geonic responsa, see Elon, *Jewish Law* 2:404, 714n6; Libson, "Halakha and Reality in the Geonic Period," 76, 82–83, and n. 39.

223. According to rabbinic legal theory, the threat of sanction that implicitly undergirds communal ordinances—namely, the "threat of excommunication by the Great Court"—is only effective as an instrument of social control if one can count on the

cooperation of all members of the society. *Ḥerem Beit Din ha-Gadol* was a legal institution and concept that extended to the local community rights and powers that had once been held only by the High Court of the Sanhedrin. It was this threat that backed a broad range of rulings enacted in post-talmudic Jewish societies—both of the geonim and of their European heirs. See Gideon Libson, *Jewish and Islamic Law : A Comparative Study of Custom during the Geonic Period* (Cambridge, Mass., 2003).

224. R. Brody, "Kelum hayu ha-geonim meḥoqeqim?" *Shenaton ha-Mishpat ha-'Ivri* 11–12 (1984–86): 290–304; Brody, *Geonim*, 62–63.

225. According to Brody, the Babylonian geonim had more circumscribed legal powers than did the amoraim; "their ability to innovate in legal matters was severely limited." Brody, *Geonim*, 39.

226. Levin, *Oẓar ha-Geonim*, Git., responsa 167. On the threatening tone of this ceremony, see Ben Sasson, *Ẓemiḥat ha-Qehilah ha-Yehudit be-Arẓot ha-Islam: Qayrawan*, 299n36. Cf. Ta Shma, "Shiput 'Ivri u-mishpat 'Ivri ba-meot ha-11–12 be-Sefarad," in *Knesset Meḥqarim* 2:243. See also Gideon Libson, "Ha-Gezerta be-tequfat ha-geonim u-vereshit yeme ha-benayyim," *Shenaton ha-Mishpat ha-'Ivri* 5 (1978): 79–154; Berachyahu Lifschitz, "Gilgulah shel shevu'at bet din be-alah," *Shenaton ha-Mishpat ha-'Ivri* 11–12 (1984–86): 393–406.

227. Thus, for example, a fourth-century church father excoriated Christians who dragged other Christian litigants into synagogues in the belief that oaths taken there were more efficacious. C. Mervyn Maxwell, *Chrysostom's Homilies against the Jews: An English translation* (Chicago, 1966), homily 5.

228. On the role of children in activities designed to preserve legal or quasi-legal records for later generations, see Bernard J. Hibbits, "Coming to Our Senses: Communication and Legal Expression in Performance Cultures," *Emory Law Journal* 41 (1992): 873–960. Examples within rabbinic tradition include the practice of *qeẓaẓa* described in both the Palestinian and Babylonian Talmuds, wherein children actively participate in an act that ostracizes a given individual from his kin. During this act, a barrel filled with foodstuffs (roasted corn, dried fruit) is broken, and the children rush to gather its spilled contents. See Ta Shma, *Minhag Ashkenaz ha-Qadmon* (Jerusalem, 1992), 45–46.

229. There were also queries that asked for clarification. Thus, for example, the late ninth-century *sidur* of Amram Gaon was composed in response to a query from Spain, and it is possible that *Seder Tannaim va-Amoraim* (885) had also been composed in response to a question. Until the time of Sa'adya Gaon, geonim only responded to queries posed and did not initiate discussion of halakhic matters of their choosing. Later geonic responsa—which are longer, more detailed, and more likely to address issues broader than those required to resolve the problem at hand—reflect a growing impulse toward systematization, but they, too, remained reactive on the whole rather than proactive. Brody, *Geonim*, 241, 251.

230. Simḥa Assaf noted certain stylistic shifts, however, suggesting that later geonic responsa attempted to diminish the "identifiability" of the case in question, by (a) omitting the formulaic "And that which you have asked" and by (b) replacing details of

geographic and personal identity with "land of the Sea" and "Reuben-Simeon." Assaf, *Tequfat ha-Geonim ve-Sifrutah*, 217; Elon, *Mishpat ha-'Ivri*, 2:1263–66; Drory, *Reshit ha-Magga'im*, 75.

231. Brody, *Geonim*, 137, 185. The earliest geonic responsa are from before 689, many decades before the *Sheiltot*, the earliest halakhic compendium of the geonic era. See Elman and Ephrat, "Orality and the Institutionalization of Tradition," 115; Assaf, *Tequfat ha-Geonim ve-Sifrutah*, 171.

232. E.g., BT Git. 34b, 66b; Ḥul. 95b; Ket. 49b; BM 114a; BB 36b, 41b,127a-b; Nid. 68a; Tem. 141-b; San. 29a; and YT Qid. 3:14. See Elon, *Mishpat ha-'Ivri*, 1213–14; J. Müller, "Briefe und Responsen in der vorgeonäischen jüdischen Literatur" (Berlin, 1886), 3–36; Epstein, *Mavo le-Nusaḥ ha-Mishna*, 699–700. However, Sussman calls for a reevaluation in "'Torah she-be-'al peh,'" 291n31a, 292n34, 293n39. According to Berachyahu Lifschitz, the questions in pre-geonic responsa were academic ones, posed by sages; they did not arise from real-life situations. B. Lifschitz, "Ma'amada ha-mishpati shel sifrut ha-she-elot ve-ha-teshuvot," *Shenaton ha-Mishpat ha-'Ivri* 9–10 (1982): 279.

233. In 235 CE, bureaucrats assumed many of the roles that jurisconsults had played previously. See Catherine Heszer, "The Codification of Legal Knowledge in Late Antiquity: The Talmud Yerushalmi and Roman Law Codes," in *The Talmud Yerushalmi and Graeco-Roman Culture*, vol. 1, ed. P. Schäfer (Tübingen, 1998), 583, 585. See also George Lang, "Jurisconsulti," in *A Dictionary of Greek and Roman Antiquities*, ed. William Smith (London, 1875); W. W. Buckland, *A Text Book of Roman Law* (Cambridge, 1932), 21–25. Among those who have noted the similarity between the ancient Jewish approach to case law and that found in the *Responsa Prudentium*, the fourth-century compilation of Latin common law, are Joel Mueller, Y. N. Epstein, and M. Elon (cited in previous note); Brody, *Geonim*, 185; and Peter Haas, *Responsa: Literary History of a Rabbinic Genre* (Atlanta, 1996), 300–304.

234. A responsum of the second- and third-century jurist Paul, which is included in Justinian's sixth-century *Digest*, calls the litigant in the case in question "Lucius Titius," the Roman equivalent of "John Doe." See Heszer, "The Codification of Legal Knowledge in Late Antiquity," 589.

235. It has been suggested that this constitutes the earliest type of Roman legal literature. See Fritz Schulz, *Prinzipien des römischen Rechts* (Berlin, 1954), 33.

236. Responsa issued by local jurisconsults were often preferred. H. F. Jolowicz, *Historical Introduction to the Study of Roman Law* (Cambridge, 1952), 86ff.

237. Perry, *Masoret veShinui: Masoret Yeda' beKerev Yehude Ma'arav Eropa beYeme ha-Beynayyim* (Tel Aviv, 2010), 151.

238. Brody, *Geonim*, 250.

239. M. San. 10:1. See Drory, *Reshit ha-Magga'im*, 63.

240. This seems to have been true for some later adjudicators, too. Compare the observation that medieval French scholars regarded responsa as necessary for dealing with exigencies of the time—and not as timeless teaching for future generations, in H. Soloveitchik, *Ha-Yayin be-Yeme ha-Benayyim: Yyen Nesekh—Pereq be-Toldot ha-Halakhah be-Ashkenaz* (Jerusalem, 2008), 23.

241. Lifschitz, "Ma'amada ha-mishpati shel sifrut ha-she-elot ve-ha-teshuvot," 287.

242. See, e.g., Ginzberg, *Geonica,* 1:31–32; Abramson, *Ba-Merkazim u-va-Tefuẓot,* 163–71; S. Abramson, *Rav Nisim Gaon,* 185; Drory, *Reshit ha-Magga'im,* 61–62; Brody, *Geonim,* 60n31.

243. Brody, *Geonim,* 43.

244. In A. Neubauer, *Mediaeval Jewish Chronicles and Chronological Notes* (Oxford, 1887), 87–88; Goitein, *Sidre Ḥinukh,* 145. Cf. Ephrat and Elman, "Orality and the Institutionalization of Tradition," 113, 125; On students' participation in court cases in talmudic times, see Y. Gafni, *Yehude Bavel be-Tequfat ha-Talmud* (Jerusalem, 1990), 226–32; Brody, *Geonim,* 46. However, not all responsa were composed at the biennial *kallah* convocations. See Brody, *Geonim,* 48.

245. In writing to the Gaon of the Academy in Palestine, Sherira Gaon wrote, "We beg of you please . . . to command that the epistle be read aloud in public, for this was done for our fathers there many times." Cited in Gil, *Malkhut Yishma'el be-Tequfat ha-Geonim,* 82–83; cf. 105. For "oral publication" in antiquity, see Lieberman, *Yevanim ve-Yevanut,* 216.

246. See, e.g., E. Eisenstein, *The Printing Press as an Agent of Change* (Cambridge, 1979), 1:10; G. Schoeler, "Writing and Publishing: On the Use and Function of Writing in the First Centuries of Islam," *Arabica* 44 (1997): 429.

247. M. Ben Sasson, "Ha-mivneh, ha-megamot ve-tokhen shel ḥibur Rav Natan ha-Bavli," in *Tarbut ve-ḥevra: Qovez Ma-amarim le-Zikhro shel Ḥaim Hillel Ben Sasson,* ed. R. Bonfil, M. Ben Sasson, and Y. Hacker (Jerusalem, 1989), 137–96.

248. See Libson, "Halakha and Reality in the Geonic Period," 87–89.

249. Brody, *Geonim,* 62. However, notes Brody, there is no reason to assume that geonic responsa were determined by majority vote.

250. Libson, "Halakha and Reality in the Geonic Period," 74. Hai Gaon's responsum to the Qayrawanese (discussed above) boldly identifies custom and consensus as standards to be used in evaluating the authoritativeness of a talmudic teaching.

251. Brody, *Geonim,* 156. The oral nature of Talmud in the geonic period has been stressed by E. S. Rosenthal, "Lishna Aḥarina," 14–15, 18–19; Epstein, *Mevo-ot le-Sifrut ha-Amoraim,* 140–41; Sussman, "'Torah she-be-'al peh,'" and Danzig, "Mi-talmud 'al peh le-talmud bekhtav."

252. See, e.g., Libson, "Terumat ha-genizah le-ḥeqer ha-monografiyyot ha-hilkhatiyot shel ha-Rav Shmuel ben Ḥofni," 189–239; Brody, *Geonim,* 262; Sklare, *Samuel ben Ḥofni*; Sklare, "R. David ben Sa'adya al-Ger ve-ḥiburo Al-Hawwi"; Stampfer, "Ha-mishpat ha-'ivri be-Sefarad ba-meah ha-11."

CHAPTER 2

1. See Chapter 1.

2. Jews may have been moved to Qayrawan immediately after its foundation in 670. H. Z. Hirschberg, *A History of the Jews in North Africa* (Leiden, 1974), 1:100, 144. On

Qayrawan as a hub in Maghreb-Mashriq trade, see Jamil M. Abun-Nasr, *A History of the Maghrib in the Islamic Period* (Cambridge, 1987), 58.

3. The Maghreb was the main channel of trans-Saharan trade between the second half of the ninth century (when the trade route connecting Sudan and Egypt declined) and the end of the fifteenth century (when Europeans began to create trade routes on coast of West Africa). Abun-Nasr, *History of the Maghrib in the Islamic Period*, 19, 29; Hirschberg, *History of the Jews in North Africa*, 1:248.

4. Because Qayrawan was near the fortified harbor city of Maḥdiyya, but far enough from the coast to be safe from sudden landings, it was a major market for the import of eastern spices and for the export, to the East, of precious metals, amber, silk, clothing, wool, hides, iron, lead, mercury, horses, mules, camels, cattle, and slaves. Ibn Hawqal, *Kitāb Sūrat al-ard,* trans. J. H. Kramers and G. Wiet as *Configuration de la Terre* (Paris-Beyrouth, 1964), 73b.

5. J. Mann, *Texts and Studies in Jewish History and Literature* (Cincinnati, 1931), 1:363; Hirschberg, *History of the Jews in North Africa*, 1:105.

6. Abun-Nasr, *History of the Maghrib in the Islamic Period*, 66. Abdul-Rahman III was unable to take them up on this offer. Though the Spanish caliph claimed the North African cities of Fez and Sijilmasa as part of the Umayyad domain, Qayrawan never did come under his rule. Hirschberg, *History of the Jews in North Africa*, 1:107.

7. Hirschberg, *History of the Jews in North Africa*, 1:254; M. Ben Sasson, *Ẓemiḥat ha-Qehilah ha-Yehudit be-Arẓot ha-Islam: Qayrawan, 800–1057* (Jerusalem, 1996), 37. Qayrawan was the primary bearer of Babylonian traditions in the Mediterranean—and even preceded southern Italy (and Egypt) in this regard. See R. Bonfil, "Bein Ereẓ Yisrael le-vein Bavel," *Shalem* 5 (1987): 1–30; R. Bonfil, "'Eduto shel Agobard me-Lyon 'al 'olamam ha-ruḥani shel yehude 'iro ba-me'ah ha-teshi'it," in *Meḥqarim ba-Qabalah, be-Filosofyah Yehudit, u-ve-Sifrut ha-Musar ve-he-Hagut: Mugashim le-Yeshayah Tishby*, ed. J. Dan and J. Hacker (Jerusalem, 1986), 327–28, 346–48, nn. 1, 64–72; A. Grossman, *Ḥakhme Ashkenaz ha-Rishonim* (Jerusalem, 1981), 426–27; E. Fleischer, "Ḥedveta bei-Rabi Avraham: Rishon le-Paytane Italya?" *Italya* 2 (1981): 21–23.

8. Judging from Harkavy's collection of responsa, more letters were sent by the Babylonian geonim to the Maghreb than anywhere else—and through the Maghreb, to Jewish communities in Europe. Hirschberg, *History of the Jews in North Africa*, 1:301, 109, 160. Names of geonim who sent reponsa to Africa appear in S. A. Posnanski, "Anshe Qayrawan," *Zikkaron le-Avraham Eliyahu Harkavy: Qevuẓat Ma-amarim be-Ḥokhmat Yisrael*, ed. D. von Günzberg and I. Markon (St. Petersburg, 1908), 179–83 (Heb.); J. Mann, "The Responsa of the Babylonian Gaonim as a Source of Jewish History," *JQR* 7 (1916–17): 477f.; J. Mann, *Texts and Studies*, 1:63f.

9. On ties between Babylonian and North African sages, see Salo Baron, *A Social and Religious History of the Jews* (New York, 1958), 6:28, 49, 53, 64f.; Louis Ginzberg, *Geonica* (New York, 1929), 1:204.

10. Hirschberg, *History of the Jews in North Africa*, 1:303.

11. M. Ben Sasson, *Ẓemiḥat ha-Qehilah ha-Yehudit be-Arẓot ha-Islam: Qayrawan*, 169.

12. Ibid., 259, 261, 265.

13. Ibid., 246, 261; Hirschberg, *History of the Jews in North Africa,* 1:219–20, 223.

14. S. Abramson, *Perush Rabbenu Ḥananel la-Talmud* (Jerusalem, 1955), 39; M. Ben Sasson, *Ẓemiḥat ha-Qehilah ha-Yehudit be-Arẓot ha-Islam: Qayrawan,* 259.

15. M. Ben Sasson, *Ẓemiḥat ha-Qehilah ha-Yehudit be-Arẓot ha-Islam: Qayrawan,* 265.

16. Ben Sasson stresses that while the weakness in the East was an incentive to the cultivation of local Qayrawanese rabbinic capabilities, the efflorescence of rabbinic culture was not intended or perceived as an anti-Babylonian revolution; R. Ya'aqov ibn Shaḥin simply facilitated the development of possibilities that were already available. Notwithstanding the community's functional intellectual independence, Jews of Qayrawan persisted in maintaining relations with the sacred centers of rabbinic leadership. The same pattern of behavior prevailed in Sicily, Spain, and other Jewish communities of the Maghreb. Ibid., xi, xii, 269.

17. Abramson, *Perush Rabbenu Ḥananel la-Talmud,* 69.

18. After the death of Hai Gaon, Rav Ḥananel of Qayrawan was accepted as the definitive halakhic authority even by Jews of Italy. See A. Grossman, *Ḥakhme Ashkenaz,* 253, 351; M. Ben Sasson, "Ifriqiyya and Italy from the Ninth to the Eleventh Centuries," *Les relations intercommunautaires juives en mediterranee et en Europe occidentale* (Paris, 1983), 34–50, esp. 43; M. Ben Sasson, *Ẓemiḥat ha-Qehilah ha-Yehudit be-Arẓot ha-Islam: Qayrawan,* 229, 292. Some North African scholars were even called "*ziqnei Bavel she-be-medinat Qayrawan,*" the elders/venerable ones of Babylonia who are in the land of Qayrawan! M. Ben Sasson, *Ẓemiḥat ha-Qehilah ha-Yehudit be-Arẓot ha-Islam: Qayrawan,* 266.

19. According to Ben Sasson, the lone geonic commentary on an entire talmudic tractate, namely, Hai Gaon's commentary on Berakhot, drew upon earlier work produced in Qayrawan. M. Ben Sasson, *Ẓemiḥat ha-Qehilah ha-Yehudit be-Arẓot ha-Islam: Qayrawan,* 239. However, in a private communication, Professor Robert Brody expressed skepticism about this claim.

20. S. Assaf, *Tequfat ha-Geonim ve-Sifrutah,* 283; Abramson, *Perush Rabbenu Ḥananel la-Talmud,* 31, 54, 55; Ta Shma, *Ha-Sifrut ha-Parshanit la-Talmud be-Eropa u-ve-Ẓefon Afriqa* (Jerusalem, 1999), 1:125.

21. See Chapter 1.

22. On talmudic manuscripts copied in Qayrawan, see references in Hirschberg, *History of the Jews in North Africa,* 1:329–30; N. Danzig, "Mi-talmud 'al peh le-talmud be-khtav," *Sefer ha-Shana Bar Ilan* 30–31 (2006): 74. A recent study of thousands of late ninth- to eleventh-century Qayrawanese manuscripts and manuscript fragments preserved in Qayrawan's mosque library illuminates the meticulousness with which legal manuscripts were copied there. For the most part, the bulk of the manuscripts are copies of locally produced Maliki jurisprudence composed by Muhammed b. Sahnun (776–854), the legist who established Malikism in Qayrawan. Described in Miklos Muranyi, *Die Rechtsbücher des Qairawaners Sahnun b. Sa'id: Enstehungsgeschichte und Werküberlieferung* (Stuttgart, 1999). According to one reviewer, Muranyi's examination of marginalia and

colophons (many of which identify the precise exemplars from which copies were made) and the sheer quantity of the manuscripts that he compared constitute "a compelling body of evidence that the transmission . . . was, in general, careful, conscientious and above all, accurate." Joseph Lowry, Review of *Die Rechtsbücher des Qairawaners Sahnun b. Sa'id: Entstehungsgeschichte und Werküberlieferung*, by Miklos Muranyi, *Journal of the American Oriental Society* 123 (2003): 438–40.

23. M. Ben Sasson, *Ẓemiḥat ha-Qehilah ha-Yehudit be-Arẓot ha-Islam: Qayrawan*, 261. R. Nisim's concern for the integrity—and authority—of the talmudic text is also evident from certain questions he posed to Hai Gaon. See, e.g., B. M. Levin, ed., *Oẓar ha-Geonim*, Ber., responsa 318.

24. See Chapter 4. According to Ta Shma, the role that R. Ḥananel played in the Mediterranean world was comparable to that played by Rashi in northern Europe. Ta Shma, *Ha-Sifrut ha-Parshanit*, 1:121.

25. Danzig, "Mi-talmud 'al peh le-talmud be-khtav," 72–74 and notes. According to Danzig, the situation changed entirely in time of the *Rishonim*, for Jewish scholars of medieval Europe referred to "books of the geonic academies" as works they had in their possession.

26. References to such *sefarim mugahim*, or "fair copies," appear, for example, in Moses ben Naḥman, *Milḥamot ha-Shem*, BK, chapter 8 (p. 31a in the commentary of Alfasi) and in R. Solomon ben Adret, *Ḥidushim* on Yeb. 24b. See Mann, "The Responsa of the Babylonian Gaonim as a Source of Jewish History," 152; Hirschberg, *History of the Jews in North Africa*, 1:258.

27. An exchange between Maimonides and his students that hinges on the absence of a fair copy manuscript of Mishnah is illuminating. See Maimonides, *Teshuvot ha-Rambam*, ed. Joshua Blau (Jerusalem, 1989), no. 442. On "fair copy" in Sefarad, see Colette Sirat, *Hebrew Manuscripts of the Middle Ages* (Cambridge, 2002), 62, 279–82. And cf. G. Schoeler, "Writing and Publishing: On the Use and Function of Writing in the First Centuries of Islam," *Arabica* 44 (1997): 429.

28. Thus, for example, R. Nisim had planned to write on allusive language and wordplays in the Talmud. Hirschberg, *History of the Jews in North Africa*, 1: 338.

29. Rav Nisim divided the Talmud's allusions ["*remazim*"] to matters mentioned elsewhere into more than 50 categories, and brought examples from each. Abramson, *Perush Rabbenu Ḥananel la-Talmud*, 56; M. Ben Sasson, *Ẓemiḥat ha-Qehila ha-Yehudit be-Arẓot ha-Islam:Qayrawan*, 265; Ta Shma, *Ha-Sifrut ha-Parshanit*, I. 139.

30. Certain exceptions, where North African scholars were unaware of *taqqanot* promulgated in Babylonia, are noted in M. Ben Sasson, *Ẓemiḥat ha-Qehila ha-Yehudit be-Arẓot ha-Islam: Qayrawan*, 246.

31. For example, R. Israel son of Samuel b. Ḥofni, who became Suran gaon in 1017, composed *On the Duty of Prayer* at the request of the Nagid of Qayrawan. Hirschberg, *History of the Jews in North Africa*, 1:215.

32. Moshe Gil, "The Babylonian Yeshivot and the Maghrib in the Early Middle Ages," *PAAJR* 57 (1990–91): 82; M. Ben Sasson, *Ẓemiḥat ha-Qehilah ha-Yehudit be-Arẓot ha-Islam: Qayrawan*, 210, 267–68.

33. On lists of responsa—and their tables of contents—compiled in Qayrawan, see S. Abramson, *'Inyanot be-Sifrut ha-Geonim* (Jerusalem, 1974), 196–97, 243–44; M. Ben Sasson, *Ẓemiḥat ha-Qehilah ha-Yehudit be-Arẓot ha-Islam: Qayrawan*, 210, 239. Evidence of this collecting activity appears in an early eleventh-century letter from Qayrawan to Fostat, cited in Moshe Gil, *Malkhut Yishma'el be-Tequfat ha-Geonim* (Jerusalem, 1997), 154.

34. According to Ta Shma, the recensions of Gemara with which Ḥananel and Nisim worked were more stable than those used by their Ashkenazi contemporaries. Ta Shma, *Ha-Sifrut ha-Parshanit*, 1:136, 141.

35. Ta Shma, *Ha-Sifrut ha-Parshanit*, 1:128 and n. 30.

36. Rabbenu Ḥananel wrote that, in the academy of Qayrawan, the study of Talmud was completed every thirty years. And in one particularly lengthy excursus of his commentary, R. Ḥananel asked for indulgence, noting that earlier rabbis had not offered clear explanations. Ta Shma, *Ha-Sifrut ha-Parshanit*, 1:124n19, 131.

37. Ibid., 1:125.

38. Abramson, *Perush Rabbenu Ḥananel la-Talmud*, 37, 147; M. Ben Sasson, *Ẓemiḥat ha-Qehilah ha-Yehudit be-Arẓot ha-Islam: Qayrawan*, 238.

39. Abramson, *Perush Rabbenu Ḥananel la-Talmud*, 147, on BT BM 33a, "*ha'oseq be-miqra.*"

40. Ibid.

41. Ibid.

42. Ibid., 39, and cf. 48, 49, 108, 146; Ta Shma, *Ha-Sifrut ha-Parshanit*, 1:130.

43. Abramson, *Perush Rabbenu Ḥananel la-Talmud*, 148–49.

44. Ibid., 34, 56–57, 78–94.

45. Ibid., 23. On medieval uses of this phrase, see I. Twersky, *Rabad of Posquieres*, (Cambridge, Mass., 1962), xx–xxiii; I. Twersky, *Introduction to the Code of Maimonides: Mishneh Torah* (New Haven, Conn., 1980), 170–75.

46. Abramson, *Perush Rabbenu Ḥananel la-Talmud*, 100.

47. Ta Shma, *Ha-Sifrut ha-Parshanit*, 1:128.

48. Ibid., 1:139.

49. Ibid.

50. In medieval writings, the term "Maghreb" was understood to designate the territory between Spain and Ifriqiyya. See, for example, G. D. Cohen, *Sefer Ha-Qabbalah: The Book of Tradition by Abraham Ibn Daud* (Philadelphia, 1967), 134n3.

51. S. Spiegel, "Le-farashat ha-polmos shel Pirqoi ben Baboi," *Harry Austryn Wolfson Jubilee Volume*, Hebrew Section, ed. Saul Lieberman (Jerusalem, 1965), 272–73. From Pirqoi's locution, it is not clear whether Torah, Talmud, or both were studied in these schools. A student of Sa'adya Gaon referred to the Jews of Qayrawan on several occasions as "students of the Bible and Mishnah, great scholars," and in 1006 R. Hai wrote to Qayrawan praising the reputation of R. Ḥushiel and expressing the wish that he had come to Babylonia. Hirschberg, *History of the Jews in North Africa*, 1:304; Abramson, *Perush Rabbenu Ḥananel la-Talmud*, 16. Skepticism about the level of learning that existed in Sefarad is expressed in S. Abramson, "Mi-torato shel Rav Shmuel HaNagid mi-Sefarad,"

Sinai 100 (1987): 20, 23–24. See now D. Sklare, "R. David ben Sa'adya al-Ger ve-ḥiburo al-Ḥawwi," *Te'udah* 14 (1998): 103–23, and Y. Ẓ. Stampfer, "Ha-mishpat ha-'ivri be-Sefarad ba-meah ha-11: Bein geonim le-rishonim ('al pi Kitab al-Hawwi le-R. David ben Sa'adya)," *Shenaton ha-Mishpat ha-'Ivri* 38 (2008): 217–36.

52. E. Ashtor, *The Jews of Moslem Spain* (Philadelphia, 1973), 2:135. According to a report by Sa'adya ibn Danan, while visiting Granada for his daughter's wedding, Rav Nisim of Qayrawan taught Shlomo ibn Gabirol. Hirschberg, *History of the Jews in North Africa*, 1:329.

53. Cited in Ta Shma, *Ha-Sifrut ha-Parshanit*, 1:139n44.

54. Hirschberg, *A History of the Jews in North Africa*, 1:14; Abramson, "Mi-torato shel Rav Shmuel HaNagid mi-Sefarad," 20.

55. There is some question about whether Alfasi had studied with Rabbenu Ḥananel as well as Rabbenu Nisim. See Abramson, "Mi-torato shel Rav Shmuel HaNagid mi-Sefarad," 21–23, 26; Ta Shma, *Ha-Sifrut Ha-Parshanit*, 1:137, 147–48. Alfasi publicized the changes he made in his *Halakhot Gedolot* (or *Halakhot Rabbati*) in responses to questioners, and he enjoined his students to make corrections. Still, the fact that there are variants of this work led to disputes among subsequent scholars (including Alfasi's students) about what the master had said. The primary source of knowledge about Alfasi's retractions and alterations come from Provençal and Spanish scholars, like Zeraḥya Halevi of Lunel, Rabad of Posquieres, R. Isaac ben Abba Mari, author of *Sefer ha-'Itur*, and Naḥmanides. See S. Shafer, *HaRif u-Mishnato* (Jerusalem, 1966), 78–88; Shamma Friedman, "Mi-tosafot ha-Rashbam la-Rif," *Qoveẓ 'al Yad* 68 (1976): 187–227; Yisrael Francus, "Hashmatot ve-ta'uyyot qedumot be-Hilkhot ha-Rif," *Tarbiẓ* 47 (1978): 30–48; Ta Shma, *Ha-Sifrut ha-Parshanit*, 1:146, 152.

56. Jonathan Decter, *Iberian Jewish Literature: Between al-Andalus and Christian Europe* (Bloomington, Ind., 2007), 6, 211.

57. Hirschberg, *History of the Jews in North Africa*, 1:151.

58. On Isaac b. Ḥalfon, a North African who relocated to al-Andalus and the first Jew who is known to have received a salary for writing poetry in the Hebrew language, see ibid., 1:311.

59. On the *Risala*, a pioneering ninth-century work in comparative philology written by Ibn Quraysh of Tahert, and its influence on later Hebrew philologists and grammarians who emigrated to Spain from North Africa, like Dunash ben Labrat and Yehudah Hayyuj, see Paul Fenton, *Introduction to Le Commentaire sur le Livre de la Creation de Dunas ben Tamim de Kairouan (Xe Siecle)*, by Georges Vajda (Leuven, 2002), 8–9.

60. Isaac Israeli (d. 955), physician to Qayrawan's last Aghlabid king (903–9) and its first Fatimid Shiite prince, served as an expert on philosophical matters for Sa'adya before the latter was appointed gaon. Israeli's disciple, Dunash b. Tamim of Qayrawan, wrote that "R. Isaac was in the habit of showing me these letters, when I was not more than some 20 years old, and I would indicate the errors (in Sa'adya's writing), which gave great pleasure to my teacher, because of my youth." Fenton, *Introduction to Le Commentaire sur le Livre de la Creation de Dunas ben Tamim de Qayrawan*, 3–4, 12; A. Altmann and

S. M. Stern, *Isaac Israeli* (Oxford, 1958); Hirschberg, *History of the Jews in North Africa*, 1:271.

61. Though occasionally misattributed, Dunash ben Tamim's commentary on *Sefer Yeẓira* was even more encyclopedic in scope than Israeli's writings. It made teachings from Stoicism, Neoplatonism, the Brethren of Purity, anatomy, medicine, astronomy, physics, Arabic grammar, and mathematics accessible to a broad range of medieval Sefardi readers, including Judah b. Barzilai, Moses b. 'Ezra, Joseph ibn Ẓaddiq, Judah Halevi, David Kimḥi, Abraham ibn Ḥasdai, Gershon b. Shlomo, and Yedaiah Bedersi. See Fenton's introduction to Georges Vajda, *Le Commentaire sur le Livre de la Creation de Dunas ben Tamim de Qayrawan*, 1–20.

62. Another edition of this work was dedicated to the third Fatimid caliph, and yet another work to the governor of Maḥdiyya in Ifriqiyya. Fenton's introduction to Georges Vajda, *Le Commentaire sur le Livre de la Creation de Dunas ben Tamim de Qayrawan*, 7, 8.

63. See Y. Sussman, "'Torah she-be-'al peh'—Peshutah ke-mashma'ah." In *Meḥqere Talmud* 3, ed. Ya'aqov Sussman and David Rosenthal (Jerusalem, 2005), 298n61, 330n32; Y. Sussman, "Ketovet hilkhatit me-'emeq Bet She-an: Seqira muqdemet," *Tarbiẓ* 43 (1974): 156n497; Y. Sussman, "Ketovet hilkhatit me-'emeq Bet She-an: Tosafot ve-tiqunim," *Tarbiẓ* 44 (1975): 195; S. 'Imanuel, *Teshuvot ha-Geonim ha-Ḥadashot: ve-'iman Teshuvot, Pesaqim u-Ferushim me-et Ḥakhme Provans ha-Rishonim* (Jerusalem, 1995), no. 118; S. Abramson, *Massekhet 'Avodah Zarah—Ketav Yad Bet ha-Midrash le-Rabanim* (New York, 1957), xiii, n. 1; D. Rosenthal, "Le-Toldot Rav Paltoi Gaon," 593, 603–9; R. Brody, *The Geonim of Babylonia and the Shaping of Medieval Jewish Culture*, 156, 157n7, 163; Elman and Ephrat, "Orality and the Institutionalization of Tradition: The Growth of the Geonic Yeshiva and the Islamic Madrasa," 115.

64. On the various passages recounting that the Jews of Spain had asked Paltoi to send "*Talmud u-fitrono*" (roughly, "Talmud and its meaning")—which he did—see B. M. Levin, ed., *Iggeret Rav Sherira Gaon* (Jerusalem, 1982), xxiii; Mordecai Margalioth, *Hilkhot ha-Nagid* (Jerusalem, 1969), 3–4; Assaf, *Tequfat ha-Geonim ve-Sifrutah*, 137ff.; S. Abramson, "Perush Rabbenu Barukh b'r Shmuel ha-Sefaradi la-Talmud," *Bar Ilan* 26–27 (1995): 17; N. Danzig, "Mi-talmud 'al peh le-talmud be-khtav," 62.

65. See M. Margalioth, *Hilkhot ha-Nagid*, 2, 93; Lewin, ed., *Iggeret Rav Sherira Gaon*, 104, n. 7; S. Abramson, *Massekehet 'Avodah Zarah*, xiii, n. 1. Bonfil suggested that, in writing the Talmud from memory for the Jews of Spain, Rav Natronai "looked like a rebel." R. Bonfil, "Mitos, retoriqa, historya? 'Iyyun be-Megilat Aḥima'aẓ," *Tarbut ve-Ḥevra be-Toldot Yisrael bi-Yeme ha-Benayyim*, ed. R. Bonfil, M. Ben Sasson, and Y. Hacker (Jerusalem, 1989), 114.

66. A tradition preserved in a rabbinic writing by Isaiah ben Mali di Trani from thirteenth-century Italy relates that all the corpora of *oral matters* were written down in antiquity, lest they be forgotten. These remarks explain the obvious disregard for (or violation of) a tannaitic ruling, and place all inscribers of *oral matters* in the company of revered predecessors.

67. Judah ben Barzilai, *Perush Sefer Yeẓirah* (Berlin, 1885), 186–87.

68. The various kingdoms of Spain had shifting borders during the Middle Ages. According to modern scholars who assumed that "*Asfamya*" referred to all of Spain, "*Qortva*" must designate a place other than Cordoba for the passage to make sense. See Aharon Oppenheimer, "Mi-Qortva le-Asfamya," in *Galut Aḥar Golah: Meḥqarim Mugashim le-Ḥayyim Beinart le-Melot 70 Shanah,* ed A. Mirsky et al. (Jerusalem, 1988), 57–63. According to another perspective, "Asfamya" refers only to a region of Spain, and so R. Isaac might well have died en route from Cordoba to Asfamya. See S. Abramson, "Asfamya she-be-Sefarad," *Sinai* 69 (1971): 42–44; Abramson, "Mi-torato shel Rav Shmuel HaNagid mi-Sefarad," 24. In a later article, however, Abramson pronounced this talmudic passage a "murky" source from which nothing clear can be learned. S. Abramson, "Perush Rabbenu Barukh b'r Shmuel haSefaradi la-Talmud," 17.

69. Thus, according to Shmuel HaNagid, the Jews of Spain "never abandoned the Targum or a single matter of the meanings of *talmud* [*ta'ame talmud*] that were arranged in their mouths from [the time of?] Yiẓḥaq the Exilarch, son of the sister of Rav Bibi, who died in Sefarad between Qortva and Asfamya." In Judah ben Barzilai, *Sefer ha-'Itim*, ed. Y. Shor (Cracow, 1902, 267, and cf. x–xi, n. 5.

70. On BT Git. 60b, see Chapter 1.

71. A variant manuscript tradition, "*eyn lemedin halakhah mi-pi talmid*," "one does not derive halakhah from a student," has been traced from Joseph ibn Migash back to Joseph bar Judah al-Barceloni. The meaning of this locution seems to be that when the pupil is seated before his master and the two come up with a particular understanding based on their reasoning, the pupil may not rely upon this as something to be implemented in practice. Ibn Migash calls attention to another ramification of Oral Torah's inscription: a change in master-student relations. Commenting on a different phrase in the same talmudic passage—the variant formulation, "one must not learn from a pupil"—Ibn Migash asserts that this prohibition had only applied before the consignment of Talmud to writing. See S. Abramson, "Berurim," *Sinai* 58 (1966): 183–85, and E. E. Urbach, *Ha-Halakhah, Meqoroteha ve-Hitpatḥuta*, (Jerusalem, 1984), 229–30.

72. Sherira's remarks about "*talmud*" are discusssed in Chapter 1, and those of later Andalusian scholars are discussed in Chapter 5. On "*talmud*" as an approach and not a literary corpus, see Judah Goldin, "Freedom and Restraint of Haggadah," in *Studies in Midrash and Related Literature*, ed. Judah Goldin, Barry L. Eichler, and Jeffrey H. Tigay (Philadelphia, 1988), 253–55.

73. Joseph ibn Migash, *Ḥidushin* on BB 130b, from a manuscript cited in N. Danzig, *Mavo le-Sefer Halakhot Pesuqot* (New York, 1993), 134, 138–39. It seems that what has been transcribed in Danzig's text as "*halakhah le-Moshe mi-Sinai*" is actually supposed to be "*halakhah le-ma'aseh*." Cf. Y. Sussman, "Ve-shuv le-Yerushalmi Neziqin," *Meḥqere Talmud* 1 (1990): 105n196.

74. Judah ben Barzilai, *Perush Sefer Yeẓira*, 186–88.

75. Maimonides' Letter to Pinḥas b. Meshullam, *dayyan* of Alexandria, in M. Maimonides, *Iggerot ha-Rambam*, ed. Yiẓḥaq Shilat (Jerusalem, 1987), 2:442. Maimonides echoed the essential elements of HaNagid's perspective, rooting the Talmud's authority in

consensus and alluding to a moment of formal talmudic closure. Like Sherira and Hai Gaon before him, Maimonides argued (in the introduction to *Mishneh Torah* and in the introduction to his *Commentary on the Mishnah*) that proof of the Talmud's authority lies in the fact that its teachings have garnered the near-universal assent of the community of Israel. Though it is not clear why Maimonides avoided the "our Talmud" theory, given his esteem for Ibn Migash, it may be that Jewish communities of the East were more wary of Karaite polemics than their Spanish counterparts. Rabbinic scholars who faced the Karaite claim that the Written Torah was the sole source of Jewish law (an early iteration of "*sola Scriptura*") may have felt it prudent to avoid mentioning that the Talmud on which Rabbanites relied was not identical to the "*talmud*" mentioned in ancient teachings.

76. As Brody insightfully noted, Maimonides understood full well that "in order to issue rulings on the basis of Talmud, one must develop a theory to the effect that the Talmud, as we have it . . . was redacted (a) with a view to conveying halakhah, and (b) enjoys special authority by virtue of an uncontested consensual tradition." Brody, *Geonim*, 179 and n. 27.

77. Meir Halevi Abulafia, *Sefer Yad Ramah: Shitah le-Mahadurah Batra* (Salonika, 1790–91; Tel Aviv, 1962) on BB, 130; and cf. S. Abramson, "Berurim," *Sinai* 58 (1966): 185. On 184n2, Abramson noted that a citation from YT Peah, preserved in a *Yad Ramah* recension in *Shitah Mequbeẓet*, says, "*ella min ha-Talmud*," not "*ve-lo min ha-Talmud*."

78. If this supposition is correct, it may also be related to the fact that far fewer rabbinic Jews were engaged in Talmud study in Spain than in northern Europe. See below.

79. While the Karaite challenge to Rabbanism gave this question heightened prominence, both the Karaite and the Rabbanite interests in epistemology should be seen within the broader context of the contemporaneous Muslim drive to evaluate the reliability of *hadith* traditions.

80. Sa'adya Gaon, beginning of the second part of his *Book on Attaining the Revealed Commandments*, in Moshe Zucker, *Perush R. Sa'adya Gaon le-Vereshit*, 13n9, trans. D. Sklare in *Samuel ben Ḥofni and His Cultural World* (Leiden, 1996), 160. Samuel ben Ḥofni's response to this question appears in his *Introduction to Mishna and Talmud*, chap. 5. See Sklare, *Samuel ben Ḥofni*, 162–63. Hai Gaon's response to this question is discussed above in Chapter 1.

81. See Chapter 1.

82. See T. Fishman, "Claims about the Mishna in Sherira Gaon's *Epistle*: Islamic Theology and Jewish History," *Border Crossings: Interreligious Interaction and the Exchange of Ideas in the Islamic Middle Ages*, ed. D. Freidenreich and M. Goldstein. (Philadelphia, forthcoming)

83. Cited in Judah ben Barzilai, *Perush Sefer Yeẓira*, 186–87.

84. G. D. Cohen, *Sefer ha-Qabbalah*, 56, emphasis added. A similar claim made by the Rhineland Pietists is discussed in Chapter 6.

85. On the attempts to get R. Ḥanokh to respond to Sherira Gaon, see Hirschberg, *History of the Jews in North Africa*, 1:316–18; M. Margalioth, *Hilkhot ha-Nagid*, 9, 22.

86. According to Margalioth, when Shmuel HaNagid was twenty-two years old, he

composed a work on difficult *sugyot* of the Talmud in which he criticized the explanations offered by Hai Gaon. M. Margalioth, *Hilkhot ha-Nagid*, 30–32; cf. 34–35. Shraga Abramson vehemently rejected this hypothesis and asserted that the material in question was actually part of HaNagid's larger work, *Hilkheta Gavrata*. Abramson, *Perush Rabbenu Ḥananel la-Talmud*, 55; Abramson, "Mi-torato shel Rav Shmuel HaNagid mi-Sefarad," 15. The broader significance of this material continues to be debated. See Ta Shma, *Ha-Sifrut ha-Parshanit*, 1:161.

87. On the claim that Ibn Gabirol celebrated the Andalusian halakhist's besting of Rav Hai in a 1035 panegyric, see M. Margalioth, *Hilkhot ha-Nagid*, 35.

88. From D. Sassoon, ed., *Diwan of Samuel ha-Nagid* (London, 1934), 13, cited in Margalioth, *Hilkhot ha-Nagid*, 65 (with the correction suggested by Harkavy).

89. Cited in Margalioth, *Hilkhot ha-Nagid*, 65–66.

90. Abramson, "Mi-torato shel Rav Shmuel HaNagid mi-Sefarad," 11, 15, 21, 22.

91. On indebtedness to geonim in writings by Shmuel HaNagid, Isaac ibn Ghiyyat, and Judah b. Barzilai of Barcelona, see Brody, *Geonim*, 133n33.

92. Ibn Daud's pro-Umayyad investment in this regional rivalry, even after 1031, is explained in terms of local politics in Cordoba, in G. D. Cohen, "The Story of the Four Captives," *PAAJR* 29 (1960–61): 68–69.

93. Cohen, *Sefer ha-Qabbalah*, 66.

94. Ibn Daud's chronicle also portrays the establishment of rabbinic centers in other lands as divinely validated. Ibid., 292–93.

95. Ibid., 135, nn. 61–62 and 74. Cf. 66, 71, 134n2.

96. Ibid., 269ff. On genizah research corroborating Ibn Daud's tendentiousness, see Brody, *Geonim*, 12–13.

97. See Cohen, *Sefer ha-Qabbalah*, 294: "Even if the Babylonian attempts to retrieve their exclusive position in Jewry were known in Spain, it is hardly likely that in the middle of the twelfth century, the Andalusians, particularly now that they were dwelling in the Christian North, would have taken the appeal and threats of Baghdad seriously. They could not have submitted to Babylonian authority even if they had wanted to."

98. Cohen, "The Story of the Four Captives," 68–69.

99. Positive assessments of the caliber of rabbinic learning in Spain are discussed in Cohen, *Sefer ha-Qabbalah*, 135, supplementary note to lines 38–39; Cohen, "Story of the Four Captives," 114ff.; Margalioth, *Hilkhot ha-Nagid*, 1f.; Danzig, "Mi-talmud 'al peh le-talmud be-khtav," 64–65, n. 57. Abramson took pains to portray the level of rabbinic learning in eleventh-century al-Andalus as far more mediocre (and less influential) than suggested by Margalioth: Abramson, "Mi-torato shel Rav Shmuel HaNagid mi-Sefarad," *Sinai* 100 (1987): esp. 12, 16–19, 21, 23, 24.

100. Ibn Daud's stylized portrait of Shmuel HaNagid appears in G. D. Cohen, *Sefer ha-Qabbalah*, 56. On his praise for benefactors who acquired and copied Jewish texts, see Nehemiah Allony, "Shire Ẓiyon be-shirato shel Rav Shmuel HaNagid," *Sinai* 68 (1971): 223–25.

101. The teacher in this poem is portrayed not only as an ignoramus, but as an ill-

mannered boor, more concerned with upholding the halakhic injunction against speaking during prayers than in observing common courtesies. Thanks to Yael Landman for sensitizing me to this point, and to the poem's misogynistic overtones. David Sklare describes "*Ha-yirhav ha-zeman*" as a poem that chastises those in the academy more for their manners and manner of speech than for the caliber of learning, in "R. David ben Sa'adya al-Ger ve-ḥiburo al-Ḥawwi," 119.

102. In this sense, HaNagid's outrage is not an expression of anti-talmudism, but a reaction to the narrowing of curricular options and to the blurring of distinctions between learners of disparate intellectual abilities. See Chapter 5.

103. Samuel HaNagid, "Shir La'ag," in *Toldot ha-Shira ha-'Ivrit be-Sefrarad u-ve-Provence*, ed. Y. Schirmann (Jerusalem, 1955), 1:147, no. 45. With the exception of the last line, the translation is that of Peter Cole, *Selected Poems of Shmuel HaNagid* (Princeton, 1996), 33. "The Gate" is a reference to one of the three talmudic tractates bearing this name: the First Gate (*Bava Qama*), the Middle Gate (*Bava Metzia*), and the Final Gate (*Bava Batra*).

104. From the superscription by HaNagid's son Yehosef, we know that "*Elohim he-erikh li peh ba-torot*" was written around 1049 after battle at Malaga.

105. The phrase is "*vi-liẓoq 'al ẓeme-ei dat u-Mishnah ve-Talmud mi-te'udat El me-tarot, u-mo'eẓot ei-feseq ha-halakhot*," from HaNagid, "*Elohim he-erikh li peh ba-torot*" in Dov Jarden, ed., *Divan Shemuel ha-Nagid: Ben Tehilim* (Jerusalem, 1966), v. 1, poem 27, p. 93.

106. Ibid., 90, lines 10–12. The phrase "six granaries" alludes to Haggai 2:19.

107. Ibid., lines 14–20. HaNagid's reference to females in the context of traditionally male rabbinic activity, both in this poem and others, warrants further exploration. In his caustic poem, "*Ha-yirhav ha-zeman*," the boorish and ignorant rabbi is unflatteringly likened to a woman.

108. Ibid., lines 20–24. While the last mentioned activity in line 33, "*lidrokh ba-teu'dah*, "might be read as an allusion to the inscription of Talmud (if "*ba-te'udah*" is taken to mean "in a documentary manner"), HaNagid frequently uses the term *te'udah* as a synonym for Torah. See, e.g., "*Alut 'Az*," in Shmuel HaNagid, *Kol Shire Rabi Shmuel HaNagid* , 1:12; as well as "*Ahuv nafshi*," 2:22, and "*Ha-nirpa ha-zeman*," 2:25.

109. HaNagid, "*Elohim he-erikh li peh ba-torot*," in Jarden, *Divan Shmuel HaNagid*, 1:90, lines 35–37. According to HaNagid, in lines 30–34, this deplorable situation "strengthens the arm of the heretics." Though Margalioth understood this as a reference to Karaite critics who ridiculed the polyphony and inconsistency of rabbinic legal voices, Abramson rejected the assumption that Karaites posed a threat in al-Andalus in this time.

110. Margalioth, *Hilkhot ha-Nagid*, 11, 16–17; Abramson, "Mi-torato shel Rav Shmuel HaNagid mi-Sefarad," 55. Though HaNagid seems to be exonerating the geonim themselves by portraying the blameworthy writings as having been altered by copyists and poor students, Margalioth feels that this is something of a trope.

111. HaNagid, "*Elohim he-erikh li peh be-torot*," in Jarden, *Divan Shmuel HaNagid*, 1:90, lines 42–46.

112. Selections of HaNagid's teachings are preserved in Judah ben Barzilai's (aka Judah al-Barceloni's) *Sefer ha'Itim*, *Peruṣh le-Sefer Yeẓirah*, and *Sefer ha-Shetarot*. It has been shown that the introduction to the Talmud ascribed to HaNagid is really an abridgment of the introduction to the Talmud written by Shmuel ben Ḥofni. See Abramson, "Mi-torato shel Rav Shmuel HaNagid mi-Sefarad," 22.

113. Margalioth, *Hilkhot ha-Nagid*, 24, 52.

114. Abramson, "Mi-torato shel Rav Shmuel HaNagid mi-Sefarad," 12, 16, 17. Strangely, Abramson speculated that HaNagid would not have undertaken a comprehensive work of this nature "so close to the end of his life". And even though the thirteenth-century Provençal scholar Menahem HaMeiri referred to a comprehensive halakhic work by HaNagid, Abramson wrote that, in this instance, HaMeiri could not be regarded as a reliable informant (13).

115. Sklare, "R. David ben Sa'adya al-Ger ve-ḥiburo al-Ḥawwi," 104; Stampfer, "Ha-Mishpat ha-'Ivri be-Sefarad ba-meah ha-11," 218.

116. Sklare, "R. David ben Sa'adya al-Ger ve-ḥiburo al-Ḥawwi," 104.

117. Ibid., 105; Stampfer, "Ha-Mishpat ha-'Ivri be-Sefarad ba-meah ha-11," 221.

118. A quote from R. David appears in Stampfer, "Ha-mishpat ha-'Ivri be-Sefarad ba-meah ha-11," 220: "Note that Scripture pointed to transmission through hearing, from the transmitter to the receiver, without reliance on any other intermediary, like a book or *diwan*. [And] regarding a remarkable heard tradition which the hearer has not heard from its original transmitter: Notice that when the sages heard some new halakhic detail from whomever said it, or some strange case from a transmitter, they made the effort to go to its initial transmitter in order to hear it directly from him."

119. R. David shows his awareness of the use of different languages for different genres: The Arabic, he wrote, was for beginners, who needed to understand the basic concepts, while the Aramaic was designed as a mnemonic prompt for people who had already studied the Talmud, understood the issues, and needed reminders about the law itself. Sklare, "R. David ben Sa'adya al-Ger ve-ḥiburo al-Ḥawwi," 122–23.

120. Quoted in Sklare, "R. David ben Sa'adya al-Ger ve-ḥiburo al-Ḥawwi," 103.

121. Ibid., 115.

122. *She-elot u-Teshuvot Rabbenu Yiẓḥaq Alfasi*, ed. Z. W. Laiter (Pittsburgh, 1954), #5, cited in Stampfer, "Ha-Mishpat ha-'Ivri be-Sefarad ba-meah ha-11," 219–20.

123. Ibid.

124. Sklare, "R. David ben Sa'adya al-Ger ve-ḥiburo al-Ḥawwi," 112–13.

125. Ibid., 113n34. This perspective is consistent with that of Abramson, who repeatedly asserted that the scholarly influence of HaNagid was minimal and who denigrated the caliber of HaNagid's rabbinic learning when compared with that of his contemporary, Rabbi Isaac ibn Ghiyyat. Unlike HaNagid, ibn Ghiyyat lived long enough to study with R. Alfasi. Abramson, "Mi-torato shel Rav Shmuel HaNagid mi-Sefarad," 16, 17, 19, 23.

126. See, e.g., Abramson, "Mi-torato shel Rav Shmuel HaNagid mi-Sefarad," 13.

127. HaNagid, "Elohim he-erikh li peh ba-torot," in Jarden, *Divan Shmuel Ha-Nagid*, 1:90, lines 39–41.

128. On this *topos* of Andalusian Hebrew writings, first articulated by Sa'adya in the *Egron*, see A. Halkin, "The Medieval Jewish Attitude toward Hebrew," in *Biblical and Other Studies*, ed. Alexander Altmann (Cambridge, Mass., 1963), 233–48.

129. In this regard, it is interesting to note that Andalusian Jews in the time of Shmuel HaNagid were censured for failing to maintain the use of Aramaic in synagogue. On HaNagid's denial of this charge, see Margalioth, *Hilkhot ha-Nagid*, 19.

130. HaNagid, "*Elohim he-erikh li peh ba-torot*," in Jarden, *Divan Shmuel ha-Nagid* (Jerusalem, 1966), 1:84: "*Be-sifri teḥezeh divre qedumim va-aḥronim ve-lo titraḥ le-ḥapes.*"

131. As Maimonides wrote in the introduction to the *Mishneh Torah*, "The gist of the matter is that one need not have need of any other composition in the world regarding a rule [*din*] of the rules of Israel. Rather, let this composition be a *summa* [*meqabbeẓ*] for the entire Oral Torah. . . . For this reason I have given this composition the title '*Mishneh Torah*.' For a person first reads Written Torah, and then reads this, and knows from it the entire Oral Torah, and has no need to read another book apart from them." Part of this passage appears in I. Twersky, *Introduction to the Code of Maimonides*, 97, though I have rendered *torah she-be-'al peh* as "Oral Torah" and not "Oral Law."

132. As Margalioth (and later Yisrael Ta Shma) noted, the celebrated codes of Jewish law—Maimonides' twelfth-century *Mishneh Torah*, R. Jacob ben Asher's fourteenth-century *Arba'a Turim*, and R. Joseph Qaro's sixteenth-century *Shulḥan 'Arukh*—were all produced by scholars in the Andalusian orbit. Margalioth, *Hilkhot ha-Nagid*, 37, 52.

133. E. E. Urbach's path-breaking article on the *Tur* and the *Siete Partidas* offers a model of the insights that can be gleaned from this sort of analysis. See E. E. Urbach, "Mi-darkhe ha-Qodifiqaẓya- 'al Sefer ha-Turim le-Rabi Ya'aqov beRabi Asher," *American Academy for Jewish Research Jubilee Volume* 46–47 (1980) Hebrew pagination, 1–14.

134. Nicole Cottart, "Mālikiyya," *Encyclopaedia of Islam*, 2nd ed., ed. P. Bearman et al., 6:278–82.

135. Ibid.

136. The assumption within Umayyad Spanish society that legal writings were, by default, prescriptive might explain, for example, why Andalusian Jews of HaNagid's generation regarded *Halakhot Gedolot* itself as a code of law (when the geonim themselves did not), and why their encounter with this text might even have served as an impetus to their own codificatory endeavors. The same cultural orientation might also shed light on the disdain for anthologization expressed by Abraham ibn 'Ezra.

137. In one of his letters to the sages of Lunel, Maimonides described the state of rabbinic studies in North Africa as unacceptable.

138. The indebtedness of Alfasi's *Halakhot* to the works of rabbinic predecessors in both Qayrawan and al-Andalus was not lost on medieval scholars of Spain, Provence, and Ashkenaz. Margalioth, *Hilkhot ha-Nagid*, 35, 42. When Alfasi's students left Lucena for many places in Spain, they displaced local traditions and introduced a uniformity of practice that came from their shared pedagogic experience and their observations of the master. Ta Shma, *Ha-Sifrut ha-Parshanit*, 154.

139. See, e.g., Maimonides, *Teshuvot ha-Rambam*, ed. J. Blau (Jerusalem, 1989), no.

442: "What is the source of our knowledge of how our Saintly Master wrote the Mishna?" The claim that all "Spanish" manuscripts of Sherira's *Epistle* are late and were subject to "heavy-handed reworking" in order to bring them into accord with the writings of Maimonides appears in Sussman, "Torah she-be'al peh—peshuta ke-mashma'a," 234n26.

140. See Levin, *Iggeret Sherira Gaon*, 59, and see Chapter 1 above.

141. This phenomenon was paralleled in Islamic culture. See the observation that the transmission of *hadith* was best accomplished through auditing (*sama'*) and not through copying, even after it was inscribed, "shackled." G. Schoeler,"Oral Torah and Hadit: Transmission, Prohibition of Writing, Redaction," *The Oral and the Written in Early Islam,* ed., James E. Montgomery (London:, 2006), 129.

142. I. Twersky, "Some Non-Halakhic Aspects of *Mishneh Torah*," in *Jewish Medieval and Renaissance Studies*, ed., Alexander Altmann (Cambridge, Mass., 1967), 109, relying on the explanation of "Mishnah" offered by Maimonides' son. Abraham Maimonides, *Perush R. Abraham ben ha-Rambam z"l 'al Bereshit u-Shemot,* trans. E. Wiesenberg, ed. D. Sassoon (London,1958), 382–84. On exposition as an oral activity, see E. Wolfson, "Beyond the Spoken Word: Oral Tradition and Written Transmission in Medieval Jewish Mysticism," in *Transmitting Jewish Traditions: Orality, Textuality, and Cultural Diffusion*, ed. Y. Elman and I. Gershoni, 193–202.

143. Maimonides, introduction to *Mishneh Torah*. Referring to the *Mishneh Torah* in a letter to his pupil, Joseph ibn 'Aqnin, Maimonides instructed him to "persist with regularity in your oral study of the composition. [*'tatmid be-limud ha-ḥibur be-'al peh'*]." Maimonides' letter to Ibn 'Aqnin, in David Baneth, *Iggerot ha-Rambam: Ḥalifat ha-Mikhtavim 'im R. Yosef ben Yehudah* (Jerusalem, 1985), 68. Wondering whether Baneth had translated this passage correctly, Abramson writes: "It seems garbled [*megumgam*] to me that Rambam would instruct his student to recite [*le-shanen*] his composition by heart." Abramson, *Rav Nisim Gaon*, 29–30. Yet, as Twersky noted, Maimonides most certainly did intend for his *Mishneh Torah* code of law to be committed to memory. I. Twersky, "Biqoret sefer: 'Ḥamishah Sefarim le-Rav Nisim Gaon,'" *Tarbiẓ* 37 (1968): 325–26. Abramson's confusion was connected with his puzzlement over the claim by R. Nisim of Qayrawan that the Talmud continued to be studied orally after it acquired its written form.

144. "It is not possible for a person to remember the entire Talmud by heart." Maimonides, introduction to *Perush ha-Mishnah,* ed. Kafaḥ (Jeusalem, 1967), 1:26. Notwithstanding Maimonides' assertion, several medieval scholars, such as Shmuel ben 'Eli and Rav Mevorakh, acquired reputations for their ability to recite all of Talmud. See E. Greenhut, *Sibuv Rabi Petaḥia me-Regensburg* (Frankfurt, 1904–5), 8; Maimonides, *Iggerot ha-Rambam,* ed. Y. Shilat (Jerusalem, 1987), 1:306; N. Danzig, "Mi-talmud 'al peh le-talmud be-khtav," 82.

145. An ancient midrashic rumination on the biblical phrase (Deut. 17:18) "*mishneh ha-torah*," "a copy of this teaching," plays on the similarity of its first word and the verb *lishanen*, review or recite: "*Mishneh Torah*—for in the future they will review [*yihyu shonin oto*] it by heart." *Sifre* Deuteronomy, *Shoftim,* noted by I. Twersky in "Biqoret sefer: 'Ḥamishah Sefarim le-Rav Nisim Gaon,'" 325–26.

146. See the passages extolling the importance of oral-memorial study cited in I. Twersky, "Biqoret sefer: 'Ḥamishah Sefarim le-Rav Nisim Gaon,'" 325–26; H. A. Wolfson, *Crescas' Critique of Aristotle* (Cambridge, Mass., 1929), 22ff. By contrast, see N. Danzig, "Mi-talmud 'al peh le-talmud be-khtav," 82.

147. Y. Qaro, introduction to *Shulḥan 'Arukh* (Venice, 1565). A facsimile of this introduction appears in Reuven Margalioth, "Defuse ha-Shulḥan 'Arukh ha-rishonim," in *Rabi Yosef Qaro*, ed. Yiẓḥaq Raphael (Jerusalem, 1969), 91.

148. If this conjecture is correct, then the conceptual understandings that arose from the variant formulations of the "Spanish" and "French" recensions of Sherira's *Epistle* may not have been dramatically different.

149. See Chapter 1.

150. The epistolary exchange is presented and analyzed in Moshe Gil and Ezra Fleischer, *Yehudah HaLevi u-Vene Ḥugo* (Jerusalem, 2001), 60–62, 302–6; on the identification of the Spaniard as Rabbi Yaacov Alcal'i, see 60.

151. Indeed, while Sefardi rabbinic scholars expressed respect for the authority of the geonim and invoked their teachings as precedents, they did not treat geonic decisions as binding. See Brody, *Geonim*, 197n49; Ta Shma, *Ha-Sifrut ha-Parshanit*, 1:149, 151.

152. Ta Shma, "Shiput 'ivri u-mishpat 'ivri ba-meot ha-11–12 be-Sefarad," reprinted in *Knesset Meḥqarim* (Jerusalem, 2004), 2:247–48

153. Ibn Migash, Responsum no. 114, cited in S. D. Goitein, *Sidre Ḥinukh be-Yeme ha-Geonim u-Vet ha-Rambam* (Jerusalem, 1962), 167; I. Twersky, "Sefer Mishneh Torah la-Rambam, megamato ve-tafqido," *Proceedings of the Israel Academy of Sciences and Humanities* 5 (1972): 3–4n12; Y. Ta Shma, "Yeẓirato ha-sifrutit shel Rabbenu Yosef Halevi ibn Migash," *Qiryat Sefer* 46 (1971): 136–46, 541–53.

154. D. Rosenthal, "Le-Toldot Rav Paltoi Gaon," 610–13 and nn. 138–40. For a partial list of medieval rabbinic scholars who differed with geonim, see S. Z. Havlin, "'Al ha-ḥatimah ha-sifrutit ke-yesod ha-ḥaluqah le-tequfot ba-halakhah," *Meḥqarim be-Sifrut ha-Talmudit*, ed. S. Z. Havlin (Jerusalem, 1983), 148ff. and n. 120. Cf. R. (Yeraḥmiel) Brody, "Kelum hayyu ha-geonim meḥoqeqim?" *Shenaton ha-Mishpat ha-'Ivri* 11–12 (1984–86): 286 and n. 3; G. Libson, "Halakha and Reality in the Geonic Period: Taqqanah, Minhag, Tradition and Consensus," in *The Jews of Medieval Islam: Community, Society and Identity*, ed. Daniel Frank (Leiden; New York, 1995), 99.

155. See, e.g., Naḥmanides' Sermon for Rosh HaShanah in *Kitve ha-Ramban*, ed. Charles Chavel (Jerusalem, 1962–63), 1:214–52. And see M. Halbertal, "Ha-minhag ve-ha-historia shel ha-halakhah be-torato shel ha-Ramban," *Ẓion* 67 (2002): 25–56.

156. Eliyahu Mizraḥi, *She-elot u-Teshuvot* (Jerusalem, 1937), no. 76, 248. Because they did not understand how Jewish law had evolved in earlier times, medieval scholars from Sefarad and Provence assumed that certain recorded practices that deviated from talmudic teachings had been enactments of the geonim. See Brody, "Kelum hayyu ha-geonim meḥoqeqim?" 286n3; and Brody, *Geonim*, 31.

157. On the clear distinction between *dayyanim* and *ba'ale hora-a* in fifteenth-century Algiers, see R. Solomon ben Simon Duran, *Sefer ha-Rashbash: She-elot u-Teshuvot*,

230. On boorish (and violent) *dayyanim* in Spain, see Y. Baer, *Toldot ha-Yehudim be-Sefarad ha-Noẓrit* (Tel Aviv, 1945), 185, 206.

158. Cf. the observation that it was possible to exempt Jewish scholars from taxes in Sefarad because the scholarly class there was much smaller than in northern Europe. E. Kanarfogel, *Jewish Education and Society in the High Middle Ages* (Detroit, 1992), 45–46.

159. Baḥya ibn Paquda, *Ḥovot ha-Levavot*, ed. Avraham Ẓifroni (Jerusalem, 1929), 1:219ff. This passage is discussed in I. Twersky, *Introduction to the Code of Maimonides*, 90–91.

160. In many places, *Hilkhot Alfasi* or *Pisqei ha-Rosh* were studied in lieu of Talmud. See Y. Ta Shma, "Rashi -Rif, ve-Rashi-Rosh," in *Rashi: 'Iyyunim be-Yeẓirato*, ed. Ẓ. Steinfeld (Ramat Gan, 1993), 209–20. *Sefer Ḥasidim* suggests that those who cannot study serve as copyists.

161. These curricular divisions were described by R. Joseph Rosh ha-Seder ben Ya'aqov ben 'Ali, a contemporary of Maimonides, who moved from Babylonia to Cairo. The three groups are respectively designated as *'amei ha-areẓ* (simple folk); *talmide ḥakhamim*, disciples of sages, and *ḥakhamim*, sages. Cited in S. D. Goitein, *Sidre Ḥinukh*, 148.

162. Of course, this expectation proved daunting. In certain times and places in France, Ashkenaz, and Italy, Jewish men fulfilled the precept of *talmud torah* by studying specific works of talmudic exegesis, and even digests of applied law. On the study of Alfasi's *Halakhot* and of *Pisqe ha-Rosh* in lieu of Talmud, see Ta Shma, "Rashi-Rif, ve-Rashi-Rosh."

163. Thus, for example, Sefardim of later centuries complained that growing emphasis on Talmud study was displacing the pursuit of other disciplines, like biblical exegesis and philology. See Chapter 5 and M. Poliak, "Merkaziyyuto shel limud ha-miqra be-arẓot ha-Islam 'al pi 'edutah shel genizat Qahir," *'Al ha-Pereq* 17 (2000): 131–41; U. Simon, "Parshane sefarad," in *Parshanut ha-Miqra ha-Yehudit*, ed. Moshe Greenberg (Jerusalem, 1983), 29–60.

164. On the description of Naḥmanides' novellae on the Talmud as the first halakhic work to transcend geographic boundaries, see M. Halbertal, "Ha-minhag ve-ha-historiah shel ha-halakhah be-torato shel ha-Ramban," *Ẓion* 67 (2002): 55–56.

165. Joseph ibn Ḥabiba, *Ḥidush le-Massekhet Berakhot*, cited in Mordecai Breuer, "Le-Ḥeqer ha-tipologia shel yeshivot ha-ma'arav bi-yeme ha-benayyim." In *Peraqim be-Toldot ha-Ḥevra ha-Yehudit be-Yeme ha-Benayyim u-va-'Et ha-Ḥadasha*, ed. I. Etkes and Y. Salmon (Jerusalem, 1980), 45n1.

CHAPTER 3

1. The claim that Sefarad was the cultural heir of Babylonia and that Ashkenaz was the cultural heir of Palestine is put forward most forcefully in Binyamin Klar's afterword to *Megilat Aḥima'aẓ* (Jerusalem, 1944–45), 144–51. See also R. Bonfil, "Beyn Ereẓ Yisrael le-veyn Bavel: Qavvim le-ḥeqer toldot ha-tarbut shel ha-yehudim be-Italya ha-deromit u-ve-Eropa ha-noẓrit be-yeme ha-benayyim ha-muqdamim," *Shalem* 5 (1987): 1–30.

2. See A. Grossman, *Ḥakhme Ashkenaz ha-Rishonim* (Jerusalem, 1981), 424–35; A. Grossman, "Ziqata shel yahadut Ashkenaz ha-qeduma el Ereẓ Yisrael," *Shalem* 3 (1981): 57–92; D. Berger, "Ḥeqer rabbanut Ashkenaz ha-qedumah," *Tarbiẓ* 53 (1984): 479–87; R. Brody, *Geonim* (New Haven Conn., 1988), 117, 120–22; H. Soloveitchik, *Ha-Yayin be-Yeme ha-Benayyim: Yeyn Nesekh—Pereq be-Toldot ha-Halakhah be-Ashkenaz* (Jerusalem, 2008), chap. 9.

3. No comparable attempt will be made here to reframe the cultural world of Sefarad. An undertaking of this magnitude would require that attention be paid not only to the heartland of the Roman Empire but to the culture of Visigothic Spain and to the cultures of the different Islamic rulers who ruled Spain and North Africa.

4. Pierre Riché, *Education and Culture in the Barbarian West, Sixth through Eighth Centuries* (Columbia, S.C., 1976), x, 49, 177.

5. Ibid., 189, 211–12.

6. The Germanic residents of Aquitaine had adopted the customs of Rome and probably its language as well. Patrick Geary, *Before France and Germany: The Creation and Transformation of the Merovingian World* (New York, 1988), 115; Riché, *Education and Culture in the Barbarian West,* 183.

7. Because the Byzantine state needed trained functionaries, Emperor Justinian reinstated the payment of salaries to teachers of grammar, rhetoric, and medicine in 554. Riché, *Education and Culture in the Barbarian West,* 140.

8. Ibid., 15.

9. Ibid., 189.

10. Geary, *Before France and Germany,* 203; Riché, *Education and Culture in the Barbarian West,* 190.

11. Riché, *Education and Culture in the Barbarian West,* 36–37.

12. Ibid., 38–39. Roman schools reopened in North Africa in the late fifth century.

13. E. R. Curtius, *European Literature and the Latin Middle Ages,* trans. Willard Trask (London, 1953), 61–68.

14. Riché, *Education and Culture in the Barbarian West,* xxxvi. It was only after having attended grammarian's school that people entered the ranks of the clergy.

15. Curtius, *European Literature and the Latin Middle Ages,* 61–68; Brian Stock, *The Implications of Literacy* (Princeton, N.J., 1983), 16, 40; E. Magnou-Nortier, "The Enemies of the Peace: Reflections on a Vocabulary, 500–1100," in *The Peace of God: Social Violence and Religious Response around the Year 1000,* ed. T. Head and R. Landes (Ithaca, N.Y., 1992), 58–72; W. C. Jordan, *Europe in the High Middle Ages* (London, 2001), 22.

16. Pierre Bonnassie, "From the Rhone to Galicia: Origins and Modalities of the Feudal Order," in *From Slavery to Serfdom in South Western Europe* (Cambridge, 1991), 104–31. On the import of papyrus, see Riché, *Education and Culture in the Barbarian West,* 179.

17. Riché, *Education and Culture in the Barbarian West,* 179.

18. Ibid., 22n34.

19. Ibid., 22–23.

20. Ibid., 178, 180. Based on close study of eleventh-century documents, Georges Duby described Burgundy as having been "ahead of other regions" in its "marked preference for written proof." G. Duby, *The Chivalrous Society,* trans. Cynthia Postan (Berkeley, 1980), 52.

21. Riché, *Education and Culture in the Barbarian West,* 178, 180–81.

22. On the activities of Euric, Gundobad, and Theodoric, compilers of legal codes for various barbarian peoples, and on the services rendered by Boethius and Cassiodorus in the court of the Ostrogothic kingdom of Italy, see Geary, *Before France and Germany,* 32; Riché, *Education and Culture in the Barbarian West,* 17; J. M. Wallace-Hadrill, *The Barbarian West: The Early Middle Ages A.D. 400–1000* (Oxford; Cambridge, 1996), 32.

23. Riché, *Education and Culture in the Barbarian West,* 61–62.

24. Ibid., 13, 183; Geary, *Before France and Germany,* 14.

25. The persistence of strong feelings for or against Rome was apparent in the allegiances forged by various Germanic tribes. According to Geary, this was among the factors that sped up ethnogenesis and led to formation of new tribal confederations and peoples. Geary, *Before France and Germany,* 58.

26. Riché, *Education and Culture in the Barbarian West,* 210; Geary, *Before France and Germany,* 90–91. In fact, Germanic law continued to borrow from Roman law throughout the Middle Ages. See Alan Watson, "The Causes of the Reception of Roman Law," in his *The Evolution of Law* (Baltimore, 1985).

27. Stock, *Implications of Literacy,* 16.

28. Riché, *Education and Culture in the Barbarian West,* 12. Cf. the observation that the *carta* (charter) was primarily a symbol of physical *traditio,* or as a Langobard charter put it, the *notitia,* a text to be retained by memory for future times. Stock, *Implications of Literacy,* 46.

29. The fact that the Merovingian king Clovis promulgated a Latin code of Salic law between 508 and 511 does not invalidate this claim. Historians understand Clovis's project as an attempt on the part of a barbarian ruler to claim that he was the legitimate ruler not simply of the Northern Franks (for whom the code would appear to have been designed), but of the entirety of the former Roman Empire. Geary, *Before France and Germany,* 90.

30. Ta Shma, *Minhag Ashkenaz ha-Qadmon* (Jerusalem, 1992), 15, 42; H. Soloveitchik, *Ha-Yayin,* 111–12.

31. Though Yisrael Ta Shma showed great awareness of the cultural differences that distinguished the heartland of the former Roman Empire from its borderlands, he failed to elaborate on its implications for the subcultures of medieval Jewry. This may have been because he was preoccupied with reconstructing what he saw as the diachronic influence of ancient Palestine on medieval Ashkenaz. See especially I. Ta Shma, "Halakhah, minhag u-masoret be-yahadut Ashkenaz ba-meot ha-11–12," *Sidra* 3 (1987): esp. 145–48, 157, 160. Some of the shortcomings of this perspective are discussed below in Chapter 5.

32. It goes without saying that any comparable study of Sefarad would need to take into account the cultures of the Spanish Visigoths and of the Muslim groups that ruled in al-Andalaus and North Africa, and not only the culture of the Roman Empire.

33. Patrick Geary, *Phantoms of Remembrance: Memory and Oblivion at the End of the First Millennium* (Princeton, N.J., 1994), 29.

34. Gerd Tellenbach, "Vom Karolingischen Reichsadel zum deutschen Reichsfürstenstand," in *Herrschaft und Staat im Mittelalter*, trans. R. F. Bennett (Darmstadt, 1956), 191–242; K. Leyser, "The German Aristocracy from the Ninth to the Early Twelfth Century: A Historical and Cultural Sketch," *Past and Present* 41 (1968): 32.

35. Leyser, "The German Aristocracy from the Ninth to the Early Twelfth Century," 28. On the market in luxury items and natural and man-made wonders, see L. Daston and K. Park, *Wonders and the Order of Nature* (New York, 1998), chap. 2, esp. 100–108.

36. During the Ottonian Renaissance (950–1050), international merchants come to wield even greater power because they could provide the aristocracy with the luxury goods they needed to make manifest their social positions. Geary, *Before France and Germany*, 102; Leyser, "The German Aristocracy from the Ninth to the Early Twelfth Century," 28, 43.

37. Leyser, "The German Aristocracy from the Ninth to the Early Twelfth Century," 30, 36–37.

38. Geary, *Phantoms of Remembrance*, 68; Leyser, "The German Aristocracy from the Ninth to the Early Twelfth Century," 37.

39. Leyser, "The German Aristocracy from the Ninth to the Early Twelfth Century," 26–27.

40. Tellenbach and his students analyzed the *Libri Memoriales* from monasteries in southern Germany, Lotharingia, and northern Italy in order to identify the largest families. Leyser, "The German Aristocracy from the Ninth to the Early Twelfth Century," 33.

41. Geary, *Before France and Germany*, 171–72, 176.

42. Stephen White, *Custom, Kinship and Gifts to Saints: The "Laudatio Parentum" in Western France, 1050–1150* (Chapel Hill, N.C., 1998), 68.

43. Geary, *Before France and Germany*, 98.

44. Ibid., 173.

45. Ibid., 178, 139–40; Riché, *Education and Culture in the Barbarian West*, 324–29. The impact of Irish monasticism's penitentialism on the lives of Christians and Jews of the medieval Rhineland is discussed in Chapter 6.

46. Geary notes that the impact of this "vigorous" northern phenomenon reversed a geographic trend of influence, for in earlier centuries it was the southern, Mediterranean strain of Christianity that had penetrated the North. Now, however, monasticism began to transform the Romanized South, and religious sites (like basilicas) that had once been controlled by bishops were remade into abbeys whose residents adopted the Benedictine rule. See Geary, *Before France and Germany*, 178, and Stephane Lebecq, "The Role of Monasteries in the Systems of Production and Exchange of the Frankish World between the Seventh and the Beginning of the Ninth Centuries," in *The Long Eighth Century*, ed. I. L. Hansen and C. Wickham (Leiden, 2000), 123–24.

47. On the older European monasteries, see Riché, *Education and Culture in the Barbarian West*, 102; Geary, *Before France and Germany*, 35.

48. Riché, *Education and Culture in the Barbarian West,* 86, 90, 121.

49. Jean Leclercq, *The Love of Learning and the Desire for God: A Study of Monastic Culture* trans., Catharine Misrahi (New York, 1961), 72; Jean Leclercq, "The Renewal of Theology," in *Renaissance and Renewal in the Twelfth Century,* ed. Robert Benson, Giles Constable, and Carol D. Lanham (Cambridge, Mass., 1982), 77.

50. Stephen Jaeger, *The Envy of Angels: Cathedral Schools and Social Ideas in Medieval Europe, 950–1200* (Philadelphia, 1994), 39, 43–44, 46–47; John Baldwin, *Masters, Princes and Merchants: The Social Views of Peter the Chanter and His Circle* (Princeton, N.J., 1970), 175–204.

51. Jaeger, *Envy of Angels,* 62–63.

52. Speaking of the period and its educational ideals, Jaeger wrote, "Its works of art are men whose 'manners' are 'composed.'" Jaeger, *Envy of Angels,* 3–4. Teaching by example was also the dominant pastoral duty of canons regular, whose houses burgeoned after the second half of the eleventh century. See Caroline Bynum, *Docere Verbo et Exemplo: An Aspect of Twelfth-Century Spirituality* (Missoula, Mont., 1978).

53. Jaeger, *Envy of Angels,* 3.

54. Ibid., 41–42.

55. Ibid., 117, 240.

56. Ibid., 81.

57. Ibid., 79–80.

58. Ibid., 106, 111, 115; C. Bynum, *Docere Verbo et Exemplo.*

59. Jaeger, *Envy of Angels,* 37. Brun of Cologne (fl. 940s–960s), brother of Emperor Otto the Great, served as imperial chancellor and ultimately as Archbishop of Cologne.

60. Brun's biography was written by his former student Ruotger of Cologne. Jaeger, *Envy of Angels,* 37.

61. Geary, *Phantoms of Remembrance,* 29, 49.

62. Duby, *Chivalrous Society,* 126. As Duby notes (125), temporal and spiritual powers had been merged in the Carolingian monarch.

63. For half a century, these Peace Councils took place only in Aquitaine and Provence; later, they spread to other locations in southern Gaul (e.g., Narbonne, Arles, Lyons, and Burgundy) and, ultimately, to northern France. See G. Duby, *Chivalrous Society,* 123–24.

64. Rodulfus (= Raoul) Glaber, *The Five Books of the Histories, and the Life of St. William,* trans. John France (Oxford, 1989), Fourth Book.

65. Duby, *Chivalrous Society,* 130–31.

66. H. E. J. Cowdrey, *The Cluniacs and the Gregorian Reform* (Oxford, 1970), 127, 134.

67. Ibid., 124–25. On Irish penitentials on the European continent, see T. Tentler, *Sin and Confession on the Eve of the Reformation* (Princeton, N.J., 1977), 3–9; J. McNeill, *The Celtic Penitentials and Their Influence on Continental Christianity* (Paris, 1923), chap. 5.

68. Cowdrey, *The Cluniacs and the Gregorian Reform,* 182. This, too, was noted by Raoul Glaber. On Christian pilgrimages to the Holy Land before the First Crusade, see

A. Grabois, *Le Pèlerin Occidental en Terre Sainte au Moyen Age* (Brussels, 1998). The Cluniac network maintained close connections with Jerusalem-based clergy through the Byzantine church's dependencies in southern French, especially the monastery at Moissac. Cowdrey, *The Cluniacs and the Gregorian Reform*, 183. This connection has been described as one that promoted spiritual and artistic preoccupation with the theme of Jerusalem—and that may have helped to prepare the seedbed for the preaching of Urban II, who issued the call to Crusade on his journey in France. See A. Gieysztor, "The Genesis of the Crusades: The Encyclical of Sergius IV (1009–1012)," *Medievalia et Humanistica* 5 (1948): 3–23; 6 (1950): 3–34.

69. According to monastery correspondence, charters, and customs, Cluny was called the *asylum poenitentium*, the refuge of those who sought deliverance from their sins. Cowdrey, *The Cluniacs and the Gregorian Reform*, 129–30.

70. Ibid., 135, 184.

71. Ibid., 171, 190.

72. Ibid., 173.

73. Rosamund McKitterick, *The Carolingians and the Written Word* (Cambridge, 1989).

74. G. Duby, *The Chivalrous Society*, 15–58. Cf. the observation that in Roman law, "the real function of the court, the jurors and the public was mediation." Stock, *Implications of Literacy*, 58.

75. Brigitte Bedos-Rezak questions Rosamund McKitterick's claim that the pattern of literacy introduced by Charlemagne continued well after the breakdown of the Carolingian Empire. See R. McKitterick, *The Carolingians and the Written Word*, chap. 2; B. Bedos-Rezak, "The Confrontation of Orality and Textuality: Jewish and Christian Literacy in Eleventh- and Twelfth-Century Northern France," in *Rashi, 1040–1990: Hommage à Efraim E. Urbach*, ed. G. Sed-Rajna (Paris, 1993), 547 and n. 38. There is no doubt that the Roman practices of inscription that were reintroduced by Charlemagne survived in northern Europe's ancient cities and in its earliest monasteries. See Riché, *Education and Culture in the Barbarian West*, 212–13; Geary, *Phantoms of Remembrance*, 24.

76. See White, *Custom, Kinship and Gifts to Saints*, 68, 72–73; Frederic Cheyette, "The Invention of State," in *Essays in Medieval Civilization*, ed. B. K. Lackner and K. R. Phillip (Austin, Tex., 1979), 143–76; F. Cheyette, "Custom, Case Law and Medieval Constitutionalism: A Re-Examination," *Political Science Quarterly* 78 (1963): 362–90; Frederic Cheyette, "Suum Cuique Tribuere," *French Historical Studies* 6 (1970): 292.

77. Stephen White, "*Pactum . . . Legem Vincit et Amor Judicium*: The Settlement of Disputes by Compromise in Eleventh Century Western France," *American Journal of Legal History* 22 (1978): 281–308.

78. Duby, *The Chivalrous Society*, 57.

79. Lon Fuller, "Human Interaction and the Law," in *The Rule of Law*, ed. R. P. Wolff (New York, 1971), 114.

80. M. T. Clanchy, "Remembering the Past and the Good Old Law," *History* 55 (1970): 165.

81. Riché, *Education and Culture in the Barbarian West,* 217–18.

82. B. J. Hibbits, "Coming to Our Senses: Communication and Legal Expression in Performance Cultures," *Emory Law Journal* 41 (1992): 873–960; B. Bedos-Rezak, "Diplomatic Sources and Medieval Documentary Practices: An Essay in Interpretive Methodology," in *The Past and Future of Medieval Studies,* ed. John Van Engen (Notre Dame, Ind., 1994), 321 and 339n23; Jacques Le Goff, "Le rituel symbolique de la vassalité," in *Pour un autre Moyen âge* (Paris, 1977), 349–419. On the importance of leaving impressions on children in marking changes in legal status, see Ta Shma's thoughtful discussion of the talmudic practice of *qeẓaẓa* in *Minhag Ashkenaz ha-Qadmon,* 44–45.

83. Le Goff, "Le rituel symbolique de la vassalité," 370–84; Stock, *Implications of Literacy,* 47.

84. Emily Zack Tabuteau, *Transfers of Property in Eleventh Century Norman Law* (Chapel Hill, N.C., 1988), 7–8, 213–19; cf. Geary, *Phantoms of Remembrance,* 124–25.

85. On the charter as a symbolic object, see M. T. Clanchy, *From Memory to Written Record* (London, 1979), 203–8; B. Bedos-Rezak, "Diplomatic Sources and Medieval Documentary Practices," 321, 339n23.

86. White, *Custom, Kinship and Gifts to Saints,* 37, 208; Tabuteau, *Transfers of Property in Eleventh Century Norman Law,* 207, 212–15. As Stephen White explains (200), the writs of *laudatio parentum* affirmed social ties or established them and testify, in a larger sense, to changes in the social and religious makeup of the region over the centuries in question.

87. Jaeger, *Envy of Angels,* 46–48.

88. Ibid., 15–16.

89. Geary, *Before France and Germany,* 201; Geary, *Phantoms of Remembrance,* 29.

90. Writing in the mid-ninth century, Bishop Agobard of Lyons described a meeting of five people, each of whom followed a different law. Cited in Paul Vinogradoff, *Roman Law in Medieval Europe* (Oxford, 1929), 25–26. Adherence to the "law of person" made the experience of Jews far more similar to that of other peoples in the early Middle Ages. See Mark Cohen, *Under Crescent and Cross: The Jews in the Middle Ages* (Princeton, N.J., 1994), 44.

91. Stock, *Implications of Literacy,* 52. On Jewry law in codes like the *Sachsenspiegel* and *Schwabenspiegel,* see Guido Kisch, *Jewry Law in Medieval Germany: Laws and Court Decisions Concerning Jews* (New York, 1949).

92. Jaeger, *Envy of Angels,* 81.

93. Ibid., 240, 203. According to Jaeger (9), twelfth-century students wistfully attempted to capture, at least symbolically, a fading charisma enjoyed in the previous age, when masters were embodied bearers of cultural ideals.

94. The three scriptural occurrences of the term "Ashkenaz" appear in Genesis 10:3, I Chronicles 1:6, and Jeremiah 51:27. The verse in Genesis names Ashkenaz as one of the sons of Gomer, and the talmudic sages seem to have associated Gomer with "*Germamia*" because of the phonetic similarities of the words. See BT Yoma 10a and Meg. 71b as well as YT Meg 1:9 and Gen. R. 37:1.

95. A. Harkavy, *Me-assef Nidaḥim: Meqorot u-Meḥqarim be-Toldot Yisrael u-ve-Sifruto* (Jerusalem, 1969), 1, 90. The appearance of the term in the mid-ninth century *Seder Rav 'Amram Gaon* has been identified as a late interpolation.

96. Ta Shma, *Minhag Ashkenaz ha-Qadmon*, 14–16, 22–27; C. Brühl, *Deutschland—Frankreich: Die Geburt zweier Völker* (Cologne and Vienna, 1990).

97. Maurice Liber, *Rashi*, trans. Adele Szold (Philadelphia, 1906), 47. Haym Soloveitchik notes that while scholars in France and Germany preferred different compositional genres, there was no major difference between approaches to learning in the two regions. H. Soloveitchik, *Ha-Yayin*, 122.

98. Avraham Reiner, "From Rabbenu Tam to R. Isaac of Vienna: The Hegemony of the French Talmudic School in the Twelfth Century," in *The Jews of Europe in the Middle Ages*, ed. Christopher Cluse (Turnhout, 2004), 273–81.

99. On the emergence of regional identities, see, e.g., M. Bloch, *Feudal Society*, trans. L. A. Manyon. (London, 1961) 139; David Herlihy, "Family Solidarity in Medieval Italian History," in *Economy, Society, and Government in Medieval Italy*, ed. David Herlihy, Robert Lopez, and Vsevolod Slessarev (Kent, Ohio, 1969), 173–84.

100. A. Grossman, *Ḥakhme Ashkenaz ha-Rishonim*, 400–439, A. Grossman, "Yiḥus mishpaḥa u-meqomo ba-ḥevra ha-yehudit be-Ashkenaz ha-qeduma," in *Peraqim be-Toldot ha-ḥevra ha-Yehudit . . . Muqdashim le-Professor Yaacov Katz* (Jerusalem, 1980), 9–23.

101. A. Grossman, *Ḥakhme Ashkenaz ha-Rishonim*, 400–401, esp. 403; Grossman, "Yiḥus mishpaḥa u-meqomo ba-ḥevra ha-yehudit biAshkenaz ha-qeduma," 12.

102. BT Pes. 108a.

103. See the assertion that an "important woman" is "one whose husband is not strict with her" in R. Elazar of Worms, *Ha-Roqeaḥ ha-Gadol* (Jerusalem, 1960), no. 283.

104. R. Samuel b. Meir, *Commentary on the Talmud*, Pes. 108a.

105. According to R. Manoaḥ, a scholar of late thirteenth- and early fourteenth-century Narbonne, an "important woman" possesses enough "manservants and maidservants, so that she need not be directly involved with household matters," whether or not the wealth was generated by "the fruits of her own labor." Cited in J. Qaro, *Kesef Mishneh* on *MT Hil. Ḥamez u-Maẓah* 7:8.

106. Ibid.

107. Ibid.

108. Tosafot on Pes. 108a; Mordecai ben Hillel, *Mordecai*, on Pes. 108a. On the topic of *nashim ḥashuvot*, see A. Grossman, *Ḥasidot u-Mordot: Nashim Yehudiyot be-Eropah be-Yeme ha-Benayyim* (Jerusalem, 2001), 326–28; T. Fishman, "A Kabbalistic Perspective on Gender-Specific Commandments: On the Interplay between Symbol and Society," *AJS Review* 17 (1992): 208–15.

109. K. Stow, "By Land or by Sea: The Passage of the Kalonymides to the Rhineland in the Tenth Century," in *Communication in the Jewish Diaspora*, ed. S. Menache (Leiden, 1996), 64. On the role of Jews in medieval European trade, see also Roberto Lopez and I.W. Raymond, *Medieval Trade in the Mediterranean World: Illustrative Documents* (New York, 1955), 30n53.

110. Michael Toch, "The Formation of a Diaspora: The Settlement of Jews in the Medieval German Reich," in his *Peasants and Jews in Medieval Germany* (Aldershot, Hampshire, 2003), chap. 9.

111. Shlomo Eidelberg, "*Ma'arufia* in Rabbenu Gershom's Responsa," *Historia Judaica* 15 (1953): 59–66.

112. M. Toch, *Die Juden im mittelalterlichen Reich* (Munich, 1998), 7.

113. Most recently, see the remarks of H. Soloveitchik in *Ha-Yayin*, 331–38. And see Lopez and Raymond, *Medieval Trade in the Mediterranean World*, 30n53; Irving Agus, *Urban Civilization in Pre-Crusade Europe: A Study of Organized Town Life in the Tenth-Eleventh Centuries Based on Responsa Literature* (New York, 1965), 1:88, 92, 104–5.

114. Because the European parties to the transaction needed to comply with local tariffs, a rabbinical court in southern Italy ruled that profits could only be calculated after these expenditures had been taken into consideration by all the associated partners. Aryeh Grabois, "The Use of Letters as Communication Medium among Medieval European Jewish Communities," in *Communication in the Jewish Diaspora*, ed. Sophia Menache (Leiden, 1996), 100.

115. A responsum of Natronai Gaon written in the mid-ninth century advised Jews in Spain and Faranjah about how they should behave when news of a Gaon's death reached them more than a year late. On Faranjah (or Afrangah) as the land of Franks, see R. Brody, *Geonim*, 133. See also Y. Brody, *Teshuvot Rav Natronai bar Hilai Gaon* (Jerusalem, 1994), 63n25, 373–74.

116. E. Kanarfogel, *Jewish Education and Society in the High Middle Ages* (Detroit, 1992) 101, 105, 195–97. On *Sefer Ḥuqqei ha-Torah*, see E. Kanarfogel, "A Monastic-like Setting for the Study of Torah," in *Judaism in Practice*, ed. Lawrence Fine (Princeton, N.J., 2001), 191–202.

117. The Pietists' perspectives might be compared with the Ashkenazi worldview exposed in I. Yuval, *Two Nations in Your Womb: Perceptions of Jews and Christians in Late Antiquity and the Middle Ages*, trans. Barbara Harshav and Jonathan Chipman (Berkeley, 2006).

118. H. Soloveitchik, "Sefer Ḥasidim: 'Olam ha-midrash ve-ha-humanizm shel ha-meah ha-12," *Tarbiẓ* 71 (2002): 533.

119. Speyer, however, did not invite Jewish settlers until 1084.

120. See Chapter 6 below.

121. On earlier Ashkenazi documentation of local practice, see Chapter 4. On the explosion of Jewish writings on custom in the twelfth century, see Chapter 5.

122. Medieval Ashkenazim were certainly not the first Jews to execute legal acts through performance; Israelites and rabbis of late antiquity did so as well. Nonetheless, the sheer quantity of rituals and the density of performative detail in medieval northern Europe is striking.

123. Because practices mentioned in *Sefer Maharil* were cited in R. Moses Isserles's sixteenth-century glosses to the *Shulhan 'Arukh* law code, they attained widespread influence in Ashkenazi life.

124. I am grateful to Professor Elḥanan Reiner for discussing this matter with me.

125. Agus, *Urban Civilization in Pre-Crusade Europe*, 672.

126. Robert Sabatino Lopez, review of *Urban Civilization in Pre-Crusade Europe* by Irving Agus, *Speculum* 42 (1967): 342.

127. Menaḥem Ben Sasson adduced ample evidence for the widespread use of written correspondence as the basis of financial transactions in the Mediterranean, where it was "simply not seen as a problem," and noted that this same practice was not permitted in Ashkenaz. M. Ben Sasson, *Ẓemiḥat ha-Qehilah ha-Yehudit be-Arẓot ha-Islam: Qayrawan, 800–1057* (Jerusalem, 1996), 79–80, 97, 102

128. Riché, *Education and Culture in the Barbarian West*, 178–80, 210; Geary, *Before France and Germany*, 90–91; Stock, *Implications of Literacy*, 16.

129. The halakhic basis for disallowing this practice is BT BK 104, and the geonic perspective appears in B. M. Levin, *Oẓar HaGeonim: Teshuvot Geone Bavel u-Ferushehem 'al pi Seder ha-Talmud* (Haifa and Jerusalem, 1928–43) *Bava Qama,* responsa 80–83.

130. The foundation myth first appeared in Elazar of Worms's commentary on prayer and was first published in Yosef Shlomo Delmedigo, *Maẓref le-Ḥokhma* (Basilea, 1669), 14b. Cf. A. Grossman, *Ḥakhme Ashkenaz*, 27–44; Y. Dan, *Torat ha-Sod shel Ḥasidut Ashkenaz* (Jerusalem, 1968), 14; R. Bonfil, "Beyn Ereẓ Yisrael," 23n81; I. Marcus, "History, Story and Collective Memory: Narrativity in Early Ashkenazic Culture," in *The Midrashic Imagination*, ed. M. Fishbane (Albany, 1993), 262–65; Haym Soloveitchik, *She-elot u-Teshuvot ke-Maqor Histori* (Jerusalem, 1990), 37. A Jewish foundation myth from a more southerly region appears in Jeremy Cohen, "Nasi of Narbonne," *AJS Review* 2 (1978): 45–76. See A. Grabois, "Le souvenir et la legende de Charlemagne dans les textes hebraiques medievaux," *Le Moyen Age* 72 (1966): 5–41.

131. See Stock, *Implications of Literacy*, 88; M. Bloch, *Feudal Society*, 139; Herlihy, "Family Solidarity in Medieval Italian History," 173–84. Even before the age of print, the emergence of regional identities was abetted by the composition of other texts, e.g., legal codes or customaries, that unified Jews of nearby settlements.

132. R. Reiner, "From Rabbenu Tam to R. Isaac of Vienna," 273–281; Y. Sussman, *Mif'alo ha-madda'i shel Professor E. E. Urbach*," in *Efraim Elimelekh Urbach- Bio-Bibliografya: Musaf Madda'ei ha-Yahadut* (Jerusalem, 1993), 1:39nn63, 83. On the claim that the rabbinic styles of Ashkenaz and France became culturally blended after the deaths of Elazar of Worms and Eliezer ben Yoel Halevi, the two figures who represented the opposite poles of Ashkenazi Jewry, see H. Soloveitchik, *"Yeynam": Saḥar be-Yeynam shel Goyim 'al Gilgulah shel Halakhah ba-'Olam ha-Ma'aseh* (Tel Aviv, 2003), 27.

133. For this reason, writes Clanchy, the Domesday Survey, a census of both people and animals conducted by William the Conqueror at the time of the Norman Conquest, was seen as a humiliation. Clanchy, *From Memory to Written Record*, 6, 262.

134. Ibid., 3.

135. Ibid., 4–5. The process of textualization in different regions of France can be traced in White, *Custom, Kinship, and Gifts to Saints*, and Tabuteau, *Transfers of Property in Eleventh-Century Norman Law*. Aspects of the textualization process in Germanic lands

are reconstructed in Fritz Kern, *Kingship and Law in the Middle Ages*, trans. S. B. Chrimes (Oxford, 1939), and in Harold Berman, *Law and Revolution: The Formation of the Western Legal Tradition* (Cambridge, Mass., 1983). Brian Stock's *Implications of Literacy* has bearing on the textualization process throughout medieval Europe.

136. Clerics were often in the vanguard of the textualization process because they fulfilled certain scribal functions at a time when lay people could not yet do this for themselves. See, for example, the observation that the "harsh exactitude of Norman and Angevin officials caused British churchmen, and ultimately laymen, to keep records of their own." Clanchy, *From Memory to Written Record*, 6, and cf. B. Bedos-Rezak, "The Confrontation of Orality and Textuality," 541–58.

137. While the case of the Babylonian geonim (discussed in Chapter 1) constitutes an obvious exception, it does not undermine or invalidate the claim itself.

138. Stock, *Implications of Literacy*, 38–42; Clanchy, *From Memory to Written Record*, 1, 6.

139. Duby, *The Chivalrous Society*, 9.

140. See Adriaan Verhulst, *The Carolingian Economy* (New York, 2002).

141. Geary, *Phantoms of Remembrance*, 114, 21.

142. Ibid., 86.

143. See Jaeger, *Envy of Angels*, 199; Duby, *Chivalrous Society*, 57.

144. Aristocrats who were concerned about the state of their souls in a time of spiritual anxiety "alienated" property through outright gifts to the church; knights ceded property to the church as penance for having violated the Peace of God.

145. B. Bedos-Rezak, "Diplomatic Sources and Medieval Documentary Practices," 323.

146. See, e.g., S. Kuttner, "The Revival of Jurisprudence," in *Renaissance and Renewal in the Twelfth Century*, ed. Robert Louis Benson, Giles Constable, and Carol D. Lanham (Cambridge, Mass., 1982), 299–323.

147. C. Radding, *The Origins of Medieval Jurisprudence: Pavia and Bologna 850–1150* (New Haven, Conn., 1988), 115–16; C. M. Radding and A. Ciaralli, *The Corpus Iuris Civilis in the Middle Ages: Manuscripts and Transmission from the Sixth Century to the Juristic Revival* (Leiden, 2006). Yisrael Ta Shma often cited Radding's thesis, which seemed to offer reinforcement for his idea that talmudic dialectic was brought to northern Europe by the Jews who came to the Rhineland from Lombardy. In this context, it should be noted that Radding's notions about medieval legal education have been subjected to significant criticism. See, e.g., Anders Winroth, *The Making of Gratian's Decretum* (New York, 2000), and Anders Winroth, "Origins of Legal Education in Medieval Europe," http://law.usc.edu/academics/assets/docs/winroth.pdf.

148. Stock, *Implications of Literacy*, 46.

149. Geary observes that a paucity of documentary evidence ought not be construed as any indication of a community's disinterest in writing; it may be a function of a previous generation's decisions about the utility of inherited written materials. Geary, *Phantoms of Remembrance*, 15.

150. Clanchy, *From Memory to Written Record*, 158. This recurring methodological issue is discussed, for example, in C. H. Lohr, "The Medieval Interpretation of Aristotle," *The Cambridge History of Later Medieval Philosophy* , ed. N. Kretzmann, A. Kenney, and J. Pinborg (Cambridge, 1982), 84; Dimitri Gutas, *Greek Thought, Arabic Culture: The Graceo-Arabic Translation Movement in Baghdad and Early Abbasid Society (8th–10th Centuries)* (London, 1998), 4.

151. Stock, *Implications of Literacy*, 55. Examples of the struggles that transpired are found, e.g., in Geary, *Phantoms of Remembrance*, 108.

152. Berman, *Law and Revolution*. The analytical scrutiny applied in the Investiture Contest benefited the church. See W. Jordan, *Europe in the High Middle Ages* (London, 2001), 127.

153. Jordan, *Europe in the High Middle Ages*, 115–16.

154. Stock, *Implications of Literacy*, 37; Clanchy, *From Memory to Written Record*, 5.

155. W. Ullman, *The Growth of Papal Government in the Middle Ages: A Study of the Ideological Relation of Clerical to Lay Power* (London, 1962), 262; G. Tellenbach, *Church, State, and Christian Society at the Time of the Investiture Contest*. Trans. R. F. Bennett. (Oxford, 1940; Stock, *Implications of Literacy*, 37. Cf. Hayden White, "The Gregorian Ideal and Saint Bernard of Clairvaux," *Journal of the History of Ideas* 21 (1960): 321–48. On the parallel development of administrative kingship, see C. Warren Hollister and John Baldwin, "The Rise of Administrative Kingship: Henry I and Philip Augustus," *American Historical Review* 83 (1978): 867–905. On bureaucratization, see Clanchy, *From Memory to Written Record*, 333.

156. This search for truth "would lead to the restoration or renewing of the authentic practices of the apostles and the primitive Church." Stock, *Implications of Literacy*, 37.

157. The notion of "socially-useful rationality" is Max Weber's. On the ways in which canonists writing prior to 1100 prepared the ground for legal analysis, see Kuttner, "The Revival of Jurisprudence." Cf. Stock, *Implications of Literacy*, 42–46.

158. Bedos-Rezak, "The Confrontation of Orality and Textuality," 543.

159. Clanchy, *From Memory to Written Record*, 19, 112.

160. Objecting to a progressive model of cultural development, and to the assumption that growing literacy represented greater sophistication, Stephen Jaeger asserted that the transition from the eleventh to the twelfth centuries played itself out in a contest between "charismatic culture" and "intellectual culture," a contest that recurs throughout history. Jaeger, *Envy of Angels*, 5–7.

161. Hollister and Baldwin, "The Rise of Administrative Kingship"; cf. Stock, *Implications of Literacy*, 9, 33, 55.

162. Tellenbach, *Church, State and Christian Society at the Time of the Investiture Contes*; H. White, "The Gregorian Ideal and Saint Bernard of Clairvaux."

163. He went on to say that "the contest between old and new learning is as much a part of twelfth century intellectual life as is the clash between new learning (e.g., Abelard and Berengar of Tours) and monastic orthodoxy." Jaeger, *Envy of Angels*, 218.

164. From Goswin of Mainz's 1065 letter to Walcher, his student, cited in ibid., 367; cf. 222.

165. Ibid., 217.

166. See the many medieval sources on this theme cited in ibid., 446n1.

167. Ibid., 66, 73.

168. Stock, *Implications of Literacy*, 41. On penances, see Chapter 6 below.

169. Ibid., 88.

170. A passage from Kern omitted in the body of this chapter reads: "We might, perhaps, suppose that the basis of this decision is the rule that customary law breaks enacted law. But this explanation is not necessarily the right one. That legal principle, it is true, was characteristic of the period which stands historically and logically intermediate between pure medieval customary law and pure modern enacted law. In later modern law, the principle is nonsensical, because customary law has become theoretically a part and parcel of enacted law, and prevails only within the limits imposed by enactment. In early medieval law, on the other hand, such a principle was inconceivable, because enacted law was nothing but recorded customary law. But even if the *Lex Salica* was not regarded as enacted law, it would seem that being old and recorded law, it ought to override less ancient and unrecorded law. The Franks, apparently, did not see it this way." Kern, "Law and Constitution in the Middle Ages," 160–61.

171. Ibid. Kern's article originally appeared as "Recht und Verfassung in Mittelalter," *Historische Zeitschrift* (1919).

172. On the apt reference to these custumals, customaries, *coutumiers,* and *livres de pratique* as "scribal museum[s]," see Stock, *Implications of Literacy*, 529 (cf. 49); White, *Custom, Kinship, and Gifts to Saints*, 83; Paul Ourliac and Jean-Louis Gazzaniga, *Histoire du droit prive francais de l'an mil au code civil* (Paris, 1985), 99–104. On the codification of customs at Cluny, see Rodulfus Glaber, *The Five Books of the Histories,* lviii.

173. This comment is made about the *Vita Geraldi* and *Vita Odonis*, in Barbara Rosenwein, *Rhinocerous Bound: Cluny in the Tenth Century* (Philadelphia, 1982), 96–97. Cf. Kassius Hallinger, *Corpus Consuetudinum Monasticarum* (Siegburg, 1963), 1:xlv-xlvii.

174. On medieval France, see Bloch, *Feudal Society*, 113–14; on Germany, see Kern, *Kingship and Law in the Middle Ages,* 149–80; Michael Toch, "Asking the Way and Telling the Law: Speech in Medieval Germany," *Journal of Interdisciplinary History* 16:4 (1986): 667–82; Helmut Feigl, "Von der mündlichen Rechtsweisung zur Aufzeichnung: Die Entstehung der Weistümer und verwandter Quellen," in *Recht und Schrift in Mittelalter,* ed. Peter Classen (Sigmaringen , 1977), 425–48. On medieval England, see T.F.T. Plucknett, *A Concise History of the Common Law* (London, 1956), 307–8; Stock, *Implications of Literacy*, 56, 529.

175. Clanchy, "Remembering the Past and the Good Old Law," 172.

176. Speaking of the remembrancer, Clanchy wrote, "The good old law . . . which he recalls will be adapted to the requirements of his hearers, rather than historically objective. . . . Judges who don't rely on writing, but rather, on that which is preserved in memory, are not restricted by precedent, because, these, being mostly unrecorded, are . . . transformed . . . the lack of writing makes it possible to give the sanction of immemorial custom to relatively new rules." Ibid., 165, 170–71.

177. And not, wrote a historian of medieval British law, as "the fossilized remains of a remote past." T.F.T. Plucknett, *Legislation of Edward I* (Oxford, 1962), 7.

178. On the remembrancer's adaptation of "the good old law" to requirements of his hearers, see Clanchy, "Remembering the Past and the Good Old Law," 165, 166, 172. And cf. Pierre Nora, "Between Memory and History: *Les Lieux de Mémoire*," *Representations* 26 (1989): 8.

179. Kern, *Kingship and Law in the Middle Ages*, 156, 179.

180. Clanchy, "Remembering the Past and the Good Old Law"; cf. Y. Ta Shma, *Minhag Ashkenaz ha-Qadmon*, 96.

181. On the inscription of custom throughout Europe, see John Gilissen, *La Coutume* (Turnhout, 1982). On the "universalizing" impact of textualization, see Stock, *Implications of Literacy*, 17–18.

182. Stock, *Implications of Literacy*, 56.

183. The term *jederzeitlichkeit* used in E. Auerbach, *Mimesis: The Representation of Reality in Western Literature*, trans. Willard Trask (New York, 1953), 188–92, was felicitously rendered as "omnitemporality," in W. W. Holdheim, *The Hermeneutic Mode: Essays on Time in Literature and Literary Theory* (Ithaca, N.Y., 1984), 215.

184. Stock, *Implications of Literacy*, 456.

185. Geary, *Phantoms of Remembrance*, 178, 21, 25.

186. These remarks closely follow ibid., 25.

187. Clanchy, *From Memory to Written Record*, 149. For example, whereas English Jews dated their documents with reference to Creation, Christians deliberated whether to situate themselves in relation to the birth of Jesus, to the Crucifixion (whose date was the subject of debate), or to the year of the king's reign. See Clanchy, *From Memory to Written Record*, 301–3; F. A. Lincoln, *The Starra: Their Effect on Early English Law and Administration* (London, 1939), 30, 32, 57.

188. Thus, for example, in the opening of his Chronicle, Rodulfus Glaber (c. 980–1046) announced his intention of bridging the gap between his age, and that of Bede and of Paul the Deacon, whom he evidently regarded as the last real historians. He asserted that he would tell the story of great men who lived after 900, until 987. Glaber, *The Five Books of the Histories*, xxxvii–xxxviii.

189. Geary, *Phantoms of Remembrance*, 115.

190. Ibid., 134–35. Cf. A. Grabois, "Le souvenir et la legende de Charlemagne dans les textes hebraiques medievaux," 5–41.

191. It is hard to judge whether those who supplied such textual pasts truly believed what they wrote. Cf. Geary, *Phantoms of Remembrance*, 116–17.

192. Mary J. Carruthers, *The Book of Memory: A Study of Memory in Medieval Culture* (Cambridge, 1990), 21.

193. Stock, *Implications of Literacy*, 149.

CHAPTER 4

1. See, for example, R. Bonfil, "Mitos, retoriqa, historya? 'Iyyun be-Megilat Aḥima'aẓ." In *Tarbut ve-Ḥevra be-Toldot Yisrael bi-Yeme ha-Benayyim*, ed. R. Bonfil, M. Ben Sasson, and Y. Hacker (Jerusalem, 1989), 114; A. Samely and P. Alexander, introduction

to "Artefact and Text: Recreation of Jewish Literature in Medieval Hebrew Manuscripts," *Bulletin of the John Rylands University Library of Manchester* 75 (1993): 8–9; Y. Ta Shma, *Ha-Sifrut ha-Parshanit la-Talmud be-Eropa u-ve-Ẓefon Afriqa* (Jerusalem, 1999), 1:32; Ivan Marcus, "The Dynamics of Jewish Renaissance and Renewal in the Twelfth Century," in *Jews and Christians in Twelfth Century Europe,* ed. M. Signer and J. Van Engen (Notre Dame, Ind., 2001), 37–38; Simḥa 'Imanuel, *Shivre Luḥot: Sefarim Avudim shel Ba'ale ha-Tosafot* (Jerusalem, 2006), 1–12. Each of these sources comments on the inscription of formerly oral traditions, but not to the broader process of textualization.

2. Samely and Alexander, introduction to *Artefact and Text,* 8.

3. M. Beit Arié, *Hebrew Codicology: Tentative Typology of Technical Practices Employed in Hebrew Dated Medieval Manuscripts* (Paris, 1976), 98; M. Beit Arié, "Ideals versus Reality: Scribal Prescriptions in *Sefer Ḥasidim* and Contemporary Scribal Practices in Franco-German Manuscripts," in *Rashi, 1040–1990: Hommage à Ephraim E. Urbach,* ed. Gabrielle Sed-Rajna (Paris, 1993), 559–66. Cf. I. Ta Shma, "The Library of the French Sages," in *Rashi, 1040–1990: Hommage à Ephraim E. Urbach,* 538.

4. Ta Shma, "The Library of the French Sages," 538.

5. According to Irving Agus, Rashi undertook to commit formerly oral teachings to writing after the destruction of the Rhineland rabbinic academies in 1096, because he feared that knowledge transmitted orally at Worms and Mainz would be lost. See I. Agus, "R. Jacob Tam's Stringent Criticism of R. Meshullam of Melun in Its Historical Setting," in *Essays on the Occasion of the Seventieth Anniversary of the Dropsie University (1909–1979),* ed. Abraham I. Katsh and Leon Nemoy (Philadelphia, 1979), 1–10.

6. As will be seen, while Rashi was a prominent agent, he did not initiate this process. His Talmud commentary (along with the rest of his oeuvre) was almost complete by the turn of the century—and it was built on earlier written commentaries composed by anonymous, eleventh-century scholars. See H. Soloveitchik, "Catastrophe and Halakhic Creativity: Ashkenaz 1096, 1242, 1306 and 1298," *Jewish History* 12 (1998): 79–80.

7. See Chapter 3 above.

8. See Chapter 3's discussion of the "accidental" recovery of Justinian's *Digest* in 1070.

9. This chapter briefly considers the impact of textualization on prayer and custom, and Chapter 6 refers to the impact of textualization on the transmission of *sod*, esoteric knowledge.

10. On these traditions, see above, Chapter 2.

11. Charles M. Radding, *The Origins of Medieval Jurisprudence: Pavia and Bologna 850–1150* (New Haven, Conn., 1988), 2–3.

12. This was debated by the *Wissenschaft des Judenthums* scholars Rappaport, Zunz, and Shadal, who attempted to draw historical information from the twelfth-century foundation account of Elazar of Worms. Over the last few decades, scholars have concluded that the responsa composed in the late tenth and early eleventh centuries by Rabbi Qalonymos b"r Meshullam were actually written from Lucca, to Jews of other Mediterranean communities, rather than those of Ashkenaz. See A. Grossman, *Ḥakhme Ashkenaz ha-*

Rishonim (Jerusalem, 1981), 47, 49–58; Haym Soloveitchik, *She-elot u-Teshuvot ke-Maqor Histori* (Jerusalem, 1990), 37.

13. Other scholars include Rashi's contemporaries, the four sons of Makhir who compiled *Ma'aseh ha-Geonim*. Scholars active in earlier generations include those responsible for compiling the Mainz Talmud commentary, Rashi's Ashkenazi teachers: R. Isaac bar Judah, R. Isaac Halevi, R. Ya'aqov b.Yaqar, and R. Yosef Tov 'Elem of France.

14. Though HaNagid's personal library was not kept together after the murder of his son, Yehosef, it was reported in the first half of the twelfth century that parts of HaNagid's private collection were in the possession of R. Isaac Ibn Migash. On Yehosef's death, see G. D. Cohen, *Sefer ha-Qabbalah: The Book of Tradition by Abraham Ibn Daud* (Philadelphia, 1967), 73, lines 11–12. The report was that of Ibn Migash's student, R. Meir Halevi Abulafia, in *Kitab al-Rasail* (Paris, 1871), 79–80, and is cited in N. Allony, "Shire Ẓion be-shirato shel Rav Shmuel HaNagid," *Sinai* 68 (1971): 225.

15. Rabbenu Gershom may also have inscribed the *Masorah*, a quintessentially oral corpus of traditions regulating the Torah scroll's scribal production. See A. Marx, "Rabbenu Gershom, Light of the Exile," *Essays in Jewish Biography* (Philadelphia, 1947), 39–60; A. Grossman, *Ḥakhme Ashkenaz ha-Rishonim*, 160. References to Rabbenu Gershom's Bible are collected in A. Berliner, "Le-toldot perushe Rashi," in *Ketavim Nivḥarim* (Jerusalem, 1949), 2:180; Yaaqov Spiegel, *'Amudim be-Toldot ha-Sefer ha-'Ivri* (Ramat Gan, 1996), 105–8. References to R. Gershom's Talmud are found in Rashi, BT Suk. 40a–b. The possibility that Rabbenu Gershom also wrote out a copy of *Sefer Yosippon* is mentioned in D. Flusser, *Sefer Yosippon* (Jerusalem, 1981), 2:3–6, though doubts about this attribution are raised in H. Soloveitchik, "Halakha, Hermeneutics and Martyrdom in Medieval Ashkenaz," *JQR* 94:2 (2004): 280.

16. Many ordinances that were actually communal were later ascribed to a person of stature. A. Grossman, *Ḥakhme Ashkenaz ha-Rishonim*, 133–40.

17. R. Moshe Rivkes (1590–1684) ascribed to Rabbenu Gershom the prohibition against clipping blank book margins for reuse in his commentary on the *Shulḥan 'Arukh, Be-er HaGolah*, YD, end of 334.

18. I. Agus, *Urban Civilization in Pre-Crusade Europe: A Study of Organized Town Life in the Tenth-Eleventh Centuries Based on Responsa Literature* (New York, 1965), 2: 533–34.

19. See R. Jacob b. Meir Tam's introduction to *Sefer ha-Yashar: Ḥeleq ha-Ḥidushim*, ed. Shimon Shlomo Shlesinger (Jerusalem, 1959). (This also appears in Moses Isserles, *Darkhei Moshe*, Tur, YD 279, discussed below.) There is no earlier evidence that Rabbenu Gershom had promulgated such an ordinance; it was not even mentioned by Provençal and Sefardi scholars who were known opponents of textual emendation. See Y. Spiegel, *'Amudim be-Toldot ha-Sefer ha-'Ivri*, 101–5. Finding it hard to imagine that people would be so audacious as to emend a text on the basis of their own reasoning, Haym Soloveitchik suggested that Rabbenu Gershom's curse was actually directed against those who emended texts based on what they saw written in other texts. H. Soloveitchik, *Ha-Yayin be-Yeme ha-Benayyim: Yeyn Nesekh—Pereq be-Toldot ha-Halakhah be-Ashkenaz* (Jerusalem, 2008),

330. However, Rabbenu Tam's own methodological guideline of regarding the *lectio dificilior* as the most likely and credible, on the grounds that emenders could never have created it themselves, suggests that he did assume that some emendations were not textually based.. See H. Soloveitchik, *Ha-Yayin*, 357. And see the comment by Y. Sussman, quoted below.

20. Hai Gaon described how scribal errors occur in A. Harkavy, ed., *Teshuvot ha-Geonim* (New York, 1959), no. 272, 137–38, cited in N. Danzig, "Mi-talmud 'al peh le-talmud be-khtav," *Sefer ha-Shana Bar Ilan* 30–31 (2006): 67.

21. See M. Beit-Arié, "Transmission of Texts by Scribes and Copyists: Unconscious and Critical Interferences," *Bulletin of the John Rylands Library of Manchester* 75 (1993): 37. On the similar attitude expressed in writings by Sa'adya and subsequent geonim, see Chapter 1.

22. See Shimon Shlomo Schlesinger, "'Al ketivat torah she-be-'al peh be-zeman ha-talmud," *Sinai* 117 (1996): 70; cf. 68. (The first footnote explains that this article circulated long before its posthumous appearance, and was cited by E. E. Urbach in a 1962 publication.) Cf. Martin Jaffee, "Oral Cultural Context of the Talmud Yerushalmi: Greco-Roman Rhetorical Paideia, Discipleship, and the Concept of Oral Torah," in *The Talmud Yerushalmi and Greco-Roman Culture*, ed. Peter Schäfer (Tübingen, 1999), 1:54.

23. Samely and Alexander, introduction to *Artefact and Text*, 8, 9.

24. Saul Lieberman's study of the Mishnah emphasizes that written rabbinic texts as we know them are layered pastiches, exhibiting "fusion and confusion of the *lemmata* with the commenting text." S. Lieberman, *Hellenism in Jewish Palestine: Studies in the Literary Transmission, Beliefs and Manners of Palestine in the I Century B.C.E.–IV Century C.E.* (New York, 1950), 99n128.

25. While the Tosefta on some tractates appears to be wholly independent of Mishnah, it presupposes the Mishnah in others. See Y. Elman, *Authority and Tradition: Toseftan Baraitot in Talmudic Babylonia* (New York, 1994).

26. Meir Ish Shalom, a nineteenth-century Viennese scholar, emphasized the prolonged snowballing process that preceded the production of Talmud, as we know it: "If the Talmud had been written with its commentaries and additions [i.e., *Tosafot*] and novellae [*Ḥidushim*] mixed in, would you find your way? Well, in fact, the Gemara you are used to already has commentaries and additions mixed in!" R. Meir Ish Shalom, Introduction to "'Al Derekh Ḥeqer ha-Sugya," 314n112, cited in S. Friedman, *Talmud 'Arukh: Pereq ha-Sokher et ha-Omanin* (Jerusalem, 1996), 8n6.

27. Thus, stresses Sussman, "we should no longer speak of the tradition of the version [*masoret ha-nusaḥ*] of the *Tosfeta*, the *Sifre* or the *Yerushalmi*, but rather, of the versions that were preserved in *our Tosefta, Sifrei* or *Yerushalmi*." Y. Sussman, "Beraita de-teḥume Ereẓ Yisrael," *Tarbiẓ* 45 (1976): 226–27.

28. Yisrael Ta Shma made this claim most pointedly in conjunction with the observation that medieval Ashkenazim had reworked earlier rabbinic compositions (such as *Midrash Tanḥuma, Eikhah Rabbati, Avot de-Rabi Natan, Midrash Shoḥer Tov, Seder Rav 'Amram Gaon, Toldot Yeshu, Ben Sira, Sefer Assaf HaRofe*, and *Seder 'Olam*). See Y. Ta

Shma, "Sifriyyatam shel ḥakhme Ashkenaz bene ha-meah ha-11–12," *Qiryat Sefer* 60 (1985): 302–8; Y. Ta Shma, "Library of the French Sages," 535–40. Describing Ashkenazic emendation as "cut off from any obligation to the legacy of earlier exegetes," Ta Shma claimed that "this aggressive Ashekanzic re-working that we are discussing has its original source on the soil of Ashkenaz, and not in Italy." Ta Shma, *Ha-Sifrut ha-Parshanit*, 33–34; Ta Shma, "Sifriyyatam shel ḥakhme Ashkenaz bene ha-meah ha-11–12," 303; cf. 308–9. According to Ta Shma, this "openness to revision" was an indication of Ashkenazic culture's "creativity," a legacy of Jewish culture in ancient Palestine. This questionable claim has been reiterated in works by a number of scholars.

29. The reworking of Italian manuscripts of *Halakhot Qeẓuvot* and of the geonic commentary on *Seder Toharot* is discussed in Y. N. Epstein, *Perush ha-Geonim le-Seder Toharot* (Jerusalem, 1982), 93, and is mentioned in Ta Shma, "Sifriyyatam shel ḥakhme Ashkenaz bene ha-meah ha-11–12," 304–5. Rabbi Yiẓḥaq b. Malki Ẓedeq of Siponto engaged in forceful emendation in southern Italy; he is said to have reworked the Talmud in order to reflect his personal opinion! See S. Lieberman, *Tosefet Rishonim* (Jerusalem, 1939), 4:20–21.

30. Though Ta Shma relied on Chaim Milikovsky's analysis of *Seder 'Olam*, Milikovsky himself disavowed Ta Shma's claim that widescale refashioning of texts was a uniquely Ashkenazic phenomenon, and drew attention to a manuscript of *Seder 'Olam* that was reworked in the East. C. Milikowsky, "Mahadurot ve-tipusei teqst be-sifrut ḥazal: Be-'iqvot ma-amaro shel Y. M. Ta Shma, 'Sifriyyatam shel ḥakhme Ashkenaz bene ha-meah a 11–12,'" *Qiryat Sefer* 61 (1987): 170n2.

31. According to Ya'aqov Sussman, all "Spanish" manuscripts of Sherira's *Epistle* were subject to "heavy-handed reworking" in order to bring them into accord with the writings of Maimonides. Sussman, "'Torah she-be-'al peh'—Peshutah ke-mashma'ah," *Meḥqere Talmud* 3 (2005): 234n26.

32. In his painstaking analysis of *Midrash Bereshit Rabbah*, Menahem Kahane demonstrated that particular medieval manuscripts of this work were heavily reworked over time through erasures, interpolations, word changes, explanations, and segues. Menahem Kahane, "Ziqat ketav yad Vatican 60 shel Bereshit Rabba le-maqbilotav," *Te'udah* 11 (1996): 18–60. Kahane's study of manuscripts of *Midrash Sifre* on Numbers revealed a similar pattern of refashioning, and demonstrated that this text's "abnormal formulations" reflect the concerted effort of the redactor(s) to merge this text with disparate traditions found in five other midrashic corpora. Menahem Kahane, "Aqdamot le-hoẓa-ah ḥadasha shel Sifre Bamidbar" (Ph.D. diss., Hebrew University, 1982), 239ff. Pinḥas Mendel concluded that those called tannaim in the geonic period had "corrected" manuscripts of *Midrash Eikha* on the basis of parallels found in other manuscripts. Pinḥas Mendel, "Ha-Sipur be-Midrash Eikha" (Ph.D. diss., Hebrew University, 1983), 208–11. Peter Schäfer's detailed study of medieval *Hekhalot* manuscripts convinced him of the inherent instability of the text and led him to posit that "most of the 'works' only reached the stage of a standardizing and structuring final redaction very late—or not at all." Peter Schäfer, "Tradition and Redaction in *Hekhalot* Literature," *Journal for the Study of Judaism* 14 (1984):

172–81. Asking whether it is possible to speak of the "original forms" of ancient texts, given their fluidity, Schäfer raised the question of whether there is any point in trying to reconstruct them. See P. Schäfer, "Research into Rabbinic Literature: An Attempt to Define the *Status Quaestionis*," *Journal of Jewish Studies* 37 (1986): 139–52; C. Milikowsky, "The *Status Quaestionis* of Research in Rabbinic Literature," *Journal of Jewish Studies* 39 (1988): 201–11; P. Schäfer, "Once Again the *Status Quaestionis* of Research in Rabbinic Literature: An Answer to Chaim Milikowsky," *Journal of Jewish Studies* 40 (1989): 89–94.

33. Or, as Peter Schäfer wrote, "Emergence, transmission and redaction overlap in various ways and overflow into one another." Schäfer, "Once Again the *Status Quaestionis* of Research in Rabbinic Literature," 89–90. Elsewhere Schäfer raised the provocative question of whether "the final redaction [of a text is] merely the more or less incidental discontinuation of the manuscript tradition." Schäfer, "Research into Rabbinic Literature: An Attempt to Define the *Status Quaestionis*," 150.

34. Mary J. Carruthers, *The Book of Memory: A Study of Memory in Medieval Culture* (Cambridge, 1990) 169.

35. C. S. Lewis, "The Genesis of a Medieval Book," *Studies in Medieval and Renaissance Literature*, ed. W. Hooper (Cambridge, 1966), 37–38. To cite one example: Both the Paris and Vienna manuscripts of the *Liber Legis Langobardorum*, a medieval collection of Lombard, Frankish, and Saxon laws, incorporate the glossatorial apparatus of Walcauso into the body of the text itself. Radding, *Origins of Medieval Jurisprudence*, 121.

36. I believe that Professor Ta Shma made this claim, but I have been unable to locate the source in writing. Cf. A. Grossman, "Shorashav shel qidush ha-shem be-Ashkenaz ha-qedumah," in *Qedushat ha-Ḥayyim ve-Ḥeruf ha-Nefesh*, ed. Isaiah M. Gafni and Aviezer Ravitzky (Jerusalem, 1992), 107.

37. See, for example, A. Grossman, *Ḥakhme Ashkenaz ha-Rishonim*, 419–20.

38. A. Epstein, "'Inyene masorah ve-diqduq," in *Mi-Qadmoniyyot ha-Yehudim* (Vienna, 1887), 253–58; Y. Ta Shma, "Sifriyyatam shel ḥakhme Ashkenaz bene ha-meah ha-11–12," 300.

39. Y. Ta Shma, "Sifriyyatam shel ḥakhme Ashkenaz bene ha-meah ha-11–12," 302–3.

40. Y. Sussman, "Masoret limud u-masoret nusaḥ shel ha-Talmud ha-Yerushalmi," in *Meḥqarim be-Sifrut ha-Talmudit: Yom 'Iyyun . . . le-Shaul Lieberman* (Jerusalem, 1983), 14n11.

41. The observations that follow draw on Berliner, "Le-toldot perushe Rashi," 2:182; Ta Shma, *Ha-Sifrut ha-Parshanit*, 1:35–40.

42. Its subsequent ascription to Rabbenu Gershom may reflect the penchant of later generations to enhance a work's stature by linking it to a towering figure. It is also in keeping with the tosafist tendency to name an academy for the scholar at its helm, and with that of Cathedral Schools, which were known for their preeminent teachers. See E. Kanarfogel, *Jewish Education and Society in the High Middle Ages* (Detroit, 1992), 71, 57; R. W. Southern, "The Schools of Paris and the School of Chartres," in *Renaissance and Renewal in the Twelfth Century*, ed. Robert Louis Benson, Giles Constable, and Carol D. Lanham (Cambridge, Mass., 1982), 113–37.

43. A. Epstein, "Der Rabbenu Gershom Meor ha-Golah zugeschriebene Talmud Commentar," in *Festschrift zum achtzigsten Geburtstage Moritz Steinschneiders* (Leipzig, 1896), 115–43; Ta Shma, "'Al perush Rabbenu Gershom Meor Ha-Golah la-Talmud," *Qiryat Sefer* 53 (1978): 356–65; A. Grossman, *Ḥakhme Ashkenaz HaRishonim* (Jerusalem, 1989), 165–74.

44. Ta Shma, "'Al perush Rabbenu Gershom Meor ha-Golah la-Talmud"; Ta Shma, *Ha-Sifrut ha-Parshanit*, 1:28.

45. See the reference to this sort of anthologization as the "contents of one's memory, set forth as a study guide," in Carruthers, *Book of Memory*, 89–91.

46. Ta Shma, *Ha-Sifrut ha-Parshanit*, 1:24.

47. As M. T. Clanchy observed, many types of medieval documents "retained—both in their physical format and their phraseology—numerous reminders that they had been developed in an earlier period, when more reliance had been put on living memory than on parchment." M. T. Clanchy, *From Memory to Written Record: England 1066–1307* (London, 1979) 327.

48. Berliner, "Le-toldot perushe Rashi," 180–81 and n. 4.

49. Ibid., 180, refers to R. Ya'aqov ben Yaqar on BT Git. 82. The claim that the term *quntres* denotes a *material* feature of the commentary, namely its distinctness from the underlying text, appears in M. Beit Arié, *Hebrew Codicology* (Paris, 1976), 44n77. See also E. M. Lifschitz, "Rashi," in *Ketavim*, ed. E. M. Lifschitz (Jerusalem, 1947), 55–67; E. E. Urbach, *Ba'ale ha-Tosafot: Toldotehem, Ḥiburehem, Shitatehem* (Jerusalem, 1980) 1:22; A. Grossman, *Ḥakhme Zorfat ha-Rishonim* (Jerusalem, 1995), 437, 450.

50. Writing in *Safah Berurah* sixty years after Rashi's death, Abraham ibn Ezra lamented the ascription of such importance to Rashi's commentary (noted in Berliner, "Le-toldot perushe Rashi," 192). And see H. Soloveitchik, "Catastrophe and Halakhic Creativity," 80; H. Soloveitchik, *Ha-Yayin*, 131–32; Ta Shma, *Ha-Sifrut ha-Parshanit* 1:157.

51. Rashi on BT Git. 60b, "*ilema mishum kavod*"; BT Ket. 7b, "*bigdata-a*." See Y. Frankel, *Darko shel Rashi be-Ferusho la-Talmud ha-Bavli* (Jerusalem, 1980), 24; Y. Sussman, "'Torah she-be-'al peh,'" 234n26.

52. Rashi on BT BM 33a, "*talmud: latet lev le-havin setumot ta'ame ha-Mishnah*." Frankel noted that just as Rashi understood that "*talmud*" referred to explanations of Mishnah, he understood the term "*sevara*" (in BT Suk. 28a) to denote explanations of Talmud. In Frankel, *Darko shel Rashi be-Ferusho la-Talmud ha-Bavli*, 17–19.

53. Rashi on BT Ber. 47b, "*she-hayyu notnim le-divre ha-Mishnah ta'am . . . vehu dugmat ha-gemara she-sidru ha-amoraim*."

54. Rashi on BT Nid. 7b.

55. Rashi on BT BM 86a, "*Ravina ve-Rav Ashi sof hora-a*."

56. His reference to the two ordering activities they performed, "arranging" (*sidur*) and "pegging" or "filing" (*qevi'a*), might be construed as referring to the physical manipulation of material texts. If this were the case, these non-official notes would presumably have been regarded as *megilot setarim*.

57. Rashi on BT BM 86a, "*sof ha-Mishnah*": "Until their days, each person said his matter in the *beit midrash*, and the pupils would recite each heard-teaching separately. And there were neither organized tractates nor Order collected after Order [of Mishnah]. And they collated that which was said in the generations before them, and arranged the tractates. And after them, very little was added." Cf. Rashi on BT BM 33b, "*be-yeme Rabi.*"

58. Frankel, *Darko shel Rashi be-Ferusho la-Talmud ha-Bavli*, 28–29.

59. Rashi on BT Hul. 49a, "*ve-eyn.*"

60. See T. Fishman, "Claims about the Mishnah in Sherira Gaon's *Epistle*: Islamic Theology and Jewish History," in *Border Crossings: Interreligious Interaction and the Exchange of Ideas in the Islamic Middle Ages*, ed. D. Freidenreich and M. Goldstein (Philadelphia, forthcoming).

61. Frankel, *Darko shel Rashi be-Ferusho la-Talmud ha-Bavli*, 31.

62. Y. N. Epstein, *Mevo-ot le-Sifrut ha-Amoraim* (Jerusalem, 1962), 613–15; Ta Shma, "Sifriyyatam shel ḥakhme Ashkenaz bene ha-meah ha-11–12," 301.

63. Rashi on BT BM 33a, "*vi-eyna midah.*" Though the standard Rom edition of the Gemara says "*be-dorot aḥaronim*" "(recent/later generations [began to write it]), the formulation cited above, "*be-doroteinu*," is found in Bodleian ms. 429; British Library ms. 412; JTS ms. (Porges collection). This is pronounced the definitive formulation in Frankel, *Darko shel Rashi be-Ferusho la-Talmud ha-Bavli*, 32n56. Cf. N. Danzig, "Mi-talmud 'al peh le-talmud be-khtav," 61n46.

64. Frankel, *Darko shel Rashi be-Ferusho la-Talmud ha-Bavli*, 31 and nn. 51–52.

65. As Yonah Frankel noted, Rashi's remarks about the formation of the ancient rabbinic corpora evince none of the angst that permeates the *Epistle*. On "envy as a historical principle," see Stephen Jaeger, *The Envy of Angels: Cathedral Schools and Social Ideas in Medieval Europe, 950–1200* (Philadelphia, 1994), 9.

66. BT BM 33a. The phrase "*midah ve-eynah midah*" might literally be rendered, "it is meritorious and not meritorious." The term "*gemara*" was substituted for "*Talmud*" by the censors.

67. Rashi on BT BM 33a, "*ve-eyna midah.*"

68. Cf. Rashi on BT Tem. 14b, "*dilmah milta ḥaddeta shanei.*"

69. Rashi on Shab. 6b, "*megilat setarim.*" Cf. Rashi on Shab. 96b, "*megilat setarim*"; on BT BM 92a, "*megilat setarim*"; on BT Git. 60b, "*devarim she-be'al peh*"; on BT Suk. 28b, "*maqrei u-matnei.*"

70. Though Rashi does not use the term *megilat setarim* in referring to it, he (like later Jews) understood *Megilat Ta'anit*, (The Scroll of Fasts)—a listing of the dates on which fasting is not permitted—as an example of ephemeral writing: Juxtaposing *Megilat Ta'anit* with other—unwritten—tannaitic creations, Rashi pointedly referred to this scroll as "a reminder": "Since the rest of Mishnah and Beraita were not written . . . and this was written as a reminder so that the days on which it is forbidden to fast would be known, therefore it was called 'scroll,' for it was written/inscribed in a scroll-book." Rashi on BT Shab. 13b, "*Megilat Ta'anit*"; cf. Rashi on BT 'Eruv. 62, "*kegon Megilat Ta'anit:*

shelo hayta devar halakha ketuva be-yemehen [shel amoraim] afilu ot aḥat ḥuẓ mi-Megilat Ta'anit." On efforts by a later Jewish scholar to reconstruct the lost pedagogic milieu of oral-memorial study, see R. Samuel de Medina, *She-elot u-Teshuvot* (Lemberg, 1862), HM 1.4; HM 265; YD 255. See Y. Aḥituv, "Mi-pi sefarim ve-lo mi-pi sofrim," *Sinai* 107 (1991): 137n13.

71. E.g., Rashi on Ket. 19b, "*sefer*"; BT Ket. 69b, "*tala*"; BT 'Eruv. 21b, "*masoret be-simanim—bein ketivot ha-Miqra, bein be-girsa shel Mishnah.*"

72. "In any place where one could be misled by the talmudic formulation, Rashi, in his great sensitivity, clarifies and emphasizes that writing, per se, is not intended." Y. Sussman, " 'Torah she-be-'al peh,' " 229n15.

73. Ibid.

74. Vered Noam, "Mesorot nusaḥ qedumot be-hagahot Rashi ba-Talmud," *Sidra* 17 (2001–2): 109–50.

75. These passages were first collected and studied by Isaac Hirsch Weiss. An overview of earlier scholarship on this matter appears in Rami Reiner, "Mumar okhel nevelot le-teavon—pasul? Mashehu 'al nusaḥ u-ferusho be-yede Rashi," in *Shimon Schwarzfuchs Jubilee Volume*, ed. J. Hacker et al. (forthcoming). I am grateful to the author for sharing this article with me prior to its publication.

76. Noam, "Mesorot nusaḥ qedumot be-hagahot Rashi ba-Talmud," 109–50.

77. Rami Reiner, "Le-hitqabluto shel Sefer Halakhot Gedolot be-Ashkenaz," in *Limud ve-Da'at be-Maḥshavah Yehudit*, ed. Ḥayyim Kreisel (Beer Sheva, 1996), 2:95–121; R. Reiner, "Mumar okhel nevelot le-teavon—pasul?"

78. On the implications of opting for a paraphrastic commentary, see Ta Shma, *Ha-Sifrut ha-Parshanit*, 1:42; Soloveitchik, *Ha-Yayin*, 342.

79. Berliner, "Le-toldot perushe Rashi," 186.

80. C. Sirat, *Hebrew Manuscripts of the Middle Ages*, ed. Nicholas de Lange (Cambridge, 2002) 277; cf. Berliner, "Le-toldot perushe Rashi," 179–226. On Rashi's multiple dictations of his pioneering commentary on tractate 'Avodah Zarah as he worked matters out, see Soloveitchik, *Ha-Yayin*, 143.

81. The enormous variation between the manuscripts of Rashi's Talmud commentary on tractate 'Avodah Zarah prompted the following comment: "It is hard to tell whether we are dealing with different recensions of the same work or with different works." Samely and Alexander, introduction to *Artefact and Text*, 8.

82. Rashi testifies to one such encounter in his comment on BT Suk. 40a, " '*eẓim de-hasaqa*," cited in R. Reiner, "Mumar okhel nevelot le-teavon—pasul?" See Berliner, "Le-toldot perushe Rashi," 188–89; S. Y. Friedman, "Perush Rashi la-Talmud: Hagahot u-mahadurot," in *Rashi: 'Iyyunim be-Yeẓirato*, ed. Z. Steinfeld (Ramat Gan, 1993), 147–76; Ta Shma, *Ha-Sifrut ha-Parshanit*, 1:54; H. Soloveitchik, "Can Halakhic Texts Talk History?" *AJS Review* 3 (1978): 166–67.

83. Berliner discusses Rashi's comments on BK 9a, BK 20a, and RH 32a in "Le-toldot perushe Rashi," 182, 185. Cf. S. Schwarzfuchs, "Reshit darko shel Rashi," in *Rashi: 'Iyunim be-Yeẓirato*, 177–83. There is no indication of whether Rashi ascribed different "weights" to the knowledge acquired in these two different ways.

84. A. Darmesteter, *Les gloses françaises dans les commentaires talmudiques de Raschi* (Paris, 1929–37).

85. Carruthers, *The Book of Memory*, 325n12. In the cases of both Bible and the law, she explains, the "ordinary gloss" was compiled from the mainly anonymous stock of preexisting glosses (159).

86. Suzanne Fleischman, "Philology, Linguistics and the Discourse of the Medieval Text," *Speculum* 65 (1990): 33.

87. Berliner, "Le-toldot perushe Rashi," 184.

88. Lifschitz, "Rashi," 1:54; Urbach, *Ba'ale ha-Tosafot*, 527–28.

89. Other expressions of the ways that tosafists continued in Rashi's footsteps are found in Urbach, *Ba'ale ha-Tosafot*, 1:22, 34; Grossman, *Ḥakhme Zorfat ha-Rishonim*, 439.

90. Theories about the name "Tosafot" appear in H. Graetz, *Geschichte der Juden von den ältesten Zeiten bis auf die Gegenwart*, 3rd ed. (Leipzig, 1897–1911), 6:143–44; Isaac Hirsch Weiss, "Rabbenu Tam," in *Beit Talmud* 3 (1882); Isaac Hirsch Weiss, *Dor Dor ve-Dorshav: Hu Sefer Divre ha-Yamim le-Torah she-be'al Peh* (Berlin, 1924), 4:336; A. Aptowitzer, *Mavo le-Sefer Ravyah* (1938): 357–66; Urbach, *Ba'ale ha-Tosafot*, 18–19; S. Friedman, "Mi-Tosafot ha-Rashbam la-Rif," *Qoveẓ 'al Yad* 18 (1976): 192–93n16. Thanks to Professor Yehuda Galinsky for bringing this last source to my attention.

91. The claim that Rabbenu Tam's *Sefer ha-Yashar* aimed at legitimating the talmudic formulations embedded in older works appears in Y. Spiegel, *'Amudim be-Toldot ha-Sefer ha-'Ivri*, 116–17, 119.

92. Moses ben Naḥman, Introduction to *Dina de-Garmei*, cited in Urbach, *Ba'ale ha-Tosafot*, 22.

93. Y. Ta Shma, "Qelitatam shel sifre ha-Rif, ha-Raḥ, ve-Halakhot Gedolot be-Ẓorfat u-ve-Ashkenaz," *Qiryat Sefer* 55 (1980): 191–201; A. Grossman, "Me-Andalusia le-Eropa: Yaḥasam shel ḥakhme Ashkenaz ve-Ẓorfat ba-meot ha-12–13 el sifre ha-halakha shel ha-Rif ve-ha-Rambam," *Pe'amim* 80 (1999): 14–32; Ta Shma, *Ha-Sifrut Ha-Parshanit*, 1:61 (cf. 138–39); Y. Ta Shma, *Rabi Zeraḥya Halevi Ba'al ha-Maor u-Vene Ḥugo* (Jerusalem, 1992), 43–44, 68–72, 106–12, 148–49.

94. See above and Chapter 3.

95. Ta Shma, *Ha-Sifrut ha-Parshanit*, 1:38.

96. This feature prompted Tchernowitz and Urbach to observe that the comments of the tosafists might have been mistaken for a part of the Gemara itself had they not been separated spatially from the body of that text. In Urbach's opinion, the tosafists revitalized intellectual approaches that had been abandoned by their more proximate chronological predecessors and reinstated the vitality of the amoraim. Urbach, *Ba'ale ha-Tosafot*, 525–26. The claim that the tosafist enterprise restored dialectic to its central place after a hiatus of 400–500 years appears in Soloveitchik, *Ha-Yayin*, 116. See also Jacob Katz, "Biqoret sefarim: Ba'ale ha-Tosafot," *Qiryat Sefer* 31 (1956): 9–16.

97. On Shmuel HaNagid's use of rabbinic formulations, see Shraga Abramson, "Divre ḥazal be-shirat HaNagid," *World Congress for Jewish Studies* 1 (Jerusalem, 1952): 274–78. The tosafists' northern European predecessors chose to compose their responsa purely in Hebrew.

98. Frankel, *Darko shel Rashi be-Ferusho la-Talmud ha-Bavli*, 31.

99. Cf. Clanchy, *From Memory to Written Record*, 118.

100. On the preeminent importance of this figure, see Rami Reiner, "R'I ha-Zaqen bein hemshekhiyut le-ḥidush: Hirhurim be-'iqvot *Yeynam* le-Ḥaym Soloveitchik," *Sidra* 12 (2006): 165–74.

101. Menaḥem ben Aharon ben Zeraḥ, cited in Urbach, *Ba'ale ha-Tosafot*, 251–52, and cf. Aḥituv, "Mi-pi sofrim vi-lo mi-pi sefarim," 137–38.

102. M. Carruthers, *Book of Memory*, 18.

103. *Sefer Ḥasidim*, ed. J. Wistinetzki and J. Freimann (Frankfurt am Main, 1924), no. 672, 177, with parallels in the Bologna edition, no. 1538, 872. The passage goes on to advise that tractates are best bound individually for purposes of lending.

104. Solomon Luria, *Yam shel Shlomo*, introduction to *Ḥulin*, cited in Urbach, *Ba'ale ha-Tosafot*, 696, and cf. 689, 715, 727, 730; Grossman, *Ḥakhme Ẓorfat ha-Rishonim*, 439; Ta Shma, *Halakhah Minhag u-Meẓiut be-Ashkenaz, 1000–1350* (Jerusalem, 1996), 21–23; H. Soloveitchik, *Ha-Yayin*, 116.

105. Commenting on Rashbam's observation (on BB 130b) that the Talmud was written down for the purpose of applied legal decisions, Shraga Abramson remarked: "But even from this perspective, the Talmud does not (except in a limited way) set forth the tools needed to arrive at applied law [*pesaq*]!" S. Abramson, *Perush Rabbenu Ḥananel la-Talmud* (Jerusalem, 1955), 148.

106. See Reiner, "Le-hitqabluto shel Sefer Halakhot Gedolot be-Ashkenaz," 2:97–99, 101. As Reiner notes, this assessment differs from that articulated by Yisrael Ta Shma, who had claimed that *Halakhot Gedolot* was important to early rabbinic scholars from both Ashkenaz and France. On R. Isaac Halevi's insistence on relying on *Sefer Halakhot Gedolot*, and his unprecedented call to follow a book of halakha, see Reiner, pp. 105–6.

107. For example, when asked whether a Jew might borrow money from another Jew on behalf of his own non-Jewish partner, Rabbenu Gershom cited a tannaitic teaching in the Talmud that prohibits this practice, but he went on to conclude that the ruling was not observed in his own time: "And in any event . . . the people are accustomed to treat this as permissible." In S. Eidelberg, ed., *She-elot u-Teshuvot Rabbenu Gershom Me-or ha-Golah* (New York, 1955), 85.

108. "In other words, halakhists of these generations set aside a clear source from which one could easily draw the desired conclusions, and instead base themselves on a text whose pertinence and applicability to the incident in question is tenuous." Soloveitchik, *She-elot u-Teshuvot ke-Maqor Histori*, 104; cf. 100.

109. Rabbenu Gershom invoked biblical prooftexts in three of his rulings. See Grossman, *Ḥakhme Ashkenaz* 429–30; A. Grossman, "Bein 1012 le-1096: Ha-reqa' ha-tarbuti ve-ha-ḥevrati le-qidush ha-shem be-1096," in *Yehudim Mul ha-Ẓelav: Gezerot 1096 be-Historia u-ve-Historiographia*, ed. Yom Tov Assis, Michael Toch, Jeremy Cohen, Ora Limor, and Aharon Kedar (Jerusalem, 2000), 51–73; Grossman, "Shorashav shel qidush ha-shem be-Ashkenaz ha-qeduma," 99–130; A. Grossman, "Yaḥase eyvah la-yehudim al

reqa' kalkali ve-ḥevrati ba-khalifut ha-muslemit," in *Sin-at Yisrael le-Doroteha*, ed. Shmuel Almog (Jerusalem, 1980), 171–87.

110. Grossman, *Ḥakhme Ashkenaz ha-Rishonim*, 73–77, 201–4; Kanarfogel, *Jewish Education and Society in the High Middle Ages*, 91.

111. Soloveitchik, *She-elot u-Teshuvot ke-Maqor Histori*, 100.

112. Though Yisrael Ta Shma argued repeatedly that northern European Jewry's valorization of custom reflected its cultural debt to ancient Palestine, the region's indebtedness to Babylonian tradition was not only no less strong, but historically more proximate. For an alternative explanation of the prominence of custom in medieval Ashkenaz, see Chapter 5.

113. This hypothesis might also explain why Rabbenu Gershom claimed, in one case, to have relied on his own powers of reasoning, and, in another, to have derived insights with supernatural assistance. See Eidelberg, *Teshuvot Rabbenu Gershom Meor ha-Golah*, no. 63, 147ff.

114. As is clear from *Seder Tannaim va-Amoraim*, Jews of the geonic period were already familiar with certain principles of adjudication, and many of the questions sent to Babylonia from Qayrawan in R. Ya'aqov Ibn Shaḥin's lifetime were designed to identify additional adjudicatory principles. See M. Ben Sasson, *Ẓemiḥat ha-Qehilah ha-Yehudit be-Arẓot ha-Islam: Qayrawan, 800–1057* (Jerusalem, 1996), 259. E. E. Urbach emphasizes that the "principles" of adjudication found in Talmud were generalizations based on statistics, and not formulated as mandates or prescriptive norms. E. E. Urbach, *Ha-Halakhah, Meqoroteha ve-Hitpatḥuta* (Jerusalem, 1984), 202–3.

115. Interestingly, Haym Soloveitchik himself made this point in 1990: "The very proliferation of *midrashim* they adduce is, in fact, a consequence of the absence of an established *halakha*—which could have served as the cornerstone of their decision." Soloveitchik, *She-elot u-Teshuvot ke-Maqor Histori*, 106.

116. In propounding this viewpoint, Haym Soloveitchik structures his synoptic overview of rabbinic culture in medieval northern Europe as a retrospective narrative that begins with the French tosafists of the twelfth century and moves backward in time, to show how their accomplishments flowed from those of their Rhenish predecessors. Soloveitchik, *Ha-Yayin*, 115–32.

117. Professor Soloveitchik offered this explanation regarding the biblical verse cited in a responsum of R. Yosef Tov 'Elem, published in *Teshuvot Maharam b"r Baruch* (Lvov), no. 423, 141c, and discussed in Soloveitchik, *She-elot u-Teshuvot ke-Maqor Histori*, 67–72.

118. A reconstruction of what "submission" to the Crusaders would have entailed is offered in D. Malkiel, *Reconstructing Ashkenaz: The Human Face of Franco-German Jewry, 1000–1250* (Stanford, Calif., 2009), chap. 3.

119. H. Soloveitchik, "Religious Law and Change," *AJS Review* 12 (1987): 205–21; Grossman, "Shorashav shel qiddush ha-shem be-Ashkenaz ha-qeduma," 130–99; Grossman, "Bein 1012 le-1096: Ha-reqa' ha-tarbuti ve-ha-ḥevrati le-qidush ha-shem be-Ashkenaz," 55–73; Y. Ta Shma, "Hitabdut ve-reẓaḥ ha-zulat 'al qidush ha-shem: Le-sheelat meqoma shel ha-aggadah be-masoret ha-pesiqa ha-Ashkenazit," in *Yehudim Mul ha-*

Ẓelav: Gezerot 1096 be-Historia u-ve-Historiographia, 150–56; Marcus, "The Dynamics of Jewish Renaissance and Renewal in the Twelfth Century," 27–45, esp. 36; E. Kanarfogel, "Realia (*Metsiut*) and Halakha in Ashkenaz: Surveying the Parameters and Defining the Limits," *Jewish Law Annual* 14 (2002): 201–16; H. Soloveitchik, "Halakhah, Hermeneutics and Martyrdom in Medieval Ashkenaz," *JQR* 94 (2004): 77–108, 278–99. On the transmission of ancient Jewish suicide narratives to the Rhenish Jews of 1096, see D. Goodblatt, "Suicide in the Sanctuary: Traditions on Priestly Martyrdom," *Journal of Jewish Studies* 46 (1995): 10–29.

120. On the widespread medieval Jewish perception of *Sefer Yosippon*'s author as a tanna, see, e.g., M. Liber, *Rashi*, 84.

121. On literary inspirations for the behaviors of 1096, see the sources cited in note 119. Some of the broader notions that may have motivated the Rhenish Jews of 1096 are discussed in Israel Yuval, *Two Nations in Your Womb: Perceptions of Jews and Christians in Late Antiquity and the Middle Ages*, trans. Barbara Harshav and Jonathan Chipman (Berkeley, 2006), chaps. 3, 4, and 6.

122. The phrase is that of H. Soloveitchik, in "Religious Law and Change," 209–10.

123. Apart from Tractate 'Avodah Zarah (discussed in the body of this work), Rashi offered applied legal decisions in his commentary on tractates Berakhot and Ḥulin. I am grateful to Dr. Rami Reiner for discussing this matter with me. Other cases in which Rashi's exegetical comments are allied with his legal decisions are discussed in Rami Reiner, "Le-hitqabluto shel Sefer Halakhot Gedolot be-Ashkenaz," 112ff., and Reiner, "Mumar okhel nevelot le-teavon—pasul? Mashehu 'al nusaḥ u-ferusho be-yede Rashi" (forthcoming). And see Grossman, *Ḥakhme Ẓorfat ha-Rishonim*, 234; Ta Shma, *Ha-Sifrut ha-Parshanit*, 1:43; Soloveitchik, *Ha-Yayin*, 228.

124. Why was the inscription of applied law performed only by his students and not by Rashi himself? While Rashi has been portrayed as a reluctant adjudicator and as one who preferred, when possible, not to impose his will upon others (see Soloveitchik, *Ha-Yayin*, 351), the explanation for this division of labor—and of genre—may be consistent with longstanding cultural assumptions. As a product of the Rhineland academies, Rashi may have continued to take seriously the tannaitic injunction against inscribing halakhot. When he gave instruction in applied law, he did so orally, as was appropriate when transmitting *oral matters*. By the same taxonomic logic, jottings of his students, the works that make up the "literature of Rashi's school," would have had the cultural status of *megilot setarim*, "phantom texts," and would not qualify as official writings. For the sake of comprehensiveness, this hypothesis would posit that Rashi thought of the responsa he wrote as texts that possessed the ephemeral status of an epistle. See the discussion in Chapter 1.

125. Soloveitchik, *Ha-Yayin*, 144, 352. In printed editions, it appears in BT AZ 61b.

126. This point is made emphatically in R. Reiner, "Le-hitqabluto shel Sefer Halakhot Gedolot be-Ashkenaz," 2:112–13, 119.

127. On the growing alignment of life with legal prescription in medieval European Christian societies, see B. Stock, *The Implications of Literacy: Written Language and Models of Interpretation in the Eleventh and Twelfth Centuries* (Princeton, N.J., 1983), 54 and nn. 197–98.

128. Ta Shma, "Qelitatam shel sifre ha-Rif ha-Raḥ ve-Halakhot Gedolot be-Ẓorfat u-ve-Ashkenaz," 191–201; Grossman, "Me-Andalusia le-Eropa," 23–24; Friedman, "Mi-tosafot ha-Rashbam la-Rif: Seder Nashim u-Massekhet Ḥulin," *Qoveẓ 'al Yad* 68 (1976): 189–226; R. Reiner, "Rabbenu Tam u-Vene Doro: Qesharim, Hashpa'ot, ve-Darkei Li-mudo ba-Talmud" (Ph.D. diss., Hebrew University, 2002), 207 and n. 61; Ta Shma, *Ha-Sifrut ha-Parshanit*, 1:61, 138–39.

129. Rashbam on BB 130b, "*'ad she-yoru halakha le-ma'aseh*." See Urbach, *Ba'ale ha-Tosafot*, 535; E. Urbach, "Masoret ve-halakhah," *Tarbiẓ* 50 (1980–81); Y. Sussman, "Ve-shuv le-Yerushalmi Neziqin," *Meḥqere Talmud* 1 (1990) 105–6 and n. 196.

130. In the words of Haym Soloveitchik ("Three Themes in *Sefer Ḥasidim*," *AJS Review* 1 [1976]: 345), the "Tosafist movement had turned a corpus into a problem."

131. On R. Barukh's *Sefer ha-Terumah*, see Soloveitchik, *Ha-Yayin*, 120.

132. On the problems posed by *Sefer ha-Yashar* (and especially the section on *Ḥidu-shim*, novellae, a work not printed until 1811), see ibid., 117.

133. See Gillian Knight, *The Correspondence between Peter the Venerable and Bernard of Clairvaux* (Ashgate, 2002), 127. In her analysis of the often vitriolic language used in a famous epistolary exchange between medieval Christians, Knight speaks of the difficulty of "penetrating the rhetorical veil" when it comes to interpreting letters. See pp. 2, 17, 34, 127, 141, 145. On playful "jesting" as a form of knightly activity, see, e.g., M. T. Clanchy, *Abelard: A Medieval Life* (Oxford, 1997), 332; J. Huizinga, *Homo Ludens: A Study of the Play-Element in Culture* (Boston, 1950), 144ff.

134. Earlier scholarly assessments of Rabbenu Tam by Ḥayyim Hillel Ben Sasson, Shalom Albeck, and Ephraim Urbach are reviewed in R. Reiner, "Rabbenu Tam u-Vene Doro," 318. Anxiety about presenting Rabbenu Tam as an adjudicator who was excessively responsive to the demands of the times and insufficiently wedded to a methodology of halakhah can be discerned in Urbach, *Ba'ale ha-Tosafot*, 70; Y. Twersky, "Biqoret sefer: 'Ba'ale ha-Tosafot,'" *Tarbiẓ* 26 (1956): 221–22, and Jacob Katz, "Biqoret sefarim: 'Ba'ale ha-Tosafot,'" *Qiryat Sefer* 31 (1956): 13.

135. Thinking along these lines, Rami Reiner posited that France and Provence constituted two schools of exegesis and adjudication, and identified four main points of systematic difference dividing the perspectives of Rabbenu Tam and R. Meshullam. R. Reiner, "Rabbenu Tam u-Vene Doro," 291–92, 318.

136. See ibid., 290–91, 304–5, 320–21.

137. Though it is clear that Abraham ben Isaac of Narbonne's *Sefer ha-Eshkol* introduced Spanish rabbinic traditions into Provence in the twelfth century, little is known about earlier channels of Andalusian influence. On *Sefer ha-Eshkol*, see Shalom Albeck, "Ma-amar Meḥoqeqe Yehudah," in *Festschrift für Israel Lewys siebzigsten Geburtstag*, ed. M. Brann and J. Elbogen (Breslau, 1911), 104–31. On the question of whether Shmuel HaNagid's *Hilkehta Gavrata* was known in Provence, see M. Margalioth, *Hilkhot ha-Nagid* (Jerusalem, 1962) 23, 35, 41, and S. Abramson, "Mi-torato shel Rav Shmuel Ha-Nagid mi-Sefarad," *Sinai* 100 (1987). On connections between Ashkenaz and Provence, see Y. Sussman, "Perush ha-Ra'abad le-massekhet Sheqalim: Ḥidah bibliografit, ba'aya historit," in *Meah She'arim*, ed. E. Fleischer et al. (Jerusalem, 2001), 155.

138. Joseph ibn Migash, *Ḥidushe ha-R'I Migash 'al Massekhet Bava Batra* (Jerusalem, 2001–2), on BB 130b; Sussman, "Ve-shuv le-Yerushalmi Neziqin," 105n196; and see Chapter 2.

139. See Chapter 5 below.

140. Ḥayyim Hillel Ben Sasson noted that, in his exchange of responsa with R. Meshullam, Rabbenu Tam was "battling . . . about the status of extra-talmudic literature." H. H. Ben Sasson, "Hanhagata shel Torah," *Beḥinot* 9 (1956): 51.

141. As Ephraim Urbach put it, "Rabbenu Tam knew that adjudication of *halakhah le-ma'aseh* could not be based solely on the interpretation of sources." Urbach, *Ba'ale ha-Tosafot,* 70.

142. Indeed, Rabbenu Tam held the emendations of R. Ḥananel in high regard, because he knew that R. Ḥananel had consulted other books. See Jacob ben Meir Tam, *Sefer ha-Yashar: She-elot u-Teshuvot,* ed. F. Rosenthal (Berlin, 1898), nos. 619–23. And cf. Meir Ish Shalom, *Sifre Deve Rav 'im Tosfot Meir 'Ayin,* part 1, *Haqdama, pereq bet* (Vienna, 1864), n.p.

143. See Urbach, *Ba'ale ha-Tosafot,* 55, 715–16. While works other than Talmud are largely introduced by Rabbenu Tam as a way to confirm or reject talmudic interpretations, the statement in *Sefer ha-Yashar* that the extra-talmudic teachings in "old books" trump those of the Talmud, even when the two conflict, led Rami Reiner to surmise that Rabbenu Tam's stance evolved over time.

144. Jacob ben Meir Tam, *Sefer ha-Yashar: She-elot u-Teshuvot,* 45:3 (to Melun). Though the printed version says "and Talmud," Shraga Abramson determined that "*Yelammedenu*" is the correct word. S. Abramson, "'Inyanot be-Sefer ha-Yashar le-Rabbenu Tam ve-haqdamato," *Qiryat Sefer* 37 (1962): 243.

145. The final words, "'*al pihem,*" might be read as emphasizing the oral nature of this transmission. In Jacob ben Meir Tam, *Sefer ha-Yashar: She-elot u-Teshuvot,* 45:3 (to Melun), cf. 47:5 and 48:5. A parallel listing of sources appears in *Sefer ha-Yashar: She-elot u-Teshuvot,* 46:4.

146. Ibid., 45:5, 84.

147. Ibid., 48:6, end.

148. Rabbenu Tam's claim here is that, by saboraic times, the traditions of Palestine and Babylonia constituted a single, unified legacy. This perspective dovetails with an observation Avraham Grossman made about the Jews of early Ashkenaz. This population, he claimed, did not feel themselves more greatly indebted to Palestine than to Babylonia. A. Grossman, "Ziqata shel yahadut Ashkenaz ha-qeduma el Ereẓ Yisrael," *Shalem* 3 (1981): 57–92.

149. See Chapter 1.

150. Jacob ben Meir Tam, *Sefer ha-Yashar: She-elot u-Teshuvot,* 48:6, end.

151. See, for example, ibid., 46:2. These traditions were sometimes accessed through mediating literary channels.

152. See, e.g., ibid., 45 (beginning) where Rabbenu Tam declared that vinegar touched by gentiles was unfit for Jewish consumption, though R. Meshullam followed the

Talmud in permitting it. The clash between Talmud and custom regarding the number of cups of wine to be used at a wedding, when two distinct blessings—for betrothal and for marriage—are recited, generated several rounds of correspondence between R. Meshullam and Rabbenu Tam. See ibid., 48:8; R. Reiner, "Rabbenu Tam u-Vene Doro," 310 and n. 90.

153. According R. Meshullam, the recitation of a blessing when none was commanded would violate the third commandment. See Y. Gilat, *Peraqim be-Hishtalshelut ha-Halakhah* (Ramat Gan, 1992), 334–44; Ta Shma, *Minhag Ashkenaz ha-Qadmon*, 125–35.

154. "I heard that Rabanit Hannah, sister of Rabbenu Tam, warned the women not to say the *berakha* over candles until the second one had been lit. For if not, and Shabbat had already been received, how could she light the second?" Via *Sefer Asufot*, cited in A. Grossman, *Ḥasidot u-Mordot: Nashim Yehudiyyot be-Eropah be-Yeme ha-Benayyim* (Jerusalem, 2001), 339n109; Urbach, *Ba'ale ha-Tosafot*, 228n8.

155. This reason is given in Bereshit Rabbah 17:8. In YT Shab. 2:6 (end), *Seder Rav 'Amram*, and *Seder Rav Sa'adya Gaon*, the precept is not specifically identified as atonement for this sin.

156. Jacob ben Meir Tam, *Sefer ha-Yashar: She-elot u-Teshuvot*, 45:4.

157. Ibid., 47:6.

158. Ibid., 48:7. The phrase "if they are not prophets, they are the children of prophets," appears in BT Pes. 66a.

159. Reiner refers to Meshullam's conception of the "self sufficiency of the talmudic text" in "Rabbenu Tam u-Vene Doro," 313. Sa'adya Gaon rejected the notion of Scripture's self-sufficiency in battling the Karaites, and Naḥmanides made a related point in his animadversion to the Second Principle of Maimonides' *Sefer ha-Miẓvot*.

160. In such situations, the Talmud was literally a "canon," in the sense of "measuring rod." See R. Reiner, "Rabbenu Tam u-Vene Doro," 320–21.

161. Jacob ben Meir Tam, *Sefer ha-Yashar: She-elot u-Teshuvot*, 44:2, 77. Urbach pointed out that much of the vituperative rhetoric hurled toward R. Meshullam by Rabbenu Tam is drawn from talmudic attacks on Boethusians. Urbach, *Ba'ale ha-Tosafot*, 73n10.

162. *Sefer Ha-Yashar, Ḥidushim*, no. 602, 355, discussed in R. Reiner, "Le-hitqabluto shel Sefer Halakhot Gedolot be-Ashkenaz," 2:120.

163. Jacob ben Meir Tam, *Sefer ha-Yashar, She-elot u-Teshuvot*, 130: "You will not find a child who has not emended."

164. See Urbach, *Ba'ale ha-Tosafot*, 528–29.

165. According to Rabbenu Tam, Rashbam emended "twenty times" more than Rashi.

166. Jacob ben Meir Tam, *Sefer ha-Yashar: She-elot u-Teshuvot*, 105.

167. Ibid., 44:2, 48:12.

168. Rabbenu Tam also had sharp exchanges about emendations with R. Eliezer of Metz and Ephraim of Regensburg. See ibid., 130, 157.

169. Ibid., 78.

170. Ibid., no. 44, part 1 (p. 75).

171. R. Reiner, "R'I ha-Zaqen: beyn hemshekhiut le-ḥidush: Hirhurim be-'iqvot *Yeynam* le-Rav Ḥaym Soloveitchik," 169–70.

172. This, claims Reiner, led to the decline of *minhag* and to the rise of Talmud as exclusive vehicle of law. Ibid., 171, 174.

173. See Ta Shma, "Library of the French Sages," 538.

174. U. Fuchs, "Darkhe ha-hakhra'a, samkhut shel teqstim u-muda'ut 'aẓmit: Hirhurim 'al darkhe ha-pesiqa bi-shalhe tequfat ha-geonim," in *Sugyot be-Meḥqar ha-Talmud: Yom 'Iyyun le-Ẓiyyun Ḥamesh Shanim le-Fetirato shel Ephraim E. Urbach* (Jerusalem, 2001), 100–124.

175. Though Andalusian rabbis may, in reality, have relied on codes or other digests of applied law for adjudication, they consistently affirmed the Talmud's identity as the source.

176. See, e.g., P. Geary, *Phantoms of Remembrance: Memory and Oblivion at the End of the First Millennium* (Princeton, N.J., 1994) 26, and elsewhere.

177. According to a recent work of scholarship, Rabbenu Tam avoided the use of historicist insights to solve halakhic problems, while his nephew, R'I ha-Zaqen, did so. See R. Reiner, "R'I ha-Zaqen: Beyn hemshekhiut le-ḥidush: Hirhurim be-'iqvot *Yeynam* le-R Haym Soloveitchik," 68.

178. Tosafot on Meg. 32a, "*ha-qoreh be-lo ne'ima.*"

179. Urbach, *Ba'ale ha-Tosafot*, 558–59.

180. Y. Elman, *Authority and Tradition: Toseftan Baraitot in Talmudic Babylonia* (New York, 1994), 47–48. Cf. Geary, *Phantoms of Remembrance*, 162.

181. Jacob ben Meir Tam, *Sefer ha-Yashar le-Rabbenu Tam, Ḥeleq ha-Ḥidushim*, introduction, 9. My translation of the last phrase, "*lo 'amdu ha-aḥronim be-shemu'atam*," is open to improvement.

182. See Ta Shma, *Ha-Sifrut ha-Parshanit*, 1:43 (notwithstanding his remarks, there, on 74).

183. A list of cases in which Rabbenu Tam retracted positions he had earlier endorsed, some in the realm of adjudication and others of purely exegetical import, appears in R. Reiner, "Rabbenu Tam u-Vene Doro," 219.

184. BT 'Eruv. 62a. See E. Kanarfogel, "Rabbinic Authority and the Right to Open an Academy in Medieval Ashkenaz," *Michael* 12 (1991): 233–50; 'Imanuel, *Shivre Luḥot*, 3–4.

185. Isaac ben Joseph of Corbeil, *Ha-Semaq mi-Ẓurikh ve-ha-sefer 'Amude Golah*, ed. Y. Har Shoshanim (Jerusalem, 1973), 1:275. The claim that R. Isaac of Dampierre did not view this as a negative development, and willingly ceded the rights of the master is found in R. Reiner, "R'I ha-Zaqen bein hemshekhiyut le-ḥidush," 171.

186. Cited in Y. Yuval, "Rishonim ve-aḥaronim, Antiqui et Moderni," *Ẓion* 57 (1992): 375.

187. Stock, *Implications of Literacy*, 86, 327.

188. See Chapter 1.

189. R. Reiner, "Rabbenu Tam u-Vene Doro," 64–65; Soloveitchik, *Ha-Yayin*, 123.

In light of observations presented in Chapter 2, I am inclined to question Reiner's claim (pp. v, vi, 66) that the Spanish/North African treatment of responsa as definitive records of decided law was in keeping with geonic precedent.

190. See, e.g., Eliezer ben Nathan, *Sefer Ra-aban*, ed. S. Albeck (Warsaw, 1905), no. 42, 31; L. Ginzberg, "Siduro shel Rav Sa'adya Gaon," in *'Al Halakha ve-Aggadah* (Tel Aviv, 1960), 171–74.

191. Abraham ben Isaac. *Sefer ha-Eshkol.* Ed. Shalom Albeck (Jerusalem, 1984) 10. Cf. Berliner, "Le-toldot perushe Rashi," 180; Y. Ta Shma, *Ha-Tefila ha-Ashkenazit ha-Qeduma* (Jerusalem, 2003), 33.

192. On the *maḥzorim* written by R. Ya'aqov ben R. Shimshon, R. Shemaiah, and R. Azriel ben Natan, see Grossman, *Ḥakhme Ẓorfat ha-Rishonim*, 395–403, 417, 532–33. On Rashi's central place in the crystallization of *Maḥzor Vitry*, compiled by Simḥa of Vitry, see Ta Shma, *Ha-Tefila ha-Ashkenazit ha-Qeduma*, 17, 50. See also Stefan Reif, "Rashi and Proto-Ashkenazi Liturgy," in *Rashi, 1040–1990: Hommage à Ephraim E. Urbach*, 445–54.

193. *Seder Rav 'Amram Gaon* and *Sidur R. Sa'adya Gaon* include instructions for practice. On this feature in medieval Christian prayer books, see E. Palazzo, *A History of Liturgical Books from the Beginning to the Thirteenth Century* (Collegeville, Minn., 1998), 214–28.

194. Mordecai on Shab. 142b, "*halakha ke-rav Huna*," no. 396. This observation was also made by a Provençal writer of the twelfth century. R. Abraham ben Isaac of Narbonne listed cases of noncompliance with the tannaitic dicta regarding the transmission of oral and written matters: the reading of a book of aggadah on Shabbat (mentioned in Talmud), the inscription of Talmud itself, and the recitation of liturgical passages that are of scriptural origin (e.g., various Psalms, "Hear O Israel," etc.)—without opening up Scripture and reading from it. "Since they saw the oppression of Exile and the deterioration of the world and the diminution of hearts from engaging in recitation, they said [BT Tem. 14b], 'Better that one letter be uprooted from Torah, that Torah not be forgotten in Israel.'" Abraham ben Isaac of Narbonne, *Sefer ha-Eshkol*, 10, and see Albeck's remarks in the volume's introduction, 68; Ta Shma, *Ha-Tefilah ha-Ashkenazit ha-Qeduma*, 30.

195. Meir HaKohen of Rothenburg, *Hagahot Maimuniyyot*, MT, Hil. Shab. 23:27b (= *shin*).

196. Grossman, *Ḥakhme Ẓorfat ha-Rishonim*, 533; See also M. M. Schmelzer, "Perush alfabetin: Perush 'al 13 piyyutim aramiyyim le-Rabi Binyamin ben Abraham min ha-'Anavim," in *Meḥqarim u-Meqorot: Me-asef le-Mada'e ha-Yahadut*, ed. H. Z. Dimitrovsky (New York, 1977), 172. Cf. Boccaccio's creation of a glossed exemplar of his own work, discussed in Carruthers, *Book of Memory*, 218.

197. See, for example, BT Men. 43b, "*ḥayyav adam le-ḥaddesh meah berakhot be-khol yom.*" Cf. E. Fleischer, *Shirat ha-Qodesh ha-'Ivrit be-Yeme ha-Benayyim* (Jerusalem, 1975), 47–56; R. Brody, *Geonim*, 107.

198. Thus, for example, Rabbi Meir of Rothenburg composed a treatise on the laws of mourning in the thirteenth century in order to consolidate instructions pertaining to this behavior in the talmudic tractate Mo'ed Qatan. Soloveitchik, *Ha-Yayin*, 129.

199. R. Isaac of Vienna was the first to elaborate on this topic in his thirteenth-century *Or Zaru'a.*

200. Y. Ta Shma, "Qavin le-ofyah shel sifrut ha-halakhah be-Ashkenaz ba-meot ha-13–14," *'Ale Sefer* 4 (1977): 26–41.

201. "An invisible scripture seemed to lurk behind everything once said. . . . What had been expressed in gestures, rituals and physical symbols became imbedded in a set of interpretive structures involving grammars, notations and lexica." B. Stock, *Listening for the Text: On the Uses of the Past* (Baltimore, 1990), 20.

202. See, for example, *Ma'aseh ha-Geonim*, ed. A. Epstein and Y. Freimann (Berlin, 1909), no. 58 and 55.

203. Stock, *Listening for the Text*, 40.

204. See I. Ta Shma, "Halakhah, minhag u-masoret be-yahadut Ashkenaz ba-meot ha-11–12," *Sidra* 3 (1987): 145, 153; Ta Shma, *Minhag Ashkenaz ha-Qadmon*, 96; Ta Shma, "Gedarav shel Sefer ha-Maor," *Shenaton ha-Mishpat ha-'Ivri* 3 (1971): 395–404; Ta Shma, *Rabi Zeraḥya HaLevi Ba'al ha-Ma-or u-Vene Ḥugo*, 86–125.

205. As Brigitte Bedos-Rezak noted, "Intense literacy in no way expunged orality as a Jewish mode of communication." She describes the written deeds inscribed by Jews as "aids to oral statements which were themselves necessary to establish that a transaction described within the document had actually occurred." B. Bedos-Rezak, "The Confrontation of Orality and Textuality: Jewish and Christian Literacy in Eleventh- and Twelfth-Century Northern France," in *Rashi, 1040–1990: Hommage à Ephraim E. Urbach*, 546–47. Cf. Agus, *Urban Civilization*, 673.

206. Soloveitchik, *Ha-Yayin*, 124. On the scriptural exegesis of the tosafists R. Yosef Qara and Eleazar of Beaugency, see S. A. Posnanski, *Perush 'al Yeḥezqel u-Tere 'Asar* (Warsaw, 1913), introduction. On tosafist involvement in Masorah studies, see Ta Shma, "Sifriyyatam shel Ḥakhme Ashkenaz bene ha-meah ha-11–12," 300n7. As Ta Shma pointed out (307), Rashi clearly knew *Sefer Yeẓira*; his teacher R. Ya'aqov ben Yaqar wrote a commentary on it. And see E. Kanarfogel, *Peering through the Lattices: Mystical, Magical, and Pietistic Dimensions in the Tosafist Period* (Detroit, 2000). In light of the above, Ta Shma's claims that the tosafists abandoned traditional material and replaced the principles of eleventh-century Ashkenaz with their "opposites" is in need of revision. Ta Shma, "Library of the French Sages," in *Rashi, 1040–1990: Hommage à Ephraim E. Urbach*, 535–40, esp. 536.

207. Thus, for example, Rabbenu Tam sharply disagreed with five Provencal rabbis who signed a responsum that permitted the liturgical reading of Torah from bound *ḥumashim* (Pentateuchs) when a scroll was not available. In his opinion, "those (Provençal Jews) who read from them [*ḥumashim* for liturgical purposes] are like those who read *be-'al peh* [from memory, or orally], though there are some who are lenient when it comes to Haftarah. For books of Prophets are hard to find." According to Rabbenu Tam, Jews who recited the blessing over the Torah when reading liturgically from a bound *ḥumash* were guilty of taking God's name in vain; they would not receive the reward connected with the properly performed miẓvah. See R. Reiner, "Rabbenu Tam u-Vene Doro," 288.

208. Soloveitchik, *Yeynam*, 25; Soloveitchik, *Ha-Yayin*, 118.

209. See Katz, "Biqoret sefarim: Ba'ale ha-Tosafot," 9–16.

210. The scene described in this classroom is quite similar to that described in *Sipur Natan HaBavli* (whose historical testimony regarding early tenth-century Sura is unfortunately also suspect). The author describes the practice of studying one tractate by means of oral recitation (*gores*), while another was "*galuy*," presumably, open for study. See above, Chapter 1.

211. Menaḥem ben Aharon ben Zeraḥ, cited in E. Urbach, *Ba'ale ha-Tosafot*, 251–52; Aḥituv, "Mi-pi sofrim vi-lo mi-pi sefarim," 137–38.

212. In "The Ashkenazi Elite at the Beginning of the Modern Era: Manuscript versus Printed Book," *Polin* 10 (1997): 87n8, Elḥanan Reiner identifies this activity as the one case in which late medieval Ashkenazi society observed the ancient prohibition against (Git. 60b) "saying oral matters in writing," and claims that the material discussed in this closed-book session was not of any legal utility. Yet Ḥayyim ben Beẓalel's anger at the adolescent boys who ferreted out his private halakhic jottings—a *megilat setarim*—from their storage place and copied them suggests that the ancient dictum did continue to have meaning for Ashkenazi Jews of the early modern period.

213. Cf. Job 28:11.

214. Eliyahu Capsali, *Seder Eliyahu Zuta*, ed. A. Shmuelovitz, S. Simonsohn, and M. Benayahu (Jerusalem, 1977), 2:246–47. A passage by R. Israel Bruna in fifteenth-century Moravia seems to offer comparable instruction (though some scholars might argue that the term "*shema'teta*" no longer refers to "aurally heard" traditions): "Where adjudicating is concerned, or permitting a prohibition: it is forbidden to decide law or to permit the forbidden unless [there are] explicit, clear, and limpid opinions derived from the plain sense of the aurally heard talmudic passage [*mitokh peshatei sugya shema'teta*], and not from [logical] analysis." *She-elot u-Teshuvot Mahar'i Bruna*, #29, cited in Urbach, *Ba'ale ha-Tosafot*, 567–68.

215. Ḥayyim ben Beẓalel, *Vikkuaḥ Mayyim Ḥayyim* (Amsterdam, 1712), 4b–5a.

216. See Y. Ta Shma, "Hilkheta ke-vatraei: Beḥinot historiyyot shel kelal mishpati," in *Halakhah, Minhag u-Meẓiut be-Ashkenaz, 1000–1350* (Jerusalem, 1996), 58–78.

217. See E. Reiner, "Temurot be-yeshivot Polin ve-Ashkenaz ba-meot ha-16–17," in *Ke-Minhag Ashkenaz u-Polin: Sefer Yovel le-Khone Shmeruk*, ed. Y. Bartal, C. Turniansky, and E. Mendelsohn (Jerusalem, 1993), 20n18; E. Reiner, "The Ashkenazi Elite at the Beginning of the Modern Era: Manuscript vs. Printed Book," *Polin* 10 (1997): 87.

218. In this context, see the claim that "the Ashkenazic halakhic tradition is understood, at least in the mid-sixteenth century, as inherently oral." E. Reiner, "The Ashkenazi Elite at the Beginning of the Modern Era," 88.

CHAPTER 5

1. On this and similar phrases, see Chapter 1.
2. See Chapter 4 above.

3. Simḥa ben Samuel, *Maḥzor Vitry* (Nurenburg, 1923), 136; Barukh ben Isaac of Worms, *Sefer ha-Terumah* (Warsaw, 1897), no. 245. On Barukh of Worms's French provenance, see Simḥa 'Imanuel, "Ve-ish 'al meqomo mevoar shemo: Le-toldotav shel R. Barukh bar Yiẓḥaq," *Tarbiẓ* 69 (2000): 423–40.

4. On cases of contemporary noncompliance with the tannaitic dicta regarding the transmission of *oral matters*, and *written matters* listed by scholars of twelfth-century Narbonne, see Chapter 4.

5. Zeraḥya Halevi, *Ba'al ha-Maor*, Shab., chap. 15, 5 (on 42b in *Halakhot* of R. Isaac Alfasi in printed editions of Talmud); Isaac ben Abba Mari, *Sefer ha'-Itur* (Jerusalem, 1970), introduction; Meshullam ben Moses of Beziers, *Sefer ha-Hashlama*, ed. Avraham Hafuta (Tel Aviv, 1961), Shab. 115a; Menaḥem HaMeiri, *Bet Ha-Beḥirah 'al Massekhet Berakhot*, ed. Samuel Dickman (Jerusalem, 1964), introduction, 24.

6. Isaac ben Moses, *Or Zaru'a* (Zhitomir, 1862), BM, *Pesaqim* no. 373; Mordecai ben Hillel, *Mordecai*, Shab. no. 396; Meir HaKohen of Rothenburg, *Hagahot Maimuniyyot* on MT, Hil. Shab. 23, letter "shin."

7. R. Meir Halevi Abulafia, *Ḥidushe ha-Ramah ve-Shitat Qadmonim 'al Massekhet Gittin*, ed. A. Shoshana (Jerusalem, 1989) 91; R. Asher b. Yeḥiel, *Hilkhot ha-Rosh*, Shab. chap. 16, no. 1.

8. R. Ẓidqiyahu ben Avraham 'Anav, *Shibole ha-Leqet* (Vilna, 1886) Hil. Shab. no. 115.

9. Asher ben Yeḥiel, *Tosafot Rosh* on BM 116a, "*Rava afiq zuga de-sarvela*"; cf. N. Danzig, "Mi-talmud 'al peh le-talmud be-khtav," *Sefer ha-Shana Bar Ilan* 30–31 (2006): 107–8.

10. BT BM 29b.

11. See Chapter 1.

12. Moses ben Naḥman, *Ḥidushe ha-Ramban* (Jerusalem, 1970) on BM 29. If the verb "to roll" is not to be understood in a figurative manner, it would seem that Ramban was speaking of a manuscript of some portion of the Talmud that was in the form of a scroll.

13. On differences in the information contained in Rashi's and Sherira's historical surveys of the formation of the rabbinic corpora, see Chapter 4.

14. Moses ben Jacob of Coucy. *Sefer Miẓvot Gadol* (Venice, 1547), introduction, 3, column A.

15. Published in S. K. Mirsky, *Sheiltot de-Rav Aḥai Gaon* (Jerusalem, 1960), 40–49; cf. N. Danzig, "Mi-talmud 'al peh le-talmud be-khtav," 62. On the circulation of R. Isaac Stein's commentary on *Sefer Miẓvot Gadol* prior to its publication, see M. Beit Arié, "Transmission of Texts by Scribes and Copyists: Unconscious and Critical Interferences," *Bulletin of the John Rylands Library* 75 (1993): 37, and M. Beit Arié, "Publication and Reproduction of Literary Texts in Medieval Jewish Civilization: Jewish Scribality and Its Impact on the Texts Transmitted," in *Transmitting Jewish Traditions: Orality, Textuality, and Cultural Diffusion*, ed. Y. Elman and I. Gershoni (New Haven, Conn., 2000), 228, 240n12.

16. See the end of Chapter 2.

17. In the Greek-speaking lands of Byzantium, medieval Jews fulfilled the commandment of *talmud torah*, engaging in Torah study, by studying the *Sheiltot*—where they encountered applied *halakhot* in conjunction with the weekly Torah portion in which the laws appeared. I. Ta Shma, "Le-toldot ha-sifrut ha-rabbanit be-Yavan ba-meah ha-14," *Tarbiẓ* 62 (1993): 102.

18. According to H. Z. Dimitrovsky, the emergence of Talmud study as a cultural ideal was the defining feature of "the Jewish Middle Ages." H. Z. Dimitrovsky, "Ha-yesh yeme ha-benayyim yehudiyyim?" in *Meḥqarim be-Mada'e ha-Yahadut*, ed. M. Bar Asher (Jerusalem, 1986), 265.

19. As is evident from the published writings of Professor Twersky's students, he himself often used the term "talmudocentrism" in teaching. The concept is discussed in *Introduction to the Code of Maimonides* (New Haven, Conn., 1980), 200–203, though the term is not used there. On "halakocentricity," see I. Twersky, "Religion and Law," in *Religion in a Religious Age*, ed. S. D. Goitein (Cambridge, Mass., 1974), 70.

20. Isaac Alfasi, *She-elot u-Teshuvot Rabenu Yiẓḥaq Alfasi z'l* (Pittsburgh, 1954), no. 223.

21. Profet Duran, *Ma'aseh Efod*, ed. J. Friedlander and J. Cohen (Vienna, 1865), 14. Under the towering influence of Naḥmanides and his students in the Barcelona yeshivah, Sefardic rabbinic culture, too, came to adopt certain curricular features of Ashkenaz. On the reception and appropriation of the tosafists by Naḥmanides and his students, see below. Another uniquely Sefardi response to the growing talmudocentrism of the curriculum was the composition of works like Isaac Canpanton's *Darkhe ha-Talmud* that attempted to present talmudic argumentation as a form of systematic logic. See Daniel Boyarin, *Ha-'Iyyun ha-Sefaradi: Le-Farshanut ha-Talmud shel Megorashe Sefarad* (Jerusalem, 1989), and now, Sergey Dolgopolski, *What Is Talmud? The Art of Disagreement* (New York, 2009).

22. BT Qid. 30a, "*le-'olam yeshalesh adam.*"

23. Accepting the variant reading, "*talmide ḥakhamim*" rather than "*talmidim.*"

24. In Yeraḥmiel Brody, ed., *Teshuvot Rav Natronai bar Hilai Gaon* (Jerusalem, 1994), 1:146–48. Brody notes that versions of this rabbinic saying are found in Lamentations Rabbah, end of chapter 10, and Canticles Rabbah 8:12.

25. Tosafot on San. 24a, "*belula.*" Cf. Simḥa ben Samuel, *Maḥzor Vitry*, 26.

26. In the wry conclusion of these remarks, Efodi radically revalues a talmudic passage: "And because engagement with the Babylonian Talmud, in its depth, is so overwhelming . . . they said . . . [BT BM 58a], '*Rav Zera sat and fasted 1000 fasts in order to forget the Babylonian Talmud.*'" Profet Duran, introduction to *Ma'aseh Efod*, 14.

27. Maimonides, MT, Hil. Talmud Torah 1:11.

28. Ibid. See the analysis of this passage in I. Twersky, "Some Non-Halakhic Aspects of the *Mishneh Torah*," in *Jewish Medieval and Renaissance Studies*, ed. A. Altmann (Cambridge, Mass., 1967), 106–11; I. Twersky, *Introduction to the Code of Maimonides*, 489–93. I have substituted the term "Torah" for "Law" in Twersky's translation. Twersky referred

to this statement as one "capable of working a silent revolution in Jewish intellectual history" (489). Cf. Twersky, "Religion and Law," 69–82.

29. This outlook is explicitly corroborated in Maimonides' introduction to the *Mishneh Torah*, in which he writes, "The gist of the matter is that one need not have need of any other composition in the world regarding a rule [*din*] of the rules of Israel. Rather, let this composition be a *summa* [*meqabbeẓ*] for the entire Oral Torah. . . . For this reason I have given this composition the title '*Mishneh Torah*.' For a person first reads Written Torah, and then reads this, and knows from it the entire Oral Torah, and has no need to read another book apart from them." Part of this passage appears in I. Twersky, *Introduction to the Code of Maimonides*, 97, though I have rendered *torah she-be-'al peh* as "Oral Torah" and not "Oral Law."

30. See for example I. Twersky, "The Beginnings of *Mishneh Torah* Criticism," in *Biblical and Other Studies*, ed. A. Altmann (Cambridge, Mass., 1963), 161–82.

31. Joseph ibn Kaspi, "Guide to Knowledge" (*Sefer ha-Musar*) translated in *Hebrew Ethical Wills*, ed. I. Abrahams (Philadelphia, 1926), 1:151–52. Cf. I. Twersky, "Joseph Ibn Kaspi—Portrait of a Medieval Jewish Intellectual," in *Studies in Medieval Jewish History and Literature* (Cambridge, Mass., 1979), 231–57.

32. Baḥya ibn Paquda, *Sefer Torat Ḥovot ha-Levavot*, trans. Y. Kafaḥ (Jerusalem, 1972), 24.

33. Ibid., 28.

34. Like contemporary Christians who deplored the misuse of dialectics, Jews criticized the pursuit of *pilpul* (casuistry) on both aesthetic and substantive grounds. Critiques of the dialectical excesses of Talmud study abound in medieval Jewish writings. Some examples are cited in E. Urbach, *Ba'ale ha-Tosafot: Toldotehem, Ḥiburehem, Shitatehem*, 2nd ed. (Jerusalem, 1980), 1:22–24, 76, 78.

35. Judah ben Samuel, *Sefer Ḥasidim'al pi Nusaḥ Ketav Yad asher be-Parma*, ed. Judah Wistinetzki and Jacob Freimann (Frankfurt, 1924), 410. The phrase used is "*gorsim qushiyyot*."

36. Elazar ben Judah of Worms, *Ḥokhmat ha-Nefesh* (Safed, 1913), 20b.

37. Jacob Moellin, *Sefer Maharil*, Hil. Tefilah (Cremona, 1558), 82a.

38. Baḥya ibn Paquda, Abraham ibn Ezra, Qalonymos b. Qalonymos, Solomon Al'ami, and Yosef Yaveẓ number among the medieval Jews who charge rabbinical students with arrogance (*yuhara*) and/or self-aggrandizement (*hitpa-arut*). See Twersky, "Religion and Law," 81n27; Twersky, *Introduction to the Code of Maimonides*, 199nn26–27.

39. Profet Duran, introduction to *Ma'aseh Efod*, 5–6. Taking a cue from Baḥya, Efodi continues: "On the whole, he has wandered away from the study of the law to things which neither benefit him nor elevate him spiritually, things the ignorance of which would not even be noticed."

40. These critiques are discussed in E. Kanarfogel, *Jewish Education and Society in the High Middle Ages* (Detroit, 1992), 75; Yisrael Ta Shma, "Miẓvat talmud torah ke-ve'aya datit ve-ḥevratit be-Sefer Ḥasidim," in his *Halakhah, Minhag u-Meẓiut be-Ashkenaz* (Jerusalem, 1996), 112–29; Urbach, *Ba'ale ha-Tosafot*, 26; E. Reiner, "Temurot be-yeshivot

Polin ve-Ashkenaz ba-meot ha-16–17," in *Ke-Minhag Ashkenaz u-Polin: Sefer Yovel le-Khone Shmeruk*, ed. Y. Bartal, C. Turniansky, and E. Mendelsohn (Jerusalem, 1993), 68–70.

41. Eliezer of Metz, introduction to *Sefer Yere-im*, cited in Y. N. Epstein, "Tosafot Ashkenaziyyot ve-Italqiyyot qedumot," *Tarbiẓ* 12 (1942): esp. 190n6.

42. Moses Taqu, in *Sefer Yeri'ah Qetana*, published in R. Solomon Luria, *Sefer Yam shel Shlomo 'al Massekhet Ḥulin* (Jerusalem, 1995), introduction.

43. Jonah ibn Janaḥ, *Sefer ha-Riqma*, ed. M. Wilensky and D. Tene (Jerusalem, 1964), 5.

44. On the mediation of the tosafist method by Naḥmanides and his students Rabbi Solomon ben Adret, R. Yom Tov Ishbili, and R. Nissim Gerondi, see S. Abramson, *Kelale ha-Talmud be-Divre ha-Ramban* (Jerusalem, 1971), 8–9; I. Ta Shma, *Ha-Sifrut ha-Parshanit la-Talmud be-Eropa u-ve-Ẓefon Afriqa* (Jerusalem, 1999), 2:38–45; Ẓvi Groner, "Darkhe hora-a shel rishonim u-geonim," in *Meah She'arim: 'Iyyunim be'Olamam ha-Ruḥani shel Yisrael be-Yeme ha-Benayyim le-Zekher Yiẓḥaq Twersky*, ed. Ezra Fleisher, Ya'aqov Blidstein, Carmi Horowitz, and Bernard Sepṭimus (Jerusalem, 2001), 267–78.

45. See Moshe Halbertal, "Ha-minhag ve-ha-historiah shel ha-halakhah be-torato shel ha-Ramban," *Ẓion* 67 (2002): 25–56.

46. Groner brings seven textual examples that illustrate the discrepancy between Naḥmanides' tosafistic deliberations in the context of study and his fidelity to geonic perspectives in adjudication. Ẓvi Groner, "Darkhe hora-a shel rishonim u-geonim," 267–78.

47. See M. Idel, "We Have No Kabbalistic Tradition on This," in *Rabbi Moses ben Naḥman: Explorations in His Religious and Literary Virtuosity*, ed. I. Twersky (Cambridge, Mass., 1983), 51–73.

48. See Halbertal, "Ha-minhag ve-ha-historiah shel ha-halakhah be-torato shel ha-Ramban," 25–56.

49. Menaḥem HaMeiri, *Bet ha-Beḥirah 'al Massekhet Baba Batra*, ed. Avraham Sofer (Jerusalem, 1971), 537.

50. Ibid.

51. It may well be that HaMeiri was drawing on the earlier comment of Rabbenu Ḥananel. In his explanation of Pes. 50a, "*ashrei mi she-ba le-khan ve-talmudo be-yado*," R. Ḥananel had written: "There is one who says [some say] that he recites it by mouth/heart, for he passed away and his recitation remained with him [*ki halakh ve-girsato 'imo*]. And another explains it to mean that he comes here [to heaven/'*olam ha-ba*] and his deeds are established, and 'his *talmud*'—for he implemented everything that he learned. And in this sense it is as if he brought his proofs with him." S. Abramson, *Perush Rabbenu Ḥananel la-Talmud* (Jerusalem, 1955) on RH, 145. However, noted Abramson, in R. Ḥananel's comment on MQ 28a, the meaning accords with the first explanation.

52. Ibid. Thus, writes HaMeiri (invoking BT Pes. 50a), "when all is said and done, *praised be the one who comes here* [*to the World-to-Come*] *with his talmud* [alternatively, "*his learning*"] *in his hand.*" Cf. the classical aphorism that a person's learning is known by what he brings with him into the bathhouse.

53. HaMeiri, *Bet ha-Beḥirah 'al Massekhet Baba Batra*, 537–39.

54. Menaḥem HaMeiri, *Bet ha-Beḥirah 'al Massekhet Avot*, ed. Binyamin Ze'ev Prag. (Jerusalem, 1964), introduction, 52.

55. Maimonides criticized *Halakhot Gedolot* in *Sefer ha-Mizvot*. See I. Twersky, *Rabad of Posquieres* (Cambridge, Mass., 1962), 217; Halbertal, "Ha-minhag ve-ha-historiah shel ha-halakhah be-torato shel ha-Ramban," 28 and n. 8.

56. On HaMeiri's debt to Rabad in this regard, see Twersky, *Rabad of Posquieres*, 221.

57. Further insulating Rav Aḥa from the suspicion that he had inscribed legal matters for purposes of adjudication, R. Yosef b"r Shaul explained that the *Sheiltot* functioned as a school book for Rav Aḥa's son: "[I]t seems to me that he [R. Aḥa] intended to say [to his son]: 'You will find the explanation [*derush*] of these *halakhot* in this place in the Talmud.' And in order to prove the veracity of what I had said, I told him to gather the explanations of the halakhot and mark down their source." R. Berlin (known as the Neẓiv), who cites this tradition, underscores the cultural import of HaMeiri's narrative: "In this regard, then, it was his intention almost to minimize the importance of this book, saying that our master [R. Aḥa] did not intend to teach Torah to the many, but only to stimulate the son's heart to analyze." R. Yosef b"r Shaul's commentary on *Sefer ha-'Itur*, in Aḥa of Shabḥa, *Sheiltot de-Rav Aḥai Gaon u-Veuro shel Naftali Ẓvi Yehudah Berlin* (Jerusalem, 1947), *Petaḥ ha'Emeq*, 1, introduction *vav*, section *dalet*, second paragraph; end of section *heh*.

58. Menaḥem HaMeiri, introduction to *Beit ha-Beḥirah 'al Massekhet Avot* (Jerusalem, 1964), 52.

59. Some scholars—e.g., L. Ginzberg, *Geonica* (New York, 1909), 1:89—rejected the historical veracity of HaMeiri's account of the origins of the *Sheiltot*, but others accepted it. See Mirsky, ed., *Sheiltot de-Rav Aḥai Gaon*, introduction, 1:17–18; N. Danzig, *Mavo le-Sefer Halakhot Pesuqot* 129–30 and n. 71.

60. Some scholars have read this passage as one that celebrates the changes mentioned, but readers might infer from their framing of these changes that the Shneur brothers saw them as unwelcome developments. A tone of lament and wistfulness would have been appropriate for scholars sympathetic to the ideas of the Rhineland Pietists. See Urbach, in *Ba'ale ha-Tosafot*, 479; Danzig, "Mi-talmud 'al peh le-talmud be-khtav," 108 and n. 236. On Evreux's connection with *Ḥasidut Ashkenaz*, see Urbach, *Ba'ale ha-Tosafot*, 1:479–81; Kanarfogel, *Jewish Education and Society in the High Middle Ages*, 74–79; E. Kanarfogel, *Peering through the Lattices* (Detroit, 2000), 26–27n1; I. Ta Shma, "Ḥasidut Ashkenaz be-Sefarad: Rabi Yonah Gerondi, ha-ish u-fo'alo," in *Galut Aḥar Golah: Meḥqarim be-Toldot 'Am Yisrael Mugashim le-Professor Ḥayyim Beinart le-melot lo Shiv'im Shana*, ed. A. Mirsky, A. Grossman, and Y. Ḳaplan (Jerusalem, 1988), 165–73, 181–88; Y. Sussman, "Masoret limud u-masoret nusaḥ shel ha-Talmud ha-Yerushalmi," in *Meḥqarim be-Sifrut ha-Talmudit* (Jerusalem, 1983), 34–35 and n. 114.

61. M. Avot 4:12 and elsewhere.

62. In his citation of this passage, Naḥman Danzig ("Mi-talmud 'al peh le-talmud be-khtav," 108 and n. 236) substituted the word "*gemarot*" for "*sefarim*," basing the

change on a sixteenth-century source, Samuel de Medina, *She-elot u-Teshuvot*, HM, no. 1. Yet, as noted in Chapter 2, Sefardi scholars were so confident that Talmud had been inscribed for the explicit purpose of giving instruction in applied law that they were astonished by geonic deviations from the Talmud's legal perspectives. Indeed, writing in the Ottoman Empire in the age of print, Samuel de Medina's framing of this passage is truly celebratory: "But now, in our days, when all *dinim* [applied laws] come from what is written in Talmud and in *ḥibburim* [codes], and in the books of *posqim* [adjudicators]—early and late, recent and old— . . . it makes no sense to impose the perspective of the minority [unwritten laws] on the majority [written laws]." Samuel de Medina, *She-elot u-Teshuvot*, HM 1.4. He makes similar references to the shift from oral reception (*kabbalah*) to transmission by book in responsa on HM 265 and YD 255, end of 47. See Y. Aḥituv, "Mi-pi sefarim ve-lo mi-pi sofrim," *Sinai* 107 (1991): 137n13. There is little reason to assume that the pietistically inclined brothers of Evreux would have shared this perspective.

63. *Midrash Tanḥuma,* Teẓaveh 9; cf. BT San. 5b and elsewhere.

64. Moshe and Shmuel Shneur, *Orḥot Ḥayyim* I, Hil. Talmud Torah, halakha 800, no. 21 (Jerusalem, 1957), 64b, cited in Urbach, *Ba'ale ha-Tosafot* (Jerusalem, 1980), 1:479.

65. On the naming of rabbinic academies for virtuoso dialecticians, see Kanarfogel, *Jewish Education and Society in the High Middle Ages*, 71, 57, and the parallel with contemporaneous developments in Christian education that Kanarfogel noted. Cf. R. W. Southern, "The Schools of Paris and the School of Chartres," in *Renaissance and Renewal in the Twelfth Century*, ed. R. L. Benson, G. Constable, and C. D. Lanham (Cambridge, Mass., 1982), 113–37; U. T. Holmes, "Transition in European Education," in *Twelfth Century Europe and the Foundations of Modern Society*, ed. M. Clagett (Madison, Wisc., 1961), 15–38.

66. Isaac of Corbeil, a student of Samuel Shneur, alluded to this change in a nonjudgmental way: "R'I said: That which we have said [BT San. 5b], 'let a student not give instruction in halakhah . . . ,' this is in the time of the tannaim and amoraim. . . . But now, the *pesaqim* and *horaot* are written, and all can look in the books and *pesaqim* and give instruction." Isaac ben Joseph of Corbeil, *Ha-Semaq mi-Ẓurikh ve-ha-sefer 'Amude Golah*, ed. Y. Har Shoshanim (Jerusalem,1973), miẓvah 111, 1:275. And see E. Kanarfogel, "Rabbinic Authority and the Right to Open an Academy in Medieval Ashkenaz," *Michael* 12 (1991): 233–50. On the saying "*mi-pi sofrim ve-lo mi-pi sefarim,*" which expresses the rabbinic preference for the living teacher, see S. Abramson, introduction to S. Y. Agnon, *Sefer Sofer ve-Sipur* (New York, 1989); Y. Aḥituv, "Mi-pi sefarim ve-lo mi-pi sofrim," 133–50.

67. S. Grayzel, *The Church and the Jews in the Thirteenth Century* (Philadelphia, 1933); A. Funkenstein, "Ha-temurot be-vikkuaḥ 'al ha-dat she-beyn yehudim le-noẓrim ba-meah ha-12," *Ẓion* 33 (1968): 125–44; Ḥ. Merḥavya, *Ha-Talmud be-Re-i ha-Naẓrut* (Jerusalem, 1970); J. Cohen, *The Friars and the Jews: The Evolution of Medieval Anti-Judaism* (Ithaca, N.Y., 1982).

68. Ḥ. Merḥavya, *Ha-Talmud be-Re-i ha-Naẓrut*, 4–5.

69. Augustine, *City of God.* Trans. Demetrius B. Zema and Gerald G. Walsh (New York, 1950–54), Book 18.

70. J. Cohen, *The Friars and the Jews,* 171. As Cohen writes (243): "Although the papacy officially protected the Jews, it was bound to protect only those who conformed to the classical Augustinian conception of the bearers of the Old Testament, and that sort of Jew no longer existed."

71. Thus, for example, the Inquisition of the Talmud headed by Bernard Gui led to its burning in the 1310s and 1320s, after the Jews had been expelled from France. Y. H. Yerushalmi, "The Inquisition and the Jews of France in the Time of Bernard Gui," *Harvard Theological Review* 63 (1970): 323; J. Cohen, *The Friars and the Jews,* 93.

72. J. Cohen, *The Friars and the Jews,* 14–16, 237; G. Kisch, ed., *Jewry Law in Medieval Germany: Laws and Court Decisions concerning Jews,* 2nd ed. (New York, 1970), 38–41, 111–28, 159–68.

73. J. Cohen, *The Friars and the Jews,* 245–46.

74. Funkenstein makes a distinction between different stages in Christian theological inquiry represented, successively, by Anselm of Canterbury, Petrus Alfonsi, Peter the Venerable, and Alain de Lille. A. Funkenstein, "Ha-temurot be-vikkuaḥ 'al ha-dat shebeyn yehudim le-noẓrim ba-meah ha-12," 125–44.

75. J. Cohen, *The Friars and the Jews,* 25. But see Cohen's observation (76) that Christian reliance on the Old Testament in polemical encounters, even after this alleged shift, continued the "literary and unreal nature of Christian-Jewish dialogue, and the lack of relevance to contemporary Judaism."

76. An attempt to identify the precise Jewish sources that were known to thirteenth-century Christians (and that had not been cited in earlier Church Fathers) was made by Ḥ. Merḥavya, *Ha-Talmud be-Re-i ha-Naẓrut,* xii and elsewhere. Cf. Pseudo-Jerome, *Quaestiones on the Book of Samuel,* ed. Avrom Saltman (Leiden, 1975); Bat-Sheva Alpert, "*Adversus Iudaeos* in the Carolingian Empire," in *Contra Iudaeos: Ancient and Medieval Polemics between Christians and Jews,* ed. Ora Limor and Guy Stroumsa (Tübingen, 1996), 119–42.

77. Ḥ. Merḥavya, *Ha-Talmud be-Re-i ha-Naẓrut,* 3.

78. Other materials, attributed to Jerome, that appear in patristic writings are small "midrashim" on subjects such as the ten names of God, names of the letters of the Hebrew alphabet, Jacob's blessings, the ten trials in the wilderness, and the Song of Deborah. Ibid., 9, 17–18, 29.

79. On the post-biblical Jewish sources invoked by Procopius of Gaza and Caesaria in the sixth century, by Olympiadorus of Alexandria in the seventh century, and by John of Damascus in the eighth century, see ibid., 4, 12.

80. Jerome's letter 121 (= PL 22:1033–34) is cited in ibid., 74.

81. The peculiar claim made by Arye Edrei and Doron Mendels, "A Split Jewish Diaspora: Its Dramatic Consequences," *Journal for the Study of the Pseudepigrapha* 16.2 (2007): 127, that this was not a manifestation of a Jewish-Christian conflict, strikes me as untenable. Amnon Linder suggests that Jews asked the Byzantine emperor to enable them

to read Torah in languages they understood (and not merely in Hebrew); Linder never claimed that Jews asked the Byzantine Emperor to abolish the transmission of *deuterosis* in the synagogues! Edrei and Mendels's ungrounded claim ignores the fact that Christians themselves had been warned about *deuterosis* one and a half centuries earlier, when they were admonished to abandon the literature of the pagans. In other words, anti-*deuterosis* decrees were known tactics implemented by Christian monarchs as part of their mission to eradicate impediments to Christian belief. Ḥ. Merḥavya, *Ha-Talmud be-Re-i ha-Naẓrut*, 7.

82. Amnon Linder, *The Jews in Roman Imperial Legislation* (Detroit, 1987), document 66.

83. The precise referent of "*deuterosis*" has been debated by a wide range of scholars. In the opinion of Merḥavya, it refers to *midrashim* (*Pesiqta, Mekhilta, Sifra, or Sifre*) that were connected with the weekly *parshiyyot*. Ḥ. Merḥavya, *Ha-Talmud be-Re-i ha-Naẓrut*, 9; cf. 14. Other theories are discussed in G. Veltri, "Die Novelle 146: Das Verbot des Targumsvortrags in Justinians Politik," in M. Hengel and A. M. Schwemer, eds., *Die Septuaginta zwischen Judentum und Christentum* (Tübingen, 1994), 116–30, and in Seth Schwartz, "Rabbinization in the Sixth Century," in *The Talmud Yerushalmi and Graeco-Roman Culture*, ed. Peter Schäfer (Tübingen, 2002), 3:93.

84. The reference is to *agraphoi kenophoniai*. See ibid., 7–8.

85. Ibid., 13, 20.

86. When codices were seized from the synagogue at Palermo in 599, Pope Gregory the Great ordered that they be returned. However, it is not clear what these codices contained. See ibid., 21; M. Orfali, *Talmud y Cristianismo: Historia y Causas de un Conflicto* (Barcelona, 1998), 121. In note 203, Orfali notes that Gregory refers to these as "codices" and not "rotulae."

87. See Jean Juster, "La condition légale des juifs sous les rois visigoths," *Etudes d'histoire juridique offertes à Paul Fréderic Girard* (Paris, 1913), 2:306n1; S. Grayzel, *The Church and the Jews in the Thirteenth Century*, 29n42a.

88. Ḥ. Merḥavya, *Ha-Talmud be-Re-i ha-Naẓrut*, 21–22.

89. Ibid., 65, 68

90. PL 117:785, cited in Ḥ. Merḥavya, *Ha-Talmud be-Re-i ha-Naẓrut*, 70.

91. In second-century Samaria, Justin Martyr wrote: "But if your teachers only expound to you why female camels are spoken of in this passage, and are not in that; or why so many measures of fine flour and so many measures of oil [are used] in the offerings; and do so in a low and sordid manner. . . . " Justin Martyr, *Dialogue with Trypho*, trans. Thomas B. Falls, ed. Michael Slusser (Washington, D.C., 2003), 112:4, cf. M. Orfali, *Talmud y Cristianismo*, 58.

92. In drawing on post-biblical Jewish sources, Rabanus Maurus (776–856), archbishop of Mainz from 847, differed both from his teacher Alcuin and from Bede. Ḥ. Merḥavya, *Ha-Talmud be-Re-i ha-Naẓrut*, 28, 43, 45, 51. On the corpus of "Pseudo-Jerome," inscribed by a convert from Judaism, see A. Saltman, "Rabanus Maurus and the Pseudo-Hieronymian *Quaestiones Hebraicae in Libros Regum et Paralipomenon*," *HTR* 66 (1973): 43–75; B. Alpert, "*Adversus Iudaeos* in the Carolingian Empire," 119–42.

93. Ḥ. Merḥavya, *Ha-Talmud be-Re-i ha-Naẓrut*, 58, 64.

94. Agobard had always shown interest in Hebrew Bible and was eager to exhibit his knowledge of Judaism. Using Jerome's *Psaltarum Gallicanum*, a Latin translation based on the Hexaplaric Greek text, he often referred to the original Hebrew. B. Alpert, "*Adversus Iudaeos* in the Carolingian Empire," 122.

95. Agobard's assistant, Archdeacon Florus of Lyons (780–860), wrote letters about the Hebrew Book of Psalms between 825 and 840. In order to correct the psalter in use at Lyons, he had consulted the Septuagint, Jerome, and "the books of the Hebrews." According to Bat-Sheva Alpert, when Florus claimed to correct from the Hebrew, he was generally wrong—except for two instances. Alpert surmises that, in these cases, he acquired help from Jews. B. Alpert, "*Adversus Iudaeos* in the Carolingian Empire," 123.

96. Ḥ. Merḥavya, *Ha-Talmud be-Re-i ha-Naẓrut*, 41, 76, 87 and note 24.

97. Ibid., 72. Agobard's anti-Jewish animus has been explained with reference to his Spanish origins. Bat-Sheva Alpert writes of an "almost fanatical Visigothic preoccupation with Judaism." See B. Alpert, "*Adversus Iudaeos* in the Carolingian Empire," 120, 125–26, 137–38. On the eve of the Muslim Conquest of 711, Spain was home to a large number of forced Jewish converts to Christianity. See Amnon Linder, *The Jews in the Legal Sources of the Early Middle Ages* (Detroit and Jerusalem, 1997), 604–5.

98. Though the Lyonnaise clerics were largely unsuccessful in this attempt, notes Alpert, they did promulgate anti-Jewish decrees at the Council of Paris-Meaux (845–46), convened after the division of the Carolingian Empire among the sons of Charlemagne. In the end, Charles the Bald listened to the magnates of his kingdom, who felt that the Lyonnaise proposals grossly interfered with their interests and with the traditional Carolingian policy toward Jews. B. Alpert, "*Adversus Iudaeos* in the Carolingian Empire," 135, 149; Ḥ. Merḥavya, *Ha-Talmud be-Re-i ha-Naẓrut*, 75.

99. Among these were the Jews' ability to obstruct the baptism of their servants, their court-afforded protection from clerics, their ability to build new synagogues, their freedom to sell their wines to bishops, and the establishment of a market day that was not on the Jewish Sabbath. B. Alpert, "*Adversus Iudaeos* in the Carolingian Empire," 136.

100. Ḥ. Merḥavya, *Ha-Talmud be-Re-i ha-Naẓrut*, 85; J. Cohen, *The Friars and the Jews*, 22–23n6; B. Alpert, "*Adversus Iudaeos* in the Carolingian Empire," 134.

101. Ḥ. Merḥavya, *Ha-Talmud be-Re-i ha-Naẓrut*, 71; R. Bonfil, "'Eduto shel Agobard me-Lyon 'al 'olamam ha-ruḥani shel yehude 'iro ba-me'ah ha-teshi'it," in *Meḥqarim ba-Qabalah, be-Filosofyah yehudit u-ve-Sifrut ha-Musar ve-he-Hagut Mugashim le-Yeshayah Tishbi*, ed. J. Dan and J. Hacker (Jerusalem, 1986), 331–32.

102. J. Tolan, *Petrus Alfonsi and His Medieval Readers* (Gainesville, Fla., 1993); Ḥ. Merḥavya, *Ha-Talmud be-Re-i ha-Naẓrut*, 93.

103. On Alfonsi's discussion of aggadot (in PL 157:541–93), see A. L. Williams, *Adversus Judaeos* (Cambridge, 1935), 233–40; H. Merḥavya, *Ha-Talmud be-Re-i ha-Naẓrut*, 93–127; J. Cohen, *The Friars and the Jews*, 26–28. According to Alfonsi, it was this same irrationality that led Jews to reject Jesus.

104. PL 157:527–672, esp. 540, 541, 543, 549, 575, in M. Orfali, *Talmud y Cristianismo*, 63.

105. PL 157:540, cf. 543; Ḥ. Merḥavya, *Ha-Talmud be-Re-i ha-Naẓrut*, 122.

106. This codicological information might be compared with the testimony of *Sefer Ḥasidim*, which juxtaposed the German and Babylonian practices of binding Talmud. See Chapter 4.

107. PL 157:575; Ḥ. Merḥavya, *Ha-Talmud be-Re-i ha-Naẓrut*, 93n1, 100.

108. Ḥ. Merḥavya, *Ha-Talmud be-Re-i ha-Naẓrut*, 94, 111, 114, 123n170.

109. In his *Tractatus adversus Judaeorum inveteratam duritem*, Peter the Venerable of Cluny (1092–1156) called the Talmud "*nephanda scriptura*." See PL 189:633, 661, 702, 709, 714. Cf. Ḥ. Merḥavya, *Ha-Talmud be-Re-i ha-Naẓrut*, 130.

110. PL 189:602; Ḥ. Merḥavya, *Ha-Talmud be-Re-i ha-Naẓrut*, 133; D. Iogna-Prat, *Order and Exclusion: Cluny and Christendom Face Heresy, Judaism and Islam (1000–1150)* (Ithaca, N.Y., 2002), 302. See also A. Funkenstein, *Perceptions of Jewish History* (Los Angeles, 1993), 119–21; Elisheva Carlebach, "Attributions of Secrecy and Perceptions of Jewry," *Jewish Social Studies* 2 (1996): 119–20.

111. Iogna-Prat, *Order and Exclusion*, 301.

112. S. Lieberman, *Sheqi'in* (Jerusalem, 1970), 27–42. In his other polemical writings, including those directed against Islam, Peter the Venerable identified his sources, but in this work he was pointedly coy. This stance may have helped him reinforce the sense of the Talmud's "occult character." Iogna-Prat, *Order and Exclusion*, 302.

113. Ḥ. Merḥavya, *Ha-Talmud be-Re-i ha-Naẓrut*, 128, 130n7.

114. The critiques of aggadah by Sa'adya, Sherira, Shmuel ben Ḥofni, and Hai Gaon are excerpted in J. Elbaum, *Le-Havin Divre Ḥakhamim* (Jerusalem, 2000), and discussed in M. Saperstein, *Decoding the Rabbis: A Thirteenth-Century Commentary on the Aggadah* (Cambridge, Mass., 1980) chap. 1; J. Harris, *How Do We Know This? Midrash and the Fragmentation of Modern Judaism* (Albany, 1995), 73–81; D. Sklare, *Samuel ben Ḥofni and His Cultural World* (Leiden, 1996), 39–48.

115. See, e.g., M. Perlmann, "The Medieval Polemics between Islam and Judaism," in *Religion in a Religious Age*, ed. S. D. Goitein (Cambridge, Mass., 1974), 103–20; M. Perlmann, "Eleventh Century Andalusian Authors on the Jews of Granada," *PAAJR* 18 (1948–49): 269–90.

116. Petrus Alfonsi, *Dialogue against the Jews,* trans. Irven M. Resnick (Washington, D.C, 2006), dialogue 5, 62, also in PL 157:602a. On the phenomenon of Jews and Christians "nurtured among the Muslims" in twelfth-century Spain, see Thomas Burman, "The *Tathlit al-wahdaniya* and the Twelfth Century Andalusian-Christian Approach to Islam," in *Medieval Christian Perceptions of Islam*, ed. John Victor Tolan (New York, 1996), 109.

117. The anti-talmudic part of Petrus Alfonsi's *Dialogues* was broadly publicized in twenty-two chapters of Vincent of Beauvais' thirteenth-century *Speculum Historiale*. Ḥ. Merḥavya, *Ha-Talmud be-Re-i ha-Naẓrut*, 125.

118. On Nicholas Donin's condemnation of the Talmud's errors in the presence of Pope Gregory IX and King Louis the Pious in Paris in 1236, see Isidore Loeb, "La controverse de 1240 sur la Talmud," *REJ* 1 (1880): 246–71; *REJ* 2 (1881): 248–73; *REJ* 3 (1881):

39–57, and above-cited works by S. Grayzel, R. Chazan, J. Cohen, and M. Orfali. Frederick II, who sat in judgment on the Fulda Blood Libel of 1235, may have known, through Donin, of the "Jewish laws called the Talmud." See I. Yuval, *Two Nations in Your Womb: Perceptions of Jews and Christians in Late Antiquity and the Middle Ages*, trans. Barbara Harshav and Jonathan Chipman (Berkeley, 2006), 280–81. Raymond Martini amplified Nicholas Donin's work in 1278. Excluded from this history of Talmud-centered Christian anti-Jewish polemics is the wholly antithetical project of showing how Talmud proves the veracity of Christianity. See J. Cohen, *The Friars and the Jews*, 165–66.

119. Amos Funkenstein noted that Christians as early as Jerome, Epiphanius, and Augustine had claimed that Jews preferred "human doctrine" to "divine doctrine," yet even the most aggressive Christian attacks on extra-biblical Jewish traditions, in his words, "never denied the subjective dependence of this literature on the Bible, that is, its exegetical character from the standpoint of Judaism. Paradigmata of *errores et superstitiones* were presented as an example of the harm which literal exegesis can do, but not more." A. Funkenstein, "Basic Types of Christian Anti-Jewish Polemics in the Later Middle Ages," *Viator* 2 (1971): 380. These earlier charges were thus different from that leveled against Judaism in the thirteenth century.

120. Peter the Venerable (PL 189:602 and 607) claimed that the Talmud was equal in weight to the Torah, but Nicholas Donin, Jeronimo de Santa Fe, and Alfonso de Espina all portrayed the Talmud as trumping the Bible in the opinion of the Jews. Ḥ. Merḥavya, *Ha-Talmud be-Re-i ha-Naẓrut*, 142–43; J. Cohen, *The Friars and the Jews*, 68 ; M. Orfali, *Talmud y Cristianismo*, 79.

121. Gregory IX, in Grayzel, *The Church and the Jews*, 240–41; J. Cohen, *The Friars and the Jews*, 66.

122. In J. M. Rosenthal, "The Talmud on Trial," *JQR* 47 (1956): 145–46.

123. Berthold of Regensburg, *Das Wirken . . . gegen die Ketzer*, cited in J. Cohen, *The Friars and the Jews*, 233.

124. Merḥavya suggested that aggadot included in the Talmud reached a level of linguistic standardization long before non-talmudic aggadot. He also stressed that Christian critics of extra-biblical Judaism targeted aggadah, rather than halakhah, and denounced "Jewish practices" rather than "Jewish laws."

125. According to one scholar, R. Meir of Rothenburg's dirge, "*She-ali serufa ve-esh*," was composed after the burning of twenty-four wagonloads of Talmud in Paris, 1244. See A. M. Haberman, ed., *Sefer Gezerot Ashkenaz ve-Ẓorfat* (Jerusalem, 1946), 180, 183–85.

126. BT Qid. 30a; AZ 19b.

127. BT Suk. 28a; cf. BB 134b.

128. Duran, *Ma'aseh Efod*, introduction, 6.

129. Ibid.

130. Italian Jews had initially known only the Jerusalem Talmud and Palestinian traditions. See Ta Shma, "Halakhah, minhag u-masoret be-yahadut Ashkenaz ba-meot ha-11–12," *Sidra* 3 (1987); Ta Shma, *Minhag Ashkenaz ha-Qadmon*, 9–10, 16, 85–88, 98–103.

131. Ta Shma, "Halakhah, minhag u-masoret be-yahadut Ashkenaz ba-meot ha-11–12," 145.

132. Ibid.

133. Ibid.

134. Ibid., 146.

135. Ibid., 157.

136. When "subjected to the test of talmudic literature and to the scrutiny of foundational halakhic concepts, general and specific, [and] the problems began to be all too obvious." Ibid., 148.

137. Ibid., 86, 147, 152.

138. Ibid., 99, 157.

139. Saul Lieberman, "Perurim," *Tarbiẓ* 2 (1941): 377; E. Z. Melamed, "Ha-Ma'aseh ba-Mishna ke-maqor le-halakhah," *Sinai* 46 (1960): 152–64.

140. Y. Ta Shma, *Minhag Ashkenaz ha-Qadmon*, 71; cf. 69–74, 85–88.

141. See A. Grossman, *Ḥakhme Ashkenaz ha-Rishonim* (Jerusalem, 1981), 424–35; A. Grossman, "Ziqata shel yahadut Ashkenaz ha-qeduma el Ereẓ Yisrael," *Shalem* 3 (1981): 57–92; D. Berger, "Ḥeqer rabbanut Ashkenaz ha-qedumah," *Tarbiẓ* 53 (1984): 479–87; R. Brody, *Geonim*, 117, 120–22; H. Soloveitchik, *Ha-Yayin be-Yeme ha-Benayyim: Yeyn Nesekh—Pereq be-Toldot ha-Halakhah be-Ashkenaz* (Jerusalem, 2008), chap. 9.

142. A number of relevant sources are cited in footnotes to H. J. Zimmels, *Ashkenazim and Sephardim: Their Relations, Differences and Problems as Reflected in the Rabbinical Responsa* (London, 1976), 4–5.

143. This point is made in the sources cited in n. 141 above.

144. Jews of ninth-century "Faranjah," Land of the Franks, wrote to Natronai Gaon of Baghdad for legal guidance. Robert Brody surmised that their inquiry as to whether they might trade at a market held on grounds named for "one of their idols" may be a reference to the fair at Saint Denis, in Paris. Brody, *Teshuvot Rav Natronai*, 63n25, 373–74.

145. Ta Shma (in *Minhag Ashkenaz ha-Qadmon*, 61–67) attempts to find support for his argument that *ma'aseh* (practice observed by a reputable figure) was a more important factor than *halakhah* (received legal teaching) in Palestinian adjudication, in the disparate Palestinian and Babylonian narratives of the encounter between Hillel and Bene Beteyra. In my examination of these versions, however, I have not found evidence for Ta Shma's claims. See, in particular, Y. Frankel, "She-elot hermeneutiyyot be-ḥeqer sipur ha-aggadah," *Tarbiẓ* 47 (1978): 139–72.

146. In the first occurrence of the phrase, which discusses a day laborer's work schedule, Mishnah BM 7:1 concludes that local custom (*minhag*) determines the hours of work, even if the custom conflicts with a received legal teaching (*halakhah*). The Palestinian amora R. Hoshaya chimes in by declaring (YT BM 7:1 = 11b): "*minhag mevattel halakhah*." In this particular context, the phrase is simply an aphorism that affirms the Mishnah's perspective. The parallel discussion in the Babylonian Talmud (BT BM 83a–b) does precisely the same thing. Though the aphorism does not appear there, none of the amoraim object to the Mishna's assertion. In short, the Babylonian and Palestinian perspectives are identical in upholding the tannaitic decision regarding determination of a laborer's working hours. The second occurrence of this phrase appears in a discussion of

the footgear used in performance of *ḥaliẓah* (literally, "un-binding"), the ceremony in which a childless widow releases her brother-in-law (or other kinsman of her deceased husband) from his obligation to wed her in levirate marriage. Mishnah Yeb. 12:1 stipulates that *ḥaliẓah* may be performed with a shoe, but not with a particular type of slipper (the *anfilia*). The Jerusalem Talmud's commentary on this passage (YT Yeb. 12:1 = 12c) in no way disturbs the mishnaic status quo: "If Elijah should come and say that *ḥaliẓah* is performed with a shoe, we listen to him. That *ḥaliẓah* is not permitted with a sandal, we don't listen to him. For it has been the practice of the public to perform *ḥaliẓah* with a sandal, and custom overrides the law." Notwithstanding the combative valence of its rhetoric, nothing in this Palestinian utterance actually challenges the halakhah, the received legal teaching—for, in fact, the halakhah says nothing at all about a sandal! As was the case in the aforementioned passage, the phrase "*minhag mevattel halakhah*" appears here simply as an aphorism; its occurrence in the Jerusalem Talmud does not in any way affect or alter the determination of applied law. Moreover, the Palestinian perspective has its direct counterpart in the Babylonian Talmud (BT Yeb. 102a), which also affirms the ineluctable power of custom to determine the footgear used in the *ḥaliẓah* ceremony. Yisrael Ta Shma himself admitted this in the course of a rather serpentine discussion. Ta Shma, *Minhag Ashkenaz ha-Qadmon*, 65.

147. When asked to explain why the *haftarah* (prophetic lection) read in the local synagogue on the festival of Simḥat Torah was not the one identified in the Talmud, R. Isaac bar Judah's reply was: "They behaved this way because this is the way they behaved. For minhag trumps/overrides halakhah." *Sefer ha-Pardes* 353, quoted in Ta Shma, *Minhag Ashkenaz ha-Qadmon*, 30.

148. The passage explains why it is proper for a *kohen* to refrain from conferring the the priestly blessing upon the congregation during his period of mourning, in keeping with custom. "It is a *miẓvah* to hold onto the custom of the Early Ones in whatever manner possible, for we have found in the Jerusalem Talmud, that *minhag* overrides *halakhah*. And we have found this, too, in our Babylonian Talmud." Ẓidqiyahu ben Avraham 'Anav, *Shibole ha-Leqet*, no. 23, cited in Ta-Shma, *Minhag Ashkenaz ha-Qadmon*, 30.

149. The phrase "*minhag avoteinu Torah hi*" was used by Rashi's teacher, R. Isaac bar Yehudah, and appears in (among other writings) *Sefer ha-Pardes*, *Sefer ha-Yashar*, and *Or Zaru'a*. In none of these sources is it used in agonistic relation to the Babylonian Talmud. See S. Abramson, *'Inyanot be-Sifrut ha-Geonim* (Jerusalem, 1974), 284; S. Abramson, *Rav Nisim Gaon* (1965): 552; D. Sperber, *Minhage Yisrael* (Jerusalem, 1989), 1:235–37.

150. Ta Shma, *Minhag Ashkenaz ha-Qadmon*; Ta Shma, *Halakhah, Minhag u-Meẓiut be-Ashkenaz, 1000–1350*; Eric Yiẓḥaq Zimmer, *'Olam ke-Minhago Noheg: Peraqim be-Toldot ha-Minhagim, Hilkhotehem ṿe-Gilgulehem* (Jerusalem, 1996); Ya'aqov Gartner, *Gilgule Minhag be-'Olam ha-Halakhah* (Jerusalem, 1995).

151. See A. Arthur Schiller, "Custom in Classical Roman Law," *Virginia Law Review* 24 (1937–38): 268–82, esp. 281–82. As was later the case in Jewish culture, custom came to be absorbed into other spheres of Roman law.

152. It seem that even Ta Shma was aware of the evidence, for after citing a passage

from Gratian's twelfth-century code, the *Corpus Juris Canonici*, Ta Shma asked: "Is it really true that Gratian thought it impossible for there to be a conflict between law and custom?" Ta Shma, "Halakhah, minhag u-masoret be-yahadut Ashkenaz ba-meot ha-11–12," 130.

153. Donald R. Kelley, "'Second Nature': The Idea of Custom in European Law, Society & Culture," in *Transmission of Culture in Early Modern Europe*, ed. A. Grafton and A. Blair (Philadelphia, 1990), 133–35.

154. Ibid., 136, and see the citation there from *Dissensiones Dominorum sive Controversiae veterum iuris romani interpretum qui gloassatores vocantur*.

155. Kelley, "'Second Nature,'" 136.

156. See Chapter 3.

157. See ibid.

158. For a comparable development in the Christian world, see Kelley, "'Second Nature,'" 138.

159. Cf. M. T. Clanchy, "Remembering the Past and the Good Old Law," *History* 55 (1970): 165–66, 172. Cf. Pierre Nora, "Between Memory and History: *Les Lieux de Mémoire*," *Representations* 26 (1989): 8; Marc Bloch, *Feudal Society*, trans. L. A. Manyon (London, 1961), 113–14; Fritz Kern, *Kingship and Law in the Middle Ages*, trans. S. B. Chrimes (Oxford, 1939), 149–80; T. F. T. Plucknett, *A Concise History of the Common Law* (London, 1956), 307–8; T. F. T. Plucknett, *The Legislation of Edward I* (Oxford, 1962), 7.

160. Y. Ta Shma, "Gedarav shel Sefer ha-Maor," *Shenaton ha-Mishpat ha-'Ivri* 3 (1971): 395–404; Y. Ta Shma, *Rabi Zeraḥya Halevi Ba'al ha-Ma'or u-Vene Ḥugo* (Jerusalem, 1992), 86–125.

161. A fourth medieval Jewish response to the new prominence of talmudic halakhah in adjudication was not specifically a northern European development. Kabbalistically oriented critiques, like the one leveled in *Sefer ha-Qanah*, a text from fifteenth-century Byzantium, targeted the errors and shortcomings of talmudic logic. See T. Fishman, "A Kabbalistic Perspective on Gender-Specific Commandments: On the Interplay between Symbol and Society," *AJS Review* 17 (1992): 199–245.

162. While Ta Shma identified Rhineland Pietism as a movement that emerged to protest the changes in northern European culture, he saw *Ḥaside Ashkenaz* as a reaction to Tosafism in particular. I. Ta Shma, "Halakhah, minhag u-masoret be-yahadut Ashkenaz ba-meot ha-11–12," 152.

163. See I. Marcus, "History, Story and Collective Memory: Narrativity in Early Ashkenazic Culture," in *The Midrashic Imagination*, ed. Michael Fishbane (Albany, N.Y., 1993), 265.

CHAPTER 6

1. The following appears in an important recent doctoral dissertation on Rabbenu Tam: "There is no question that phenomena like the appearance of the Rhineland Pietists, the development of kabbalah in Provence and the codification of *halakhah* in Sefarad are

all related, in some way or another, to the revolution of the twelfth century, and for this reason, research into Jewish culture in this century cannot cut itself off from general research [*ha-meḥqar ha-kelali*]." Avraham Reiner, "Rabbenu Tam u-Vene Doro: Qesharim, Hashpa'ot, ve-Darkei Limudo be-Talmud" (Ph.D. diss., Hebrew University, 2002), 18. Compare the following claim: "The sudden outburst of the different mystical and Pietistic trends in northern France, Germany, Provence, and northern Spain in the twelfth and thirteenth centuries is a phenomenon that has never been fully explained historically." Elliot Wolfson, *Through a Speculum That Shines: Vision and Imagination in Medieval Jewish Mysticism* (Princeton, N.J., 1994), 272. Moshe Idel established a cogent link between the widespread dissemination of Maimonides' *Guide for the Perplexed* and the rise of Kabbalah in studies like "Maimonides' *Guide of the Perplexed* and the Kabbalah," *Jewish History* 18 (2004): 197–226.

2. The following citations are hardly exhaustive: Moshe Idel, "Transmission in Thirteenth Century Kabbalah," in *Transmitting Jewish Traditions: Orality, Textuality, and Cultural Diffusion*, ed. Y. Elman and I. Gershoni (New Haven, Conn., 2000), 138–65; Elliot Wolfson, "Beyond the Spoken Word: Oral Tradition and Written Transmission in Medieval Jewish Mysticism," in *Transmitting Jewish Traditions: Orality, Textuality, and Cultural Diffusion*, 166–224; Ḥaviva Pedaya, *Ha-Shem ve-ha-Miqdash be-Mishnat R. Yiẓḥaq Sagi Nahor: 'Iyyun Mashveh be-Khitve Rishone ha-Mequbalim* (Jerusalem, 2001); Daniel Abrams, "Ketivat ha-sod be-Ashkenaz ve-ha-ma'avar le-Sefarad," *Maḥanayyim* 6 (1994): 94–105; Moshe Halbertal, *'Al Derekh ha-Emet: Ha-Ramban ve-Yeẓiratah shel Masoret* (Jerusalem, 2006).

3. On Rhineland Pietism as a "movement," see Haym Soloveitchik, *Ha-Yayin be-Yeme ha-Benayyim: Yeyn Nesekh—Pereq be-Toldot ha-Halakhah be-Ashkenaz* (Jerusalem, 2008), 125. On Tosafism, see Haym Soloveitchik, "Three Themes in *Sefer Ḥasidim*," *AJS Review* 1 (1976): 318. On the relationship of the two, see Soloveitchik's assertion in the 1976 essay that the "Tosafist movement . . . was in consonance with the deepest drives of the pietists," and that Rhineland Pietists were "committed to the dynamics" of the tosafists. More recent ruminations on the common cultural pursuits of Pietists and tosafists (along with a summary of older perspectives) appear in E. Kanarfogel, *Peering through the Lattices: Mystical, Magical, and Pietistic Dimensions in the Tosafist Period* (Detroit, 2000), 22–31.

4. While the first generation of tosafists were French, subsequent tosafists came from Germany. See Avraham Reiner, "From Rabbenu Tam to R. Isaac of Vienna: The Hegemony of the French Talmudic School in the Twelfth Century," in *The Jews of Europe in the Middle Ages*, ed. Christopher Cluse (Turnhout, 2004), 273–81; H. Soloveitchik, *Ha-Yayin,* 127.

5. On the question of whether Jews may sell non-kosher animals to non-Jews, R. Isaac of Dampierre is reported to have taught: "[If] one is stringent in this matter, seeking to be cunning in awe [for the Divine], may he be blessed" (*Ve-ha-maḥmir ha-ba lihyot 'arum be-yirah, tavo 'alav berakha*). In *Tosafot Rabbenu Elḥanan* 15/14b, "*eyn,*" cited in H. Soloveitchik, *Ha-Yayin*, 361. In note 63, Soloveitchik states that the ending of this passage is "*mi-pi rabi,*" meaning that it was a teaching of R. Elḥanan's teacher, R. Isaac.

6. The talmudic recommendation that one be "cunning" in one's fear and awe of God, "*'arum bi-yirah*" (BT Ber. 17a), is a recurring exhortation in Samuel the Pietist's programmatic remarks that launch the printed edition of *Sefer Ḥasidim*, ed. Judah Wistinetzki and Jakob Freimann (Frankfurt am Main, 1924) 1–3.

7. Soloveitchik, "Three Themes in *Sefer Ḥasidim*," 318; Y. Ta Shma, "*Mizṿat talmud torah ke-be'aya datit ve-ḥevratit be-Sefer Ḥasidim*," in *Halakhah, Minhag u-Meẓiut be-Ashkenaz, 1000–1350* (Jerusalem, 1996), 121; Ta Shma, *Minhag Ashkenaz ha-Qadmon* (Jerusalem, 1992), 95.

8. Cf. Patrick Geary, *Phantoms of Remembrance: Memory and Oblivion at the End of the First Millennium* (Princeton, N.J., 1994), 7–8.

9. In the words of one scholar, "the present itself became a sort of recycled, updated past." M. Carruthers, *Book of Memory: A Study of Memory in Medieval Culture* (Cambridge, 1990) 21.

10. The suggestion that the Rhineland Pietists' emphasis on asceticism and on the cultivation of humility be examined with reference to monastic practices was first made by Y. Baer, "Ha-megama ha-datit ḥevratit shel Sefer Ḥasidim," *Ẓion* 3 (1948): 10. Cf. David Berger, *The Jewish-Christian Debate in the High Middle Ages: A Critical Edition of the Niẓaḥon Vetus* (Philadelphia, 1979), 27n71; E. Kanarfogel, *Jewish Education and Society in the High Middle Ages* (Detroit, 1992) 63, 70–71; T. Fishman, "The Penitential System of *Ḥaside Ashkenaz* and the Problem of Cultural Boundaries," *Journal of Jewish Thought and Philosophy* 8 (1999): esp. 219–23.

11. See, e.g., J. Leclercq, *The Love of Learning and the Desire for God: A Study of Monastic Culture* (New York, 1960), 89–91, 188–90.

12. D. E. Luscombe, *The School of Peter Abelard* (London, 1969), 103–42.

13. Monasticism's emergence has been linked to governmental recognition of Christianity as a licit religion. Once there was no opportunity for martyrdom, Christians who sought to express their faith through rejection of this world and emulation of the self-sacrifice of Jesus chose to retreat from the distractions of the polis.

14. On this issue in pagan cultures of antiquity, see, e.g., Plato, *Phaedrus*; D. Frankfurter, "The Magic of Writing and the Writing of Magic," *Helios* 21 (1994): 179–221. Rabbinic expressions of the tension between pneumatic/inspired authority and scholastic authority in both antiquity and the Middle Ages are discussed in E. Urbach, "Halakhah u-Nevuah," *Tarbiẓ* 18 (1946–47): 1–27; A. J. Heschel, "'Al ruaḥ ha-qodesh be-yeme ha-benayyim," *Alexander Marx Jubilee Volume* (New York, 1950), 175–208; Ta Shma, "Shee-lot u-teshuvot min ha-shamayim," *Tarbiẓ* 57 (1987–88): 51–66. On this issue in medieval Christian cultures, see, e.g., E. R. Curtius, *European Literature and the Latin Middle Ages*, trans. Willard Trask (London, 1953), 304; M. T. Clanchy, *From Memory to Written Record: England 1066–1307* (London, 1979), 6, 52, 262, 296. On expressions of preference for oral transmission within Muslim culture, see G. Schoeler, "Oral Torah and Hadit: Transmission, Prohibition of Writing, Redaction," in *The Oral and the Written in Early Islam*, ed. James E. Montgomery (London, 2006), 111–41; Jonathan P. Berkey, *The Transmission of Knowledge in Medieval Cairo* (Princeton, N.J., 1992), 26.

15. There are two recensions of *Sefer Ḥasidim*: the Parma edition was published in Berlin, 1891, and the Bologna edition was published in Jerusalem, 1960. References to SḤ in this chapter are to the Parma edition unless otherwise noted. On the dating of this work, see H. Soloveitchik, "Li-ta-arikh ḥiburo shel Sefer Ḥasidim," in *Tarbut ve-Ḥevra be-Toldot Yisrael be-Yeme ha-Benayyim*, ed. M. Ben Sasson, R. Bonfil, and J. Hacker (Jerusalem, 1989), 383–88.

16. See, e.g., SḤ 761 (referring to YT Eruv. 1:1; cf. Ber. 28a); SḤ 762, 763, 750, 770, 748. And see the remarks of E. E. Urbach and Y. Dan on *'Arugat ha-Bosem*, cited below.

17. On *memoria* culture, see Mary Carruthers, *The Book of Memory*. On the Pietists' engagement of corpora of oral matters (e.g., liturgy, Masorah) by performing acts of associative linkage, see below.

18. Cf. the description of the different approaches of Abelard and Bernard in Raymond Klibansky, "Peter Abailard and Bernard of Clairvaux," *Medieval and Renaissance Studies* 5 (1961): 1–27.

19. E. Kanarfogel, *Jewish Education and Society in the High Middle Ages*, 70–72; H. Soloveitchik, "Three Themes in *Sefer Ḥasidim*," 342–43, 348–49. On the monastic preference for the synthetic *collatio* over the more decisive and selective *lectio* of the scholastic, see J. J. Leclercq, "The Renewal of Theology," in *Renaissance and Renewal in the Twelfth Century*, ed. Robert Louis Benson, Giles Constable, and Carol D. Lanham (Cambridge, Mass., 1982), 77. Rhineland Pietists seem to have conceived of the talmudic tractates as products of amoraic oral-memorial culture: "Therefore it is called '*massekhet*,' using the language of weaving . . . for it collects everything into one matter; this is a *massekhta*." SḤ 667, and see 176n2 for variant explanations of the term "*massekhet*."

20. The Rhineland Pietists' critique of pride is discussed below. An early eleventh-century chronicle recounts that Hervé of Tours had rejected an education in classics on the grounds that it would inevitably lead to pride. Rodulfus Glaber, *The Five Books of the Histories*, 3, iv, 14, and Introduction, xxii, n.5.

21. S. Jaeger, *The Envy of Angels*, 81.

22. E. Kanarfogel, *Jewish Education and Society in the High Middle Ages*, 76, 91; E. Kanarfogel, *Peering through the Lattices*, 23; A. Grossman, *Ḥakhme Ashkenaz ha-Rishonim* (Jerusalem, 1981), 165–70; H. Soloveitchik, "Three Themes in *Sefer Ḥasidim*," 345–54, 350; M. Beit Arié, "Ideals versus Reality: Scribal Prescriptions in *Sefer Ḥasidim* and Contemporary Scribal Practices in Franco-German Manuscripts," in *Rashi, 1040–1990: Hommage à Ephraim E. Urbach*, ed. Gabrielle Sed-Rajna (Paris, 1993), 559–66; G. Scholem, *Major Trends in Jewish Mysticism* (New York, 1946), 81; Ivan Marcus, *Piety and Society* (Leiden, 1981), 4–8; Yosef Dan's review of Ivan Marcus, *Piety and Society*, in *Tarbiẓ* 51 (1981–82): 324–25. Ta Shma, on the other hand, describes the Rhineland Pietists as those who "continued the path" of eleventh-century Ashkenazic predecessors. Y. Ta Shma, *Minhag Ashkenaz ha-Qadmon*, 89.

23. The short life of Rhineland Pietism is stressed in H. Soloveitchik, "Piety, Pietism and German Pietism: *Sefer Ḥasidim* I and the Influence of *Ḥaside Ashkenaz*," *JQR* 92.3–4 (2002): 455–93.

24. Ivan Marcus pointedly rejected the portrait of *Ḥasidut Ashkenaz* as (nothing but) a reaction to the rise of Tosafism. I. Marcus, "History, Story and Collective Memory: Narrativity in Early Ashkenazic Culture," in *The Midrashic Imagination*, ed. Michael Fishbane (Albany, New York, 1993), 265.

25. The author of the *'Arukh* referred to anonymous rabbis whose teachings are preserved in *Perushe Magenza* by several names. See Y. Ta Shma, "'Al perush Rabbenu Gershom Meor HaGolah la-Talmud," *Qiryat Sefer* 53 (1978): 357; A. Berliner, "Le-toldot perushe Rashi," in *Ketavim Nivḥarim*, ed. Abraham Berliner (Jerusalem, 1949), 2:181.

26. The term *ḥasidim* is used to designate Jews of the Second Temple period who were devotees of certain stringent practices. See, e.g., M. Ber. 5:1; BT Ned. 10a; BT Men. 40b–51a.

27. Cecil Roth, ed., *The Dark Ages: Jews in Christian Europe, 711–1096* (New Brunswick, N.J., 1966), 61–63, 106; Y. Dan, *Torat Ha-Sod shel Ḥasidut Ashkenaz* (Jerusalem, 1968), 12–24; R. Bonfil, "Beyn Ereẓ Yisrael le-veyn Bavel: Qavvim le-ḥeqer toldot ha-tarbut shel ha-yehudim be-Italya ha-deromit u-ve-Eropa ha-noẓrit be-yeme ha-benayyim ha-muqdamim," *Shalem* 5 (1987): 21–22; R. Bonfil, "Can Medieval Storytelling Help Understanding Midrash? The Story of Paltiel," *The Midrashic Imagination* (Albany, N.Y., 1993), 228–54.

28. M. Ben Sasson, *Ẓemiḥat ha-Qehilah ha-Yehudit be-Arẓot ha-Islam: Qayrawan, 800–1057* (Jerusalem, 1996), 150n230; see 276 for another term that appears in Qayrawanese sources, "*anshe ha-yir-ah*," "men of awe."

29. On the Rhineland Pietists' depiction of famous historical personages as *ba'ale sod* (masters of esoteric mysteries), see Y. Dan, *Torat ha-Sod shel Ḥasidut Ashkenaz*, 80. Dan (80–81) points out that only earlier sages warrant this label. The distinguished of their own generation were designated as "*ha-qadosh*," "*ha-navi*"—which was the designation for Samuel the Pietist (and R. Neḥemiah); "*ha-kohen ha-gadol*"—as R. Avraham haKohen was designated, and especially "*he-ḥasid*," which correponds to "*ha-nazir*," a label given to individuals in Provence. Yosef Dan, "Ḥug ha-keruv ha-meyuḥad be-tenu'at ḥasidut Ashkenaz," *Tarbiẓ* 35 (1966): 349–72. Thus, for example, some *ḥasidim* were associated with *Sefer ha-Navon* and others with "*ha-keruv ha-meyuḥad*" (the Special Cherub). R. Avraham, author of a Pietist prayer commentary, was familiar with the teachings of the mystic R. Ya'aqov HaNazir. See Avraham ben 'Azriel, *'Arugat ha-Bosem*, ed. E. Urbach (Jerusalem, 1963), 4:119–26.

30. References to "*ḥaside Ẓorfat*," "*ḥaside Provinza*," and "*ḥaside Alemania*" appear in Abraham b. Nathan (HaYarḥi), *Sefer ha-Manhig* (Jerusalem, 1978), 363, 460, 607, 626. Salo Baron alluded to the broader geographical scope of this phenomenon when he speculated that *Ḥuqqei ha-Torah*, an anonymous medieval syllabus and manual of ascetic conduct, was produced either by Jewish elitists of Provence or by Rhineland Pietists. S. Baron, *A Social and Religious History of the Jews* (New York, 1952–58), 6:140–41, 395; I. Twersky, *Rabad of Posquieres* (Cambridge, Mass., 1962), 25–29; E. Kanarfogel, *Jewish Education and Society in the High Middle Ages*, appendix A. In *Ba'ale ha-Tosafot: Toldotehem, Ḥiburehem, Shitatehem* (Jerusalem, 1980), 131n41. E. Urbach drew attention to the phenomenon in

southern France described by G. Scholem, *Reshit ha-Qabbalah* (Jerusalem, 1948), 84–91. Cf. M. Saperstein, "Christians and Christianity in the Sermons of Jacob Anatoli," *Jewish History* 6 (1992): 225–42.

31. On uses of the terms *parush* (withdrawn one), *nazir* (Nazirite), and *ḥasid* (Pietist) to refer to particular Jews in medieval Provence, see G. Scholem, *Origins of the Kabbalah*, ed. R. J. Zwi Werblowsky, trans. Allan Arkush (Philadelphia, and Princeton, N.J., 1987), 229–33; I. Twersky, *Rabad of Posquieres*, 25–27. Other terms that might be considered in this context are *navi* (prophet) and *qadosh* (consecrated one). See A. J. Heschel, "'Al Ruaḥ ha-qodesh be-yeme ha-benayyim"; M. Idel, *Kabbalah: New Perspectives* (New Haven, Conn., 1988), 43; E. Wolfson, *Through a Speculum That Shines*, 298.

32. These references to the ascetic behavior—and in some cases, visionary practices—of twelfth- and thirteenth-century Jewish elites in Provence as well as Ashkenaz (bracketing Egypt for the moment) might now be seen as indicative of a pan-European Jewish phenomenon, whose common core of Pietism assumed different doctrinal and practical expressions.

33. Speaking of the modesty of his teacher, R. Ya'aqov ben Yaqar, Rashi wrote, "He comported himself like a trodden threshold and acted as if he were the dregs of the dregs [*shirei shirayyim*] and his heart was never inflated to [assume] the crown that it deserved—to innovate any matter in his generation." In *Sidur Rashi*, ed. S. Buber (Berlin, 1911), 80; cf. A. Grossman, *Ḥakhme Ashkenaz ha-Rishonim*, 246–49.

34. Grossman, *Ḥakhme Ashkenaz ha-Rishonim*, 247.

35. Other customs of *persuhim*—mentioned in *Sefer ha-Pardes* and *Shibbole ha-Leqet*—include eating the placenta after childbirth. See Y. Ta Shma, *Minhag Ashkenaz ha-Qadmon*, 53–54. Even before the emergence of Rhineland Pietism, some Jews observed the stringent custom of having two-year-old children refrain from food on fast days. Noted in I. Marcus, "The Dynamics of Jewish Renaissance and Renewal in the Twelfth Century," in *Jews and Christians in Twelfth Century Europe*, 38–39.

36. Grossman notes that the giving of priestly gifts in Ashkenaz bore witness to the recipients' certainty that their family lineages were untainted. A. Grossman, "Yiḥus mishpaḥah u-meqomo ba-ḥevra ha-yehudit be-Ashkenaz ha-qedumah," in *Peraqim be-Toldot ha-Ḥevra ha-Yehudit . . . Muqdashim le-Professor Yaacov Katz*, ed. E. Etkes and Y. Salmon (Jerusalem, 1980), 19–20. On the reference to a particular subgroup of Jewish kinfolk as "the Levites of Worms," see N. Wieder, "Yismaḥ Moshe: Hitnagdut ve-sanegorya," in *Meḥqarim be-Aggadah, Tirgumim u-Tefila le-Zekher Yosef Heinemann*, ed. E. Fleischer and J. Petuchowski (Jerusalem, 1981), 83.

37. On this reference in *Shibbole ha-Leqet*, see A. Grossman, *Ḥakhme Ashkenaz ha-Rishonim*, 370.

38. The subject of Ashkenazi self-image is treated in H. Soloveitchik, *Halakhah, Kalkalah, ve-Dimui 'Aẓmi* (Jerusalem, 1985), 112–13, 118–19; H. Soloveitchik, "Religious Law and Change," *AJS Review* 12 (1987): 205–21; H. Soloveitchik, *Ha-Yayin*, 362ff. It is not clear whether Jews from other places also referred to the Jews of Ashkenaz in this manner. See I. Marcus, "History, Story and Collective Memory Narrativity in Early Ash-

kenazic Culture," 270–71. On the Mainz Jews' perception of their town as "holy," see Y. Yuval, "Heilige Städte-Heilegen Gemeinden: Mainz als das Jerusalem Deutschlands," in *Judische Gemeinden und Organisationformen von der Antike bis zum Gegenwart* (Vienna, Cologne, Weimar, 1996), 91–101.

39. B. Stock, *Listening for the Text: On the Uses of the Past* (Baltimore, 1990), 40.

40. Pietists even inscribed esoteric teachings (*sod*), though only in a manner that made them virtually unusable unless the text was orally clarified. See below.

41. See below. The exception to this is *Sefer Ḥasidim*, a work that enables readers to hear "ideas muted in other [Pietist] genres." E. Baumgarten, *Mothers and Children: Jewish Family Life in Medieval Europe* (Princeton, N.J., 2004), 163.

42. S. Jaeger, *Envy of Angels*, 9.

43. Ibid., 14.

44. Ibid.

45. The critique was also leveled against copyists who signed their names. See SḤ 706, SḤ Bologna 136.

46. SḤ 1945. A similar rebuke appears in SḤ 1052: "The one who composed *Torat Kohanim*, and the books of *Mekhilta* [or and *Sifre* and *Mekhilta*] and *beraitot* and *midrashim* and *aggadot* and *tiqqune ha-'olam*, like *Massekhet Sofrim*—they did not write in their books, 'I so and so, son of so and so, wrote this book.'" Cf. SḤ 1620.

47. Cf. the explanation of why a righteous person might die early, in SḤ 648.

48. SḤ 1052. Cf. SḤ 1945 (end): "For they knew that if they had done this, their hearts would benefit and they would receive their reward in this world. Therefore, they didn't wish to do so."

49. For this reason, if one is asked to what he attributes his good fortune or long life, he is permitted to answer verbally, but must not inscribe any document or monument that could be construed as self-praise or as praise for one's living forbears or children.

50. SḤ 706.

51. The modesty of these predecessors is praised, for example, in SḤ 1528: "Some of the early ones did not wish to mention their names in the *piyyutim* that they established [*she-yasdu*], in order that their hearts not derive benefit, and their offspring not swell with pride, saying that their fathers did such and such—for example [the composer of the *piyyut* for Rosh HaShanah] *Ahallela Elohai*. And even though they would have blessed his memory, had they known, they said, better that they not become proud and engage in self-aggrandizement." Cf. SḤ 1620. Another *piyyut* praised for its anonymity is *Efḥad be-ma'asai anusa le-'ezra*, in SḤ 1945, SḤ 1620.

52. *Sefer Ḥasidim* notes with disdain that some paytanim even alter words in order to inscribe their names.

53. In point of fact, not all tosafistic compositions were named for individuals; some were designated by the location of the academy in which they were produced.

54. SḤ 746.

55. Several scholars have noted that *Sefer Ḥasidim* only objects to wrong uses of *pilpul*, casuistry. I. Marcus, *Piety and Society* (Leiden, 1981), 103–5; Y. Ta Shma, "Miẓvat

talmud torah ke-be'aya datit ve-ḥevratit be-Sefer Ḥasidim"; E. Kanarfogel, *Jewish Education and Society in the High Middle Ages*, 75, 89.

56. SḤ 752: "*limud shel niẓahon, kegon shnayyim she-mitvakkḥim kedei le-nazeaḥ zeh et zeh.*"

57. SḤ 1707.

58. SḤ 648.

59. SḤ 747: "*talmid ḥakham ha-mimaes et torato.*" It is not clear from the context whether this judgment is based on the individual's failure to comport himself in a manner befitting a scholar, or whether the phrase refers to the scholar's actual derision of his subject matter.

60. SḤ 1375 refers to the wicked one (*rasha'*) as *mefulpal yoter*, "more" or "most casuistical." Other references to those who are rabbinically learned without possessing commensurate personal qualities appear in SḤ 814, 811, 1075, 1093. The intemperate references to "wicked" Jews should undoubtedly be viewed within the context of a culture that generated a rich rhetoric of opprobrium, and perhaps as "the wish dream of an embattled mentality." Cf. S. Jaeger, *Envy of Angels*, 233.

61. SḤ 752. While this term testifies to at least a modicum of Jewish familiarity with trends in contemporary Christian pedagogy, the literary context suggests that the Pietists may have applied the epithet *goy* (gentile) to any act undertaken from improper motives. Having referred to "*dialeqtiqa shel goyyim*," *Sefer Ḥasidim* goes on to explain the meaning of the term *she-lo lishma*, study that is not undertaken for its own sake: " 'Not for its own sake'—meaning, [not] from awe. But to call [such a student] 'rabbi'! He is an outright *goy*!" (SḤ 753).

62. Indeed, even R. Elazar of Worms engaged in dialectic, though not for the purpose of drawing halakhic conclusions. H. Soloveitchik, "*Yeynam*": *Saḥar be-Yeynam shel Goyim 'al Gilgulah shel Halakhah ba-'Olam ha-Ma'aseh* (Tel Aviv, 2003), 27.

63. SḤ 664; SḤ 1026.

64. SḤ 1739.

65. See H. Soloveitchik, "Three Themes in *Sefer Ḥasidim*," 318. Pietists recognized that this type of study was not for everyone, however, and particularly not in their own era of diminished cultural standards: "And these days, when there is not much wisdom, the teacher must explain everything" (SḤ 801).

66. SḤ 801.

67. See J. Leclercq, *Love of Learning*, 142, 202, and citations there. Though Roman sources stressed the importance of memory for the discipline of rhetoric, Aristotle said more about memory's importance for the discipline of dialectics. See R. Sorabji, *Aristotle on Memory* (Providence, 1972), 27, 28, 31, 35, 36.

68. SḤ 745: "*keyvan she-'oseq ba-Torah u-meḥaddesh bah, ke-ilu hi shelo, u-mimenu ba-ah.*" Cf. Rabba's explanation of Ps. 1:2 in BT AZ 19a.

69. Cf. S. Jaeger, *Envy of Angels*, 7, 15. In an environment that privileges charisma, writes Jaeger, education is transmitted, above all, by a kind of body magic.

70. S. Ẓfatman, "Ma'aseh Bukh: Qavim le-demuto shel zhaner be-sifrut Yiddish ha-

yeshanah," *Ha-Sifrut* 28 (1979): 146. Ẓfatman notes that the hagiographic repetoire of tales pertaining to R. Judah the Pietist was fixed by the early fifteenth century. (She also explains [132] that while the tales were originally told in Yiddish, they were inscribed in Hebrew before they were inscribed in Yiddish.)

71. Though in her analysis of *Sefer Ḥasidim*'s "Tale of the Three Penitents" (discussed below), Tamar Alexander assumed that the *rosh yeshivah* occupied a more exalted place in the Pietist hierarchy than the *ḥakham*, I would suggest that the ranking in this particular tale reflects the ideological shift that took place within Rhineland Pietism under the leadership of R. Elazar of Worms. See T. Alexander, "Li-darkhe 'iẓuv ha-sipur ha-Ḥasidi-Ashkenazi," *Studies in Aggadah and Jewish Folklore* 7 (1983): 197–223; T. Fishman, "The Penitential System of *Ḥaside Ashkenaz* and the Problem of Cultural Boundaries," n. 17.

72. Cited in Avraham Epstein, *Kitve Avraham Epstein*, ed. A. M. Haberman (Jerusalem, 1949–57), 1:252n14 (from *Sefer Ma'asiyyot* in Bruell, *Jahrbikher* 9:32, which differs slightly from *Mayesebukh* [Roedelheim, 1753], 45c). Cf. R. Bonfil, "Bein Ereẓ Yisrael le-vein Bavel," 26–27.

73. On Rabbenu Tam's perspective, see Chapter 4. On Mishnah study among Pietists, see Y. Sussman, "Kitve yad u-mesorot nusaḥ shel ha-mishnah," *Proceedings of Seventh World Congress of Jewish Studies* (Jerusalem, 1981), 3:235–36; E. Kanarfogel, *Jewish Education and Society in the High Middle Ages*, 90–91.

74. SḤ 745. This passage has been used—anachronistically—to reconstruct geonic attitudes to halakhic compilations.

75. On the scope of the talmudic curriculum in northern European academies, see Chapter 4.

76. So important is this obligation that a *kohen* (priest) may even defile himself to perform it. On *met miẓvah* and its obligations, see *Sifre*, Num. 26; BT Meg. 26b; Tur, YD 360; Bet Yosef on YD 374:3. The Pietists refigure the (ungrammatical) term "miẓvah of the dead [who has none to attend to him]" to mean something like "abandoned miẓvah [which has none to attend to it]."

77. SḤ 1, 2. See Ta Shma, *Ha-Sifrut ha-Parshanit,* 33.

78. It is not known to me whether this curricular policy was implemented in Speyer. On the relationship between the rabbinic academy at Evreux and the Rhineland Pietists, see Chapter 5.

79. Y. Sussman, "Kitve yad u-mesorot nusaḥ shel ha-Mishnah," 3:235–36; E. Kanarfogel, *Jewish Education and Society in the High Middle Ages,* 90–91.

80. Examples of Ashkenazi invocation of aggadah in decision making are cited in N. Wieder, "Yismaḥ Moshe: Hitnagdut ve-sanegorya," 91; S. Spitzer, "She-elot u-teshuvot Rabbenu Yehudah heḤasid be-'inyene teshuvah," *Sefer ha-Zikaron le-Rav Shmuel Barukh Verner* (Jerusalem, 1996), 202.

81. M. Zucker, *Perushe Rav Sa'adya Gaon le-Ve-reshit*, 180–84 and notes; Brody, *The Geonim of Babylonia and the Shaping of Medieval Jewish Culture* (New Haven, 1998), 245. I argued in Chapter 1 that the geonim also regarded the talmudic corpus as an (unwritten)

text that lacked self-sufficiency and required complementation by living tradition in order to be adequate as a source of legal authority.

82. Taqu's programmatic opposition to reliance on "extraneous" books (which he labels "*sefarim ḥiẓonim*," using the term for Apocrypha!) appears in his "*Ketav Tamim*," ed. Raphael Kircheim, in *Oẓar Neḥmad* 4 (1860): 62–63. See E. Urbach, *Ba'ale ha-Tosafot*, 424; J. Dan's introduction to the facsimile of Taqu, *Ketav Tamim: Ketav Yad Paris* H711 (Jerusalem, 1984). Other figures targeted by Taqu (65, 73, 95) are Maimonides and Abraham ibn Ezra.

83. On the Pietist concept of *reẓon ha-Bore*, see H. Soloveitchik, "Three Themes in *Sefer Ḥasidim*," 313, 315, and note 8.

84. Y. Ta Shma, "Sifriyyatam shel ḥakhme Ashkenaz bene ha-meah ha-11–12," *Qiryat Sefer* 61 (1987): 298–309; Y. Ta Shma, "The Library of the French Sages," in *Rashi, 1040-1990*, 535–40.

85. Though the earliest known manuscripts of this—awkwardly composite—version of the Jerusalem Talmud's tractate *Sheqalim* are from eleventh-century Italy, this version has been described as "the accepted and authoritative version for sages of Ashkenaz" in the twelfth and thirteenth centuries, and Pietists were among the few early rabbis to write commentaries on it. Y. Sussman, "Masoret limud u-masoret nusaḥ shel ha-Talmud ha-Yerushalmi," in *Meḥqarim ba-Sifrut ha-Talmudit* (Jerusalem, 1983), 34–35 and n. 114.

86. Ibid., 39; cf. 42n130.

87. SḤ 1, 2. On the compilation of *Sefer Ḥasidim*, see I. Marcus, "The Recensions and Structure of *Sefer Ḥasidim*," *PAAJR* 45 (1978): 131–53; H. Soloveitchik, "Le-ta-arikh ḥiburo shel Sefer Ḥasidim," in *Tarbut ve-ḥevra be-Toldot Yisrael be-Yeme ha-Benayyim*, ed. R. Bonfil et al. (Jerusalem, 1989), 383–88.

88. A prominent example from late antiquity is an order issued by Emperor Justinian in 524, in which he exhorted the jurists charged with compiling the *Digest* from three older codes of law to "reshape" anything incorrectly expressed. H. Jolowicz, *Historical Introduction to the Study of Roman Law* (Cambridge, 1952), 491n1. Shraga Abramson compiled a list of geonic (and later medieval) texts that echo the sentiment of Rav Natan Av ha-Yeshiva, who had written, "Whomever encounters this compiled book [*ha-sefer ha-zeh ha-mequbbaẓ*] and sees in it some blemish [*pegam*], let him fill it in/close it up. Or if [he sees] a clear explanation, let him add to it." Shraga Abramson, "Mehem u-vahem," in *Sefer Sivan: Minḥat Zikkaron le-Shalom Sivan*, ed. A. Even-Shoshan (Jerusalem, 1979), 3–7.

89. B. Stock, *The Implications of Literacy: Written Language and Models of Interpretation in the Eleventh and Twelfth Centuries* (Princeton, N.J., 1983), 523; cf. 7.

90. "For this reason, *Sefer Ḥasidim* was written: to know what to do, and of what to be wary." SḤ 27.

91. Cf. B. Stock, *Implications of Literacy*, 90.

92. S. Spiegel, "Me-Aggadot ha'aqedah: Piyyut 'al sheḥitat Yiẓḥaq u-teḥiyyato le-Efrayim mi-Buna," *Alexander Marx Jubilee Volume* (New York, 1950), 471–574; rendered in English by Judah Goldin, *The Last Trial* (New York, 1967). Spiegel claimed somewhat

enigmatically (119 and cf. 120n158) that "the Jews had obviously gotten the habit anew from their neighbors."

93. I. Marcus, *Rituals of Childhood: Jewish Acculturation Medieval Europe* (New Haven, Conn., 1996).

94. Ibid., 16.

95. Ibid., 26–28.

96. On the impact of Pietist penitential theory and practice on subsequent Ashkenazi culture, see Y. Baer, "Ha-megama ha-datit ha-ḥevratit shel Sefer Ḥasidim," *Ẓion* 3 (1938): 50; J. Dan, "Goralah ha-histori shel torat ha-sod shel Ḥaside Ashkenaz," in *Meḥqarim ba-Qabbalah u-ve-Toldot ha-Datot Mugashim le-Gershom Scholem*, ed. R. J. Z. Werblowsky, C. Wirszubski, and E. E. Urbach (Jerusalem, 1968), 97–99; J. Elbaum, *Teshuvat ha-Lev ve-Qabbalat Yisurim* (Jerusalem, 1992), 12. Outside of Ashkenaz, the penitential teachings of *Ḥaside Ashkenaz* found their way into the writings of R. Aharon HaKohen of Lunel, R. Isaac of Corbeil, R. Israel Al-Naqqawa, R. Jacob b. Judah Ḥazan of London, R. Elijah da Vidas, R. Elazar Aziqri, R. Solomon Alqabeẓ, and R. Moses Cordovero, and into Sefardi *maḥzorim* of the sixteenth century. See Elbaum, *Teshuvat ha-Lev ve-Qabbalat Yisurim,* 37–40; Y. Dinari, *Ḥakhme Ashkenaz be-Shalhe Yeme ha-Benayyim* (Jerusalem, 1984), 85–93.

97. Y. Baer, "Ha-megama ha-datit ha-ḥevratit shel Sefer Ḥasidim," 18; G. Scholem, *Major Trends in Jewish Mysticism*, 96, 104–5; A. Rubin, "The Concept of Repentance among the *Ḥasidey Ashkenaz*," *Journal of Jewish Studies* 16 (1965): 161–76. While his remarks are oblique to the topic at hand, Ephraim E. Urbach noted the compatibility between the Rhineland Pietists' approach to self-mortification and their conception of martyrdom, and he upheld Baer's claim that "some new spirit" infused Jewish martyrology in medieval Ashkenaz. E. Urbach, "Eskesis ve-yisurim be-torat ḥazal," *Sefer Yovel le-Yiẓḥaq Baer* (Jerusalem, 1961), 67n99.

98. I. Marcus, *Piety and Society*, 150n54; I. Marcus, "Hierarchies, Religious Boundaries and Jewish Spirituality in Medieval Germany," *Jewish History* 1 (1986): 25n34; I. Marcus, "History, Story and Collective Memory: Narrativity in Early Ashkenazi Culture," 276n45; J. Dan, "Toratam ha-musarit ve-ha-ḥevratit shel Ḥaside Ashkenaz," *Tarbiẓ* 51 (1982): 319n5; J. Dan, "Le-toldot torat ha-teshuvah shel Ḥaside Ashkenaz," *Yovel Orot: Haguto shel HaRav Avraham Yiẓḥaq HaKohen Kook* (Jerusalem, 1985), 227; P. Schäfer, "The Ideal of Piety of the Ashkenazi Ḥasidim and Its Roots in Jewish Tradition," *Jewish History* 4 (1990): 10, 18. Cf. A. Grossman, "Ziqata shel yahadut Ashkenaz ha-qedumah el Ereẓ Yisrael," *Shalem* 3 (1981): 57–92; A. Grossman, *Ḥakhme Ashkenaz ha-Rishonim*, 424–35; Y. Ta Shma, review of the preceding volume, *Qiryat Sefer* 56 (1981): 344–52; Y. Ta Shma, *Minhag Ashkenaz ha-Qadmon*, 98 (esp. n.143), 102–3; R. Bonfil, "Bein Ereẓ Yisrael le-veyn Bavel," 21–22; R. Bonfil, "Can Medieval Storytelling Help Understanding Midrash? The Story of Paltiel," In *The Midrashic Imagination,* ed. Michael Fishbane (Albany, 1993), 234.

99. E. Urbach, "Eskesis ve-yisurim be-torat ḥazal," 48–68; M. Berr, "'Al ma'ase kapparah shel ba'ale teshuva be-sifrut ḥazal," *Ẓion* 46 (1981): 150–81; S. Fraade, "Ascetical

Aspects of Ancient Judaism," in *Jewish Spirituality*, ed. A. Green (New York, 1986), 1:253–88. Urbach asserts that these extreme acts should be seen as responses to specific historical events, and not as vestiges of ancient ascetic teachings. Notwithstanding tannaitic efforts to suppress extreme behaviors, ascetic tendencies proliferated in the wake of the destruction of the Second Temple and at the time of the Hadrianic persecutions.

100. SḤ 19. SḤ combines the talmudic account of Adam's three stages of penance, each lasting 130 years (BT 'Eruv. 18b), with *Pirqe de-Rabi Eliezer*'s account of Adam's penance in the river, where he stood for seven weeks "until his body became as porous as a sieve" (*Pirqe de-Rabi Eliezer*, 20). The latter motif is found in the Apocrypha of many regions, though both the duration of the penance (which was also undergone by Eve, who stood in a different river) and the identity of the rivers vary. See, e.g., "The Penance of Adam," in *Irish Biblical Apocrypha Irish Biblical Apocrypha: Selected Texts in Translation*, ed. Maire Herbert and Martin McNamara (Edinburgh, 1989), 8–11; "The Life of Adam and Eve," in *The Apocryphal Old Testament*, ed. H. F. D. Sparks (Oxford, 1984), 147–48. In light of its late dating, *Pirqe de-Rabi Eliezer*'s relationship to apocryphal traditions regarding the penance of Adam (and the direction of cultural influence) requires further study.

101. SḤ 38; BT Ber. 56a. And see the discussion of exile's effect on atonement in BT San. 37b.

102. SḤ 18. On Naḥum of Gamzu, see BT Ta'an. 21a; on Yaqim of Ẓerorot who subjected himself to the four death penalties, see BR 65:27, 742, in the Theodor-Albeck edition. Baer observed that medieval Pietists consciously modeled themselves on the early *ḥasidim* mentioned in classical rabbinic sources.

103. This question directly parallels one posed by Marcus in his challenge to Baer's hypothesis of Christian influence on Ashkenazi Pietism. Observing that Latin penitentials had been in existence for centuries and were used in many lands, Marcus wondered why Christian penitential practices would have had such influence only on Jewish culture in the specific time and place that Rhineland Pietism flourished. Marcus, *Piety and Society*, 150n54; J. Dan, "Toratam ha-musarit ve-ha-ḥevratit shel Ḥaside Ashkenaz," 310n5.

104. T. Alexander, "Le-darkhei 'iẓuv ha-sipur ha-Ḥasidi-Ashkenazi," 197–223.

105. A. Rubin, "The Concept of Repentance among the *Ḥasidey Ashkenaz*," 165–66.

106. BT Yom. 86b and SḤ 43.

107. The quote is from SḤ 43, in A. Rubin, "The Concept of Repentance among the *Ḥasidey Ashkenaz*," 164–65. It is perhaps for similar reasons that Maimonides (MT, Hil. Teshuva, 2:1) understood *teshuvah ha-ba-ah* as the fullest form of repentance, calling it "*teshuvah gemurah*."

108. According to BT AZ 17b, when R. Ḥanina and R. Jonathan reached a fork in the road and were forced to choose between walking past a place of idolatry or a place of harlotry, one sage opted for the former route, since the appetite for idolatry was reputed to have been eradicated. However, the other sage (whose opinion held sway) suggested that they walk past the place of harlotry in order to be able to "defy our inclination and have our reward." In a similar vein, it is possible that a midrashic passage defining the

ability to withstand enormous sexual temptation as a standard of faith could conceivably have been transformed into a test of faith: "And the greatest of the faithful, who is he? . . . A bachelor who lives in the neighborhood of prostitutes and does not sin." *Midrash Tanḥuma Yelammedenu* on Gen. 40:1.

109. G. W. H. Lampe, *A Patristic Greek Lexicon* (Oxford, 1961).

110. L. Gougaud, "Mulierum Consortia: Etude sur le Syneisaktisme chez les Ascetes Celtiques," *Eriu* 9 (1921–23), 155.

111. See, for example, the twelfth-century biographies of S. Aldhelm of Malmesbury (d. 709), a bishop of Sherbourne in contact with the Irish, which describe his heroic chastity. L. Gougaud, "Mulierum Consortia: Etude sur le Syneisaktisme chez les Ascetes Celtiques," 147–56. Gougaud (152 and n. 3) traced the origins of *syneisaktism*, like most other eyebrow-raising medieval Christian penances, to older Irish penitential practices. Cf. P. Brown, *The Body and Society: Men, Women, and Sexual Renunciation in Early Christianity* (New York, 1988), 266–67.

112. The testimonies of Marbode, Bishop of Rennes, and of Geoffrey, Abbot of Trinité de Vendôme (both of which appear in Migne's *PL*), are cited in L. Gougaud, "Mulierum Consortia: Etude sur le Syneisaktisme chez les Ascetes Celtiques," 147–56. And see E. Werner, "Zur Frauenfrage und Frauenkultur im Mittelalter: Robert von Arbrissel und Fontevrault," *Forschungen und Fortschritte* 29 (1955): 272; E. McLaughlin, "Equality of Souls, Inequality of Sexes: Women in Medieval Theology," *Religion and Sexism*, ed. R. Ruether (New York, 1974), 240.

113. David of Augsburg, *De Exterioris et Interioris Hominis Compositione*, trans. Dominic Devas in *Spiritual Life and Progress* (London, 1937), 2:9, cited in A. Rubin, "The Concept of Repentance among the *Ḥasidey Ashkenaz*," 166n21.

114. Burchard's *Decretum* was executed with the help of Bishop Walter of Speyer. Prior to his appointment as Bishop of Worms in the year 1000, Burchard was in the service of the Archbishop of Mainz. F. J. Schaefer, "Burchard of Worms," *Catholic Encyclopedia* (New York, 1908), 3:64.

115. Over the course of four hundred years (from the seventh through the eleventh centuries), the Church officially opposed penitential literature, which had begun infiltrating the European mainland from Ireland around the year 600. Irish penitential tracts represented—and successfully propagated—an approach to penance that deviated in a number of ways from the older, ecclesiastically formulated system of canonical penance. On the place of Irish penitentials on the European continent, see T. N. Tentler, *Sin and Confession on the Eve of the Reformation* (Princeton, N.J., 1977), 3–9; J. T. McNeill, *The Celtic Penitentials and Their Influence on Continental Christianity* (Paris, 1923), chap. 5.

116. E.g., where Burchard took up a text on fornication found in the Bede-Egbert Double Penitential (2:135), he inscribed it as "*ex concilio Meledensi.*" *Decretum* 9:68; PL 140.826D, cited in Pierre Payer, *Sex in the Penitentials: The Development of a Sexual Code, 550–1150* (Toronto, 1984), 73, 82. Irish monks (among them an eleventh-century monk-historian who spent his final years as an *inclusus* in Mainz) appear to have been well-known figures in many cities in the Rhineland where they controlled churches in the

tenth and eleventh centuries. On Marianus Scottus (= Mael-Brigte), see J. F. Kenney, *Sources for the Early History of Ireland I: Ecclesiastical* (New York, 1929), 615; K. Hughes, *The Church in Early Irish Society* (Ithaca, N.Y., 1966), 254; Anne-Dorothee von den Brincken, "Marianus Scottus als Universalhistoriker iuxta veritatem evangelii," *Die Iren und Europa im fruheren Mittelalter*, ed. H. Lowe (Stuttgart, 1982), 2:97–109. On Irish monks in Ratisbone, Cologne, Fulda, Wurzburg, and Mainz, see Kenney, *Sources for the Early History of Ireland*, 608–18; D. A. Binchy, "Irish Benedictine Congregation in Medieval Germany," *Studies* 18 (1929): 194–210; A. Gwynn, "Irish Monks and the Cluniac Reform," *Studies* 29 (1940): 409–30.

117. The work itself, in the words of one researcher, "reflects northern Europe's accommodation to the laxity of the penitentials." T. N. Tentler, *Sin and Confession on the Eve of the Reformation*, 17n15.

118. "The *Decretum* was not simply one collection among many; it tended to dominate the canonical tradition of the eleventh century." Payer, *Sex in the Penitentials: The Development of a Sexual Code*, 83.

119. Payer, *Sex in the Penitentials: The Development of a Sexual Code*, 189n54; P. Fournier, "De quelques collections canoniques issues du Decret de Burchard," *Melange Paul Fabre: Etudes d'histoire du moyen age* (Paris, 1902), 189–214. Robert Grossteste's thirteenth-century work contains an interrogatory which depends on Burchard.

120. See E. J. Hobsbawm and T. Ranger, ed., *The Invention of Tradition* (Cambridge, 1992).

121. SḤ 673. It is not clear to me whether, in this locution, *Sefer Ḥasidim* intends to refer to the earlier use of "phantom texts."

122. M. Beit Arié, "Ideals versus Reality: Scribal Prescriptions in *Sefer Ḥasidim* and Contemporary Scribal Practices in Franco-German Manuscripts," in *Rashi, 1040–1990*, 560; C. Sirat, ed., *La Conception du Livre chez les Piétistes Ashkenazes du Moyen Âge* (Geneva, 1996). Cf. C. Sirat, "Les rouleaux bibliques de Qumran au Moyen Age: Du livre au Sefer Tora, de l'oreille a l'oeil," *Comptes rendus de l'Academie des Inscriptions et Belles Lettres* (1991): 415–32; C. Sirat, "Orality/Literacy, Languages, Alphabets: Example of the Jewish People," *Proceedings of the Workshop on Orality vs. Literacy: Concepts, Methods and Data*, ed. C. Pontecorvo and C. Blanche-Benveniste, *ESF Scientific Networks* (1993), 49–88.

123. Some of this material is collected in units with the subheadings "The Subject of Books" and "More on the Subject of Books," in the Freimann-Wistinetzki edition, based on the Parma manuscript of *Sefer Ḥasidim*, 171–89, secs. 638–746; 417, 1739–63.

124. Among the details that emerge, for example are that scribes read aloud while copying from another manuscript, and that copyists were paid by the quire.

125. See SḤ 1748 regarding rented manuscripts of Talmud. SḤ 868 (and cf. SḤ 603) refer to an environment in which Christians pledged Latin books when they borrowed from Jewish moneylenders, and Jews left Hebrew books as collateral when they procured loans from Christians. On the presence of Hebrew promissory jottings in Latin books and of Latin promissory jottings in medieval Hebrew manuscripts, see C. Sirat, *La Conception du Livre chez les Piétistes Ashkenazes du Moyen Âge* (Geneva, 1996), 13. Jews learned the

craft of binding in monastic ateliers, and bound Latin books during their apprenticeship. Pietists were suspicious that Christian binders of Hebrew books might trim parchment margins in order to use them for writing their own *sefarim pesulim* (improper books), but these fears did not prevent them from employing expert Christian journeymen for this purpose, as is seen in SḤ 681–82 and SḤ 668. SḤ 513 stipulates that, when arranging a pack animal's saddlebags, one may not place *sefarim* on one side in order to balance out the load of *sefarim pesulim* on the other, nor may *sefarim* and *sefarim pesulim* be placed in the same book cabinet.

126. SḤ 710 prohibits the practice of inverting the order of words by writing an *aleph* over one word and a *bet* over another—to indicate needed corrections.

127. SḤ 700, 703, 705, 706, 707. See M. Beit Arié, "How Scribes Disclosed Their Names by Means of Their Copied Text," in *Meah She'arim: 'Iyyunim be-'Olamam ha-Ruḥani shel Yisrael bi-Yeme ha-Benayyim, le-Zekher Yizḥaq Twersky*, ed. Ezra Fleisher, Yaaqov Blidstein, Carmi Horowitz, and Bernard Septimus (Jerusalem, 2001), 113–29; M. Beit Arié, "Ideals versus Reality," 563–64.

128. See, e.g., BT Ber. 19b; Shab. 21b; Shab. 94b; 'Eruv. 41b; Meg. 3b; Men. 38a; BK 79b. The author of *Sefer Ḥuqqei ha-Torah*, a medieval work that describes a quasi-monastic pedagogic environment, emphasizes the importance of this principle, as cited in *Beit Yosef* on YD 282. On *Sefer Ḥuqqei ha-Torah*, see E. Kanarfogel, *Jewish Education and Society in the High Middle Ages*, 101–5; E. Kanarfogel, "A Monastic-like Setting for the Study of Torah," in *Judaism in Practice*, ed. L. Fine (Princeton, N.J., 2001), 191–202.

129. Among these are stipulations that both a *sefer* and its case must be saved from a conflagration that breaks out on the Sabbath, when a fire may not be extinguished, and that just as worn-out Torah scrolls must be handled in a particular manner, so must their wrappings, cases, and other accoutrements. Rabbinic sources of antiquity enumerate the conditions under which a Torah scroll may be sold, and what may be purchased in its stead; the requisite number and types of coverings in which a scroll must be sheltered if taken into an inappropriate place (e.g., a lavatory, bathouse, or cemetery), and the physical distance from the dead that must be maintained when ritually reading from a Torah scroll. One is forbidden to sit on a bed on which a Torah scroll lies or to have sexual intercourse in a house that contains one, unless the scroll is encased in extra covers that were not explicitly designed for its containment, or unless it is ensconced behind a sheltering wall of a particular height. One whose hands are dirty may not touch the Torah before washing, but the ritually impure (e.g., menstruants) are permitted to hold the Torah scroll and to read from it (!), since "matters of Torah do not contract ritual impurity." The Torah scroll must be housed in a dedicated space appropriate to its grandeur, and it must be transported with dignity. Jews must stand upon seeing it raised or carried, and, whenever in its presence, comport themselves with modesty and reverence. The Talmud also conveys a sense of the hierarchy of sanctity in stipulating, for example, that an inscription of prophetic writings may not be placed upon an inscription of Pentateuch (BT Meg. 27). See the material collected in S. Assaf, "'Am ha-sefer ve-ha-sefer," in *Be-Ohole Ya'aqov* (Jerusalem, 1943), 1–26.

130. In an era that witnessed the growing use of codices, the late eighth- or ninth-century tractates *Massekhet Sefer Torah* and *Massekhet Sofrim* added a number of prescriptions that range from regulations regarding the creation of ritually valid Torah scrolls to the stipulation that only the right hand may be used in passing *sefarim* from one to another. Cf. R. Langer, "Shelavim qedumim be-hitpatḥuta shel hotza-at ha-torah ve-hakhnasata be-vet ha-knesset be-yeme ha-benayyaim: 'Iyyun be-teqasim shel Seder Rav 'Amram Gaon u-Massekhet Sofrim," *Kenishta* 2 (2003): 99–118. The debate over whether Jews used codices before the Moslem conquest is helpfully summarized in C. Hezser, *Jewish Literacy in Roman Palestine* (Tübingen, 2001), 143–44. Colette Sirat, Stephan Reif, and Malachi Beit Arié have posited that Jews refrained from the use of codices prior to the Moslem conquest in order to distinguish their writings from those of Christians, while Meir Bar Ilan claims that Jews did use codices in earlier centuries, though only for *megilot setarim*.

131. The prescriptions that had accrued through the twelfth century are codified in Maimonides, *Mishneh Torah*, Hil. Sefer Torah, chap. 10. On R. Judah the Pietist's familiarity with Maimonides' *Mishneh Torah*—from which SḤ quotes verbatim—see S. Assaf, "'Am ha-sefer," in *Be-Ohole Ya'aqov*, 17.

132. Other passages in *Sefer Ḥasidim* warn against behaviors that display disrespect for *sefarim*. Thus, for example, SḤ 661 instructs the reader not to place one book upon another to keep its pages open, lest he derive benefit from *bizayon ha-sefer*. Though SḤ 665 does not refer explicitly either to *kevod ha-sefer* or to *bizayon ha-sefer*, it cautions against utter disparaging remarks about the quality or price of a *sefer* when surveying it for possible purchase.

133. On Abraham ibn Daud's claim that Mishnah and Talmud "are also sacred writings," see Chapter 2.

134. Y. Sussman has affirmed this point in "'Torah she-be-'al peh'—peshutah ke-mashma'ah: Koḥo shel qoẓo shel yod," *Meḥqere Talmud* 3 (2005): 209–384.

135. C. Wilke, "Les degrés de la sainteté des livres," in C. Sirat, ed., *La Conception du Livre chez les Piétistes Ashkenazes du Moyen Âge*, 47. Among these are the prohibitions against sitting on a bench on which a *sefer* lies and against resting a *sefer* on the ground, and the injunctions to pick up a fallen *sefer* and to right an overturned one and kiss it. When passing a *sefer* to another, one must extend it in his right hand, rather than his left, and when two people pass through an entryway, the one carrying a *sefer* must proceed first. *Sefarim* must be rescued from fire or flood before other precious objects. See SḤ 275, 523, and cf. BT Ber. 43b; Yom. 39a, *Massekhet Sofrim* 3:10; *Liqutei Maharil*, 118b; R. Yosef Qaro, *Beit Yosef*, YD 282; R. Moses Isserles, *Shulḥan 'Arukh*, YD 282.

136. According to SḤ 487 and SḤ 1745, just as myrrh and other fragrant herbs are to be placed in the ark containing the Torah scroll and under the scroll's mantle, so they are to be placed in one's bookshelf .

137. SḤ 698.

138. A talmudic passage (BT Meg. 27a) prescribing which texts may and may not be placed upon which others articulates a clear hierarchy of sanctity, ranging from the Torah scroll on top to the Pentateuch to compilations of the Prophets and Hagiographa.

139. Distinctions between the treatment to be accorded scriptural writings found in scroll form and in codex form were discussed by R. Asher ben Yeḥiel, R. Solomon ben Adret, R. Meshullam of Beziers, and his student R. Manoaḥ, the Mordecai, and the fourteenth-century author of the *Hagahot Maimunmiyyot*. See *Beit Yosef*, Tur, YD 282, 246–47.

140. Interestingly, the same passage sets forth an inverted hierarchy of scholarship, declaring that talmudists take precedence over students of Scripture ("*ba'ale Talmud qodmin le-lomed miqra*").

141. A discussion of the propriety of placing texts of Gemara and of its commentaries in a cabinet that had held a Torah scroll also appears in rabbinic writings of Provence. See the citation from the Provençal scholar, R. Elazar of Tarasconne, in N. Danzig, "Mi-talmud 'al peh le-talmud be-khtav," *Sefer ha-Shana Bar Ilan* 30–31 (2006): 108.

142. It is for this very reason that Rabbi Judah the Pietist pointedly refers to *Sefer Ḥasidim* as a "*sefer*" (SḤ 27). His own compilation is authoritative, he writes, not because it is a written communication aid, but because it is inherently sacred.

143. The fifteenth-century kabbalistic text *Sefer ha-Qanah*, a dialogue between pupil and teacher, offers a particularly stark expression of this logophobic perspective. Its learned excurses expose the logical inconsistencies of amoraic dialectics to vicious ridicule, in order to demonstrate that the Talmud's semantic dimension could not possibly have anything to do with its authority. Rather, claims the teacher, Oral Torah is authoritative because of its ontological status, its origins in the Celestial Academy. See T. Fishman, "A Kabbalistic Perspective on Gender-Speecific Commandments: On the Interplay between Symbol and Society," *AJS Review* 17 (1992): 199–245.

144. Cf. the suggestive remarks in S. Jaeger, *Envy of Angels*, 190–92.

145. Scholarship pertaining to the *Maysebukh* is cited above.

146. Drawing on ancient traditions like those recorded in BT Ber. 56a and San. 37b, SḤ 38 identified voluntary, self-imposed exile as a form of penance. This practice, along with other extreme forms of atonement, was targeted by the thirteenth-century Provençal rabbi Jacob Anatoli, who decried it as alien to Judaism. Jacob Anatoli, *Sefer Malmad ha-Talmidim* (Lyck, 1866), 174b, and cf. M. Saperstein, "Christians and Christianity in the Sermons of Jacob Anatoli," 232. Irish monks conceived of the practice of voluntary exile as "an attempt to live out the image of the Christian life as a journey in an alien land between birth and death." P. Geary, *Before France and Germany: The Creation and Transformation of the Merovingian World* (New York, 1988), 170.

147. This appears (in English translation) in Moses Gaster, *Ma'aseh Book* (Philadelphia, 1934), 317–19, and is cited in I. Marcus, "History, Story and Collective Memory: Narrativity in Early Ashkenazic Culture," 266. Cf. S. Ẓfatman, "Ma'aseh Bukh: Qavim le-demuto shel zhaner be-sifrut yiddish ha-yeshanah," *Ha-Sifrut* 28 (1979): 132.

148. The inclusion of charters in tactile and auditory rituals (like placing the pen, ink, and parchment on the land to be sold, or recitation of the charter by the donors) imbued the documents in question with sacred authority. B. Bedos-Rezak, "The Confrontation of Orality and Textuality: Jewish and Christian Literacy in Eleventh- and Twelfth-

Century Northern France," in *Rashi, 1040–1990*, 549; B. Bedos-Rezak, "Diplomatic Sources and Medieval Documentary Practices: An Essay in Interpretive Methodology," in *The Past and Future of Medieval Studies*, ed. John Van Engen (Notre Dame, Ind., 1994), 321–24, 339n23.

149. Though the strategies are analogous, the case of the Pietists is probably not similar to that of Christian monks, for the latter's sacralization of mundane documents seems to have been intertwined with the loss of their monopoly on inscription. When the Cathedral Schools established at the time of the Gregorian Reform offered non-monastic clerics training in the skills of book copying and book production, monks were deprived of an important power base. See the articles by B. Bedos-Rezak cited in the previous note. At this stage of research there is no reason to assume that Rhineland Pietists (or their predecessors) had played any analogous role as the copyists or book producers within Jewish society.

150. On the *maḥzorim* written by R. Ya'aqov ben R. Shimshon, R. Shemaiah, and R. Azriel ben Natan, see A. Grossman, *Ḥakhme Ẓorfat ha-Rishonim* (Jerusalem, 1995), 395–403, 417, 532–33. Rashi's central place in the crystallization of *Maḥzor Vitry*, compiled by Simḥa of Vitry in the 1130s, is emphasized in Y. Ta Shma, *Ha-Tefilah ha-Ashkenazit ha-Qedumah* (Jerusalem, 2003), 17, 50. See also S. Reif, "Rashi and Proto-Ashkenazi Liturgy," in *Rashi, 1040–1990*, 445–54.

151. On prayer's locus within the category of *oral matters*, see YT Shab. 15c; BT Shab. 115b.

152. See Chapter 4.

153. According to Ta Shma, the Pietist attack was directed specifically against *Maḥzor Vitry*. Ta Shma, *Ha-Tefilah ha-Ashkenazit ha-Qedumah*, 27, 51, and elsewhere.

154. See the Bologna recension of Judah ben Samuel, *Sefer Ḥasidim*, ed. R. Margalioth (Jerusalem, 1957), 81.

155. Isaac b"r Moshe, *Sefer Or Zaru'a* (Zhitomir, 1862), 1:115.

156. SḤ 785. Cf. Y. Ta Shma, *Ha-Tefilah ha-Ashkenazit ha-Qedumah*, 33–34.

157. Speculating about the focus of this arcane prayer praxis, Yosef Dan asked what engaged worshippers were supposed to do in order for their prayers to be ritually effective. Y. Dan, "Sefer 'Arugat ha-Bosem le-Rabi Avraham b"r 'Azriel," in Y. Dan, *'Iyyunim be-Sifrut Ḥasidut Ashkenaz* (Ramat Gan, 1975), 66. Yisrael Ta Shma wondered why this "numeric method" was articulated and preserved only in the circles of Rabbi Judah the Pietist. Y. Ta Shma, *Ha-Tefilah ha-Ashkenazit ha-Qedumah*, 47–51.

158. SḤ 1575.

159. The time-consuming nature of this practice is corroborated in a query posed to Rabbi Judah the Pietist by Rabbi Barukh of Mainz. Sensitive to the fact that proper performance of the Pietist technique breached the halakhically prescribed times of prayer (not to mention social etiquette), Rabbi Barukh was particularly concerned about its unwanted consequences during specific occasions of communal worship, specifically Pesaḥ, Shavuot, and weddings. "For sometimes," wrote Rabbi Barukh, "*qeriat shema*' lasts three hours [when performing this praxis], and thus the proper time for reciting *qeriat shema*'

passes!" Preserved by Shimshon b"r Ẓadoq, cited in Meir ben Barukh, *Teshuvot Pesaqim u-Minhagim*, ed. Y. Z. Kahana (Jerusalem, 1967), 1:146, sec. 50.

160. First and second-century Romans who allude to this practice include Plautus, Juvenal, Quintilian, Pliny, Suetonius, Apuleius, and Sidonius Apollinarus. Jerome and Augustine were among the Christians of the Roman Empire who referred to finger-reckoning in their theological writings. For sources, see E. Bechtel, "Finger-Counting among the Romans in the Fourth Century," *Classical Philology* 4 (1909): 25–31. Early evidence of finger-reckoning outside the Roman world is discussed in a prodigiously cross-cultural study of systems used for numeric notation and computation. S. Gandz, "The Origin of the Ghubar Numerals, or the Arabian Abacus and the Articuli," *Isis* 16 (1931): 393–424. On the persistence of this practice in the Middle Ages, see Riché, *Education and Culture in the Barbarian West, Sixth through Eighth Centuries* (Columbia, 1976), 476–77nn192–93; W. Levison, "St. Boniface and Cryptography," in *England and the Continent in the Eighth Century*, ed. Wilhelm Levison (Oxford, 1946), 290–94; B. Bischoff, "Übersicht über die nichtdiplomatischen Geheimschriften des Mittelalters," *Mitteilungen Institut für österreichische Geschichtsforschung* (*MIOEG*) 62 (1954): 1–27; Charles W. Jones, ed., *Bedae: Opera de Temporibus* (Cambridge, Mass., 1943), 329; M. C. Welborn, "Lotharingia as a Center of Arabic and Scientific Influence in the Eleventh Century," *Isis* 17 (1932): 260–63.

161. Riché, *Education and Culture in the Barbarian West*, 476–77; E. M. Sanford, "De loquela digitorum," *Classical Journal* 23 (1928): 588–93.

162. The work proposed a novel method for determining the much-disputed date of Easter. On early Christian controversies over the date of Easter, see Jones, ed., *Bedae: Opera de Temporibus*, introduction, 3–122.

163. C. W. Jones, *Bedae Pseudepigrapha* (Ithaca, N.Y., 1939), reprinted in C. W. Jones, *Bede, the Schools and the Computus* (Brookfield, Vermont, 1994), appendix, 53–54; Jones, *Bedae: Opera de Temporibus*, 329–30.

164. Charles Jones describes 133 manuscripts of Bede's *De Temporum Ratione* in *Bedae: Opera de Temporibus*, 140–61. On the manuscripts that contained only the first chapter of this work, see C. W. Jones, *Bede, the Schools and the Computus*, 54.

165. Bede the Venerable, *Bedae: Opera de Temporibus*, 179–82; I. Grattan-Guiness, *The Norton History of the Mathematical Sciences* (New York, 1998), 129; G. Friedlein, *Die Zahlzeichen und das elementare Rechnen der Griechen und Römer und des christlichen Abendländes vom 7. bis 13. Jahrhundert* (Erlangen, 1869).

166. See S. Gandz, "The Origin of the Ghubar Numerals, or the Arabian Abacus and the *Articuli*," 401; J. Ruska, "Arabische Texte über das Fingerrechnen," *Der Islam* 10 (1920): 87–119.

167. G. Sarton, *Introduction to the History of Science* (Baltimore, 1962), 1:529.

168. These circumstances account for many of the rabbinic deliberations discussed in two recent books by Haym Soloveitchik: *Yeynam* and *Ha-Yayin be-Yeme ha-Beinayyim*.

169. In Judah ben Barzilai, *Perush Sefer Yeẓirah*, ed. S. J. Halberstamm (Berlin, 1885), 142–43. The next sentence in ben Barzilai's (=al-Barceloni's) commentary is particularly intriguing: "Since no masters of computation, like managers [*gizbarin*], and business ac-

countants [*sofre melakhot*], and treasurers [*u-memunei oẓarot*] and geometers [*ve-khol ba'ale handasa*] have the right to add upon one hundred thousand, which are ten myriads." This passage appears in a slightly different English translation in S. Gandz, "The Origin of the Ghubar Numerals, or the Arabian Abacus and the Articuli," 397–98n16. Gandz notes (397) that while al-Barceloni also refers to use of the abacus (*Perush Sefer Yeẓirah*, 140), this computational method should not be confused or conflated with finger-reckoning.

170. See J. Dan, "The Emergence of Mystical Prayer," *in Studies in Jewish Mysticism*, ed. J. Dan and F. Talmage (Cambridge, Mass., 1982), 88–89. Cf. J. Dan, "Le-demuto ha-historit shel Rabi Yehudah he-Ḥasid," in *Tarbut ve-Ḥevrah: Qoveẓ Ma-amarim le-Zikhro shel Ḥayyim Hillel Ben Sasson* (Jerusalem, 1989), 389–98; Y. Ta Shma, "Quntres Sodot ha-Tefilah le-Rabi Yehudah HeḤasid," *Tarbiẓ* 65 (1996): 65–77; Y. Ta Shma, *Ha-Tefilah ha-Ashkenazit ha-Qedumah*, 50. And see Elazar ben Judah, *Perushe Sidur ha-Tefilah la-Roqeaḥ*, ed. Moshe and Yehudah Hershler (Jerusalem, 1992). (This volume, a pastiche of various manuscripts, conveys the flavor of Pietist prayer interpretation, but is not a critical edition.) On the identity of this work, see A. Grossman, *Ḥakhme Ashkenaz ha-Rishonim*, 346–48. On the relationship between this work and Rabbi Judah the Pietist's larger oeuvre of prayer commentary, see J. Dan, "Sefer ha-Ḥokhmah le-Rav Elazar mi-Vorms u-mashma'uto le-toldot torato shel Ḥasidut Ashkenaz," in *'Iyyunim be-Sifrut Ḥasidut Ashkenaz* (Ramat Gan, 1975), 50n33.

171. Elazar ben Judah, *Perushe Sidur ha-Tefilah la-Roqeaḥ*, 312. The reference to "hooks and clasps" is from Ex. 26:10–11 (where it describes the linking hardware on the portable tabernacle) and it recurs in the writings of Rabbi Judah the Pietist. See Y. Dan, *Torat ha-Sod shel Ḥasidut Ashkenaz* 76–77; I. Marcus, "Exegesis for the Few and for the Many: Judah He-Ḥasid's Biblical Commentaries," *Meḥqere Yerushalayim be-Maḥshevet Yisrael* 8 (1989): 17–18.

172. The former is a commentary on both the fixed prayers (*tefilot qeva'*) and the *piyyutim*, the novelty liturgical poems artfully crafted in Palestine sometime between the late sixth and the eighth centuries, in conformance with occasion and form-specific conventions. The latter is primarily a commentary on the *piyyutim*. See Y. Ta Shma, *Ha-Tefilah ha-Ashkenazit ha-Qedumah*, 49.

173. There are actually nineteen blessings. See C. Adler, "Shemoneh Esreh," in *Jewish Encyclopedia* (New York, 1901–6), vol. 11. http://www.jewishencyclopedia.com/view.jsp?artid = 612&letter = S

174. I am unable to explain the numerical error in the italicized phrase.

175. *Gen. R.* 69:7.

176. Elazar ben Judah, *Perushe Sidur ha-Tefilah la-Roqeaḥ*, 1:365–66.

177. In describing a Pietist work that applies *gematria* to biblical studies, Yisrael Ta Shma noted its "method of weaving from one matter to another—from any given saying, scriptural or rabbinic, to matters of magic, demons and spirits and other widespread beliefs, and from there to matters of aggadah and their explanation—by tying them to some *gematria* value." Y. Ta Shma, introduction to *Sefer Gematriyyot le-Rabi Yehudah he-Ḥasid*, ed. Daniel Abrams (Los Angeles, 1998), 19–20.

178. Y. Dan, "Sefer 'Arugat ha-Bosem le-Rabi Avraham b"r 'Azriel," in Y. Dan, *'Iyyunim be-Sifrut Ḥasidut Ashkenaz*, 65.

179. Avraham ben 'Azriel, *'Arugat Ha-Bosem*, ed. E. E. Urbach, 4:91; cf. 102.

180. On the construction of mnemonic springboards in ancient Jewish tradition, see S. Naeh, "Omanut ha-zikkaron: Mivnim shel zikkaron ve-tavniyyot shel teqst be-sifrut ḥazal," *Meḥqere Talmud* 3 (2005): 543–89. On this activity in Christian culture, see M. Carruthers, *The Book of Memory*; M. Carruthers, *The Craft of Thought* (New York, 1998).

181. M. Carruthers, *The Craft of Thought*, 34.

182. On the numerical exegesis of Jerome and Augustine, see E. Bechtel, "Finger Counting among the Romans in the Fourth Century," 25–31. Isidore of Seville's seventh-century *Liber Numerorum* appears in *PL* 83; 179–180; 82: 155.

183. J. Leclercq, *Love of Learning*; M. Carruthers, *The Book of Memory*; M. Carruthers, *The Craft of Thought*. See also Meyvaert, "Medieval Monastic Claustrum," *Gesta* 12 (1973): 53–59.

184. M. Carruthers, *Craft of Thought*, 34.

185. Bible scholars are of the opinion that the word *ravḥati* may be the result of a scribal error in which the initial letter *ẓadi* was replaced by a *resh*. According to this hypothesis, the intended word was "*le-ẓavḥati*," "to my scream." Attempts have also been made to explain *ravḥati* as "expiration," from the root "ruaḥ." On these possibilities, see *Enẓiqlopedya 'Olam ha-Tanakh* (Tel Aviv, 1982), vol. 164, 148. I am grateful to Professor Jeff Tigay for this reference.

186. The hapax legomenon *ravḥati* (my groan) may also be related to "space," in that exhalation creates space in the lungs. See, e.g., Ex. 8:11, "And Pharaoh saw that there was *harvaḥa*" (in the JPS translation, "relief").

187. Rhineland Pietists inscribed the *Shi'ur Qoma* traditions, thereby making these and other esoteric traditions accessible to subsequent generations of Jews who were not privy to their oral transmission. On this topic, see K. Hermann, "Re-Written Mystical Texts: The Transmission of the Heikhalot Literature in the Middle Ages," *Bulletin of the John Rylands University Library* 75 (1993): 97–116; D. Abrams, "*Ma'aseh Merkabah* as a Literary Work: The Reception of *Hekhalot* Traditions by the German Pietists and Kabbalistic Reinterpretation," *JSQ* 5 (1998): 329–45.

188. Michael Fried, "Art and Objecthood," *Artforum* 5 (1967): 15.

189. See the reflections on exaggeration and its meaning in Susan Stewart, *On Longing* (Durham, N.C., 1993), 3–36, 70–103.

190. M. Carruthers, *Craft of Thought*, 23, 272.

191. In a posthumously published essay, Gerson Cohen claimed that Ashkenazic commentary on liturgical poems ("non-classical texts," as he pointed out) brought a "virtually new genre of Hebrew literature" into being. G. Cohen, "The Hebrew Crusade Chronicles and the Ashkenaz Tradition," *Minḥah le-Naḥum: Biblical and Other Studies Presented to Naḥum M. Sarna*, , ed. M. Brettler and M. Fishbane (Sheffield, 1993), 46–47.

192. For example, in his commentary on Qalir's *siluq*, "*Elohim al dami lakh ke-qol mayyim rabim*," Menaḥem b"r Ḥelbo referred to a particular verse from Psalms by invok-

ing its word count: seventeen. This *siluq* appears in *Sefer 'Avodat Yisrael*, ed. R. Isaac Seligmann Baer (Rödelheim, 1868), 669–72. Menahem b"r Ḥelbo's commentary is discussed in A. Grossman, *Ḥakhme Ẓorfat ha-Rishonim*, chaps. 6 and 9, esp. 528.

193. The following brief example is from a comment on the *'Amidah* prayer: "When you count all the blessings [in the *'Amidah*], from [the opening] '*Barukh*' [of the first blessing] to the end of the blessing, such as 'Blessed are You God, Shield of Abraham,' 'Blessed are You God, Resurrector of the dead,' 'Blessed are You God, the consecrated Lord,' and so all the others, it [the total] will be 113 words, which corresponds to [the number of words] from [1 Sam 2:1] "*my heart exults*" until [1 Sam. 2:10] '*the horn of His annointed one*'—which is 113 words. And the word 'heart' appears 113 times in the Pentateuch, in order that the heart give intent to prayer." Elazar ben Judah, *Perushe Sidur ha-Tefilah la-Roqeaḥ*, 364.

194. As Urbach pointed out, Judah the Pietist was actually a liturgical innovator, given his criticism of prayer variants that had been used in Ashkenaz since geonic times, and his attack on a prayer formulation authorized by his father, Rabbi Samuel. Avraham ben Azriel, *Sefer 'Arugat ha-Bosem*, ed., E. E. Urbach, 4:147–49.

195. Cited in ibid., 4:97; J. Dan, "The Emergence of Mystical Prayer," 88–89. Cf. J. Dan, "Le-demuto ha-historit shel R. Yehudah he-Ḥasid," 389–98; Y. Ta Shma, "Quntres Sodot ha-Tefilah le-Rabi Yehudah HeḤasid," 65–77; Y. Ta Shma, *Ha-Tefilah ha-Ashkenazit ha-Qedumah*, 50. See Elazar ben Judah, *Perushe Sidur ha-Tefilah la-Roqeaḥ*, 287–88. On the identity of this work, see A. Grossman, *Ḥakhme Ashkenaz ha-Rishonim*, 346–48. The Pietist's final dig warrants further analysis: "For if this were not so, then our prayer, God forbid, would be like the melody [*zemer*] of the uncircumcised gentiles." Avraham b. 'Azriel, *Sefer 'Arugat ha-Bosem*, ed. Urbach, 4:97. Cf. SḤ 550, end, 154.

196. In BT Meg. 31b, the rabbis declared prayer a substitute for sacrifice in the Temple's absence, in keeping with Hosea 14:3, "Instead of bulls, we will offer [the offering of] our lips."

197. See Y. Ta Shma, *Ha-Tefilah ha-Ashkenazit ha-Qedumah*, 50.

198. M. Jennings, "Tutivillus: The Literary Career of the Recording Demon," *Studies in Philology* 74 (1977): 5. M. T. Clanchy, *From Memory to Written Record*, 187. Cf. SḤ 733.

199. Yiẓḥaq Shimshon Lange corrected the impression that R. Meir of Rothenburg (mid-fourteenth century) was the earliest known tradent of Masorah commentary (having taught it to R. Asher ben Yeḥiel, who transmitted it to his son, Jacob Ba'al HaTurim). Judah ben Samuel, *Ta'ame Masoret ha-Miqra le-Rabi Yehudah he-Ḥasid*, ed. Y. S. Lange (Jerusalem, 1980), 11; cf. Jacob ben Asher, *Perush Ba'al HaTurim 'al ha-Torah*, ed., Y. Reinitz (Bene Brak, 1971), 15. I am inclined to assume that Pietists did not create these traditions but only inscribed them.

200. Judah ben Samuel, *Ta'ame Masoret ha-Miqra le-Rabi Yehudah he-Ḥasid*, 32.

201. Ibid., 66.

202. Ibid.

203. Cf. M. Carruthers, *Craft of Thought*, 26, 30.

204. I. Marcus, "History, Story and Collective Memory: Narrativity in Early Ashkenazic Culture," 265, 272.

205. See the articles by Klaus Hermann and Daniel Abrams cited in n. 187..

206. Nonetheless, around 1508–1509, the Ashkenazic author, Asher Lemlein Reutlingen, wrote in defense of the region's *gematria*-infused approach to prayer. See E. Kupfer, "Ḥezyonotav shel R. Asher ben Meir, ha-mekhuneh Lemlein Reutlingen," *Qoveẓ 'al Yad* 68 (1976), esp. 397–402.

207. Tur, OḤ 113. See G. Scholem, *Major Trends in Jewish Mysticism*, 99; Y. Tishby, *Mishnat ha-Zohar* (Jerusalem, 1957), 2:252.

208. Cited in *Beit Yosef* on Tur, OḤ 113.

209. See Ẓ. Malachi, "Rashi and His Disciples in Relation to the Old Paytanim," in *Rashi, 1040–1990*, 457–60; A. Grossman, *Ḥakhme Ẓorfat ha-Rishonim*, 525–26.

210. See Rav Shemaiah's remarks on the *piyyut* by Qalir, "*Tal zu ba'am zo le-haḥadot*," cited in A. Grossman, *Ḥakhme Ẓorfat ha-Rishonim*, 525n80. Unfortunately, since the passage in which Rashi's amanuensis recorded this stance is garbled, we are left wondering whether Rashi was reticent (a) because he thought that the traditions expounded by others did not have a hallowed pedigree, or (b) because he felt that such matters were not to be taught in general, or (c) because he objected to the technique itself—given the almost infinite plasticity and malleability of number interpretation. Regarding *piyyut* commentary, see A. Grossman, "Ẓemiḥat parshanut ha-piyyut," in *Sefer Yovel le-Shlomo Simonsohn*, ed. Aharon Oppenheimer (Tel Aviv, 1993), 55–72; A. Grossman, "Exegesis of the Piyyut in Eleventh Century France," in *Rashi et la Culture Juive en France du Nord au Moyen Age*, ed. Gilbert Dahan and Gerard Nahon (Paris and Louvain, 1997), 261–77. See T. Fishman, "Rhineland Pietist Approaches to Prayer and the Textualization of Rabbinic Culture in Medieval Northern Europe," *Jewish Studies Quarterly* 11 (2004): 313–31. And compare speculations about Naḥmanides' later reticence to disclose esoteric teachings in writing in, e.g., M. Idel, "We Have No Kabbalistic Tradition on This," in *Rabbi Moses ben Naḥman: Explorations in His Religious and Literary Virtuosity*, ed. I. Twersky (Cambridge, Mass., 1983), 51–73.

211. See Chapter 2.

212. See T. Fishman, "The Penitential System of *Ḥaside Ashkenaz* and the Problem of Cultural Boundaries," 205n17.

213. Elazar ben Judah, *Sefer ha-Roqeaḥ* (Brooklyn, 1998), introduction, 1–5. Cf. H. H. Ben Sasson, "Ḥaside Ashkenaz 'al ḥaluqat qinyanim ḥomriyyim u-nekhasim ruḥniyyim ben bene ha-adam," *Ẓion* 35 (1970): 75–79. See, too, D. Abrams, "Ketivat ha-sod be-Ashkenaz ve-ha-ma'avar le-Sefarad," 94–105.

214. The Hebrew word for oil, described in Ex. 30:25 as an "expertly blended compound," and his own name, Elazar ben Yehudah, are numerically equivalent; both terms add up to 390.

215. According to R. Elazar, *Midrash Tadsheh* conceals the name of Pinḥas ben Yair, *Bereshit Rabbah* conceals the name of R. Oshayya Rabba and *Seder 'Olam* conceals the name of R. Yossi.

216. *Sefer ha-Ḥokhma* is printed at the beginning of *Perush ha-Roqeaḥ 'al ha-Torah*, ed. S. Kanivsky (Bene Brak, 2000), 11–51. On this work, see J. Dan, "Sefer ha-Ḥokhmah le-Rabbenu Elazar mi-Vorms u-mashma'uto le-toldot toratah ve-sifrutah shel ḥasidut Ashkenaz," *Ẓion* 29 (1964): 168–81; J. Dan, "The Ashkenazi Ḥasidic Gates of Wisdom," in *Hommage à George Vajda: Ètudes d'histoire et de pensée juives*, ed. G. Nahon and C. Touati (Louvain, 1980), 183–89.

217. On the death of Elazar's son, see Elazar's chronicle in A. Haberman, ed., *Sefer Gezerot Ashkenaz ve-Ẓorfat* (Jerusalem, 1946), 164.

218. This may refer to Talmud itself.

219. In Elazar of Worms, *Perush ha-Roqeaḥ 'al ha-Torah*, 11.

220. A. Neubauer, "Abou Ahron, le Babylonien," *REJ* 23 (1891): 230–37. But see the discussions in I. Marcus, *Piety and Society*, 68, 109–20; D. Abrams, "Ketivat ha-sod be-Ashkenaz ve-ha-ma'avar le-Sefarad," 94–105.

221. See H. Soloveitchik, "Three Themes in *Sefer Ḥasidim*," 318, 350. A parallel pattern may be observed in Christian culture where, even prior to the composition of Burchard's *Corrector*, penitential practices initially prescribed for monks (an elite subculture) ultimately became widespread.

222. See the claim that "by the end of the first quarter of the thirteenth century, there was no longer a distinct German halakhic culture." H. Soloveitchik, *Ha-Yayin*, 127. On the persistence of Pietist attitudes and practices in the elaborate system of penances and commutations articulated by Ashkenazi rabbis of the fourteenth and fifteenth centuries, see J. Elbaum, *Teshuvat ha-Lev ve-Qabbalat Yisurim*, 12, 19–27. An enigmatic text of the mid-fourteenth century may preserve another reference to some form of "Neo-Pietism." The anonymous treatise *Sefer 'Alilot Devarim* rants against God Fearers (*yirei Elohim*) who do that which they were not commanded to do in order to increase their reward, and who say (M. Avot 5:22) "the reward is commensurate with the suffering." (This was certainly a slogan of *Ḥaside Ashkenaz*.) The people singled out for criticism in *Sefer 'Alilot Devarim* devote their labors to harmonizing discrepancies they encounter in the writings of the talmudic glossators. See Joseph ben Meshullam, *Sefer 'Alilot Devarim*, in *Oẓar Neḥmad* 4 (Vienna, 1863), 197, lines 21–24, and R. Bonfil, "Sefer 'Alilot Devarim: Pereq be-toldot he-hagut ha-yehudit ba-meah ha-14," *Eshel Beer Sheva* 2 (1980): 237–39, 248–50.

EPILOGUE

1. I. Twersky, "The Beginnings of *Mishneh Torah* Criticism," in *Biblical and Other Studies*, ed. A. Altmann (Cambridge, Mass., 1963), 161–82.

2. See, e.g., Amnon Raz-Krakotzkin, *The Censor, the Editor, and the Text: The Catholic Church and the Shaping of the Jewish Canon in the Sixteenth Century*, trans. Jackie Feldman (Philadelphia, 2007), 189–91; Simḥa Assaf, "Le-polmos 'al hadpasat sifre qabbalah," *Sinai* 5 (1939): 360–68; Y. Tishby, "Ha-vikkuaḥ 'al hadpasat ha-zohar be-Italia," *Peraqim* 1 (1967–68): 131–81.

3. Ḥayyim ben Beẓalel, *Vikkuaḥ Mayyim Ḥayyim* (Amsterdam, 1712), 5b.

4. Ibid., 2b, principle 3. E. Reiner, "The Ashkenazi Elite at the Beginning of the Modern Era: Manuscript vs. Printed Book," *Polin* 10 (1997): 87.

5. Ḥayyim ben Beẓalel, *Vikkuaḥ Mayyim Ḥayyim*, 4a.

6. Ibid., 3a, principle 4. Ḥayyim ben Beẓalel likens the makers of halakhic books in his time to makers of coins who find that the mines have been depleted of all metal. Unable to unearth any new material, they melt down older coins in order to produce new ones of inferior quality. Ibid., 4b.

7. E. Reiner, "The Ashkenazi Elite at the Beginning of the Modern Era," 87.

8. See Chapter 5.

9. Haym Soloveitchik, "Rupture and Reconstruction: The Transformation of Contemporary Orthodoxy," *Tradition* 28 (1994): 64–130.

10. S. Lieberman, *Hellenism in Jewish Palestine: Studies in the Literary Transmission, Beliefs and Manners of Palestine in the I Century B.C.E.-IV Century C.E.* (New York, 1950) 99n128.

11. "If the Talmud had been written with its commentaries and Tosafot and novellae mixed in [rather than in its designated spatial location on the page], would you find your way?" R. Meir Ish Shalom, cited in Shamma Friedman, "Mavo 'al derekh ḥeqer ha-sugya," in *Meḥqarim u-Meqorot*, ed. H. Z. Dimitrovsky (New York, 1978), 314n112; S. Friedman, *Talmud 'Arukh: Pereq ha-Sokher et ha-Omanin* (New York and Jerusalem, 1996), 8n6.

12. E. S. Rosenthal, "'Iyyunim be-toldot ha-nusaḥ shel ha-talmud ha-bavli," in *Sefer ha-Yovel le-khvod Mordecai Breuer*, ed. M. Bar Asher (Jerusalem, 1992), 571–91. Cf. Y. Sussman, "Ve-shuv le-Yerushalmi Neziqin," *Meḥqere Talmud* 1 (1990): 109n205.

13. Y. Sussman, "Ve-shuv le-Yerushalmi Neziqin," 109n205; cf. Sussman, "'Torah she-be-'al peh': Peshutah ke-mashma'ah: Koḥo shel qoẓo shel yod," *Meḥqere Talmud* 3 (2005): 211n9 and 212; 345n61; 349–50n85a.

14. Elman and Gershoni, "Transmitting Tradition: Orality and Textuality in Jewish Cultures," in *Transmitting Jewish Traditions: Orality, Textuality, and Cultural Diffusion*, 8.

15. See Chapter 1.

16. Rina Drory, *Reshit ha-Magga'im shel ha-Sifrut ha-Yehudit 'im ha-Sifrut ha-'Aravit ba-Meah ha-'Asirit* (Tel Aviv, 1988).

17. I have alluded to this briefly in Chapter 3.

18. Yisrael Ta Shma, who presented medieval Ashkenaz as a cultural colony of ancient Palestine, did notice this—and was visibly perturbed. After discussing the fact that Hai Gaon, like the earlier Babylonians, Yehudai Gaon and Pirqoi ben Baboi, privileged traditions transmitted orally over those transmitted in writing, Ta Shma wrote: "Were it not for the fact that it [Hai's responsum] is ascribed to him with certainty, I would say, speculatively, that it was written by one of the early scholars of Ashkenaz." I. Ta Shma, "Halakhah, minhag u-masoret be-yahadut Ashkenaz ba-meot ha-11–12," *Sidra* 3 (1987): 133–34.

19. M. Halbertal, "Ha-minhag ve-ha-historia shel ha-halakhah be-torato shel ha-Ramban," *Ẓion* 67 (2002): 25–56.

20. A. Grossman, "Ziqata shel yahadut Ashkenaz ha-qeduma el Ereẓ Yisrael," *Shalem* 3 (1981): 57–92.

21. Cf. Elizabeth Eisenstein, *The Printing Press as an Agent of Change* (Cambridge, 1979), 1:117–18; David Herlihy, "Family Solidarity in Medieval Italian History," in *Economy, Society, and Government in Medieval Italy*, ed. David Herlihy, Robert Lopez, and Vsevolod Slessarev (Kent, Ohio, 1969), 173–84; M. Bloch, *Feudal Society*, trans. L. A. Manyon (London, 1961), 139; Georges Duby, "Lineage, Nobility and Knighthood," in *The Chivalrous Society*, trans. Cynthia Postan (Berkeley, 1980), 59–80.

22. B. Stock, *The Implications of Literacy: Written Language and Models of Interpretation in the Eleventh and Twelfth Centuries* (Princeton, N.J, 1983), 88.

BIBLIOGRAPHY

Avraham ben 'Azriel. *'Arugat ha-Bosem.* Vol. 4. Ed. E. E. Urbach. Jerusalem: Meqiẓe Nirdamim, 1963.

Abraham ben Isaac. *Sefer ha-Eshkol.* Ed. Shalom Albeck. Jerusalem: H. Vagshal, 1984.

Abraham ben Nathan (HaYarḥi). *Sefer ha-Manhig.* Ed. Yiẓḥaq Raphael. Jerusalem: Mosad ha-Rav Kook, 1978.

Abrahams, Israel. *The Book of Delight and Other Papers.* Philadelphia: Jewish Publication Society, 1912.

Abrams, Daniel. "Hashpa'ot sufiyut al ha-qabbalah be-Ẓefat." *Maḥanayyim* 6 (1993): 170–79.

———. "Ketivat ha-sod be-Ashkenaz ve-ha-ma'avar le-Sefarad." *Maḥanayyim* 6 (1994): 94–105.

———. "*Ma'aseh Merkabah* as a Literary Work: The Reception of *Hekhalot* Traditions by the German Pietists and Kabbalistic Reinterpretation." *JSQ* 5 (1998): 329–45.

Abramson, Shraga. "Asfamya she-be-Sefarad." *Sinai* 69 (1971): 42–44.

———. *Ba-Merkazim u-va-Tefuẓot be-Tequfat ha-Geonim.* Jerusalem: Mosad ha-Rav Kook, 1965.

———. "Berurim." *Sinai* 58 (1966): 181–92.

———. "Divre ḥazal be-shirat HaNagid." *World Congress for Jewish Studies* 1 (Jerusalem, 1952): 274–78.

———. "'Inyanot be-Sefer ha-Yashar le-Rabbenu Tam ve-haqdamato." *Qiryat Sefer* 37 (1962): 241–48.

———. *'Inyanot be-Sifrut ha-Geonim.* Jerusalem: Mosad ha-Rav Kook, 1974.

———. "'Iyyunim: Shne munaḥe shetarot ba-teshuvah shel Rav Naḥshon Gaon." *Sinai* 75 (1974): 4–19.

———. *Kelale ha-Talmud be-Divre ha-Ramban.* Jerusalem: Mosad ha-Rav Kook, 1971.

———. "Ketivat ha-Mishnah." In *Tarbut ve-Ḥevra be-Toldot Yisrael be-Yeme ha-benayyim,* ed. M. Ben Sasson, R. Bonfil, and J. Hacker. 27–52. Jerusalem: Merkaz Shazar, 1989.

———. *Massekhet 'Avodah Zarah- Ketav Yad Bet ha-Midrash le-Rabanim.* New York: Jewish Theological Seminary, 1957.

———. "Mehem u-vahem." In *Sefer Sivan: Minḥat Zikkaron le-Shalom Sivan,* ed. A. Even-Shoshan. 3–21. Jerusalem: Qiryat Sefer, 1979.

———. "Mi-torato shel Rav Shmuel HaNagid mi-Sefarad." *Sinai* 100 (1987): 7–73.

———. "Perush Rabbenu Barukh b'r Shmuel ha-Sefaradi la-Talmud." *Bar Ilan* 26–27 (1995): 17–115.

———. *Perush Rabbenu Ḥananel la-Talmud.* Jerusalem: H. Vagshal, 1955.

———. *Rav Nisim Gaon, Ḥamishah Sefarim.* Jerusalem: Meqiẓe Nirdamim, 1965.

———. "Ẓerufe teshuvot geonim." In *Sefer ha-Yovel Minḥah le-I"sh: Mugash le-ha-Rav Avraham Yeshayahu Dolgin.* Ed. Itamar Varhaftig. Jerusalem: Bet ha-Knesset Bet Ya'a-qov, 1991.

Abulafia, Meir Halevi. *Ḥidushe ha-Ramah ve-Shitat Qadmonim 'al Massekhet Gittin.* Ed. A. Shoshana. Jerusalem: Mekhon Or ha-Mizraḥ, 1989.

———. *Kitab Alrasa'il, Meturgam be-'Ivrit.* Paris: Brill, 1871.

———. *Sefer Yad Ramah: Shitah le-Mahadura Batra.* New York: Da'at, 1945.

Abun-Nasr, Jamil M. *A History of the Maghrib in the Islamic Period.* Cambridge: Cambridge University Press, 1987.

Adler, Cyrus. "Shemoneh 'Esreh." *Jewish Encyclopedia.* Vol. 11. New York: Funk and Wagnalls, 1901–6.

Adler, Michael. "A Medieval Bookworm." In *The Bookworm* 2:251. London: E. Stock, 1890.

Agnon, S. Y. *Sefer Sofer ve-Sipur.* New York: Schocken Books, 1989.

Agus, Irving A. "R. Jacob Tam's Stringent Criticism of R. Meshullam of Melun in Its Historical Setting." In *Essays on the Occasion of the Seventieth Anniversary of the Dropsie University (1909–1979),* ed. Abraham I. Katsh and Leon Nemoy. 1–10. Philadelphia: Dropsie University, 1979.

———. "Rashi and His School." In *The World History of the Jewish People,* vol. 11, ed. Cecil Roth. 210–30. New Brunswick, N.J.: Rutgers University Press, 1966.

———. *Urban Civilization in Pre-Crusade Europe: A Study of Organized Town Life in the Tenth-Eleventh Centuries Based on Responsa Literature.* 2 vols. New York: Yeshiva University Press, 1965.

Aḥa of Shabḥa. *Sheiltot de-Rav Aḥai Gaon u-Veuro shel Naftali Ẓvi Yehudah Berlin.* 3 vols. Jerusalem: Mosad ha-Rav Kook, 1947.

Aḥituv, Yosef. "Mi-pi sefarim ve-lo mi-pi sofrim." *Sinai* 107 (1991): 133–50.

Alashqar, Moses. *She-elot u-Teshuvot.* Jerusalem: Y. D. Shtitsberg, 1958.

Albeck, Hanokh. *Mavo u-Maftehot le-Midrash Bereshit Raba.* Berlin: Ha-Akademyah le-Mada'e ha-Yahadut, 1931–36.

Albeck, Shalom. "Ma-amar Meḥoqeqe Yehudah." In *Festschrift für Israel Lewys siebzigsten Geburtstag,* ed. M. Brann and J. Elbogen. 104–31 (Hebrew section). Breslau: M. & H. Marcus, 1911.

———. "Yaḥaso shel Rabbenu Tam le-va'ayot zemano." *Ẓion* 19 (1954): 104–41.

Alexander, Tamar. "Li-darkhe 'iẓuv ha-sipur ha-Ḥasidi-Ashkenazi." *Studies in Aggadah and Jewish Folklore* 7 (1983): 197–223.

Alfasi, Isaac. *She-elot u-Teshuvot Rabbenu Yiẓḥaq Alfasi z'l.* Ed. Zeev Woolf Laiter. Pittsburgh: Mekhon HaRambam, 1954.

Allony, Neḥemia. "Shire Ẓiyon be-shirato shel Rav Shmuel HaNagid." *Sinai* 68 (1971): 210–34.

Alon, Gedaliah. *Meḥqarim be-Toldot Yisrael be-Yeme Bayit Sheni u-ve-Tequfat ha-Mishnah ve-ha-Talmud.* 2 vols. Tel Aviv: Ha-Qibbuẓ ha-Meuḥad, 1957.

Alpert, Bat-Sheva. "*Adversus Iudaeos* in the Carolingian Empire." In *Contra Iudaeos: Ancient and Medieval Polemics between Christians and Jews*, ed. Ora Limor and Guy Stroumsa. 119–42. Tübingen: Mohr, 1996.

———. *Medieval Studies: In Honor of Avrom Saltman.* Ramat Gan: Bar Ilan University Press, 1995.

Altmann, A., and S. M. Stern. *Isaac Israeli.* Oxford: Oxford University Press, 1958.

Anatoli, Jacob. *Sefer Malmad ha-Talmidim.* Lyck: Meqiẓe Nirdamim, 1866.

Aptowitzer, Avigdor. *Mavo le-Sefer Ravyah.* Jerusalem: Meqiẓe Nirdamim, 1938.

Asher b. Yeḥiel. *Hilkhot ha-Rosh.* Printed in standard editions of the Talmud.

———. *Tosafot Rosh.* Printed in standard editions of the Talmud.

Ashtor, Eliayhu. *The Jews of Moslem Spain.* 2 vols. Philadelphia: Jewish Publication Society, 1973.

Assaf, Simḥa. *Be-Ohole Ya'aqov.* Jerusalem: Mosad ha-Rav Kook, 1943.

———. "Le-polmos 'al hadpasat sifre qabbalah." *Sinai* 5 (1939): 360–68.

———. "Le-ẓemiḥat ha-merkazim ha-yisraeliyyim be-tequfat ha-geonim." *Ha-Shiloaḥ* 35 (1918).

———. *Meqorot le-Toldot ha-Ḥinukh.* 4 vols. Tel Aviv: Devir, 1924.

———. *Mi-Sifrut ha-Geonim: Teshuvot ha-Geonim u-Seridim mi-Sifre ha-Halakhah mi-tokh Kitve-yad shel ha-Genizah u-Meqorot Aḥerim.* Jerusalem: Darom, 1933.

———. "Sefer Megilat Setarim le-Rav Nisim bar Ya'aquv me-Qayrawan." *Tarbiẓ* 11 (1940): 229–59.

———. *Tequfat ha-Geonim ve-Sifrutah.* Jerusalem: s.n., 1955.

———. *Teshuvot ha-Geonim.* Jerusalem: s.n., 1927.

Attenborough, F. L. *The Laws of the Earliest English Kings.* New York: Cambridge University Press, 1922.

Auerbach, Erich. *Mimesis: The Representation of Reality in Western Literature.* Trans. Willard Trask. Garden City, N.Y.: Doubleday, 1953.

Augustine. *City of God.* Trans. Demetrius B. Zema and Gerald G. Walsh. 3 vols. New York: Fathers of the Church, 1950–54.

Avinery, Isaac. *Hekhal Rashi.* Vol. 1. Tel Aviv: Ha-Meḥaber, 1949.

Avot de-Rabi Natan. Ed. Solomon Schechter. New York: Feldheim, 1945.

Azulai, Ḥayyim Yosef David. *Shem ha-Gedolim.* Vilna: Y. R. Rom, 1852.

Baer, Y. "Ha-hatḥalot ve-hayesodot shel irgun ha-qehilot ha-yehudiyot be-yeme ha-benayyim." *Ẓion* 15 (1950): 1–41.

———. "Ha-megama ha-datit-ḥevratit shel Sefer Ḥasidim." *Ẓion* 3 (1938): 1–50.

———. *Toldot ha-Yehudim be-Sefarad ha-Noẓrit.* 2 vols. Tel Aviv: 'Am 'Oved, 1945.

Baldwin, John W. *Masters, Princes and Merchants: The Social Views of Peter the Chanter and His Circle.* Princeton, N.J.: Princeton University Press, 1970.

Bamberger, Yiẓḥaq Dov. *Sha'are Simḥa la-Rav Yitẓḥaq ben Għiyyat.* 2 vols. Fuerth: Yura Sommer, 1861.

Baneth, David. *Iggerot ha-Rambam: Ḥalifat ha-Mikhtavim 'im R. Yosef ben Yehudah.* Jerusalem: Magnes Press, 1985.

Banitt, Menaḥem. *Peshuto shel Miqra be-Ferush Rashi.* Tel Aviv: Tel Aviv University, 1985.

Baron, Salo W. *A Social and Religious History of the Jews.* 18 vols. New York: Columbia University Press, 1952–58.

Barukh ben Isaac (of Worms). *Sefer ha-Terumah.* Warsaw: Ya'aqov Zev Unterhendler, 1897.

Baumgarten, Elisheva. *Mothers and Children: Jewish Family Life in Medieval Europe.* Princeton, N.J.: Princeton University Press, 2004.

Baumgarten, J. M. "The Unwritten Law in the Pre-Rabbinic Period." *Journal for the Study of Judaism* 3 (1972): 7–29.

Bechtel, Edward A. "Finger Counting among the Romans in the Fourth Century." *Classical Philology* 4 (1909): 25–31.

Bedos-Rezak, Brigitte. "Civic Liturgies and Urban Records in Northern France, 1100–1400." In *City and Spectacle in Medieval Europe,* ed. Barbara A. Hanawalt and Kathryn L. Reyerson. 34–55. Minneapolis: University of Minnesota Press, 1994.

———. "The Confrontation of Orality and Textuality: Jewish and Christian Literacy in Eleventh- and Twelfth-Century Northern France." In *Rashi, 1040–1990: Hommage à Ephraim E. Urbach,* ed. Gabrielle Sed-Rajna. 541–58. Paris: Editions du Cerf, 1993.

———. "Diplomatic Sources and Medieval Documentary Practices: An Essay in Interpretive Methodology." In *The Past and Future of Medieval Studies,* ed. John Van Engen. 313–43. Notre Dame, Ind.: University of Notre Dame Press, 1994.

Beer, Moshe. "'Iyyunim le-Iggeret Sherira Gaon." *Shenaton Bar Ilan* 4–5 (1967): 181–95.

Beit-Arie', Malachi. *Hebrew Codicology: Tentative Typology of Technical Practices Employed in Hebrew Dated Medieval Manuscripts.* Paris: CNRS, 1976.

———. "How Scribes Disclosed Their Names by Means of Their Copied Text." In *Meah She'arim: 'Iyyunim be-'Olamam ha-Ruḥani shel Yisrael be-Yeme ha-Benayyim, le-Zekher Yiẓḥaq Twersky,* ed. Ezra Fleisher, Yaaqov Blidstein, Carmi Horowitz, and Bernard Septimus. 113–29. Jerusalem: Magnes Press, 2001.

———. "Ideals versus Reality: Scribal Prescriptions in *Sefer Ḥasidim* and Contemporary Scribal Practices in Franco-German Manuscripts." In *Rashi, 1040–1990: Hommage à Ephraim E. Urbach,* ed. Gabrielle Sed-Rajna. 559–66. Paris: Editions du Cerf, 1993.

———. "Publication and Reproduction of Literary Texts in Medieval Jewish Civilization: Jewish Scribality and Its Impact on the Texts Transmitted." In *Transmitting Jewish Traditions: Orality, Textuality, and Cultural Diffusion,* ed. Y. Elman and I. Gershoni. 225–47. New Haven, Conn.: Yale University Press, 2000.

———. "Transmission of Texts by Scribes and Copyists: Unconscious and Critical Interferences." *Bulletin of the John Rylands University Library* 75 (1993): 33–51.

Ben Sasson, Ḥayyim Hillel. "Hanhagata shel Torah." *Beḥinot* 9 (1956): 39–53.

———. "Ḥaside Ashkenaz 'al ḥaluqat qinyanim ḥomriyyim u-nekhasim ruḥaniyyim beyn bene ha-adam." *Ẓion* 35 (1970): 61–79.

———. "Yeme ha-benayyim ha-yehudiyyim: Mah hem?" in *Reẓef u-Temurah,* ed. J. Hacker. 359–78. Tel Aviv: 'Am 'Oved, 1984.

Ben Sasson, Menaḥem. "Ha-mivneh, ha-megamot ve-tokhen shel ḥibur Rav Natan ha-Bavli." In *Tarbut ve-Ḥevra: Qoveẓ Ma-amarim le-Zikhro shel Ḥayyim Hillel Ben Sasson,* ed. R. Bonfil, M. Ben Sasson, and J. Hacker. 137–96. Jerusalem: Merkaz Shazar, 1989.

———. "Ha-Qehilah ha-Yehudit be-Ẓefon Afriqah—Ḥevrah u-Manhigut: Qayrawan 800–1057." Ph.D. diss., Hebrew University, 1983.

———. "Italy and Ifriqiyya from the Ninth to the Eleventh Centuries." In *Les relations intercommunautaires juives en Mediterranee et en Europe occidentale,* ed. J. L. Miege. 34–50. Paris, 1984.

———. "Seridim mi-Sefer ha-'Edut ve-ha-Shetarot la-Rav Sa'adya Gaon." *Shenaton ha-Mishpat ha-'Ivri* 11–12 (1984–86): 135–278.

———. "Shivre iggerot me-ha-genizah: Le-toldot ḥidush ha-qesharim shel yeshivot Bavel 'im ha-ma'arav." *Tarbiẓ* 56 (1987): 171–209.

———. *Ẓemiḥat ha-Qehilah ha-Yehudit be-Arẓot ha-Islam: Qayrawan, 800–1057.* Jerusalem: Magnes Press, 1996.

Ben Shammai, Haggai. "Al 'Mudawwin', 'orekh sifre ha-miqra be-farshanut ha-miqra ha-'aravit ha-yehudit." In *Rishonim ve-Aḥaronim: Meḥqarim be-Toldot Yisrael Mugashim le-Avraham Grossman,* ed. J. Hacker, B. Z. Kedar, and Y. Kaplan. 73–110. Jerusalem: Merkaz Shazar, 2010.

Berger, David. "Ḥeqer rabbanut Ashkenaz ha-qedumah." *Tarbiẓ* 53 (1984): 479–87.

———. *The Jewish-Christian Debate in the High Middle Ages: A Critical Edition of the Niẓaḥon Vetus.* Philadelphia: Jewish Publication Society, 1979.

Berkey, Jonathan P. *The Transmission of Knowledge in Medieval Cairo.* Princeton, N.J.: Princeton University Press, 1992.

Berliner, Abraham. "Le-toldot perushe Rashi." In *Ketavim Nivḥarim,* ed. Abraham Berliner. 2:179–226. Jerusalem: s.n., 1949.

Berman, Harold J. *Law and Revolution: The Formation of the Western Legal Tradition.* Cambridge, Mass.: Harvard University Press, 1983.

Berr, Moshe. "'Al ma'ase kappara shel ba'ale teshuvah be-sifrut ḥazal." *Ẓion* 46 (1981): 150–81.

Binchy, D. A. "The Irish Benedictine Congregation in Medieval Germany." *Studies* 18 (1929): 194–210.

Bischoff, B. "Übersicht über die nichtdiplomatischen Geheimschriften des Mittelalters." *Mitteilungen Institut für österreichische Geschichtsforschung* (*MIOEG*) 62 (1954): 1–27.

Blau, Yehudah Aryeh. "Shemot ha-ḥiburim shel Torah she-be'al peh." *Sefer Zikaron le-khevod ha-Doktor Shemuel Avraham Poznanski.* 1927. Reprint, Jerusalem: s.n., 1968.

Bloch, Marc. *Feudal Society.* Trans. L. A. Manyon. London: Routledge & Kegan Paul, 1961.

Bonfil, Roberto (Reuven). "Beyn Ereẓ Yisrael le-veyn Bavel: Qavvim le-ḥeqer toldot ha-tarbut shel ha-yehudim be-Italya ha-deromit u-ve-Eropa ha-noẓrit be-yeme ha-benayyim ha-muqdamim." *Shalem* 5 (1987): 1–30.

———. "Can Medieval Storytelling Help Understanding Midrash? The Story of Paltiel."

In *The Midrashic Imagination,* ed. Michael Fishbane. 228–54. Albany: SUNY Press, 1993.

———. "'Eduto shel Agobard me-Lyon 'al 'olamam ha-ruḥani shel yehude 'iro ba-meah ha-teshi'it." In *Meḥqarim ba-Qabalah, be-Filosofyah Yehudit, u-ve-Sifrut ha-Musar ve-he-Hagut Mugashim le-Yeshayah Tishbi,* ed. J. Dan and J. Hacker. 327–48. Jerusalem: Magnes Press, 1986.

———. "Mitos, retoriqa, historya? 'Iyyun be-Megilat Aḥima'aẓ." In *Tarbut ve-Ḥevra be-Toldot Yisrael be-Yeme ha-Benayyim,* ed. R. Bonfil, M. Ben Sasson, and J. Hacker. 99–135. Jerusalem: Merkaz Shazar, 1989.

———. "Sefer 'Alilot Devarim: Pereq be-toldot he-hagut ha-yehudit ba-me-ah ha-14." *Eshel Beer Sheva'* 2 (1980): 224–64.

Bonnassie, Pierre. "From the Rhone to Galicia: Origins and Modalities of the Feudal Order." In *Slavery to Feudalism in South Western Europe,* ed. Pierre Bonnassie. 104–32. Cambridge: Cambridge University Press, 1991.

Bossy, John. *Disputes and Settlements: Law and Human Relations in the West.* Cambridge: Cambridge University Press, 1983.

Boullata, Issa."The Rhetorical Interpretation of the Qur'an: *I'jaz* and Related Topics." In *Approaches to the History of the Interpretation of the Qur'an,* ed. Andrew Rippin. 139–57. Oxford: Clarendon Press, 1988.

Bousquet, G. H. "La Mudawwana, Index." *Arabica* 17 (1970): 113–50.

Boyarin, Daniel. *Border Lines: The Partition of Judeo-Christianity.* Philadelphia: University of Pennsylvania Press, 2004.

———. *Ha-'Iyyun ha-Sefaradi: Le-Farshanut ha-Talmud shel Megorashe Sefarad.* Jerusalem: Yad Ben Ẓvi, 1989.

———. *Socrates and the Fat Rabbis.* Chicago: University of Chicago Press, 2009.

Boyce, Mary. *A History of Zoroastrianism.* 3 vols. Leiden: Brill, 1975.

Bregman, Marc. "Mishnah ke-mysterion." *Meḥqere Talmud* 3 (2005): 101–9.

Breuer, Mordecai. "Le-Ḥeqer ha-tipologia shel yeshivot ha-ma'arav bi-yeme ha-benayyim." In *Peraqim be-Toldot ha-Ḥevra ha-Yehudit be-Yeme ha-Benayyim u-va-'Et ha-Ḥadasha,* ed. I. Etkes and Y. Salmon. 45–55. Jerusalem: Magnes Press, 1980.

Brin, Gershon. "'Iyyun be-ferush Rabi Yehudah he-Ḥasid la-Torah." *Sinai* 88 (1981): 1–17.

Brody, Robert (Yeraḥmiel). *The Geonim of Babylonia and the Shaping of Medieval Jewish Culture.* New Haven, Conn.: Yale University Press, 1998.

Brody, Yeraḥmiel (Robert). "Kelum hayu ha-geonim meḥoqeqim?" *Shenaton ha-Mishpat ha-'Ivri* 11–12 (1984–86): 297–315.

———. *Le-toldot Nusaḥ ha-Sheiltot.* New York: Ha-Akademyah le-Mada'e ha-Yahadut, 1991.

———. "Meḥqar sifrut ha-halakhot mi-tequfat ha-geonim." *Tarbiẓ* 64 (1994): 139–52.

———. "Sifrut ha-geonim ve-ha-teqst ha-talmudi." *Meḥqere Talmud* 1 (1990): 237–303.

———. *Teshuvot Rav Natronai bar Hilai Gaon.* 2 vols. Jerusalem: Mekhon Ofek, 1994.

Brown, Peter. *The Body and Society: Men, Women, and Sexual Renunciation in Early Christianity.* New York: Columbia University Press, 1988.

Brühl, Carlrichard. *Deutschland—Frankreich: Die Geburt zweier Völker*. Cologne and Vienna: Bohlau, 1990.
Brüll, N. "Die Enstehungsgeschichte des Babylonischen Talmuds als Schriftwerkes." *Jahrbücher für Jüdische Geschichte und Literatur* 2 (1876): 1–123.
Bruna, Israel. *She-elot u-Teshuvot*. Stettin: s.n., 1860.
Buckland, W. W. *A Text Book of Roman Law*. Cambridge: Cambridge University Press, 1932.
Burman, Thomas. "The *Tathlit al-wahdaniya* and the Twelfth Century Andalusian-Christian Approach to Islam." In *Medieval Christian Perceptions of Islam*, ed. John Victor Tolan. 109–28. New York: Garland, 1996.
Bynum, Caroline W. *Docere Verbo et Exemplo: An Aspect of Twelfth-Century Spirituality*. Missoula, Mont.: Scholars Press, 1978.
Capsali, Eliyahu. *Seder Eliyahu Zuta*. Ed. A. Shmuelovitz, S. Simonsohn, and M. Benayahu. 2 vols. Jerusalem: Ben Ẓvi, 1977.
Carlebach, Elisheva. "Attributions of Secrecy and Perceptions of Jewry." *Jewish Social Studies* 2 (1996): 115–36.
Carruthers, Mary J. *The Book of Memory: A Study of Memory in Medieval Culture*. Cambridge: Cambridge University Press, 1990.
———. *The Craft of Thought*. New York: Cambridge University Press, 1998.
Cassel, David. *Teshuvot Geonim Qadmonim*. Berlin: Fridlendershe bukhdrukerai, 1848.
Cerquiglini, Bernard. *Éloge de la variante: Histoire critique de la philologie*. Paris: Seuil, 1989.
Chazan, Robert. "Condemnation of the Talmud Reconsidered (1239–1248)." *PAAJR* 55 (1988): 11–30.
Cheyette, Frederic. "Custom, Case Law and Medieval Constitutionalism: A Reexamination." *Political Science Quarterly* 78 (1963): 362–90.
———. "The Invention of the State." In *Essays on Medieval Civilization: Walter Prescott Webb Memorial Lectures*, ed. B. K. Lackner and K. R. Phillip. 143–76. Austin: University of Texas Press, 1979.
———. "*Suum Cuique Tribuere*." *French Historical Studies* 6 (1970): 287–99.
Clanchy, M. T. *Abelard: A Medieval Life*. Oxford: Blackwell, 1997.
———. *From Memory to Written Record: England 1066–1307*. London: Edward Arnold, 1979.
———. "Remembering the Past and the Good Old Law." *History* 55 (1970): 165–76.
Cohen, Boaz. "The Classification of Law in the Mishneh Torah." *JQR* 25 (1935): 519–40.
Cohen, Gerson D. "The Hebrew Crusade Chronicles and the Ashkenazic Tradition." In *Minḥah le-Naḥum: Biblical and Other Studies Presented to Naḥum M. Sarna*, ed. Marc Brettler and Michael Fishbane. 36–53. Sheffield: Journal for the Study of the Old Testament, 1993.
———. *Sefer ha-Qabbalah: The Book of Tradition by Abraham Ibn Daud*. Philadelphia: Jewish Publication Society, 1967.
———. "The Story of the Four Captives." *PAAJR* 29 (1960–61): 55–131.

Cohen, Jeremy. *The Friars and the Jews: The Evolution of Medieval Anti-Judaism*. Ithaca, N.Y.: Cornell University Press, 1982.

———. "Nasi of Narbonne." *AJS Review* 2 (1978): 45–76.

Cohen, Mark R. *Jewish Self-Government in Medieval Egypt*. Princeton, N.J.: Princeton University Press, 1980.

———. *Under Crescent and Cross: The Jews in the Middle Ages*. Princeton, N.J.: Princeton University Press, 1994.

Cole, Peter. *Selected Poems of Shmuel HaNagid*. Princeton, N.J.: Princeton University Press, 1996.

Cook, Michael. "The Opponents of the Writing of Tradition in Early Islam." *Arabica* 44 (1997): 437–530.

Cottart, Nicole. "Mālikiyya." *Encyclopaedia of Islam*. 2nd ed. Ed. P. Bearman, Th. Bianquis, C. E. Bosworth, E. van Donzel, and W. P. Heinrichs. 6:278–82. Leiden: Brill, 2002.

Coulson, Noel J. *A History of Islamic Law*. Edinburgh: Edinburgh University Press, 1964.

Cowdrey, H. E. J. *The Cluniacs and the Gregorian Reform*. Oxford: Clarendon Press, 1970.

Curtius, E. R. *European Literature and the Latin Middle Ages*. Trans. Willard Trask. London: Routledge and Kegan Paul, 1953.

Dan, Yosef (Joseph). "The Ashkenazi Ḥasidic Gates of Wisdom." In *Hommage à George Vajda: Ètudes d'histoire et de pensée juives*, ed. Gerard Nahon and Charles Touati. 183–89. Louvain: Peeters, 1980.

———. "Ashkenazi Ḥasidism, 1941–1991: Was There Really a Ḥasidic Movement in Medieval Germany?" In *Gershom Scholem's Major Trends in Jewish Mysticism 50 Years After*, ed. Peter Schäfer and Joseph Dan. 87–101. Tübingen: J. C. B. Mohr, 1993.

———. "*Biqoret sefer*: Ivan Marcus, *Piety and Society*." *Tarbiẓ* 51 (1981–82): 324–25.

———. "The Emergence of Mystical Prayer." In *Studies in Jewish Mysticism*, ed. J. Dan and F. Talmage. 85–120. Cambridge, Mass.: Association for Jewish Studies, 1982.

———. "Goralah ha-histori shel torat ha-sod shel Ḥaside Ashkenaz." In *Meḥqarim ba-Qabbalah u-ve-Toldot ha-Datot Mugashim le-Gershom Scholem*. Ed. R. J. Z. Werblowsky, C. Wirszubski, and E. E. Urbach. 87–99. Jerusalem: Magnes Press, 1967.

———. *Ḥasidut Ashkenaz be-Toldot ha-Maḥshavah ha-Yehudit*. Vol. 2. Ramat Aviv: Open University Press, 1990.

———. "Ḥug ha-keruv ha-meyuḥad be-tenu'at ḥasidut Ashkenaz." *Tarbiẓ* 35 (1966) 349–72.

———. *'Iyyunim be-Sifrut Ḥasidut Ashkenaz*. Ramat Gan: Masadah, 1975.

———. "Le-demuto ha-historit shel Rabi Yehudah he-Ḥasid." In *Tarbut ve-Ḥevrah: Qoveẓ Ma-amarim le-Zikhro shel Ḥayyim Hillel Ben Sasson*, ed. R. Bonfil, M. Ben Sasson, and J. Hacker. 389–98. Jerusalem: Merkaz Shazar, 1989.

———. "Le-toldot torat ha-teshuvah shel Ḥaside Ashkenaz." In *Yovel Orot: Haguto shel ha-Rav Avraham Yiẓḥaq ha-Kohen Kook*, ed. B. Ish-Shalom and S. Rosenberg. 221–28. Jerusalem: Avi Chai, 1985.

———. "Sefer ha-Ḥokhmah le-R. El'azar mi-Vorms u-mashma'uto le-toldot toratah ve-sifrutah shel ḥasidut Ashkenaz." *Ẓion* 29 (1964): 168–81.

———. *Sifrut ha-Musar ve-ha-Derush.* Jerusalem: Keter, 1975.

———. "Toratam ha-musarit ve-ha-ḥevratit shel Ḥaside Ashkenaz." *Tarbiẓ* 51 (1982): 319–25.

———. *Torat ha-Sod shel Ḥasidut Ashkenaz.* Jerusalem: Mosad Bialik, 1968.

Danzig, Naḥman. "Mi-talmud ʿal peh le-talmud be-khtav." *Sefer ha-Shana Bar Ilan* 30–31 (2006): 49–112.

———. *Mavo le-Sefer Halakhot Pesuqot.* New York: Jewish Theological Seminary, 1993.

Darmesteter, Arseʿne. *Les gloses françaises dans les commentaires talmudiques de Raschi.* Paris: Champion, 1929–37.

Daston, Lorraine, and Katharine Park. *Wonders and the Order of Nature.* New York: Zone Books, 1998.

David of Augsburg. *De Exterioris et Interioris Hominis Compositione.* In *Spiritual Life and Progress.* Vol. 2. Trans. Dominic Devas. London: Burns, Gates, and Washbourne, 1937.

Decter, Jonathan. *Iberian Jewish Literature: Between Al-Andalus and Christian Europe.* Bloomington: Indiana University Press, 2007.

Delmedigo, Yosef Shlomo. *Maẓref le-Ḥokhma.* Basilea, 1669.

Dimitrovsky, Ḥayyim Zalman. "Al derekh ha-pilpul." In *Salo Wittmayer Baron Jubilee Volume,* ed. Saul Lieberman. 3:111–81 (Hebrew section). Jerusalem: American Academy for Jewish Research, 1974.

———. "Ha-yesh yeme benayyim yehudiyyim?" In *Meḥqarim be-Mada'e ha-Yahadut,* ed. M. Bar Asher. 257–65. Jerusalem: Ha-Makhon le-Mada'e ha-Yahadut, 1986.

Dinari, Yedidya. *Hakhme Ashkenaz be-Shalhe Yeme ha-Benayyim.* Jerusalem: Mosad Bialik, 1984.

Dolgopolski, Sergey. *What Is Talmud? The Art of Disagreement.* New York: Fordham University Press, 2009.

Dozy, R. P. A. *The History of the Almohades, Preceded by a Sketch of the History of Spain, From the Times of the Conquest till the Reign of Yusof ibn-Ta'shifin, and of the History of the Almoravides. By Abdo-'l-Wahid al-Marre'kuoshi.* Leiden: S. & J. Luchtmans, 1847.

Drory, Rina. *Reshit ha-Magga'im shel ha-Sifrut ha-Yehudit 'im ha-Sifrut ha-'Aravit ba-Meah ha-'Asirit.* Tel Aviv: Ha-Qibbuẓ ha-Meuḥad, 1988.

———. "'Words Beautifully Put': Hebrew vs. Arabic in Tenth Century Jewish Literature." In *Genizah Research after Ninety Years: The Case of Judeo-Arabic,* ed. J. Blau and S. Reif. 53–66. Cambridge: Cambridge University Press, 1992.

Duby, Georges. *The Chivalrous Society.* Trans. Cynthia Postan. Berkeley: University of California Press, 1980.

———. *The Early Growth of the European Economy: Warriors and Peasants from the Seventh-Twelfth Century.* Trans. Howard Clark. Ithaca, N.Y.: Cornell University Press, 1974.

———. "The Middle Ages." In *A History of French Civilization,* ed. G. Duby and Robert Mandrou. 32–58. New York: Random House, 1964.

Duran, Profet. *Ma'aseh Efod.* Ed. J. Friedlander and J. Cohen. Vienna: Holzwarth, 1865.

Duran, Solomon ben Simon. *Sefer ha-Rashbash: She-elot u-Teshuvot.* Livorno: A. Ben Rafa, 1742.

Eckhardt, Karl August. *Lex Salica.* Weimar: H. Bolhaus Nachf., 1953.

Eidelberg, Shlomo. "*Ma'arufia* in Rabbenu Gershom's Responsa." *Historia Judaica* 15 (1953): 59–66.

———. *She-elot u-Teshuvot Rabbenu Gershom Me-or ha-Golah.* New York: Yeshiva University Press, 1955.

Eisenberg, Saadia R. "Reading Medieval Religious Disputation: The 1240 'Debate' Between Rabbi Yehiel of Paris and Friar Nicholas Donin." Ph.D. diss., University of Michigan, 2008.

Eisenstein, Elizabeth L. *The Printing Press as an Agent of Change.* 2 vols. Cambridge: Cambridge University Press, 1979.

Elazar ben Judah. *Ḥokhmat ha-Nefesh.* Safed: n.s., 1913.

———. *Ha-Roqeaḥ ha-Gadol.* Jerusalem: s.n., 1960.

———. *Perush ha-Roqeaḥ 'al ha-Torah.* Ed. S. Kanivsky. Bene Brak: J. Klugmann and Sons, 2000.

———. *Perushe Sidur ha-Tefilah la-Roqeaḥ.* Vol. 1. Ed. Moshe and Yehudah Hershler. Jerusalem: Makhon ha-Rav Hershler, 1992.

———. *Sefer ha-Roqeaḥ.* Ed. Y. E. Rosenfeld. Brooklyn: Rosenfeld, 1998.

Elbaum, Jacob. *Le-Havin Divre Ḥakhamim.* Jerusalem: Mosad Bialik, 2000.

———. *Teshuvat ha-Lev ve-Qabbalat Yisurim.* Jerusalem: Magnes Press, 1992.

Elfenbein, Yisrael. *Teshuvot Rashi.* Jerusalem: s.n., 1968.

Eliezer ben Nathan. *Sefer Ra-aban.* Ed. S. Albeck. Warsaw: A. Boimritter, 1905.

Elman, Yaakov. *Authority and Tradition: Toseftan Baraitot in Talmudic Babylonia.* New York: Ktav, 1994.

———. "Middle Persian Culture and Babylonian Sages: Accommodation and Resistance in the Shaping of Rabbinic Legal Tradition." In *The Cambridge Companion to Rabbinic Cambridge Literature,* ed. C. E. Fonrobert and M. S. Jaffee. 165–97. Cambridge: Cambridge University Press, 2007.

———. "Orality and Redaction in the Babylonian Talmud." *Oral Tradition* 14 (1999): 52–99.

———. "Order, Sequence, and Selection: The Mishnah's Anthological Choices." In *The Anthology in Jewish Literature,* ed. David Stern. 53–80. Oxford: Oxford University Press, 2004.

Elman, Yaakov, and Daphna Ephrat. "Orality and the Institutionalization of Tradition: The Growth of the Geonic Yeshiva and the Islamic Madrasa." In *Transmitting Jewish Traditions: Orality, Textuality, and Cultural Diffusion,* ed. Y. Elman and I. Gershoni. 107–37. New Haven, Conn.: Yale University Press, 2000.

Elman, Yaakov, and Israel Gershoni. "Transmitting Tradition: Orality and Textuality in Jewish Cultures." In *Transmitting Jewish Traditions: Orality, Textuality, and Cultural Diffusion,* ed. Y. Elman and I. Gershoni. 1–26. New Haven, Conn.: Yale University Press, 2000.

Elon, Menaḥem. *Jewish Law: History, Sources, Principles*. Trans. Bernard Auerbach and Melvin J. Sykes. 4 vols. Philadelphia: Jewish Publication Society, 1994.

———. "Le-mahutan shel taqanot ha-qahal ba-mishpat ha-'Ivri." In *Meḥqere Mishpat le-Zekher Avraham Rosenthal*, ed. Guido Tedeschi. 1–55. Jerusalem: Magnes Press, 1964.

———. *Mishpat ha-'Ivri: Toldotav, Meqorotav, 'Eqronotav*. 3 vols. Jerusalem: Magnes Press, 1973.

Emery, Richard W. "New Light on Profayt Duran 'The Efodi.'" *JQR* 58 (1967–68): 328–37.

Epstein, Abraham. "Der Rabbenu Gershom Meor ha-Golah zugeschriebene Talmud Commentar." *Festschrift zum achtzigsten Geburtstage Moritz Steinschneiders*. 115–43. Leipzig, 1896.

Epstein, Avraham. *Kitve Rav Avraham Epstein*, ed. A. M. Haberman. 2 vols. Jerusalem: Mosad ha-Rav Kook, 1949–57.

———. "'Inyene masorah ve-diqduq." In *Mi-Qadmoniyyot ha-Yehudim*. 253–58. Vienna: Kommissionsverlag von H. D. Lippe, 1887.

Epstein, Y. N. *Mavo le-Nusaḥ ha-Mishnah*. Jerusalem: Magnes Press, 1963.

———. *Mevo-ot le-Sifrut ha-Amoraim*. Jerusalem: Magnes Press, 1962.

———. *Mevo-ot le-Sifrut ha-Tannaim*. Jerusalem: Magnes Press; Tel Aviv: Devir, 1957.

———. *Perush ha-Geonim le-Seder Toharot*. Ed. E. Z. Melamed. Jerusalem: Devir-Magnes, 1982.

———. "Tosafot Ashkenaziyyot ve-Italqiyyot qedumot." *Tarbiẓ* 12 (1941): 190–204.

Faur, José. *'Iyyunim be-Mishneh Torah le-ha-Rambam*. Jerusalem: Mosad ha-Rav Kook, 1978.

———. "The Legal Thinking of Tosafot." *Dine Israel* 6 (1975): xliii–lxxii.

Feigl, Helmut. "Von der mündlichen Rechtsweisung zur Aufzeichnung: Die Entstehung der Weistümer und verwandter Quellen." In *Recht und Schrift in Mittelalter*, ed. Peter Classen. 425–48. Sigmaringen: J. Thorbecke , 1977.

Fenton, Paul. Introduction to *Le Commentaire sur le Livre de la Creation de Dunas ben Tamim de Kairouan (Xe Siecle)*, by Georges Vajda. Leuven: Peeters, 2002.

Finkelstein, Louis. *Jewish Self-Government in the Middle Ages*. New York: Jewish Theological Seminary, 1924.

Fischer, Katherine. *The Burgundian Code: Liber constitutionum sive Lex Gundobada; Constitutiones extravagantes*. Philadelphia: University of Pennsylvania Press, 1949.

———. *The Lombard Laws*. Philadelphia: University of Pennsylvania Press, 1973.

Fishbane, Michael A. *Biblical Interpretation in Ancient Israel*. Oxford: Clarendon Press, 1985.

Fishman, Talya. "Claims about the Mishna in Sherira Gaon's *Epistle*: Islamic Theology and Jewish History." In *Border Crossings: Interreligious Interaction and the Exchange of Ideas in the Islamic Middle Ages*, ed. D. Freidenreich and M. Goldstein. Philadelphia: University of Pennsylvania Press, forthcoming.

———. "Forging Jewish Memory: *Besamim Rosh* and the Invention of Pre-Emancipation Jewish Culture." In *Jewish History and Jewish Memory*, ed. Elisheva Carlebach, John

M. Efron, and David N. Myers. 70–88. Hanover, N.H.: University Press of New England, 1998.

———. "Guarding Oral Transmission: Within and Between Cultures." *Oral Tradition* 25:1 (2010): 41–56.

———. "A Kabbalistic Perspective on Gender-Specific Commandments: On the Interplay between Symbol and Society." *AJS Review* 17 (1992): 199–245.

———. "The Penitential System of *Ḥaside Ashkenaz* and the Problem of Cultural Boundaries." *Journal of Jewish Thought and Philosophy* 8 (1999): 201–29.

———. "Rhineland Pietist Approaches to Prayer and the Textualization of Rabbinic Culture in Medieval Northern Europe." *Jewish Studies Quarterly* 11 (2004): 313–31.

———. "The Rhineland Pietists' Sacralization of Oral Torah." *JQR* 96 (2006): 9–16.

Fleischer, E. "Ḥedveta bei-Rabi Avraham: Rishon le-paytane Italya?" *Italya* 2 (1981): 21–23.

Fleischer, Ezra. *Shirat ha-Qodesh ha-'Ivrit be-Yeme ha-Benayyim.* Jerusalem: Keter, 1975.

Fleischman, Suzanne. "Philology, Linguistics and the Discourse of the Medieval Text." *Speculum* 65 (1990): 19–37.

Flusser, David. *Sefer Yosippon.* Jerusalem: Mosad Bialik, 1981.

Fournier, Paul. "De quelques collections canoniques issues du Decret de Burchard." In *Mélanges Paul Fabre,* ed. Paul Fabre.189–214. Paris: A. Picard et fils, 1902.

Fraade, S. "Ascetical Aspects of Ancient Judaism." In *Jewish Spirituality*, ed. Arthur Green. 1:253–88. New York: Crossroad, 1986.

Fraade, Steven D. *From Tradition to Commentary: Torah and Its Interpretation in the Midrash Sifre to Deuteronomy.* Albany: State University of New York Press, 1991.

Francus, Yisrael "Hashmatot ve-ta'uyyot qedumot be-Hilkhot ha-Rif." *Tarbiẓ* 47 (1978): 30–48.

Frankel, Yonah. *Darko shel Rashi be-Ferusho la-Talmud ha-Bavli.* Jerusalem: Magnes Press, 1980.

———. "She-elot hermeneutiyyot be-ḥeqer sipur ha-aggadah." *Tarbiẓ* 47 (1978): 139–72.

Frankfurter, David. "The Magic of Writing and the Writing of Magic." *Helios* 21 (1994): 179–221.

Fried, Michael. "Art and Objecthood." *Artforum* 5 (1967): 12–23.

Friedlein, Gottfried. *Die Zahlzeichen und das elementare Rechnen der Griechen und Römer und des christlichen Abendländes vom 7. bis 13. Jahrhundert.* Erlangen: n.s., 1869.

Friedman, Mordecai A. "'Al ta'anat Pirqoi ben Baboi be-divre meẓiat sefarim genuzim shel ha-Yerushalmi." *Sinai* 82–83 (1977–78): 250–51.

———. "'Al terumat ha-genizah le-ḥeqer ha-halakhah." *Mada'e ha-Yahadut* 38 (1993): 277–301.

Friedman, S. Y. "Perush Rashi la-Talmud: Hagahot u-mahadurot." In *Rashi: 'Iyyunim be-Yeẓirato,* ed. Z. Steinfeld. 147–76. Ramat Gan: Bar Ilan University Press, 1993.

Friedman, Shamma. "Le-hithavut shinuyye ha-girsaot ba-Talmud ha-Bavli." *Sidra* 7 (1991): 68–102.

———. "Mavo 'al derekh ḥeqer ha-sugya." In *Meḥqarim u-Meqorot,* ed. H. Z. Dimitrovsky. 1:275–441. New York: Jewish Theological Seminary, 1978.

———. "Mi-Tosafot ha-Rashbam la-Rif: Seder Nashim u-Massekhet Ḥulin." *Qoveẓ 'al Yad* 68 (1976): 187–227.

———. *Talmud 'Arukh: Pereq ha-Sokher et ha-Omanin.* Jerusalem: Jewish Theological Seminary, 1996.

Fuchs, Uziel. "Darkhe ha-hakhra'a, samkhut shel teqstim u-muda'ut 'aẓmit: Hirhurim 'al darkhe ha-pesiqa be-shalhe tequfat ha-geonim." In *Sugyot be-Meḥqar ha-Talmud: Yom 'Iyyun le-Ẓiyyun Ḥamesh Shanim le-Fetirato shel Ephraim E. Urbach.* 100–124. Jerusalem: Akademyah ha-Le-umit ha-Yisraelit le-Mada'im, 2001.

Fuller, Lon. "Human Interaction and the Law." In *The Rule of Law*, ed. R. P. Wolff. 171–217. New York: Simon and Schuster, 1971.

Funkenstein, Amos. "Basic Types of Christian Anti-Jewish Polemic in the Later Middle Ages." *Viator* 2 (1971): 373–82.

———. "Ha-temurot be-vikkuaḥ 'al ha-dat she-beyn yehudim le-noẓrim ba-meah ha-12." *Ẓion* 33 (1968): 125–44.

———. *Perceptions of Jewish History.* Los Angeles: University of California Press, 1993.

Gafni, Isaiah. "Concepts of Periodization and Causality in Talmudic Literature." *Jewish History* 10 (1996): 21–38

———. *Land, Center and Diaspora: Jewish Constructs in Late Antiquity.* Sheffield: Sheffield Academic Press, 1997.

———. Review of David Goodblatt, "Hitpatḥuyyot ḥadashot be-ḥeqer yeshivot Bavel." *Ẓion* 46 (1981): 52–56.

———. *Yehude Bavel be-Tequfat ha-Talmud.* Jerusalem: Merkaz Shazar, 1990.

———. "Yeshiva u-metivta." *Ẓion* 43 (1978): 12–37.

Gandz, Solomon. "Dawn of Literature: Prolegomena to a History of Unwritten Literature." *Osiris* 7 (1939): 261–522.

———. "The Origin of the Ghubar Numerals, or the Arabian Abacus and the Articuli." *Isis* 16 (1931): 393–424.

Gartner, Ya'aqov. *Gilgule Minhag be-'Olam ha-Halakhah.* Jerusalem: s.n., 1995.

Gaster, Moses. *Ma'aseh Book.* Philadelphia: Jewish Publication Society, 1934.

Geary, Patrick J. *Before France and Germany: The Creation and Transformation of the Merovingian World.* New York: Oxford University Press, 1988.

———. *Phantoms of Remembrance: Memory and Oblivion at the End of the First Millennium.* Princeton, N.J.: Princeton University Press, 1994.

Gerhardssohn, Birger. *Memory and Manuscript: Oral Tradition and Written Transmission in Rabbinic Judaism and Early Christianity.* Copenhagen: Ejnar Munksgaard, 1961.

Gevaryahu, Gilead. *Ma'aseh Sofrim ba-Miqra: Osef Ma-amarim shel Ḥayyim Moshe Yiẓḥaq Gevaryahu.* Jerusalem: Gevaryahu, 2000.

Gieysztor, Alexander. "The Genesis of the Crusades: The Encyclical of Sergius IV (1009–1012)." *Medievalia et Humanistica* 5 (1948): 3–23; 6 (1950): 3–34.

Gil, Moshe. "Rav Aharon ha-Cohen Gaon ben Yosef u-vanav 'Eli ve-Avraham." *Sefunot* n.s. 1/ o.s. 16 (1980): 9–23.

———. "The Babylonian Yeshivot and the Maghrib in the Early Middle Ages." *PAAJR* 57 (1990–91): 69–120.

———. *Malkhut Yishma'el be-Tequfat ha-Geonim*. Jerusalem: Mosad Bialik, 1997.

Gil, Moshe, and Ezra Fleischer. *Yehudah HaLevi u-Vene Hugo*. Jerusalem, 2001.

Gilat, Yiẓḥaq D. *Peraqim be-Hishtalshelut ha-Halakhah*. Ramat Gan: Bar Ilan University Press, 1992.

Gilissen, John. *La Coutume*. Turnhout: Brepols, 1982.

Ginzberg, Louis. *'Al Halakhah ve-Aggadah*. Tel Aviv: Devir, 1960.

———. *Geonica*. 2 vols. New York: Jewish Theological Seminary, 1909.

———. *Ginze Shekhter*. 3 vols. New York: Jewish Theological Seminary, 1929.

Glaber, Rodulfus. *The Five Books of the Histories, and the Life of St. William*. Trans. John France. Oxford: Oxford University Press, 1989.

Goitein, S. D. *Sidre Ḥinukh be-Yeme ha-Geonim u-Vet ha-Rambam*. Jerusalem: Ben-Ẓvi, 1962.

Goldin, Judah. "The Freedom and Restraint of Haggadah." In *Studies in Midrash and Related Literature*, ed. Judah Goldin, Barry L. Eichler, and Jeffrey H. Tigay. 253–70. Philadelphia: Jewish Publication Society, 1988.

Goodblatt, David. "Hitpatḥuyot ḥadashot be-ḥeqer yeshivot Bavel." *Ẓion* 46 (1981): 14–38.

———. "Suicide in the Sanctuary: Traditions on Priestly Martyrdom." *Journal of Jewish Studies* 46 (1995): 10–29.

Gougaud, Louis. "Mulierum Consortia: Etude sur le Syneisaktisme chez les Ascetes Celtiques." *Eriu* 9 (1921–23): 147–56.

Grabois, Aryeh. *Le Pélerin Occidental en Terre Sainte au Moyen Âge*. Brussels: De Boeck Université, 1998.

———. "Le souvenir et la legende de Charlemagne dans les textes hebraiques medievaux." *Le Moyen Age* 72 (1966): 5–41.

———. "The Use of Letters as a Communication Medium among Medieval European Jewish Communities." In *Communication in the Jewish Diaspora*, ed. Sophia Menache. 93–106. Leiden: Brill, 1996.

Graetz, Heinrich. *Geschichte der Juden von den ältesten zeiten bis auf die gegenwart*. 3rd ed. 11 vols. Leipzig: O. Leiner, 1897–1911.

Grafton, Anthony. "Introduction: Notes from Underground on Cultural Transmission." In *The Transmission of Culture in Early Modern Europe*, ed. A. Grafton and A. Blair. 1–7. Philadelphia: University of Pennsylvania Press, 1990.

Grattan-Guiness, Ivor. *The Norton History of the Mathematical Sciences*. New York: W. W. Norton, 1998.

Grayzel, Solomon. *The Church and the Jews in the Thirteenth Century*. Philadelphia: Dropsie College, 1933.

Greenhut, E. *Sibuv Rabi Petaḥya me-Regensburg*. Jerusalem: A. M. Luntz; Frankfurt: J. Kauffmann, 1904–5.

Groner, Ẓvi. "Darkhe hora-a shel rishonim u-geonim." In *Meah She'arim: 'Iyyunim be'Olamam ha-Ruḥani shel Yisrael be-Yeme ha-Benayyim le-Zekher Yiẓḥaq Twersky*, ed. Ezra Fleisher, Ya'aqov Blidstein, Carmi Horowitz, and Bernard Septimus. 267–78. Jerusalem: Magnes Press, 2001.

———. *The Legal Methodology of Hai Gaon*. Chico, Calif.: Scholars Press, 1985.

———. "Ha-Maghreb ve-yeshivot ha-geonim be-Bavel be-re-i ha-she-elot u-teshuvot ba-meot ha-9–11." *Pe'amim* 38 (1989): 49–57.

Grossman, Avraham. "Bein 1012 le-1096: Ha-reqa' ha-tarbuti ve-ha-ḥevrati le-qidush ha-shem be-1096." In *Yehudim Mul ha-Ẓelav: Gezerot 1096 be-Historia u-ve-Historiographia*, ed. Yom Tov Assis, Michael Toch, Jeremy Cohen, Ora Limor, and Aharon Kedar. 51–73. Jerusalem: Magnes Press, 2000.

———. "Exegesis of the Piyyut in Eleventh Century France." In *Rashi et la Culture Juive en France du Nord au Moyen Age*, ed. Gilbert Dahan and Gerard Nahon. 261–77. Paris and Louvain: Peeters, 1997.

———. *Ḥakhme Ashkenaz ha-Rishonim*. Jerusalem: Magnes Press, 1981.

———. *Ḥakhme Ẓorfat ha-Rishonim*. Jerusalem: Magnes Press, 1995.

———. *Ḥasidot u-Mordot: Nashim Yehudiyyot be-Eropah be-Yeme ha-Benayyim*. Jerusalem: Merkaz Shazar, 2001.

———. "Ha-ziqa bein ha-mivneh ha-ḥevrati le-yeẓirah ha-ruḥanit be-qehilot Yisrael be-tequfat ha-geonim." *Ẓion* 53 (1988): 259–72.

———. "Me-Andalusia le-Eropa: Yaḥasam shel ḥakhme Ashkenaz ve-Ẓorfat ba-meot ha-12–13 el sifre ha-halakhah shel ha-Rif ve-ha-Rambam." *Pe'amim* 80 (1999): 14–32.

———. "Shorashav shel qidush ha-shem be-Ashkenaz ha-qedumah." In *Qedushat ha-Ḥayyim ve-Ḥeruf ha-Nefesh*, ed. Isaiah M. Gafni and Aviezer Ravitzky. 99–130. Jerusalem: Merkaz Shazar, 1992.

———. "Yaḥase eyvah la-yehudim al reqa' kalkali ve-ḥevrati ba-khalifut ha-muslemit." In *Sin-at Yisrael le-Doroteha*, ed. Shemuel Almog. 171–87. Jerusalem: Merkaz Shazar, 1980.

———. "Yiḥus mishpaḥah u-meqomo ba-ḥevra ha-yehudit be-Ashkenaz ha-qedumah." In *Peraqim be-Toldot ha-Ḥevra ha-Yehudit . . . Muqdashim le-Professor Yaacov Katz*, ed. E. Etkes and Y. Salmon. 9–23. Jerusalem: Magnes Press, 1980.

———. "Ẓemiḥat parshanut ha-piyyut." In *Sefer Yovel le-Shlomo Simonsohn*, ed. Aharon Oppenheimer. 55–72. Tel Aviv: Tel Aviv University Press, 1993.

———. "Ziqata shel yahadut Ashkenaz ha-qedumah el Ereẓ Yisrael." *Shalem* 3 (1981): 57–92.

Gruenwald, Ithamar. "A Preliminary Critical Edition of *Sefer Yetsira*." *Israel Oriental Studies* 1 (1971): 135–36.

———. *Rituals and Ritual Theory in Ancient Israel*. Leiden: Brill, 2003.

Gutas, Dimitri. *Greek Thought, Arabic Culture: The Graeco-Arabic Translation Movement in Baghdad and Early Abbasid Society (8th–10th Centuries)*. London: Routledge, 1998.

Gwynn, A. "Irish Monks and the Cluniac Reform." *Studies* 29 (1940): 409–30.

Haas, Peter J. *Responsa: Literary History of a Rabbinic Genre*. Atlanta: Scholars Press, 1996.

Haberman, Abraham, ed. *Sefer Gezerot Ashkenaz ve-Ẓorfat*. Jerusalem: Sifre Tarshish, 1946.

Halbertal, Moshe. *'Al Derekh ha-Emet: Ha-Ramban ve-Yeẓiratah shel Masoret*. Jerusalem: Makhon Shalom Hartman, 2006.

———. "Ha-Minhag ve-ha-historiah shel ha-halakhah be-torato shel ha-Ramban." *Ẓion* 67 (2002): 25–56.

———. *People of the Book: Canon, Meaning, and Authority.* Cambridge, Mass.: Harvard University Press, 1997.

Halevy, Isaac. *Dorot ha-Rishonim. Divre ha-Yamim le-Vene Yisrael.* 4 vols. Frankfurt: s.n., 1897.

Halivni, David Weiss. *Meqorot u-Mesorot.* Tel Aviv: Devir, 1968.

———. *Peshat and Derash: Plain and Applied Meaning in Rabbinic Exegesis.* New York: Oxford University Press, 1991.

———. "The Reception Accorded to Rabbi Judah's Mishna." In *Jewish Christian Self-Definition,* ed. E. P. Sanders, Al Baumgarten, and Alan Mendelsohn. 204–12. Philadelphia: Fortress Press, 1981.

Halkin, Abraham. "The Medieval Jewish Attitude toward Hebrew." In *Biblical and Other Studies,* ed. Alexander Altmann. 233–48. Cambridge, Mass.: Brandeis University Texts and Studies, 1963.

Halkin, Hillel. *Grand Things to Write a Poem On: A Verse Autobiography of Shmuel Ha-Nagid.* Jerusalem: Gefen, 2000.

Hallinger, Kassius. *Corpus Consuetudinum Monasticarum.* Siegburg: F. Schmitt, 1963–present.

HaNagid, Samuel. *Kol Shire Rabi Shmuel HaNagid.* Ed. A. M. Haberman and S. Abramson. 5 vols. Tel Aviv: s.n., 1944, 1945–52, 1953.

Ḥananel ben Ḥushiel. Perushe Rabenu Ḥananel ben Ḥushiel la-Talmud, ed. David Metzger. Jerusalem: Mekhon Lev Sameaḥ, 1995.

Haran, Menaḥem. *Ha-Asupah ha-Miqra'it.* Jerusalem: Mosad Bialik; Magnes Press, 1996.

———. "Mi-ba'ayot ha-qanonizaẓya shel ha-miqra." *Tarbiẓ* 25 (1956): 245–71.

Harkavy, Avraham. *Ha-Sarid ve-ha-Palit.* St. Petersburg: Berman and Rabinowitz, 1891.

———. *Me-assef Nidaḥim: Meqorot u-Meḥqarim be-Toldot Yisrael u-ve-Sifruto.* Reprint of 1878. Jerusalem: Qedem, 1969.

———. *Teshuvot ha-Geonim.* Facsimile of vol. 4 of *Zikkaron la-Rishonim ve-gam le-Aḥaronim* (Berlin, 1887), New York: Menorah, 1959.

———. *Zikkaron la-Rishonim ve-gam la-Aḥronim.* Vol. 1. Berlin, 1887.

Harris, Jay. *How Do We Know This? Midrash and the Fragmentation of Modern Judaism.* Albany: State University of New York Press, 1995.

Havlin, Shlomo Z. "'Al ha-ḥatimah ha-sifrutit ke-yesod ha-ḥaluqah le-tequfot ba-halakhah." In *Meḥqarim be-Sifrut ha-Talmudit,* ed. S. Z. Havlin. 148–92. Jerusalem: Israel Academy of Sciences, 1983.

Ḥayyim ben Beẓalel. *Vikkuaḥ Mayyim Ḥayyim.* Amsterdam: Propis, 1712.

Ḥayyot, Ẓvi Hersch. *Kol Sifre Mahari"ẓ Ḥayyot.* Jerusalem: Divre Ḥakhamim, 1958.

Ḥazan, Yisrael Moshe. *Iyye ha-Yam* Gloss on *She-elot u-Teshuvot ha-Geonim: Sha'are Teshuvah.* Livorno, 1869.

Heil, Johannes. "Deep Enmity and/or Close Ties? Jews and Christians before 1096: Sources, Hermeneutics and Writing History in 1996." *Jewish Studies Quarterly* 9 (2002): 259–306.

Heinemann, Yiẓḥaq. *Darkhe ha-Agadah.* Jerusalem: Magnes Press, 1949.

Heinrichs, W. "An Evaluation of *Sariqa.*" *Quaderni di Studi Arabi* 5–6 (1987–88): 357–68.

Herbert, Maire, and Martin McNamara, eds. "The Penance of Adam." In *Irish Biblical Apocrypha: Selected Texts in Translation.* 8–11. Edinburgh: T&T Clark, 1989.

Herlihy, David. "Family Solidarity in Medieval Italian History." In *Economy, Society, and Government in Medieval Italy*, ed. David Herlihy, Robert Lopez, and Vsevolod Slessarev. 173–84. Kent, Ohio: Kent State University Press, 1969.

———. *Medieval Households.* Cambridge, Mass.: Harvard University Press, 1985.

Hermann, Klaus. "Re-Written Mystical Texts: The Transmission of the Heikhalot Literature in the Middle Ages." *Bulletin of the John Rylands University* 75 (1993): 97–116.

Herr, M. D. "Le-mashma'uto shel ha-munaḥ 'yeme ha-benayyim' be-toldot Yisrael." In *Tarbut ve-Ḥevra*, ed. R. Bonfil, M. Ben Sasson, and J. Hacker. 83–97. Jerusalem: Merkaz Shazar, 1989.

Heschel, Abraham Joshua. "'Al ruaḥ ha-qodesh be-yeme ha-benayyim." In *Alexander Marx Jubilee Volume*, 175–208. New York: Jewish Theological Seminary, 1950.

———. *Torah min ha-Shamayyim ba-Aspaqlaryah shel ha-Dorot.* 3 vols. London: Soncino, 1962–65.

Heszer, Catherine. "The Codification of Legal Knowledge in Late Antiquity: The Talmud Yerushalmi and Roman Law Codes." In *The Talmud Yerushalmi and Graeco-Roman Culture,* ed. Peter Schäfer. 1:581–641. Tübingen: Mohr-Siebeck, 1998.

———. *Jewish Literacy in Roman Palestine.* Tübingen: Mohr Siebeck, 2001.

Hibbits, Bernard J. "Coming to Our Senses: Communication and Legal Expression in Performance Cultures." *Emory Law Journal* 41 (1992): 873–960.

Hildesheimer, Ezriel, and Naḥum Rakover. *Ha-Qehilah: Irgun ve-Hanhagah, Taqanot u-Pinqese Qahal.* Jerusalem: Merkaz Shazar, 1978.

Hildesheimer, Ezriel, ed. *Halakhot Gedolot.* Jerusalem: Meqiẓe Nirdamim, 1971.

Hirschberg, H. Z. *A History of the Jews in North Africa.* Vol. 1. Leiden: Brill, 1974.

Hobsbawm, Eric, and Ranger, Terence. *The Invention of Tradition.* Cambridge: Cambridge University Press, 1992.

Holdheim, W. Wolfgang. *The Hermeneutic Mode: Essays on Time in Literature and Literary Theory.* Ithaca, N.Y.: Cornell University Press, 1984.

Hollister, C. Warren, and John Baldwin. "The Rise of Administrative Kingship: Henry I and Philip Augustus." *American Historical Review* 83 (1978): 867–905.

Holmes, U. T. "Transition in European Education." In *Twelfth Century Europe and the Foundations of Modern Society*, ed. Marshall Clagett. 15–38. Madison: University of Wisconsin Press, 1961.

Horowitz, Ḥayyim Meir. *Sefer Tosefta 'Atiqta.* Frankfurt: H. M. Horowitz, 1889.

Hughes, Kathleen. *The Church in Early Irish Society.* Ithaca, N.Y.: Cornell University Press, 1966.

Huizinga, Johan. *Homo Ludens: A Study of the Play-Element in Culture.* Boston: Beacon Press, 1950.

Hunt, R. W. "Studies in Priscian in the Twelfth Century II: The School of Ralph of Beauvais." *Mediaeval and Renaissance Studies* 2 (1950): 1–56.

Ibn Ezra, Abraham ben Meir. *Safah Berurah*. Fuerth, 1839.

Ibn Hawqal. *Configuration de la Terre*. Trans. J. H. Kramers and G. Wiet. Paris-Beyrouth: UNESCO, 1964.

Ibn Janaḥ, Jonah. *Sefer ha-Riqmah*. Ed. M. Wilensky and D. Tene. Jerusalem: Ha-Akademyah le-Lashon ha-'Ivrit, 1964.

Ibn Kaspi, Joseph. "Guide to Knowledge." (*Sefer ha-Musar*). In *Hebrew Ethical Wills*, ed. I. Abrahams. 1:127–62. Philadelphia: Jewish Publication Society, 1926.

Ibn Migash, Joseph Halevi. *Ḥidushe ha-R'I Migash 'al Massekhet Bava Batra*. Jerusalem: Hoẓa-at ha-Mosad le-'Idud Limud ha-Torah, 2001–2.

Ibn Paquda, Baḥya. *Sefer Torat Ḥovot ha-Levavot*. Trans. Judah Ibn Tibbon. Ed. Avraham Ẓifroni. Tel Aviv: Hoẓa-at Omanut, 1929.

Ibn Yaḥya, Gedaliah. *Sefer Shalshelet ha-Qabbalah*. Lemberg: Druck v M.F. Poremba, 1864.

Idel, Moshe. *Kabbalah: New Perspectives*. New Haven, Conn.: Yale University Press, 1988.

———. "Maimonides' *Guide of the Perplexed* and the Kabbalah." *Jewish History* 18 (2004): 197–226.

———. "Transmission in Thirteenth Century Kabbalah." In *Transmitting Jewish Traditions: Orality, Textuality, and Cultural Diffusion*, ed. Y. Elman and I. Gershoni. 138–65. New Haven, Conn.: Yale University Press, 2000.

———. "We Have No Kabbalistic Tradition on This." In *Rabbi Moses ben Naḥman: Explorations in His Religious and Literary Virtuosity*, ed. I. Twersky. 51–73. Cambridge, Mass.: Harvard University Press, 1983.

'Imanuel, Simḥa. *Shivre Luḥot: Sefarim Avudim shel Ba'ale ha-Tosafot*. Jerusalem: Magnes Press, 2006.

———. *Teshuvot ha-Geonim ha-Ḥadashot: Ve-'iman Teshuvot, Pesaqim u-Ferushim me-et Ḥakhme Provans ha-Rishonim*. Jerusalem: Sifriyat Fridberg, 1995.

———. "Ve-Ish 'al meqomo mevoar shemo: Le-toldotav shel R. Barukh bar Yiẓḥaq." *Tarbiẓ* 69 (2000): 423–40.

Iogna-Prat, Dominique. *Order and Exclusion: Cluny and Christendom Face Heresy, Judaism and Islam (1000–1150)*. Trans. Graham Robert Edwards. Ithaca, N.Y.: Cornell University Press, 2002.

Isaac ben Abba Mari. *Sefer ha-'Itur*. Ed. Meir Jonah Glanovsky. Jerusalem: s.n., 1970.

Isaac ben Joseph of Corbeil. *Sefer Miẓvot Qatan: Sefer 'Amude Golah*. Jerusalem: Yerid ha-Sefarim, 2005.

———. *Ha-Semaq mi-Ẓurikh ve-ha-sefer 'Amude Golah*. Ed. Y. Har Shoshanim. Jerusalem: s.n., 1973.

Isaac ben Moses. *Sefer Or Zaru'a*. Zhitomir: Shapira, 1862.

Ish Shalom, Meir. *Sifre Deve Rav 'im Tosfot Meir 'Ayin*. Vienna, 1864.

Jacob ben Asher. *Perush Ba'al ha-Turim 'al ha-Torah*. Ed. Ya'aqov Reinitz. Bene Brak: s.n., 1971.

Jacob ben Meir Tam. *Sefer ha-Yashar: Ḥeleq ha-Ḥidushim*. Ed. Shimon Shlomo Shlesinger. Jerusalem: Qiryat Sefer, 1959.

———. *Sefer ha-Yashar: She-elot u-Teshuvot.* Ed. F. Rosenthal. Berlin: Ittskovski, 1898.

Jacobs, Louis. *Principles of the Jewish Faith: An Analytical Study.* London: Vallentine, Mitchell, 1964.

Jaeger, Stephen C. *The Envy of Angels: Cathedral Schools and Social Ideas in Medieval Europe, 950–1200.* Philadelphia: University of Pennsylvania Press, 1994.

Jaffee, Martin S. "Oral Cultural Context of the Talmud Yerushalmi: Greco-Roman Rhetorical Paideia, Discipleship, and the Concept of Oral Torah." In *The Talmud Yerushalmi and Greco-Roman Culture*, ed. Peter Schäfer. 1:7–61. Tübingen: Mohr Siebeck, 1999.

———. *Torah in the Mouth: Writing and Oral Tradition in Palestinian Judaism, 200 BCE–400 CE.* Oxford: Oxford University Press, 2001.

Jarden, Dov, ed. *Divan Shmuel HaNagid: Ben Tehilim.* Jerusalem: Hebrew Union College Press, 1966.

Jennings, Margaret. "Tutivillus: The Literary Career of the Recording Demon." *Studies in Philology* 74 (1977): 1–95.

Jolowicz, Herbert Felix. *Historical Introduction to the Study of Roman Law.* Cambridge: Cambridge University Press, 1952.

Jones, Charles W. *Bedae: Opera de Temporibus.* Cambridge: Mediaeval Academy of America, 1943.

———. *Bedae: Pseudepigrapha.* Ithaca, N.Y.: Cornell University Press, 1939.

———. *Bede, the Schools and the Computus.* Brookfield, Vermont: Variorum, 1994.

Jordan, William C. *Europe in the High Middle Ages.* London: Penguin Press, 2001.

Joseph ben Meshullam. *Sefer 'Alilot Devarim.* In *Oẓar Neḥmad.* 4:179–214. Vienna: Y. Knepfelmakhars Bukhhandlung, 1863.

Judah ben Barzilai. *Perush Sefer Yeẓirah.* Ed. S. J. Halberstamm. Berlin, 1885.

———. *Sefer ha-'Itim.* Ed. Ya'aqov Shor. Cracow: Y. Fisher, 1902.

———. *Sefer ha-Shetarot.* Ed. S. J. Halberstamm. Berlin, 1898.

Judah ben Samuel. *Perush ha-Torah.* Ed. Yiẓḥaq Shimshon Lange. Jerusalem: Lange, 1975.

———. *Sefer Ḥasidim.* Ed. Reuven Margalioth. Jerusalem: Mosad ha-Rav Kook, 1957.

———. *Sefer Ḥasidim 'al pi Nusaḥ Ketav Yad asher be-Parma.* Ed. Judah Wistinetzki and Jacob Freimann Frankfurt: M. A. Varmann, 1924.

———. *Ta'ame Masoret ha-Miqra le-Rabi Yehudah he-Ḥasid.* Ed. Yiẓḥaq Shimshon Lange. Jerusalem: Lange, 1980.

Juster, Jean. "La condition legale des juifs sous les rois visigoths." *Études d'histoire juridique offertes à Paul Fréderic Girard.* 2:275–313. Paris: Paul Geuthner, 1913.

Justin Martyr. *Dialogue with Trypho.* Trans. Thomas B. Falls. Ed. Michael Slusser. Washington, D.C.: Catholic University of America Press, 2003.

Kahane, Menaḥem. "Mahadurot biqortiyot shel Mekhilta de-Rabi Yishmael le-or seride genizah." *Tarbiẓ* 55 (1985–86): 489–93.

———. "Ziqat ketav yad Vatican 60 shel Bereshit Rabbah le-maqbilotav." *Te'udah* 11 (1996): 18–60.

Kalmin, Richard. "The Formation and Character of the Babylonian Talmud." In *The*

Cambridge History of Judaism, vol. 4, *The Late Roman Rabbinic Period*, ed. Steven Katz. 843–52. Cambridge: Cambridge University Press, 2006.

Kanarfogel, Ephraim. "German Pietism in Northern France: The Case of R. Isaac of Corbeil." In *Ḥazon Naḥum: Studies in Jewish Law, Thought, and History Presented to Dr. Norman Lamm on the Occasion of His Seventieth Birthday*, ed. Y. Elman and J. Gurock. 207–28. New York: Yeshiva University Press, 1977.

———. *Jewish Education and Society in the High Middle Ages*. Detroit: Wayne State University Press, 1992.

———. "A Monastic-like Setting for the Study of Torah." In *Judaism in Practice*, ed. Lawrence Fine. 191–202. Princeton, N.J.: Princeton University Press, 2001.

———. *Peering through the Lattices: Mystical, Magical, and Pietistic Dimensions in the Tosafist Period*. Detroit: Wayne State University Press, 2000.

———. "Progress and Tradition in Medieval Ashkenaz." *Jewish History* 14 (2000): 287–316.

———. "Rabbinic Authority and the Right to Open an Academy in Medieval Ashkenaz." *Michael* 12 (1991): 233–50.

———. "Realia (*Metsiut*) and Halakha in Ashkenaz: Surveying the Parameters and Defining the Limits." *Jewish Law Annual* 14 (2002): 201–16.

Kaplan, Julius. *The Redaction of the Babylonian Talmud*. Jerusalem: Maqor, 1973.

Kasher, M. *Gemara Shelema: Massekhet Pesaḥim min Talmud Bavli*. Jerusalem: Mif'al Gemara Shelemah, 1960.

Katz, Jacob. "Alterations in the Time of the Evening Service (*Ma'ariv*): An Example of the Interrelationship between Religious Customs and their Social Background." In *Divine Law in Human Hands: Case Studies in Halakhic Flexibility*. 88–127. Jerusalem: Magnes Press, 1998. Originally published as "Ma'ariv be-zemano ve-shelo be-zemano: Dugma le-ziqah bein minhag, halakhah, ve-ḥevra," in *Halakhah ve-Kabbalah*, ed. Jacob Katz, 175–200 (Jerusalem: Magnes Press, 1984).

———. "Biqoret sefarim: Ba'ale ha-Tosafot." *Qiryat Sefer* 31 (1956): 9–16.

———. *Exclusiveness and Tolerance*. London: Oxford University Press, 1961.

———. "Meqomam shel yeme ha-benayyim be-toldot Yisrael." In *Meḥqarim be-Mada'e ha-Yahadut*, ed. M. Bar Asher. 209–25. Jerusalem: Hebrew University, ha-Makhon le-Mada'e ha-Yahadut, 1986.

Kelley, Donald R. "'Second Nature': The Idea of Custom in European Law, Society and Culture." In *Transmission of Culture in Early Modern Europe*, ed. A. Grafton and A. Blair. 131–72. Philadelphia: University of Pennsylvania Press, 1990.

Kenney, J. F. *Sources for the Early History of Ireland*. Vol. 1. *Ecclesiastical*. New York: Columbia University Press, 1929.

Kern, Fritz. *Kingship and Law in the Middle Ages*. Trans. S. B. Chrimes. Oxford: Blackwell, 1939.

Klibansky, Raymond. "Peter Abailard and Bernard of Clairvaux." *Medieval and Renaissance Studies* 5 (1961): 1–27.

Khadduri, Majid. Trans and Ed. *Islamic Jurisprudence: Shafi'i's Risala*. Baltimore: Johns Hopkins University Press, 1961.

Kisch, Guido. *Jewry Law in Medieval Germany: Laws and Court Decisions concerning Jews.* New York: American Academy for Jewish Research, 1949; 2nd ed., New York, 1970.

Kister, Menaḥem. "Marginalia Qumranica." *Tarbiẓ* 57 (1988): 315–16.

Klar, Binyamin. *Megilat Aḥima'aẓ.* Jerusalem, n.s., 1944–45.

Knight, Gillian. *The Correspondence between Peter the Venerable and Bernard of Clairvaux: A Semantic and Structural Analysis.* Aldershot, England; Burlington, Vt.: Ashgate, 2002.

Kraemer, David. *Reading the Rabbis: The Talmud as Literature.* New York: Oxford University Press, 1996.

Kraemer, Joel L. *Humanism in the Renaissance of Islam: The Cultural Revival during the Buyid Age.* Leiden: Brill, 1986.

Kupfer, E. "Hilkhot ha-get asher yasad Rabbenu Yiẓḥaq b"r Shemuel." *Qoveẓ 'al Yad* 6/68 (1966): 131.

Kupfer, Ephraim. "Ḥezyonotav shel R. Asher ben R. Meir, ha-mekhuneh Lemlein Reutlingen." *Qoveẓ 'al Yad* 68 (1976): 387–423.

———. *Teshuvot u-Pesaqim.* Jerusalem: *Meqiẓe* Nirdamim, 1973.

Kuttner, Stephen. "The Revival of Jurisprudence." In *Renaissance and Renewal in the Twelfth Century*, ed. Robert Louis Benson, Giles Constable, and Carol D. Lanham. 299–323. Cambridge, Mass.: Harvard University Press, 1982.

Lamm, Norman. *Torah Lishmah: Torah for Torah's Sake in the Works of Rabbi Ḥayyim of Volozhin and His Contemporaries.* Hoboken, N.J.: Ktav, 1989.

Lampe, G. W. H. *A Patristic Greek Lexicon.* Oxford: Clarendon, 1961.

Lang, George. "Jurisconsulti." In *A Dictionary of Greek and Roman Antiquities*, ed. William Smith. London, 1875.

Langer, Ruth. "Shelavim qedumim be-hitpatḥutah shel hotza-at ha-Torah ve-hakhnasatah be-vet ha-knesset be-yeme ha-benayyaim: 'Iyyun be-teqasim shel Seder Rav 'Amram Gaon u-Massekhet Sofrim." *Kenishta* 2 (2003): 99–118.

Langmuir, Gavin I. *Toward a Definition of Antisemitism.* Berkeley: University of California Press, 1990.

Lassner, Jacob. *The Shaping of Abbasid Rule.* Princeton, N.J.: Princeton University Press, 1980.

———. *The Topography of Baghdad in the Early Middle Ages.* Detroit: Wayne State University Press, 1970.

Lazarus-Yafeh, Ḥava. "Ezra-'Uzayr: The Metamorphosis of a Polemical Motif." In *Intertwined Worlds: Medieval Islam and Bible Criticism*, ed. Hava Lazarus-Yafeh. 50–74. Princeton, N.J.: Princeton University Press, 1992.

Lazarus-Yafeh, Ḥava, ed. *The Majlis: Interreligious Encounters in Medieval Islam.* Wiesbaden: Harrassowitz, 1999.

Le Goff, Jacques. "Le rituel symbolique de la vassalité." In *Pour un autre Moyen âge*, ed. Jacques Le Goff. 349–419. Paris: Gallimard, 1977.

———. *Time, Work, and Culture in the Middle Ages.* Chicago: University of Chicago Press, 1980.

Lea, H. C. *A History of Auricular Confession and Indulgences in the Latin Church*. Vol. 2. Philadelphia: Lea Brothers & Co., 1896.

Lebecq, Stephane. "The Role of Monasteries in the Systems of Production and Exchange of the Frankish World between the Seventh and the Beginning of the Ninth Centuries." In *The Long Eighth Century*, ed. I. L. Hansen and C. Wickham. 121–48. Leiden: Brill, 2000.

Leclercq, Jean. *The Love of Learning and the Desire for God: A Study of Monastic Culture.* New Trans., Catharine Misrahi. York: New American Library, 1961.

———. "The Renewal of Theology." In *Renaissance and Renewal in the Twelfth Century*, ed. Robert Benson, Giles Constable, and Carol D. Lanham. 68–87. Cambridge, Mass.: Harvard University Press, 1982.

Lecrivain, Charles. "Remarques sur l'interpretation de la *Lex Romana Visigothorum.*" *Annales du Midi* 1 (1889): 145–82.

Levenson, Jon D. "The Eighth Principle of Judaism and the Literary Simultaneity of Scripture." *Journal of Religion* 68 (1988): 205–25.

Levin, B. M. *Ginze Qedem: Ma-asef Madda'i le-Tequfat ha-Geonim.* Vol. 5. Haifa: Ginze Qedem, 1944.

———. "Mi-seride ha-genizah 'B': Ma'asim le-vene Yisrael." *Tarbiẓ* 2 (1931): 383–410.

———. *Oẓar Ḥiluf Minhagim bein Bene Ereẓ Yisrael u-vein Bene Bavel.* Jerusalem: Maqor, 1972.

———, ed. *Iggeret Rav Sherira Gaon: Mesuderet be-Shne Nusḥa-ot: Nusaḥ Sefarad ṿe-Nusaḥ Ẓorfat 'im Ḥilufe Girsaot.* Haifa: Godeh Itzkowitz, 1921.

———, ed. *Oẓar ha-Geonim: Teshuvot Geone Bavel u-Ferushehem 'al pi Seder ha-Talmud.* 13 vols. Haifa and Jerusalem: Hebrew University, 1928–43.

Levison, Wilhelm. "St. Boniface and Cryptography." In *England and the Continent in the Eighth* Century, ed. Wilhelm Levison. 290–94. Oxford: Clarendon Press, 1946.

Lewis, C. S. "The Genesis of a Medieval Book." In *Studies in Medieval and Renaissance Literature*, ed. W. Hooper. 18–40. Cambridge: Cambridge University Press, 1966.

Leyser, K. "The German Aristocracy from the Ninth to the Early Twelfth Century: A Historical and Cultural Sketch." *Past and Present* 41 (1968): 25–53.

Liber, Maurice. *Rashi.* Trans. Adele Szold. Philadelphia: Jewish Publication Society, 1906.

Libson, Gideon. "Ha-gezerta be-tequfat ha-geonim u-ve-reshit yeme ha-benayyim." *Shenaton ha-Mishpat ha-'Ivri* 5 (1978): 79–154.

———. "Halakha and Reality in the Geonic Period: Taqqanah, Minhag, Tradition and Consensus." In *The Jews of Medieval Islam: Community, Society and Identity*, ed. Daniel Frank. 67–100. Leiden: Brill, 1995.

———. *Jewish and Islamic Law: A Comparative Study of Custom during the Geonic Period.* Cambridge, Mass.: Islamic Legal Studies Program, Harvard Law School, 2003.

———. "Terumat ha-genizah le-ḥeqer ha-monografiyyot ha-hilkhatiyyot shel ha-Rav Shemuel ben Ḥofni." *Te'udah* 15 (1999): 189–239.

Lieberman, Saul. "Biqoret Sifre." *Qiryat Sefer* 14 (1937–38): 323–36.

———. *Greek in Jewish Palestine: Studies in the Life and Manners of Jewish Palestine in the II-IV centuries C.E.* New York: Jewish Theological Seminary, 1942.

———. *Hellenism in Jewish Palestine: Studies in the Literary Transmission, Beliefs and Manners of Palestine in the I Century B.C.E.–IV Century C.E.* New York: Jewish Theological Seminary, 1950.

———. "Perurim," *Tarbiẓ* 2 (1941): 377–79.

———. *Sheqi'in.* Jerusalem: Sifre Vahrman, 1970.

———. *Tosefet Rishonim.* Vol. 4. Jerusalem: Bamberger et Vahrman, 1939.

———. *Tosefta ke-Feshutah.* Jerusalem: Jewish Theological Seminary, 1992–2001.

———. *Yevanim ve-Yevanut be-Ereẓ Yisrael.* Jerusalem: Mosad Bialik, 1962.

Lifschitz, Berachyahu. "Ma'amada ha-mishpati shel sifrut ha-she-elot ve-ha-teshuvot." *Shenaton ha-Mishpat ha-'Ivri* 9–10 (1982): 265–300.

Lifschitz, E. M. "Rashi." In *Ketavim,* ed. E. M. Lifschitz. Vol. 1, 9–196. Jerusalem: Mosad ha-Rav Kook, 1947.

Lincoln, Fredman A. *The Starra: Their Effect on Early English Law and Administration.* London: Oxford University Press, 1939.

Linder, Amnon. *The Jews in the Legal Sources of the Early Middle Ages.* Detroit: Wayne State University Press; Jerusalem: Israel Academy of Sciences and Humanities. 1997.

———. *The Jews in Roman Imperial Legislation.* Detroit: Wayne State University Press; Jerusalem: Israel Academy of Sciences and Humanities, 1987.

Loeb, Isidore. "La controverse de 1240 sur la Talmud." *REJ* 1 (1880): 246–71; 2 (1881): 248–73; 3 (1881): 39–57.

Lohr, C. H. "The Medieval Interpretation of Aristotle." In *The Cambridge History of Later Medieval Philosophy,* ed. N. Kretzmann, A. Kenney, and J. Pinborg. 80–98. Cambridge: Cambridge University Press, 1982.

Lopez, R., and I. W. Raymond. *Medieval Trade in the Mediterranean World: Illustrative Documents.* New York: Columbia University Press, 1955.

Lopez, Robert Sabatino. Review of *Urban Civilization in Pre-Crusade Europe* by Irving Agus. *Speculum* 42 (1967): 342.

Lowry, Joseph. Review of *Die Rechtsbücher des Qairawaners Sahnun b. Sa'id: Entstehungsgeschichte und Werküberlieferung* by Miklos Muranyi. *Journal of the American Oriental Society* 123:2 (2003): 438–40.

Lowry, Joseph E. *Early Islamic Legal Theory: The Risāla of Muḥammad ibn Idrīs al-Shāfi'ī.* Leiden: Brill, 2007.

Lucas, Scott. "Where Are the Legal *Hadith*? A Study of the *Musannaf* of Ibn Abi Shayba." *Islamic Law and Society* 15 (2008): 283–314.

Luria, Solomon. *Sefer Yam shel Shlomo 'al Massekhet Ḥullin.* Jerusalem: Mekhon Mishnat Dayid, 1995.

Luscombe, D. E. *The School of Peter Abelard.* London: Cambridge University Press, 1969.

Ma'aseh ha-Geonim. Ed. Abraham Epstein and Ya'aqov Freimann. Berlin: Meqiẓe Nirdamim, 1909.

Magnou-Nortier, Elisabeth. "The Enemies of the Peace: Reflections on a Vocabulary, 500–1100." In *The Peace of God: Social Violence and Religious Response around the Year 1000,* ed. T. Head and R. Landes. 58–79. Ithaca, N.Y.: Cornell University Press, 1992.

Molin, Jacob. *Sefer Maharil.* Cremona, 1558.

Maimonides, Abraham. *Perush R. Abraham ben ha-Rambam z"l 'al Bereshit u-Shemot.* Trans. E. Wiesenberg. Ed. D. Sassoon. London: s.n., 1958.

Maimonides, Moses. *Iggerot ha-Rambam.* Ed. Yiẓḥaq Shilat. 2 vols. Jerusalem: Hoẓa-at Ma'aliyot, 1987.

———. *Iggerot ha-Rambam, Mikhteve Rabenu Moshe ben Maimon u-Mikhteve Bene Doro Elav.* Ed. D. Z. Baneth. Jerusalem: Meqiẓe Nirdamim, 1946.

———. *Mishnah'im Perush Rabenu Moshe ben Maimon.* Ed. Yosef Kafiḥ. Jerusalem: Mosad ha-Rav Kook, 1967.

———. *Mishneh Torah 'al pi Kitve Yad Teman 'im Perush Maqif.* Ed. Yosef Kafiḥ. 23 vols. Tel Aviv: Mekhon Mishnat ha-Rambam, 1983–84.

———. *Sefer ha-Miẓvot.* Trans. Yosef Kafiḥ. Jerusalem: Mosad ha-Rav Kook, 1971.

———. *Teshuvot Ha-Rambam.* Ed. Joshua Blau. Jerusalem, 1989.

Malachi, Ẓvi. "Rashi and His Disciples in Relation to the Old Paytanim." In *Rashi, 1040–1990: Hommage à Ephraim E. Urbach*, ed. Gabrielle Sed-Rajna. 455–62. Paris: Editions du Cerf, 1993.

Malkiel, David. *Reconstructing Ashkenaz: The Human Face of Franco-German Jewry, 1000–1250.* Stanford, CA.: Stanford University Press, 2009.

Malter, Henry. *Saadia Gaon: His Life and Works.* Philadelphia: Jewish Publication Society, 1942.

Mann, Jacob. "'Inyanim shonim le-ḥeqer tequfat ha-geonim." *Tarbiẓ* 5 (1934): 148–79.

———. "The Responsa of the Babylonian Gaonim as a Source of Jewish History." *JQR* 7 (1916): 457–90; 8 (1917–18): 339–66; 9 (1918–19): 139–79.

———. *Texts and Studies in Jewish History and Literature.* Vol. 1. Cincinnati: Hebrew Union College Press, 1931.

Marcus, Ivan."The Dynamics of Jewish Renaissance and Renewal in the Twelfth Century." In *Jews and Christians in Twelfth Century Europe,* ed. M. Signer and J. Van Engen. 27–45. Notre Dame, Ind.: University of Notre Dame Press, 2001.

———. "Exegesis for the Few and for the Many: Judah He-Ḥasid's Biblical Commentaries." *Meḥqere Yerushalayyim be-Maḥshevet Yisrael* 8 (1989): 1–24.

———. "Ḥibure ha-teshuvah shel Ḥaside Ashkenaz." In *Meḥqarim be-Qabalah, be-Filosofya Yehudit u-ve-Sifrut ha-Musar ve-he-Hagut,* ed. J. Dan and J. Hacker. 369–84. Jerusalem: Magnes Press, 1986.

———. "Hierarchies, Religious Boundaries and Jewish Spirituality in Medieval Germany." *Jewish History* 1 (1986): 7–26.

———. "History, Story and Collective Memory: Narrativity in Early Ashkenazic Culture." In *The Midrashic Imagination,* ed. Michael Fishbane. 255–79. Albany: State University of New York Press, 1993.

———. *Piety and Society: The Jewish Pietists of Medieval Germany.* Leiden: Brill, 1981.

———. "The Recensions and Structure of *Sefer Ḥasidim.*" *PAAJR* 45 (1978): 131–53.

———. *Rituals of Childhood: Jewish Acculturation in Medieval Europe.* New Haven, Conn.: Yale University Press, 1996.

Margalioth, Mordecai, ed. *Hilkhot Ereẓ Yisrael Min ha-Genizah*. Jerusalem: Mosad ha-Rav Kook, 1973.

———. *Hilkhot ha-Nagid*. Jerusalem: Keren Yehudah Leb ve-Mini Epshtayn, 1962.

Margolioth, Reuven. "Defuse ha-Shulḥan 'Arukh ha-rishonim." In *Rabi Yosef Qaro*, ed. Yiẓḥaq Raphael. 91. Jerusalem: Mosad ha-Rav Kook, 1969.

Margoliouth, G. "A *Fihrist* of Works by the Gaon Samuel ben Hofni." *JQR* 14 O.S. (1902): 311.

Margulies, Mordecai. *Ha-Ḥiluqim she-beyn Anshe Mizraḥ u-Vene Ereẓ Yisrael*. Jerusalem: Reuven Mass, 1938.

Martin, Richard C. "Inimitability." In *Encyclopaedia of the Qur'an*, ed. J. D. McAuliffe. 526–36. Leiden: Brill, 2001.

———. "The Role of the Basran Mu'tazila in Formulating the Doctrine of the Apologetic Miracle." *Journal of Near Eastern Studies* 39 (1980): 175–89.

Martini, Raymund. *Ordinis Praedicatorum Pugio fide adversus Mauros et Judaeos*. Farnborough, England: Gregg Press, 1967.

Marx, Alexander. "Rabbenu Gershom, Light of the Exile." In *Essays in Jewish Biography*, ed. Alexander Marx. 39–60. Philadelphia: Jewish Publication Society, 1947.

McCormick, Michael. *Origins of the European Economy: Communications and Commerce, A.D. 300–900*. Cambridge: Cambridge University Press, 2001.

McKitterick, Rosamund. *The Carolingians and the Written Word*. Cambridge: Cambridge University Press, 1989.

McLaughlin, Eleanor. "Equality of Souls, Inequality of Sexes: Women in Medieval Theology." In *Religion and Sexism*, ed. Rosemary Ruether. 213–66. New York: Simon and Schuster, 1974.

McNeill, J. T., and H. Gamer, eds. *Medieval Handbooks of Penance: A Translation of the Principal Libri Poenitentiales*. New York: Octagon Books, 1965.

McNeill, John T. *The Celtic Penitentials and Their Influence on Continental Christianity*. Paris: É. Champion, 1923.

Medina, Samuel de. *She-elot u-Teshuvot*. Lemberg: P. M. Balaban, 1862.

Melamed, E.Z. "Ha-Ma'aseh ba-Mishna ke-maqor le-halakhah." *Sinai* 46 (1960): 152–64.

Meir ben Barukh. *Sha'are Teshuvot*. Ed. M. A. Bloch. Berlin: Itzkowski, 1891.

———. *Teshuvot Pesaqim u-Minhagim*. Ed. Y. Z. Kahana. 4 vols. Jerusalem: Mosad ha-Rav Kook, 1967.

Meir ha-Kohen of Rothenburg. *Hagahot Maimuniyyot*, In Maimonides, *Mishneh Torah*.

Meiri, Menaḥem ben Solomon. *Bet ha-Beḥirah 'al Massekhet Avot*. Ed. Binyamin Ze'ev Prag. Jerusalem: Mekhon ha-Talmud, 1964.

———. *Bet ha-Beḥirah 'al Massekhet Baba Batra*. Ed. Avraham Sofer. Jerusalem: Kedem, 1971.

———. *Bet ha-Beḥirah 'al Massekhet Berakhot*. Ed. Samuel Dickman. Jerusalem: Mosad ha-Talmud ha-Yisraeli ha-Shalem, 1964.

———. *Bet ha-Beḥirah 'al Massekhet Shabat*. Ed. Y. S. Lange. Jerusalem: s.n., 1976.

———. *Ḥibur ha-Teshuvah*. New York: Shulsinger, 1950.

Melchert, Christopher. "Ibn Mujahid and the Establishment of Seven Qur'anic Readings." *Studia Islamica* 91 (2000): 5–22.

Menache, Sophia. "Communication in the Jewish Diaspora: A Survey." In *Communication in the Jewish Diaspora*. Leiden: Brill, 1996.

Merḥavya, Ḥen. *Ha-Talmud be-Re-i ha-Naẓrut*. Jerusalem: Mosad Bialik, 1970.

Meshullam ben Moses of Beziers. *Sefer ha-Hashlama*. Ed. Avraham Hafuta. 11 vols. Tel Aviv: Yeshivat ha-Rambam, 1961.

Metsger, Itamar. *Seder Tannaim va-Amoraim*. Jerusalem: Mekhon Neve Asher, 2001.

Meyvaert, P. "Medieval Monastic Claustrum." *Gesta* 12 (1973): 53–59.

Milikowsky, Chaim. "Mahadurot ve-tipusei teqst be-sifrut ḥazal: be-'iqvot ma-amaro shel Y. M. Ta Shma, 'Sifriyyatam shel ḥakhme Ashkenaz bene ha-meah ha-11–12.'" *Qiryat Sefer* 61 (1987): 169–70.

———. "The *Status Quaestionis* of Research in Rabbinic Literature." *Journal of Jewish Studies* 39 (1988): 201–11.

Mirsky, Samuel K. *Haqdama la-Mishna*. New York: Yeshiva University Press, 1965.

———. ed. *Sheiltot de-Rav Aḥai Gaon*. 5 vols. Jerusalem: Sura, 1959.

Mizraḥi, Eliyahu. *She-elot u-Teshuvot*. Jerusalem: Hoẓa-at Sefarim Darom, 1937.

Moses ben Jacob of Coucy. *Sefer Miẓvot Gadol ha-Shalem*. Jerusalem: Makhon Jerusalem, 1993.

Motzki, Harald. "The Author and His Work in the Islamic Literature of the First Centuries: The Case of Abd al-Razzaq's *Musannaf*." *Jerusalem Studies in Arabic and Islam* 28 (2003): 1–31.

Müller, Joel. *Briefe und Responsen in der Vorgeonäischen Judischen Literatur*. Berlin: Bernstein, 1886.

———. *Vierter Bericht über die Lehranstalt für die Wissenschaft des Judenthums*. Berlin: s.n., 1886.

Muranyi, Miklos. *Die Rechtsbücher des Qairawaners Sahnun b. Said: Enstehungsgeschichte und Werküberlieferung*. Stuttgart: Deutsche Morgenlandische Gesellschaft -Kommissionsverlag, F. Steiner, 1999.

Naeh, Shlomo. "'Aseh libkha ḥadre ḥadarim: 'Iyyun nosaf be-divre ḥazal 'al ha-maḥloqet." In *Meḥuyyavut Yehudit Meḥudeshet: 'Al 'Olamo ve-Haguto shel David Hartman*, ed. Z. Zohar and A. Sagi. 851–75. Tel Aviv: Mekhon Shalom Hartman, 2001.

Naeh, Shlomo. "Omanut ha-zikkaron: Mivnim shel zikkaron ve-tavniyyot shel teqst be-sifrut ḥazal." *Meḥqere Talmud* 3 (2005): 543–89.

Naḥalon, Aharon. *Qahal ve-Taqanot Qahal be-Toratam shel ha-Geonim*. Jerusalem: Hebrew University Press, ha-Makhon le-Ḥeqer ha-Mishpat ha-'Ivri, 2001.

Naḥmanides, Moses. *Ḥidushe HaRamban*. Multiple volumes. Jerusalem: Mekhon ha-Talmud ha-Yis're'eli ha-Shalem, 1970–.

———. *Kitve ha-Ramban*. Ed. Charles Chavel. 2 vols. Jerusalem: s.n., 1962–63.

Nathan ben Jehiel. *'Arukh ha-Shalem*. Ed. Alexander Kohut. New York: Pardes, 1955.

Natronai Gaon. *Teshuvot Rav Natronai bar Hilai Gaon*. Ed. Yeraḥmiel (Robert) Brody. 2 vols. Jerusalem: Mekhon Ofek, 1994.

Netanyahu, B. "Alfonso de Espina: Was He a New Christian?" *PAAJR* 43 (1976): 124–65.

Neubauer, Adolf. "Abou Ahron, le Babylonien." *REJ* 23 (1891): 230–37.

———. *Mediaeval Jewish Chronicles and Chronological Notes*. Oxford: Clarendon Press, 1887.

Neusner, Jacob. *A History of the Jews in Babylonia*. Vol. 5. Atlanta: Scholars Press, 1999.

———. *What, Exactly, Did the Rabbinic Sages Mean by "The Oral Torah"? An Inductive Answer to the Question of Rabbinic Judaism*. Atlanta: Scholars Press, 1998.

Nichols, Stephen G. "Introduction: Philology in a Manuscript Culture." *Speculum* 65 (1990): 1–10.

Nissi ben Noah. *Bitan ha-Maskilim ve-ha-Nevonim*. Ashdod: Mekhon Tiferet Yosef, 2000.

Noam, Vered. "Mesorot nusaḥ qedumot be-hagahot Rashi ba-Talmud." *Sidra* 17 (2001–2): 109–50.

Nora, Pierre, "Between Memory and History: *Les Lieux de Mémoire*." *Representations* 26 (1989): 7–24.

Notopoulos, James A. "Mnemosyne in Oral Literature." *Transactions and Proceedings of the American Philological Association* 69 (1938): 465–93.

Ó Cróinin, Dáibhi. "The Irish as Mediators of Antique Culture on the Continent." In *Science in Western and Eastern Civilization in Carolingian Times*, ed. P. L. Butzer and D. Lohrmann. 42–51. Basel: Birkhauser Verlag, 1993.

Oakley, T. P. "Commutations and the Redemptions of Penance in the Penitentials." *Catholic Historical Review* 18 (1932): 341–51.

Oppenheimer, Aharon. *The 'Am ha-Aretz: A Study in the Social History of the Jewish People in the Hellenistic-Roman Period.* Trans. I. H. Levine. Leiden: Brill, 1977.

———. "Mi-Qorteva le-Asfamya." In *Galut Aḥar Golah: Meḥqarim Mugashim le-Ḥayyim Beinart le-Mlot 70 Shanah*, ed. A. Mirsky, A. Grossman, and Y. Kaplan. 57–63. Jerusalem: Mekhon Ben-Zvi, 1988.

Orfali, Moshe. "Jerónimo de Santa Fe y la polémica cristiana contra el Talmud." *Annuario di studi Ebraici* 10 (1984): 157–78.

———. *Talmud y Cristianismo: Historia y Causas de un Conflicto*. Barcelona: Riopiedras, 1998.

Ourliac, Paul, and Jean-Louis Gazzaniga. *Histoire du droit privé francais de l'an mil au code civil.* Paris: Albin Michel, 1985.

Ovadia b. Abraham Maimuni. *The Treatise of the Pool.* Trans. Paul Fenton. London: Octagon Press, 1981.

Palazzo, Eric. *A History of Liturgical Books from the Beginning to the Thirteenth Century*. Collegeville, Minn.: Liturgical Press, 1998.

Payer, Pierre. *Sex and the Penitentials: The Development of a Sexual Code, 550–1150*. Toronto: University of Toronto Press, 1984.

Pedaya, Ḥaviva. *Ha-Shem ve-ha-Miqdash be-Mishnat R. Yiẓḥaq Sagi Nahor: 'Iyyun Mashveh be-Khitve Rishone ha-Mequbalim*. Jerusalem: Magnes Press, 2001.

Pedersen, Johannes. *The Arabic Book*. Princeton, N.J.: Princeton University Press, 1984.

Perlmann, Moshe. "Eleventh Century Andalusian Authors on the Jews of Granada." *PAAJR* 18 (1948–49): 269–90.

———. "The Medieval Polemics between Islam and Judaism." In *Religion in a Religious Age*, ed. S. D. Goitein. 103–20. Cambridge, Mass.: Harvard University Press, 1974.

Petrus, Alfonsi. *Dialogue against the Jews*. Trans. Irven M. Resnick.Washington, D.C.: Catholic University of America Press, 2006.

Petuchowski, Jakob J. "The Supposed Dogma of the Mosaic Authorship of the Pentateuch." *Hibbert Journal* 57 (1959): 356–60.

Pinsker, Simḥa. *Lickute Kadmoniot: Zur Geschichte des Karaismus und der karäischen Literatur*. 2 vols. 2nd ed. Vienna, 1860; Jerusalem, 1968.

"*Pirqoi ben Baboi.*" In *Geonica*, ed. Louis Ginzberg. 2:48–53. New York: Jewish Theological Seminary, 1909.

Plucknett, T. F. T. *A Concise History of the Common Law*. London: Butterworth, 1956.

———. *The Legislation of Edward I*. Oxford: Oxford University Press, 1962.

Poliak, Meira. "Merkaziyyuto shel limud ha-miqra be-arẓot ha-Islam 'al pi 'edutah shel genizat Qahir." *'Al ha-Pereq* 17 (2000): 131–41.

Posnanski, Shemuel Avraham. "Anshe Qayrawan." *Zikkaron le-Avraham Eliyahu Harkavy: Qevuẓat Ma-amarim be-Ḥokhmat Yisrael*, ed. D. von Günzberg and I. Markon. 175–220 (Hebrew section). St. Petersburg, 1908.

———. *Perush 'al Yeḥezqel u-Tere 'Asar*. Warsaw: H. Epfelberg, 1913.

Pseudo-Jerome. *Quaestiones on the Book of Samuel*. Ed. Avrom Saltman. Leiden: Brill, 1975.

Qaro, Yosef. *Shulḥan 'Arukh*. Venice: Frentsoni-Bragadin, 1565.

Rabbinovicz, Raphael Nathan Nata. *Ma-amar 'al Hadpasat ha-Talmud: Toldot Hadpasat ha-Talmud*. Ed. A. M. Haberman. Jerusalem: Mosad ha-Rav Kook, 2005.

Radding, Charles M. *The Origins of Medieval Jurisprudence: Pavia and Bologna, 850–1150*. New Haven, Conn.: Yale University Press, 1988.

Radding, Charles M., and Antonio Ciaralli. *The Corpus Iuris Civilis in the Middle Ages: Manuscripts and Transmission from the Sixth Century to the Juristic Revival*. Leiden: Brill, 2006.

Rahman, Yusuf."The Miraculous Nature of Muslim Scripture: A Study of Abd al-Jabbar's *Ijaz al-Quran*," *Islamic Studies* 35 (1996): 409–24.

Rapoport, S. *Sefer 'Erekh Milin*. Warsaw, 1920.

Raspe, Lucia. *Jüdische Hagiographie im mittelalterlichen Aschkenas*. Tübingen: Mohr Siebeck, 2006.

Raz-Krakotzkin, Amnon. *The Censor, the Editor, and the Text: The Catholic Church and the Shaping of the Jewish Canon in the Sixteenth Century*. Trans. Jackie Feldman. Philadelphia: University of Pennsylvania Press, 2007.

Reif, Stefan C. "Rashi and Proto-Ashkenazi Liturgy." In *Rashi, 1040–1990: Hommage à Ephraim E. Urbach*, ed. Gabrielle Sed-Rajna. 445–54. Paris: Editions du Cerf, 1993.

Reiner, Avraham (Rami). "From Rabbenu Tam to R. Isaac of Vienna: The Hegemony of the French Talmudic School in the Twelfth Century." In *The Jews of Europe in the Middle Ages*, ed. Christopher Cluse. 273–81. Turnhout: Brepols, c. 2004.

———. "Le-hitqabluto shel Sefer Halakhot Gedolot be-Ashkenaz." In *Limud ve-Da'at be-Maḥshavah Yehudit*, ed. Ḥayyim Kreisel. 2:95–121. Beer Sheva: Ben Gurion University, 2006.

———. "Mumar okhel nevelot le-teavon—pasul? Mashehu 'al nusaḥ u-ferusho be-yede Rashi." In *Shimon Schwarzfuchs Jubilee Volume*, ed. J. Hacker et al. Forthcoming.

———. "Rabbenu Tam: Rabbotav (ha-Ẓorfatiyyim) ve-Talmidav Bene Ashkenaz." M.A. thesis, Hebrew University, 1997.

———. "Rabbenu Tam u-Vene Doro: Qesharim, Hashpa'ot, ve-Darke Limudo ba-Talmud." Ph.D. diss., Hebrew University, 2002.

———. "R'I ha-Zaqen bein hemshekhiyut le-ḥidush: Hirhurim be-'iqvot *Yeynam* le-Ḥaym Soloveitchik." *Sidra* 12 (2006): 165–74.

Reiner, Elḥanan. "The Ashkenazi Elite at the Beginning of the Modern Era: Manuscript versus Printed Book." *Polin* 10 (1997): 85–98.

———. "Temurot be-yeshivot Polin ve-Ashkenaz ba-meot ha-16–17." In *Ke-Minhag Ashkenaz u-Polin: Sefer Yovel le-Khone Shmeruk*, ed. Y. Bartal, C. Turniansky, and E. Mendelsohn. 9–80. Jerusalem: Merkaz Shazar, 1993.

Rembaum, Joel. "The Talmud and the Popes: Reflections on the Talmud Trials of the 1240's." *Viator* 13 (1982): 203–23.

Riché, Pierre. *Education and Culture in the Barbarian West, Sixth through Eighth Centuries.* Columbia: University of South Carolina Press, 1976.

Robson, James, trans. *An Introduction to the Science of Tradition* by Muhammad ibn Abd Allah Hakim al-Nisaburi. London: Royal Asiatic Society of Great Britain and Ireland, 1953.

Rosenberg, Shalom. "Ḥeqer ha-miqra ba-maḥshavah ha-yehudit ha-datit ha-ḥadashah." In *Ha-Miqra va-Anaḥnu*, ed. Uriel Simon. 86–119. Ramat Gan: Devir, 1979.

Rosenthal, David. "Le-toldot Rav Paltoi Gaon." *Shenaton ha-Mishpat ha-'Ivri* 11–12 (1984–86): 359–653.

———. "Lishna de-kalla." *Tarbiẓ* 52 (1982–83): 273–308.

———. *Mishnah Avodah Zarah, Mahadurah Biqortit be-Ẓeruf Mavo.* Jerusalem: s.n., 1980.

Rosenthal, E. S. "'Iyyunim be-toldot ha-nusaḥ shel ha-talmud ha-bavli." In *Sefer ha-Yovel le-khvod Mordecai Breuer*, ed. M. Bar Asher. 571–91. Jerusalem: Aqademon, 1992.

———. "Le-leshonoteha shel Massekhet Temura." *Tarbiẓ* 58 (1989): 317–56.

———. "Lishna aḥarina." *Proceedings of the Second World Congress of Jewish Studies* (1957): 14–15 (Hebrew); 18–19 (English).

———. "Toldot ha-nusaḥ u-va'ayot 'arikha be-ḥeqer ha-talmud ha-bavli." *Tarbiẓ* 57 (1988): 1–39.

Rosenthal, J. M. "The Talmud on Trial." *JQR* 47 (1956): 58–76, 145–69.

Rosenwein, Barbara H. *Rhinoceros Bound: Cluny in the Tenth Century*. Philadelphia: University of Pennsylvania Press, 1982.

Roth, Cecil, ed. *The Dark Ages: Jews in Christian Europe, 711–1096.* New Brunswick, N.J.: Rutgers University Press, 1966.

Rouse, Richard and Mary. *Manuscripts and Their Makers: Commercial Book Producers in Medieval Paris, 1200–1500.* 2 vols. Turnhout: Harvey Miller Publishers, 2000.

Rubenstein, Jeffrey. "The Rise of the Babylonian Rabbinic Academy: A Re-Examination of the Talmudic Evidence." *Jewish Studies: An Internet Journal* 1 (2002): 55–68.

Rubin, Asher. "The Concept of Repentance among the Ḥasidey Ashkenaz." *Journal of Jewish Studies* 16 (1965): 161–76.

Ruska, Julius. "Arabische Texte über das Fingerrechnen." *Der Islam* 10 (1920): 87–119.

Sa'adya Gaon. *The Book of Beliefs and Opinions.* Trans. Samuel Rosenblatt. New Haven, Conn.: Yale University Press, 1948.

———. *Mishle 'im Tirgum u-Ferush ha-Gaon Sa'adya ben Yosef Fayumi.* Trans. and ed. Yosef Kafiḥ. Jerusalem: Ha-Va'ad le-Hoza'at Sifre Rasag, 1975–76.

———. *Sefer Yeẓirah.* Trans and ed. Yosef Kafiḥ. Jerusalem: Ha-Va'ad le-Hoẓa'at Sifre Rasag, 1972.

———. "Rabanus Maurus and the Pseudo-Hieronymian *Quaestiones Hebraicae in Libros Regum et Paralipomenon.*" *Harvard Theological Review* 66 (1973): 43–75.

Samely, Alexander, and Philip Alexander. "Artefact and Text: Recreation of Jewish Literature in Medieval Hebrew Manuscripts." *Bulletin of the John Rylands University Library* 75 (1993): 5–17.

Samuel HaNagid. "Shir La'ag." In *Toldot ha-Shira ha-'Ivrit be-Sefarad u-ve-Provence*, ed. Y. Schirmann. 1:147. Jerusalem: Magnes Press, 1955.

Sanford, E. M. "De loquela digitorum." *Classical Journal* 23 (1928): 588–93.

Saperstein, Marc. "Christians and Christianity in the Sermons of Jacob Anatoli." *Jewish History* 6 (1992): 225–42.

———. *Decoding the Rabbis: A Thirteenth Century Commentary on the Aggadah.* Cambridge, Mass.: Harvard University Press, 1980.

Sarna, Naḥum M. "The Modern Study of the Bible in the Framework of Jewish Studies." In *Proceedings of the Eighth World Congress of Jewish Studies.* 19–27. Jerusalem: World Union of Jewish Studies, 1983.

Sarton, George. *Introduction to the History of Science.* Baltimore: Williams and Wilkins, 1962.

Sassoon, David S., ed. *Diwan of Samuel HaNagid.* London: Oxford University Press, 1934.

Schacht, Joseph. *Introduction to Islamic Law.* Oxford: Clarendon Press, 1964.

Schaefer, F. J. "Burchard of Worms." *The Catholic Encyclopedia.* New York: Appleton, 1908.

Schäfer, Peter. "Das 'Dogma' von der mündlichen Torah im rabbinischen Judentum." In *Studien zur Geschichte und Theologie des Rabbinischen Judentums*, ed. Peter Schäfer. 166–79. Leiden: Brill, 1978.

———. "The Ideal of Piety of the Ashkenazi Ḥasidim and Its Roots in Jewish Tradition." *Jewish History* 4 (1990): 9–23.

———. "Once Again the *Status Quaestionis* of Research in Rabbinic Literature: An Answer to Chaim Milikowsky." *Journal of Jewish Studies* 40 (1989): 89–94.

———. "Research into Rabbinic Literature: An Attempt to Define the *Status Quaestionis.*" *Journal of Jewish Studies* 37 (1986): 139–52.

———. "Tradition and Redaction in *Hekhalot* Literature." *Journal for the Study of Judaism* 14 (1984): 172–81.

Schechter, Solomon. *Saadyana.* Cambridge: Deighton and Bell, 1903.
Schepansky, Israel. *Rabbenu Ephraim: Talmid Ḥaver shel ha-Rif.* Jerusalem: Mosad ha-Rav Kook, 1976.
Schiller, A. Arthur. "Custom in Classical Roman Law." *Virginia Law Review* 24 (1937–38): 268–82.
Schlesinger, Shimon Shlomo. "'Al ketivat torah she-be-'al peh be-zeman ha-talmud." *Sinai* 117 (1996): 41–70.
Schlueter, M. "Was the Mishna Written? The Answer of Rav Sherira Gaon." In *Rashi, 1040–1990: Hommage à Ephraim E. Urbach,* ed. G. Sed-Rajna. 213–18. Paris: Editions du Cerf, 1993.
Schmelzer, Menaḥem H. "Perush alfabetin: Perush 'al 13 piyyutim aramiyyim le-Rabi Binyamin ben Abraham min ha-'Anavim." In *Meḥqarim u-Meqorot: Me-asef le-Mada'e ha-Yahadut,* ed. H. Z. Dimitrovsky. 1:167–274. New York: Jewish Theological Seminary, 1977.
Schoeler, Gregor. "Oral Torah and Hadit: Transmission, Prohibition of Writing, Redaction." In *The Oral and the Written in Early Islam,* ed. James E. Montgomery. 111–41. London: Routledge, 2006.
———. "Writing and Publishing: On the Use and Function of Writing in the First Centuries of Islam." *Arabica* 44 (1997): 423–35.
Scholem, Gershom G. *Major Trends in Jewish Mysticism.* New York: Schocken Books, 1946.
———. *Origins of the Kabbalah.* Ed. R. J. Zwi Werblowsky. Trans. Allan Arkush. Philadelphia: Jewish Publication Society; Princeton: Princeton University Press, 1987.
———. *Reshit ha-Qabbalah.* Jerusalem: Schocken, 1948.
Schönbach, Anton E. *Studien zur Geschichte der altdeutschen Predigt, 3: Das Wirken Bertholds von Regensburg gegen die Ketzer.* Vienna: s.n., 1904.
Schulz, Fritz. *History of Roman Legal Science.* Oxford: Clarendon Press, 1946.
———. *Prinzipien des Römischen Rechts.* Berlin: Duncker and Humblot, 1954.
Schwartz, Seth. "Rabbinization in the Sixth Century." In *The Talmud Yerushalmi and Graeco-Roman Culture.* Ed. Peter Schäfer. 3:55–69. Tübingen: Mohr-Siebeck, 2002.
Schwarzfuchs, S. "L'opposition Ẓarfat-Provence: La formation du Judaisme du nord de la France." In *Hommage à Georges Vajda: Ètudes d'histoire et de pensée juives,* ed. G. Nahon and C. Touati. 135–50. Louvain: Peeters, 1980.
———. "Reshit darko shel Rashi." In *Rashi: 'Iyyunim be-Yeẓirato,* ed. Z. Steinfeld. 177–83. Ramat Gan: Bar Ilan University Press, 1993.
Scott, S. P. *The Visigothic Code.* Littleton: F. B. Rothman, 1910.
Sefer 'Avodat Yisrael. Ed. Isaac Seligmann Baer. Rödelheim, 1868.
Sefer ha-Eshkol: Kolel Teshuvot u-Fisqe Dinim. Ed. Ḥayyim Yehudah Ehrenreich. Budapest: Katzburg Brothers, 1923.
Sefer Ḥasidim. Ed. Judah Wistinetzki and Jakob Freimann. Frankfurt am Main, 1924.
Sefer Ḥemdah Genuzah. Ed. Schneur Zalman Schneurson and Ze'ev Wolf Wolfenson. Jerusalem: Yisrael Bek, 1863.

Septimus, Bernard. "Maimonides on Language." In *The Culture of Spanish Jewry,* ed. Aviva Doron. 35–54. Israel: Levinsky College of Education, 1994.

Shafer, S. *Ha-Rif u-Mishnato.* Jerusalem: Yefeh-Nof, 1966.

Shapiro, Marc. *The Limits of Orthodox Theology: Maimonides' Thirteen Principles Reappraised.* Oxford: Littman Library of Jewish Civilization, 2004.

Sherira ben Ḥanina, Gaon. *Iggeret Rav Sherira Gaon.* Ed. B. M. Lewin. Reprint of 1921, Jerusalem: Maqor, 1982.

———. *Iggeret Rav Sherira Gaon.* Ed. David Metsger. Jerusalem: Mekhon Neve Asher, 2001.

Shinan, Avigdor, and Zakovitch, Yair. "Midrash on Scripture and Midrash within Scripture." In *Scripta Hierosolymitana* 31: *Studies in Bible,* ed. Sara Japhet. 257–77. Jerusalem: Magnes Press, 1986.

Sidur Rashi: Kolel Pisqe Dinim Ve-Halakhot. Ed. Shlomo Buber. Berlin: Meqiẓe Nirdamim, 1911.

Sifre 'al Sefer Devarim. Ed. Eliezer Finkelstein. New York: Jewish Theological Seminary, 1969.

Sifre: A Tannaitic Commentary on the Book of Deuteronomy. Trans. Reuven Hammer. New Haven, Conn.: Yale University Press, 1986.

Simḥa ben Samuel. *Maḥzor Vitry.* Ed. S. Horowitz. Nuremberg: Y. Bulka, 1923.

Simon, Uriel. "Parshane Sefarad." In *Parshanut ha-Miqra ha-Yehudit,* ed. Moshe Greenberg. 29–60. Jerusalem: Mosad Bialik, 1983.

Sirat, Colette. *Hebrew Manuscripts of the Middle Ages.* Trans. Nicholas de Lange. Originally *Du Scribe au Livre: Les Manuscrits He'braux au Moyen Age.* Paris: CNRS éditions, 1994. Cambridge: Cambridge University Press, 2002.

———. *La Conception du Livre chez les Piétistes Ashkenazes du Moyen Age.* Geneva: Droz, 1996.

———. "Les rouleaux bibliques de Qumran au Moyen Age: Du livre au Sefer Tora, de l'oreille a l'oeil." *Comptes rendus de l'Academie des Inscriptions et Belles Lettres* (1991): 415–32.

———. "Orality/Literacy, Languages, Alphabets: Example of the Jewish People." In *Proceedings of the Workshop on Orality vs. Literacy: Concepts, Methods and Data,* ed. C. Pontecorvo and C. Blanche-Benveniste. 49–88. ESF Scientific Networks, January 1993.

Sklare, David. "R. David ben Sa'adya al-Ger ve-ḥiburo Al-Ḥawwi." *Te'udah* 14 (1998): 103–23.

Sklare, David Eric. *Samuel ben Ḥofni Gaon and His Cultural World.* Leiden: Brill, 1996.

Soloveitchik, Haym. "Can Halakhic Texts Talk History?" *AJS Review* 3 (1978): 153–96.

———. "Catastrophe and Halakhic Creativity: Ashkenaz —1096, 1242, 1306 and 1298." *Jewish History* 12 (1998): 71–85.

———. "Halakha, Hermeneutics, and Martyrdom in Medieval Ashkenaz." *JQR* 94:1 (2004): 77–108; 94:2 (2004): 278–99.

———. *Halakhah, Kalkalah, ve-Dimui 'Aẓmi.* Jerusalem: Magnes Press, 1985.

———. *Ha-Yayin be-Yeme ha-Benayyim: Yeyn Nesekh—Pereq be-Toldot ha-Halakhah be-Ashkenaz.* Jerusalem: Merkaz Shazar, 2008.

———. "Le-ta-arikh ḥiburo shel Sefer Ḥasidim." In *Tarbut ve-Ḥevra be-Toldot Yisrael be-Yeme ha-Benayyim*, ed. M. Ben Sasson, R. Bonfil, and J. Hacker. 383–88. Jerusalem: Merkaz Shazar, 1989.

———. "Piety, Pietism and German Pietism: *Sefer Ḥasidim* I and the Influence of Ḥaside Ashkenaz." *JQR* 92:3–4 (2002): 455–93.

———. "Religious Law and Change." *AJS Review* 12 (1987): 205–21.

———. "Rupture and Reconstruction: The Transformation of Contemporary Orthodoxy." *Tradition* 28 (1994): 64–130.

———. "Sefer Ḥasidim: 'Olam ha-midrash ve-ha-humanizm shel ha-meah ha-12." *Tarbiẓ* 71 (2002): 531–36.

———. *She-elot u-Teshuvot ke-Maqor Histori.* Jerusalem: Merkaz Shazar, Hebrew University, 1990.

———. "Three Themes in *Sefer Ḥasidim.*" *AJS Review* 1 (1976): 311–58.

———. *"Yeynam": Saḥar be-Yeynam shel Goyim 'al Gilgulah shel Halakhah ba-'Olam ha-Ma'aseh.* Tel Aviv: Am 'Oved, 2003.

Sorabji, Richard. *Aristotle on Memory.* Providence: Brown University Press, 1972.

Southern, R. W. "The Schools of Paris and the School of Chartres." In *Renaissance and Renewal in the Twelfth Century*, ed. Robert Louis Benson, Giles Constable, and Carol D. Lanham. 113–37. Cambridge, Mass.: Harvard University Press, 1982.

Sparks, H. F. D. "Jerome as Biblical Scholar." In *The Cambridge History of the Bible*, ed. P. R. Ackroyd and C. F. Evans. 1:510–41. Cambridge: Cambridge University Press, 1970.

———, ed. "The Life of Adam and Eve." In *The Apocryphal Old Testament.* 147–48. Oxford: Clarendon Press, 1984.

Sperber, Daniel. *Minhage Yisrael.* Vol. 1. Jerusalem: Mosad ha-Rav Kook, 1989.

Spiegel, Gabrielle. "History, Historicism and the Social Logic of the Text." *Speculum* 65 (1990): 59–86.

Spiegel, Shalom. *The Last Trial.* Trans. Judah Goldin. New York: Pantheon Books, 1967.

———. "Le-Farashat ha-polmos shel Pirqoi ben Baboi." In *Harry Austryn Wolfson Jubilee Volume*, ed. Saul Lieberman. 243–74 (Hebrew section). Jerusalem: American Academy for Jewish Research, 1965.

———. "Me-Aggadot ha-'aqedah: Piyyut 'al sheḥitat Yiẓḥaq u-teḥiyato le-Efrayim mi-Buna." In *Alexander Marx Jubilee Volume.* 471–574. New York: Jewish Theological Seminary, 1950.

Spiegel, Yaaqov. *'Amudim be-Toldot ha-Sefer ha-'Ivri.* Ramat Gan: Bar Ilan University Press, 1996.

———. "Leshonot perush ve-hosafot meuḥarot ba-talmud ha-bavli." *Te'udah* 3 (1983): 91–112

Spinoza, Benedictus de. *Theological-Political Treatise.* Trans. Samuel Shirley. Indianapolis: Hackett Publishing Company, 2001.

Spitzer, Shlomo. "She-elot u-teshuvot Rabbenu Yehudah he-Ḥasid be-'inyene teshuvah." In *Sefer ha-Zikaron le-R. Shmuel Barukh Verner*, ed. Y. Buksboim, 199–205. Jerusalem: Moriah, 1996.

Stampfer, Yehudah Ẓvi. "Ha-Mishpat ha-'ivri be-Sefarad ba-meah ha-11: Bein geonim le-rishonim ('al pi Kitab al-Ḥawwi le-R. David ben Sa'adya)." *Shenaton ha-Mishpat ha-'Ivri* 38 (2008): 217–36.

Steiner, Richard. "A Jewish Theory of Biblical Redaction from Byzantium: Its Rabbinic Roots, Its Diffusion and Its Encounter with the Muslim Doctrine of Falsification." *Jewish Studies Internet Journal* 2 (2003): 123–67.

Stewart, Susan. *On Longing*. Durham, N.C.: Duke University Press, 1993.

Stock, Brian. *The Implications of Literacy: Written Language and Models of Interpretation in the Eleventh and Twelfth Centuries*. Princeton, N.J.: Princeton University Press, 1983.

———. *Listening for the Text: On the Uses of the Past*. Baltimore: Johns Hopkins University Press, 1990.

———. "Tradition and Modernity: Models from the Past." *Modernité au Moyen Age: le défi du passé*. Ed. Brigitte Cazelles and Charles Méla. 33–44. Geneva: Droz, 1990.

Stow, Kenneth. "By Land or by Sea: The Passage of the Kalonymides to the Rhineland in the Tenth Century." In *Communication in the Jewish Diaspora*, ed. Sophie Menache. 59–72. Leiden: Brill, 1996.

Strack, Hermann L. *Einleitung in Talmud und Midrasch*. Munich: Beck, 1921.

Strauss, Leo. *Persecution and the Art of Writing*. Glencoe: Free Press, 1952.

Sussman, Ya'aqov. "Beraita de-teḥume Ereẓ Yisrael." *Tarbiẓ* 45 (1976): 213–57.

———. "Ketovet hilkhatit me-'Emeq Bet She-an: Seqira muqdemet." *Tarbiẓ* 43 (1974): 158–88.

———. "Ketovet hilkhatit me-'Emeq Bet She-an: Tosafot ve-tiqunim." *Tarbiẓ* 44 (1975): 193–95.

———. "Kitve yad u-mesorot nusaḥ shel ha-Mishnah." *Proceedings of the Seventh World Congress of Jewish Studies* (1981): 215–50.

———. "Masoret limud u-masoret nusaḥ shel ha-Talmud ha-Yerushalmi." In *Meḥqarim ba-Sifrut ha-Talmudit*. 12–76. Jerusalem: Ha-Akademyah ha-Leumit ha-Yisraelit le-Mada'im, 1983.

———. "Mif'alo ha-madda'i shel Professor E. E. Urbach." *Ephraim Elimelekh Urbach-Bio-Bibliografya: Musaf Mada'e ha-Yahadut* 1 (1993): 7–117.

———. "Perush ha-Raabad le-massekhet Sheqalim: Ḥidah bibliografit, ba'aya historit." In *Meah She'arim*, ed. Ezra Fleisher, Yaaqov Blidstein, Carmi Horowitz, and Bernard Septimus. 151–61. Jerusalem: Magnes Press, 2001.

———. "Pirqe Yerushalmi." *Meḥqere Talmud* 2 (1993): 220–83.

———. "'Torah she-be-'al peh'—peshutah ke-mashma'ah: Koḥo shel qoẓo shel yod." *Meḥqere Talmud* 3 (2005): 209–384.

———. "Ve-shuv le-Yerushalmi Neziqin." *Meḥqere Talmud* 1 (1990): 55–133.

Swartz, Michael. *Scholastic Magic: Ritual and Revelation in Early Jewish Mysticism*. Princeton, N.J.: Princeton University Press, 1996.

Ta Shma, Yisrael M. "'Al perush Rabbenu Gershom Meor ha-Golah la-Talmud." *Qiryat Sefer* 53 (1978): 356–65.

———. "Gedarav shel Sefer ha-Maor." *Shenaton ha-Mishpat ha-'Ivri* 3 (1971): 361–406.

———. 'Halakhah, minhag u-masoret be-yahadut Ashkenaz ba-meot ha-11–12." *Sidra* 3 (1987): 85–161.

———. *Halakhah, Minhag u-Meẓi'ut be-Ashkenaz, 1000–1350*. Jerusalem: Magnes Press, 1996.

———. *Ha-Nigleh she-ba-Nistar*. Tel Aviv: Ha-Qibbuẓ ha-Meuḥad, 1995.

———. "Ḥasidut Ashkenaz be-Sefarad: R. Yonah Gerondi—ha-ish u-fo'alo." In *Galut Aḥar Golah: Meḥqarim be-Toldot 'Am Yisrael Mugashim le-Professor Ḥayyim Beinart le-melot lo Shiv'im Shana*, ed. A. Mirsky, A. Grossman, and Y. Kaplan. 165–94. Jerusalem: Yad Ben-Ẓvi, 1988.

———. *Ha-Sifrut ha-Parshanit la-Talmud be-Eropa u-ve-Ẓefon Afriqa*. 2 vols. Jerusalem: Magnes Press, 1999.

———. *Ha-Tefilah ha-Ashkenazit ha-Qedumah*. Jerusalem: Magnes Press, 2003.

———. "Hilkheta ke-vatraei: Beḥinot historiyyot shel kelal mishpati." *Shenaton ha-Mishpat ha-'Ivri* 6–7 (1979–80): 405–23. Also published in *Halakhah, Minhag u-Meẓiut be-Ashkenaz, 1000–1350*, 58–78 (Jerusalem: Magnes Press, 1996).

———. "Hitabdut ve-reẓaḥ ha-zulat 'al qidush ha-shem: Le-she-elat meqoma shel ha-aggadah be-masoret ha-pesiqa ha-Ashkenazit." In *Yehudim Mul ha-Ẓelav: Gezerot 1096 be-Historia u-ve-Historiographia*, ed. Yom Tov Assis, Michael Toch, Jeremy Cohen, Ora Limor, and Aharon Kedar. 150–56. Jerusalem: Magnes Press, 2000.

———. *Knesset Meḥqarim: 'Iyyunim be-Sifrut ha-Rabanit be-Yeme ha-Benayyim*. 2 vols. Jerusalem: Mosad Bialik, 2004.

———. "Le-toldot ha-sifrut ha-rabbanit be-Yavan ba-meah ha-14." *Tarbiẓ* 62 (1993): 101–14.

———. "The Library of the French Sages." In *Rashi, 1040–1990: Hommage à Ephraim E. Urbach*, ed. Gabrielle Sed-Rajna. 535–40. Paris: Editions du Cerf, 1993.

———. *Minhag Ashkenaz ha-Qadmon*. Jerusalem: Magnes Press, 1992.

———. "Miẓvat Talmud Torah ke-ve'aya datit ve-ḥevratit be-Sefer Ḥasidim." *Shnaton Bar Ilan* 14–15 (1977): 98–113. Also published in *Halakhah, Minhag u-Meẓiut be-Ashkenaz, 1000–1350*, 112–29 (Jerusalem: Magnes Press, 1996).

———. "The 'Open Book' in Medieval Hebrew Literature: The Problem of Authorized Editions." *Bulletin of the John Rylands University Library* 75 (1993): 15–24.

———. "Qavin le-ofyah shel sifrut ha-halakhah be-Ashkenaz ba-me-ot ha-13–14." *'Ale Sefer* 4 (1977): 26–41.

———. "Qelitatam shel sifre ha-Rif, ha-Raḥ, ve-Halakhot Gedolot be-Ẓorfat u-ve-Ashkenaz." *Qiryat Sefer* 55 (1980): 191–201.

———. "Quntres Sodot ha-Tefilah le-Rabi Yehudah he-Ḥasid." *Tarbiẓ* 65 (1996): 65–77.

———. *Rabi Zeraḥya Halevi Ba'al ha-Maor u-Vene Ḥugo*. Jerusalem: Mosad ha-Rav Kook, 1992.

———. "Rashi-Rif, ve-Rashi-Rosh." In *Rashi: 'Iyyunim be-Yeẓirato*, ed. Ẓvi Steinfeld. 209–20. Ramat Gan: Bar Ilan University, 1993.

———. Review of *Ḥakhme Ashkenaz ha-Rishonim* by Avraham Grossman. *Qiryat Sefer* 56 (1981): 344–52.
———. Introduction to *Sefer Gematriyyot le-Rabi Yehudah he-Ḥasid*, ed. Daniel Abrams. Los Angeles: Hoẓa'at Keruv, 1998.
———. "She-elot u-teshuvot min ha-shamayyim." *Tarbiẓ* 57 (1987–88): 51–66.
———. "Shiput 'ivri u-mishpat 'ivri ba-meot ha-11–12 be-Sefarad." In idem, *Knesset Meḥqarim: 'Iyyunim be-Sifrut ha-Rabanit be-Yeme ha-Benayyim*. 2: 239–260. Jerusalem: Mosad Bialik, 2004. Reprinted from *Shnaton ha-Mishpat ha-'Ivri* 1 (1974): 353–72.
———. "Sifriyyatam shel Ḥakhme Ashkenaz bene ha-meah ha-11–12." *Qiryat Sefer* 60 (1985): 298–309.
———. "Yeẓirato ha-sifrutit shel Rabbenu Yosef Halevi Ibn Migash." *Qiryat Sefer* 46 (1971): 136–46, 541–53.
Tabuteau, Emily Zack. *Transfers of Property in Eleventh-Century Norman Law*. Chapel Hill: University of North Carolina Press, 1988.
Taqu, Moshe. *Ketav Tamim*. Ed. Raphael Kircheim. *Oẓar Neḥmad* 4 (1860): 58–99.
———. *Ketav Tamim: Ketav Yad Paris H711*. Introduction by Joseph Dan. Jerusalem: Merkaz Dinur, 1984.
Tellenbach, Gerd. *Church, State, and Christian Society at the Time of the Investiture Contest*. Trans. R. F. Bennett. Oxford: Blackwell, 1940.
———. "Vom Karolingischen Reichsadel zum deutschen Reichsfürstenstand." In *Herrschaft und Staat im Mittelalter*, ed. Hellmut Kämpf. 191–242. Darmstadt: H. Gentner, 1956.
Tentler, Thomas N. *Sin and Confession on the Eve of the Reformation*. Princeton, N.J.: Princeton University Press, 1977.
Tishby, Yeshayahu. "Ha-vikkuaḥ 'al hadpasat ha-zohar be-Italia." *Peraqim* 1 (1967–68): 131–81.
———. *Mishnat ha-Zohar*. Vol. 2. Jerusalem: Mosad Bialik, 1957.
Toch, Michael. "Asking the Way and Telling the Law: Speech in Medieval Germany." *Journal of Interdisciplinary History* 16:4 (1986): 667–82.
———. *Die Juden im mittelalterlichen Reich*. Munich: R. Oldenbourg,1998.
———. *Peasants and Jews in Medieval Germany*. Aldershot, Hampshire: Ashgate Variorum, 2003.
Tolan, John. *Petrus Alfonsi and His Medieval Readers*. Gainesville: University Press of Florida, 1993.
Toorawa, Shawkat Mahmood. *Ibn Abī Ṭāhir Ṭayfūr and Arabic Writerly Culture: A Ninth-Century Bookman in Baghdad*. London: Routledge Curzon, 2005.
Twersky, Isadore. "The Beginnings of *Mishneh Torah* Criticism." In *Biblical and Other Studies*, ed. A. Altmann. 161–82. Cambridge, Mass.: Harvard University Press, 1963.
———. "Biqoret sefer: 'Ba'ale ha-Tosafot.'" *Tarbiẓ* 26 (1956): 221–22.
———. "Biqoret sefer: 'Ḥamishah Sefarim le-Rav Nisim Gaon.'" *Tarbiẓ* 37 (1968): 325–26.

———. *Introduction to the Code of Maimonides.* New Haven, Conn.: Yale University Press, 1980.

———. "Joseph Ibn Kaspi—Portrait of a Medieval Jewish Intellectual." In *Studies in Medieval Jewish History and Literature,* ed. I. Twersky. 231–57. Cambridge, Mass.: Harvard University Press, 1979.

———. *Rabad of Posquieres.* Cambridge, Mass.: Harvard University Press, 1962.

———. "Religion and Law." In *Religion in a Religious Age,* ed. S. D. Goitein. 69–82. Cambridge, Mass.: Association for Jewish Studies, 1974.

———. "Sefer Mishneh Torah la-Rambam, megamato ve-tafqido." *Proceedings of the Israel Academy of Sciences and Humanities* 5 (1972): 1–22.

———. "Some Non-Halakhic Aspects of the *Mishneh Torah.*" In *Jewish Medieval and Renaissance Studies,* ed. A. Altmann. 95–119. Cambridge, Mass.: Harvard University Press, 1967.

Ullmann, Walter. *The Growth of Papal Government in the Middle Ages: A Study of the Ideological Relation of Clerical to Lay Power.* London: Methuen, 1962.

Urbach, Ephraim Elimelech. *Ba'ale ha-Tosafot: Toldotehem, Ḥiburehem, Shitatehem.* 2 vols. 2nd ed. Jerusalem: Mosad Bialik, 1980.

———. "Eskesis ve-yisurim be-torat ḥazal." *Sefer Yovel le-Yiẓḥaq Baer,* ed. S. Ettinger. 48–68. Jerusalem: Ha-Ḥevra ha-Historit ha-Yisraelit, 1960.

———. *Ha-Halakhah, Meqoroteha ve-Hitpatḥuta.* Jerusalem: Yad la-Talmud, 1984.

———. "Halakhah u-nevuah." *Tarbiẓ* 18 (1946–47): 1–27.

———. "Masoret ve-halakhah." *Tarbiẓ* 50 (1980–81): 136–63.

———. "Mi-darkhe ha-Qodifiqaẓya- 'al Sefer ha-Turim le-Rabi Ya'aqov beRabi Asher." *American Academy for Jewish Research Jubilee Volume* 46–47 (1980): Hebrew pagination, 1–14.

Van Acker, L. *Corpus Christianorum Continuatio Mediaevalis* 52. Turnhout: Brepols, 1981.

Van Berkum, W. J. "The Hebrew Grammatical Tradition in the Exegesis of Rashi." In *Rashi, 1040–1990: Hommage à Ephraim E. Urbach,* ed. Gabrielle Sed-Rajna, 427–35. Paris: Editions du Cerf, 1993.

Veltri, Giusepppe. "Die Novelle 146: Das Verbot des Targumsvortrags in Justinians Politik." In *Die Septuaginta zwischen Judentum und Christentum,* ed. M. Hengel and A. M. Schwemer. 116–30. Tübingen: J. C. B. Mohr, 1994.

Verhulst, Adriaan E. *The Carolingian Economy.* New York: Cambridge University Press, 2002.

Vinogradoff, Paul. *Roman Law in Medieval Europe.* Oxford: Clarendon Press, 1929.

Von den Brincken, Anne-Dorothee. "Marianus Scottus als Universalhistoriker iuxta veritatem evangelii." In *Die Iren und Europa im fruheren Mittelalter,* ed. H. Lowe. 2:97–109. Stuttgart: Klett-Cotta, 1982.

Wallace-Hadrill, J. M. *The Barbarian West, 400–1000.* Oxford: Basil Blackwell, 1996.

Watkins, Oscar D. *A History of Penance.* London: Longman, Green, and Co., 1920.

Watson, Alan. *Evolution of Law.* Baltimore: Johns Hopkins University Press, 1985.

Weiss, Isaac Hirsch. *Dor Dor ve-Dorshav: Hu Sefer Divre ha-Yamim le-Torah she-be'al Peh.* 5 vols. Berlin: Platt & Minkus, 1924.

———. "Rabbenu Tam." *Beit Talmud* 3 (1882): 33–36, 129–38, 161–69, 193–201, 225–33, 257–61, 289–95.

Welborn, Mary C. "Lotharingia as a Center of Arabic and Scientific Influence in the Eleventh Century." *Isis* 17 (1932): 260–63.

Werner, Ernst. "Zur Frauenfrage und Frauenkultur im Mittelalter: Robert von Arbrissel und Fontevrault." *Forschungen und Fortschritte* 29 (1955): 269–76.

White, Hayden. "The Gregorian Ideal and Saint Bernard of Clairvaux." *Journal of the History of Ideas* 21 (1960): 321–48.

White, Stephen D. *Custom, Kinship, and Gifts to Saints: The "Laudatio Parentum" in Western France, 1050–1150.* Chapel Hill: University of North Carolina Press, 1998.

———. "*Pactum . . . Legem Vincit et Amor Judicium*: The Settlement of Disputes by Compromise in Eleventh Century Western France." *American Journal of Legal History* 22 (1978): 281–308.

Wieder, N. "Hashpa'ot islamiyot 'al ha-pulḥan ha-yehudi." *Melilah* 2 (1946): 37–120.

———. "Yismaḥ Moshe: Hitnagdut ve-sanegorya." In *Meḥqarim be-Aggadah, Tirgumim u-Tefilah le-Zekher Yosef Heinemann*, ed. E. Fleischer and J. Petuchowski. 75–99. Jerusalem: Magnes Press, 1981.

Wilke, Carsten. "Les degrés de la sainteté des livres." In *La Conception du livre chez les piétistes ashkénazes*, ed. Colette Sirat. 37–63. Geneva: Droz, 1996.

Wilken, Robert L. *John Chrysostom and the Jews: Rhetoric and Reality in the Late Fourth Century.* Berkeley: University of California Press, 1983.

Williams, A. Lukyn. *Adversus Judaeos.* Cambridge: Cambridge University Press, 1935.

Winroth, Anders. "Origins of Legal Education in Medieval Europe." http://law.usc.edu/academics/assets/docs/winroth.pdf.

———. *The Making of Gratian's Decretum.* New York: Cambridge University Press, 2000.

Wolfson, Elliot R. "Beyond the Spoken Word: Oral Tradition and Written Transmission in Medieval Jewish Mysticism." In *Transmitting Jewish Traditions: Orality, Textuality, and Cultural Diffusion*, ed. Y. Elman and I. Gershoni. 166–224. New Haven, Conn.: Yale University Press, 2000.

———. *Through a Speculum That Shines: Vision and Imagination in Medieval Jewish Mysticism.* Princeton, N.J.: Princeton University Press, 1994.

Wolfson, Harry Austryn. *Crescas' Critique of Aristotle.* Cambridge, Mass.: Harvard University Press, 1929.

Wyrick, Jed. *The Ascension of Authorship.* Cambridge, Mass.: Harvard University Press, 2004.

Yassif, Eli. "Rashi Legends and Medieval Popular Culture." In *Rashi, 1040–1990: Hommage à Ephraim E. Urbach*, ed. Gabrielle Sed-Rajna, 483–92. Paris: Editions du Cerf, 1993.

———. *Sipure Ben Sira be-Yeme ha-Benayyim.* Jerusalem: Magnes Press, 1984.

Yassif, Eli, and Jacqueline Teitelbaum. *Hebrew Folktales: History, Genre, Meaning.* Bloomington: Indiana University Press, 1999.

Yeivin, Y. "Hat-amat ha-torah she-be'al-pe be-te'amim." *Leshonenu* 24 (1960): 47–69, 167–78, 207–31.

Yerushalmi, Y. H. "The Inquisition and the Jews of France in the Time of Bernard Gui." *Harvard Theological Review* 63 (1970): 317–76.

Yuval, Israel Jacob (Yisrael). "Heilige Städte-Heiligen Gemeinden: Mainz als das Jerusalem Deutschlands." In *Jüdische Gemeinden und Organisationformen von der Antike bis zum Gegenwart*, ed. Robert Jütte and Abraham Kustermann. 91–101. Vienna, Cologne, Weimar: Böhlau, 1996.

———. "Rishonim ve-Aḥaronim, Antiqui et Moderni." *Ẓion* 57 (1992): 369–94.

———. *Two Nations in Your Womb: Perceptions of Jews and Christians in Late Antiquity and the Middle Ages*. Trans. Barbara Harshav and Jonathan Chipman. Berkeley: University of California Press, 2006.

Zacuto, Abraham ben Samuel. *Sefer Yuḥasin ha-Shalem*, ed. Ẓvi Fillipowski. London and Edinburgh: Ḥevrat Me'orere Yeshenim, 1857.

Zeraḥya Halevi. *Ba'al ha-Maor*. Printed with *Halakhot* of R. Isaac Alfasi in Rom edition of Talmud.

Ẓfatman, Sara. "Ma'aseh Bukh: Qavim le-demuto shel zhaner be-sifrut Yiddish ha-yeshanah." *Ha-Sifrut* 28 (1979): 126–52.

Ẓidqiyahu ben Avraham 'Anav. *Shibole ha-Leqet*. Ed. Salomon Buber. Vilna, 1886.

Zimmels, H. J. *Ashkenazim and Sephardim: Their Relations, Differences and Problems as Reflected in the Rabbinical Responsa*. London: Marla Publications, 1976.

Zimmer, Eric Yiẓḥaq. *'Olam ke-Minhago Noheg: Peraqim be-Toldot ha-Minhagim, Hilkhotehem ve-Gilgulehem*. Jerusalem: Merkaz Shazar, 1996.

Zlotnick, Dov. *The Iron Pillar—Mishnah: Redaction, Form and Intent*. New York: Ktav, 1988.

———. "Memory and the Integrity of the Oral Tradition." *JANES* 16–17 (1984–85): 229–41.

———. *The Tractate Mourning*. New Haven, Conn.: Yale University Press, 1966.

Ẓucker, Moshe. *Perushe Rav Sa'adya Gaon le-Vereshit*. New York: Jewish Theological Seminary, 1984.

———. "Qeta'im mi-Kitab Taḥsil al-Shara'i al-Sama'iyah." *Tarbiẓ* 41 (1972): 373–410.

INDEX

ACKNOWLEDGMENTS

The University of Pennsylvania has proven a wonderful academic environment in which to complete this work. My thinking has been enriched by conversations with my students at Penn, undergraduates as well as graduates. Colleagues in the Department of Religious Studies and in the Seminar on the History of the Book have contributed to my reading and thinking; they have also enabled me to sustain the belief that the best academic inquiry is neither inaccessible nor divorced from life concerns. My colleagues in the Jewish Studies program share my commitment to integrating Judaica into the humanities, and Professors David Ruderman and David Stern, the two colleagues whose interests most closely overlap with my own, have served as sounding boards, coaches, and friends.

I wish to express particular thanks to an anonymous reader of this manuscript who offered astute criticisms and suggestions and to the scholars who generously read and offered feedback on chapters at various stages of their formation. Professor Yisrael Yuval read the entire manuscript. Professor Robert Brody and Dr. David Sklare read versions of Chapter 1, and Professor Yehudah Galinsky and Dr. Rami Reiner read versions of Chapter 4. Each corrected errors, pointed me to additional bibliography, and challenged my thinking in various ways. Professor Haym Soloveitchik was an unusually gracious and helpful reader of Chapter 4; his sharp criticisms led me to rethink (and jettison) earlier claims that I had made—though certain perspectives with which he disagrees remain in this version. The aforementioned scholars have collectively helped to make this a less flawed work, and I am enormously grateful to each for manifesting patience and ungrudging collegiality.

I also benefited greatly from the stimulating questions, challenges, and conversations that followed my presentation of work-in-progress in a number of academic venues: the Department of Religious Studies, the Program in Jewish Studies, and the Oriental Club of the University of Pennsylvania; the Jewish Studies Seminar at the University of Toronto; the Seminar für Judaistik of the Johann Wolfgang Goethe-Universität, Frankfurt-am-Main; the Jüdische Hochshule of Heidelberg; the Seminar für Judaistik/Jüdische Studien of the Martin-Luther-Universität, Halle-Wittenberg; and the Institut für Judaistik at the Freie Universität, Berlin.

Some of the themes in Chapter 6 were the subjects of articles: "The Penitential System of Hasidei Ashkenaz and the Problem of Cultural Boundaries," *Journal of Jewish Thought and Philosophy* 8 (1999): 201–29; "Rhineland Pietist Approaches to Prayer and the Textualization of Rabbinic Culture in Medieval Northern Europ, *Jewish Studies Quarterly* 11 (2004): 313–31, and "The Rhineland Pietists' Sacralization of Oral Torah, *Jewish Quarterly Review* 96 (2006): 9–16.

While working on this project, I was a recipient of fellowships from the Stanford Humanities Center, the University of Pennsylvania's Center for Advanced Judaic Studies, the American Council of Learned Societies, the National Endowment for the Humanities, and the Guggenheim Foundation. The first two experiences offered the camaraderie of an intellectual community, and each fellowship afforded me research time whose value cannot be overstated and for which I am enormously grateful.

Staff members of the Van Pelt Library and the Center for Advanced Judaic Studies Library of the University of Pennsylvania helped me acquire hard-to-find materials. Thanks to Dr. Arthur Kiron, Judith Leifer, and Josef Gulka for their many kindnesses, and to the interlibrary loan staff at the Van Pelt Library. Thanks, too, to Jason Watkins for his graciousness in addressing computer problems. For permission to reproduce images in their holdings, thanks to the Universitäts- und Landesbibliothek Darmstadt, the Bibliothèque Municipale de Rouen, and the British Library. I am particularly indebted to Dr. Rina Talgam, Director of the Center for Jewish Art of the Hebrew University, and to Michal Sternthal, Head of the Section of Hebrew Illuminated Manuscripts at that Center, who graciously shared their knowledge of relevant images.

At different stages in this work's evolution, I received valuable assistance from a number of former Penn students: (then) undergraduate students Yael Landman, David Shyovitz, and Jonathan Winer, and (then) graduate student Yaacob Dweck. It was an honor and privilege to work with each of them.

Special thanks to Dr. Jerry Singerman of the University of Pennsylvania Press for expressing early enthusiasm about this project and for ongoing forbearance—and to Erica Ginsburg, Caroline Winschel, and Eric Schramm for shepherding this book through production with care. Joseph Kamm helped with index preparation.

The steadfast friendship and support of a number of people have sustained me over the years of this book's composition: Marcia and Larry Arem, Lena Boski, Jane Eisner and Marc Berger, David Fishman, Leora Fishman, Roy Gould, Paige and Bernard Kaplan, Margaret Kaufman, Sharon Leibhaber and Alan Iser (who also gave valuable feedback on a draft of this work), Ben Nathans, the greater Posner family, Adena Potok, Sheila and Dan Segal, Mindy Seidlin, Esther and Barry Sherman, Susanna Sirkin, Karen Strauss, Susan Tachau, Helene and Jeff Tigay, Beth Wenger, Maitkie and Marvin Winer, and Lisa and Jonny Wurtele.

The gestation of this work was punctuated by the loss of both teachers and parents. I cannot know whether my late teacher, Professor Yitzhak Twersky, of blessed memory, would have agreed with all the formulations set forth in this book, but his interests and concerns, reflected most strongly in much of Chapter 5 and part of Chapter 2, nurtured both this work and its author. The internalized voices of my mother, Priscilla Block Fishman, and my father, Hertzel Fishman, of blessed memory, continue to guide, goad, and inspire me—in all arenas of my life.

Happily, the very living and audible voices of our children—Elisheva, Leah, Jessica and Mikey, Sam and Jennifer—and of our grandchildren help to focus my priorities on a daily basis. Neither our textured lives—nor this work—would have been possible without the love and companionship of my husband, Max Apple, who helps to make the impossible imaginable.

CPSIA information can be obtained
at www.ICGtesting.com
Printed in the USA
JSHW021436181122
33436JS00001B/2

9 780812 222876